GOVERNING BY FAKE NEWS

ISBN : 978-2-315-01071-4

Jacques Baud

GOVERNING BY FAKE NEWS

30 Years of Fake News in the West

L'INCONNU

CONTENT

GOVERNING BY FAKE NEWS FOREWORD

Taken together, my notes and analyses from thirty-five years of working in international security on three continents, in the service of security and peace, in national and international settings, would have saved just over 470,000 lives. But nothing was done! Fear of deviating from prevailing opinions, prejudice, refusal to see a problem from a different angle have been convenient loopholes, often hiding incompetence and lack of curiosity. This is what is known as the 'deep state' or 'permanent state': a bureaucracy that lives for itself and seeks to satisfy its own interests, to the detriment of the general interest.

Working for the United Nations and NATO, I have been in contact with soldiers from all countries during several crises, both in the field and at headquarters level (in the Congo, Sudan, during the Libyan, Ukrainian and Syrian crises). I have seen the weakness of the higher echelons of command: the inability to understand the logic of the adversary, the lack of general culture, the absence of sensitivity to the holistic dimension of conflicts, a total lack of imagination in finding alternatives to the use of force to solve sometimes simple problems, cowardice when it comes to advising the political level based on facts and an almost total absence of a sense of responsibility. Wars are won by soldiers, but certainly not by generals.

Diplomats are not much better. Generally more educated, they are often corrupt, lack courage and imagination. Locked into institutional thinking, they share with the military an inability to understand asymmetric phenomena. Frequently the complacent victims of rumours, they favour administrative discipline over common sense and solve problems more out of duty than out of concern for efficiency… even if it means 'twisting the neck' of the truth.

What are the facts that allow one to say that "*the Islamic State is seeking to create a civil war in France*[1]"? What are the facts that allowed Nicolas Sarkozy to claim that Iran "*calls for the destruction of Israel*[2]" or Emmanuel Macron to

1. Nicolas Truong, "Islamic State seeks to unleash a civil war", *lemonde.fr*, November 14, 2015
2. Speech by President Sarkozy to the Knesset, *Le Figaro*, June 20, 2008

claim that Vladimir Putin is "*obsessed with interference in our democracies*[3]" or that "*Russia invaded Ukraine*[4]"? Literally none... but it is enough to establish a foreign policy, to strike and kill innocent people.

In fact, our perception of events is very partial, and therefore biased. We believe we have objective and complete information, but this is not the case: slight omissions, simplifications and other distortions modify in a subtle way our way of understanding the world. The phenomenon is all the more pronounced when it is fuelled by emotion - as in the case of terrorism - or by fears that are deeply rooted in the mind - for example, the Russian threat. Thus, suppositions become certainties and prejudices become realities, verbs in the conditional tense are rephrased in the indicative tense, and the prudence of the intelligence services is ignored in favour of more categorical messages. To the point that the intelligence services are castigated when they provide facts that contradict the political discourse[5]!

Even war seems to escape all rationality. People engage in it without any strategy or precise objectives, destroying societies permanently for short-term reasons. By analogy, we attribute to others (such as Russia, Syria or Iran) the same willingness to engage in conflicts without objectives, simply out of a desire for conquest or glory... Yet the facts tend to contradict our prejudices. We do not understand war, so we cannot understand peace. With simulacra of strategy, which are only an erratic series of tactical actions, we seek solutions to our perceptions, and not to the reality on the ground, as in the Democratic Republic of Congo, Darfur or South Sudan, which was enthusiastically welcomed at the United Nations in 2011, and which is today one of the main providers of refugees[6].

The mistreatment of a small cat arouses more emotion on social networks than the massacre of children in Iraq by Western air forces... The death of the "500,000" Iraqi children[7] in the 1990s, or of 40,000 Venezuelans in 2017-2018[8], because of Western sanctions, has not provoked any reaction in Europe: no one has taken to the streets, and those responsible have never been sought or sanctioned! There are demonstrations for migrants, but not against the Western

---

3. "President Macron on relations with the US, Syria and Russia", *Fox News/YouTube*, 22 April 2018, (12'40")

4. Emmanuel Macron, during his press conference at the end of the G7, on 27 May 2017 ("Ukraine: Macron promises a 'demanding' exchange without 'concessions' with Putin", *Europe 1*, 27 May 2017); "Putin - Macron: les dossiers qui fâchent", *BFMTV*, 29 May 2017; "Vladimir Putin: Emmanuel Macron, prêt à engager un 'rapport de force'", *Le Point*, 29 May 2017

5. John Bowden, "Senate Democrat says he is concerned intelligence community is 'bending' Soleimani presentations", *The Hill*, 14 January 2020

6. *Global Trends - Forced Displacement In 2018*, UNHCR, 18 June 2019

7. *60 Minutes* program, "Madeleine Albright," *newmedia7/YouTube*, 5 August 2016. (In reality, the figure would be more like 130,000 dead children).

8. Mark Weisbrot & Jeffrey Sachs, *Economic Sanctions as Collective Punishment: The Case of Venezuela*, Center for Economic and Policy Research, Washington DC, April 2019, p. 11

strikes that drive them into exile. We demonstrate for sustainable development, but we plunder the main resource of developing countries: people. A modern form of colonialism, where the victims are complacent and participate in the plunder. Millions of people have taken to the streets to demonstrate their anger at terrorism, but how many demonstrated *before* the strikes provoked the violence, when the likely consequences were known?

The cause of these dysfunctions is information that is most often deliberately truncated in order to protect poorly thought-out decisions that support individual postures or respond to short-term visions.

This book does not claim to establish or re-establish truths, but seeks to inspire 'reasonable doubt' about the way we are informed. It shows that what we take for granted is an often crude deception: official reports and the international press demonstrate that the information is there, available, provided that one takes the trouble to look for it. In the information jungle, the intelligence services have an essential role in providing an objective picture of the situation, a sort of 'yardstick', which should enable political or military decision-makers to decide. We shall see where they have failed… well before terrorism and wars…

J. Baud

1. THE PERVERSE EFFECT OF FALSE TRUTHS

A liar says: "I lie! Is he lying?
(Epimenides, 550 BC)

Our perception of the environment is truncated by information that conceals false truths - often fuelled by cultural bias - which tend to shift our frame of reference and distort our reading.

The Christchurch killer in March 2019 justified his massacre of 51 Muslims with the theory of 'great replacement'. Yet in New Zealand, the Muslim population constitutes barely 1% of the total population, while the Maori and Asian populations make up 15% and 6.5% of the population respectively. This suggests that this sense of 'great replacement' has been artificially generated; perhaps not deliberately, but through carelessness and clientelism. By associating - *volens nolens* - Islamists with Muslims, we have created the conditions for inter-community violence and given real meaning to the word 'Islamophobia'.

Our reductive vision of things tends to generate 'false truths', which have entered the 'normal' reading of things and - for various reasons - are no longer questioned. We then enter the realm of 'post-truths', where reality becomes the product of perception and no longer of objective facts. The problem is that these 'post-truths' condition the way we see problems and solve them.

Western strategic decisions are based on assumptions, prejudices and, in the best cases, clues, but very rarely on proven facts. When Donald Trump struck Syria with 59 cruise missiles in April 2017, the media and the European political establishment applauded and followed suit, even though there was no evidence to justify an act of war against a sovereign country, without being threatened and without a UN mandate[9].

9. See, for example: Frédéric Autran, "Frappes en Syrie: Trump cible directement le régime de Bachar al-Assad", *liberation.fr*, 7 April 2017; "Syrie: Donald Trump met ses menaces à exécution", *lefigaro.fr*, 7 April 2017

As soon as it is conveyed by the "traditional media", the information becomes a "truth", and all the more so if it confirms our prejudices. Ironically, the political or military action induced by these 'truths' is precisely the source of the terrorism that is killing us. We ourselves create the conditions for our insecurity. Most of the victims caused by terrorism in France between 1990 and 2017 could easily have been avoided if we had wanted to understand objectively the terrorists' motives. If the latter are obviously guilty of their acts, politicians, journalists and other "terrorism experts" who seek to impose their own interpretation of the phenomenon, excluding the reasons given by the terrorists themselves (under the pretext of not "proving them right") objectively become accomplices. In fact, they distort the understanding of the phenomenon and provoke inappropriate responses.

The search for 'truth' is a complex undertaking. Lies and omissions are the basic elements of "founding myths": rightly or wrongly, they have often helped to create a consensual basis and to smooth out potential conflicts, thus contributing to the stabilisation of societies and the facilitation of living together. Buddha, Moses, Jesus Christ, William Tell, Joan of Arc and many others probably fuelled "fake news" in their time, yet they have become moral references or symbols of unity. But they have also justified massacres, genocides and injustices...

Today, we claim to be fighting terrorism in the name of "Western values": respect for human rights or the rule of law. But is this true? We start wars in defiance of international law, lie to multilateral organisations, threaten the families of recalcitrant diplomats with reprisals, practice torture, bomb sovereign countries without UN approval, support countries that commit massacres, support jihadist movements that use women and children as human shields, support the assassinations conducted by Western countries against diplomatic emissaries of countries with which they are not at war, accept military forces that deliberately shoot children with impunity, etc. In July 2019, a report by the UN Assistance Mission in Afghanistan shows that Western coalition forces are killing more civilians than the Islamic State[10]!

In November 2018, in an interview with the BBC, Mike Pompeo presented the US sanctions and announced that the Iranian government would have to do the right thing "*if they want their people to eat*[11]". This way of threatening the civilian population in order to force the government to

10. *Midyear Update on the Protection of Civilians in Armed Conflict: January 1st to June 30, 2019*, United Nations Assistance Mission in Afghanistan (UNAMA), July 30, 2019, p. 12; Amy Woodyatt & Arnaud Siad, "More civilians are being killed by Afghan and international forces than by the Taliban and other militants," *CNN*, July 31, 2019
11. "Interview With Hadi Nili of BBC Persian", *Michael R. Pompeo - Secretary of State*, Washington DC, November 7, 2018; Brendan Cole, "Mike Pompeo Says Iran Must Listen To U.S. 'If They Want Their People To Eat'", *Newsweek*, November 9, 2018.

act as the US wishes, corresponds precisely to the definition of... terrorism, namely:

The use or threat of force to achieve political change[12].

But to justify these wars, it has been necessary to present the enemy as worse than us. For example, the term "*Bashar al-Assad's regime forces*[13]" or "*loyalist forces*[14]" is often used instead of "*Syrian army*[15]", implying that it is a faction and not a state institution (Christian militias are "*loyalist forces*"). When referring to Russia, "*power*" becomes synonymous with "*government*[16]", the Russian army becomes "*Putin's forces*[17]", while "*arrests*" become "*arrests*[18]". It is thus accepted as an indisputable fact that Vladimir Putin, invariably described as the "*master of the Kremlin*[19]", is a "*dictator*[20]" or a "*muscular autocrat*[21]", or that Bashar al-Assad is "*massacring his people*[22]", in such a way that it is no longer necessary to demonstrate this. Are we talking about the "*forces of Macron's regime*" or "*the master of the Élysée*" deployed on the Champs-Élysées? In fact, this terminology is not innocent and is part of a subtle conditioning to legitimise Western actions. In 2016, NATO's Centre of Excellence for Strategic Communication (STRACOM), based in Latvia, even published a document that sought to show a kinship between the Islamic State's communication strategy and that of the Russian government[23]!

The revelations of official documents show that in Afghanistan, Libya, Syria and Iraq, Westerners have thrown themselves "headlong" into conflicts presented as indispensable to our security, without any strategy, without any knowledge of the adversary and without foreseeing the consequences at home. We are silent

12. Biran Jenkins, advisor to the RAND Corporation (in Charles-Philippe David & Benoît Gagnon, *Repenser le Terrorisme*, Éditions PUL, Université de Laval (Canada), 2007, p. 35
13. "Syria: 71 fighters killed in clashes between jihadists and regime forces", *L'Obs/AFP*, July 11, 2019; Hala Kodmani, "Idlib, ultime creuset du conflit syrien", *liberation.fr*, August 20, 2019
14. See article "Syrian Civil War", *Wikipedia*
15. Caroline Roux in the programme "C dans l'air", "Syria: le coup de force de Poutine #cdanslair 28-09-2016", YouTube, September 28, 2016 (09'30")
16. "Demonstrators arrested in Moscow: 'We are witnessing a tightening of Russian power'", *France24*, July 29, 2019 (updated July 30, 2019)
17. Jérôme Fenoglio, "Les frontières invisibles de Narva", *Le Monde*, 14 May 2014; "Vous pensiez à la Syrie? La 3e Guerre mondiale pourrait plutôt commencer dans la Baltique (et on y entendre de plus en plus de bruits de bottes)", *Atlantico.fr*, November 4, 2016
18. For example: *France24*, 1pm news of August 3, 2019
19. For example: Marion Pignot, "Russia: Vladimir Putin reinstated as Kremlin leader on Monday", *20minutes.fr*, May 7, 2018
20. "Carte blanche au dictateur Poutine", *Courrier International*, March 19, 2018
21. Sara Daniel, "What does Russia look like under Vladimir Putin?", *L'Obs*, March 8, 2018
22. "Quand on massacre son peuple": la cinglante réplique de Le Drian à el-Assad", *L'Express*, December 18, 2017
23. *The Kremlin and DAESH Information Activities*, NATO Strategic Communications Centre of Excellence, Riga, October 2016

on the fact that we deliberately created these conflicts and that their horrors are the result of our irresponsibility. But no one calls for accountability. Even the victims seem to be willing…

2. DEFINING FAKE NEWS

Translated into French by the term "infox" - which combines the words "information" and "intoxication", and presupposes that its purpose is to deceive - the expression "fake news" is a legacy of Donald Trump's election campaign. Used to castigate his opponents, the expression quickly went viral and has marked the political vocabulary since 2016. However, if we intuitively understand its meaning, its definition remains unclear. Is it falsified information? Transformed? Inauthentic? False? Unreal? Unrealistic? Inaccurate ? Exaggerated ? Undocumented ? Incomplete? Altered intentionally (misinformation) or unintentionally (misinformation)? Is it the result of ignorance, malice or didactic simplification? Conversely, what criteria determine whether information is true? How many people believe it? What is the standard by which we decide that a piece of information is true?

Rumours about the banning of Chips in Belgium[24] or about the development of a sushi tree in Japan[25] are obviously more a matter of humour than a desire to cause harm. Some fake news can be generated by Internet users themselves. For example, Google's success comes from the way it searches for information: it attributes a relevance value to the results of a search according to the number of links that lead to it, on the assumption that Internet users make a rational choice between the various answers offered to them. Thus, the relevance of a search result is not directly related to its content, but to the number of visits by Internet users. In an extreme case, if they choose a stupid answer as the result of their search, Google will consider it the most relevant. Jokers have used this principle to create fakes - called "*Google bombing*" - by "bombarding" wacky answers with links. For example, typing in "*miserable failure*" led inexorably to *George W. Bush*, or "*French military victories*" yielded no results, and suggested searching under "*French military defeats*"[26]. Today, Google has put in place corrective mechanisms

24. B.T., "After their Belgian counterparts, the chip shops of the North threatened by the European Commission?, *La Voix du Nord*, June 19, 2017

25. https://www.journaldemourreal.com/des-chercheurs-japonais-developpent-un-arbre-a-sushis/

26. Patrick Langridge, "The 11 Most Infamous Google Bombs In History", www.screamingfrog.co.uk, October 18, 2012; Barry Schwartz, "George Bush 'Miserable Failure' Google Bomb Back, This Time In Knowledge Graph", *Search Engine Land*, June 12, 2013

that prevent such manipulations. This being said, the very nature of algorithms does not exclude that similar situations can be provoked in a more subtle way. This is the anecdotal aspect of "fake news".

At the top of the pyramid is fake news, which manipulates facts to create a false coherence around an appearance of truth, in order to distort an audience's perception and push them to support a policy. They lead to the notion of 'post-truth'. These are the "real" fake news: the most perverse, the most dangerous, but the most difficult to detect.

A quick look shows that there are very few verifiable and irrefutable facts to support our picture of countries like Russia, Iran, Syria, etc. Gaddafi was probably a dictator, but where are the mass graves of the massacres attributed to him? Omar Bashir was probably a dictator too, but where are the mass graves of the 400,000 deaths in Darfur between 2003 and 2006? By having created and accepted these lies without batting an eyelid, we have generated hundreds of thousands of other deaths and an immigration that we can no longer control...

3. WESTERN INTERVENTIONS: LIES AS COVER FOR DEMOCRACY

Long before the start of the "Arab Spring" of 2010-2012, the US had a plan to overthrow 7 governments in the Near and Middle East. In March 2007, US General Wesley Clark, former NATO *Supreme Allied Commander Europe*, revealed a conversation he had at the Pentagon just after 9/11:

> *One of the generals [...] picks up a piece of paper on his desk: "I just received this memo today from the floor above, from the office of the Secretary of Defense, which describes how we are going to take down 7 countries in five years: starting with Iraq, Syria, Lebanon, Libya, Somalia, Sudan, and ending with Iran[27]!"*

A little less than twenty years later, all these countries are in crisis or at war. In all of them, the unrest began as a manoeuvre for influence and led to a regional crisis. All these crises have the involvement of the US, France and Israel in common; all will encourage the development of jihadist terrorism and all will be steeped in myths carefully nurtured by the mainstream media. All follow the same Hegelian pattern.

	Principle	Example: Libya	Example: Venezuela
1	Create the *problem* by arming or provoking a group or a party, and push it into a violent posture.	Provoking demonstrations by relying on Islamists. Arm the rebels (clandestinely).	Paralyse economic activity through sanctions. Preventing any possibility of funding to address the precariousness of the situation.

27. *Democracy Now!* interview ("1. Gen. Wesley Clark, Democracy Now! interview, 2007", *Democracy Now! / YouTube*, June 27, 2013). Full interview: "General Wesley Clark speaks to Democracy Now! (March 2, 2007)", *YouTube*, January 30, 2015

2	Generate a *reaction* in public opinion and in the political class through disinformation or by demonising the government to make it particularly odious.	Accusing the government of massacring its population. Accusing it of employing "highly paid" mercenaries. Accusing the government of inciting the rape of women.	Create the image of an unscrupulous dictatorship. To give the image of a government that seeks to starve its population in the face of common sense and prevents international humanitarian aid.
3	Propose a *solution* to the problem (military intervention, establishment of a state of emergency, curtailment of fundamental rights or freedoms, etc.)	Adoption of a resolution for the protection of civilians. Supporting the Islamist opposition materially (officially).	To give the image of a unanimous opposition. Recognition of an alternative president. Offer humanitarian aid. Half-hearted threats of military intervention.

Table 1- How a crisis is made

3.1 "It was the Soviet invasion of Afghanistan that led to the creation of al-Qaeda[28]"

Fuelled by the prevailing 'Russophobia', the myth that the Soviet intervention in Afghanistan is at the origin of jihadism is still alive and well. It is still frequently evoked by specialists in terrorism, such as Rik Coolsaet[29], politicians, such as former Prime Minister Manuel Valls[30] or journalists such as François Clémenceau:

> *One of the reasons why we have seen the emergence of Al Qaeda is because in Afghanistan the Russians came and invaded, occupied the country and in a way created Al Qaeda*[31]

But this is not true! Robert Gates, director of the CIA from 1991 to 1993, explains in his memoirs that the Soviet intervention was itself a response to the

28. Pierre Servent, *Extension du domaine de la guerre*, Robert Laffont, Paris, 2016, p. 116
29. Rik Coolsaet, *Terrorism and radicalisation in the post-Daech era*, International Journal of Criminology and Forensic Science, no. 3/19, Egmont Institute, October 10, 2019
30. Interview "envoyé spécial - 13 novembre: ce que l'on n'a pas su voir", *France 2*, November 3, 2016 (14'50")
31. François Clémenceau in the programme "C dans l'air", "Syria: advantage Putin #cdanslair 29-09-2015", *YouTube*, September 29, 2015 (42'20")

American attempt to destabilise the pro-Soviet regime in Kabul with jihadist movements six months earlier[32].

In April 1979, two months after taking power in Iran, Ayatollah Khomeini had the CIA's TACKSMAN I (in Behchahr) and TACKSMAN II (in Kabkan) electronic listening stations closed. Located in the north of Iran, they ensured the surveillance of the south of the USSR. At the same time, in Afghanistan, land reform provoked growing discontent against President Taraki. But despite repeated requests, the USSR refused to intervene to restore order. There was therefore an opportunity for the Americans to encourage an Islamic rebellion in Afghanistan in order to overthrow the regime and keep Soviet influence in the region at bay. Incidentally, the CIA is considering redeploying a listening station there, which would take over the tasks of the old TACKSMAN stations.

Thus, on July 3, 1979, President Carter signed a directive authorising the CIA to support the mujahideen in Afghanistan through clandestine psychological operations and material support. This was the beginning of Operation CYCLONE, which had a budget of 4 billion dollars[33] and allowed the CIA to arm the Afghan Islamists. On the same day, Zbigniew Brzezinski, National Security Advisor, sent a note to President Jimmy Carter to draw his attention to the fact that "*this aid would lead to Soviet military intervention*[34]". In January 1998, in an interview with the *Nouvel Observateur*, he explained:

> *We did not push the Russians to intervene, but we knowingly increased the likelihood that they would do so*[35].

In September 1979, the brutal rise of Islamist violence pushed Hafizullah Amin to take power in Kabul. But it also had an effect on the southern republics of the USSR, which had a Muslim tradition and had been in chronic struggle against Moscow's power since the 1920s. After several attacks by Islamist groups, the USSR felt directly threatened and decided to intervene in Afghanistan in December 1979.

Initially, it deployed its 40th Army at short notice, but configured for conventional warfare and ill-prepared for counter-insurgency combat, its losses were high and its results meagre. This suggests that the Soviets had not planned this intervention for a long time, but they learned quickly. The 40th Army was completely restructured and reconfigured: its armoured units were reduced

32. Robert M. Gates, *From the Shadows: The Ultimate Insider's Story of Five Presidents and How They Won the Cold War*, Simon and Schuster, December 20, 2011, p. 608, p. 132.
33. "The CIA's "Operation Cyclone" - Stirring The Hornet's Nest Of Islamic Unrest", *Rense.com*, February 27, 2010 (rense.com/general31/cyc.htm).
34. Vincent Jauvert, "Brzezinski: "Oui, la CIA est entrée en Afghanistan avant les Russes…", *Le Nouvel Observateur*, January 15 to 21, 1998, p. 76
35. Ibid.

and its backbone was now made up of artillery (nothing moves faster on the battlefield than fire), signals units, small special forces units ('spetsnaz'), and helicopters.

In a second phase (from 1983), new operational concepts were applied: the emphasis was placed on air-mobile combat, with tactics reminiscent of those of the French army in Algeria twenty-five years earlier. The autonomy of small independent units was increased and the operational integration of combat means was improved. The ability to act on the basis of individual initiative - a concept that had been very limited in the Soviet army until then - was encouraged. The implementation of the 'Reconnaissance-Rapid Complex' (RUK), which shortened the decision-making circuit between combat units and support formations, very quickly brought spectacular results accompanied by a drastic reduction in losses[36].

The effectiveness of these new concepts was such that the United States decided in 1986 to provide the Afghan resistance with portable Stinger anti-aircraft missiles, which were, at that time, highly sensitive, classified and sparingly shared.

Contrary to what the West would later claim, the Soviets were considerably more effective and efficient than Nato and the US. While the latter would try to change society (and fail to do so), the Soviets sought only to keep the government in place: a considerably more reasonable goal, and one which they achieved. As always, the weakness of the Western military is the use of tactics as a substitute for strategy.

The resistance that the Americans supported politically, financially and materially was an amalgam of scattered, poorly coordinated groups with no unifying doctrine. A picture as disparate as the Resistance in France in the years 1940-1942. Far-left movements rubbed shoulders with royalists, Shiites worked with Sunnis with a single adversary: the Soviet occupier. There was no talk of a global jihad or of attacking Western countries. The objective was not to propagate a faith, but to overthrow a government considered corrupt. This is why, once back in their countries of origin (Algeria, Egypt or Libya), foreign fighters will take up the same struggle against their respective governments.

What is known as "al-Qaeda" is only a military base (*al-qa'ida al-'askariyya*[37]) of the Afghan resistance. It was dismantled in 1989: no terrorist group of this name was created, neither by Osama bin Laden (OBL) nor by anyone else. He himself confirmed this in an interview given to *Al-Jazeera* on October 21, 2001, which was not widely broadcast in the West (removed from *YouTube*), a

36. Lester W. Grau, *Mine Warfare and Counterinsurgency: The Russian View*, Foreign Military Studies Office, Fort Leavenworth, KS, 1999.

37. Don Rassler & Vahid Brown, *The Haqqani Nexus and the Evolution of al-Qa'ida*, Harmony Program, The Combating Terrorism Center, West Point, July 14, 2011, p. 24.

transcript of which is available on the *Terrorism.net* website[38]. The rumour that OBL was an American agent is simply not true: he was only one of the multiple beneficiaries of American support through the Pakistani services, but American officials only really knew about his existence in the 1990s[39].

After the departure of the Soviets and without a unifying enemy, Afghanistan and its capital are left to rival factions struggling for power. Lynchings and public executions - sometimes with great cruelty - are a daily occurrence[40]. The problem is that the Americans were not concerned with rebuilding a new Afghanistan, but simply with fighting the Soviets. Thus, unlike in the Second World War, the Americans have not been able to put in place a "De Gaulle" or a "Jean Moulin" who would federate the efforts of the resistance into a strategic coherence. In fact, the Taliban will fulfil this role, as will the Islamic State thirty years later in Iraq and Syria… the Westerners have learned nothing!

It is in this atmosphere that the Taliban ("students of religion") are taking hold. Of Sunni origin, their movement appeared in September 1994. It aims to federate the different ethnic groups, religious tendencies, political families and factions that had made up the Afghan resistance. Starting from the region of Kandahar, in the south of the country, it quickly conquered, practically without fighting, the whole country, except for the north which remained in the hands of the Northern Alliance, led by the Tajik Ahmed Shah Massoud.

As soon as they came to power, the Taliban established a strict regime, the aim of which was to restore civil peace and order, suppress factionalism and enable the management of the state. The Shariah regime - Islamic law - is imposed and enforced severely. Their government enjoys fairly broad popular support, mainly because it provides a form of security and eliminates the anarchy and arbitrariness that prevailed with the militias. However, it failed to gain the international recognition that would allow the country to develop[41]. The West refuses to deal with the regime; an intransigence that has the effect of discrediting the moderate fringe of the movement, which is in favour of reforms in exchange for international recognition, in order to develop the country.

The Taliban are not 'global jihadists' and have never aimed to spread their doctrine around the world. On the other hand, they support - more out of religious conviction than political or territorial ambition - the efforts of Islamist fighters in the region[42], especially in Jammu and Kashmir. The conflict then drains Islamist fighters from all over the world, settled in the 'tribal areas' on the

38. "Document - The unreleased interview with Usamah bin Laden - October 21st, 2001", *terrorism.net*, August 19, 2002

39. State Department Cable, "Osama Bin Laden: Taliban Spokesman Seeks New Proposal For Resolving Bin Laden Problem," November 23, 1998, (SECRET) (Number 5)

40. According to eyewitness accounts sent directly to the author.

41. The Taliban government has only been recognised by Saudi Arabia, the United Arab Emirates and Pakistan.

42. Report from the US Embassy in Islamabad to the State Department, October 22, 1998 (SECRET).

border between Afghanistan and Pakistan. These fighters, captured at the end of 2001, beginning of 2002 by the American special forces, constituted the first contingent of prisoners at Guantanamo; which the Americans had to free a few years later… after having transformed them into global jihadists!

In fact, the Taliban's efforts are absorbed by domestic problems and rivalries between local jihadist leaders:

> *The Taliban and Mullah Omar, in fact, have often defined themselves against other Afghan leaders whom they consider to represent radical pan-Islamic thought. The Taliban mocked these Muslims, who include Gulbuddin Hekmatyar and Abdul Rassoul Sayyaf, as "Ikhwanis[43]", their term for radical pan-Islamists[44].*

The American strikes of August 1998 brought the Taliban closer to the pan-Islamic jihadists around a defence of Islam[45], without however pushing them into the global jihad. On the other hand, they will create a feeling of injustice and cowardice that will lead to "9/11".

3.1.1 "The Taliban refuse to hand over Bin Laden[46]"

Since September 11, the names 'Al Qaeda' and Bin Laden have been on everyone's lips, but what concrete evidence was there to make this claim? In reality: none. To this day, his guilt remains speculative and there is no evidence to suggest that he was actually involved in the attacks, as we have seen.

After the June 1996 attack on the Khobar Towers in Saudi Arabia, OBL was expelled from Sudan under pressure from the United States. The first accusations against him were formulated on 10 June 1998, in a document that remained classified SECRET, and concerned his alleged involvement in the death of American soldiers in Somalia in 1993. He then took refuge in Afghanistan, in the Kandahar region, where he continued his fight against the American presence in Saudi Arabia and organised training camps for the fighters of Jammu-Kashmir. But his freedom of action is not total: in 1998, Mullah Omar, the Taliban leader, imposes on him not to undertake any terrorist act as a condition to stay in the country[47], and there is no indication that he has broken this agreement.

43. NdA: In this region, the term *Ikhwani* refers to followers of the *Muslim Brotherhood*.
44. Report of the American Embassy in Islamabad, *op. cit.*
45. Ibid.
46. "Les Taliban refuse to hand over Bin Laden", *L'Humanité*, 20 August 1998; Pascal Riche, "Bush declares war on the Taliban", *Libération*, September 22, 2001; Tensions and Conflicts: The War on Terrorism, Cycle 2, *Teacher's Guide*, École secondaire d'Anjou, Anjou, Québec (Canada)
47. Mark Matthews, "U.S. sets conditions for killing terrorist Cohen says bin Laden may be hit in line of fire", *The Baltimore Sun*, August 24, 1998

After the August 7, 1998 attacks on the American embassies in Dar es Salaam and Nairobi, the Americans became more pressing and asked for his extradition. However, there is no proof and the American accusation is based solely on suspicions, themselves based on his fatwa of February 1998. But in reality, we don't know anything about it: on a note concerning these attacks, President Bill Clinton scribbles to Sandy Berger, his National Security Advisor:

> *Sandy, if this article is correct, the CIA has certainly exaggerated the facts presented to me. What are the facts*[48]*?*

The Taliban's position is clear: they are ready to hand him over, but demand proof of his guilt[49]. The Americans provided evidence, but the Afghan High Court of Justice ruled that it did not prove his involvement and refused to hand him over. The Taliban then asked the Americans to make a "*constructive proposal*" to resolve the crisis[50]. But this request was never reported as such in the Western media and the Americans did not respond.

Yet the Taliban sought a solution. On February 21, 2001, they offered to extradite him to the United States in exchange for an agreement on the sanctions affecting the country, but for reasons that were never fully clarified, the US government refused.

After 9/11, the issue of OBL's extradition came up again and the Taliban envoy told the US chargé d'affaires in Islamabad that if the US provided evidence of his responsibility, the "*problem could be easily solved*[51]".

But in reality, the evidence of OBL's involvement is of little interest to the Americans, as they had already decided to intervene in Afghanistan long before '9/11'. On September 4, 2001, exactly one week before 9/11, the National Security Presidential Directive 9 (NSPD9)[52] was submitted to President George W. Bush for signature. Classified SECRET, it is entitled *Defeating the Terrorist Threat to the United States*[53], and in a TOP SECRET classified annex, it directs the Secretary of Defense to plan military options "*against Taliban targets in*

---

48. "*Sandy - If this article is right, the CIA sure overstated its case to me - what are the facts?*" quoted in David Martosko, "Bill Clinton doubted CIA's intelligence on Osama bin Laden After his own 1998 'Wag the Dog' cruise missile strikes in Afghanistan and Sudan", *Daily Mail*, July 19, 2014.

49. Brian Whitaker, "Taliban agreed Bin Laden handover in 1998", *The Guardian*, November 5, 2001

50. State Department Cable, 'Osama Bin Laden: Taliban Spokesman Seeks New Proposal For Resolving Bin Laden Problem', November 23, 1998, (SECRET) (Figures 6-10).

51. "Afghanistan: Taliban Refuses To Hand Over Bin Laden", *RFEL*, September 21, 2001; Alex Strick van Linschoten & Felix Kuehn, *An Enemy We Created: The Myth of the Taliban / Al-Qaeda Merger in Afghanistan, 1970-2010*, C Hurst & Co Publishers Ltd, January 18, 2012.

52. National Security Presidential Directive-9 (NSPD-9)

53. www.fas.org/irp/offdocs/nspd/nspd-9.pdf

Afghanistan, including leadership, command control, air defence, ground forces and logistics[54]". It was approved on October 25, 2001.

But the President must have the approval of Congress. To get around this problem, on September 14, 2001, Congress passed a Joint Resolution on the Authorisation for the Use of Military Force (AUMF), which stipulated that the President must have the approval of Congress...

> *That the President is authorized to use all necessary and appropriate force against those nations, organizations, or persons that he determines planned, authorized, committed, or aided the terrorist attacks of September 11, 2001, or harbored such organizations or persons, in order to prevent any future acts of international terrorism against the United States by such nations, organizations, or persons*[55].

It provides the legal basis for the 'perpetual wars' waged by the US since then, and explains why Iraq, Venezuela and Iran will later be accused of supporting international terrorism...

On 7 October, with US forces ready to strike, the Afghan government offers to try OBL, but President Bush refuses the offer[56] and launches bombing raids which, even at this stage, affect the civilian population. A week later, the Afghan deputy prime minister, Haji Abdul Kabir, confirmed that the Taliban were ready to hand over OBL, if proof of his "involvement" (not even his "responsibility") was provided and in exchange for a halt to the bombing. This position is also relayed by the Taliban ambassador to Pakistan[57] ; but the Americans refuse to enter into it[58]. The *Independent* newspaper even states that the US President "*peremptorily refused to provide evidence that Mr Bin Laden was behind the September 11 attacks*[59]"; probably simply because at that stage - as up to now - such evidence did not exist.

In fact, the Americans provided them with a file[60], a copy of which was sent to Tony Blair. On 4 October 2001, the British government published a 70-point summary for Parliament. The press saw it as a tissue of "*conjectures, suppositions and assertions of fact*[61]" and "*almost worthless from a legal point of view*[62]": the accusations are essentially speculations on the 1998 attacks and very few concern

54. www.fas.org/irp/offdocs/nspd/nspd-9.htm
55. *2001 Authorization for Use of Military Force (AUMF)*, S.J.Res 23(107th), September 14, 2001
56. "U.S. rejects Taliban offer to try bin Laden", *CNN.com*, October 7, 2001
57. Mullah Abdul Salaam Zaeef, Taliban Ambassador to Pakistan, *Times*, September 22, 2001
58. "Bush rejects Taliban offer to hand Bin Laden over", *The Guardian*, October 14, 2001 ;
59. *The Independent*, September 22, 2001, p. 1.
60. "White House warns Taliban: 'We will defeat you', *CNN*, September 21, 2001
61. *The Independent*, October 7, 2001, p. 7.
62. *The Guardian*, October 5, 2001, p. 23.

"9/11". One can read, for example, that Bin Laden was involved in drug trafficking (which was never the case, either closely or remotely); this will serve as a pretext for Tony Blair to intervene in Afghanistan.

On October 16, 2001, the Taliban once again proposed to the US government to extradite OBL, without even demanding proof of his involvement, in exchange for a halt to the bombings affecting the civilian population[63]. But once again, the American government refused.

3.1.2. A poorly defined enemy and objectives

In 2019, after 18 years of war, some 17,000 troops still deployed for Nato's RESOLUTE SUPPORT mission, billions of dollars spent, nearly 200,000 dead and an equal number seriously wounded, and millions displaced[64], little thought has been given to why the West intervened in Afghanistan. The Americans, and then Nato, through their total lack of understanding of the theatre of war and their negligence, created the conditions for the development of a jihadism that did not exist before 2001.

No foreign power has been able to control Afghanistan. However, close examination shows that the Soviets were able to maintain greater operational coherence[65] than Nato[66]. They retained control of politically and economically important areas of the country, and 'abandoned' others. Conversely, Nato was unable to prioritise its engagement and even alienated areas that were more favourable to it. You can't embrace too much. In 1987, the CIA estimated the cost of Soviet involvement at $50 million, or 75% of what the Americans had spent on Vietnam[67]. After 16 years of war, the US has spent about $1 trillion - 200 times more - not to mention the human cost, for a defeat it cannot manage[68].

On September 7, 2019, Donald Trump announces that he is ending the negotiations with the Taliban that had been going on since 2018 and which seemed to be on the verge of an agreement. He justifies this by accusing the Taliban of wanting to increase the pressure on the United States with an attack two days earlier[69]. But what he does not say is that between April and September 2019, US strikes increased by more than 50 per cent, reaching their highest level since October 2010[70]. In fact, Trump is applying the same "strategy" as

63. Rory McCarthy, 'New offer on Bin Laden', *The Guardian,* October 17, 2001.
64. Neta C. Crawford, *Update on the Human Costs of War for Afghanistan and Pakistan,* 2001 to mid-2016, Boston University, August 2016
65. "The Afghan War (1979-1989): The Soviet invasion", *Tactical Survey,* November 13, 2010
66. Dawood Azami, "Why Afghanistan is more dangerous than ever", *BBC News,* September 14, 2018
67. "The Cost of Soviet Involvement in Afghanistan", *Intelligence Directorate, CIA,* February 1987
68. Neta C. Crawford, *United States Budgetary Costs of the Post-9/11 Wars Through FY2019: $5.9 Trillion Spent and Obligated,* Watson Institute, Brown University, November 14, 2018
69. "Afghanistan: Trump ends talks with Taliban", *AFP,* September 8, 2019
70. Jessica Purkiss, 'US strikes in Afghanistan rose by half before Taliban peace talks collapsed', *The Bureau of Investigative Journalism,* September 11, 2019; Gareth Jennings, 'US records highest airstrike rate in Afghanistan for a

with Iran: put the adversary under maximum pressure in order to force him to negotiate. A method dear to mafias.

On December 9, 2019, the *Washington Post* publishes around 2,000 pages of declassified documents on the war in Afghanistan. This is a file compiled as part of a feedback project by the Special Inspector General for Afghanistan Reconstruction (SIGAR), which confirms two things. The first is that, as early as 2001, the United States had no idea why it was fighting this war, what its enemy was and what its objective was. In February 2015, Lieutenant General Douglas Lute, the White House 'Afghanistan Czar', admitted in 2015 about the war in Afghanistan:

> *We had no idea what we were doing*[71].

The second is that the American military and political leaders have lied to their people and their parliamentary representatives for 18 years[72]. But the Americans are not the only ones: the other countries involved on their side have also lied to their public opinions! But the French press did not even notice it. Behind the 'good work' of the contingents lies a total lack of strategy and objective: soldiers died for nothing, in the literal sense of the term. The same thing is happening in the Sahel today. We have learned nothing: the staffs, parliaments and public opinion have failed miserably for lack of critical thinking and analysis and continue to do so…

3.2 "Darfur: A genocide of 300,000 Victims[73]"

3.2.1. The context

In 2005-2006, the author was head of the Joint Mission Analysis Center *(JMAC) of the* United Nations Mission in Sudan (UNMIS), the first (and largest) civilian-military strategic intelligence structure in a UN peacekeeping mission. Although Darfur was not part of the UNMIS mandate, it was the responsibility of the Special Representative of the Secretary General, who was responsible for coordinating UN activities in the country.

---

decade', *Jane's Defence Weekly*, January 27, 2020

71. *Interview with Ambassador Douglas Lute, NATO Permanent Rep, former Director Iraq/ Afghanistan, NSC 2007-2014*, Office of the Special Inspector General for Afghanistan Reconstruction, February 20, 2015

72. Jeff Schogol, "US government officials are encouraged to lie about progress in Afghanistan, special inspector general says", *Task & Purpose*, January 15, 2020

73. "Darfur: a genocide of 300,000 victims", *Euronews*, February 18, 2015

The Darfur crisis illustrates both one of humanity's oldest causes of war and a conflict linked to global warming. For many years, the Sahara has been expanding southwards, severely affecting the fragile Sahel zone: between the late 1970s and the early 2000s, the desert advanced by almost 200 kilometres in Darfur. It has gradually covered the territory of nomadic pastoralist tribes - in particular the Zaghawa and Jimir - pushing them into the lands of sedentary farming tribes, including the Four ("Dar Four").

This slow, one-way migration should not be confused with the seasonal migrations of herders moving their herds from north to south and vice versa according to the seasons. The latter are also a source of contention, but are effectively managed by traditional mechanisms, which define and allocate transhumance routes.

In Sudan, as in many Muslim countries, land does not belong to anyone. The allocation and use of land is governed by traditional mechanisms, specific to each tribe, according to sometimes complex rules, called *hawakir* or *hakura*. However, the arrival of new populations in areas where natural resources are scarce has disrupted these rules, leading to violent clashes that are at the root of the Darfur conflict.

From the 1990s onwards, in order to calm the situation and bring about a lasting solution, the government in Khartoum tried to redefine the mechanisms of land allocation and to impose a uniform method throughout Darfur. But this 'intervention' by the central government infringes on tribal prerogatives and provokes violent reactions: it is interpreted as a marginalisation of local authorities, and some tribes are protesting against the new rules that give newcomers the same rights as indigenous populations. International and development organisations will interpret the crisis in a 'Western' way and accuse Khartoum of abandoning Darfur, when the opposite is true...

The Sudanese government soon found itself isolated between those who wanted compensation for their lost land and those who refused to change the traditional hawakir. In 2002, Abdul Wahed Mohammed Nour brought these two sources of discontent together and created the Darfur Liberation Movement (DLM).

This is the beginning of the politicisation of the conflict in Darfur. It is not accidental and coincides with the adoption of a new strategy by John Garang, leader of the Sudan's People Liberation Movement/Army *(SPLM/A)* in Southern Sudan. The strategy is to 'encircle' the government in Khartoum, creating insurgent pockets in all parts of the country to force it to negotiate. It threatens Khartoum from the East with its New Sudan Brigade (NSB), stationed in Eritrea. From 2001, with US support, it joined forces with the MLD (which became the Sudan Liberation Movement - SLM - in 2003) and began arming the Darfur rebels to create a threat in the West. Contrary to popular belief, John

Garang was not in favour of southern independence, but for 'one country and two nations', overthrowing the Sudanese government. It was only later, after his death and the advent of Salva Kiir, that the separatist tendency took over in Southern Sudan.

In addition to the tribal tensions between farmers and pastoralists, there are 'raids' by Chadian and Libyan groups. Known as '*cattle raiders*', they carry out raids over several hundred kilometres to seize entire herds and sell them in Chad. Well organised and well armed, they do not hesitate to attack the army. Boko Haram, which appeared much later in Nigeria, is the Islamist variant of the same phenomenon, which can be found throughout the Sahel.

Darfur is about the size of France and has an estimated population of about 6 million people, mostly in small, scattered villages. There is no evidence to support the claim that the government is trying to eliminate its population. A close look at the violence shows attacks on individuals, families, even parts of villages or small hamlets, but hardly ever on entire tribes or ethnic groups.

Until 2002, the clashes in Darfur were seen as a local phenomenon. But after 9/11, the Americans thought that the Sahel had become a favourite hideout for jihadists. They set up the Trans Sahara Counterterrorism Initiative (TSCTI)[74] which includes most of the Sahel countries[75], where special forces are deployed under the leadership of Special Operations Command Europe *(SOCEUR)*; and the Combined Joint Task Force - Horn of Africa (CJTF-HOA), based in Djibouti under the authority of the Central Command (CENTCOM), to cover North-East Africa. Their only shadow is Sudan. In the 1990s, it had hosted OBL - then in disgrace - and the Americans were convinced that it was the weak point of their system. It is therefore necessary to put pressure on it to accept the deployment of a military force in Darfur. Accusations and fanciful figures on crimes and massacres in Darfur are multiplying.

But after Iraq and Afghanistan, the Sudanese government fears that a peacekeeping mission in Darfur is a prelude to an operation to overthrow it. In 2004, however, it agreed to the deployment of an African Union peacekeeping mission (AMIS) in Darfur. It is funded by the European Union, while NATO provides logistical support and deploys intelligence elements. From the beginning of 2005, American special forces operated clandestinely on Sudanese territory in the Darfur region in order to detect possible Islamist groups… and found nothing.

---

74. The TSCTI was then developed on the basis of a smaller initiative, the *Pan Sahel Initiative (PSI)*, which was reportedly initiated in November 2002, but whose implementation was accelerated by the GSPC's action.
75. Namely the PSI countries: Mali, Mauritania, Niger and Chad, plus Algeria, Morocco, Tunisia, Senegal, Ghana and Nigeria.

3.2.2. The "Janjaweed" Militias

Accusations against the Sudanese government invariably refer to the 'Janjaweed' militia. But here again, ignorance meets misinformation.

During the 1980s and 1990s, the Sudanese army was at war in the south of the country, and had no forces to respond to the tribal violence in Darfur. The government adopted the same strategy as the British and French in Africa and Asia: it armed the tribes it could rely on. Unfortunately, it did not establish sufficient mechanisms to manage and co-ordinate these militias, and they gradually slipped out of its control to conduct completely independent tribal operations. These militias are known as *Murahalin* in Bahr el-Ghazal, *Shahama* in Abyei and *Janjaweed* in Darfur.

In 1989, in order to regain control of the situation, the government created the Popular Defence Forces (PDF): territorial units composed of locally recruited soldiers, armed, equipped and trained by the army. Poorly equipped, lacking heavy equipment and with very little mobility, the PDFs played an essentially defensive and local role, while the dynamic dimension of maintaining order was devolved to the troops of the Ministry of the Interior.

The term 'Janjaweed' is typically Darfurian and refers to a bandit. While in the West it is associated with government militias, in common parlance it refers to anyone who carries a weapon (including Chadian rebels who take refuge in Sudanese territory). In fact, the cross-checking of testimonies shows that it refers primarily to organised gangs ('cattle raiders') and independent tribal militias, but also to the rebel movements themselves.

Furthermore, precise and confirmed information indicates that since at least March 2005, the Sudanese government has ceased all support to the tribal militias. So much so that in 2005, there were numerous clashes between "Janjaweed" militias and Sudanese security forces, including a siege of its garrison in El-Geneina that lasted several days.

3.2.3. Chemical Weapons

In 2016, Amnesty International (AI) published a report accusing the Sudanese army of using chemical weapons against rebels in the Jebel Marra region[76]. This type of accusation has reappeared regularly since the late 1990s, but none of the verification missions sent to the area have been able to confirm it[77].

The Amnesty report raises many questions and the German government has expressed doubts about its relevance: the small number of rebels in Darfur does not seem to require the use of such extreme means and the small number of

76. *Scorched Earth: Poisoned Air - Sudanese Government Forces Ravage, Jebel Marra, Darfur*, Amnesty International, 2016

77. *Reporting on Conflict in Darfur: The Importance of Access, Research and Evidence*, Chatham House, October 28, 2016

'witnesses' tends to reinforce these doubts. Furthermore, the UN Mission in Darfur (UNAMID) claims that it has not seen the use of chemical weapons and that no victims have been treated in its hospitals[78].

Moreover, the photos of the victims show symptoms that can be explained by common ailments in the region[79]; as for the combination of horse attacks and chemical bombing[80], it seems surreal to say the least!

Apart from the fact that no evidence was found on the ground, it is not clear why such weapons would have been used in Darfur in 2016, when they are known to be a justification for international interventions, and when the Sudanese armed forces have not used them in considerably larger battles in the south of the country.

In reality, we find here the same phenomenon as in Syria: the attempt by some to provoke a Western military intervention.

3.2.4. The War of Numbers

Due to the size of the country, low operational mobility and small numbers, Sudanese forces are unable to control a situation that is considered an internal security problem. As a result, the 12,000 regular army personnel stationed in Darfur are only rarely engaged. Counter-insurgency operations are normally carried out by internal security forces. However, the ISAF - while seemingly large - are grossly under-equipped with weapons and transport, and are not configured to fight an insurgency. They are clustered in the main towns of Darfur (El-Fasher, Nyala and El-Geneina) and patrol the main roads (between these three towns) without robust means to operate in the intervening area.

The massive 'bombing' of populations by 'Antonovs' reported by refugees and the press at the time was often spurious. In 2005, the Sudanese air force had five Antonov-24s *and* Antonov-26s for transport, which were not equipped to drop bombs and which were already widely used to ensure the logistics of its military garrisons spread over 2.5 million km2 and in regions that can often only be reached by air. By comparison, the United Nations has a fleet of more than 50 aircraft to provide logistics for UNMIS (about 30,000 people) in the same area. A review of the reported incidents and observations on the ground do not confirm the use of these aircraft to bomb civilian populations. In fact, the word "Antonov" is used for anything that flies, including Mi-24 (or more rarely Mi-8) helicopters equipped with rockets, used to fight armed groups.

Unguided air-to-surface rockets are usually the most frequently misfired munitions. However, field surveys conducted by international demining experts

---

78. Dagmar Dehmer, "Berlin questions authenticity of claims Sudan used chemical weapons", *Der Tagesspiegel*, November 2, 2016

79. JP Zanders, "Allegation of chemical warfare in Darfur", *the-trench.org*, February 1st, 2017

80. http://darfurconflict2016.amnesty.org/report/7

commissioned by the UN in 2006 and 2007 found that the most common munitions remnants encountered in Darfur in combat areas are RPG-7 hand grenades and anti-tank grenades. In some areas, remnants of surface-to-air rockets are found. As for the remains of aerial bombs, the teams sent to the battle sites in early 2006 by the UN found none!

All this does not prove anything, but it does cast serious doubt on Western accusations of genocide and systematic destruction of the population…

That said, after the Western intervention in Libya, the security landscape of the region is profoundly altered: weapons recovered from both sides (including those supplied by European countries despite the UN embargo) find their way into northern Sudan/Darfur and fuel tribal conflicts from the borders of Chad to central Darfur.

Claims that the government is trying to '*Arabise*[81]' Darfur are simply not true. First of all, the government has never claimed such a policy and it is not clear what its objective could be. Even the North-South conflict, which is often presented as a religious war between Islamists and Christians/animists, was tribal in nature. This is why it persists after the independence of Southern Sudan. In Darfur, the populations of Arab and African origin have become closely intermingled over time and it is virtually impossible to differentiate between them. In religious terms, unlike in Southern Sudan, the population is homogeneous and almost exclusively Muslim. In reality, the clashes are between Arabs, non-Arabs, farmers and herders in all possible combinations. It is this diversity of 'conflicts' that is the source of the problem:

a) Contrary to a widely held view in the West, most violence is tribal or criminal in nature. The number of "political" movements remains very marginal. The number of "political" movements remains very marginal: 3-4 in 2005, they are 27 in 2007 due to splits: undermined by internal rivalries and quarrels, they do not constitute a real threat to the government. Moreover, they do not demand independence, but greater regional autonomy.

b) The government in Khartoum has never really equipped itself with the means to fight unrest that is endemic in this part of the world. It has limited itself to treating the issue as a domestic problem, relying on traditional tribal rivalries, without any real counter-insurgency strategy or adequate leadership structures.

Stigmatised by many NGOs and the US administration, the 'systematic massacre' of the Darfur population by the Sudanese government, like what happened in Rwanda ten years earlier, has not been confirmed by the facts. The number of studies carried out on mortality in Darfur testifies to the unease that reigns around the figures.

---

81. Pawan Haulkory, "Political Islam and Arabization of Sudan as the source of conflict", *wordpress.clarku.edu/id252-sudan/*, November 4, 2014

At the outset of the Darfur crisis, the UN Office for the Coordination of Humanitarian Affairs (OCHA) mentioned the figure of 180,000 dead[82]. By early 2005, when the UN mission was established, the most common estimate was 200,000 dead. During this period, when the author had a very good overview of the situation and collaborated with the main Western intelligence services, no major clashes took place and humanitarian access was generally good. However, in 2008, Jan Egeland, the then OCHA coordinator, stated that 400,000 was closer to the reality[83]. However, ten years later, the figure most often put forward is 300,000 dead, while remaining purely speculative. Despite numerous rumours and the claims of some humanitarian NGOs, no mass graves, mass graves or evidence of massacres on this scale have been found[84].

In fact, these figures are derived from statistical estimates and projections based on unverified and unverifiable testimony. But this does not prevent the international community from accusing the Sudanese government of 'genocide'. To justify this accusation, two notions are played on alternately: mortality due to the *consequences of violence* (lack of hygiene, lack of water and food, etc.) and mortality due to the *acts of violence* themselves. In fact, they are mixed. In addition, the role of local armed actors is deliberately minimised in order to attribute their violence to the government.

Between early 2005 and mid-2006, at the request of the head of UNMIS, the mission's intelligence unit (JMAC) carried out four studies on violent mortality in Darfur. All available sources are used: international (such as WHO and ICRC) and non-governmental organisations, the African Union mission (AMIS), the UN security service (UN DSS), Sudanese security services, Western intelligence services and the rebel groups themselves. In most cases, there are photographic documents or detailed reports (police, medical, military, and/or human rights bodies). The results are surprising:

Period	Number of deaths1 (See bibliography)
June 2004 - March 2005	400
April 2005 - July 2005	1,200
August 2005 - January 2006	500
February 2006 - July 2006	400
Total (June 2004 - July 2006)	2500

Table 2- Victims of violence in Darfur (2004-2006)

82. Eric Reeves, *DARFUR MORTALITY UPDATE: June 30, 2005*, August 30, 2005
83. "Death toll of 200,000 disputed in Darfur", *Associated Press/NBCNews.com*, March 28, 2008
84. Rebecca Hamilton & Mary Beth Sheridan, "U.S. Government Cannot Confirm Mass Graves in Sudan", *The Washington Post*, July 21, 2011

These figures are probably still too high, but they include *all* forms of violence, from simple crime to tribal skirmishes. In the same order of magnitude as those periodically reported to the Security Council[85], they are very far from those proclaimed by the Western media... But the reports will be buried... and at the end of 2006, there is talk of 400,000 deaths[86]. We went from 200,000 to 400,000 deaths in a year and a half. Where do they come from? No answer!

As for the burnt hamlets, widely reported in the press, internal information from OCHA in Sudan in 2005 shows that it is the displaced people, attracted by better living conditions in the UN displacement camps, who burn their huts themselves by "inventing" attacks, so as not to be turned away by aid organisations.

On 11 April 2019, on *France 24*, columnist Gauthier Rybinski literally creates a fable around the situation in Darfur and oil. Claiming that in addition to the 300,000 killed, President Omar Bashir has sought to prevent the survivors from surviving by poisoning water wells. He also claims that the government has deliberately abandoned people living in oil-free areas[87]. Why and for what purpose? This is simply not true: it is an assembly of scattered and unverified information into a conspiracy-like construct. Moreover, he does not fail to point out that Sudan has been one of the sponsors of international terrorism, as it hosted the terrorist Carlos between 1991 and 1994. An accusation that would be just as relevant for France, which has been harbouring Italian terrorists from the 1960s-1980s for almost 50 years[88].

As we will see later in the case of Syria, the accusation of genocide in Darfur is based entirely on the assumption that the Sudanese government is trying to eliminate part of its population... For what reasons? Why now and not before? No one can say! Some have suggested that oil is the reason, but until 2007[89], the epicentre of the violence was in the west and north of Darfur, while the oil-producing areas are in the south-east.

In reality, the problems in Darfur are due more to the impotence of the Sudanese government than to the opposite. Its good faith has been systematically rejected by a West locked in a logic of fighting Islamism. Today, a plethora of humanitarian aid has drawn the people of Darfur into refugee camps (exactly

85. See "UN Documents for Sudan (Darfur): Secretary-General's Reports" (www.securitycouncilreport.org)
86. *DARFUR CRISIS - Death Estimates Demonstrate Severity of Crisis, but Their Accuracy and Credibility Could Be Enhanced*, Report to Congressional Requesters, United States Government Accountability Office, November 2006 (GAO-07-24)
87. Le Journal de 12 heures, *France 24*, April 11, 2019
88. Thibaut Cavaillès, "Salvini wants to hunt down Italian 'terrorists' who have found refuge in France", *France Inter*, January 14, 2019; Matthieu Lasserre, "Les terroristes des années de plomb, pommes de discorde dans les relations Italie-France", *La Croix*, 12 February 2019; Aude Le Gentil, "Qui sont les anciens terroristes italiens vivant en France et que Rome veut extrader?", *Le Journal du Dimanche*, February 13, 2019.
89. NdA: From 2007-2008, the border issue between Kordofan and Bahr el-Gazal will be a new source of conflict and violent clashes between tribes.

as in Chad 25 years ago), creating a population that is completely dependent on international aid, where local crafts and agricultural know-how have totally disappeared. From a habitat of small scattered hamlets, the population has gathered in camps of several thousand people where food is distributed by the international community and then sold, giving rise to flourishing trafficking.

By analysing the issue on the basis of prejudices and the "tourist reports" of philosophers and film actors, we have created lasting problems without reducing violence. On the contrary: by creating a mercantile economy in the IDP camps, where money circulates more, we have *ipso facto* encouraged the development of organised crime. This has resulted in a loss of influence of traditional tribal crisis management mechanisms. All this was visible - and predictable - already in 2005...

3.3 Conclusions for Western interventions

Built on lies, the war in Iraq is a disaster. Not only is it criminal, but it has been conducted in a stupid way from the start: it has only strengthened the United States' main enemy, Iran. In 2019, a 1,300-page study by the US Army commissioned by General Ray Odierno, former Chief of Staff of the Army, concludes:

> *By the time this project is completed in 2018, an emboldened and expansionist Iran appears to be the only winner*[90].

Darfur is an example of a crisis that the international community - and in particular the humanitarian organisations - has literally created, under pressure from the United States. The problem is that our lies have completely inhibited our ability to learn from the past. For example, Bernard-Henri Lévy's 'report' on the situation in northern Nigeria, published in *Paris Match* in December 2019, reveals exactly the same lack of understanding as for Darfur. His 'conclusions' are severely criticised[91]. They are based on a simplistic analysis of events, which seems logical for someone who moves seamlessly and very temporarily from Parisian salons to African realities like a tourist[92], but insufficient to address the problem.

---

90. Todd South, "Army's long-awaited Iraq war study finds Iran was the only winner in a conflict that holds many lessons for future wars", *Army Times*, January 18, 2019
91. "Au Nigeria, on massacre les chrétiens", le SOS de Bernard-Henri Lévy", *Paris Match*, December 5, 2019
92. "TRUE OR FAKE Violences in central Nigeria: Bernard-Henri Lévy's analysis contested by specialists", *TV-5MONDE*, January 17, 2020

The author has seen first-hand in NATO and Afghanistan that Americans - and a fortiori Westerners - are simply not intellectually, culturally and doctrinally prepared to understand a different way of waging war than their own. Limited general knowledge and poor quality senior officers explain why their military successes are only tactical and rarely strategic, and achieved at considerable human and material cost. All Western interventions have followed the same pattern of disinformation. In order to convince the public, the data of the problem has been truncated. Inappropriate solutions have therefore been found.

The failures in Afghanistan[93], Iraq[94], Libya[95], Syria[96] and in the fight against terrorism were perfectly predictable and are largely due to Western intellectual rigidity.

93. Craig Whitlock, 'At war with the truth', *The Washington Post*, December 9, 2019; R. D. Ward, 'Lies, Damned Lies, and Statistics: The Politics of the Afghanistan Papers', *War on the Rocks*, December 18, 2019; Thomas Gibbons-Neff, 'The Lies the Generals Told About Afghanistan', *The New York Times*, December 20, 2019

94. Jared Keller, "America Lost the Iraq War. These Cables Show How," *The New Republic*, November 25, 2019

95. Alan Kuperman, "Lessons from Libya: How Not to Intervene", *Belfer Center*, September 2013; Emadeddin Zahri Muntasser & Dr Mohamed Fouad, "How the West and the UN Failed Libya", *Atlantic Council*, July 3, 2018

96. Deirdre Shesgreen, 'Trump's troop withdrawal caps failed US policy in Syria, experts say', *USA Today*, December 16, 2019

4. IRAN

4.1. The context

Iran is a country traditionally sympathetic to the West. Ethnically distinct from the Arabs, its population is strongly influenced by Indian culture and practices a less strict Shiite Islam than the Sunni Islam of Saudi Arabia. Iran has no tradition of warlike expansion and has not attacked any country since 1798.

After the overthrow of Prime Minister Mohammad Mossadegh in 1953 by a joint operation of the British MI-6 and the American CIA (Operation AJAX), and until the beginning of the 1980s, Iran was the main ally of Israel and the West in the region. As a country bordering the Soviet Union, it was an essential part of the United States' apparatus, both for its regional policy and its intelligence capabilities. Despite this, Iran maintained a non-aligned security policy: its armaments came in equal parts from Eastern and Western countries: Soviet T-72 tanks rubbed shoulders with British Chieftain tanks[97].

From 1976, the priority of the Carter government on human rights issues pushed the Shah to diversify his alliances and to increase his military cooperation with Israel. Documents seized from the American embassy in Tehran in 1979 even revealed that Israel was planning to sell a nuclear missile to Iran (Operation TZOR)[98].

In 1979, the arrival of Khomeini in power did not erase 25 years of military and intelligence cooperation with Israel. Iran had suffered a war provoked by Iraq and chemical attacks carried out with the blessing of the United States[99]: Israel was then a precious ally "on the back" of the Arab countries. For its part, Israel sees Iran as a kind of "strategic counterweight" to Arab pressure and supports it. In particular, it struck the Tuwaitha research centre near Baghdad

97. See, for example, *The Military Balance 1990-1991*, International Institute for Strategic Studies, London, Autumn 1990

98. Ronen Bergman, *The Secret War with Iran*, Oneworld, Oxford, 2008 (p. 5)

99. Shane Harris & Matthew M. Aid, "Exclusive: CIA Files Prove America Helped Saddam as He Gassed Iran", *Foreign Policy*, August 26, 2013.

(September 30, 1980), then the Iraqi nuclear power station of Osirak (June 7, 1981). At that time, Israel's enemy was Iraq, which had been hosting several Palestinian movements since the mid-1970s.

The negotiations for the release of the 52 hostages of the American embassy in Tehran lead to the Algiers agreements of January 19, 1981, which stipulate, among other things, that:

> *The United States pledges that from now on its policy will be not to intervene, directly or indirectly, politically or militarily, in Iran's internal affairs*[100].

... a commitment that the Americans will never honour.

A few months later, in order to finance the Nicaraguan Contras, President Reagan secretly authorised the sale of arms to Iran. This was the beginning of 'Irangate', in which Israel played a central role by discreetly delivering arms to Iran. But Israel will 'double-cross' the US by supplying Iran with unapproved weapons. This prompted the Americans to launch Operation STAUNCH in the spring of 1983 to stop the arms deliveries.

On 3 July 1988, the Airbus of Iran Air Flight 655 was shot down by a sea-to-air missile fired by the US cruiser USS Vincennes, killing 290 people, including 66 children. Later investigations by the International Civil Aviation Organization (ICAO) and the US Navy confirmed that the cruiser was in Iranian territorial waters and had detected a civilian aircraft in the process of climbing. After initially denying and then lying that the USS Vincennes was in international waters and that the Airbus was in a dive against the ship, the US government justified the shooting as a "mistake". But this too was a lie: Captain William C. Rogers III had convinced himself that he was under attack by an Iranian F-14[101]! At the end of the engagement, the ship's crew was awarded the *Combat Action Ribbon for* "*active participation in combat actions*", while the officer in charge of coordinating the aerial combat was awarded the *Navy Commendation Medal* for "*repeated heroic or meritorious acts*"[102]! Finally, international justice[103] condemns the United States to compensate the families of the victims and to apologise. But President George H. Bush (Sr.) says:

100. *Algiers Accords - Declaration of the Government of the Democratic and Popular Republic of Algeria*, January 19, 1981, para 1

101. Jeremy R. Hammond, "The 'Forgotten'US Shootdown of Iranian Airliner Flight 655", *Foreign Policy Journal*, July 3, 2017

102. See Wikipedia article "Iran Air Flight 655

103. John F. Burns, 'World Aviation Panel Faults U.S. Navy on Downing of Iran Air', *The New York Times*, December 4, 1988

I will never apologise for the United States of America. I will never do that. I don't care about the facts[104].

... which the Western media will fail to recall after the tragedy of Ukraine Airlines Flight 752 in January 2020[105].

Since the end of the Cold War, Iran has tried to improve its relations with the West. Its neutrality during the first Gulf War (1990-91) was a key to the success of the international coalition. In this changing geostrategic balance, Iran took advantage of the opportunity to reach out to the Europeans, but under American pressure, they did not seize it.

After 9/11, the government of President Mohammed Khatami expressed its condolences to the American people and supported the American intervention in Afghanistan. After the Taliban assassination of nine Iranian diplomats in 1998, tensions between the two countries had increased and Iran provided significant intelligence support to the Americans in the early days of Operation ENDURING FREEDOM. Iran also funded and trained Ahmed Shah Massoud's Northern Alliance, which overthrew the Taliban and seized power in Kabul on November 14, 2001. In December 2001, at the Bonn conference, the American negotiator James Dobbins thanked Iran for having convinced its Afghan allies to join the coalition of national unity[106]... But one month later, on January 29, 2002, during his State of the Union speech, the American President, as a thank you, included Iran in the "axis of evil"!

As early as 2001, it was Western mistakes and lack of strategic vision that gave Iran its role as a regional power, as confirmed by former Israeli Foreign Minister Shlomo Ben-Ami:

Iran supported the US in the first Gulf War, but was left out of the Madrid conference. Iran also sided with the US administration in the war against the Taliban in Afghanistan. And when US forces routed Saddam Hussein's army in the spring of 2003, the defensive Iranians proposed a "comprehensive pact" that would put all points of contention on the table, from the nuclear issue to Israel, from Hezbollah to Hamas. The Iranians also pledged to stop obstructing the Arab-Israeli peace process. But American neo-conservative arrogance - "We don't talk to the axis of evil" - prevented a pragmatic response to the Iranian approach[107].

104. "When America Apologizes (or Doesn't) for Its Actions", *The New York Times*, December 6, 2011
105. For example: "19 h 30", RTBF, January 11, 2020
106. Arshad Mohammed, "U.S., Iran have history of contact since cutting ties", *Reuters*, March 10, 2007
107. Shlomo Ben-Ami, former Israeli Foreign Minister, *Le Figaro*, September 19, 2007.

By intervening in Iraq in 2003, with the support of the country's Shiite majority, American strategists did not understand that they were creating a continuous axis between Iran and Lebanon, which they reinforced by isolating Syria after 2005. They thus generated a feeling of encirclement among the Gulf monarchies, as evidenced by a SECRET message from the American embassy in Ryadh, dated March 22, 2009[108]. This is what will later push Saudi Arabia and Qatar to reassert Sunni influence through the revolutions, which affected secular Arab countries. The West perceived them as democratic outbursts, whereas they were essentially a defensive reaction of the Gulf monarchies that felt threatened. This is all the more true since most of their oil wealth is located in areas where their Shiite minorities are in the majority.

In the early 2000s, relations between Iran and Israel changed radically. The Hebrew state sees American support as a sine qua non condition for its survival. However, this support is a function of the threats it faces. With the disappearance of Iraq as the main threat, Israel aligns itself with its protector and adopts Iran as its "favourite enemy". Its paranoia was unfounded in the case of Iraq, and it is just as unfounded today with regard to Iran.

Iran is in the crosshairs of the United States, which wants to impose regime change on it[109]. On April 21, 2004, President George Bush declared that he would "*deal with Iran*[110]". This led Iran to announce in February 2005 that it was starting preparations to fight a possible US aggression. According to Philip Giraldi, a former CIA official, the Americans then had a plan for a nuclear and conventional attack, with 450 targets to be destroyed in Iran[111]. This uninformed policy created a spiral of tension. Despite the opposition to the mullahs' regime, national unity strengthened in favour of the "hardliners" and to the detriment of the reformers: Mahmoud Ahmadinejad thus became president on August 3, 2005.

In 2006, the United States began its subversion operations in Syria with a view to regime change. For Tehran, Syria is a kind of last bastion, the only ally in the region capable of avoiding a strategic encirclement: the Damascus-Tehran axis is strengthened.

In 2007, President George W. Bush signed an executive order authorising clandestine operations in Iran[112], and Congress voted $400 million to bring about regime change[113]. These operations are based on the Iranian Baluchi and Ahwazi separatist movements, as well as other dissident organisations, and include active

---

108. *Saudi Intelligence Chief Talks Regional Security With Brennan Delegation*, March 22, 2009 (https://wikileaks.org/plusd/cables/09RIYADH445_a.html)

109. "Sharon says U.S. should also disarm Iran, Libya and Syria", *Haaretz*, September 30, 2004.

110. Mike Allen, 'Iran 'Will Be Dealt With,' Bush Says', *The Washington Post*, April 22, 2004.

111. Philip Giraldi, "Deep Background," *The American Conservative*, August 1st, 2005.

112. Brian Ross & Richard Esposito, "Bush Authorizes New Covert Action Against Iran", *ABC News*, May 23, 2007

113. Seymour M. Hersh, "Preparing the Battlefield", *The New Yorker*, June 29, 2008

support (delivery of arms and equipment, training of troops, etc.) to terrorist movements. This is the case of the Free Life Party of Kurdistan (PJAK) (on the Treasury Department's list of terrorist movements since February 4, 2009[114]) or the *Modjahedin-e-Khalq* (MeK), which was responsible for the death of Americans in the 1970s (on the State Department's list of terrorist movements since August 10, 1997[115]) and is cited as an example of Iraq's collusion with terrorism[116]! These operations coincide with an upsurge in terrorist attacks in Iran (notably in Ahvaz on June 12 and October 15, 2005 and on January 24, 2006), including the assassination of Iranian scientists, for which the Iranian government has confirmed the responsibility of the United States and Britain[117].

After Ayatollah Khomeini came to power (which they had failed to anticipate), the United States set out to convince Western public opinion that Iranian power was irrational and hegemonic. This justified the application of sanctions that kept adding up, until they became a kind of sterile "background noise" that the Iranians learned to circumvent on a daily basis.

4.2 "Iran is the most dangerous country in the world and in fact much more dangerous than the Islamic State[118]"

4.2.1. Does Iran want to destroy Israel?

A widely spread urban legend maintained by Western propaganda[119] and Israel is that Iran seeks to "*destroy Israel*". It began on October 26, 2005, when President Mahmoud Ahmadinejad quoted the Ayatollah Khomeini at a conference entitled "A World Without Zionism":

> *As the Imam said, the regime that occupies Jerusalem must be erased from the page of history*[120].

But the sentence is mistranslated by the translation service of the Iranian News Agency (IRNA), and becomes:

---

114. "U.S. brands anti-Iran Kurdish group terrorist", *Reuters*, February 4, 2009

115. *Foreign Terrorist Organizations*, Bureau of Counterterrorism, US Department of State (http://www.state.gov/j/ct/rls/other/des/123085.htm)

116. *Saddam Hussein's Support for International Terrorism*, The White House, (http://georgewbush-whitehouse.archives.gov/infocus/iraq/decade/sect5.html). The MeK will be removed from the US State Department's list of terrorist movements on September 28, 2012 to allow the US and Britain to collaborate with it to carry out clandestine actions in Iran.

117. Seymour Hersh, "Preparing the Battlefield", *The New Yorker*, July 7, 2008.

118. "Nucléaire: Israël juge l'Iran "plus dangereux que l'EI"", *lexpress.fr/AFP*, July 5, 2015

119. "Iran: at the heart of the tensions - Behind the scenes", *YouTube/Arte*, September 21, 2019

120. See memri.org/bin/articles.cgi?Page=archives&Area=sd&ID=SP101305

As the Imam said, Israel must be wiped off the map[121].

Yet serious commentators recognise that Ahmadinejad never said this, either in spirit or in letter[122]. For example, he did not mention the State of Israel, but only its *government* (which obviously cannot be erased from a map!) and did not refer to a geographical concept ("map"), but to history. His quote was accompanied by three examples: the Soviet regime, the regime of the Shah of Iran and the regime of Saddam Hussein. Even *the* Washington-based Middle East Media Research Institute (MEMRI) confirms this mistranslation[123]. The Iranians will try to restore a more accurate translation, but it is too late…

In 2005, in the midst of the war against the "axis of evil", with the Shiite resistance in Iraq - and the suspicion of a nuclear weapon in Iran - the translation error came at the right time with considerable impact. Thus, President Nicolas Sarkozy, then visiting Israel, declared:

> *Those who outrageously call for the destruction of Israel will always find France standing in their way*[124].

It remains today the main key to reading the Iranian position for many Western politicians and feeds a catastrophist discourse, very largely maintained by the Israeli government. It has become a real tool of manipulation that hinders any constructive dialogue. While most traditional Western media continue to propagate the false translation, such as *RT France* (which is readily accused of being pro-Iran)[125], few media, such as the *Guardian*, regularly attempt to correct it[126].

The mullahs' regime is not unanimously supported by Iranians, who are generally pro-Western and who could very well turn against the regime. But in the face of what is understood in the Middle East as a Western "crusade", aggravated by repeated Israeli strikes against Iranian units deployed in Syria, many Iranians feel that their country could be the next target of the United States. The government in Tehran is thus pushed by its public opinion into a "verbal jihad" that is very misunderstood in the West. Through its aggressive rhetoric against Israel, the Iranian government is generating a strong enough

---

121. "En voie de radicalisation, l'Iran veut " rayer " Israël de la carte ", *Le Monde*, October 27, 2005
122. Jonathan Steele, "Lost in Translation", *The Guardian*, June 22, 2006
123. *memri.org*, op. cit.
124. Speech by President Sarkozy to the Knesset, *Le Figaro*, June 20, 2008.
125. "Meyer Habib: "The United States has only one objective: that Iran is not nuclear", *YouTube/RT France*, June 20, 2019 (02'54")
126. "Corrections and clarifications", *The Guardian*, 28 July 2007; "Corrections and clarifications", *The Guardian*, April 23, 2009

American reaction to maintain national unity, but without giving a tangible pretext for military intervention.

We are so used to waging wars without concrete objectives that we lend the same foolishness to others. What could be Iran's objectives in waging war against Israel? With no common borders, no territorial claims, no ethnic ties and no specific political disputes, with a Jewish minority that is not persecuted, that even feels respected[127] and is represented in parliament, it is difficult to see what the Iranian government would seek in such an adventure. Not to mention that it would undoubtedly trigger a Western military response.

After having generated a threat that would push Syria to ask for Iran's help, Israel feels threatened by it. In the programme "C dans l'air" of May 11, 2018, Ms Mahnaz Shirali accuses Iran of provocation, saying that "it is *known*" that Iran was behind a missile attack on Israel on May 10[128]. This is not true. In reality, it was a Syrian retaliation, *following* an Israeli missile attack on the village of Baath[129], which is not mentioned at any point in the programme. In fact, the Iranian military in Syria are very clearly engaged in the fight against the jihadists (partly armed by Israel) and are neither equipped nor positioned to pose a threat to the Jewish state. Moreover, on May 14, 2019, during a teleconference with the Pentagon, Major General Christopher Ghika, second in command of the Western coalition (Operation INHERENT RESOLVE) states:

> *No, there is no increased threat from the presence of pro-Iranian forces in Iraq and Syria. Clearly, we are aware of that presence; and we are monitoring them with others, because that is our environment. We are monitoring the Shiite militias [...] carefully; and if the threat level seems to be increasing, then we will increase our protective measures accordingly*[130].

4.2.2. Anti-Semitism and Holocaust Denial

Shortly after the "Mohammed cartoons" crisis in Norway and Denmark in late 2005, President Ahmadinejad proposed a conference on December 11-12, 2006 in Tehran entitled *Review of the Holocaust: Global Vision.* It was preceded in February 2006 by a Holocaust cartoon competition organised by the Iranian

127. Kim Hjelmgaard, "Iran's Jewish community is the largest in the Mideast outside Israel - and feels safe and respected", *USA Today*, September 1st, 2018

128. Mahnaz Shirali, in the programme "C dans l'air", "Iran/Israel: the escalation...until where? #cdanslair 11.05.2018 ", *France 5/YouTube*, May 11, 2018 (08'05")

129. David M. Halbfinger & Isabel Kershner, "Israel and Iran, Newly Emboldened, Exchange Blows in Syria Face-Off," *The New York Times*, May 10, 2018

130. "U.S. pulls most personnel from Iraq as U.S. officials say Iranian military likely behind tanker attacks," *CBS News*, May 15, 2019; Tyler Durden, "Top British Commander in Rare Public Dispute With US Over Iran Intelligence," *Antimedia.com*, May 15, 2019

newspaper *Hamshahri*. As expected by the Iranians, the conference triggered a wave of protests in the West.

However, contrary to what has been reported in the West, its objective was not to contest the reality of the Holocaust. Indeed, it was attended by Orthodox Jews who certainly do not deny the reality of the Holocaust, but do challenge its political exploitation[131]. Labelled "antisemitic" and "revisionist" in the Western press, the conference was a trap. Not against Jews, but against Westerners, by highlighting their contradictions on freedom of expression[132].

After the Charlie Hebdo attacks in 2015, a similar competition was organised by the Iranian *Sarcheshmeh Cultural Complex*[133]. Three questions then guide the cartoonists:

> *1-If the West knows no limits to freedom of expression, why does it not allow scholars and historians to discuss the Holocaust?*

> *2-Why should the oppression of the Palestinians compensate for the Holocaust? People who played no part in the Second World War?*

> *3- We are concerned about other holocausts such as the nuclear holocaust (holocaust in Iraq, Syria and Gaza)*[134].

As can be seen, none of them denied the historical fact in any way. Moreover, the victor did not dispute the existence of the Holocaust, quite the contrary, since - rightly or wrongly - he compared it to the present situation of the Palestinians[135].

Whether these contests were in "good taste" is irrelevant here. In fact, for Iran - like the Muslim world in general - the reality of the Holocaust is neither a concern nor an issue. Indeed, in September 2013, President Hassan Rohani told CNN's Christiane Aman that "*the crime committed by the Nazis against Jews and non-Jews was reprehensible and condemnable*[136]", thus acknowledging the reality of the Holocaust. Yet Iran is still regularly referred to as a "Holocaust *denier*"[137].

---

131. "Ahmadinejad meets anti-Zionist Jews", *AP Archive/YouTube*, July 23, 2015

132. "Why are Jews at the 'Holocaust denial' conference?", *BBC News*, December 13, 2006.

133. The deadline to enter was April 1st, 2015 and the first prize was $12,000 (*The Times of Israel*, "Iran Holocaust cartoon contest draws 839 entries - Over 300 artists, including from France, Turkey and Brazil, turn in works for competition derided by UNESCO", April 7, 2015.

134. http://www.irancartoon.com/the-second-holocaust-international-cartoon-contest-2015/

135. See *Wikipedia*, article "International Holocaust Cartoon Competition".

136. Josh Levs & Mick Krever, "Iran's new president: Yes, the Holocaust happened", *CNN*, September 25, 2013

137. "Meyer Habib: "The United States has only one objective: that Iran is not nuclear", *YouTube/RT France*, June 20, 2019 (01'52")

4.2.3. The Nuclear Program

On September 6, 2019, Axel de Tarlé opens the programme "*C dans l'air*" on *France 5* by claiming that Iran has resumed its nuclear programme with the "*unstated goal - to hold the atomic bomb*[138]". This is disinformation.

After the war with Iraq in 1988, Iran definitively abandoned the idea of exporting its model of Islamic revolution and sought to strengthen its defensive capabilities. It had suffered chemical attacks (with the help of the Americans[139]) and envisaged a defensive strategy based on dissuasion. It therefore launched the AMAD Project, a research programme to study *the feasibility of* acquiring nuclear weapons. The aim was not to attack the United States or Israel, but to deal with the Iraqi threat[140].

In February 2000, in order to find out the nature and progress of the AMAD project, the Americans decided to carry out an operation under a false banner: this was Operation MERLIN[141]. They provided Iran with plans for a TBA-480 nuclear bomb fuse, to enable the CIA and NSA to "trace" the development of the bomb. The plans contain imperceptible errors to prevent the construction of a functional weapon. But the operation failed: the Iranians suspected a deception and dismantled an entire CIA network in Iran[142]. There is no confirmation that Iran is developing a nuclear weapon, but the Western media will continue to spread this disinformation[143].

In May 2005, the US Intelligence Community estimated that Iran is "*committed to developing nuclear weapons*[144]". But in November 2007, in their National Intelligence Assessment (NIA), the Office of the Director of National Intelligence and the National Intelligence Council revised their judgment and confirmed that "*Tehran halted its nuclear weapons programme in the fall of 2003*[145]". The *New York Times* writes:

138. "Nucléaire: l'Iran défie Trump #cdanslair 06.09.2019, C dans l'air", *YouTube/France 5*, September 7, 2019 (00'23")

139. Shane Harris & Matthew M. Aid, "Exclusive: CIA Files Prove America Helped Saddam as He Gassed Iran", *Foreign Policy*, August 26, 2013

140. Robert Czulda, "The Defensive Dimension of Iran's Military Doctrine: How Would They Fight?", *Middle East Policy Council*, Volume XXIII, No. 1, Spring 2016

141. James Risen, *State of War: The Secret History of the CIA and the Bush Administration*, Free Press, October 24, 2006

142. James Risen, "George Bush insists that Iran must not be allowed to develop nuclear weapons. So why, six years ago, did the CIA give the Iranians blueprints to build a bomb?", *The Guardian*, January 5, 2006

143. See, for example, the "19 h 30" of RTBF's *La Première* (January 6, 2010)

144. Gregory F. Treverton, *Support to Policymakers: The 2007 NIE on Iran's Nuclear Intentions and Capabilities*, Center for the Study of Intelligence, Central Intelligence Agency, Washington, DC, May 2013, p. 19

145. *National Intelligence Estimate - Iran: Nuclear Intentions and Capabilities*, Office of the Director of National Intelligence & National Intelligence Council, November 2007; Gregory F. Treverton, *The 2007 National Intelligence Estimate on Iran's Nuclear Intentions and Capabilities*, RAND Corporation, May 2013

Despite repeated smear campaigns, the IAEA has stood firm and repeatedly concluded that since 2002 there is no evidence of an undeclared nuclear weapons programme in Iran[146].

In early 2012, the CIA and Mossad agreed that Iran had never taken the decision to build a nuclear weapon[147]. Iran is therefore not a threat.

But, by the admission of the US intelligence services[148], a pretext is being sought to overthrow Ahmadinejad. This is why the Security Council renewed the sanctions regime against Iran in June 2012[149]. In September 2012, Benjamin Netanyahu told the UN General Assembly that Iran would have a nuclear weapon by summer 2013[150]. But he is lying again: a Mossad memo sent a few weeks later to the South African intelligence services states that...

Iran, at this stage, is not engaged in the activities necessary for the production of nuclear weapons[151].

On 14 July 2015, the United States, Russia, China, France, the United Kingdom, Germany, the European Union (EU) and Iran signed the Vienna Agreement (better known by its English abbreviation: JCPOA). In short, in exchange for the lifting of Western sanctions, Iran committed itself to:

to reduce its stockpile of 97% enriched uranium and to stop enriching uranium for military purposes;

to limit the number of its centrifuges to 5,060 and not to modernise its installations;

cease operations at the Arak plant, which produced plutonium that could eventually be used for military purposes;

accept inspections by the International Atomic Energy Agency (IAEA) to verify the implementation of the agreement.

On 16 January 2016, the UN lifts its sanctions, but the JCPOA signatories drag their feet. Despite the fact that the IAEA has verified Iran's compliance

146. Elaine Sciolino, "Europeans See Murkier Case for Sanctions", *The New York Times*, December 4, 2007

147. Mark Mazzetti & James Risen, "U.S. Agencies See No Move by Iran to Build a Bomb", *The New York Times*, February 25, 2012; "Mossad, CIA Agree Iran Has Yet to Decide to Build Nuclear Weapon", *Haaretz*, March 18, 2012.

148. Karen DeYoung & Scott Wilson, 'Goal of Iran sanctions is regime collapse, U.S. official says', *Washington Post*, January 13, 2012.

149. http://www.un.org/press/en/2012/sc10666.doc.htm

150. "Netanyahu diagrams Iran's nuclear status", *CNN/YouTube*, September 27, 2012

151. Note of October 22, 2012, para. 9 (https://static.guim.co.uk/ni/1424713149380/Mossad-On-Iran-Nuclear-Stat.pdf)

with the treaty on 15 occasions[152], Western countries are not living up to their commitments and their sanctions are not lifted.

On 30 April 2018, in a theatrical display, Benjamin Netanyahu "reveals" "*secret archives*" relating to Iran's nuclear programme stolen "*a few weeks earlier*" near Tehran. He claims that Iran is lying and pursuing the development of nuclear weapons. But in reality, it is he who is lying. The documents presented date from 2002, ten years before the CIA and Mossad concluded that Iran had never undertaken to build a bomb. Moreover, the experts quickly note that the "unveiled" documents had already been submitted by Iran to the IAEA in... 2005[153] and already published in large part in November 2011[154] ! This will not prevent MP Meyer Habib from repeating this lie in June 2019 on *RT France*[155] using the expression "*Islamic State*" to refer to Iran[156], in order to maintain a confusion!...

In fact, Netanyahu addresses only one person: Donald Trump, who announces a week later the American withdrawal from the JCPOA and the reinstatement of sanctions[157]. He will "tweet" his reasons on 10 July 2019:

> *Iran has long secretly "enriched", in total violation of the terrible $150 billion deal signed by John Kerry and the Obama administration. Remember that this agreement was due to expire in a few years*[158]. *[...]*

In a few words, he manages to lie on three points. Concerning enrichment activities, it should be remembered that for military use, uranium must be enriched to 90%. Iran never exceeded 20% before the JCPOA. With the treaty, Iran had agreed to limit itself to 3.67% for a period of 15 years; and in its report of 31 May 2019, the IAEA confirms that Iran has kept to these limits[159]. Moreover, in January 2019, during her hearing before the *Senate Intelligence Committee*, CIA Director Gina Haspel confirmed that Iran had complied with the JCPOA, thus contradicting Trump[160].

---

152. Daniel Larison, "IAEA Confirms Iranian Compliance for the Fifteenth Time", *The American Conservative*, May 31, 2019
153. Oliver Holmes & Julian Borger, "Nuclear deal: Netanyahu accuses Iran of cheating on agreement", *The Guardian*, April 30, 2018
154. *Implementation of the NPT Safeguards - Agreement and relevant provisions of Security Council resolutions in the Islamic Republic of Iran*, IAEA Board of Governors, November 8, 2011 (GOV/2011/65)
155. "Meyer Habib: 'The United States has only one objective: that Iran is not nuclear'", *YouTube/RT France*, June 20, 2019 (04'58")
156. "Meyer Habib: 'The United States has only one objective: that Iran is not nuclear'", *YouTube/RT France*, June 20, 2019 (00'50")
157. Mark Landler, "Trump Abandons Iran Nuclear Deal He Long Scorned", *The New York Times*, May 8, 2018
158. https://twitter.com/realDonaldTrump/status/1148958770770382849
159. *Verification and monitoring in the Islamic Republic of Iran in light of United Nations Security Council resolution 2231 (2015)*, IAEA Board of Governors, May 31, 2019, (GOV/2019/21)
160. "CIA Director: Iran 'Technically' In Compliance with Nuclear Deal", *C-Span*, January 29, 2019

As for the $150 billion, this is not the amount paid by the US, but the total of Iranian assets that should be "unfrozen", and the total is probably much lower. In August 2015, in an audit to the Senate Finance Committee, Adam J. Szubin, Treasury Undersecretary for Financial Intelligence and Terrorism, estimated the amount at "*just over $50 billion*[161]". Another lie.

Finally, as far as the timetable is concerned, Donald Trump seems not to have read (or understood) the JCPOA. He claims that:

> *In seven years, this agreement will have expired and Iran will be free to create nuclear weapons. This is not acceptable. Seven years is tomorrow*[162].

This is another lie. While some of the treaty's provisions do indeed expire in 2025 (e.g. on centrifuge development), the most significant clauses (e.g. on the prohibition of nuclear weapons development, nuclear fuel reprocessing or the application of IAEA safeguards) do not have a time limit[163].

In fact, Trump wants to renegotiate the treaty on its terms and, in June 2019, he is offering to be "*Iran's best friend, if it gives up nuclear weapons*[164]". An offer that Iran cannot accept, since it already gave up nuclear weapons in 2003... These seemingly incoherent manoeuvres are probably less irrational than they appear. In fact, Trump is applying a mechanism proposed in 2009 by the Brookings Institution to bring about regime change by force in Iran:

> *The best way to minimise international disapproval and maximise support (however reluctantly or covertly) is to strike only if the world is convinced that the Iranians have been offered a superb deal but have rejected it - a deal so good that only a regime bent on acquiring nuclear weapons, and for the wrong reasons, would reject it. In these circumstances, the US (or Israel) could present their operation as one of regret, not anger, and at least some members of the international community would conclude that the Iranians provoked it by turning down a very good deal*[165].

The idea is to show that Iran is the "bad guy". However, the media fall for it and castigate the Iranian refusal, like *L'Express*[166] and many others.

161. *Written Testimony of Adam J. Szubin, Acting Under Secretary of Treasury for Terrorism and Financial Intelligence United States Senate Committee on Banking, Housing, And Urban Affairs*, Department of the Treasury, Press Center, August 5, 2015
162. Donald Trump, White House Press Conference, April 30, 2018
163. Jon Greenberg, "Donald Trump says wrongly the Iran nuclear deal expires in 7 years", *Politifact*, May 2, 2018
164. "Trump says he will be Iran's 'best friend' if it renounces nuclear arms", *The Times of Israel*, June 22, 2019
165. Kenneth M. Pollack, et al, "Which Path to Persia? Options for a New American Strategy toward Iran", Analysis Paper Nr 20, *Saban Center for Middle East Policy, The Brookings Institution*, June 2009
166. "Iran rejects Trump's dialogue proposal", *LEXPRESS.fr/AFP*, August 1st, 2018

The withdrawal of the United States and the non-compliance of the West with the JCPOA led Iran to question the framework it had accepted. First of all, it should be understood that under Article IV of the Nuclear Non-Proliferation Treaty (NPT), to which the JCPOA refers, countries have an "*inalienable right... to develop research, production and use of nuclear energy for peaceful purposes*". The problem is that the US does not recognise this "*inalienable right*" for Iran (while it recognises it for Israel, which is not a party to the NPT!)

In exchange for the dismantling of sanctions, Iran thus agreed to stay far below the NPT limits, giving up its right to enrich uranium under the NPT, and storing only 300 kg of uranium enriched to the 3.67% limit. The problem is that the enrichment process cannot be stopped, and to keep its stockpile at 300 kg, Iran was allowed to sell its enriched uranium on the market. But the new American sanctions forbid it to access this market! Very logically, it is therefore condemned to go beyond the limits of the JCPOA and to return to its rights under the NPT, in order to push the Europeans to implement solutions.

Therefore, in November 2019, Iran increases its uranium enrichment capacity. The French press went wild: the idea that Iran was seeking to produce nuclear weapons was propagated. Patrick Cohen on *France 5*, for example, insinuated that it was "*getting closer to it*[167]". A few days later, in the programme "C dans l'air", François Clémenceau went further in the same direction, stating that Iran sees "*no limit to* [its] *desire to enrich uranium in order to gain access to what will enable* [it] to *have the bomb*[168]". In reality, there is no concrete evidence that Iran *intends to* produce nuclear weapons. The daily *La Croix* states that "*Iran has reduced a little more (...) its international nuclear commitments*[169]". *Le Figaro* recalls the terms of the JCPOA... but carefully avoids mentioning Article 26[170], although it is very clear:

> *Iran has stated that it will treat any such reintroduction or re-imposition of the sanctions specified in Annex II, or any such imposition of new nuclear-related sanctions, as grounds for full or partial termination of the implementation of its commitments under the present JCPOA*[171].

Thus, Iran only implemented a provision of the JCPOA, which it had included because it already knew that the West would not keep its word!

167. Patrick Cohen in the programme "C à vous", "USA - Iran: la tension monte - C à Vous - 6 janvier 2020", *France 5/YouTube*, January 7, 2020 (01'50")
168. "Crash du Boeing 737: l'Iran accusé #cdanslair 10.01.2020 ", *France 5/YouTube*, January 11, 2020, (28'20")
169. "Nucléaire: l'Iran relaunches des activités d'enrichissement d'uranium gelées", *La Croix*, November 5, 2019
170. "Iran has resumed uranium enrichment at its Fordo plant", *Le Figaro/AFP*, November 8, 2019.
171. *Joint Comprehensive Plan of Action*, Vienna, July 14, 2015, Article 26, p.14

For Europe had many tools and options - which it did not use - to respond to Trump[172], starting with the application of rules it had adopted in 1996 to combat the extraterritoriality of US laws[173]; but it did not do so. On the other hand, other means of pressure exist, such as support (more political than military) for coalitions in Iraq and Afghanistan, for example. Showing that, despite the declarations, our principles and values take a back seat to our interests...

In January 2020, Israel claims that Iran "*could have the bomb by the end of the year*[174]". But this too is disinformation. Apart from the fact that Iran has not enriched uranium to 90%, designing a bomb requires converting that uranium into a weapon, which Iran has never done, nor has it acquired the capability to do. Moreover, before a nuclear weapon can be used, it has to work! One recalls the debates in France on nuclear tests simply to maintain an existing capacity... Moreover, it has never been demonstrated that Iran decided to acquire nuclear weapons. So we are very far from the Israeli claims...

But this is not a contradiction in terms, since in an official statement of July 1st, 2019 on the JCPOA, the White House states that "There is *little doubt that even before the agreement was concluded, Iran had violated its terms*[175]"! Welcome to Absurdity!

In late April 2020, the *New York Times* reported that the US was seeking to re-enter the agreement. Not for the sake of multilateralism, but to use a clause in the JCPOA that would allow the reinstatement of pre-signature sanctions.[176]

In the face of Western (and Israeli) irrationality and despite provocative verbal deviations, Iranian leaders have been very rational in their choices. Spectacular statements against Israel and the United States should often be taken for what they are: rhetoric, aimed at expressing resistance ('verbal jihad') and satisfying an Iranian public that no longer understands the government's resilience. Speaking about the possibility of Iranian nuclear action, the former director of Mossad, Israel's strategic intelligence service, Meir Dagan, confirms:

> *The regime in Iran is a very rational regime [...] There is no doubt that they are aware of all the implications of their actions and that they would pay a very high price... and I think at this stage the Iranians are very cautious on this issue*[177].

172. Ellie Geranmayeh, "Europe Must Fight to Preserve the Iran Deal", *Foreign Policy*, January 23, 2018

173. *Council Regulation (EC) No 2271/96 of 22 November 1996 protecting against the effects of the extra-territorial application of legislation adopted by a third country, and actions based thereon or resulting therefrom*, Official Journal L 309, November 29, 1996 (eur-lex.europa.eu)

174. Alisa Odenheimer, "Israel Report Says Iran Could Have Uranium for Bomb by Year-End", *Bloomberg*, January 15, 2020

175. *Statement from the Press Secretary*, www.whitehouse.gov, 1 July 2019

176. David E. Sanger, "To Pressure Iran, Pompeo Turns to the Deal Trump Renounced", *The New York Times*, April 26, 020

177. Watch Stahl, 'Ex-Mossad chief: Iran rational; don't attack now', *CBS News*, March 11, 2012.

Our perception of Iran is maintained by media that are heavily influenced by Israeli domestic politics and do not provide any analytical or critical input[178]. Benjamin Netanyahu exploits the servility of some Western journalists, while former Mossad directors like Efraim Halevy warn against this overdramatisation[179]. In fact, our traditional media tend to become propaganda organs, just like *Pravda* in the Soviet Union.

4.3 "Iran Remains a Major Sponsor of International Terrorism[180]"

Because we do not honestly try to understand the reasons for Islamist terrorism, we end up associating it with anyone. Thus, on January 17, 2015, on the programme "On n'est pas couché", Michel Onfray claimed that "*Iran rejoiced*" after the January 2015 attack on Charlie Hebdo[181]. This is not true. In fact, on January 9, Iranian President Rouhani clearly condemned the fact that *"people are killing in the name of Islam*[182]". But this lie 'confirms' our prejudices.

Shortly after Donald Trump took office, the new Secretary of Defense James Mattis - a former US Marine Corps general and nicknamed "*Mad Dog*" - accused Iran of being "*the world's largest state sponsor of terrorism*[183]". This statement will be repeated in 2018 to justify the US withdrawal from the JCPOA and possible strikes on Iran. Thus, before the Senate Foreign Relations Committee, Mike Pompeo declared:

> *The factual question about Iran's relationship with al-Qaeda is very real. They have hosted al-Qaeda, they have allowed al-Qaeda to transit through their country. [...]*
>
> *There is no doubt that there is a link between the Islamic Republic of Iran and al-Qaeda. Full stop. Full stop*[184].

But Pompeo is lying. Today's jihadist terrorism is a response to Western interventions. That is why it remains essentially Sunni. Thus, if we cannot exclude

178. "Iran nuclear power, most serious global threat, says Netanyahu", *rtbf.be/AFP*, September 30, 2014
179. Raphael Ahren, "Is a nuclear Iran really an existential threat to Israel?", *The Times of Israel*, February 28, 2015
180. Rex W. Tillerson, Secretary of State, April 18, 2017 (www.state.gov/secretary/remarks/2017/04/270315.htm)
181. "Michel Onfray, Charlie Hebdo, Islam and France - On n'est pas couché January 17, 2015 #ONPC", *France5/YouTube*, January 17, 2015 (17'05")
182. "Charlie Hebdo: Iran's Rouhani condemns killing in name of Islam", *AFP/Dawn*, January 9, 2015
183. Rachael Revesz, "Iran is 'world's biggest sponsor of state terrorism', says US Defense Secretary James Mattis", *Independent*, February 4, 2017 (http://www.independent.co.uk/news/world/americas/iran-worlds-biggest-sponsor-terrorism-us-donald-trump-james-mattis-nuclear-test-missile-sanctions-a7563081.html)
184. "Pompeo says Iran tied to Al-Qaeda, declines to say if war legal", *France24*, April 10, 2019

that people associated with "Al-Qaeda" could have been on Iranian territory, it is without the knowledge of the authorities[185]. The study of Bin Laden's documents discovered in Abbottabad in 2011 confirms the total absence of complicity between 'Al Qaeda' and Iran[186].

In reality, Pompeo is seeking to invoke the AUMF[187], legislation that allows the president to strike at the perpetrators of '9/11' without congressional approval. This is why, in 2003, the US accused Iraq of supporting 'Al Qaeda'[188]. In total, the AUMF was used to justify 41 military operations in 19 countries. As early as 2004, the Bush administration tried the same stratagem to attack Iran[189] and prepare plans to attack[190]. As soon as he took office, Donald Trump continued along the same lines. Concerned about the consequences of an irrational policy, Congress is seeking to repeal the AUMF as early as May 2019. After the assassination of General Qassem Soleimani on January 3, 2020, the House of Representatives decided to repeal the AUMF on January 30, and passed a law requiring the president to seek congressional authorisation to go to war with Iran[191]. The Senate - albeit with a Republican majority - followed suit on February 13[192].

4.3.1. The Context and the Attacks of October 23, 1983

The main reason for linking Iran to international terrorism is its support for Lebanese Hezbollah. But these accusations are fuelled more by our ignorance than by hard facts.

The Israeli intervention in 1982 was the reason for the creation of Hezbollah. After the 1967 war and the events of September 1970 in Jordan, some 300,000 Palestinian refugees settled in South Lebanon. This presence destabilised the local economy and affected the Shiite population, which lived in peace with its Israeli neighbour. The installation of the PLO command in Beirut and the frequent incursions of Feddayin on the Lebanese border pushed Israel to intervene in

---

185. Seth G. Jones et al, *The Evolution of the Salafi-Jihadist Threat Current and Future Challenges from the Islamic State, Al-Qaeda, and Other Groups*, Center for Strategic & International Studies, November 2018

186. Nelly Lahoud, *Al-Qa'ida's Contested Relationship with Iran The View from Abbottabad*, New America, September 2018

187. *2001 Authorization for Use of Military Force (AUMF)*, S.J.Res 23(107th), September 14, 2001

188. Steven Kull, 'The American Public On International Issues - Misperceptions, The Media And The Iraq War', *The Program On International Policy Attitudes (PIPA)/Knowledge Networks Poll*, October 2, 2003

189. *CNN*, 'Bush: U.S. probes possible Iran links to 9/11', July 19, 2004.

190. James Fallows, "Will Iran Be Next?", *The Atlantic*, December 2004.

191. David Roza, "House passes bills to repeal 2002 AUMF and require Congress to approve any war with Iran", *Task & Purpose*, January 30, 2020; Joe Gould & Leo Shane III, "House votes to curb Trump's military action on Iran", *Defense News*, January 30, 2020

192. *Senate Joint Resolution 68 - A joint resolution to direct the removal of United States Armed Forces from hostilities against the Islamic Republic of Iran that have not been authorized by Congress*, 116th Congress (2019-2020), February 13, 2020

Lebanon in June 1982. Operation PEACE IN GALILEE targets Yasser Arafat's Palestine Liberation Organisation (PLO).

The Lebanese Shiite population welcomed the Israelis with enthusiasm and "*a shower of rice*[193]". But instead of relying on this population and the intra-Arab dissensions to fight against the PLO, the Israelis fought indiscriminately against Lebanese Shiites and Palestinian Sunnis, quickly creating unanimity against them. The Israeli intelligence does not understand the situation and the troops are caught in a spiral of violence[194]. The result was a negative reaction from the American Jewish community, which threatened to stop supporting Israeli policy[195]. This is where - according to intelligence sources - the Rue des Rosiers attack in Paris (9 August 1982) took place, a special operation to recreate unity around Israeli policy.

In September 1982, after the cease-fire agreements between Israel and the PLO, a Multinational Security Force (MNF) was deployed in Beirut. It was based on Security Council Resolution 521, which provided for assistance to the Lebanese government to protect the population. In the following year, the American forces were the target of a series of skirmishes attributed to Israeli commandos[196]. On April 18, 1983, a bomb attack against the American embassy in Beirut caused 63 victims. It was claimed by the Islamic Jihad Organisation (IJO).

On October 23, 1983, two attacks hit the Multinational Security Force (MNF) in Beirut: the first one killed 241 people at the US Marines' headquarters, and the second one, two minutes later, destroyed the "Drakkar", killing 58 French paratroopers. The most diverse motives were evoked, such as the delivery of Super-Etendard planes to Iraq by France a few days earlier. The official discourse blames Hezbollah and makes Westerners the victims of Iranian terrorism. But this is not true: Iran is far from Lebanon and the reasons lie in the way the West interprets its mandate. A delicate subject...

The MNF was a security force, supposed to be impartial, but the Westerners were not quite so. France conducts joint patrols with the Lebanese Army: although it does not take part in combat operations, it thus becomes a protagonist in the conflict[197]. As for the Americans, their presence is ambiguous. First of all, it should be remembered that American legislation forbids an American soldier to obey any authority other than that of the President of the United

193. Greg Myre, "Israelis in a Shiite Land: Hard Lessons From Lebanon", *The New York Times*, April 27, 2003

194. Ronen Bergman, *The Secret War with Iran*, Oneworld, Oxford, 2008 (p. 58)

195. Dov Waxman, *Trouble in the Tribe: The American Jewish Conflict over Israel*, Princeton University Press, 2016 (pp. 316)

196. Donald Neff, "Israel Charged with Systematic Harassment of U.S. Marines", *Washington Report on Middle East Affairs*, March 1995, pp. 79-81.

197. Alain Brouillet, "La seconde force multinationale à Beyrouth (24 septembre 1982-31 mars 1984)", *Annuaire français de droit international*, volume 31, 1985. pp. 115-166

States. This results in hybrid leadership structures when an American force is in a multinational structure. In Lebanon, in parallel to their participation in the MNF (under UN mandate), US forces supported the Lebanese Army. In April 1983, without much consultation within the administration, Robert McFarlane, the President's Special Representative to the Middle East, committed the battleship USS New Jersey off the coast of Lebanon to bomb Lebanese villages occupied by the opposition - causing about a thousand innocent civilian casualties. This was the reason for the retaliatory bombing on October 23. With a very American naivety, the US command had waived the raising of the alert level of its MNF contingent, in order to emphasise that they were separate from the US forces otherwise fighting in Lebanon[198]. A legal subtlety that the terrorists obviously did not grasp. The Americans would make exactly the same mistake in Mogadishu, Somalia, ten years later, and in Afghanistan thirty years later.

Although Italy supplied arms to Iraq during the war[199], its contingent, deployed between the Americans and the French, remained in its original role and was not targeted by attacks. Victor Ostrovsky, a former Mossad agent, later revealed that the Israelis knew about the attack but did not inform the Americans, in order to push them into the conflict[200].

The two attacks were immediately attributed to the ODI (like the April attack), but they were claimed by the Free Islamic Revolution Movement (FIRM)[201], which was unknown until then. The Americans associated it with Iran, but had no proof: it was the enemy of the moment. Only later, in order to put the blame on a known entity, Israel and several Western countries, including the United States and Britain, will accuse Hezbollah, claiming that it was founded in 1982.

In fact, in 1983, Hezbollah did not exist[202] and publications on terrorism from 1982-1984 do not mention it[203]. Therefore, apart from a handful of Western countries, which align their foreign policy with Washington - and thus with Israel - most countries do not consider it a terrorist organisation. Its creation is marked by the establishment of its Charter on February 16, 1985[204], while Israel was completing the first phase of its withdrawal from Lebanon[205].

198. Nir Rosen, 'Lesson Unlearned', *Foreign Policy*, October 29, 2009 (http://foreignpolicy.com/2009/10/29/lesson-unlearned/).

199. "La prima guerra del golfo: Iran-Iraq (1980-1988)", *archivio900.it*, August 8, 2006

200. Ostrovsky, Victor & Claire Hoy, *By Way of Deception*, New York, St. Martin's Press, 1990, p. 321.

201. Journal télévisé de 20 heures, *Antenne 2*, October 23, 1983; William E. Farrell, "Unanswered Question: Who Was Responsible?", *The New York Times*, October 25, 1983

202. Nir Rosen, "Lesson Unlearned", *Foreign Policy*, October 29, 2009

203. See, for example, Samuel M. Katz & Lee E. Russell, *Armies in Lebanon 1982-84*, Osprey Publishing Ltd, London, 1985

204. https://www.cia.gov/library/readingroom/docs/DOC_0000361273.pdf; Jonathan Masters & Zachary Laub, "Hezbollah", *Council on Foreign Relations*, January 3, 2014; "Profile: Lebanon's Hezbollah movement", *BBC News*, March 15, 2016

205. Jean-Jacques Mével, "L'UE place le Hezbollah sur la liste noire du terrorisme", *lefigaro.fr*, July 22, 2013

Prior to this date, no Lebanese armed group referred to or defined itself in relation to the *Party of God* (*Hezbollah*). The main Shiite resistance group was then the ODI, a vague entity whose contours were never precisely known, a bit like "Al-Qaeda" twenty years later. Antidating the creation of Hezbollah made it possible to associate individuals suspected of being linked to the ODI, such as Imad Mougnieh[206], with an identifiable structure. American jurists would use the same device twenty years later with "al-Qaeda", in order to use their legislation. We will come back to this.

In September 2001, Caspar Weinberger, who was Secretary of Defense in 1983, said in an interview:

> *(…) We still don't know who carried out the bombing of the Marine barracks at Beirut airport, and we certainly didn't know it at the time*[207].

In 2009, President Obama was criticised for not mentioning Hezbollah when commemorating the attack[208]. But the reason for this 'omission' is very simple: to this day, no one knows exactly who carried it out.

4.3.2. Hezbollah

Hezbollah is a resistance organisation created during the departure of the Israelis from Lebanon in 1985. Its aim is to restore the integrity of the Lebanese territory before the 1982 intervention.

Since 1985, the Israelis have never returned all the territory taken during the operation. Meyer Habib's claim that Israel "*got out of Lebanon to the last square inch*[209]" is false. Israel retained the "Shebaa Farms" area, a territory of some 25 km^2 on the borders of Israel, Lebanon and Syria; as well as many small portions of territory along the Israeli-Lebanese border, behind the Blue Line. These tiny territories are the source of almost every incident between the two countries. Not to mention the maritime borders, which Israel has recently extended to include newly discovered underwater hydrocarbon reserves!

There are several border lines between Lebanon and Israel: the 1923 line (for the partition between France and Great Britain), which was largely taken up again in 1949 to mark the "official" border ("green border"); the 1978 Israeli withdrawal line, and the 2000 withdrawal "Blue Line". However, these lines do not coincide exactly. Although the Blue Line was drawn with the help of the

206. He was mysteriously assassinated in Damascus in 2008, probably by an Israeli commando.
207. *Frontline - Target America,* Interview: Caspar Weinberger, (http://www.pbs.org/wgbh/pages/frontline/shows/target/interviews/weinberger.html) (accessed August 16, 2019)
208. http://archive.defense.gov/home/features/2008/1008_beirut/
209. "Habib: "We don't call for a boycott of a friendly country!", *Europe 1/YouTube,* June 4, 2015 (03'40")

United Nations, Lebanon still disputes 13 sectors of it[210]. In July 2006, it was in one of these sectors, unilaterally annexed by Israel but considered as Lebanese, that Hezbollah arrested Israeli soldiers on patrol, thus triggering the war ("Harb Tamouz"). Similarly, the tunnels discovered in 2018 connect these disputed areas to Lebanon and not the "real" Israeli territory as claimed. Naturally, the Western media systematically fails to mention these unduly annexed territories[211], thus allowing Hezbollah to be blamed.

Presented in the West as terrorist, Hezbollah is a complex organisation. It includes a social aid structure, the *Mou'assat al-Shahid* ("Institution of the Martyr"), which helps the victims of Israeli interventions, and a structure for the reconstruction of infrastructures destroyed by Israel, the *Jihad al-Binah* ("Effort for Reconstruction"), mainly financed by Iran[212]. Hezbollah had rebuilt the road network in southern Lebanon, built and managed 5 hospitals, 14 clinics and 12 schools, before the Israelis destroyed them in 2006.

Its military wing is essentially a territorial resistance ("*al-Muqawamah*") and is neither structured nor equipped as an invasion force. Israel had a bitter experience of this in 2006: convinced that Hezbollah is an offensive organisation, its military intelligence service, AMAN, had failed to detect the complex network of trenches and concrete forts built for defensive combat. The Israelis were thus forced to retreat, but not without retaliating with massive bombing of Lebanese civilian infrastructure. The *Muqawamah* was formed with the assistance of instructors from the Al-Quds units. Better known as the *Pasdaran*, these are elite units of the Iranian Revolutionary Guards, whose role is to ensure territorial defence and the fight against terrorism, a bit like the troops of the Russian Ministry of the Interior.

The US also blames Hezbollah for the hijacking of TWA Flight 847 in Beirut, which was aimed at the release of 700-800 Shiites detained in Israel in violation of the Geneva Conventions[213]. But in fact, no one knows the identity of the terrorists, who claimed to be from the Organisation of the Oppressed of the Earth. At the time, the press only spoke of "*Shiite Muslims*[214]" and even mentioned the Amal militia, led by Nabih Berri[215].

---

210. Amos Harel, "Thirteen Israeli Border Points Raising Tensions With Lebanon", *Haaretz*, February 27, 2018
211. Nicolas Falez, "Ten years after the Israeli withdrawal from southern Lebanon, tensions persist", *RFI*, May 24, 2010
212. *Jihad al-Bina Association in Lebanon: A Hezbollah social foundation engaged in construction and social projects among the Shiite community, being a major component in Hezbollah's civilian infrastructure*, The Meir Amit Intelligence and Terrorism Information Center, June 23, 2019
213. The 1949 Geneva Convention relative to the Protection of Civilian Persons in Time of War prohibits a state from transferring captured combatants to its territory. Despite international and International Red Cross protests, Israel has obviously denied violating international law. But President Reagan, in his press conference of June 18, 1985, acknowledged that Israel had violated the Convention.
214. Rosenberg, Howard, Terrorism as Theater: TV Covers a Hijacking, *Los Angeles Times*, June 18, 1985
215. "Document - Hijacking, June 18, 1985, Transcript", *danratherjournalist.org*

On March 10, 2005, less than a month after the attack on Rafik Hariri in Beirut, in a resolution adopted by 473 votes to 33, the European Parliament "*considers that there is irrefutable evidence of terrorist action by Hezbollah and that the Council should take all necessary measures to put an end to this action*[216]". But here again, decisions are made on the basis of supposition alone. In fact, the investigation will show the good personal relations between Hassan Nasrallah, Secretary General of Hezbollah and Rafik Hariri, who met on numerous occasions and created a joint committee in view of the 2005 parliamentary elections[217], making the accusation extremely fragile and purely speculative[218].

After the attack of July 18, 2012 in Bourgas (Bulgaria), which targeted Israeli tourists, Hezbollah was immediately accused, without any proof. France, through its Minister of Foreign Affairs, Laurent Fabius, then declared the armed wing of Hezbollah as terrorist and asked for its inclusion on the EU list of terrorist organisations[219], which was done in July 2013[220]. But in 2018, the investigation conducted by the Bulgarian prosecutor's office was unable to find any evidence of Hezbollah's involvement, and removed it from the indictment[221]. This does not prevent the *Arte* channel in a documentary broadcast in 2019, entitled *Lebanon, hostage of the Middle East,* from affirming that it is responsible for the attack[222]! One acts on the basis of rumours, without proof and without integrity, in order to justify policies that are too aligned with that of Israel…

In 2012, with the emergence of Sunni militias on the Lebanese border, Hezbollah deployed troops to Syria to support the Syrian government. Presented by the Israelis as a threat, this expeditionary force does not have the capacity to carry out major offensive operations independently.

In February 2019, in order to justify US interference, Secretary of State Mike Pompeo claims that Hezbollah has an office in Venezuela[223]. This is a lie. The accusation has been recurrent since the early 2000s: attacks have indeed been carried out by a group or groups operating under the name 'Hezbollah'. But these were Marxist groups, which had no connection with Lebanon, or even

---

216. Pascal Priestley, "Lebanon: Hezbollah, the state within the state", *information.tv5monde.com*, January 31, 2011 (updated 7 April 2013)

217. *Bulletin of the Special Tribunal for Lebanon*, December 2014 - January 2015, Information and Communication Section of the Special Tribunal for Lebanon, (www.stl-tsl.org/fr/media/stl-bulletin/3795-stl-bulletin-december-2014-january-2015).

218. Nicholas Blanford, "Did Hezbollah Kill Hariri?", *Foreign Policy*, April 1st, 2010.

219. "For Paris, Hezbollah's armed wing is a terrorist group", *AFP/France* 24, May 23, 2013

220. Benjamin Barthe and Philippe Ricard, "Le Hezbollah classé organisation terroriste par l'UE", *Le Monde*, July 23, 2013

221. Yonah Jeremy Bob, "Hezbollah role unmentioned in charges for 2012 Bulgaria terrorist attack", *The Jerusalem Post*, January 31, 2018

222. Michael Richter, "Le Liban, otage du Moyen-Orient", www.arte.tv, (12'50") (broadcast on Arte on September 24, at 10:25 pm) (withdrawn on December 22, 2019)

223. Jon Sharman, "Trump's secretary of state Pompeo says Hezbollah is active in Venezuela", *The Independent*, February 7, 2019; Colin P. Clarke, "Hezbollah Is in Venezuela to Stay", *Foreign Policy*, February 9, 2019

with Islam, and in all likelihood used this nickname to cover their tracks. That said, it is likely that Hezbollah has supporters in Latin America (the triangle on the borders of Paraguay, Brazil and Argentina is often mentioned), but no direct criminal activity[224].

The 1992 and 1994 Buenos Aires bombings are cited as examples of the international nature of Iranian terrorism. Without going into the details of the investigations - which were marred by corruption and multiple twists and turns - let us simply mention that the Argentine authorities' investigation indicated '*with 99 per cent certainty*' that the explosion of March 17, 1992 was caused by explosives placed *inside* the Israeli embassy and not by a car bomb that forced its way into the building[225]. The Israeli government rejected these conclusions and the case remained unsolved. As for the attack of July 18, 1994, '*no evidence of Iranian involvement*' could be found according to the former US ambassador to Argentina[226]. In fact, some Western services tend to point the finger at Israel or the United States: the attacks would have been linked to the delivery of equipment for the construction of a nuclear power plant in Syria, and the transfer to Iran of the Condor 2 missile technology, developed jointly by Argentina, Egypt and Iraq. An agreement was signed in January 2013 between Argentina and Iran to establish a joint commission of enquiry. But in December 2015, it was denounced by the Macri government, which declared - under American pressure - Hezbollah a "terrorist organisation"[227] in July 2019.

In reality, we don't know: Hezbollah's responsibility has never been proven and it is not clear what its objective could be in taking the fight to this part of the world. The accusations against Hezbollah are more the result of credulous and manipulable politicians than of factual elements. That said, it is possible that Hezbollah has harboured or still harbours individuals who participated in terrorist attacks under other organisations in the 1970s-1980s. This does not make it a terrorist organisation, otherwise the US or French governments could just as easily be called terrorist organisations!

4.3.3. The Tanker War

In 2019, the Persian Gulf is the scene of several incidents against ships. On May 12, just after the adoption of new US economic sanctions against Iran, four ships (*Al Marzoqah, Andrea Victory, Amjad, A Michel*) are targeted by mysterious "acts of sabotage" off the port of Fujairah, United Arab Emirates. John Bolton,

224. Geoffrey Ramsey, "Hezbollah in Latin America: An Over-Hyped Threat?", *InSight Crime*, January 13, 2012
225. *Notisur*, August 16, 1996
226. *The Nation*, January 18, 2008
227. "Cristina Fernandez de Kirchner will return to Argentina's government with election victory by left-wing party", *Jewish Telegraphic Agency*, October 28, 2019

the US National Security Adviser, says it was "*almost certainly Iranian sea mines*". In fact, we don't know. A joint five-nation mission[228] investigated and issued a statement on 6 June, which envisaged "*most likely a state actor*" but did not mention Iran[229].

The photos taken by drones do not identify the people, what they are doing, or the nature of what they are handling, which is assumed to be a magnetic mine. This does not prevent the Pentagon from attributing the attacks to the Revolutionary Guards[230]. Thus, the ships were sabotaged with magnetic mines ("limpet mines") attached to the hull, but the Pentagon has no explanation as to how they were laid and by whom.

On June 11, Iran releases a US national suspected of espionage as a sign of appeasement. Bloomberg notes that diplomacy tends to resume[231]. But on June 12, a new attack is reported in the Strait of Hormuz against a Norwegian ship (*Front Altair*) and a Japanese ship flying the Panamanian flag (*Kokuka Courageous*). Once again, the perpetrators cannot be identified. But during a press conference, Mike Pompeo already accuses Iran:

> *The US assessment is that the Islamic Republic of Iran is responsible for the attacks [...] It is based on intelligence, the weapons used, the level of expertise required to execute the operation, recent similar Iranian attacks on the merchant marine and the fact that no actor operating in the region has the resources and expertise for such a sophisticated action*[232].

He refers in no particular order to attacks in Afghanistan (where the Taliban and the main rebel factions are Sunni, remember) and the suspicion that Iran has mounted sophisticated sea-to-sea missiles on traditional fishing boats ("dhows")! But he provides no evidence or facts. Yet Jeremy Hunt, the British Foreign Secretary, states:

> *We will do our own independent assessment, we have our own processes for that, (but) we have no reason to doubt the American analysis, and our instinct is to believe them because they are our closest allies*[233].

228. These are the three countries concerned (Saudi Arabia, United Arab Emirates and Norway) with technical assistance from the United States and France.
229. *Joint Press Statement of the United Arab Emirates, the Kingdom of Norway and Kingdom of Saudi Arabia*, New York, June 6, 2019 (see Wikipedia article "May 2019 Gulf of Oman incident")
230. "Pentagon accuses Iran's Revolutionary Guards over tanker attacks, *Reuters*, May 24, 2019
231. Ladane Nasseri, "Iran Frees U.S. Resident as Diplomacy Gathers Steam," *Bloomberg*, June 11, 2019
232. "Secretary of State Michael R. Pompeo Remarks to the Press," *Press Briefing Room, State Department*, Washington, DC, June 13, 2019
233. "Britain backs U.S. in blaming Iran for tanker attacks, *Reuters*, June 14, 2019

It should be noted that the Foreign Office website does not retain this last remark. Instead, it states that Iran's responsibility is justified because "*no other actor, state or otherwise, could plausibly have been responsible*[234]". In other words: "We have no proof".

On *France 5*, Pierre Servent, a military expert, illustrates quite well the Western way of approaching things: he confirms that he has no proof, but he is "*convinced*" that the attacks against the oil tankers were carried out by the Iranian secret services. He adds:

> *For a very long time, since the Iraq-Iran war, the Iranians in the Persian Gulf have been building mini secret bases in areas where you have sandbanks that are flush with the surface of the water [...] the Iranians would have, for a very long time, built small watertight bunkers underneath these areas, but large enough to house teams of combat swimmers on extremely fast RIBs with a strike and return capacity*[235].

It's the return of the famous Osama bin Laden caves in Afghanistan... pure fantasy!

It is not clear why Iran would attack a Japanese ship in June 2019: Japanese Prime Minister Shinzo Abe is on an official visit to Iran at the time, precisely to offer his services in resolving the crisis and to push the Americans back into the JCPOA. Iran has no interest in such an operation and no convincing explanation has been put forward.

Indeed, the US business media *Bloomberg Opinion* tweets that "*Iran would have little to gain by attacking oil tankers in the Arabian Sea*[236]". As Julian Lee notes:

> *For a country to perceive minute tangible signs of an easing of crippling US sanctions would be particularly bad timing. But this is understandable if the ultimate goal is to derail any signs of détente between the two countries, and push for regime change in Tehran. Whoever is behind these attacks is no friend of Iran*[237].

The observation is relevant and suggests interference by a third power. Indeed, every time there is a sign of 'warming' between Iran and the US, a new

---

234. "UK Government statement following the attacks on tankers in the Gulf of Oman", *Foreign & Commonwealth Office*, June 14, 2019

235. Pierre Servent, in the programme "C dans l'air", "États-Unis / Iran: la guerre... à 10 minutes près #cdanslair 21.06.2019", *France 5/YouTube*, June 22, 2019 (08'30")

236. https://twitter.com/bopinion/status/1139217212802240512

237. Julian Lee, "Iran Has Little to Gain From Oman Tanker Attacks", *Bloomberg*, June 13, 2019

'attack' occurs. A provocation from outside is plausible. Conspiracy? Not really: in 2009, the *Brookings Institution* had already sketched out a scenario:

> *[...] it would be much better if the United States would invoke an Iranian provocation to justify the air strikes before launching them. Obviously, the more outrageous, lethal and unprovoked the Iranian action, the better for the US. Of course, it would be very difficult for the United States to induce Iran to carry out such a provocation without the rest of the world detecting the scheme, which would undermine it. (One method that might be successful would be to revive efforts at covert regime change in the hope that Tehran would retaliate overtly, or even indirectly, which could then be described as an unprovoked act of Iranian aggression.)*[238].

The hypothesis of a third actor, who could benefit from a conflict without paying the price, is not incongruous. A plausible answer exists: the *Modjahedin-e-Khalq* (MeK). The MeK is an Iranian opposition movement with Marxist tendencies. It helped the Islamists overthrow the Shah in 1979, and was used as a pretext to accuse Saddam Hussein of supporting international terrorism[239]. In 2002, the MeK accused Iran of developing nuclear weapons and made public documents it had received from Mossad[240]. From 2005, the group's fighters are trained in Iraq by the Joint Special Operations Command (JSOC) to carry out attacks in Iran[241]. However, it has been on the US list of terrorist movements since 1997 and was only removed from it in 2012[242], after an intense lobbying campaign[243]. Despite its numerous crimes against human rights[244], its attacks and assassinations, the MeK is not considered as terrorist in France; perhaps because Israel uses it to carry out terrorist activities in Iran, notably for the assassination of nuclear engineers in Iran between 2007 and 2010[245]. Israel's use of the MeK

---

238. Kenneth M. Pollack, et al, "Which Path to Persia? Options for a New American Strategy toward Iran", Analysis Paper No. 20, *Saban Center for Middle East Policy, The Brookings Institution,* June 2009, p. 84

239. Saddam Hussein's Support for International Terrorism (https://georgewbush-whitehouse.archives.gov/infocus/iraq/decade/sect5.html)

240. Gareth Porter, "Guess who credits the Mossad with producing the 'laptop documents?'", *Middle East Eyes,* December 18, 2014

241. Seymour M. Hersh, "Our Men in Iran?", *The New Yorker,* April 5, 2012.

242. https://www.state.gov/foreign-terrorist-organizations/

243. Glenn Greenwald, "Israel, MEK and state sponsor of Terror groups", *Salon.com,* February 10, 2012

244. *No Exit - Human Rights Abuses Inside the MKO Camps,* Human Rights Watch, May 2005; *Statement on Responses to Human Rights Watch Report on Abuses by the Mojahedin-e Khalq Organization (MKO),* February 14, 2006

245. Ilan Ben Zion, "NBC: US officials say Mossad has been training group killing Iranian scientists," *The Times of Israel,* February 9, 2012; "Israel's Mossad Trained Assassins of Iran Nuclear Scientists, Report Says," *Haaretz,* February 9, 2012; "Israel-MEK relationship 'intricate and close'," NBC News, February 9, 2012; Daniel Larison, "NBC Report: Israel and the MEK Responsible for Deaths of Iranian Nuclear Scientists", *The American Conservative,* February 9, 2012; Ronen Bergman, "When Israel Hatched a Secret Plan to Assassinate Iranian Scientists", *Politico,* March 5, 2018

to carry out its dirty work against Iran was met with disapproval in the United States[246], but has received renewed attention with the Trump administration[247].

On July 4, 2019, the *Grace 1,* an Iranian oil tanker flying a Panamanian flag and carrying 2.1 million barrels of oil, was arrested off Gibraltar by the UK authorities. They suspect that the cargo is destined for Syria and invoke EU sanctions[248]. The problem is that while the EU prohibits *its members from* supplying oil to Syria, it does not have a policy of enforcing sanctions on third states. It will appear that the Gibraltar authorities acted under pressure from Washington 48 hours before the event and urgently drafted legislation to allow them to board the ship[249]. Finally, the tanker was released on August 15, despite repeated pressure from the United States, which even went so far as to try to bribe the ship's captain with $15 million to hand over his vessel[250].

4.4 "General Qassem Soleimani was preparing imminent attacks against the United States[251]"

4.4.1. The assassination

The assassination of General Soleimani is rooted in Donald Trump's claim to American authority over Iraqi oil, in payment for investments in the country! In order to put pressure on Iraq, Trump proposed to Prime Minister Adil Abdul-Mahdi to complete the reconstruction of the country's infrastructure in exchange for the transfer of 50% of the oil. But Abdul-Mahdi refuses and prefers to sign a deal with China in September 2019. Trump then asked him to cancel the agreement, otherwise he threatened to provoke popular demonstrations to overthrow the regime; he even threatened to use US Marines gunmen to eliminate demonstrators in order to escalate the situation[252]. True or not, the fact remains that in October 2019, violent protests erupted in Baghdad, with 63% of the calls coming from Saudi Arabia, 5% from the Emirates, 2% from Germany and 1% from Switzerland[253] and creating an explosive climate in the country.

246. Robert Wright, 'Israel and Proxy Terrorism', *The Atlantic*, February 13, 2012
247. "Iran group tied to Trump advisers rallies in Washington to demand regime change," *AP/The Times of Israel*, June 22, 2019
248. Jonathan Saul & Parisa Hafezi, 'Tehran fumes as Britain seizes Iranian oil tanker over Syria sanctions', *Reuters*, July 4, 2019
249. Kim Sengupta, 'UK finds itself in diplomatic maelstrom with Iran and Spain after seizure of Syria-bound oil-tanker', *The Independent UK*, July 5, 2019
250. "US offers cash to tanker captains in bid to seize Iranian ships", *Financial Times*, September 4, 2019
251. Veronica Stracqualursi & Jennifer Hansler, "Pompeo: Strike on Soleimani disrupted an 'imminent attack' and 'saved American lives'", *CNN*, January 3, 2020
252. Adil Abdul-Mahdi's speech to the Iraqi parliament, January 5, 2020.
253. https://twitter.com/aseyedp/status/1179852662449135616

The spark comes on December 27, 2019: Iranian-made 107mm FAJR-1 rockets strike the K-1 military base in Kirkuk, which houses Iraqi and US units dedicated to fighting the Islamic State. One US mercenary is killed. The perpetrators of the attack are not known, but the United States immediately attributes it to the Kataeb Hezbollah *(*Hezbollah Phalanx*), an* Iraqi Shiite organisation (with no links to the Lebanese Hezbollah), which is represented in the Iraqi parliament and which had fought the Islamic State with the Kurds. The American president accused Iran and the Revolutionary Guards, and retaliatory strikes were carried out on December 29, in Syria and against a military base of its Iraqi ally, which shelters Iraqi soldiers and Kataeb troops[254]. These strikes provoked riots that led to the intrusion into the American embassy in Baghdad on December 31, giving Trump a pretext to shoot General Qassem Soleimani on January 3, 2020.

In February 2020, the New York Times revealed that the American decision had not been subject to any consultation with Iraqi intelligence. It was based on the identification of the rockets used as being of Iranian origin. But in fact, Iran had supplied them to Iraq to fight the Islamic State, and a number were known to have been stolen from Iraqi army depots. Moreover, physical evidence recovered after the December 27 incident indicates that the shooting was carried out by the Islamic State[255].

On January 3, 2020, the Iranian Major General Qassem Soleimani was eliminated in Baghdad on the orders of Donald Trump, who accused him of preparing operations against 4 American embassies in the Middle East: an "*imminent threat*". The intelligence is provided by Israel[256]. In fact, Trump's decision is based on three elements[257]: Soleimani's visits to Shiite militias in Syria and Iraq; an unknown communication to the Iranian president that could just as easily be a request for leave; and the context of tension in Baghdad, where an American contractor was killed in a riot. The idea of the assassination was suggested by Richard Goldberg, a member of the National Security Council, but also - at the same time - an advisor to the Foundation for Defense of Democracy (FDD)[258], a body financed by the Israeli government.

---

254. Julian E. Barnes, "U.S. Launches Airstrikes on Iranian-Backed Forces in Iraq and Syria," *The New York Times*, December 29, 2019

255. Alissa J. Rubin, "Was U.S. Wrong About Attack That Nearly Started a War With Iran?", *The New York Times*, February 6, 2020

256. "Pompeo, Netanyahu discuss Iran's 'malign influence' after Soleimani strike", *The Times of Israel*, January 4, 2020

257. https://twitter.com/rcallimachi/status/1213421769777909761

258. www.fdd.org/analysis/2020/01/02/u-s-kills-irans-qods-force-commander-and-iraqs-deputy-pmf-leader-in-strike-in-baghdad

Simultaneously, the Americans attempt to shoot down Abdul Reza Shahlai, the Houthi leader, in Yemen, but miss[259]. This attempt tends to discredit the '*imminent threat*' justification. The presidential team is clearly playing with the facts, as evidenced by its refusal to provide Congress with the supporting evidence[260]. Vice President Mike Pence even claims that Soleimani had helped the terrorists prepare for '9/11'[261]. He relays a legend that the Americans love: the involvement of Iran. Yet the report of the Parliamentary Commission on 9/11 notes that there is no indication that Iran was involved:

> *[...] there is strong evidence that Iran facilitated the transit of Al Qaeda members to and from Afghanistan prior to 9/11... We have found no evidence that Iran or Hezbollah was aware of the planning of what would become the 9/11 attack*[262].

Clearly, it can be blamed for the same mistake as Germany, far below the responsibility of the United States itself (which knew, but did not act!). Moreover, the report does not mention Soleimani once.

So, as usual Trump, Pompeo and Pence lied. They are trying to justify an illegal action under US law. Indeed, Executive Order 12333, signed by President Ronald Reagan in 1981[263] defines the roles and missions of the US intelligence community and states that *"no person employed or acting on behalf of the United States Government shall be engaged in, or conspire to be engaged in, assassinations"*, thus formalising a policy already established by President Gerald Ford in 1976.

The Anglo-Saxon media - of all stripes - questioned the notion of an '*imminent threat*', which justified the assassination, as it was being eroded with each passing day[264]. On January 12, Mark Esper, Secretary of Defense, told *CBS* that he had not seen any information on these threats[265], as had the State Department administration[266]. Questioned on *France 24* about Israel's participation in the operation, Lieutenant-Colonel Jonathan Conricus, spokesman for the Israeli

---

259. Eric Schmitt, Edward Wong & Julian E. Barnes, 'U.S. Unsuccessfully Tried Killing a Second Iranian Military Official', *The New York Times*, January 10, 2020

260. Rebecca Klar, 'Esper: Gang of 8 'did not think' further intelligence on Iranian threat should be shared with Congress', *The Hill*, January 12, 2020

261. Steve Benen, 'Why Pence's falsehood about Soleimani and 9/11 matters', *MSNBC News*, January 6, 2020

262. *The 9/11 Commission Report (Authorized Edition)*, Norton & Company, New York, July 22, 2004, p. 241

263. *Executive Order 12333 - United States Intelligence Activities* (As Amended by Executive Orders 13284 (2003), 13355 (2004) and 13470 (2008), December 4, 1981, para 2.11 (www.cia.gov/about-cia/eo12333.html)

264. Aaron Blake, "Trump's 'four embassies' claim utterly falls apart", *MSN News*, January 13, 2020

265. Valerie Volcovici, 'Pentagon chief says no specific evidence Iran was plotting to attack four U.S. embassies', *Reuters*, January 12, 2020; Robert Burns, 'Defense Secretary Mark Esper Says He 'Didn't See' Evidence That 4 U.S. Embassies Were Under Threat From Iran', *Time/AP*, January 12, 2020; Peter Baker & Thomas Gibbons-Neff, 'Esper Says He Saw No Evidence Iran Targeted 4 Embassies, as Story Shifts Again', *The New York Times*, January 12, 2020.

266. Sonam Sheth, "State Department was reportedly unaware of an 'imminent threat' to 4 US embassies, blowing a hole through Trump's claims", *Business Insider*, January 13, 2020

army, got out of it by saying that the operation was directed by the United States and that Israel was not part of it. This is only part of the truth, as the intelligence about the "*imminent threat*" came from Israel[267]. And on January 13, Mike Pompeo confessed:

> *A series of imminent attacks were planned by Qassem Soleimani, but we don't know precisely when or where, but it was real*[268].

On the same day, Donald Trump confessed that this "*imminent threat*" was not the problem, but rather the general's "*horrible past*[269]"!

He is referring to his alleged responsibility for the death of 600 American soldiers in Iraq since 2003. An accusation relayed in France by the pro-Israeli media, like *Dreuz.info*[270]. But it is false: the Pentagon spokesman confesses that he "*has no study, no documentation, no data to provide to journalists that could confirm these figures*[271]." Unverified, the number of 600 was not originally attributed to Soleimani, but to Iran[272]. This is also a lie: it originated in January 2007, when US Vice President Dick Cheney was looking for pretexts to strike Iran. After the generals of the Joint Chiefs of Staff unanimously and categorically refused to strike Iranian nuclear capabilities about which there was no intelligence[273], Cheney claimed that Iran had supplied directional anti-vehicle mines (responsible for the deaths in question)[274]. Another lie: the devices were made in Iraq[275], with equipment purchased from the United Arab Emirates, as confirmed by the very serious *Jane's Intelligence Review*[276].

In France, the media are divided between their hatred of Donald Trump and their blind support for his Middle Eastern policy, but the message of the Trump administration is relayed rather slavishly. In the programme "C dans l'air" on January 3, the journalist François Clémenceau asserts that General Soleimani is

---

267. "Israeli intel helped US carry out strike that killed Iran's Soleimani - report", *The Times of Israel*, January 12, 2020
268. Mike Pompeo to Laura Ingraham, *FOX News*, January 9, 2020
269. https://twitter.com/realDonaldTrump/status/1216754098382524422
270. "Report: Iran Killed 600 U.S. Soldiers in the Iraq War," *The National Interest*, April 3, 2019; Jean-Patrick Grumberg, "More important than Bin Laden and Baghdadi, Iranian military leader Qasem Soleimani has been eliminated," *dreuz.info*, January 3, 2020.
271. Gareth Porter, 'Lies About Iran Killing US Troops in Iraq Are a Ploy to Justify War', *Truthout.org*, July 9, 2019
272. Kyle Rempfer, 'Iran killed more US troops in Iraq than previously known, Pentagon says', *Military Times*, April 4, 2019
273. Gareth Porter, 'Military Resistance Forced Shift on Iran Strike', *Inter Press Service News Agency*, October 18, 2007.
274. NdA: In fact, these are *Explosive Forged Penetrators (EFP)* designed to penetrate the ever-thickening armour of military vehicles.
275. Gareth Porter, "U.S. Military Ignored Evidence of Iraqi-Made EFPs", *Inter Press Service News Agency*, October 25, 2007
276. Michael Knights, 'Struggle for Control', *Jane's Intelligence Review*, January 2007, pp 18-23

"[a] *central figure who has been confronting the United States permanently and for a very long time, not only since the beginning of the Iraq war in 2003 but before*[277]." In fact, he is relaying a tweet from Trump[278], but this is disinformation. Not only had Iran supported the US in Afghanistan through its good relations with the Hazara community, but it had helped them during the Herat uprising in 2001:

> *The US special operations teams consisted of US Army Rangers and Delta Force, under the command of CENTCOM General Tommy Franks. The Iranian forces consisted of al-Quds Force operatives under the command of Major General Yahya Rahim Safavi, Commander of the Revolutionary Guards and Major General Qassem Soleimani, Commander of Iran's al-Quds Force*[279].

The *Courrier international* even headlines *Good riddance*[280], without congratulating or blaming the Americans. Ironically, this is the same position that the EI takes in its propaganda magazine *Al-Naba*[281]!... In 2015, Iran had supported the international coalition in Iraq in its fight against the EI. During the recapture of the city of Tikrīt, Iranian-backed forces even received US air support. *Newsweek* magazine reports General Dempsey as saying:

> *[...] Without Iranian assistance and Soleimani's advice, the offensive on Tikrit would not have been possible*[282].

The role of Iran is bathed in an atmosphere of distortion of the facts, aligned with Israeli rhetoric. For example, *France 5* states that in the summer of 2006 General Soleimani "*fought alongside Hezbollah*[283]" against Israel. This is not true. Soleimani was in Lebanon for a few days as an observer[284], which is not incongruous given Israel's regular strikes outside its borders, but he did not take part in the fighting (nor is it clear why he would have done so). Lists of Soleimani's "crimes" are circulating[285], but these are only assemblages of rumours.

---

277. François Clémenceau in the programme "C dans l'air", "Trump / Iran: la guerre est-elle déclarée ? #cdanslair 03.01.2019 ", *France5/YouTube*, January 4, 2020, (06'16")
278. https://twitter.com/realDonaldTrump/status/1213096352072294401
279. Wikipedia, page "*2001 uprising in Herat*
280. "Bête noire. La mort de Soleimani vue du Golfe: bon débarras", *Courrier international*, January 3, 2020
281. https://twitter.com/Minalami/status/1215558269588201472
282. Jack Moore, "Iranian Military Mastermind Leading Battle to Recapture Tikrit From ISIS", *Newsweek*, March 5, 2015
283. "Crash du Boeing 737: l'Iran accusé #cdanslair 10.01.2019 ", *France5/YouTube*, January 11, 2020 (48'48")
284. "Shadowy Iran commander gives interview on 2006 Israel-Hezbollah war", *France24.com*, January 10, 2019
285. Jean-Patrick Grumberg, "La liste terrifiante des activités terroristes et criminelles de Qassem Soleimani", *dreuz.info*, January 7, 2020

Soleimani was eliminated with Abu Mahdi al-Mohandes, presented by *France 24* as Soleimani's "lieutenant" in Iraq[286]. In reality, he has no organic link with the Iranian Revolutionary Guards, but was leading the Iraqi Popular Mobilisation Units (PMU). The PMUs were created to make up for the Iraqi army's deficiencies in fighting the Islamic State in the north of the country. Described as "pro-Iranian militias" in the Western press, their Iraqi character is downplayed[287], but they reflect the composition of the country: they include a majority of Shiites, with Sunnis, Turkmen, Kurds and Yazidis.

In fact, on January 5, 2020, during the debates in the Iraqi Parliament on the maintenance of the foreign military presence, Adil Abdul-Mahdi, the Iraqi Prime Minister, revealed that Soleimani was on a diplomatic peace mission at the time: he was to meet him on January 3 to convey Iran's response to an Iraqi-negotiated easing of tensions with Saudi Arabia. This is why he had travelled to Baghdad on a scheduled flight and passed through immigration with his diplomatic passport, which makes the idea of preparing a clandestine action rather implausible. In fact, the American services were most probably aware of this peace initiative and opposed to this elimination, which would explain why the Pentagon communiqué of January 2 emphasises the presidential origin of the decision[288]. But no French mainstream media relayed this information.

On January 6, disappointingly, the joint statement by Germany, France and Britain (signatories of the JCPOA) mentions Iran's '*negative role*' in the Middle East, but not the assassination[289]. Moreover, France does not condemn the assassination of an emissary on a diplomatic mission, but only the Iranian reaction[290]. In July 2020, the UN will condemn this attack as unjustified and illegal[291]. As far as the Middle East is concerned, the mainstream media tend to follow a rather pro-Trump line, contrary to the values and respect for international law that they profess.

Whatever one thinks of General Soleimani, the problem here is that we accept the principle that "the end justifies the means": this is exactly the same thinking as that of the Islamic State terrorists and it goes against the "values" that we claim to defend. In fact, the only people who really welcomed the killing - apart from the Americans and Israelis, which is not very surprising - were the jihadists in

286. Journal de 12h30, *France 24*, January 24, 2020

287. Wikipedia, article "Hashd al-Shaabi"

288. *Statement by the Department of Defense*, January 2, 2020, (www.defense.gov/Newsroom/Releases/Release/Article/2049534/statement-by-the-department-of-defense/)

289. *Joint statement by the President of the French Republic, the Federal Chancellor of Germany and the Prime Minister of the United Kingdom*, Elysee.fr, January 6, 2020

290. "After Soleimani's death, Macron wants to 'avoid a dangerous escalation'", *Reuters*, January 3, 2020

291. "US strike 'illegal and arbitrary', says UN expert", www.20min.ch, July 7, 2020

the Idlib pocket in Syria[292] and the Islamic State[293]. The Pakistani Ministry of Defence website even mentions that this elimination could lead to a revival of the Islamic State[294]! As usual, Western leaders favour short-term policies based on actions that are as ill-considered and spectacular as they are unnecessary.

4.4.2. The disaster of flight PS752

Quite logically, the assassination of General Soleimani triggered the anger of the Iranians, who announced retaliatory measures. The Americans took fright and - on January 4 - sent Iran, through the Swiss embassy in Tehran, an imploring message:

> *If you want revenge, take it in proportion to what we have done*[295].

The next day, Trump tried to intimidate and deter Iran by threatening to "*strike very quickly and very hard*" at 52 targets, including cultural property, which had already been selected[296].

On 8 January, a Boeing 737-800 of Ukraine International Airlines (PS752) crashed shortly after take-off from Tehran. After initially denying responsibility, Iran admits three days later that it accidentally shot down the plane with an anti-aircraft missile and apologises, announcing that those responsible will be punished.

In fact, what happened was certainly accidental, but - paradoxically - probably not human error: the operators were probably led to a situation where they could no longer avoid firing the missile. On January 8, Iran carried out a series of strikes against two US bases in Iraq from which the aircraft that killed General Soleimani had allegedly departed. At the same time, the Iranian command expected a US strike and placed its air defence forces on the highest level of alert, "3", applied in the event of war. According to the official account of the Revolutionary Guard Command[297], the information that cruise missiles have been fired against Iran is spreading. The origin of the information is still

292. https://twitter.com/naveedkhizer/status/1213145880250998784

293. Ryan Fahey, "ISIS welcomes the death of Iran's Qaseem Soleimani and declare it an act of 'divine intervention' that will let them regroup in Iraq", *Daily Mail*, January 10, 2020; Jeremy Bowen, "Qasem Soleimani: Why his killing is good news for IS jihadists", *BBC News*, January 10, 2020; Jeremy Bowen, "Qasem Soleimani's assassination is good news for the 'Islamic State' group", *BBC News*, January 10, 2020

294. "ISIS praises US assassination of Iranian general Soleimani as 'divine intervention' that will help them rise again", *defence.pk*, January 11, 2020

295. "Iranian general killed in Iraq - Washington's 'ridiculous message' delivered by Berne", *20minutes.ch/ATS*, January 4, 2020

296. Jeremy Diamond, Caroline Kelly & Greg Clary, "Trump warns Iran if it hits any Americans or American assets 'we have targeted 52 Iranian sites'", *CNN*, January 5, 2020.

297. "IRGC Releases Details of Accidental Downing of Ukrainian Plane", *Iran Front Page*, January 11, 2020

undetermined, but could be the result of American jamming manoeuvres (active measures) as part of a reconnaissance activity[298].

In fact, the investigation conducted by the Cyber Space Lab of the University of Tehran will show that the operators were misled by a "cyber attack" against the Iranian networks[299]. Indeed, in June 2019, Donald Trump had authorised "*cyber attacks to disable Revolutionary Guard Corps computer systems used to control rocket and missile launches*"[300]. On January 8, it is likely to be a more subtle manoeuvre, using the experience gained from these 'cyber attacks'. Thus, in preparation for their strikes, the Americans applied electronic reconnaissance measures to identify the driving networks and the way they operate, as well as the electronic protection measures of the air defence. This is done by sending a decoy or simulating an attack in virtual form to make the opponent react.

This probably explains why two hours before the PS752 crash, the US government issued a NOTAM (Notice To AirMen) forbidding US aircraft to fly over Tehran due to a "*potential miscalculation or identification*"[301]. This would also explain why the Iranians fired a second anti-aircraft missile "into the void" 23 seconds after the one that shot down the Boeing; as well as the presence of F-35 stealth aircraft over Iran for electronic reconnaissance[302].

In fact, this type of manoeuvre is not new and was already practised regularly during the Cold War. This is what led to the destruction of Korean Airlines Flight 007 (KAL007) in September 1983: a US KC-135 spy plane had 'hidden' in the 'electronic shadow' of KAL007 in order to record Soviet air defence electronic activities while flying over Kamchatka; the Soviets thus shot down a civilian aircraft by 'mistaking' it for the US Air Force plane. In September 2018, a similar situation led to Syria shooting down a Russian aircraft behind which an Israeli reconnaissance plane was "hiding"[303].

In Iran, the situation is technically different, but operationally similar. The PS752 was in the ascent phase and had the same speed as a cruise missile (about 400 km/h), leaving the operator only a few seconds to react. Communications were apparently disrupted, forcing the duty officer to make the decision to fire the missile himself. So this is probably not a 'mistake' by the Iranian command, but the tragic consequence of a cluster of indications created - intentionally or not - by the US in preparing the retaliation announced by Trump. It is probably

298. "US 'launched cyber-attack on Iran weapons systems'", *BBC News*, June 23, 2019

299. https://twitter.com/Citnanewsagency/status/1216753568864182274

300. Zak Doffman, "U.S. Attacks Iran With Cyber Not Missiles -- A Game Changer, Not A Backtrack," *Forbes*, June 23, 2019; "US launched cyber attack on Iranian rockets and missiles - reports," *Associated Press/The Guardian*, June 23, 2019

301. https://twitter.com/ConflictsW/status/1215429983021228032

302. "Russia says Iran was spooked by reports of US F-35s when it downed airliner, *Reuters/Task & Purposes*, January 17, 2020

303. "Russia blames Israel after military plane shot down off Syria", *BBC News*, September 18, 2018

wrong to say at this stage that the Americans had foreseen the catastrophe, but they deliberately increased the probability of it happening.

The French media castigate the delay in Tehran's confession. But obviously, unlike their Anglo-Saxon counterparts, they do not recall that in 1988, after the incident of Iran Air Flight 655, the Americans lied about the position of their ship, about the trajectory of the aircraft, the fact that their warnings were sent on a military frequency inaccessible to the crew of the aircraft, the fact that they waited for the judgment of an international tribunal to admit their error, that they never apologised and that they decorated and promoted those responsible[304]...

Curiously, no sooner had the Iranian authorities admitted their responsibility than new demonstrations broke out, blaming the government's "lies". The portraits of General Soleimani - whom tens, even hundreds of thousands of people had mourned the day before - were suddenly torn up in the streets. This discrepancy is difficult to explain with certainty. However, one can assume that the Americans and the British expected the Iranian government to firmly and permanently deny responsibility[305]. It is thus likely that 'words of command' were given, but arrived at the wrong time, triggering limited protests.

4.5. Conclusions on the Iranian threat

The Iranian threat is artificial. Fuelled by a deep sense of revenge on the part of the Americans who had failed to anticipate the 1979 revolution, it now serves a single purpose: to fracture the Tehran-Damascus axis, created by the American-British intervention in Iraq and which frightens the Gulf monarchies. As for the threat to Israel, it is just as artificial and has no historical basis. On the other hand, it feeds on both sides a muscular discourse, intended to create national unity for domestic political purposes. In this context, the regional instability serves Benjamin Netanyahu who is struggling to gather a majority around him for the 2019-2020 elections. This is why he launches repeated provocations against his Palestinian and Syrian neighbours and Iran[306].

The West has still not understood anything about Iran and the functioning of the Middle East: their policies have only had effects contrary to their objectives. Sanctions, direct or indirect clandestine actions with the support of

304. Jeremy R. Hammond, "The 'Forgotten'US Shootdown of Iranian Airliner Flight 655", *Foreign Policy Journal*, July 3, 2017

305. Raf Sanchez, "Iran may never admit shooting down the Ukraine flight because of another air disaster 32 years ago", *The Telegraph*, January 10, 2020

306. Dahlia Scheindlin, 'Netanyahu Needs Conflict to Survive', *Foreign Policy*, May 16, 2018; Bel Trew, 'Netanyahu's gamble with Gaza may save his political career but spark a complex drawn-out conflict', *The Independent*, November 13, 2019

terrorist groups have only served to close the ranks of the population. With a very pro-Western Iranian population, a regime change could be brought about almost immediately by relaxing all sanctions on the country and encouraging its prosperity... But the West is too locked into its prejudices. In May 2019, then visiting Baghdad, Ali Khamenei, Supreme Leader of the Revolution, declared:

Thanks be to God, who gave us such stupid enemies[307]*!*

French policy towards Iran is clearly influenced by the US and the powerful Iranian opposition lobby in France. After the assassination of General Soleimani, while the Anglo-Saxon media took a critical approach to the American action, the French media remained divided between "anti-Trump" and "anti-Iranian" postures: criticising the American president, while tending to justify the assassination.

On *France 5* or *France 24,* only representatives of the Iranian opposition appear and give a biased view of the problem. On *TV5 Monde,* the sociologist Mahnaz Shirali states that his death has provoked "*an explosion of joy, a jubilation because Soleimani really embodies the most rejected, most criticised part of the Islamic Republic*[308]". This is not true. A study, conducted by the University of Maryland in October 2019[309], states that General Soleimani was the most popular figure in Iran, with 80 per cent approval; that 81 per cent of Iranians surveyed thought the Revolutionary Guards had increased Iran's security. Despite videos from several Iranian cities showing huge crowds for General Soleimani's funeral, it downplays by claiming that they only gather "*3,000-4,000*[310]" people. This is bad faith next to disinformation. Furthermore, it refers to the "*murder of 1,500 Iranians in the streets of Tehran*[311]" during the suppression of the riots in late 2019. In fact, these are the figures propagated by the MeK[312] and the Trump administration. The exact figures will probably never be known, but Amnesty International instead suggests a figure of 300 for the whole country (not just the capital)[313].

---

307. https://afaq.tv/contents/view/details?id=87510.

308. Mahnaz Shirali "Mort de Soleimani: les Américains fédèrent les Iraniens et leurs alliés contre eux", *TV5 Monde*, January 5, 2020 (00'23")

309. Nancy Gallagher, Ebrahim Mohseni & Clay Ramsay, *Iranian Public Opinion under "Maximum Pressure"*, Center for International and Security Studies at Maryland (CISSM), October 2019

310. Mahnaz Shirali "Mort de Soleimani: les Américains fédèrent les Iraniens et leurs alliés contre eux", *TV5 Monde*, January 5, 2020 (01'28")

311. Mahnaz Shirali "Mort de Soleimani: les Américains fédèrent les Iraniens et leurs alliés contre eux", *TV5 Monde*, January 5, 2020 (04'00")

312. *Iran Protests - Over 1,500 Killed in the Iranian People's Nationwide Uprising Names of 504 Martyrs Released*, National Council of Resistance of Iran (NCRI), December 15, 2019

313. Negar Mortazavi, 'Iran protests: Over 300 killed and thousands arrested in violent crackdown, Amnesty says', *The Independent*, December 16, 2019

Ms Shirali claims that only 5% of the population supports the regime. In reality, the figure is a little less than 5%, but it is misleading. The US survey shows that only 42% of Iranians think that signing the JCPOA was a good thing, 74% approve of exceeding the JCPOA's limits in response to the US withdrawal and 69% think that the European signatories will not fulfil their obligations. 70% think the government should not make any more concessions and 48% would like Iran to establish itself as a regional power, while only 42% think a more conciliatory attitude should be taken. 92% think it is important to develop a ballistic programme and 72% think it is very important. A majority (68%) of Iranians see their economy deteriorating, and condemn rampant corruption. But they attribute this to sanctions by Western countries, whose image is deteriorating: countries such as Japan, Russia, China and Germany have a favourable image, while countries such as France, Great Britain and the United States have a negative image. In other words, the 5% support hides the fact that the remaining 95% of the population is overwhelmingly more extreme than the government, and that it is at great risk of being overrun by its right wing.

This opposition to the Islamic government does not imply that they think like us or that they want to overthrow it. This is why - as in Syria[314] - demonstrations have to be provoked from outside through social networks: the US has set up a whole system of servers and applications to facilitate the mobilisation of the discontented in Iran[315]. This explains the Internet filtering carried out by the Iranian authorities after Soleimani's assassination.

Despite the difficult living conditions, the Iranian government's support for a tougher policy towards the West remains quite broad. Unlike Western countries, it does not need to hide behind clandestine operations: on the contrary, it would be in its interest to show that it is acting, as with its strikes against two American bases in Iraq. This could explain why the "attacks" on oil tankers in the Persian Gulf were probably not carried out by Iran, but by a third power, which does not want Iran to normalise its relations with the international community.

As with the 'red line' in Syria, French journalists - more than their Anglo-Saxon colleagues - deplore the reluctance to use violence against Iran. Thus, in January 2020, Armelle Charrier said on *France 5* that Trump had made a "false step" by not striking Iran after the destruction of an American drone over its territory[316]. She sees it as an admission of weakness, which would have

314. Robert Reuel Naiman, "WikiLeaks Reveals How the US Aggressively Pursued Regime Change in Syria, Igniting a Bloodbath," *truthout.org*, October 9, 2015

315. Katrina Manson, "US boosts funding of tech companies to help anti-Tehran protests", *Financial Times*, January 20, 2020

316. Armelle Charrier in the programme "C dans l'air", "Iran / États-Unis: un pas de plus vers la guerre ? #cdanslair 02.01.2020", *France 5/YouTube*, January 3, 2020 (10'15")

pushed Iran to be more reckless. It has not understood anything: this reading of international relations through power relations and muscular policies is totally out of step with the reality of the region. This is exactly why the West has been failing there.

In fact, Trump's refusal to strike Iran in September 2019 showed the Saudis that he was not ready to engage in a new conflict in the region, and pushed them to seek a negotiated solution with Iran. Therefore, in the following weeks, the Saudis started a process of discreet negotiations through Iraq and Pakistan[317]. It was in this context that General Qassem Soleimani was in Iraq in early January 2020, and it was for this very reason that he was shot. Indeed, the only country that had no interest in these negotiations was Israel... which then provided false intelligence to the Americans.

---

317. Farnaz Fassihi & Ben Hubbard, 'Saudi Arabia and Iran Make Quiet Openings to Head Off War', *The New York Times*, October 4, 2019

5. JIHADIST TERRORISM

5.1. The context

Since the late 1990s, Western explanations for jihadist attacks have had a common thread of systematically ignoring our actions. Thus, in June 2017, Hugo Micheron, a researcher in the field of terrorism, even asserted that "DAECH" was seeking to "*interfere*" in British legislatures[318]. To what end? From individual madness to a plot to dominate the world, the "experts" are turning their professions of faith and suppositions, based on fragmentary information, into certainties. They look for explanations in the Koran, but systematically exclude what the terrorists tell us.

Middle Eastern jihadism began with the maintenance of American forces in Saudi Arabia after the Gulf War (1990-1991), to monitor Iraq. This presence worried the Saudi authorities because it fuelled a radical opposition that was beginning to emerge and threaten the regime. In fact, since the 1950s, the American presence in Saudi Arabia has been criticised in the Muslim world and, as early as 1960, Prince Faisal asked President John F. Kennedy - without success - to withdraw his troops from the Dhahran base[319]. In reality, the illegitimacy of this presence in Saudi Arabia is more a matter of sensitivity and national pride than of religion, but it is enough to provoke jihadist reflexes.

On 25 June 1996, an attack targeted the living quarters of US forces in Saudi Arabia, the Khobar Towers, near Dhahran. But the United States ignored the warning, and the Islamists increased the pressure: on August 7, 1998, two attacks simultaneously hit their embassies in Nairobi and Dar-Es-Salam.

The United States responds with two groups of strikes (Operation INFINITE REACH) to be executed on August 20, 1998, using 79 cruise missiles fired from ships in the Persian Gulf. They targeted four training camps in the Khost-Jalalabad region of Afghanistan and the Al-Shifa pharmaceutical complex near

318. "Daech wanted to interfere in the British election campaign explains Hugo Micheron", *franceinfo*, June 4, 2017

319. Gresh Alain, "Les grands écarts de l'Arabie saoudite", *Le Monde Diplomatique*, June 2003.

Khartoum, Sudan. Based on unverified and outdated information, they do not affect terrorists, but cause several dozen civilian casualties. In Sudan, according to Werner Daum, then German ambassador in Khartoum, the destruction of the Al-Shifa complex - the main drug production centre for Sudan - caused "*the death of several tens of thousands of civilians*[320]".

In 1999, a report by *the* US Department of Energy's Office of Intelligence and Counterintelligence (OICI) estimated that these strikes...

was questionable justice, as it only affected innocent people;

had a questionable impact on al-Qaeda's operational capabilities;

tended to show that the US was afraid to confront the terrorists directly;

had given rise to more terrorist projects;

had hit the Taliban, who probably had no responsibility for the terrorist activities given their limited authority in the territory[321].

These strikes therefore only affected innocent people, who were not remotely connected to the attacks in Nairobi and Dar-es-Salam. But there will be no apology or compensation[322]. A few days after the strikes, *The Economist* magazine prophesied that the bombing had '*created 10,000 new fanatics where none would have existed*[323]'. While Louis Freeh, Director of the Federal Bureau of Investigation (FBI), stated that after the strikes "there *will probably be more [terrorist] attacks and more deaths*[324]".

Quickly forgotten in the West, these indiscriminate bombings, carried out from a great distance, without allowing for parrying and without the perpetrators exposing themselves physically, were perceived as an act of cowardice:

> *The [1998] attacks did not improve America's image among the mujahideen I interviewed, who describe Tomahawk missiles as cowardly weapons, too afraid to risk their lives in battle or look their enemy in the eye*[325].

They will provide the jihadists with the motive and template for "9/11", which they consider "*the biggest special operation of all time*[326]. Indeed, on August 6,

320. Werner Daum (German Ambassador to Sudan 1996-2000), *Universalism and the West - An Agenda for Understanding*, Harvard International Review, 2001.
321. *Osama Bin Laden: A Case Study*, Sandia National Laboratories, US Department of Energy, Livermore (CA), 1999.
322. Lacey Marc, "Look at the Place! Sudan Says, 'Say Sorry,' but U.S. Won't," *The New York Times*, October 20, 2005 (accessed October 1st, 2015).
323. Editorial, 'Punish and Be Damned', The Economist, August 29, 1998.
324. Ronald K. Noble, "A Neglected Anti-Terror Weapon", *New York Times*, September 9, 1998.
325. Jessica Stern, "Being Feared Is Not Enough to Keep Us Safe", *Washington Post*, September 15, 2001.
326. *Inspire Magazine*, No. 7, Fall 2011.

2001, a CIA memo to President Bush[327] entitled *Bin Laden Determined to Strike in the US* indicated that an attack was being prepared in response to the August 1998 strikes[328].

Just as twenty years later in France, by minimising the consequences of the 1998 'indiscriminate' strikes, the reading of jihadist terrorism was distorted by making it appear as a hegemonic, irrational project, totally independent of our actions in the Near and Middle East. This opened the door to the most fanciful theories.

The US - and other Western countries that follow them - have not understood that they are already trapped in an asymmetric logic. Their show of force only showed their weakness in the eyes of the Islamists: a) by demonstrating that they were not willing to put their fighters on the line (the Somali failure is still close) b) because they had not been able to know where the "blows were coming from" and c) because they had not been able to recognise their mistake. Not to mention that by indiscriminately hitting civilian populations, the West is putting itself in the same position as the terrorists it wants to fight. The terrorists are thus at liberty to denounce their failure to respect international law: they interfere in the internal affairs of countries; they attack them without an international mandate or valid reason; they try to appropriate natural resources by force; they practice torture, commit war crimes and lock up those who denounce them (such as Julian Assange)... He who sows the wind reaps the storm...

5.2 "The Purpose of Terrorism is just That, to Terrorise People[329]"

The Western interventions in Afghanistan and Iraq in 2001 and 2003 bring a concrete rationality to the jihadists' fight. They provide them with a strategic coherence, by placing terrorism in a logic of armed resistance to clearly illegal and illegitimate invasions.

A month before the start of the Iraq war, the UK Joint Intelligence Committee (JIC) sent a summary dated February 10, 2003 to Tony Blair, the Prime Minister, which stated:

> *I. The threat from Al Qaeda will increase from the outset of any military action against Iraq. They will target coalition forces and other Western interests in the Middle East. Attacks on Western interests elsewhere in the world*

327. This is a daily intelligence brief called the *Presidential Daily Brief* (PDB). Until 2004, it was produced by the CIA with contributions from the entire intelligence community. The *Intelligence Reform and Terrorism Prevention Act* gives this responsibility to the *Director of National Intelligence* (DNI).
328. The memo was declassified on April 10, 2004 ("Transcript: Bin Laden determined to strike in US", *CNN.com*, April 10, 2004)
329. Tony Blair, "In full: Blair on bomb blasts", *BBC News*, July 7, 2005

are also likely, particularly in the US and UK, for maximum impact. The global threat from other terrorist groups and Islamist individuals will increase significantly.

[...]

18. Al Qaeda and associated groups will continue to pose by far the greatest terrorist threat to Western interests, and this threat will be enhanced by military action against Iraq. The wider threat from Islamist terrorists will also increase in the event of war, reflecting the intensification of anti-American and anti-Western sentiment in the Muslim world, including among Muslim communities in the West[330].

This report shows that it was known that engaging in this war would generate a terrorist surge in Europe. The pivotal event was the Madrid bombing (March 11, 2004). Spain was in the middle of an election period and the population was strongly opposed to participating in the war in Iraq. The elections brought the opposition to power, which decided to withdraw from Iraq, provoking the withdrawal from Honduras.

This withdrawal was not intended to satisfy the terrorists (whose motives are not understood at this stage), but public opinion, which was opposed to the war *before* the attacks. In fact, the Spaniards were overwhelmed by their reading of the attacks and did not know how to dissociate the attack from their withdrawal in their strategic communication. Unintentionally, the Spanish made the "M-11" a source of inspiration for the jihadists, who saw it as a strategic success, later conceptualised as the "*deterrence operation*[331]". It led to the London bombings (July 7 and 21, 2005)[332] and - much later - to the Paris attacks.

This is why, in 2005, Tony Blair's government sought to 'disconnect' the attacks and attempted attacks from the war in Iraq and to present the terrorists as victims of mental and social disorders[333]. However, the video of Mohammed Siddique Khan's claim of responsibility[334], explains very clearly that the attack of July 7 was motivated by the war in Iraq:

330. *International Terrorism: War With Iraq*, JIC Assessment, February 10, 2003 (TOP SECRET - Declassified), pararaphs I and 18

331. Abu Mu'sab al-Suri, "The Jihadi Experience - The Strategy of Deterring with Terrorism", *op.cit.*

332. Abu Mu'sab al-Suri, 'The Jihadi Experience - The Strategy of Deterring with Terrorism', *Inspire Magazine*, No. 10, Spring 2013, p. 23.

333. *Report of the Official Account of the Bombings in London on 7th July 2005*, Ordered by the House of Commons to be printed 11th May 2006, The Stationery Office, London [HC 1087].

334. "Mohammed Siddique Khan's 'martyrdom video', *YouTube*, October 19, 2010, (https://www.youtube.com/

[Your democratically elected governments continually perpetrate atrocities against my people around the world. And your support for them makes you directly responsible, as I am directly responsible for protecting and avenging my Muslim brothers and sisters.

Until we feel safe, you will be our targets, and as long as you bomb, gas, imprison and torture my people, we will not stop this fight.

We are at war and I am a soldier. Now you too can appreciate the reality of the situation[335] *[…]*

Published a year later by the *Al-Jazeerah* channel, the video of another terrorist of 7 July 2005, Shehzad Tanweer, repeats exactly the same themes, addressing the British:

You may wonder why you deserve this. You and your government are the ones who, to this day, oppress our women and children, our brothers and sisters, from East to West, from Palestine, Afghanistan, Iraq and Chechnya. Your government supported the massacre of some 50,000 innocent people in Fallujah […] you are directly responsible for the problem in Palestine and in Iraq to this day. […] We are 100% committed to the cause of Islam. We love death as you love life. We ask you to stop supporting the British government and the so-called "War on Terror". Ask yourself why thousands of men are willing to give their lives for the cause of Muslims[336] *[…]*

In March 2003, during the debates on intervention in Iraq, Scottish MP Tam Dalyell challenged the UK government:

Could there be a more effective way to act as a recruiting sergeant for a young generation across the Arab and Islamic world than to launch 600 cruise missiles - or anything else - at Baghdad and Iraq[337]*?*

watch?v=jHXLaio8G3I)

335. "London bomber: Text in full", *BBC News Channel*, September 1st, 2005, (accessed June 22, 2015).

336. "Shehzad Tanweer's 'martyrdom video', *YouTube*, July 21, 2012 (https://www.youtube.com/watch?v=F-G6a26uX1eA)

337. House of Commons Debate (Column 769), March 18, 2003, www.parliament.uk

The question was prescient. In 2016, during the parliamentary enquiry into the British war in Iraq, Ms Eliza Manningham-Buller, Director General of MI5, said:

> *In 2003-2004 we received increasing reports of terrorist activity in the UK... our involvement in Iraq radicalised - for want of a better term - part of a generation... saw our involvement in Iraq, alongside our involvement in Afghanistan, as an attack on Islam*[338].

Asked about the impact of the intervention in Iraq on the increase of the terrorist threat, she replies:

> *I think we can produce evidence because of the amount of the number of incidents, the number of leads, the number of people identified, and their correlation with Iraq and the statements of individuals as to why they were involved... So I think the answer to your... question: yes*[339].

On April 13, 2005, in a TOP SECRET classified report entitled *International Terrorism: Impact of Iraq*, the British Joint Intelligence Committee noted:

> *I. The conflict in Iraq has exacerbated the threat of international terrorism and will continue to have a long-term impact. It has strengthened the conviction of extremists that Islam is under attack and must be defended by force. It has strengthened the resolve of those terrorists already prepared to attack the West and motivated those who were not.*
>
> *[...]*
>
> *V. Iraq is likely to be an important motivating factor for the radicalisation of British Muslims for some time to come and for extremists who see attacking the UK as legitimate*[340].

Indeed, recent jihadist attacks in Europe have consistently occurred *after the* countries concerned have been involved in the international coalition in Iraq and Syria:

---

338. Patrick Wintour, "Intelligence files support claims Iraq invasion helped spawn Isis", *The Guardian*, July 6, 2016
339. Patrick Wintour, "Intelligence... (op.cit.)
340. JIC Assessment, *International Terrorism: Impact of Iraq, Joint Intelligence Committee*, April 13, 2005, TOP SECRET (declassified in January 2011)

Country	First armed engagement in Iraq or Syria	First Islamist attack (claimed by the Islamic State)
Germany	Iraq - December 4, 2015 (Decision)	Würzburg - July 18, 2016
Australia	Iraq - October 2014	Sydney - December 15 to 16, 2014
Belgium	Iraq - September 2014 (Withdrawn in July 2015) Recovery in Iraq and Syria - January 2016	Verviers (map) - January, 15 2015 Brussels - March, 22 2016
Canada	Iraq - October 7, 2014 (Decision)[2] (see bibliography)	Montreal - October 22, 2014
Denmark	Iraq - October 2014 (Withdrawal in August 2015, then resumption in March 2016) 1st strike in Syria - August 2016	Copenhagen - February 14 to 15, 2015 Copenhagen - September 2, 2016
Spain	Iraq - September 2014[3] (see bibliography)	Barcelona - August 17, 2017
Finland	Iraq - September 2014[4] (see bibliography)	Turku - August 18, 2017
France	Iraq - September 19, 2014 Syria - September 24, 2015	Paris - January 7 to 9, 2015 Paris - November 13, 2015
United Kingdom	Syria - December 2015[5] (see bibliography)	London - March 22, 2017
Sweden	Iraq - August 2014	Stockholm - April 7, 2017

Table 3- Causality between armed engagements in the Near and Middle East and terrorist acts

Thus, it is known that repeated Western interventions against Muslim countries create the feeling of a crusade against Islam. However, in France, the idea of a causality between military actions and terrorist acts is seen as conspiratorial, as the documentary *Complotisme: les alibis de la terreur* made by *France 3* in 2018[341] attempts to demonstrate. The psychiatrist Serge Hefez goes even further by evoking the fanciful concept of "*ancestral jihad*[342]". It is also claimed that "*the argument of self-defence is at the heart of the discourse held by terrorists on their own actions*[343]". While it is true that some perpetrators, such as Chérif Kouachi on 9 January 2015, claim to act out of '*revenge*', this is not the case with jihad theorists and Islamic State publications, which refute '*self-defence*' (admittedly for rather confused reasons)[344]: their aim is to dissuade us from intervening.

But the West has adopted the Israeli rhetoric that removes any reason for terrorism other than hatred of the West and its freedoms, and makes it an inescapable phenomenon. The result is a form of denial, the perverse effect of which is to prevent us from dealing with terrorism strategically. Thus, "9/11" was seen as the beginning of a new war. This was obviously wrong. The jihadists see it as a battle in a war that the West had started much earlier:

341. Georges Benayoun and Rudy Reichstadt, "Complotisme: les alibis de la terreur", *France 3*, January 23, 2018 (47'25")
342. Ibid (44'40")
343. Ibid (47'00")
344. "Attacks on the Prophetic Way", *Dar al-Islam Magazine*, No. 8, January 2016 (rabi al-thani 1437), (pp. 9, 11,29, 30).

9/11 was neither the beginning of a war between Muslims and the West nor the end. It was simply an episode in a long war[345] *[...]*

With a few words, this is exactly the explanation the author gave on Swiss television on September 12, 2001... Terrorist acts are always part of a logical process, "do not fall from the sky" and are basically predictable. Although the tactical aspects (location, mode of action, operational objective, etc.) are difficult to anticipate, it is possible to predict the onset of a campaign of attacks. According to Michael Scheuer, former head of the unit responsible for tracking down Osama bin Laden (OBL) from 1996 to 1999, our wars are the real cause of Islamic terrorism[346].

Indeed, indirectly we recognise this: it is the main reason why the US goes to great lengths to build international coalitions. Their aim is not to get help (for they play the leading role and often pay their partners a lot of money to participate), but to dilute the terrorist threat that would result from these engagements across the coalition membership.

To think that individuals decide to sacrifice themselves simply to "*divide France*" or "*just to terrorise*" is naivety and foolishness. In reality, we have adapted the Israeli discourse to our situations, which places terrorism in a fatality that excludes any questioning of our policies and decisions. The consequence is that - like Israel - we do not deal with terrorism strategically and limit ourselves to the operational level. In other words, we let it take the initiative.

5.3 "The United States created Al Qaeda"

The claim that the United States created "Al Qaeda" is both right and wrong. If one believes that it created and clandestinely funded an organisation to carry out attacks around the world, then it is false. Hillary Clinton's admission on *FOX News* and *CNN*[347], often cited as evidence, is a smoke and mirrors. On the other hand, through ignorance, incompetence and stupidity, they have created a context conducive to the development of a jihadist ideology: "Al-Qaeda" is not the result of a Machiavellian calculation - as the conspiracy theorists claim - but of a way of waging war as it was a century ago, without understanding it.

After the Iraqi defeat in 1991, the stationing of American forces in Saudi Arabia worried the Saudi authorities, as it fuelled a radical opposition that began

345. Yahya Ibrahim, "Letter from the Editor", *Inspire Magazine*, No. 7, Fall 2011 (1432), p. 3
346. Dana Priest, "Former Chief of CIA's Bin Laden Unit Leaves", *Washington Post*, November 12, 2004
347. "Hillary Clinton ADMITS The CIA Started & Funded Al Qaeda", *YouTube*, June 22, 2014

to threaten the regime. For the fundamentalists, Saudi territory is considered sacred, and the American presence is seen as a provocation.

OBL is the most publicised figure of this trend and will act as a 'lightning rod'. In June 1996, he was expelled from Sudan under pressure from the United States. He took refuge in Afghanistan, in the Kandahar region, where he continued his struggle against the American presence in Saudi Arabia. At the beginning of 1998, he created a movement called World Islamic Front for the fight against Jews and Crusaders *(Al-Jabhah al-Islamiya al-'Alamiyah li-Qital al-Yahud wal-Salibiyyin)*, which brings together several jihadist groups.

Its motivations are set out in a declaration ("fatwa") of February 23, 1998, which constitutes the doctrinal basis of what will later be called "Al-Qaeda". The attacks attributed to OBL that followed showed great strategic coherence with this declaration, from which the main claims of future jihadists could already be identified:

the withdrawal of the American presence from the territory of Saudi Arabia (because non-believers cannot occupy all or part of the sacred land of Arabia);

the lifting of the embargo against Iraq, as it was seen as a manifestation of Western arrogance against a Muslim country (it was not a question of supporting Saddam Hussein, who was considered a "traitor" because of his secularism);

the cessation of support for the State of Israel, as it is seen as a tool to divide the Arab nation (reference to the Yinon plan, reworked by an American think tank for the benefit of Benjamin Netanyahu in 1996, published under the title *A Clean Break*[348], which calls for the fragmentation of the Middle East. We will come back to this).

There is no global ambition to expand Islam, no Caliphate, no holy war against Christianity in the world, nor against the Western world, but only resistance against a US presence in the Middle East, perceived as invasive, arrogant and destabilising. The message was simple, clear and coherent, but it was deliberately misused by Western countries to hide the strategic errors of their interventions.

The name 'Al Qaeda' (which OBEI himself has never claimed) to describe this nascent jihadist movement was created by the American authorities[349]. This is neither a plot nor a Machiavellian calculation, but a simple legal artifice. In January 2001, when the United States was preparing to try the perpetrators of the February 1993 attack on the World Trade Center (WTC), it had no anti-terrorism legislation. The only instrument available was the *RICO Act* ([350]), which

348. "To Clean Break: A New Strategy for Securing the Realm", *The Institute for Advanced Strategic and Political Studies*, July 1996, (http://www.informationclearinghouse.info/article1438.htm)

349. Jason Burke, *Al-Qaeda - The True Story of Radical Islam*, Cahiers libres, March 2005, pp. 324.

350. Racketeer Influenced and Corrupt Organizations Act (RICO Act), October 15, 1970

allowed for the indictment of those who sponsored criminal acts abroad, but only if their organisation had a name[351]. The protagonists of the 1993 attack did not act within the framework of a known organisation[352]. But they were said to have links - which were never proven - with OBL. American lawyers therefore simply imagined that OBL was running an organisation, which they arbitrarily named after its former Afghan base (*al-qa'ïda al-'askariyya*): 'al-Qa'ida[353]'.

In 1996, the CIA created a special unit to track down OBL, the "*Bin Laden Issue Station*" (not "*Al Qaeda Station*"!) which was dismantled at the end of 2005[354]. Its head, Michael Scheuer, confirms that 'Al Qaeda' never existed, but that it is a simple and easily understandable way for the public to refer to Islamic terrorists[355]. This obscure origin has been exploited by conspiracists of all stripes. Some have interpreted it as evidence that 'Al Qaeda' was a CIA creation for some obscure plot, which is false; while others have used this 'conspiracy theory' to claim that there is an 'Al Qaeda' organisation, which is conspiracy and equally false.

The name "Al-Qaeda" has been used so much in the West that it has become a symbol of jihadism and a real "label", which has been claimed little by little by certain terrorist groups, more for reasons of branding than structural membership. Thus, from 2005 onwards, the expression "*Qaidat al-Jihad*" (*Base of Jihad*) became widely used in various countries to designate a core of armed resistance. Names such as "Al Qaeda in the Islamic Maghreb" (AQIM) or "Al Qaeda in the Arabian Peninsula" (AQAP) are inaccurate translations, promoted by Western countries, to accredit the existence of a multinational terror organisation with its "subsidiaries. Their real names are "Qaidat al-Jihad fi'l-Maghrib al-Islamiy - Base of Jihad in the Islamic Maghreb" and "Qaidat al-Jihad fi'l-Jazirah al-Arrabiyyah - Base of Jihad in the Arabian Peninsula", which do not imply any functional relationship with a hypothetical central structure[356]. There has been talk of 'franchises' and even claims that OBL has '*lost control of the al-Qaeda organisation*[357]'. But in reality, nothing was known about this. Documents recovered from Abbottabad during the US raid to eliminate OBL in 2011 showed no functional or structural links between OBL and the various jihadist groups[358].

351. The RICO Act will be complemented by the PATRIOT Act, adopted just after the 9/11 attacks.
352. Indeed, Islamists see this attack as a precursor to 'individual terrorism'. See Abu Mu'sab al-Suri, 'The Jihadi Experience: The Schools of Jihad', *Inspire Magazine*, No. 1, Summer 2010 (1431).
353. BBC, *The Power of Nightmare*, (Series of three films), Autumn 2004.
354. Mark Mazzetti, 'C.I.A. Closes Unit Focused on Capture of bin Laden', *The New York Times*, July 4, 2006.
355. "CIA Agent Exposes How Al-Qaeda Doesn't Exist", *YouTube*, November 16, 2011 (https://www.youtube.com/watch?v=-8CqUJoEWBs)
356. Kangil Lee, "Does Al Qaeda Central Still Matter?", *UNISCI Journal*, No. 37, International Center for Political Violence and Terrorism Research, January 2015
357. *CNN*, July 7, 2008.
358. Nelly Lahoud et al, *Letters from Abbottabad: Bin Ladin Sidelined?* The Combating Terrorism Center, West

To hide the fact that our military interventions have created jihadist terrorism, it has been necessary to literally invent a sprawling organisation with global ambitions and written into the Koran. This is not true. Precious energy has been wasted searching for command structures that did not exist. Without understanding the genesis, functioning, logic and motivations of terrorism, we have not been able to put in place strategies to control it. We react to it emotionally, without reflection and without strategy: exactly as the terrorists want. That is why terrorism has only grown, and no war or technology has stopped it. We have even sacrificed (unnecessarily) the values that make democracy great, such as individual freedom, the right to privacy, or freedom of expression.

5.4 "Bin Laden is responsible for the attacks of September 11, 2001"

In their programme on the "*mechanisms of conspiracy*" on *France-Culture*, in order to demonstrate that alternative theories are conspiracy theories, Roman Bronstein and Rudy Reichstadt claim that "9/11" was "*claimed by Al-Qaeda*" and "*orchestrated by Osama bin Laden*[359]". This is not true. Since 2001, hundreds of "experts" who have suddenly become specialists in terrorism and intelligence continue to hold OBL responsible for the attacks. And yet…

Although it appeared that OBL's emulators were the most likely culprits in the aftermath of the attacks, there was no evidence that they belonged to an organisation ("Al Qaeda") and that OBL had planned and given the orders.

On September 12, 2001, Lord Robertson, Nato's Secretary General, announced that - for the first time since 1949 - the North Atlantic Council (NAC) was prepared to invoke Article 5 of its Charter "*if it is determined that the attack was directed from abroad against the United States*"[360]. It states that "*… an armed attack against one or more of them… shall be considered an attack against all of them…*" and allows for the use of force under Article 51 of the UN Charter on self-defence. This article had been established for the case where a member of the Alliance had been the victim of aggression by another state. But in 2001, it was a question of intervening against a state, in response to an aggression carried out by individuals of Saudi nationality, who had prepared their attacks in Germany and the United States, and whose links with the Afghan government were only supposed. By this logic, we could just as easily have attacked Germany or Saudi Arabia!

Point, www.ctc.usma.edu, May 3, 2012.

359. Roman Bornstein, "Mécaniques du complotisme - Réécouter Le 11 Septembre, épisode 1. Les théoriciens", *France-Culture*

360. "North Atlantic Council Statement, Press Release (2001) 124, *Nato*, September 12, 2001

However, at this stage, there is no evidence that the attacks were decided or directed by OBL or an organisation. The explanation will only come on October 2, 2001. On that day, Ambassador Frank Taylor, Coordinator for Counterterrorism at the US State Department, briefed the members of the NAC on the basis of a SECRET cable dated October 1st, 2001, addressed to all US representations and whose content could only be disseminated orally. Lord Robertson used the entire text in his press release to justify the decision to apply Article 5 of the Charter[361]:

> *The facts are clear and convincing. The information presented points to an al-Qaeda role in the 9/11 attacks. We know that the perpetrators of these attacks were part of the global Al Qaeda terrorist network, led by Osama bin Laden and his top lieutenants and protected by the Taliban*[362].

It was only in 2009 that this document was quietly published by *Intelwire*[363]. As expected, it does not provide any concrete evidence of Afghan or OBL involvement, but only conjectures and vague extrapolations. Indeed, Part III, which is supposed to demonstrate the links between the attacks and "al-Qaeda", begins by stating that "*the investigation of these attacks is still in its infancy*" and that "there are *still gaps in our knowledge*". He does not provide any factual evidence, but only circumstantial elements. For example, he notes that the attacks bear similarities to previous attacks because of their "*meticulous planning, the desire to inflict mass casualties (including non-Americans) and multiple suicide attacks*".

It is meagre, but it is enough to invoke Article 5 of the Atlantic Charter and commit to Afghanistan, in what will be the longest conflict in American history. How Alliance members could accept such simplistic claims on such a tenuous set of evidence remains a mystery. The explanation certainly lies in the emotion of the moment, but also in the foolishness and servility of governments and the weakness of their intelligence services, which had no visibility of jihadist terrorism! We have not changed much since then.

In fact, we know who carried out the hijackings, but not whether or not anyone or anyone gave them the order to do so. Even today, OBL's responsibility is only a hypothesis. On 16 September 2001, he stated in a press release:

> *After the last explosions in the United States, some Americans point to me, but I deny it because I didn't do it... Again, I repeat that I didn't do it...*[364]

361. *Statement by NATO Secretary General, Lord Robertson*, NATO HQ, October 2, 2001 (www.nato.int/docu/speech/2001/s011002a.htm)

362. "September 11: Working Together to Fight the Plague of Global Terrorism and the Case Against Al-Qa'ida", October 1st, 2001 and *Statement by NATO Secretary General, Lord Robertson*, October 2, 2001.

363. "10/2/2001: Secret Post-9/11 Briefing To World Leaders", *Intelwire*, April 5, 2009

364. "Afghanistan: Bin Laden Denies Involvement in Terrorist Attacks in US", *Peshawar Afghan Islamic Press News*

Naturally, one can assume that he is trying to exonerate himself. But to what end? In fact, there is every reason to believe so. Firstly, because the raison d'être of terrorism is that its actions and objectives are known: it is about exerting pressure to achieve something. Secondly, because the fact of assuming an act (violent or not) is part of the very essence of the notion of jihad, since one is ready to sacrifice one's life to it. This is why most jihadist attacks are "over-claimed" and why some terrorists even take credit for attacks in which they were never involved[365].

Moreover, OBL has never been formally indicted or charged for 9/11[366]. Simply because there is no factual evidence linking him to the attack. That is why the FBI's wanted poster - issued and revised in November 2001 - does not mention this charge[367].

In April 2002, Robert Mueller, then Director of the FBI, stated:

> *In the course of our investigation, we have not discovered a single piece of paper - either in the US or in the treasure trove of information found in Afghanistan and elsewhere - that mentions any aspect of the 9/11 plot*[368].

In June 2006, Rex Tomb, head of FBI public relations, confirmed:

> *The reason why '9/11' is not mentioned on the Osama bin Laden wanted notice is that the FBI has no evidence linking bin Laden to '9/11'*[369].

The most frequently cited evidence of his responsibility for '9/11' is his 'confession' recorded on a video shot on 9 November 2001 and 'found' in Jalalabad on 13 December. A second video, released on 27 December - apparently shot on 19 November - shows a different OBL, whose beard has turned white (in 10 days!). However, these videos, and several others that followed, were fakes, produced by the US CIA in order to discredit him (including to make him look homosexual), as their "authors" admitted in 2010[370].

Agency, September 16, 2001 in: "Compilation of Usama Bin Laden Statements, 1994 - January 2004", *Foreign Broadcast Information Service*, January 2004; "Taleban to decide Bin Laden fate", *BBC News*, September 17, 2001

365. http://mayday.blogsome.com/2007/03/19/khalid-sheikh-mohammed-the-wally-world-of-wickedness/
366. Osama Bin Laden, *trialinternational.org*, April 23, 2006 (modified June 8, 2016)
367. https://www.fbi.gov/image-repository/usama-bin-laden_poster.jpg/view
368. Lecture by Robert S. Mueller, III, Director of the FBI, at the Commonwealth Club of California (San Francisco, California), April 19, 2002 (archives.fbi.gov/archives/news/speeches/partnership-and-prevention-the-fbis-role-in-homeland-security). He repeated the same words at a Senate committee hearing (Robert S. Mueller, "Reforming the FBI in the 21st Century: Reorganizing and Refocusing the Mission", Hearing before the Senate Judiciary Committee, May 8, 2002)
369. http://www.historycommons.org/entity.jsp?entity=rex_tomb_1
370. Jeff Stein, "CIA unit's wacky idea: Depict Saddam as gay", *Washington Post*, May 25, 2010

To conclude that 9/11 was the result of a CIA (or other) plot is certainly wrong. But we have to admit that, contrary to appearances, we don't know much about the genesis of '9/11'. The most likely version is that the 19 terrorists - perhaps with other as yet unknown accomplices - organised and carried out the attacks on their own. They were certainly inspired by jihadist militancy and driven by revenge for the August 1998 strikes against innocent civilians, but there is no evidence that they were associated with a central organisation. Instead, as with the Islamic State fifteen years later, the haphazard and tactical response of the West has made 'Al Qaeda' a myth and a reference point for future attacks.

5.5. " The attacks of September 11, 2001 were organized by Israel"

The drama of 9/11 suggested that the attacks had been the subject of sophisticated planning by a powerful organisation. "Al Qaeda" was immediately "identified", but some elements, quietly passed on the media, cast suspicion on Israel. Some, such as the renewal of the World Trade Center (WTC) insurance contract in June 2001 by Larry Silverstein, its new owner, are possible, but unlikely; others are rumours, such as the fact that the Jewish staff of the towers were informed in advance and did not go to work that day. There is also talk of stock market anomalies just before the attacks, but these have been (at least partially) explained by the Congressional Inquiry Committee[371] and do not constitute 'proof' of involvement.

As in conspiracy theories, one starts from the conclusion and looks for the elements that corroborate it. Thus, the idea that the attacks could only benefit Israel was largely built around a statement by Benjamin Netanyahu about their impact on Israeli-American relations:

> *It's very good... I mean... It's not very good, but it will generate immediate sympathy [for Israel]*[372].

On the one hand, it is hard to see what objective could justify the risk of Israel compromising its ties with the United States. On the other hand, with Hezbollah, Hamas, Iran and Syria, the Hebrew state has more than enough to keep the support of the United States, without imagining spectacular attacks!

371. "Final Report of the National Commission on Terrorist Attacks upon the United States", 9-11commission.gov, July 22, 2004, (p. 499).
372. James Bennet, 'A DAY OF TERROR: THE ISRAELIS; Spilled Blood Is Seen as Bond That Draws 2 Nations Closer', *The New York Times*, September 12, 2001; 'Report: Netanyahu Says 9/11 Terror Attacks Good for Israel', *Haaretz Service/Reuters*, April 16, 2008.

Nevertheless, there are a number of facts that make one wonder. This is the case of the five Israeli citizens, positioned in a New Jersey car park at 8 a.m., who observed and photographed the attack on the World Trade Center while "dancing", congratulating each other and exchanging *high-fives*[373]. Interested the same day, the police will establish that they had come to reconnoitre the site the day before and that two of them were on the joint CIA/FBI list of Israeli Mossad agents. A US intelligence official told *The Forward* newspaper that they were considered to be on a mission for the Israeli services[374]. After 71 days of detention and an agreement with Israel, they were expelled from the United States. A few weeks later, they confessed on Israeli television that they had been sent to New York to "*document the event*[375]", suggesting that Israel was aware of the preparations for an attack.

In the days following the attacks, more than 60 Israeli citizens living in the United States were questioned by the FBI. Among them were active military personnel and individuals who had failed a lie detector test about espionage activities. But there is no evidence that they were involved in the attacks[376].

In January 2014, the Justice Department had claimed that the 76 photos taken by the Israelis had been destroyed. But on 7 May 2019, the FBI released 14 of them, under the Freedom of Information Act (FOIA)[377]. They are heavily redacted: although the faces are already known, they are masked so that their expressions, which the FBI report described as "*visibly joyful*[378]", are not visible.

It is therefore very likely that the Israelis knew about a possible attack in New York on 11 September, but did not know the details. This would explain why they sent agents to "*document*" it. In this hypothesis, it is not unthinkable that the information could have 'leaked' into certain New York Jewish business circles, even if there is no concrete indication of this. Whether the Israelis informed their American counterparts remains an open question. According to *The Telegraph*, Israel sent two agents to Washington in August 2001 to discuss the matter, but this is not confirmed by the American side[379].

However, a certain cynicism on the part of Israel would not have been new. In 1954, the Israelis had carried out a series of terrorist attacks against their Western allies in Egypt, in order to push them into involvement in the Middle

373. FBI report (then classified SECRET/ORCON/NOFORN) dated September 14, 2001

374. Marc Perelman, "Spy Rumors Fly on Gusts of Truth", *The Forward*, March 15, 2002 (web.archive.org/web/20030413184526/http://www.forward.com/issues/2002/02.03.15/news2.html)

375. Inside Israel" programme, November 2001

376. Tamar Lewin & Alison Leigh Cowan, "A Nation Challenged: The Detainees; Dozens of Israeli Jews Are Being Kept in Federal Detention", *The New York Times*, November 21, 2001

377. "FOIA Release of 9/11 Dancing Israelis thru the FBI", *Scribd*, May 12, 2019; Whitney Webb, "Newly Released FBI Docs Shed Light on Apparent Mossad Foreknowledge of 9/11 Attacks", *Mint Press News*, May 17, 2019

378. https://archive.org/details/DancingIsraelisFBIReport/page/n19

379. David Wastell & Philip Jacobson, "Israeli security issued urgent warning to CIA of large-scale terror attacks", *The Telegraph*, September 16, 2001

East ("Lavon Affair[380]"). In 1982, according to intelligence sources, the Rue des Rosiers attack in Paris on 9 August (the only attack that was never claimed by a Palestinian organisation) was aimed at recreating unity around Israel, whose "cleansing" operations in Beirut threatened the support of the American Jewish community[381]. In 1983, according to Victor Ostrovsky, a former Mossad officer, the Israeli services had deliberately withheld information from the Americans about the preparations of the October 23 attack in Beirut, in order to incite them to become more involved in Lebanon[382].

5.6 "Conspiracy - The Alibis of Terror[383]"

In January 2018, *France 3* broadcast a documentary entitled *Complotisme, les alibis de la terreur*[384], its aim is to disprove the justifications that place jihadist terrorism as a response to an anti-Muslim plot. In fact, he dismantles two conspiracy theories:

the idea that terrorist acts are fabricated by Western services;

the idea that terrorist acts are a response to a Judeo-Crusader plot against Islam.

... To create a third one: the idea that terrorist acts are the expression of a will to Islamise the world. To this end, the report starts from a fundamental falsification that makes terrorism a doctrine in its own right, like totalitarianism[385], by lending it attributes of a messianic, conspiratorial and apocalyptic nature "*grafted into the tradition of Islam*[386]". This is false and intellectually dishonest.

5.6.1 "Terrorist Acts are Organized by the Security Services"

The documentary discusses the sometimes romantic theories about "9/11", the Mohammed Merah affair in March 2012, the January 2015 attacks in Paris and the Strasbourg attack in December 2018. Let's say it right away: despite a sometimes strange crisis management, nothing indicates that Western secret services were involved in their unfolding. All of them fit into the jihadist logic,

380. See Wikipedia, article "Lavon Affair".

381. Connie de Boer, 'The Polls: Attitudes Toward the Arab-Israeli Conflict', *The Public Opinion Quarterly*, Vol. 47, No. 1, Spring 1983, pp. 121-131

382. Ostrovsky, Victor & Claire Hoy, *By Way of Deception*, New York, St. Martin's Press, 1990, p. 321.

383. www.conspiracywatch.info/complotisme-les-alibis-de-la-terreur-teaser.html

384. Rudy Reichstadt & Georges Benayoun, "Complotisme, les alibis de la terreur", *YouTube*, January 24, 2018, (www.youtube.com/watch?v=d8e18NIqWiI)

385. Pierre-André Taguieff in "Complotisme, les alibis de la terreur", *YouTube*, January 24, 2018 (07'00")

386. Jacob Rogozinski in "Complotisme, les alibis de la terreur", *YouTube*, January 24, 2018 (10'00")

and some were even the subject of an after-action analysis by the terrorists themselves.

That said, the idea that attacks have been 'inspired' or 'instigated' by the security services is not incongruous. A 2014 Human Rights Watch study[387] finds that the top terrorist operations uncovered in the US involve government agents[388]! As of 2012, of 22 attempted attacks tried in the US, 14 - or two-thirds - had been "provoked" by the FBI[389] !

Developed to fight organised crime, this practice ("*sting operation*") consists of infiltrating agents and inciting potential criminals to perform illegal acts in order to catch them "red-handed". The aim is to "bring potential terrorists out of the woodwork", not to destabilise the state as implied by "conspiracy" theories.

Practised by several Western countries - including France - it is essentially a bureaucratic drift designed to show results, driven by a mentality that places security above the rule of law. It is highly questionable on moral, ethical and legal grounds. For what Conspiracy Watch conceals is that it has led to the imprisonment of relatively simple-minded, often unemployed individuals who had - originally - no intention of carrying out violent actions, who had no political aspirations or contacts to mount attacks and who posed no threat to national security, simply lured by sums of up to $250,000[390].

Two problems plague the security services. The first is their misunderstanding of jihadist terrorism, which leads them to treat it as a 'normal' (symmetrical) criminal act. The second is that ethics tend to be overshadowed by bureaucratic logic. The aim is more to "make numbers" than to improve security[391]. For example, in the United States, an FBI agent who had infiltrated a group of pacifist activists and had not discovered a terrorist project decided to create one by trying to get the group to send money to the Popular Front for the Liberation of Palestine (PFLP) and the Colombian Revolutionary Armed Forces (FARC)[392].

This being the case, there is a clear willingness on the part of the security establishment to overestimate the terrorist threat in order to extend their rights and privileges, even at the cost of undermining trust in the authorities[393].

---

387. *Illusion of Justice: Human Rights Abuses in US Terrorism Prosecutions*, Human Rights Watch, July 21, 2014.

388. Spencer Ackerman, "Government agents 'directly involved' in most high-profile US terror plots", *The Guardian*, July 21, 2014.

389. David K. Shipler, "Terrorist Plots, Hatched by the F.B.I.", *The New York Times*, April 29, 2012

390. "Report finds government agents 'directly involved' in many U.S. terror plots," *Police State USA*, July 31, 2014. (http://www.policestateusa.com/2014/report-finds-fbi-plans-its-own-terror-plots/)

391. Paul Harris, "Fake terror plots, paid informants: the tactics of FBI 'entrapment' questioned", *The Guardian*, November 16, 2011

392. Kevin Gosztola, "Undercover FBI Agent Tried to Get Activists to Send Money to PFLP, a US-Designated Terrorist Organization," *shadowproof.com*, February 28, 2014

393. John-Pierre Maeli, "When 30% of Terrorist Plots Are Created By The FBI Is Terrorism Really That Big of a Threat?", *medium.com*, January 22, 2016

5.6.2 "Terrorist Acts are a Response to a Judeo-Crusader Plot against Islam"

They try to explain that jihadist terrorism has no rational basis and is linked to a paranoia inherent in Islam. In the *France 3* documentary, Serge Hefez, a psychiatrist, even speaks of an "*ancestral jihad*"[394]. The concept is fanciful, but it allows terrorism to be presented as inescapable and linked to the very nature of Islam.

It is true that the publications of the Islamic State glorify the heroes of the Crusades and give a romantic image of their struggle. Jihadists draw parallels with the world today and like to talk about a '*crusader plot*'. In their defence, it must be admitted that the obvious lies and the absence of real and valid reasons for intervening in Afghanistan, Iraq or Libya tend to support this discourse. The language of those who started them leaves no room for doubt:

> *President Bush vowed on Sunday to "rid the world of evil", and warned: "This crusade, this war on terror, will take time"*[395].

But this is not a simple error of vocabulary! In June 2003, in Sharm el-Sheikh, George W. Bush told a Palestinian delegation:

> *I am guided by a mission from God. God told me, George, go and fight those terrorists in Afghanistan. And I did. Then God told me, George, go and end that tyranny in Iraq. And I did.*

In 2009, it was learned that Donald Rumsfeld, Secretary of Defense, regularly peppered his messages to the troops in Iraq with biblical quotations; a practice that had been instigated by Major General Glen D. Shaffer, then Director of Military Intelligence (J2). Shaffer, then Director of Military Intelligence (J2)[396].

As for Tony Blair, John Burton, who worked with him for twenty-four years, said:

> *Tony's Christian faith is part of him, right down to his cotton socks. At the time, he was firmly convinced that intervention in Kosovo, Sierra Leone and also Iraq was part of a Christian struggle. Good must overcome evil and make life better*[397].

---

394. Serge Hefez in "Complotisme, les alibis de la terreur", *YouTube*, January 24, 2018 (44'40")
395. Peter Waldman & Hugh Pope, "'Crusade' Reference Reinforces Fears War on Terrorism Is Against Muslims", *The Wall Street Journal*, September 21, 2001. See also: '9/11 George Bush - This Crusade Is Gonna Take A While', *YouTube*, September 17, 2001
396. Alex Spillius, "Donald Rumsfeld covered Iraq briefing papers with Biblical texts", *The Telegraph*, May 17, 2009
397. Jonathan Wynne-Jones, "Tony Blair believed God wanted him to go to war to fight evil, claims his mentor", *The Telegraph*, May 23, 2009

Erik Prince, founder and director of the private security company Blackwater, which carried out the dirty work of the US military in Iraq, and indicted - but never convicted - for the murders caused by his employees, declared himself to be a "*Christian crusader charged with wiping out Muslims and the Muslim faith from the face of the earth*"[398]

This notion of a "crusade" is relayed within the American armed forces by organisations such as the Officer's Christian Fellowship (OCF), which brings together some 17,000 senior officers and whose leader, Lieutenant General Bruce Fister, defines the American forces as "*ambassadors of Christ in uniform*[399]". This idea is echoed by Lieutenant General Jerry Boykin, Deputy Under Secretary of Defense, who believes that George Bush was chosen by God to fight terrorism:

> *Our spiritual enemy will only be defeated if we go and fight him in the name of Jesus*[400].

In 2011, the Joint Forces Staff College in Norfolk even offered a course on '*total war against Islam*', which emphasised the invalidity of the Geneva Conventions in this context and called for the destruction of cities such as Medina and Mecca with nuclear weapons[401]. Prepared with the help of a consultancy close to the Republican Party - the Strategic Engagement Group - the course was finally withdrawn from the curriculum in April 2012, after complaints from students[402]. In April, at an FBI counter-terrorism seminar, a speaker said that fighting 'al-Qaeda' is a waste of time and that Islam as a whole should be targeted[403].

US Special Forces were recruiting volunteers for Iraq under the slogan "*A Mission for God and Country*[404]". Following the intervention of moderate religious organisations, the Pentagon stopped the distribution of "*Freedom Packages*" to troops deployed in Iraq: Bibles, religious propaganda material in English and Arabic, and a millenarian game ("*Left Behind: Eternal Forces*") featuring "*Soldiers of Christ*[405]". Trijicon, which supplies sights for assault rifles, has engraved the

398. "Erik Prince and the last crusade", *The Economist*, August 6, 2009.
399. Alan Cooperman, 'Marching as to War', *The Washington Post*, July 16, 2006
400. William M. Arkin, 'The Pentagon Unleashes a Holy Warrior', *Los Angeles Times*, October 16, 2003
401. http://www.documentcloud.org/documents/355983-dooley-counter-jihad-op-design-v11.html
402. Pauline Jelinek & Robert Burns, "Joint Forces Staff College Class Suspended After Teaching America's Enemy Is Islam," www.huffingtonpost.com, July 10, 2012
403. Spencer Ackerman & Noah Shachtman, "FBI Trainer Says Forget 'Irrelevant' al-Qaeda, Target Islam," *wired.com*, September 20, 2011
404. Mikey Weinstein, "US Army Special Forces Officially Recruit for 'Mission for God'", *truthout.org*, January 24, 2015
405. Michael L. Weinstein & Reza Aslan, "Not so fast, Christian soldiers", *Los Angeles Times*, August 22, 2007

ACOG sights supplied to the US army with references to the Gospels; so much so that in Afghanistan they have been dubbed "*Jesus rifles*"[406]!

The perception of a 'Judeo-crossroads' plot is obviously accentuated by individuals like Bernard-Henri Lévy, when he says of Libya: "It is as a *Jew that I participated in this political adventure*[407]". A statement echoed by Mike Pompeo who considers it "*possible*" that Trump was chosen by God to "*help save the Jewish people from the Iranian threat*[408]"!

Obviously, the *France 3* report does not mention any of this. Yet, while the idea of a *conspiracy* is certainly false, the fact that those who started the wars in the Middle East had a Crusade in mind is a reality. In any case, we have never put in place policies and communication that could lead to another interpretation:

> *The emperor of the Romans in our time, Bush, has announced it several times: it is a crusading war*[409].

The *France 3* report shows that this conspiracy theory stems from our refusal to provide a rational and coherent explanation for terrorism. In fact, it espouses the same rhetoric that the Israeli government uses against the Palestinians: anti-semitism is the main driver of jihadist terrorism. This is simply not true. Jihadists are most likely anti-Semitic, but that does not prevent them from cooperating with Israel against the Syrian government. Moreover, Israel does not perceive the Islamic State as its main threat, as we shall see. Anti-Semitism is neither a cause nor a trigger for Jihadist terrorism, although it does play a role in the choice of its targets.

By never being able to explain our military interventions in Afghanistan, Iraq, Syria and Libya, other than with proven lies, we have created the perception of a conspiracy ourselves. In addition, these interventions do not respect international law. So how can we expect the Muslim community to trust our good faith? By refusing to understand the real reasons behind the terrorists, we are only making it easier for them to do so...

406. Deliberate references to "John 8:12" and "2 Corinthians 4:6" on Trijicon ACOG sights have caused a stir in the United States, where secularism is the rule in the military. (Joseph Rhee, Tahman Bradley & Brian Ross, "U.S. Military Weapons Inscribed With Secret 'Jesus' Bible Codes", *ABC News*, January 18, 2010)

407. Bernard-Henri Lévy: "It is as a Jew that I participated in the political adventure in Libya", www.crif.org, November 21, 2011

408. Noga Tarnopolsky, "Answering Purim question, Pompeo suggests Trump is on mission from God to save Jewish people" *Los Angeles Times*, March 22, 2019

409. "Paths to Victory", *Rumiyah*, No. 2, October 2016 (Muharram 1438), p. 12.

5.6.3 "Terrorist Acts are an Expression of a Will to Islamize the World"

The *France 3* report repeats a common conspiracy theory, which places anti-Semitism and the desire to impose an Islamic world order at the centre of the jihadists' determination:

> *A world where jihadism kills every day, eating away at the foundations of our open and democratic societies. Murderers who hate our freedoms and want to force us to change our way of living and looking to the future*[410].

This is a way of explaining "jihadist conspiracy" by another conspiracy and linking jihadist terrorism to the Holocaust[411]! Obviously, at no time does the *France 3* report mention the perception generated by the conflicts in Palestine, Afghanistan, Iraq, Libya or Syria, which are systematically mentioned in the claims of the attacks.

The real cause of jihadist terrorism is indeed Western interventionism. But it has become unreadable because of fancifully assembled explanations to give another logic to a phenomenon that we do not want to understand:

> *Fundamentally, what is the cause of all this? (...) I think there are other elements that are much more fundamental than the rather circumstantial element that constitutes the commitment of France and other countries against Daech in Syria and Iraq. (...) I have made an in-depth study on these causes. We have to go back to the basics. We are faced with organisations that for thirty years, practically since Abdul Azzam, have had a fundamental political agenda, which is to destroy the West and our values. It's a fight against our values. That's what's important, because they want to substitute their values for ours (...) Today, what they want to destroy is democracy. There is no doubt about it. Because they cannot accept it. The only acceptable, legitimate law is Sharia law*[412].

It is true that the fundamentalists recognise Sharia law as the only acceptable law, but this does not mean that the Islamists want to impose it on the West. Yet the idea is persistent. Jean-Frédéric Poisson, president of the Christian Democratic Party, proclaims that there is a project to "*make Sharia dominate the Western world*[413]". This is not true. It is based on a document drawn up by the Islamic Educational, Scientific and Cultural Organisation (IESCO)

410. "Complotisme, les alibis de la terreur", *YouTube*, January 24, 2018 (01'40")
411. "Complotisme, les alibis de la terreur", *YouTube*, January 24, 2018 (10'20")
412. Jean-Louis Bruguière, Le Grand Référendum, *Sud-Radio*, April 19, 2017
413. "On the page!" The plan for the Islamization of the West unveiled by Jean-Frédéric Poisson!", *YouTube*, December 28, 2018 (02'10")

entitled *Strategy for Islamic Cultural Action outside the Islamic World*[414], the aim of which is to strengthen the conscience of Muslims abroad and make them less "vulnerable" to the secularisation of Western societies. This is not a proselytising and conquering project, but a desire to maintain moral standards in the Muslim diaspora.

In France, probably because of a Marxist culture that colours the perception of secularism across the political spectrum, religious practice tends to be perceived as destabilising. Curiously enough, however, the observations made in Great Britain are exactly the opposite. Indeed, the *British* Security Service (MI5) notes that a well-established religious identity protects against violent radicalisation[415].

The idea of a Muslim plot to take over Europe has been growing in recent years, in the wake of the book *Eurabia*[416]. Written by a Jewish woman expelled from Egypt with her family in 1956 after the Lavon affair[417], it outlines an Arab plot to dominate the Western world. It is referenced by the Norwegian right-wing extremist Anders Behring Breivik (who killed 77 people in Utoya on July 22, 2011), its scenario is taken up by all the major far-right movements in Europe[418] and is featured in the *France 3* film[419].

This highly emotional and fact-free discourse has spread from the far right to the entire political spectrum. For example, on RTL, the Belgian far-right MP Darya Safai said that the EI was seeking to "*conquer the whole world and [...] wanted to destroy Western civilisation*[420]", which is not found in the EI's writings. In fact, she echoes the words of Manuel Valls, then Prime Minister, who sketched out the idea of an Islamist plot behind terrorism:

> *[We cannot lose this war because it is basically a war of civilisation. It is our society, our civilisation, our values that we are defending*[421].

> *The Islamic State wants to destroy our democracies*[422].

414. *Strategy for Islamic Cultural Action outside the Islamic World - Strategy adopted by the Ninth Islamic Summit Conference held in Doha, State of Qatar, 2000*, Islamic Educational, Scientific and Cultural Organization, 2009

415. Alan Travis, "MI5 report challenges views on terrorism in Britain", *The Guardian*, August 20, 2008 (www.theguardian.com/uk/2008/aug/20/uksecurity.terrorism1). (Accessed November 13, 2016).

416. Bat Ye'or, *Eurabia*, Éditions Jean-Cyrille Godefroy, Paris, 2006

417. See Wikipedia, article "Lavon Affair".

418. Raphaël Liogier, "The myth of the Arab-Muslim invasion", *Le Monde diplomatique*, May 2014, pp. 8-9

419. Jacob Rogozinski in "Complotisme, les alibis de la terreur", *YouTube*, January 24, 2018 (31'20")

420. Darya Safai in the programme "C'est pas tous les jours dimanche", *RTL-TVI*, December 8, 2019

421. "Valls: the fight against terrorism is a 'war of civilisation'", *leparisien.fr*, June 28, 2015

422. "Manuel Valls: 'We will destroy the terrorists, but there will be new innocent victims'", *La Croix*, July 17, 2016; Cécile Amar, "Manuel Valls: 'We will win this war'", *Le Journal du Dimanche*, July 17, 2016 (updated on June 21, 2017)

In our societies, in Belgium as in France, we have thousands of individuals who are in prison or outside who are radicalised and who want to impose their vision of a political, radicalised, jihadist Islam within Islam and which represents a danger for Islam and a danger for our values [...].[423]

If we add to this the tendency to establish a continuum between Islam and Islamism, as Manuel Valls does:

[To say that it has nothing to do with Islam is to take away the responsibility of Islam[424].

... or certain journalists, such as Mohammed Sifaoui:

The veil is not Islamic, (...) the veil is Islamist[425]

Not to mention the controversies over the burkini - which has never been an Islamic garment and has even been condemned by the EI - an "*official truth*" has been created[426] that makes Muslims the attackers of the West. We have all the ingredients to generate a "*fear of Islam*" (in French, literally: *islamophobie*).

Thus, whether it is intended or not, a link is created between the consequences of two distinct phenomena: the practice of religion and its nationalistic expression as a result of our interventions in the Near and Middle East. This perception serves as an alibi for decades of poorly managed, clientelist immigration policies, which have given the impression of an "invasion", reinforcing the idea of a form of conquest. As for refugees, in 2018 they came mainly from Afghanistan and Syria (two countries where the West is seeking regime change) and from South Sudan (largely supported financially by the West).[427]

5.7. Conclusions for Jihadist Terrorism

Since 9/11, security has become a flourishing economic sector, an extension of the activities of the arms industry. Terrorism has become a convenient alibi for strengthening state control over the private lives of individuals. The principles we defended against communism during the Cold War are now forgotten: the

423. Arthur Lejeune with Thomas Gadisseux, "Manuel Valls: 'I took everything for others'", *RTBF.info*, March 8, 2018.
424. Manuel Valls, "Grand Jury" programme, *RTL, LCI and Le Figaro*, November 26, 2017
425. Mohammed Sifaoui in the programme "On a tellement de choses à se dire" "'Le voile n'est pas islamique' mais 'islamiste' selon Mohamed Sifaoui", *RTL /YouTube*, September 25, 2019 (06'30")
426. Alain Rebetez, *Journal de 19 h 30*, Télévision Suisse Romande, May 22, 2017
427. *Global Trends - Forced Displacement In 2018*, UNHCR, June 18, 2019

use of torture, the merging of foreign and domestic intelligence resources, the return of censorship and the denial of international law are taking us further away from democracy.

Today, the Islamic State has become a pretext for intervention in the Middle East. After being declared defeated in November 2017[428], December 2018[429] and March 2019[430], it remains the main reason for maintaining a multinational force in Iraq and Syria in 2020. When that is no longer enough, a Shiite or Iranian threat is created. According to Major General Alex Grynkewich, Chief of Operations and Intelligence for Operation INHERENT RESOLVE, the main threat to US forces would be the Iraqi Shiite militias[431]... who enabled the victory against the EI. In fact, the threat is being created as we go along in order to keep troops in place. We still do not know the adversary we are fighting, so we still do not have a coherent strategy to defeat it; but above all, we are maintaining a threat that no longer has any basis...[432]

---

428. Thomas Liabot, "Defeat of Daech in Syria and Iraq: 5 questions that arise", *Le Journal du Dimanche*, November 10, 2017; Maher Chmaytelli & Ahmed Aboulenein, "Islamic State's defeat proclaimed in Iraq", *Reuters*, December 9, 2017; "One year after the defeat of the terrorist group Islamic State, what is happening to its ex-capital?", *RTBF*, October 16, 2018

429. "Donald Trump announces defeat of Islamic State group in Syria", *rts.ch*, December 20, 2018

430. "Syria. "100% territorial defeat" of Daech", *Courrier International*, March 23, 2019

431. Jeff Schogol, "US forces in Iraq are facing more attacks from Shiite militias than ISIS, commander says", *Task & Purpose*, January 22, 2020

432. David Corn & Matt Cohen, "With a War Against Iran Brewing, Don't Listen to the Hawks Who Lied Us Into Iraq," *Mother Jones*, January 3, 2020; Will Bunch, "The folks who lied about Iraq and Afghanistan are lying about Iran. We must stop a new war', *The Philadelphia Inquirer*, January 5, 2020

6. THE WAR IN SYRIA

6.1. The context

The Syrian regime is the heir to the Arab nationalist movements of the 1950s. It combines nationalism and socialism and follows an evolution comparable to that of Tunisia and Egypt. In the 1970s, it faced a revolt organised by the Muslim Brotherhood in Syria (*Ikhwan al-Muslimin fil-Suriya*). The insurrection took a terrorist form: on June 16, 1979, between 32 and 83 Syrian army cadets were massacred[433]. It culminated in an assassination attempt on Hafez al-Assad on June 26, 1980. At the beginning of July, the government adopts Law No. 49, which punishes members of the Ikhwan by death, but grants life to repentant members[434]. In October 1980, the Ikhwan created the "*Islamic Front*" and engaged in an armed revolutionary process, described in November 1980 in a document entitled *The Islamic Revolution in Syria and its Charter*. Community tensions led to a 27-day siege of the city of Hamah in 1982, which resulted in the eradication of the Ikhwan in Syria. The number of victims has never been precisely known and estimates vary between 5,000[435] and 40,000[436] including more than 2,000 dead among the forces of order. At the time, the Cold War was in full swing: Damascus was aligned with Moscow and Western propaganda was pushing the issue. In reality, we know nothing about it; but the event will leave the image of a brutal regime, which persists to this day, despite the change of presidents.

At the end of the Cold War, deprived of the economic and political support of the USSR, Syria tried to get closer to the West. In 1990, it joined the Western coalition against Iraq and deployed 14,500 troops in Operation Desert Storm

433. The figures for this massacre are controversial. See Patrick Seale, "Asad, the Struggle for the Middle East", *University of California Press*, 1989.
434. Dr Liad Porat, "The Syrian Muslim Brotherhood and the Asad Regime", *Middle East Brief*, Brandeis University, No 47, December 2010
435. Mariam Karouny, "Syria's Hama honors victims of massacre after 30 years", *Reuters*, February 2, 2012
436. "The 1982 Hama Massacre", *Middle East Monitor*, February 12, 2018

to obtain the support of the United States to resolve the Golan Heights issue. But it was not understood (or wanted to be understood) that Syria was asking for it and that an opportunity existed to restore normal relations in that part of the world.

In the late 1990s, under President Bill Clinton, a peace process between Syria and Israel was initiated at the instigation of Hafez al-Assad. But his death in June 2000, the start of the second Intifada in Israel in September, the election of President Bush in the United States in November, the arrival of Ariel Sharon in power in Israel in March 2001 and, finally, September 11 all combined to nip these peace attempts in the bud and freeze anti-Syrian positions in the West.

Bashar al-Assad continues his father's efforts. After "9/11", Syria actively cooperates in the fight against radical Islamist and jihadist movements ("Al-Qaeda") with the American Special Operations Command. As early as 2002, it informed the Western services about the activities of the Muslim Brotherhood in Syria and Germany. It participates in the secret detention programme of the American CIA and takes in the prisoners it delivers to it[437]. The CIA admits that "*the quality and quantity of information from Syria has exceeded the Agency's expectations*" and stresses that Syria "*has received little in return*[438]".

In January 2002, George W. Bush did not include Syria in his "axis of evil". However, the State Department continues to describe it as a "*state sponsor of terrorism*", while stressing that Syria "has not been *directly involved in terrorist operations since 1986*[439]". In fact, it is blamed for harbouring the leaders of some Palestinian Marxist groups from the 1970s-1980s, whose importance and influence have become almost nil[440]. But on 6 May 2002, in an address to the Heritage Foundation (a conservative right-wing think-tank), John Bolton - then Undersecretary of State - added Syria to the axis of evil on his own initiative[441].

In 2003, the US sought to build a coalition against Iraq, but struggled to find allies to join the fight. Syria had participated in the coalition against Iraq in 1990, and US Secretary of State Colin Powell tried to pressure Bashar al-Assad to present an Arab ally. But the latter has perceived the risk of an intervention:

> *I told the Americans how to fight Al Qaeda after 9/11. That you should not go to war. That you cannot fight terrorism if you are at war. War only does the*

437. Seymour Hersh, 'Military to Military', *London Review of Books*, Vol. 38 No. 1, January 7, 2016.
438. Seymour Hersh, "The Syrian Bet", *The New Yorker*, July 27, 2003.
439. *Country Reports on Terrorism 2007*, Department of State, April 2008 (p.175).
440. As of the 2012 edition of the State Department's annual reports on terrorism, links with the Palestinian resistance are no longer mentioned, and have been replaced by those with the Lebanese Hezbollah (which is not recognised as a terrorist by a vast majority of countries).
441. "US expands 'axis of evil', *BBC News*, May 6, 2002

terrorists a favour. It's like a cancer, instead of removing the whole tumour, you are going to cut it out. When you cut it out the cancer spreads[442].

Syria did not join the coalition, but it suffered the consequences: it hosted between 1 and 1.5 million Iraqi refugees. They are essentially Sunni and largely radicalised by the American-British intervention. This presence accentuates the confessional imbalance of the country and will be exacerbated by the drought of 2005-2010, which affects the rural population (mostly Sunni). It is on this ground that the destabilisation led by the United States[443] will develop from 2006.

On 14 February 2005, the attack against the former Lebanese Prime Minister Rafic Hariri in Beirut placed Syria - opportunely - in the crosshairs of the international community and precipitated its departure from Lebanon. The international tribunal in charge of investigating the attack accuses Syria, before turning to the Lebanese Hezbollah. But its accusations are fragile and remain unverified to this day. In fact, other likely perpetrators of the assassination have been ruled out from the outset, including Israel, which is the main beneficiary and is accustomed to this type of action against its enemies and friends. While there are many technical and political elements that tend to demonstrate its involvement[444], the investigation will never move in this direction. However, since 2011, the State Department has not mentioned the Hariri case in its annual report on Syria.

The idea of the fragmentation of Syria emerged in February 1982, with the Yinon Plan, published under the aegis of the World Zionist Organisation, under the title *A Strategy for Israel in the 1980s*[445]. In its original form, this "plan" was never an official part of Israeli policy, but it sheds light on how Israel understands its strategic environment:

The dissolution of Syria and later Iraq into ethnically and religiously unique areas, as in Lebanon, is Israel's primary long-term objective on its eastern front, while the dissolution of the military power of these states is a primary objective in the short term. Syria will break up according to its ethnic and religious structures into several states, as is currently the case in Lebanon, with a Shiite Alawite state along the coast, a Sunni state in the Aleppo region, another Sunni state in Damascus, hostile to its northern neighbour, and the Druze establishing their state, perhaps even in our Golan Heights, in the

442. Bashar Al-Assad, Dictator or Democratic Visionary, op.cit.
443. Joe Romm, 'Human-Caused Warming Helped Trigger Current Syrian Conflict and Rise of ISIS', *thinkprogress.org*, March 3, 2015.
444. Jürgen Cain Külbel, *Mordakte Hariri. Unterdrückte Spuren im Libanon*, Kai Homilius Publishing, 2006.
445. Oded Yinon, "A Strategy for Israel in the Nineteen Eighties", KIVUNIM (Directions), *A Journal for Judaism and Zionism*; Issue No, 14--Winter, 5742, Department of Publicity/The World Zionist Organization, Jerusalem, February 1982

Hauran and in northern Jordan. This configuration will guarantee peace and security in the long term and this goal is already achievable today[446].

It was the basis for another document prepared in 1996 by an American think tank for Israeli Prime Minister Benjamin Netanyahu, which outlined an Israeli strategy[447]: destabilisation of the region, including the overthrow of the Iraqi and Syrian governments, instead of a comprehensive peace; increased right of pursuit and intervention in the Palestinian territories; and enhanced cooperation with the United States. This plan, too, will never be officially adopted by Netanyahu. But its authors, widely represented in the Bush administration, would later use it to shape US policy in the Middle East[448].

Indeed, in July 1986, an internal CIA memo examined various options for bringing about regime change in Syria and concluded that "*American interests would be best served by a Sunni regime, controlled by moderates guided by business*[449]".

As early as 2005, the Bush and then Obama administrations funded opposition groups and clandestine activities in Syria[450]. The interview with Bashar al-Assad by Christiane Amanpour, CNN's star journalist, shows that the project to destabilise Syria was then openly known and discussed[451]:

> *AMANPOUR: Mr. President, you know that the rhetoric of regime change is aimed at you from the United States. They are actively looking for a new Syrian leader. They are granting visas and visits to Syrian opposition politicians. They talk about isolating you diplomatically and perhaps a coup or the collapse of your regime. What do you think about this?*[452]

By overthrowing Saddam Hussein, the Americans created a continuous Shiite space between Iran and the Lebanese Hezbollah. The Israelis see this as the reason for their failure in Lebanon in 2006, more than their disastrous management of the operations. The idea of disrupting this space emerged and led to a joint US-Israeli strategy, adopted in 2007 and unveiled by the American journalist

---

446. Oded Yinon, *A Strategy for Israel in the Nineteen Eighties*, Association of Arab-American University Graduates, Inc. Belmont, Massachusetts, 1982, Special Document No. 1 (ISBN 0-937694-56-8)

447. "To Clean Break: A New Strategy for Securing the Realm", *The Institute for Advanced Strategic and Political Studies*, July 1996,

448. Brian Whitaker, 'Playing skittles with Saddam', *The Guardian*, September 3, 2002.

449. *Syria: Scenarios of Dramatic Political Changes*, Director of Global Issues, Directorate of Intelligence, CIA, July 28, 1986 (p. 24)

450. "U.S. secretly backed Syrian opposition groups, cables released by WikiLeaks show", *The Washington Post*, April 18, 2011

451. "Syria Regime Change Plans in 2005! Christiane Amanpour (CNN) interview with Assad", *CNN/YouTube*, April 28, 2018

452. "Al-Assad: 'Syria has nothing to do with this crime', *CNN.com*, October 12, 2012

Seymour Hersh - who is very close to military and intelligence circles - to topple the Iranian and Syrian regimes using Iraqi Sunni militias[453].

Diplomatic messages between the US embassy in Damascus and Washington, published by WikiLeaks, document the US administration's efforts to destabilise the Syrian government as early as 2006[454], outlining a range of possible operations to support a strategy of subversion aimed at creating a situation that would put "*Bashar personally in a situation of anxiety, which would cause him to act irrationally*"[455]. The aim was therefore to push Bashar al-Assad to commit crimes, in order to use this as a pretext for intervention.

In 2006 the US government began funding the Justice and Development Movement (JDM), an opposition organisation inside and outside Syria. Between 2006 and 2010, the US spends $6.3 million to fund *Barada TV*, a TV channel designed to spread anti-regime news, and another $6 million is used to train Syrian journalists and activists[456]. Based in London, it began broadcasting messages in support of an overthrow of the regime in April 2009. It will play a key role in 2011 through its coverage of the riots at the start of the revolution and its messages designed to inflame public opinion by disseminating false information about the reaction of Syrian law enforcement agencies, relayed by the Western media[457].

In April 2009, the US ambassador to Damascus expressed doubts about the ability of the United States to control opposition movements in Syria in a secret cable sent to Washington:

> *With the reassessment of Syria policy, and with the apparent collapse of the main external Syrian opposition organisation*[458]*, one thing becomes clear: US policy should place less emphasis on 'regime change' and move more towards encouraging 'reform behaviour'. If this assumption is borne out, then a reassessment of current support programmes for anti-government factions inside and outside Syria may prove more productive*[459].

He expresses concern that Syrian intelligence is suspicious of Washington's support for the opposition:

453. Seymour M. Hersh, 'The Redirection', *The New Yorker*, March 5, 2007
454. Adam Zagorin, "Syria in Bush's Cross Hairs", *Time Magazine*, December 19, 2006
455. "Influencing the SARG in the End of 2006", December 13, 2006 (SARG = Syrian Arab Republic Government) (https://WikiLeaks.org/plusd/cables/06DAMASCUS5399_a.html)
456. "U.S. admits funding Syrian opposition", CBC News, April 18, 2011
457. Craig Whitlock, "WikiLeaks: U.S. secretly backed Syria opposition", *Washington Post*, November 18, 2011.
458. This is the MJD.
459. Diplomatic cable of April 28, 2009 from the US Embassy in Damascus to Washington (SECRET), 09DAMASCUS306 (https://WikiLeaks.org/plusd/cables/09DAMASCUS306_a.html)

> *It is not clear to what extent [Syrian] intelligence has understood that US government funding is flowing into Syria and through which organisations. [...] What is clear, however, is that Security is increasingly interested in this issue*[460].

This casts doubt on the sincerity - or ignorance - of Alain Juppé, in January 2012, who responded to accusations of Western involvement by saying that Assad was in '*denial*[461]'. Yet at the same time, after a meeting with US officers and French and British liaison officers at the Pentagon, a representative of the US think-tank Stratfor reported that special forces - "*obviously*" from France, Britain, the US and Turkey - were training rebels on Turkish territory[462].

The Americans - and some French intellectual circles - have tried to link the Syrian government to the rise of terrorism in the Middle East. This idea is widely propagated by pro-Israeli circles, such as the Investigative Project Terrorism (IPT), directed by Steven Emerson:

> *Three Americans - Laurence Michael Foley, Sr, Keith Matthew Maupin and Kristian Menchacha - were killed in separate attacks by members of the terrorist group led by Zarqawi in Iraq and Jordan. In April 2011, the families of the victims filed a complaint against the Syrian Arab Republic, its President Bashar al-Assad, the Syrian Military Intelligence Service and its former chief, Assif Sahwkat, who was killed in a 2012 suicide attack in Damascus. Expert testimony and evidence show the Syrian government's complicity in aiding terrorist groups like Zarqawi's by allowing them to "move freely into neighboring countries, such as Iraq and Jordan, for the express purpose of killing Americans*[463]*."*

It is difficult not to see such statements as an expression of imbecility and bad faith. In reality, in order not to become a sanctuary for the Iraqi resistance and to give the Americans a pretext to intervene in Syria, the Syrians have agreed to their request to close the border. Many jihadists will thus find themselves on Syrian territory as refugees, as will the vast majority of "Syrian" refugees in Europe ten years later...

---

460. Ibid.

461. "400 deaths in Syria since the beginning of the Arab League mission", *Le Monde / AFP / Reuters*, January 10, 2012

462. https://wikileaks.org/gifiles/docs/16/1671459_insight-military-intervention-in-syria-post-withdrawal.html

463. Abha Shankar, "Syrian Regime Held Liable for Americans' Murders", *IPT News*, May 2, 2017 (https://www.investigativeproject.org/6069/syrian-regime-held-liable-for-americans-murders)

6.2 "The Conflict in Syria was Triggered in 2011 Because of the Repression of Peaceful Demonstrations[464]"

It has become commonplace to portray Bashar al-Assad as a criminal, whose aim is to eliminate his own population. Yet, during the previous decade, demonstrations that involved a "heavy-handed" response by law enforcement agencies only had a record comparable to that of the "Yellow Vests" crisis in France. According to a Human Rights Watch report, Kurdish demonstrations between 2005 and 2009 were repressed with tear gas and the intervention of riot units, with many arrests, but - despite the death of three demonstrators in March 2008 - this was a far cry from the repression described by the Western media in 2011[465].

The massacre in Qamishli, in the Kurdish area, which left about 50 people dead in March 2004, is sometimes mentioned. However, it was not a demonstration against the government, but an altercation between football fans that degenerated: many had entered the stands with weapons. According to witnesses, clashes between supporters of Saddam Hussein and pro-American supporters escalated after a local radio station reported that children had died. But according to human rights organisations, witness accounts seem to confirm that the police did not intervene with firearms, but with the usual tear gas and riot gear[466].

Thus, it is difficult to see why, in the midst of the "Arab Spring", in a very tense period in the Middle East and at a time when it was foreseeable that the situation would degenerate, the Syrian president would suddenly change his tactics and decide to use violence to repress peaceful demonstrations.

The answer is in the West: after Libya, the United States and France already have their eye on Syria. With the start of the so-called 'citizens' revolutions' of 2010-2012, Saudi and US interests seem to be coming together. The planned nature of the Syrian revolution - and the absence of a popular dimension - is confirmed by Roland Dumas, former Minister of Foreign Affairs, who stated in 2013 that he had been contacted by the British secret services, two years before the Syrian crisis, with a view to an operation to overthrow the government. Thus, in 2010, Britain was already preparing, with the United States, an insurgency aimed at bringing to power a dissident faction of the Syrian army[467].

---

464. Etienne Jacob, "Guerre en Syrie: sept ans après, les chiffres chocs d'une 'tragédie colossale'", *Le Figaro*, March 14, 2018

465. "Group Denial - Repression of Kurdish Political and Cultural Rights in Syria", *Human Rights Watch*, 2009

466. *Report 4 - The "Al-Qamishli Uprising" - The beginning of a "new era" for Syrian Kurds?* KurdWatch, Berlin, December 2009

467. Interview with Roland Dumas on Radio Courtoisie, September 24, 2013. "Syria: Roland Dumas says it all! (October 2013)", *YouTube*, November 12, 2013 (https://www.youtube.com/watch?v=Is8o-wiRY4s) and "Roland Dumas: les Anglais préparaient la guerre en Syrie deux ans avant les manifestations en 2011", *YouTube*, June 20,

In fact, these are Islamist elements, linked to the Syrian Muslim Brotherhood movement, because the bulk of the Syrian army - mostly Sunni - has remained loyal to Bashar al-Assad.

In the West, there is talk of a popular insurrection. This is not true. In Syria, discontent was not enough to trigger an insurrection. This is why, unlike in other Arab countries, the Syrian revolution was piloted from outside the country from the start. This is the case of *the* Free Syrian Army (FSA) - an offshoot of the Syrian Muslim Brotherhood that took refuge in Turkey - supported by Turkish, American and French special services. This is why there is a huge number of foreign fighters, many of whom arrived in Syria with the help of Western services, long before the emergence of the Islamic State. Like the Kurds, the bulk of whose People's Protection Units (YPG) come from Turkey and Iraq. In 2014, foreign fighters already number almost 75,000[468]. If we add the Sunni rebels who came from Iraq in 2003-2005, we can see that the 'popular' dimension of the Syrian rebellion is very relative. As soon as Gaddafi fell, Libyan rebels contacted the Syrian opposition to provide them with weapons[469] and troops[470]. In 2012, a crowdfunding account for the Syrian revolution was even opened on the Kickstarter platform[471].

Moreover, the Western media remain discreet about the fact that, unlike the Tunisian and Egyptian revolutions (which started in the big cities, thanks to students and social networks), the Syrian revolution started in the countryside ("Rif Dimachq") and in popular suburban areas ("shaabi"), without the support of social networks. This indicates that there were other channels to mobilise the insurgents and that their target audience was not in the cities, but in rural areas, mostly Sunni. This explains why the Syrian government did not feel the need to interrupt access to the Internet and social networks.

Symptomatically, on the Facebook page of the Syrian revolution, the starting point of the insurrection is placed at 18 January 2011[472], i.e. two months before the Daraa demonstrations, indicating that they were not as spontaneous as the Western media would have us believe. Presented in the West as "peaceful", these demonstrations were in fact particularly violent at the hands of the demonstrators, as reported by the Israeli newspaper *Arutz Sheva*[473]. Moreover, a jihadist

---

2013 (https://www.youtube.com/watch?v=HI23UkYl3Eo)

468. Combined sources: www.algerie1.com, www.lepoint.fr, www.lalibre.be, lefigaro.fr

469. Ruth Sherlock, "Libya's new rulers offer weapons to Syrian rebels", *The Telegraph*, November 225, 011

470. Ruth Sherlock, "Leading Libyan Islamist meets Free Syrian Army opposition group", *The Telegraph*, November 27, 2011

471. The account will be closed by the platform a month later, on 21 August 2012. (Spencer Ackerman, "New Kickstarter Pitch: 'Join the Syrian Uprising'", *Wired*, August 21, 2012)

472. https://www.facebook.com/photo.php?fbid=10151232961170727&set=a.10150308582340727.567536.420796315726&type=3&theater (accessed February 28, 2016)

473. Gabe Kahn, "Syria: Seven Police Killed, Buildings Torched in Protests", *Israel National News/Arutz Sheva*, March 21, 2011.

later confessed to *TIME* magazine that the Islamist group *Ahrar al-Sham* had begun training its phalanxes just "*after the Egyptian revolution*" and well before the official start of the revolution in Syria[474].

Despite Syria's unequivocal condemnations, little is known about the details of the first weeks of the insurgency. While the deaths are systematically attributed to the government, the available information tends to incriminate the opposition. Dutch Jesuit Father Frans van der Lugt[475], who has lived in Syria since the 1960s, is an eyewitness to the first demonstrations in Syria in 2011. He writes:

> *From the beginning, the demonstrations were not purely peaceful. From the very beginning, I saw armed demonstrators marching with the other demonstrators, shooting at the police first. Very often, the violence of the security forces was a reaction to brutal acts of violence by the rebels*[476].

The strategy used is very "Western". Provocateurs among the demonstrators seek to eliminate police officers in order to escalate the repression, with the aim of generating a popular insurrection and blaming the government:

> *Moreover, from the beginning there was the problem of armed groups, which are also part of the opposition... The street opposition is much stronger than any other form of opposition. And this opposition is armed and frequently uses brutality and violence, so that the government is blamed. Many government officials have been tortured and killed by them*[477].

Yet the Syrian government has shown great restraint from the start. In September 2011, the American analysis group Stratfor, often considered an offshoot of the CIA and specialising in strategic conflict analysis, wrote about the situation in Syria:

> *The opposition has to find a way to maintain the 'Arab Spring' discourse, so a flood of information about the brutality of the regime and the value of the opposition is to be expected. While it is certain that demonstrators and civilians have been killed, there is no clear evidence of massive brutality, as there was in*

474. Rania Abouzeid, "TIME Exclusive: Meet the Islamist Militants Fighting Alongside Syria's Rebels", *TIME Magazine*, July 26, 2012
475. Father Frans van der Lugt was murdered on 7 April 2014 in Homs because he refused to hand over to (moderate!) Islamists property entrusted to him by Syrians (Eva Bartlett, lecture at St. Matthew's Syrian Orthodox Church, West Roxbury, MA, December 11, 2016)
476. John Rosenthal, 'An Eyewitness to the Syrian Rebellion: Father Frans in His Own Words', *The BRICS Post*, April 19, 2014.
477. Ibid.

1982 or in other restorations in the region. Stratfor found no evidence of heavy weapons being used to massacre civilians or create significant combat damage, although 12.7mm machine guns mounted on armoured vehicles were used to disperse the crowd[478].

On 4 February 2012, as the Security Council was preparing to vote on a resolution calling for the resignation of President Assad, the press reported the massacre of 260 civilians in Homs[479]. But on the same day, the *Guardian* in London mentions "only" 217 deaths[480], and the *BBC* 55[481]. However, in its chronology of events established in 2016, *the* French Office for the Protection of Refugees and Stateless Persons (OFPRA) retains the number of 260 without expressing the slightest reservation[482]: the situation must be dramatised.

In fact, in early 2012, Homs was in thc hands of two phalanxes, which "officially" belonged to the ASL, including the al-Farouq Phalanx (formerly the "Baba Amr militia"). In March 2012, one of its "executors" confessed to a *Spiegel* journalist and explained how the militia tortures and eliminates civilians favourable to the government[483]. He thus confirms the accusations of the Syrian Christian Orthodox Church, which reports ethnic cleansing of the city's Christian population, which supports the Syrian regime[484]. The problem is that this phalanx was supported by France, but the French media did not mention it.

In February 2012, Robert Ford, the US ambassador to Syria, posted a note on Facebook entitled *Escalation of security operations in Homs*[485] with aerial photographs showing the deployment of Syrian artillery to pound the protests in the city, which is known to be very anti-government. It is intended to prove that the government is deliberately attacking the civilian population with artillery. However, an examination of the images shows that all the photos depict units deployed in their barracks or on training grounds not far from the city. The spots described as 'shell craters' are in fact brownish areas in sports fields, which can

478. "Syria Opposition, take half", *Stratfor*, September 14, 2011 (published on 11 March 2013 by *WikiLeaks* in *The Global Intelligence Files*)

479. "SYRIA. A night of massacre in Homs, 260 dead", *L'Obs/AFP*, February 4, 2012

480. Damien Pearse & agencies, "Fury over Homs massacre as UN security council gathers for Syria vote", *The Guardian*, February 4, 2012

481. "Syria Assad: Army massacres 'scores' in city of Homs", *BBC News*, February 4, 2012

482. "Chronology of the conflict in the province and city of Homs from March 2011 to March 2016", *Office Français de Protection des Réfugiés et Apatrides*, April 5, 2016

483. Ulrike Putz, "An Executioner for Syria's Rebels Tells His Story", *Spiegel Online*, March 29, 2012

484. Frank Crimi, "Ethnic Cleansing Of Syrian Christians", *FrontPageMag.com*, March 28, 2012 (http://www.frontpagemag.com/fpm/127087/ethnic-cleansing-syrian-christians-frank-crimi)

485. "À note from Ambassador Ford on recent events in Syria", Facebook, February 9, 2012 (ww.facebook.com/photo.php?fbid=10150600575457649&set=pu.48261722648&type=1&theater)

also be found in the earlier Google Earth imagery[486]. This is therefore purely and simply misinformation.

In fact, under the guise of a popular revolution, the objective is the dismemberment of Syria, in order to reduce Iranian influence, generated by the American war in Iraq, and to guarantee the security of Israel. The problem is that the West has not understood the complexity of the context: the "moderate rebels" they support are in fact Islamists from the start. This will become apparent a little late in October 2019, when Turkey intervenes and uses these elements to fight the Kurds. By downplaying these errors of judgement, the Western media has contributed greatly to the development of violence in the region and the emergence of the Islamic State.

6.3 "President Bashar al-Assad is Illegitimate"

The image we have of Syria is that of a totalitarian state. It was shaped during the Cold War under the dictatorship of Hafez al-Assad, Bashar's father, and has come down to us mainly through the prism of Israel, which strives to give its neighbours a threatening image. But the reality is more nuanced.

Bashar al-Assad, who came to power in spite of himself, is not the bloodthirsty man he is usually described as. Trained as a doctor who had studied and lived in the West, he immediately sought to dust off and reform the regime he had inherited, and with which he had to operate. He developed the digitalisation of Syrian society and access to social networks. At the beginning of the 2000s, his efforts to continue the attempts at openness initiated by his father are real[487]. But the international context was not favourable to him, and the world was dominated by leaders who were "war-mongering" and of dubious rationality: Ariel Sharon in Israel, George W. Bush in the United States, Tony Blair in Great Britain.

An American Marine who spent time in Syria before the conflict gives us a diametrically different picture from the one the media is giving us today[488]. Moreover, since the beginning of the conflict, the mainstream media has ignored the population living - voluntarily - in government zones. This being the case, Syria is not a democratic state in the sense that we understand it in Europe and undoubtedly requires reforms, just like Tunisia and Egypt. But neither is it a methodical and ruthless tyranny as Europe experienced in the early 20th century.

486. "The State Department Lies With Its Satellite Pictures Of Syria - No Artillery 'Deployed'", *moonofalabama.org*, February 11, 2012
487. "*Bashar Al-Assad, Dictator or Democratic Visionary?*", YouTube, November 10, 2013
488. "ISIS in Syria are CIA backed trained and funded", *YouTube*, November 18, 2015

As soon as the revolts in Tunisia and Egypt began, the possibility of a contagion in Syria was raised. In January 2011, a Facebook page entitled *Syria Revolution 2011* was created by the Muslim Brotherhood (from Sweden[489]) and announced "*Days of Rage*" on 4 and 5 February. The government reacted by cutting off access to Facebook. But the success of the call was limited: participants chanted more against the Libyan regime than against the Syrian government[490]. Access to Facebook was restored on February 8, 2011 and social networks have been functioning normally without interruption since. The opposition tried a new action in early March, but without real success, as reported by the American magazine *TIME:*

> *Even critics agree that Assad is popular and close to the country's huge youth cohort, both emotionally, ideologically and, of course, in age*[491].

The journalist confirms her finding in another article:

> *(...) Although there have been calls on Facebook for protests in Syria, the country's youth, who make up the majority of the country's 22 million citizens (65% under the age of 30), have largely ignored the internet activists*[492].

In February 2012, as the situation hardened, Russia proposed a three-point plan to Western countries for the departure of Bashar al-Assad. It was discussed by Vitalii Churkin, Russian ambassador to the United Nations, and Martti Ahtisaari, Nobel Peace Prize winner and former Finnish president[493]:

> *One: we must not give weapons to the opposition. Two: we must set up a dialogue between the opposition and Assad now. Three: we must find an elegant way for Assad to withdraw*[494].

So from the start there was a solution for the departure of Bashar al-Assad without resorting to violence. But the West refused: their objective was not to replace Bashar al-Assad, but to dismantle Syria, which Israel - and therefore the United States - perceived as an advanced bastion of Iran. They therefore

489. Joshua Landis, "The Man behind 'Syria Revolution 2011' Facebook-Page Speaks Out", *Syria Comment*, April 24, 2011

490. Aryn Baker, "Syria Is Not Egypt, but Might It One Day Be Tunisia?", *Time Magazine*, February 4, 2011

491. Rania Abouzeid, "Sitting Pretty in Syria: Why Few Go Bashing Bashar", *Time Magazine*, March 6, 2011

492. Rania Abouzeid, "The Youth of Syria: The Rebels Are on Pause", *Time Magazine*, March 6, 2011

493. Julian Borger & Bastien Inzaurralde, "West 'ignored Russian offer in 2012 to have Syria's Assad step aside'", *The Guardian*, September 15, 2015.

494. Fanny Arlandis, "En 2012, la France et ses alliés auraient ignororé un plan prévoyant le départ de Bachar el-Assad", *Slate.fr*, September 15, 2015

need to insert a Sunni obstacle into the Tehran-Beirut axis. They thus seek to militarise the conflict by clandestinely distributing arms to Sunni militants[495]. This explains Israel's support for the Syrian Islamists and its good relations with the Islamic State, as we will see below.

In 2013, based on surveys by independent humanitarian organisations, Nato itself found that Bashar al-Assad had the support of 70% of the Syrian population, mainly because the Islamists had taken over the Western-backed revolution[496]. The reason why the West - led by the US and France - is reluctant to hold a popular election to find a successor to Bashar al-Assad is that he may well win such an election[497]!

This could explain - at least in part - the perverse game played by France and the United States, which have done everything to empty Syria of its Shiite and Christian elements, generally favourable to the regime, by supporting Sunni Islamist militias and the ASL, the armed wing of the Muslim Brotherhood in Syria. This probably also explains why, during the Syrian presidential elections of June 3, 2014, France, Germany and Switzerland banned Syrian nationals from participating in the vote in embassies[498]. Despite the incongruity of such a ballot being held in a country at war (even though, at that time, the government controlled most of the inhabited areas of the country), it is surprising that Western democracies lack confidence in the foresight of the Syrian people, particularly on European territory, beyond the reach of pressure from the government.

6.4 "Daech is Bashar's Frankenstein Creature[499]"

After the Paris attacks in January and November 2015, the French government will repeat over and over again that the Islamic State (IS) is an ally of President Bashar al-Assad's regime, or was even created by him[500]. Already in January 2014, Laurent Fabius, then Minister of Foreign Affairs, stated in Geneva:

> *I believe that there is an objective alliance between Bashar al-Assad and the terrorists. An objective alliance, why? It is the other side of the same coin*[501].

495. "Syria: France delivered arms to Syrian rebels", *20 Minutes/AFP*, August 21, 2014 (updated August 22, 2014).
496. "NATO data: Assad winning the war for Syrians' hearts and minds, *WorldTribune.com*, May 31, 2013 (http://www.worldtribune.com/nato-data-assad-winning-the-war-for-syrians-hearts-and-minds/)
497. Jonathan Steele, 'Most Syrians back President Assad, but you'd never know from western media', *The Guardian*, January 17, 2012.
498. "Syria: Paris and Berlin ban voting in their embassies", *Lefigaro.fr/AFP*, May 12, 2014
499. Sofia Amara, "L'invité" programme, *TV5Monde*, October 15, 2015
500. *L'Express*, "Hollande to the UN: in Syria, 'Assad is part of the problem, not the solution'", published on September 28, 2015, updated on September 29, 2015. (www.lexpress.fr/actualite/politique/hollande-a-l-onu-en-syrie-assad-est-une-partie-du-probleme-pas-de-la-solution_1720366.html)
501. "Syria - Interview by Mr Laurent Fabius, Minister of Foreign Affairs and International Development", *BFM*

On August 22, 2014, speaking about the EI, he told Jean-Jacques Bourdin on *BFMTV*:

> *His objective is not only to create a caliphate, i.e. to control Iraq, Syria, Jordan, Lebanon and Palestine, but to kill and eliminate all those who do not think like him. And so, when we say Iraq is important... Yes, but it is a threat to the whole region, to Europe and it is a threat to the world. [...]*

> *The Islamic State was born largely in Syria and Bashar al-Assad helped it to be born, since a number of the leaders of the Islamic State are people who were prisoners and whom Bashar al-Assad freed. They were born in Syria. In particular they developed in a city called Raqqa. Then, under their theory of the Caliphate, they came to Iraq; and there they routed the Iraqi army*[502].

He is lying from start to finish. In fact, he was preparing public opinion for the French intervention in Syria. We already know, at that time, that it will provoke terrorist acts in France, but the stakes must be as high as the risk incurred.

This theory was taken up by Bernard-Henri Lévy[503] in 2015, and by the political scientist Frédéric Encel, who suggests that the Syrian government supports the EI[504]. Some go even further and imagine convoluted scenarios, explaining the creation of the Islamic EI as a 'counter-fire' to the Syrian opposition[505]. In 2017, Jean-Yves Le Drian, then Minister of Foreign Affairs, declared:

> *When you were the first to free the jihadists of Daech, you don't give lessons*[506].

In reality, all these accusations are based on a method that comes under the heading of conspiracy[507]: facts are assembled in such a way that they correspond to a message. In this case, it is the amnesties decreed in March, May and June 2011 by the Syrian government, concerning some 1,000 political prisoners

TV - RMC, 2 March 2015 (il.ambafrance.org/Syria-Entretien-de-M-Laurent-12573); Syria - Geneva II Conference (Montreux, January 22, 2014), *France Diplomatie* (www.diplomatie.gouv.fr/fr/dossiers-pays/syrie/conference-geneve-ii/article/syrie-conference-de-geneve-ii)

502. "Bourdin Direct: Laurent Fabius - 22/08", *BFMTV/YouTube*, August 22, 2014

503. "Bernard Henri-Lévy "Bashar al-Assad created Daesh"", *C News/YouTube*, September 8, 2015 (04'15")

504. Frédéric Encel in the programme "C dans l'air", "Aleppo: Putin makes Bashar triumph #cdanslair 08-12-2016", *YouTube/France 5*, December 8, 2016 (29'45")

505. Coralie Muller, *Enquête sur l'État islamique*, Éditions du Moment, Paris, 2015, p. 160.

506. "Jean-Yves Le Drian responds to Bashar al-Assad's accusations", *AFP/YouTube*, December 19, 2017

507. Raniah Salloum, "Former Prisoners Fight in Syrian Insurgency," *Der Spiegel*, October 10, 2013; Simon Speakman Cordall, "How Syria's Assad Helped Forge Isis," *Newsweek*, June 21, 2014; Roy Gutman, "Assad Henchman: Here's How We Built ISIS," *The Daily Beast*, January 12, 2016 "Bashar al-Assad's man's shocking confessions: 'Here's how we created the Islamic State,'" December 2, 2016

(mostly Islamists). For the "expert" Pierre Servent, the aim of this release was to *"scare the West so that they do not arm the rebellion*[508]*"* (!). Not only is this idiotic, but it is nothing more or less than disinformation. Moreover, if one follows this conspiracy logic, it is hard to understand why a regime that would so openly seek to eliminate its own civilian population would be so fussy about placing its crime within a legal framework! That said, it is not only in France that this conspiracy theory has developed. Magazines such as *Newsweek*, *Der Spiegel* and *The Independent*, which are well known, also claim this[509].

In fact, the Syrian government did not do otherwise than Muammar Gaddafi in March 2010[510], the Tunisian government in January 2011[511], President Mubarak in Egypt in February 2011[512]. This is simply a recurring tactic of authoritarian regimes in the face of a revolutionary movement: releasing political prisoners as a sign of appeasement, in order to lower tension.

In Syria, this was one of several concessions and appeasement measures (such as allowing the wearing of the niqab and closing casinos[513]) adopted by the government in early 2011 to try to calm the situation. It was done in the context of a general amnesty called for by the opposition[514]. The reason why there were so many Islamists among the released prisoners was simply because there was no secular opposition. But taken too late, these measures were overwhelmed by the dynamics of the rebellion. A phenomenon that is reminiscent - all things considered! - President Macron's reaction to calm the "Yellow Vests", in December 2018, or the measures adopted by the Hong Kong government to calm the rioters. These decisions must be taken before the rebellion reaches a critical threshold, or they will be totally ineffective. This is the role of strategic intelligence…

What the 'experts' hide is that in Syria, as in Libya[515], once liberated, these Islamists were promptly recuperated and armed by Western special services[516] to

508. Pierre Servent in the programme "C dans l'air", "Syria: advantage Putin #cdanslair 29-09-2015", *YouTube/ France 5*, September 29, 2015 (37'50")
509. Raniah Salloum, 'Former Prisoners Fight in Syrian Insurgency', *SpiegelOnline*, October 10, 2013; Simon Speakman Cordall, 'How Syria's Assad Helped Forge Isis', *Newsweek*, June 21, 2014; Ian Birrell, 'Assad fanned the flames of extremism: The Syrian dictator is already responsible for more deaths than Isis', *The Independent UK*, December 6, 2015
510. "Libya: 202 Prisoners Released But Hundreds Still Held Arbitrarily", *Human Rights Watch*, March 25, 2010
511. "The release of political prisoners in Tunisia is an encouraging first step", *Amnesty International*, January 20, 2011
512. Maamoun Youssef, "Egypt recognizes moderate Islamic party, promises to release political prisoners", *The Associated Press*, February 19, 2011
513. "Syria lifts niqab ban, shuts casino, in nod to Sunnis", *Reuters*, April 6, 2011
514. Zeina Karam, "Syria offers general amnesty", www.washingtonpost.com, May 31, 2011
515. Daniel Iriarte, "Islamistas libios se desplazan a Siria para "ayudar" a la revolución", *ABC.es*, December 17, 2011; Jomana Karadsheh, "Libya rebels move onto Syrian battlefield", *CNN*, July 18, 2012
516. Aron Lund, "Jaish al-Sham: An Ahrar al-Sham Offshoot or Something More?", *Carnegie Middle East Center*, October 16, 2015

form the backbone of an armed opposition. This is the case of *Ahrar al-Sham* and *Jaish al-Islam*, which John Kerry designates as affiliated with *Jabhat al-Nosrah* and the Islamic State[517] (and which commit the same atrocities, as we shall see below), but which the United States, Great Britain and France will refuse to put on the United Nations list of terrorist organisations[518].

Moreover, it should be remembered that in 2011 'Daech' did not exist, and its predecessor ('Islamic State of Iraq') was confined to Iraq. Already in March 2007, the British Joint Intelligence Committee (JIC) stated that it was the result of Western policy in Iraq[519]. In Iraq, as in Afghanistan, the (Sunni) resistance against foreign occupation has turned into a resistance against the (Shiite) government set up by the Americans.

The militarisation of the Syrian revolution by the West forced the government to concentrate its forces in the west of the country. The result was a security vacuum in the east, which allowed the joining of Iraqi and Syrian Islamist forces, and the transformation of the 'Islamic State in Iraq' into the 'Islamic State in Iraq and the Levant'. A dynamic map of the Syrian war[520] shows that the Islamic State has grown from Iraq and the Turkish border and has established itself on Syrian territory in the wake of armed groups, such as the Free Syrian Army (FSA), supported by France and the United States[521].

Taken up by the British Parliament's Committee of Inquiry (Chilcot Report), the JIC's report thus denies *ex ante* Laurent Fabius' false assertions. This confirms that he was trying to deceive the public.

The accusations of collusion between the EI and the Syrian government are purely and simply lies, which disinform the French population in order to hide the illegality of French actions in Syria. They are based on Israeli rhetoric and, more concretely, on a 2014 infographic, produced jointly by the US news channel CBS and London's Jane's Terrorism & Insurgency Center (JTIC), which tends to show that the Syrian government and the EI 'ignore' each other. It claims that only 6% of Syrian counter-terrorism operations involve the EI, while only 13% of EI attacks involve Syrian government forces, showing collusion[522].

Picked up in a *franceinfo* debunkage[523], this infographic is a perfect example of disinformation and manipulation. Firstly, it omits a large number of actors in

---

517. Juan Cole, "Is Kerry Right? Are Freemen of Syria and Army of Islam Radical Terrorists?", *Informed Comment*, July 13, 2016

518. "U.S., Britain, France block Russia bid to blacklist Syria rebels", *Reuters*, May 11, 2016

519. Josh Lowe, "What the Chilcot Report Reveals About ISIS", *Newsweek*, July 7, 2016.

520. "Syrian Civil War and Spillover: Every Day," *NY Mapper/YouTube*, March 15, 2019

521. "The Syrian Civil War, every day", *Lyria Mapping/YouTube*, October 19, 2017

522. Matthew Henman, "Syrian military and ISIS have been 'ignoring' each other on the battlefield", *CBS & IHS Jane's Terrorism and Insurgency Centre - Jane's Intelligence Review*, December 11, 2014

523. Antoine Krempf, "The Syrian opposition is not fighting the Islamic State?", *Radio France/franceinfo*, November 26, 2015

the field, suggesting that there is no other Islamist opposition than the EI. This representation prevents the very logical prioritisation of the Syrian government from being seen and understood. The harsh reality will emerge in October 2019, when these Islamists begin to attack the Western-allied Kurds.

Secondly, it suggests that the only armed non-state actors are the '*democratic opposition*': this is not true! There are a huge number of local and village self-defence militias that are not governmental, but Christian, Assyrian, Shiite, Alawite, etc. that are often, by necessity, in direct contact with the Islamic State. Ignoring them is a dishonest reduction of the problem.

Thirdly, if we go back to our dynamic map[524] we can see that the Syrian government is indeed fighting the Islamic State. But unlike the West, which strikes on the basis of opportunity, it operates methodically. Starting from the Alawite areas where it was cornered, it is making a broad "sweeping" movement from west to east, with the primary objective of maintaining an open corridor between the Mediterranean and Damascus, in order to guarantee its supplies.

It is also important to understand that the EI is not so much at war with other jihadist factions as in competition with them. All jihadist groups have the same origin and purpose: resistance to Western influence. Indeed, while it was claimed that the Islamic State was "*openly waging war*[525]" against "al-Qaeda", the Paris attacks of January 2015 showed precisely the cooperation between these groups. Even if these rivalries have sometimes resulted in local fighting (often for personal rather than ideological reasons), there is more often than not a congruence between these groups, who lend or rent each other their heavy weapons according to need[526].

6.5 "Bashar al-Assad is Massacring his Own People"

From the beginning of the Syrian crisis, as it did in Afghanistan, Iraq and Libya, the West has tried to propagate the idea that President Bashar al-Assad is obsessed with destroying his people. To what end? Why "only" in 2011 and not before? No answer.

There are similarities with the arguments that seek to justify that the Syrian government would use its chemical weapons - very "costly" politically - to kill women and children rather than combatants! This is an absurdity and a manipulation designed to fuel the idea that Western intervention is legitimate and that the solution is inevitably to overthrow the government in place. This posture, which

524. "Syrian Civil War and Spillover: Every Day," *NY Mapper/YouTube*, March 15, 2019

525. "Al-Qaeda vs Islamic State: four keys to understanding the opposition", *RTBF.be*, August 26, 2014

526. Jamie Dettmer, "Western, Gulf Weapons Supplied to Syria Rebels Leaked to Islamic State", *Voice of America*, December 13, 2017

has created the idea of "good violence" and "bad violence", has only encouraged "false-banner" crimes designed to make the Syrian army responsible for massacres.

In July 2012, a *BBC* journalist tweeted that the Syrian air force was bombing civilians in East Aleppo, and stated in an article that these were MiGs "made in Russia", while the victims were transported to various hospitals in the city. It does not indicate any source or document proving its claim[527]. The Western press seized the opportunity to attack the Syrian government. The British daily *The Telegraph* comments:

> *Fighter jets have reportedly bombed Aleppo, Syria's second largest city, and if confirmed, this would be the first time Assad's forces have used the air force against civilians*[528].

In reality, it will turn out that they were not combat "MiGs", but Su-25s or Aero L-39s (which look similar, but are radically different from MiGs), which are not equipped with bombs and did not attack civilian populations[529]. In fact, the *BBC is* trying to repeat with Syria the manipulation that led France and then Britain to intervene in Libya.

Furthermore, the silence of the mainstream media on the massacres by Sunni and Kurdish militias of Syriac, Shiite, Christian, Alawite, Kurdish, Assyrian, Ismaili and other minorities can be seen[530]. They are supported by the Syrian government and despite the denunciations of Amnesty International[531], they avoid speeches that would weaken the rebels.

6.5.1. The "Dictatorship" of a Minority

It should be recalled here that Syria is the cradle of the oldest forms of Christianity, where very diverse communities have coexisted in harmony for centuries, some of which have managed to accommodate Muslim and Christian cults.

The power held by the Alawite minority (12% of the population) is perceived in the West as the oppression of a minority over the majority[532]. The reality is very different. At the beginning of the twentieth century, it was the French who promoted this small, poor and uninfluential community into the machinery of power. Not out of altruism, but out of pragmatism. In fact, they adopted a

527. Ian Pannell, "Aleppo: BBC journalist on Syria warplanes bombing city", *BBC News*, July 24, 2012
528. Barney Henderson, "Syria: 'war planes bomb Aleppo'", *The Telegraph*, July 24, 2012
529. Tony Cartalucci, "BBC Rides with Al Qaeda in Aleppo, Syria", *Land Destroyer*, July 25, 2012
530. Huma Haider, *The Persecution of Christians in the Middle East*, University of Birmingham, K4D Helpdesk (Department for International Development - UK, February 16, 2017
531. Background - Religious Minorities in Iraq Face Persecution, Amnesty International, (http://www.amnestyusa.org/our-work/countries/middle-east-and-north-africa/iraq/background-religious-minorities-in-iraq-face-persecution)
532. Pierre Servent, *Extension du domaine de la guerre*, Robert Laffont, Paris, 2016, p. 115

solution that is quite common in Africa and the Middle East, in environments (local or national) where several large communities are fighting each other. It consists in leaving power to a minority that is not in a position to impose itself by force against the others, and will be forced to a certain neutrality in the management of affairs. Such a system limits the risk of power struggles and - at least in theory - combats corruption, which tends to favour dominant ethnic groups. At the time, in Syria, the aim was to create a balance between Sunni Muslims - numerous, but with a relatively low level of education - and Christians - less numerous, but with a higher level of education.

Similar systems worked in Libya and Iraq, where Muammar Gaddafi[533] and Saddam Hussein[534] did not come from the most important tribes, so as to maintain the balance between the big tribes. A logic that is radically different from the Western logic... which is being tried in these countries and which contributes to the current disaster.

In Syria, the head of state is Alawite, but most of his ministers - including the Minister of Defence - are Sunni, as are the bulk of the armed forces themselves[535]. If the small Alawite community really did impose its will by force, as is claimed in the West, there would have been a military coup long ago. Yet the armed forces have remained remarkably loyal to the regime. As Henry Kissinger and Zbignew Brzezinski have noted, popular support for Bashar al-Assad is considerably higher than the media claims[536]. In fact, the legitimacy of our interventions - and of an eventual overthrow of power - rests entirely on the assumption that the Syrian president has no popular support[537].

6.5.2. The Reliability of Information

In order to justify its intervention in Syria, the French government has oversimplified the situation on the ground, separating the actors into two main categories: the government and the opponents, which are subdivided into the Islamic State ('Daech'), moderate Islamists and the Kurds. Since the opposition is by definition considered legitimate, and the war was provoked by the Syrian government, all losses are thus attributed to it.

Very early on, the lack of precise and reliable figures on the total number of victims in the Syrian conflict became a political tool in America and Europe.

533. Abdulsattar Hatitah, "Libyan Tribal Map: Network Of Loyalties That Will Determine Gaddafi's Fate", *Asharq Al-Awsat*, February 24, 2011 (https://www.cetri.be/Libyan-Tribal-Map-Network-of?lang=fr)

534. Christopher Hitchens, "Tribal Ignorance - What you think you know about Iraq's factions is all wrong", *slate.com*, October 17, 2005

535. *Syria Under Bashar (II): Domestic Policy Challenges*, ICG Middle East Report N°24, Amman/Brussels, February 11, 2004

536. Kamal Alam, "Why Assad's Army Has Not Defected", *The National Interest*, 12 February 2016

537. "BHL guest on France Info, la matinale, July 6, 2012", YouTube, July 9, 2012, (www.youtube.com/watch?v=MxVBMxGpudY)

Logically enough, the Syrian government does not make announcements about its losses in order not to demoralise its troops and the absence of an international presence makes the assessment of the number of dead extremely hazardous, thus opening the door to propaganda and disinformation.

In fact, from the outset, the main source of information for the West was *the* Syrian Observatory for Human Rights (SOHR). An ambitious name that hides a very modest reality. Based in a two-room flat in London, the OSDH is run by a single individual, Rami Abder Rahman, a former Sunni opponent of the Syrian regime, who runs a clothing shop[538]. The relative quality of the OSDH's information is noted by the former head of security intelligence at the DGSE, Alain Chouet[539]:

> *If you read about Syria in the written and audiovisual media, particularly in France, you will have noticed that all the information about the situation is sourced under the name "Syrian Observatory for Human Rights" (OSDH) or, more laconically, "NGO", which amounts to the same thing, the NGO in question always being the Syrian Observatory for Human Rights.*

> *The Syrian Observatory for Human Rights is a name that sounds good to Western ears, and it has become the privileged, if not the only source of information. However, it has nothing to do with the respectable International League for Human Rights. It is in fact an offshoot of the Muslim Brotherhood Association, which is run by Islamist activists, some of whom were once convicted of violent activism, in particular its founder and first president, Mr. Ryadh el-Maleh. The OSDH was set up in the late 1980s in London under the benevolent guidance of the Anglo-Saxon services and operates almost entirely on Saudi and now Qatari funds*[540].

The complete lack of analysis and cross-checking capacity has not bothered the Western media and intelligence services at all, which have unverifiably quantified the repression of Bashar al-Assad's government, thus justifying their policy towards the regime. Democratic Congresswoman Tulsi Gabbard, a member of the House Armed Services Committee and 2020 presidential candidate, points out:

538. "A Very Busy Man Behind the Syrian Civil War's Casualty Count", *New York Times*, April 9, 2013, (accessed June 26, 2014).
539. Alain Chouet was Head of the Security Intelligence Service at the Directorate General of External Security (DGSE) (2000-2001).
540. http://blog.lefigaro.fr/malbrunot/2012/09/alain-chouet-nos-ministres-son.html

The stories that are being told about Assad now are the same stories that were told about Gaddafi, are the same stories that were told about Saddam Hussein, by those who were defending the United States to overthrow those regimes. If this were to happen in Syria, we would end up with a situation of much greater suffering, much more persecution of religious minorities and Christians in Syria, and our enemy would become considerably more powerful[541].

In the UN Security Council, the discussion is blocked. Russia and China, who felt deceived in 2011 by France and its Western allies with Resolution 1973 on Libya, are no longer willing to accept interventions without a long-term strategy and the Western policy of fait accompli, which results in chaos, as in Libya. Especially since Laurent Fabius' comments in August 2012 leave little to the imagination and clearly show that France's objective is to overthrow the Syrian government:

The Syrian regime must be brought down, and quickly [...] Bashar al-Assad does not deserve to be on earth[542].

The French press was happy to rage against Russia and its "vetoes", but remained surprisingly silent on the casualness with which the West implemented the Security Council decisions on Libya, which led to blockages on the Syrian issue.

6.5.3. The "Manufactured" Massacres

From the beginning of the war, the objective of the West is neither democracy nor human rights, but the overthrow of the Syrian government. The aim is to portray it as bloodthirsty and merciless to its own population.

In August 2011, the media reported that the Syrian government had cut off the electricity to the incubators of the maternity hospital in Hamah, causing the death of several dozen babies (the figures vary according to the media). The Gulf media are having a field day[543] and are relayed by the Western media, such as the *Daily Mail*[544] or *CNN*, without analysis[545]. But the pictures of the 'victims' are nothing more than babies sleeping peacefully in a maternity hospital in Cairo[546].

541. Seymour Hersh, 'Military to Military', *London Review of Books*, vol. 38 No. 1, January 7, 2016.

542. lepoint.fr, 'Fabius: "The Syrian regime must be brought down, and quickly"', *AFP*, August 17, 2012.

543. Duraid Al Baik, "Syrian crackdown kills 30 babies in three hospitals", *Gulf News*, September 2, 2011

544. Stephen Wright, "The bloodiest 24 hours yet: '18 premature babies die in Homs hospital after power cut caused by fifth day of shelling by Assad troops'", *Daily Mail*, February 9, 2012

545. "Rights group: 8 babies die after power cut to Syrian hospital", *CNN*, August 7, 2011

546. Ali Abunimah, "How CNN helped spread a hoax about Syrian babies dying in incubators", *The Electronic Intifada / Media Watch*, August 8, 2011

The case is eerily similar to the accusations against the Iraqi army in Kuwait City in 1990, but no Western media reacted...

On 25 May 2012, the massacre in al-Houla, near Homs, was attributed to the Syrian government. Initially, 300 deaths were reported, but the figure was reduced to 108 and then to 92[547], including 49 children. The UN press release of May 27 spoke of "*shelling and attacks by artillery and tanks*" as well as the "*killing of civilians at close range*[548]", suggesting the responsibility of the Syrian military. The government denies any involvement and accuses terrorist groups.

For the Western media, it is clear that the government is responsible. *Franceinfo* slavishly repeated the information published by the Syrian Observatory for Human Rights[549] and published a video of the event. But in fact, we see practically nothing: no place, no person, no weapon or date is identifiable[550]. The daily newspapers *Le Monde* and *La Croix*[551] reported the event, avoiding direct accusations against the Syrian government, but suggesting that it was the author[552]. On May 30, *Belgian Radio-Television* was much less nuanced and very clearly pointed to the Syrian government as the culprit[553]. On his blog, the journalist Georges Malbrunot evokes a revenge of the Syrian government for the attempted poisoning of Assad's brother-in-law; Why in Houla? Mystery[554]!...

On June 8, on *ABC News*, the American journalist Christiane Amanpour referred to a "high-ranking" Syrian personality to state:

> *What is emerging is a campaign of ethnic cleansing. The Syrian president is exploiting these massacres to expel populations that are disloyal to him and to reinforce control over what could become a divided Syria*[555].

The guilt of the Syrian government reinforces the official discourse, which the mainstream media repeat without verifying it. When in doubt, the UN observers' report accuses the "*pro-government militias*" ("Shabiha").

As later, the accusations against the government are circumstantial: it is held responsible because it is the only one to have weapons. But this is not

547. "Syria: Kofi Annan condemns the "indiscriminate crime" of Houla", *Le figaro.fr*, May 26, 2012 (updated May 27, 2012)
548. "Security Council press statement on the attacks in Houla, Syria", *Security Council*, May 27, 2012, (SC/10658); Khaled Yacoub Oweis & Louis Charbonneau, "U.N. Security Council condemns Syria over massacre", Reuters, May 27, 2012, "Houla massacre - Security Council condemns Damascus", *Libération*, May 28, 2012
549. "Syria: what we know about the Houla massacre", *franceinfo*, May 29, 2012 (updated on June 7, 2012)
550. "VIDEO. The Houla massacre filmed by Syrian opponents", *franceinfo*, May 29, 2012
551. Agnès Rotivel, "Le massacre de Houla défie le plan de paix en Syrie", *La Croix*, May 28, 2012
552. "Syria: the Houla massacre recounted by child survivors", *lemonde.fr*, May 30, 2012
553. "Houla massacre: Syrian regime targets international condemnation", *AFP/rtbf.be*, May 25, 2012 (updated May 27, 2012)
554. Georges Malbrunot, "Syria: Shawkat, Assad's brother-in-law, survives poisoning", *blog.lefigaro.fr*, May 28, 2012
555. archive.org/details/KGO_20120609_003000_ABC_World_News_With_Diane_Sawyer/start/600/end/660

true: the United States (Operation TIMBER SYCAMORE) and France were already supplying arms to the Sunni rebels in May[556]. Moreover, in an interview on February 12 with the BBC, Hillary Clinton confirmed that organisations considered as terrorists by the United States - such as 'Al-Qaeda' and Hamas - were cooperating with the opposition they supported, at the risk of creating a civil war[557].

The al-Houla massacre is a major event, as it sets the tone for Western rhetoric about a "bloodthirsty" government, which is "*the murderer of its people*[558]". The Human Rights Council condemned the Syrian government and several countries such as Germany, Belgium, the United States, France, Great Britain, Italy and Switzerland expelled Syrian diplomats from their territories or declared them "persona non grata"[559]. The United States and France talk about military intervention, and oil is poured on the fire to pave the way.

But at the beginning of June, Rainer Hermann, a journalist from the *Frankfurter Allgemeine Zeitung*, did what his Western colleagues did not: he investigated. He interviewed witnesses (members of the peaceful opposition to the Assad government[560]) and found that all the victims in Al-Houla (a predominantly Sunni area) were Alawites or Sunnis who had converted to Shi'ism; yet it would seem surprising that the government would attack minorities who support it. In fact, the massacre is said to have taken place during an attack on an army barracks by Sunni rebels[561].

On July 12, in response to a request from members of the Bundestag for clarification, the government provided a response prepared by the Foreign Intelligence Service (BND):

> *The victims of the Houla event were killed mainly with bladed weapons [literally: cut and thrust], as well as firearms, at close range. No evidence of large-calibre weapons (artillery, etc.) was found*[562].

Thus, the German services do not confirm the use of heavy weapons mentioned by the UN, which is not very surprising since the observers did not

556. "US helping funnel arms into Syria, report says", *France 24*, May 17, 2012
557. "Clinton: Syria risking civil war, *BBC News*, February 26, 2012
558. Céline Lussato, "SYRIA. After the Houla massacre, is a way out of the crisis in sight?", L'Obs, May 30, 2012
559. "In response to the Houla massacre, Washington expels Syrian chargé d'affaires", France 24, May 29, 2012; "Les Occidentaux durcissent le ton et expulsent les ambassadeurs syriens", *RTS Info*, 30 May 2012
560. Chris Marsden, "Houla massacre carried out by Free Syrian Army, according to Frankfurter Allgemeine Zeitung", *wsws.org*, June 13, 2012
561. Rainer Hermann, "Abermals Massaker In Syrien", *Frankfurter Allgemeine Zeitung*, June 7, 2012; Rainer Hermann, "Syrien: Eine Auslöschung", *Frankfurter Allgemeine Zeitung*, April 1st, 2017
562. *Kleine Anfrage der Abgeordneten Sevim Dagdelen, Heike Hänsel u.a. und der Fraktion DIE LINKE (BT-Drs. 17/10206): Kenntnisstand und Positionierung der Bundesregierung zu den Vorfällen am 25./26. May 2012 bei El-Houleh/Syria*, Berlin, June 26, 2012 (Document 17/10333) (Question 1)

visit the scene for their report[563]. As for the participation of the Shabiha militia, the BND report admits that the available information '*does not allow conclusions to be drawn about their involvement*'[564]. Six weeks after breaking off diplomatic relations with Syria, the German government admits that "*at this stage, the perpetrators cannot be clearly identified*[565]".

The day after the attack, videos were circulating showing the victims in al-Houla and a nearby village being killed with knives. Alastair Crooke, a former British intelligence officer, said:

> *[...] the methodology of this type of killing - beheadings, throat cutting, also of children, as well as mutilation of bodies - is not a characteristic of Levantine Islam, nor of Syria, nor of Lebanon, but of what we have seen in the Iraqi province of Anbar. So this seems to indicate groups associated with the war in Iraq against the United States, who may have returned to Syria, or perhaps Iraqis who came from Anbar to take part in it... But this whole process of mutilation goes so far against the tradition of Levantine Islam that I think it's very difficult to think that this is coming from soldiers, or others who would have wanted revenge*[566] *[...]*

This suggests that the majority of casualties were caused by so-called 'moderate' rebels, but the Western mainstream media avoids the subject. It therefore seems that the victims were rather the result of community rivalries or even criminal settlements of accounts[567].

The fragility of the UN report and the Western conclusions led some media to revise their judgment of the massacre. On June 7, Jon Williams, a *BBC World News* columnist, backed down and published an article encouraging more caution and circumspection in reporting events about which almost nothing is known[568]. On the same day, Paul Danahar wrote:

> *In Damascus, many diplomats, international officials and opponents of President Assad feel that his regime would no longer be able to permanently and fully control the few militia groups accused of massacring civilians. The world has seen the Syrian conflict in very black and white terms over the past 15 months. It must now admit that there are shades of grey that are emerging*[569].

---

563. Rainer Hermann, "Abermals Massaker In Syrien", *Frankfurter Allgemeine Zeitung*, June 7, 2012
564. *Kleine Anfrage der Abgeordneten Sevim Dagdelen,* op.cit (Question 23).
565. *Kleine Anfrage der Abgeordneten Sevim Dagdelen (op.cit.)* (Question 1)
566. "The Houla Massacre", *medialens.org*, May 31, 2012 (updated November 22, 2013)
567. Frédéric Pichon, *Syria: Why the West got it wrong*, Éditions du Rocher, 2014, p.58
568. Jon Williams, "Reporting conflict in Syria", *BBC World News*, June 7, 2012
569. Paul Danahar, "New 'massacre' reported in Syria's Hama province - Analysis", *BBC News*, June 7, 2012

UN observers will have to stop and then withdraw because of the rebels threatening them. Former British ambassador Oliver Miles says on *Al-Jazeerah*:

> *Until very recently, it was possible to believe that this was simply a case of a tyrannical government being resisted by protesters. But it is no longer possible to see it in these terms*[570].

On July 12, history repeated itself in Tremseh. The preacher Hani Ramadan even sees "*fruits of Zionism*"[571]. In fact, the Western media created certainties out of suspicions by dismissing information that did not fit their prejudices. But the real perpetrators of the al-Houla massacre are likely to remain unknown, while the clues and interests at stake tend to point to the responsibility of the armed opposition, notably the Free Syrian Army (FSA), which was dominant in this area.

The idea that Bashar al-Assad is massacring his people will be found in the issue of chemical weapons, which we shall see below. It will be found in early 2020, when the Syrian army is engaged in the reconquest of the Idlib area, to which the rebels had retreated. In February 2020, in the newspaper *Le Temps*, Agnès Levallois accuses the Syrian government and Russia of not having respected the Sochi agreement (September 17, 2018) which was supposed to make the Idlib pocket a demilitarised zone[572]. As usual, his judgement is based more on prejudice than on facts.

6.6. "France Supports the Moderate Rebels"

6.6.1 Western Intervention in Syria

The official discourse claims that Western countries (mainly the US and France) are in Syria to support the fight for democracy and human rights against dictatorship and tyranny. The reality is more nuanced.

The US involvement is a consequence of its mistakes in Iraq, as we shall see. But France's motives are hard to explain, other than an attempt to bolster the government's popularity, as strikes against Syria were being considered as early as 2012, well before the emergence of the Islamic State[573]. Moreover, as we

570. "Inside Syria - Has the UN observer mission failed in Syria?", YouTube/ Al Jazeera English, June 17, 2012 (01'50")
571. "The fruits of Zionism: massacres in Syria" July 17, 2012 (http://haniramadan.blog.tdg.ch/archive/2012/07/15/les-fruits-du-sionisme-massacres-en-syrie.html)
572. Marc Allgöwer, "Agnès Levallois: " Le président Erdogan s'est piégé en Syrie ", *Le Temps*, February 28, 2020
573. Jean Guisnel, "Armes chimiques: Paris préparait une action militaire en Syrie depuis début 2012", *Le Point.fr*, September 20, 2013

have seen, regime change was possible without violence[574]. But the West seems reluctant to a democratic transition. Not only because it could well give victory to... Bashar al-Assad[575], but because their objective is not to install democracy in Syria, but to fragment its territory into small antagonistic entities, incapable of allying themselves against Israel, thus breaking the Tehran-Beirut axis.

Efforts to establish a Kurdish state in the north-east of the country (in areas they have never historically occupied), and an Islamist zone in the south-east, in order to confine the Shiite, Alawite and Christian populations to the west of the country, follow the broad lines of the Israeli Yinon plan. This would explain Israeli support for the Islamist opposition, including the Islamic State (EI)[576].

This strategy places Western countries in triangular relationships, which destabilise the country, to the detriment of Christian minorities, as American and European organisations had prophesied very early on:

> *The problem for Syria is that if there is interference from foreign governments, it is the Christians and other minorities who will suffer most*[577].

In the United States, it was the political leadership that pushed for war, while the military - and the public - were generally opposed to intervention. In July 2013, in a presentation to Congress, General Martin E. Dempsey, Chairman of the Joint Chiefs of Staff, recommended against intervention in the Syrian conflict and argued that attempts to overthrow Assad would only lead to a deterioration of the security situation[578]. The confidential analysis he relied on confirmed that aid to 'moderate' rebels had turned into aid to radical jihadist movements such as Jabhat al-Nosrah and *the* Islamic State in Iraq and the Levant (ISIL)[579].

Thus, the West fights the jihadists in Afghanistan, but becomes their objective ally in Syria, to overthrow the government[580]. At first, France[581] and the United States[582] tend to encourage - or even support - those who want to go and fight in Syria. These will only become a problem two and a half years later, after the emergence of the EI.

---

574. See Chapter 9.3

575. Jonathan Steele, 'Most Syrians back President Assad, but you'd never know from western media', *The Guardian*, January 17, 2012.

576. Elizabeth Tsurkov, "Inside Israel's Secret Program to Back Syrian Rebels", *Foreign Policy*, September 6, 2018

577. Kaley Payne, "Syrian Christians fear overturn of Assad regime", http://www.biblesociety.org.au, 2012.

578. Mark Landler and Thom Shanker, 'Pentagon Lays out Options for U.S. Military Effort in Syria', *The New York Times*, July 22, 2013.

579. Seymour Hersh, 'Military to Military', *London Review of Books*, vol. 38 No. 1, January 7, 2016.

580. Joseph Wakim, "Al-Qaeda now a US ally in Syria", The Sydney Morning Herald, September 11, 2012 (http://www.smh.com.au/federal-politics/alqaeda-now-a-us-ally-in-syria-20120910-25oby.html)

581. Tristan Quinault-Maupoil, "Un député UMP accuse la France d'avoir "encouragé" le départ de djihadistes en Syrie", *lefigaro.fr*, April 24, 2014

582. Julian Pecquet, "Who is paying for America's plan to train and equip Syrian rebels?", Al-Monitor, December 4, 2014

In December 2017, the *BBC* broadcast a report on British assistance programmes to the Syrian opposition, including the training of a "free Syrian police", which revealed that not only did the funds paid go directly to jihadist groups, such as Nour al-Din al-Zinki in Aleppo, but also that the police officers trained had to be approved by Jabhat al-Nosrah[583]. Despite the denials of the bodies in charge of managing these programmes[584], the government decided in August 2018 to stop these activities[585].

In June 2018, in order to develop a policy towards its Western allies engaged in Syria, the German parliament commissioned a study of the legal situation of the various actors in the conflict[586]. The study shows unequivocally that the only country whose engagement is in line with international law is Russia. The self-defence (Article 51 of the UN Charter) invoked by the United States and France does not apply here (without even mentioning that they were involved long before the emergence of the EI in Syria), particularly because of the non-state nature of the terrorists, and that it is therefore Syria's responsibility. As for the Israeli "*early defence*" strikes[587] in Syria against Hezbollah, Iranian or Syrian forces, they can only be explained by Israel's will to maintain tension in the region, probably for electoral purposes.

Thus, not only did the West intervene in defiance of international law and the laws of war, but it was overwhelmed - from the end of 2012 - by the situation it had created. Blinded by the objective of overthrowing the Syrian government, they were gradually led to deliberately support the Islamists, at the risk of provoking the emergence of the EI. The latter is the result of the negligence of Western governments, and was predictable... and foreseen, as we shall see below[588].

6.6.2. Distinction between Extremists and Moderates

Since the beginning of the Syrian crisis, Western aid has been justified by the 'moderate' nature of the rebels and the Syrian government's desire to '*eliminate all opposition*[589]' by force. The "experts" who intervene on the Syrian question maintain a rather systematic blurring of the lines between "opposition" and

583. BBC, "Jihadis You Pay For", (www.bbc.co.uk/programmes/b09j0fql)
584. Daniel Boffey, "BBC in row over 'false claims' of cash for Syrian police being paid to jihadists", *The Guardian*, December 3, 2017
585. Jessica Elgot, "Britain to axe funding for scheme supporting Syrian opposition", *The Guardian*, August 20, 2018
586. *Völkerrechtliche Bewertung der russischen, amerikanischen und israelischen Beteiligung am Syrienkonflikt, Deutscher Bundestag*, WD 2 - 3000 - 029/18, June 28, 2018
587. Anticipatory Self-Defence
588. John Kerry, Wikileaks recording of a meeting on September 22, 2016 ("Leaked audio of John Kerry's meeting with Syrian revolutionaries/UN (improved audio)", *YouTube*, October 4, 2016)
589. "Chemical" attack in Syria: "We gave a right to kill" to Bashar al-Assad", *Europe1.fr*, April 4, 2017 (updated on April 5, 2017)

"armed opposition"[590]. However, contrary to what they claim, the government is not fighting the *entire* opposition militarily, but only the armed opposition. It is often overlooked that many 'loyalist' militias do not share the government's position, but are opposed to the jihadists.

From the beginning of the revolution, the influence of the Islamists was decisive. The atrocities[591], the beheadings of Christians[592] put the Westerners in the middle of a "ménage à trois", where they are no longer able to choose their partners and to whom to supply arms. Western services have limited visibility on the ground and put efficiency before values. This phenomenon is accentuated by the total lack of understanding of the realities on the ground by Western politicians[593].

As in Libya, the West has failed to understand the dynamics that bind the protagonists of the conflict. In September 2014, the battle of Kobane (Ain al-Arab) was seen as a success of Western strikes. However, while the latter did indeed allow the Kurds to temporarily free themselves from the Islamist threat, it also had the strategic effect of giving rival Islamist factions (in particular Jabhat al-Nosrah and the EI) a common enemy and led them to join forces[594]. The following year, the fiery speeches of François Hollande and Manuel Valls had exactly the same effect and provided unexpected propaganda for the EI.

In August 2012, *France 24* published an article on the ASL, which stated from the outset that

> *Two armies are currently fighting in Syria: the regular forces on the one side, loyal to President Bashar al-Assad, and the Free Syrian Army (FSA) on the other, a force initially made up mainly of deserters, which supports the revolution*[595].

This is a lie. Not only is the existence of Islamist forces hidden, but the idea of a "moderate" ASL is maintained. However, while its excesses indicate a growing influence of Islamists within it[596]. Moreover, according to a DIA SECRET report dated August 5, 2012, the insurgency is led by the Salafists, the Muslim

590. See the programme "C dans l'air", "Syria: Putin's power grab #cdanslair 28-09-2016", *YouTube/France 5*, September 28, 2016

591. Nick Fagge, "Syria rebels 'beheaded a Christian and fed him to the dogs' as fears grow over Islamist atrocities", *Daily Mail*, December 30, 2015.

592. Cheryl K. Chumley, "Syrians behead Christians for helping military, as CIA ships in arms", *The Washington Times*, June 27, 2013.

593. Jeff Stein, "Inside the CIA's Syrian Rebels Vetting Machine", *Newsweek*, November 10, 2014

594. Reyhanli & Urfa, "The War against Islamic State - Unintended consequences?", *The Economist*, 4 October 2014

595. In collaboration with Sarra Grira, "Ideology, financing, armament: focus on the Free Syrian Army", *Les Observateurs de France 24*, August 10, 2012

596. "An amateur video points out the abuses of the Free Syrian Army", *Les Observateurs de France 24*, January 18, 2012

Brotherhood and Al Qaeda in Iraq[597] (which will become the EI). Charles Shoebridge, a terrorism specialist with the London Metropolitan Police, will note:

> *In the early years of the Syrian crisis, the US and British governments, and the Western mainstream media, almost universally portrayed the Syrian rebels as moderate, liberal, secular, democratic, and thus deserving of Western support. Since [this report] totally contradicts this assessment, it is significant that the Western media today almost entirely ignores it, despite its immense importance*[598].

Long before the emergence of the EI in Syria, France and the United States had militarised the 'Syrian Spring' by militarily supporting factions, which were already no longer 'moderate' and far from representing humanist values. On December 12, 2012, during a press conference, French Foreign Minister Laurent Fabius declared[599] regretting that the United States had put Jabhat al-Nosrah[600] on the list of terrorist organisations[601]!

The problem is that 'moderate' fighters are deserting their units to swell the ranks of more determined and combative Islamist militias. The term 'moderate' becomes simply a front for legitimising verbal, political or material support for the opposition. In Anglo-Saxon countries, independent think-tanks and academic circles have a more critical and realistic reading of the situation. In December 2015, a report by the British "Tony Blair" Foundation noted the impossibility of distinguishing between "moderates" and "extremists":

> *This shows that all attempts by international powers to distinguish between acceptable "moderates" and unacceptable "extremists" are incoherent. The overlaps are endless. In a battle in Jisr al-Shughour this year, al-Nosrah Front forces were used as shock troops, with fire support from Western-backed rebels. Meanwhile, a US-backed and verified Free Syrian Army group has been reported to have lied about working with the al-Nosrah Front*[602].

---

597. http://www.judicialwatch.org/wp-content/uploads/2015/05/Pg.-291-Pgs.-287-293-JW-v-DOD-and-State-14-812-DOD-Release-2015-04-10-final-version11.pdf

598. Quoted in Nafeez Ahmed, "Pentagon report predicted West's support for Islamist rebels would create ISIS", *Insurge Intelligence*, May 22, 2015

599. Isabelle Maudraud, "Pression militaire et succès diplomatique pour les rebelles syriens", *Le Monde*, December 13, 2012

600. Editor's note: The Foreign Minister is even credited with saying that the al-Nosrah Front was "*doing a good job*". In the absence of the verbatim of the minister's statement, due to the lack of clarity of the quotes mentioned in the press, we will leave the reader to judge. (*Le Monde*, December 13, 2012, *op. cit.*)

601. NdA: The al-Nosrah Front was placed on the US State Department's list of terrorist organisations on December 11, 2012, and on the UN's list on May 30, 2013.

602. *If the Castle Falls*, Tony Blair Faith Foundation, December 2015, p. 8.

The West (i.e. the US and France) tends to maintain the fiction of a secular opposition in Syria in order to justify their desire to overthrow the government. But in the United States, support for the Syrian "rebels" raises questions in Congress, such as those of Republican Senator Rand Paul:

> *There's a great irony here, in that if you wanted to believe in a broad definition of the 2001 Authorisation for the Use of Military Force [AUMF]*[603]*, which authorises fighting Al Qaeda and its associated forces... Well, Al Qaeda and its associated forces are opposing Assad. So, assuming a broad definition of the 2001 AUMF, you might think that you could actually support Assad with weapons. The original AUMF would, in fact, justify giving weapons to Assad. I'm not saying that, but I am saying that you are giving weapons to the side fighting Assad that includes elements of al-Qaeda. There is a great irony here. I'm also saying that in our rush to engage in Syria, you may be giving weapons to Islamic rebels who are killing Christians. There are about one to two million Christians in Syria. They have been largely protected by Assad. I'm not saying that Assad is a good guy. I am saying that they have been a minority protected by Assad for decades [...]*[604].

Indeed, foreign fighters have been flowing into Syria long before the emergence of the EI[605]. Some journalists[606] and parliamentarians[607] have noted that at the beginning of the war, the French government was even more likely to encourage them to go to Syria. The aim was to overthrow Bashar al-Assad, but the West was quickly overwhelmed. Beheadings and other atrocities associated with the strict application of Sharia law appeared long before the EI[608], with the 'blessing' (and help) of the West. In 2013, Didier Reynders, then Belgian Foreign Minister, declared:

> *[...] If others are in terrorist or jihadist groups, they will have to be prosecuted on the basis of the law on terrorism, [...] but there may be others who will commit themselves ideally to the Syrian Liberation Army, which we*

603. AUMF 2001, adopted by the Congress on September 14, 2001

604. Senator Rand Paul, Senate Foreign Relations Committee, "Syrian Transition Support Act of 2013 Amendments, Hearing and Vote (SD-419)", May 21, 2013. ("The United States is Arming, Funding Al-Qaeda, Syrian Rebels", *YouTube*, May 28, 2013)

605. Ulrike Putz, "Foreign Fighters Join Syrian Rebels: Jihadists Declare Holy War Against Assad Regime", *Der Spiegel*, March 30, 2012

606. See David Thomson on France24, April 23, 2014 ("Djihadistes Français en Syrie: présentation d'un plan d'action en Conseil des ministres", YouTube, April 23, 2014)

607. "Alain Marsaud: "France must have encouraged some French jihadists to go to Syria", *RFI/YouTube*, April 24, 2014

608. Ulrike Putz, "The Burial Brigade of Homs - An Executioner for Syria's Rebels Tells His Story", *Der Spiegel*, March 29, 2012

support. They may be given a monument in a few years' time, so I really hope that we examine each case individually, that we do not confuse the two[609].

From the end of 2014, the virulence of the Western discourse (particularly French) against the EI made it the main bearer of the jihadist fight and contributed to the recruitment of its fighters. According to a United Nations report, the number of foreign volunteer fighters increased by 71% between the summer of 2014 and March 2015[610]. Initially, Islamist fighters leave their phalanxes to join it. In this way, the EI 'phagocytises' other groups without fighting and expands rapidly.

From the end of 2014, Western strikes had unexpected effects: fighters left the EI to join other factions. What appears to be a success is not: they do not reject the EI, but seek to increase their chances of survival. The barbaric practices that seemed to be specific to the EI thus tend to become widespread and trigger a real surge in violence. The Western strategy of "divide and rule" tends to cause a scattering of armed groups, but a greater homogeneity of their behaviour. Partisan rivalries ("hizbiyya") are no longer doctrinal, but become fights between leaders. A poorly thought-out strategy that solves nothing and makes the situation worse.

On February 19, 2015, Americans and Turks agreed to coordinate the training of Syrian rebels in the Turkish base of Kirsehir, with the dual aim of fighting the EI and changing the regime in Syria[611]. But they do not understand the nature of these rebels. The "30th Division", reputedly "moderate", armed, trained and supported by the United States, joined the ranks of Jabhat Fath al-Sham (formerly Jabhat al-Nosrah) in September 2015, just after leaving its Turkish base[612]. Moreover, in 2016, Jabhat Fath al-Sham considers the West to be on its side[613]. In East Aleppo, it will turn out that *all* the armed groups - verbally and militarily supported by the West - are Islamists. But the West also supports other militias, only some of which can be mentioned here for reasons of confidentiality:

609. "Didier Reynders is guest on Matin Première", *rtbf.be*, April 17, 2013 (https://www.rtbf.be/lapremiere/article/detail_didier-reynders-est-l-invite-de-matin-premiere?id=7974066)

610. S/2015/358, *Letter dated May 19, 2015 from the Chair of the Security Council Committee pursuant to resolutions 1267 (1999) and 1989 (2011) concerning Al-Qaida and associated individuals and entities addressed to the President of the Security Council*, UN, New York, May 19, 2015.

611. "Turkey and US agree to train and arm Syrian rebels in fight against Isis, *Associated Press/The Guardian*, February 19, 2015

612. Nabih Bulos, "US-trained Division 30 rebels 'betray US and hand weapons over to al-Qaeda's affiliate in Syria'", *The Telegraph*, September 22, 2015

613. Jürgen Todenhöfer, "Interview mit Al Nusra-Kommandeur 'Die Amerikaner stehen auf unserer Seite'", *Kölner Stadt-Anzeiger*, September 26, 2016

the *Omar al-Farouq Phalanx* (*Katibat Omar al-Farouq*), whose commander Abu Sakkar ate the still warm hearts of slain Syrian soldiers[614];

the *Fursan al-Haqq Brigade* (*Liwa Fursan al-Haqq*), which carries out kidnapping for ransom;

the *Dawoud Brigade* (*Liwa Dawoud*), which kidnapped the American journalist James Foley and handed him over to the EI[615];

the *Army of Islam* (*Jaish al-Islam*) - supported by Saudi Arabia, the United States and France - which locks Christians in cages mounted on vehicles to expose them as mobile human shields against Western and Russian strikes[616];

the French-backed and armed *Khalid Bin al-Walid Phalanx* (*Katibat Khalid Bin al-Walid), which* has been part of the EI since 2014[617];

Tajammu Fastaqim Kama Umirt, who, during the siege of East Aleppo in 2016, claimed that he would not split from the Islamists of *Jabhat Fath al-Sham* (formerly: *Jabhat al-Nosrah*)[618];

the *Nur al-Din al-Zinki Movement*, which has received TOW anti-tank missiles[619] and whose members - who are also members of the "White Helmets" - appear in videos showing the beheading of children with knives[620];

the *Eagles of the Levant Movement* (*Harakat Ahrar al-Sham*), which massacres women and children in Zara[621] and starves the civilian population in Madaya to make a profit from the humanitarian food aid provided by the international community[622].

Virtually all these groups will be in the Idlib pocket by the end of 2016, protected by the international coalition. The crimes of the "moderate" rebels are systematically concealed by Western propaganda, such as *France 24*, where

614. Syrian rebel commander eating heart of dead soldier (www.youtube.com/watch?v=UXhEiZUBBrQ) (video removed)

615. Patrick Poole, "U.S.-Funded Free Syrian Army Unit Shows Off Its Kidnapping Skills in New Training Video", *The Counter Jihad Report*, July 24, 2015

616. Robert Mackey & Maher Samaan, "Caged Hostages From Syrian President's Sect Paraded Through Rebel-Held Suburb", *The New York Times*, November 1st, 2015

617. "Khalid Bin Al-Waleed Brigade - one of the largest brigades in Homs splits from FSA and IS frees 3 Syrians in Lebanon", *LiveLeak*, August 2, 2014

618. OGN TV, "Will other Rebel Groups Turn their Backs on JFS (Nusra)", *YouTube*, September 17, 2016 (www.youtube.com/watch?v=CEmutmLr_Gs)

619. Patrick Poole, "'Vetted Moderate' Syrian Rebel Group Officially Partners with Al-Qaeda", *PJ Media*, January 28, 2017; https://twitter.com/thomasjoscelyn/status/825373171599675393/photo/1

620. Patrick Poole, "Video Shows Syrian 'Rebel' Group That Beheaded Child Still Using CIA-Provided TOW Missiles," *PJMedia*, November 22, 2016

621. Michael Doran, William McCants, and Clint Watts, "The Good and Bad of Syria's Ahrar al-Sham", *Brookings*, January 23, 2014

622. Gordon Duff, "Hoax: Madaya, the Imaginary Syrian Holocaust", *Veterans Today*, January 10, 2016

journalist Vanessa Burggraf tries to silence Bassam Tahhan, of the Union of Syrian Patriots, even though he denounces them[623]. In 2019, the Kurds will pay dearly for the dilettantism of Western journalists…

Ironically, in early 2019, after the official "defeat" of the Islamic State in Syria, France will be reluctant to claim "its" fighters. In fact, there are fears of situations like in London in June 2015, where Bherlin Gildo, a Swedish 'terrorist' on trial for being a 'foreign fighter' in Syria had his trial stopped, because the phalanx in which he operated was armed and supported by… Britain[624] !

6.6.3. The Free Syrian Army (FSA)

From the outset, the Syrian revolution was different from the Tunisian and Egyptian uprisings. After numerous political and social concessions from the government, the initial demands for the democratisation of the regime were quickly abandoned and the focus shifted to the overthrow of the government on April 7, 2011. At the end of July 2011, the creation of the SLA by former Syrian army officers with the support of the Muslim Brotherhood exiled in Turkey[625], and its arming by the United States and France heralded the militarisation and escalation of the conflict.

Its command is based in Turkey and has little command of the operational and tactical situations in Syria itself. A study by the American Institute for the Study of War, published in March 2012 on the basis of observations made at the end of 2011, casts doubt on its reality: its 'units' claim actions that are also claimed by other (Islamist) rebel groups or in areas where no rebel activity is known[626]. Its militias are short-lived and their desertion rate is very high; most often to Salafist groups[627].

Since 2011, the Western media has tried to make people believe that the rebellion is controlled by the ASL. This is false[628]. For several reasons. The first is that the ASL remains unclear: it is essentially a headquarters, claimed by different entities; no less than 9 different structures are known to claim the same name[629]. Secondly, its "units" on the ground are most often independent of any

623. "Presidential election in Syria: Bashar Al-Assad, act 3 (Part 2) - #DébatF24", *France 24/YouTube*, June 4, 2014 (06'18")

624. Richard Norton-Taylor, "Terror trial collapses after fears of deep embarrassment to security services", The Guardian, June, 1st 2015

625. Yehuda U. Blanga, "The Role of the Muslim Brotherhood in the Syrian Civil War", *Middle East Policy Council*, Volume XXIV, Autumn 2017, Nr 3, Tel Aviv

626. Joseph Holliday, *Syria's armed opposition*, Institute for the Study of War, March 2012, p. 15

627. Mona Mahmood & Ian Black, "Free Syrian Army rebels defect to Islamist group Jabhat al-Nusra", *The Guardian*, 8 May 2013; Adam Lucente & Zouhir Al Shimale, "Free Syrian Army decimated by desertions", *Al Jazeerah*, November 11, 2015

628. "Q&A: Nir Rosen on Syria's armed opposition", *Al Jazeera*, February 13, 2012

629. Aron Lund, "The Free Syrian Army Doesn't Exist", *Syria Comment*, March 16, 2013

command structure and behave like militias[630]; this explains the large number of atrocities. As for their "moderate" character, it appears from the start that the few operational ASL units owe their "efficiency" only to the fact that they are backed by jihadist groups. We will come back to this.

Very quickly, information on the exactions of the ASL against the civilian population multiplied. Its fighters slit the throats of Christian families, as witnessed by Sister Agnès-Mariam de la Croix, a nun based in Syria[631]. It carries out terrorist attacks with car bombs, as its leader, Colonel Riad al-Asaad, openly boasts in 2012[632], and quickly drifts towards Islamism[633].

On July 18, 2012, a bomb attack kills Daoud Rajha, Minister of Defence, in Damascus. It was claimed by the ASL and the Liwa al-Islam, an Islamist group. But the traditional press, which tends to relay the governmental message, such as *France 24*[634] or *the Express*[635], fails to mention the claim; *Le Monde* goes even further by suggesting that it could be a "*manipulation*" organised by the Syrian government[636]!

Since at least mid-2012, it has been known that the ASL is dominated by Islamists[637] and that Western weapons systematically arrive in the hands of jihadists[638]. Moreover, several ASL units change their logos and adopt Islamist symbolism to gain better visibility with Saudi and Qatari backers[639]. Quite quickly, the Western-backed and armed ASL is guilty of crimes that foreshadow those of the Islamic State[640].

In 2012, the very conservative US Council on Foreign Relations reported that:

> *The Syrian rebels would be infinitely weaker today without al-Qaeda in their ranks. Overall, the Free Syrian Army (FSA) battalions are tired, divided, chaotic and ineffective. Feeling abandoned by the West, the rebel forces are increasingly demoralised when confronted with the Assad regime's professional army and its better equipment. Al Qaeda fighters, however,*

630. William Van Wagenen, "There is No FSA, There is Only Al-Qaeda", *The Libertarian Institute*, December 27, 2017

631. Agnès-Mariam De La Croix, "Dernières nouvelles de Homs et de Kusayr", *Le Grand Soir*, April 1st, 2012

632. "Free Syrian Army admits responsibility for Aleppo bombing to FRANCE 24 - Syria Truth", *YouTube*, February 10, 2012.

633. "Syrian rebels elect Islamist-dominated unified command", *Reuters*, December 7, 2012

634. "Defence minister killed in suicide attack in Damascus", *France24*, July 18, 2012

635. "Syria: Defence Minister and brother-in-law of al-Assad killed in an attack", *lexpress.fr*, July 18, 2012

636. Benjamin Barthe, "Et si l'attentat du 18 juillet à Damas était une manipulation?", *lemonde.fr*, July 25, 2012

637. Reuters, "Syrian rebels elect Islamist-dominated unified command", December 8, 2012.

638. David E. Sanger, "Rebel Arms Flow Is Said to Benefit Jihadists in Syria", *The New York Times*, October 14, 2012; Jared Keller, "The US Funneled Weapons Into The Fight Against ISIS. They Only Ended Up Making The Militants Stronger", *Task & Purpose*, December 14, 2017.

639. *Deterring the Hypocrites - Exposing the Sahawat Alliance*, Islamic State in Iraq and the Levant, May (?) 2014

640. C. J. Chivers, "Brutality of Syrian Rebels Posing Dilemma in West", *The New York Times*, September 5, 2013

can help boost morale. The jihadists' contribution brings discipline, religious fervour, combat experience in Iraq, funding from Sunni sympathisers in the Gulf and, most importantly, lethal effect. In short, the SLA needs al-Qaeda now[641].

In reality, the Western services deployed on the ground to support the rebel groups do not know them:

There are fake Free Syrian Army brigades that pretend to be revolutionaries and sell the weapons they receive on the market[642].

By early 2013, the ASL was only a front[643] and even NATO considered that only the Islamists were fighting Assad[644]. The Pentagon is concerned about the growing presence of radical Islamists with the SLA and sees this as a regional problem[645]. Photos of SLA and Islamic State in Iraq and the Levant fighters side by side in Raqqa in 2013 confirm this cooperation[646]. Yet the myth of 'moderate rebels' persists, as it legitimises Western policy in Syria.

Obsessed with the overthrow of Bashar al-Assad, the Western media support the SLA. Taking refuge in the Idlib pocket and protected from Russian and Syrian attacks, the ASL - renamed the Syrian National Army (SNA) - allies itself with Turkey during its offensive in October 2019. The "experts" of "C dans l'air" present it as "*auxiliaries*" of the Turkish army, and an "official" of the US Department of Defense describes its militias as "*deranged and unreliable*[647]". Yet 21 of its 28 militias were trained, supported, armed and protected by the West (including France and Belgium)[648]! To the great displeasure of the West, it is precisely these militias that massacred the Kurdish activist Havrin Khalaf... It is also in this pocket of Idlib protected by the West that Abu Bakr al-Baghdadi, leader of the EI, was hiding!

641. Ed Husain, "Al-Qaeda's Specter in Syria", *Council on Foreign Relations*, August 6, 2012

642. Michael Bb Kelley, "How CIA-Aided Arms Shipments To Syria Keep Ending Up In Radical Hands", *Business Insider*, March 25, 2013

643. Aron Lund, "The Free Syrian Army Doesn't Exist", *Syria Comment*/www.joshualandis.com, March 16, 2013

644. "NATO: Assad, Russia and Iran are prevailing in Syria", *WorldTribune.com*, July 21, 2013.

645. Richard Engel, Jim Miklaszewski, Ghazi Balkiz and Robert Windrem, "Extremist element among Syrian rebels a growing worry", *NBC News*, September 10, 2013.

646. "FSA Cooperation with ISIS 2013, *Syrian War Blog*, April 15, 2019

647. "Trump orders withdrawal of U.S. forces from northern Syria, days after Pentagon downplays possibility", *The Washington Post*, October 13, 2019

648. Ömer Özkizilcik, *Uniting The Syrian Opposition - The Components Of The National Army And The Implications Of The Unification*, Foundation for Research in Politics, Economics and Society (SETA), Istanbul, October 2019

6.6.4. The Kurdish Forces

As the etymology of their name suggests, the Kurds were essentially a nomadic people until after the First World War. The territory that the 1920 Treaty of Sèvres provided for them was about 50 km north of the Syrian border[649]. Their settlement in Syria dates from the late 1970s, when they became refugees from Turkey, and then from Iraq, from 2003-2005. Ethnically close to the Persians, they are not originally from this region and occupy a thin strip along the Turkish border which serves as their sanctuary[650]. Thus, contrary to what some people claim, these territories do not "belong" to them: they are only the occupants.

During the Cold War, Syria supported the Kurdish Workers' Party (PKK) against Turkey. But at the end of the 1990s, it sought to draw closer to the United States, which was ready to support normalisation with Israel. It then banned the PKK, which the United States had just put on the list of terrorist organisations[651] and signed the Adana Agreement with Turkey on October 20, 1998. Syria undertook to prevent Kurdish incursions across the border and Turkey was authorised to intervene on Syrian territory against the PKK[652]. It will be of great importance twenty years later.

In 2003, the PKK structured its presence in Syria by creating the Democratic Union Party (Partiya Yekîtiya Demokrat - PYD). In 2012, it created its armed wing, the Kurdish People's Protection Units (YPG). In 2013, taking advantage of the ceasefire with the Turkish government, it moved fighters to Syria to strengthen the PYD/YPG.

In 2014, the battle of Kobane revealed the Kurdish fighters. The West decided to support and arm them instead of the 'moderate' Syrian opposition, which had not been the hoped-for catalyst for a general uprising against Bashar al-Assad. The YPG then become the "*boots on the ground*" that the Coalition does not want to deploy. Their doctrine is Marxist, but their secular approach to society makes them precious and reliable allies. They will be reinforced by French far-left fighters (some linked to the "zadists" of Notre-Dame-des-Landes)[653].

---

649. *Map: Kurds and Armenians, from the Treaty of Sèvres (1920) to the Treaty of Lausanne (1923)*, lhistoire.fr (accessed October 19, 2019)

650. https://fanack.com/syria/population/

651. Since October 8, 1997 (*Country Reports on Terrorism 2017*, Department of State, September 19, 2018; "Turkey hails US stance on PKK leaders, seeks same in Syria", *Associated Press/Stars & Stripes*, November 7, 2018)

652. *Statement Made By İsmail Cem, Foreign Minister, On The Special Security Meeting Held Between Turkey And Syria October 20, 1*998 (Unofficial Translation), Ministry of Foreign Affairs of Turkey (http://www.mfa.gov.tr/_p_statement-made-by-ismail-cem_-foreign-minister_-on-the-special-security-meeting-held-between-turkey-and-syria_br_october-20_-1998_br__unofficial-translation___p_.en.mfa)

653. "International volunteers join mass mobilization to defend Afrin", *People's defense units (ypgrojava.org)*, January 26, 2018; "Des Occidentaux avec les Kurdes à Afrin: l'ultra-gauche monte au front (1/2)", *France 24*, February 22, 2018 (updated on 19 March 2018)

The problem is that the European Union[654] and NATO[655] also consider the PKK a terrorist organisation. Not simply because of its ideology, but because it kills: with 110 deadly attacks between 2003 and 2013 according to the Global Terrorist Database[656], it is the main domestic threat in Turkey. By supporting its Syrian branch, France and the United States clearly show a lack of consistency and loyalty to their ally. In search of a political solution, the Turkish government starts secret negotiations in Norway[657], which the PKK breaks off in 2011. A ceasefire was agreed in March 2013, but was broken off again by the PKK in July 2015[658]. In fact, reinvigorated by Franco-American support in Syria, the PKK resumed armed struggle. Between 2014 and 2016, the PKK carried out 226 deadly attacks in Turkey; ten times more than the EI, which carried out 'only' 21[659]. This is why the American decision to supply arms to the Kurds in May 2017 worries Turkey, which sees these dangerous liaisons as contrary to the spirit of the Atlantic alliance.

To reassure its ally, the United States specified that this collaboration was of a "*temporary, transactional and tactical* nature[660]". In other words, it was to be based on exchanges of services (not values) and remains limited to certain areas. Furthermore, they promise to take up arms again after the defeat of the EI. This they will not do[661]. On the advice of the US Special Operations Command, the YPG allied itself with other groups and adopted the name of Syrian Democratic Forces (SDF), to hide its links with the PKK and its armed wing, the Hêzên Parastina Gel (HPG)[662]. Photos and videos of US soldiers wearing YPG insignia triggered official protests from Turkey[663], and were removed from *YouTube*[664].

In December 2018, Donald Trump baffled Europe by announcing the withdrawal of US forces from Syria. In fact, we are in the midst of "Trumpophobia".

---

654. Since July 15, 2008 (Wikipedia, article "Kurdistan Workers' Party")
655. "NATO urges restraint from Turkey over Iraq", *Reuters*, October 17, 2007
656. *Global Terrorism Database*, www.start.umd.edu/gtd/
657. "Who are Kurdistan Workers' Party (PKK) rebels?", *BBC News*, November 4, 2016
658. "KCK: Ateşkes tutumunun istismar edilmesini artık kabul etmeyeceğiz", *anfturkce.net*, July 11, 2015
659. *Global Terrorism Database*, www.start.umd.edu/gtd/
660. Jonathan Cohen, Deputy Assistant Secretary of State, Department of State, Middle East Institute, Washington DC, May 17, 2017, quoted in Cansu Çamlıbel, 'US: Relations with YPG temporary, transactional, tactical', *Hürriyet Daily News*, May 19, 2017.
661. Lolita C. Baldor, "Mattis: US arms for Syrian Kurds will continue after Raqqa," *Associated Press/Military Times*, June 27, 2017.
662. General Raymond Thomas, Commander of the US Special Operations Command (USSOCOM) at the Aspen Institute Security Forum, July 21, 2017, in "American General Explains Rebranding the YPG Away From the PKK", *YouTube*, July 22, 2017
663. "US soldiers with YPG insignias unacceptable, says Turkish FM", *Hürriyet Daily News*, May 27, 2016; Natasha Bertrand, "Turkey slams 'unacceptable' photos of US troops wearing Kurdish patches while they fight ISIS", *Business Insider*, May 27, 2016.
664. "YPG emblem American terrorists", (www.youtube.com/watch?v=gh04xp3sNUo) and "America's PKK YPG PYD Terrorist Support", (www.youtube.com/watch?v=o9KcYTqSp40) (videos removed)

In April 2016, Republican Senator Lindsey Graham, had called working with the Kurds "*the stupidest idea in the world*[665]" because it offended the Turkish ally; exactly the same words he uses in December 2018, to describe Trump's decision to abandon the Kurds[666]. So there is no strategy, but only party politics.

Same problem in Europe. Once again, the programme "C dans l'air", on *France 5*, plays its role as a sounding board for the official discourse. Only the journalist Jean-Dominique Merchet shows intellectual honesty by recalling that the intervention in Syria was not popular[667] and that the president is only applying his electoral programme[668]. Trump then suspended his decision. Contrary to what Patrice Franceschi would later assert, he did not "*retrograde*[669]", but gave his allies (including France) time to make the necessary arrangements[670]. What they will not do: they neither send troops nor establish any mechanism or agreement with the Kurds, to provide guarantees to Turkey after the withdrawal.

In October 2019, the Turks intervene in Syria as soon as the Americans leave (Operation SOURCE OF PEACE), in order to push Kurdish militias back 30 km from the Turkish border, triggering a thunder of protests. The media speak of a "*pretext*[671]", and carefully avoid mentioning the increase of Kurdish terrorism in southern Turkey and the approximately 3,000 deaths[672] it caused between July 2015 and July 2017 in Turkey. In the European Parliament, MEP Frédérique Ries speaks of an "*illegal operation*[673]". But this is inaccurate: she forgets the Adana agreement, which explains the soft reactions of Syria and Russia[674].

The Trump administration is trying to make people believe that the PKK/HPG is distinct from the PYD/YPG[675]. A myth carefully maintained in the West, especially in France, where the Kurdish people's struggle is very popular[676]. Playing with

665. "U.S. Senator Graham Criticizes U.S. Military Strategy in Syria", *YouTube/C-SPAN*, May 5, 2016

666. Cristina Maza, "Lindsey Graham Said Trump Withdrawing From Syria Is 'The Dumbest F***ing Idea I've Ever Heard'," *Newsweek*, February 20, 2019

667. Andy Sullivan, "U.S. public opposes Syria intervention as Obama presses Congress", *Reuters*, September 3, 2013

668. Jean-Dominique Merchet in the programme "C dans l'air", "La dernière surprise de Trump #cdanslair 20.12.2018", *YouTube/France 5*, December 21, 2018 (06'00")

669. "Syria: Trump abandons the Kurds - C à Vous - 08/10/2019", *France 5/YouTube*, October 8, 2019 (02'40")

670. Brett McGurk, "Hard Truths in Syria", *Foreign Affairs*, May/June 2019

671. Henri Vernet in "Syria: why the Turkish offensive against the Kurds is "immoral and dangerous" for France", *Le Parisien/YouTube*, October 10, 2019 (00'35")

672. Berkay Mandiraci, "Turkey's PKK Conflict Kills almost 3,000 in Two Years", *International Crisis Group*, July 20, 2017

673. "Plenary debate on the illegal Turkish invasion in Syria - Frédérique Ries 23 October 2019", *Frédérique Ries/YouTube*, October 23, 2019 (00'23")

674. Jared Szuba, "Syria will cooperate on Adana counter-terror agreement if Turkey withdraws forces", *The Defense Post*, January 28, 2019

675. Edward Hunt, 'The Kurdish Dilemma', *jacobinmag.com*, accessed November 9, 2019

676. Armelle Charrier in "Syria: Turkey threatens to attack the Kurdish area", *France 24/YouTube*, October 9, 2019 (00'45")

words, the Belgian MP Georges Dallemagne states that the PYD does not operate in Turkey[677]. This is incorrect: the YPG and the HPG have the same command structure, sharing and exchanging fighters on both sides of the border, as needed, as reported by the *Washington Post*[678]. Indeed, after the recapture of Raqqa, the YPG immediately hoisted the PKK flag and portraits of Abdullah Ocalan, the joint leader of the PKK/HPG and the PYD/YPG, in the centre of the city[679]. The testimonies of PKK commanders[680] are confirmed by the 2016 EUROPOL Annual Report, which notes that the two organisations are linked[681], as shown by the arrests of PKK activists in Spain[682]. On April 28, 2016, at a hearing before the Senate Armed Services Committee, Ashton Carter, then US Secretary of Defense, confirmed that the PYD/YPG are linked to the PKK[683].

Before the fall of the EI, the Kurds and the Syrian garrison in Qamishli coexisted without major friction. Therefore, in October 2019, the SDF could easily have transferred custody of jihadist prisoners to the Syrian army. However, they did not do so, preferring to use these prisoners to put pressure on the West[684].

In fact, the possible resurgence of the EI is being played on to induce the US to stay: its presence is illegal in the eyes of international law, its only legal justification being the AUMF 2001[685]. Therefore, the withdrawal of the US military to the oil-rich area of Deir ez-Zor becomes illegal in every respect. The writer Patrice Franceschi claims - without providing any evidence - to have "*seen [...] permanently, a Turkish support*" to the EI fighters for 7 years[686]. Turkey would thus have helped the EI, which carried out 21 attacks and caused 319 deaths on its territory between 2014 and 2017[687]? To what end? And why would the EI attack such a valuable ally? No explanation. In fact, he bases his accusation on the proximity between Erdogan and the Muslim Brotherhood... who are considered the "moderate rebels" in Syria!...

677. Georges Dallemagne in the programme "C'est pas tous les jours dimanche", *RTL-TVI*, October 13, 2019
678. *The Washington Post*, October 9, 2019
679. "Kurdish forces raise large banner of jailed PKK leader Abdullah Ocalan in iconic Raqqa square", *alaraby.co.uk*, October 19, 2017
680. Patrick Cockburn, "War against ISIS: PKK commander tasked with the defence of Syrian Kurds claims 'we will save Kobani'", *The Independent*, November 11, 2014
681. *TE-SAT 2016 - EU Terrorism Situation and Trend Report*, European Police Office, 2016, p. 35
682. Daniel Iriarte, 'PKK, ¿una amenaza para España? Nueve detenidos en Madrid, Valencia y Bilbao', *El Confidencial*, January 27, 2016
683. "American Defense Secretary Ashton Carter confirms "substantial ties" between the PYD/YPG and PKK", *YouTube*, July 23, 2017
684. Rod Nordland & Hwaida Saad, 'Kurdish Fighters Discuss Releasing Almost 3,200 ISIS Prisoners', *The New York Times*, December 20, 2018; Samuel Osborne, 'Isis militants break out of prison in Syria after bombing by Turkey', *The Independent*, October 11, 2019
685. AUMF 2001, adopted by the Congress on September 14, 2001
686. "Syria: Trump abandons the Kurds - C à Vous - 08/10/2019", *France 5/YouTube*, October 8, 2019 (08'10")
687. Kuang Keng Kuek Ser, "These three charts will help you understand Turkey's recent terrorist attacks", *Public Radio International*, 30 June 2016 (updated January 3, 2017)

They are trying to dramatise the situation: Caroline Fourest theatrically claims that the Kurds "*sacrificed themselves to defend us*[688]" against the EI, Patrick Cohen claims that "*they alone went to the front line to confront the jihadists*[689]". This is not true: they fought for two reasons. First, because so many Kurdish youths had joined the ranks of the EI and were threatening their own people[690]. Secondly, they expect the West to give them the territories taken from the indigenous Syrian populations: 'Rojava', east of the Euphrates River[691].

Moreover, while Turkish interventions west of the Euphrates, in 2016 (Operation EUPHRATE BOUCLIER) and 2018 (Operation RAMEAU D'OLIVIER) had not triggered any reactions, the French media went wild in October 2019. The explanation is that Operation SOURCE OF PEACE concerns the east of the Euphrates; an area where the American neo-conservatives seek to create a Kurdish state, in order to fragment Syria. The West fears an alliance between the Kurds and the Syrian government, which would allow it to restore the integrity of the country[692]. For the Kurds were not really opposed to the government of Bashar al-Assad. In April 2011, he had granted Syrian citizenship to 300,000 stateless Kurds[693], and in 2012, he concluded an informal non-aggression pact with the PYD/YPG[694]. In October 2019, their goals converge to fight Western-backed jihadists (including the Islamic State)[695].

According to Bernard-Henri Lévy, the Kurds have a "*rather unique democratic culture*[696]". However, in spite of Patrick Cohen's opinion[697], they "*are not angels*[698]". They recruit underage children[699], especially in the Kobane region, and use them as frontline fighters[700]. So much so that in Christian Assyrian areas, this practice has led to the closure of schools[701]. In fact, the Kurds are not the majority in the territories they control militarily. In order

688. "Kurds: the anger of Caroline Fourest - C l'hebdo - 12/10/2019", *France 5/YouTube*, October 12, 2019 (01'30")
689. "Syria: Trump abandons the Kurds - C à Vous - 08/10/2019", *France 5/YouTube*, October 8, 2019 (01'10")
690. Rebecca Collard, "Kurdish men are joining ISIS to kill their own people", www.pri.org, January 28, 2015
691. "The Kurds will expect a reward for their sacrifice against Isil", *The Telegraph*, January 28, 2015
692. "What Donald Trump's decision to abandon Kurdish fighters in Syria means for the Kurds, Assad and Russia", *The Conversation*, October 8, 2019
693. "Stateless Kurds in Syria granted citizenship", *CNN*, April 8, 2011
694. *Syria's Kurds: A Struggle Within a Struggle*, Crisis Group Middle East Report N°136, International Crisis Group, January 22, 2013, p.35
695. "Syrian army responds to Kurdish call and enters Minbej town", *rts.ch*, December 28, 2018
696. "Bernard Henri-Lévy "Bashar al-Assad created Daesh"", *CNEWS/YouTube*, September 8, 2015
697. "War in Syria: Trump facing Erdogan - C à Vous - 16/10/2019", *France 5/YouTube*, October 16, 2019 (01'05")
698. "For Trump, the Kurds "are not angels"", Le Figaro / AFP, October 16, 2019
699. "SYRIA - Military Service, Mandatory Self-Defence Duty and Recruitment to the YPG", *Danish Immigration Service*, Copenhagen, February 26, 2015; "'Ayn al 'Arab: YPG recruits two primary school students", *KurdWatch.org*, May 25, 2016
700. "Syria: Armed Group Recruiting Children in Camps", *Human Rights Watch*, August 3, 2018
701. Marlo Safi, "Closure of Syrian Schools: Another Bleak Sign for Christians in Syria", *National Review*, September 25, 2018

to do so, they are forcibly taking over land they have never occupied before[702], practicing ethnic cleansing by expelling Christian Assyrian populations[703] and Arabs[704] and torturing the children they capture[705]. In France, the media and the authorities turn a blind eye to these abuses. But this is not the case of the British Parliament, which has repeatedly expressed its concern about the situation of the Christian populations in the areas occupied by the Kurds[706]. This is why, on October 9, the World Council of Arameans applauded the American departure and the arrival of the Turkish army, which liberates them from the Kurds and their exactions[707].

The problem is the total lack of a comprehensive strategy. By trying to fight the Syrian government on all fronts, the West has failed to anticipate the problems, unlike the Syrian government[708]. The problem here is not that we are withdrawing from the conflict, but that we entered it!

6.6.5. Arms Deliveries and Logistical Support

In early 2012, President Obama signed a SECRET Executive Order authorising the CIA to provide weapons to Syrian rebels. He also established a secret command centre in Adana, Turkey, from which support for the Syrian opposition was coordinated[709]. Transports organised by the CIA and carried out by Saudi, Croatian, Jordanian and American aircraft to the Turkish air base of Esenboga, transport hundreds of tons of equipment and weapons to the Syrian rebels. These deliveries increased from November onwards - after the presidential elections - and included collective anti-tank weapons and portable anti-aircraft missiles from Libya[710].

---

702. "Kurds Confiscating Ancestral Lands of Indigenous Assyrians," *Assyrian Information Management (AIM)*, October 1st, 2012 (updated May 20, 2016); Matt Bradley, Ayla Albayrak & Dana Ballout, "Kurds declare 'federal region' in Syria, says official," *The Wall Street Journal*, March 17, 2016
703. Wladimir van Wilgenburg, "Tensions soar between Syrian Kurds and Christians", *Middle East Eye*, January 29, 2019
704. Hannah Lucinda Smith, 'Thousands of Arabs driven out by Kurds' ethnic cleansing', *The Times*, June 1st, 2015; Richard Spencer, 'Syrian Kurds accused of ethnic cleansing and killing opponents', *The Telegraph*, May 18, 2016
705. *Kurdistan Region of Iraq: Detained Children Tortured*, Human Rights Watch, January 8, 2019
706. "British Parliament on Assyrian Persecution - Kurds Stealing Assyrian Land!", *YouTube*, June 26, 2009; "Assyrians Demand International Support to End Kurdish Land Theft & Occupation of Assyrian Lands", *YouTube*, April 15, 2016
707. https://www.facebook.com/wca1983/photos/a.367398243336286/2494161193993303/?type=3&theater; "Syrian Christians Proclaim "Trump is right on Syria!" YPG Kurds are responsible for escalation in Northeast Syria," *World Council of Arameans (Syriacs)*, October 9, 2019; https://twitter.com/iraqschristians/status/1182810833254002688, October 11, 2019
708. "Syrian army responds to Kurdish call and enters Minbej town", *rts.ch*, December 28, 2018
709. "EXKLUSIV-Geheime Waffenlieferungen an syrische Rebellen", *Reuters*, July 27, 2012; Mark Hosenball, "Exclusive: Obama authorizes secret U.S. support for Syrian rebels", *Reuters*, August 1st, 2012
710. C. J. Chivers and Eric Schmitt, "Arms Airlift to Syria Rebels Expands, With Aid from C.I.A.", *New York Times*, March 24, 2013.

But Europeans are not left out. In May 2011[711], the European Union decreed an arms embargo on Syria, which France and Great Britain sought to have lifted in March 2013[712]. In order to reassure public opinion, President Hollande states:

> *There can be no delivery of arms at the end of the embargo [...] if there is no certainty that these arms will be used by legitimate opponents free of terrorist influence [...] For the moment, we do not have this certainty.*

And he adds:

> *Today, there is an embargo, we respect it [...] [but this rule is] violated by the Russians who send arms to Bashar al-Assad, this is a problem*[713].

But he is lying. In May 2014, he will admit that France started delivering arms to Syrian rebels as early as 2012, violating the EU arms embargo[714].

In September 2012, a Defense Intelligence Agency (DIA) SECRET/NOFORN[715] report details deliveries to Syrian rebels from Libya in August: 500 sniper rifles, 100 anti-tank rocket launchers with three rounds each, and 400 howitzers of 125 and 155 mm. Thousands of tons of ammunition and weaponry are being delivered to the Syrian rebellion[716], despite the fact that the weapons are known to arrive directly into the hands of the jihadists[717]. In May 2013, the Americans even supplied them with 4 BM-21 GRAD multiple rocket launchers, with 20,000 122 mm rockets[718].

In early 2014, the Americans officially announced that they would deliver BQM-71 TOW-2 anti-tank missiles to certain '*moderate*' and '*carefully selected*' groups. The appearance of these missiles in the Syrian theatre of operations raises some questions. Not only is there now evidence that some of these missiles (with a useful range of 4.2 km) have been regularly engaged from Turkish territory over the border against Syrian fortified positions and armoured vehicles, but the rebel units that received them - declared "moderate" by the Americans, such as Harakat al-Hazm - regularly collaborate with and lend their weapons to considerably more radical rebel formations, such as Jabhat al-Nosrah. In early 2015,

711. Xavier Panon, *Dans les coulisses de la diplomatie française*, L'Archipel, May 2014.
712. Catherine Gouëset, "Arms for Syria: who does what?", www.lexpress.fr, March 15, 2013
713. "Syria: has Hollande retropalated on the delivery of arms to the rebels?", *lexpress.fr*, March 29, 2013.
714. http://www.sipri.org/databases/embargoes/eu_arms_embargoes/syria_LAS/eu-embargo-on-Syria
715. SECRET/NOFORN = Secret and cannot be distributed to outsiders.
716. "(S/NF) Former-Libya Military Weapons Shipped to Syria via the Port of Benghazi, Libya", *Defense Intelligence Agency*, October 5, 2012 (declassified April 2015)
717. David E. Sanger, "Rebel Arms Flow Is Said to Benefit Jihadists in Syria", *The New York Times*, October 14, 2012
718. Gareth Porter, "How America Armed Terrorists in Syria", *The American Conservative*, June 22, 2017

following a dispute, al-Hazm was absorbed into Jabhat al-Nosrah, which then seized the American missiles. The French MILAN anti-tank missiles will suffer a similar fate[719].

In fact, Westerners know very little about the dynamics of the Syrian conflict. On our television screens, "experts" support rebels who are real serial war criminals, while the authorities supply arms that are passed from hand to hand according to the rule of the highest bidder. It has been known since 2012 that the rebellion is unstable and that the weapons supplied to the "moderates" have reached the Islamic State[720].

6.6.6. Western Military Instructors and Advisors

As early as 2011, France joined American, Israeli, Saudi and Qatari efforts to destabilise Syria. Former CIA agent Philip Giraldi, deputy director of the Council for National Interest, reports that:

> *French and British special forces instructors are on the ground, assisting the Syrian rebels, while the CIA and US special operations provide communications and intelligence to support the rebel cause, allowing fighters to avoid areas where Syrian soldiers are concentrated*[721].

In March 2012, Lebanese newspapers mention the capture by the Syrian army of 13 French soldiers in the Baba Amr district in Homs[722], until then held by the Al-Farouq and Khalid Bin al-Walid phalanges, which were then part of the ASL and supported by France. They will later join the jihadist ranks, and then the EI.

In June 2016, *Radio Free Europe/Radio Liberty* reported that the United States had asked Russia to avoid striking Jabhat al-Nosrah[723]; a request already made by the 'moderate' rebels in February 2016[724]. In France, no traditional media will relay this information: it would undermine the official discourse. The main objective is to overthrow the Syrian government.

On 19 December 2016, at a press conference, the Syrian ambassador to the UN gave the names of 14 foreign intelligence officers who had been surrounded in East Aleppo by Syrian special forces. Among them are 1 American officer,

---

719. *Islamic State Weapons in Kobane*, Conflict Armament Research, April 2015.
720. *Weapons of the Islamic State*, Conflict Armament Research, London, December 2017
721. Philip Giraldi, "NATO vs. Syria", *The American Conservative*, December 19, 2011
722. Henry Samuel & Amy Willis, "Thirteen French soldiers 'captured by Syrian Army'", *The Telegraph*, March 5, 2012
723. Vladimir Isachenkov, "US asks Russia not to hit Nusra Front in Syria, Moscow says", *Associated Press*, June 3, 2016; "U.S., Russia in Dispute over Strikes on Syrian Al-Qaeda Branch", *RFE/RL*, June 4, 2016
724. "Syrian opposition says temporary truce possible, but deal seems far off", *Reuters*, February 21, 2016

1 Israeli, 1 Turk and 8 Saudis[725]. Thus, Western officers are said to have supported the rebels, who - let us remember - have all joined the ranks of the jihadists.

As in Libya, the West's support for the Syrian opposition has not brought about a moralisation of the conflict, nor a greater respect for the laws of war, nor a contribution of the values it proclaims: the so-called 'moderate' groups have hardly any more consideration for human rights than the others[726]. As one rebel fighter confessed:

> *They trained us to ambush enemy regime vehicles and cut off roads [...] They also trained us to attack vehicles, search them, find information, weapons or ammunition and finish off soldiers still alive after an ambush*[727].

... which tends to show that it is neither our values nor our principles that motivate Western involvement. However, the traditional Western press - particularly in France - remains very uncritical of this engagement and its modus operandi. Moreover, practically all the candidates in the 2017 presidential elections came out clearly in favour of a withdrawal from Syria or to denounce the ineffectiveness of the international coalition in the Syrian crisis, except for... Emmanuel Macron.

6.7. Photos of "Caesar" and Sednaya Prison

Since 2011-2012, the United States and France have had the declared objective of overthrowing the Syrian government. However, at this stage, their action remained clandestine (supplying arms, financing and training the rebels) and nothing allowed them to intervene openly without a UN Security Council resolution. The aim is to demonstrate that the rebels are fighting for a just cause and that the Syrian government is massacring its own people, in order to justify an external intervention under the "responsibility to protect" (R2P).

On June 10, 2014, Foreign Minister Laurent Fabius sends a video message to participants at the Human Rights Council meeting in Geneva. He presented a report on the crimes committed in Syrian prisons. His allegations are based on 53,275 photos of some 11,000 detainees[728], who are alleged to have been tortured by the government. These files were allegedly provided by a former

725. "Syria Names Foreign Secret Agents Trapped in Aleppo", *YouTube*, December 19, 2016
726. Joshua Hersh, "'He Knew That Death Was Coming': Survivors Mourn After A Massacre By Syrian Rebels", *Huffington Post*, 10 March 2014 (updated December 6, 2017)
727. Nancy A. Youssef McClatchy, "Syrian Rebels Describe U.S.-Backed Training in Qatar", *Frontline*, May 26, 2014
728. *À Report into the credibility of certain evidence with regard to Torture and Execution of Persons Incarcerated by the current Syrian regime*, Carter-Ruck and Co. Solicitors, London, January 2014 (CONFIDENTIAL)

Syrian security officer, codenamed "CESAR". While in the service of the Syrian government, he was allegedly tasked with photographing the dead in Syrian prisons and took the pictures with him when he fled to Europe in July 2013. In order to protect him, his true identity has never been revealed[729]. However, the number of Syrian security officers who have had the same mission is probably quite small, so if CESAR is really who he says he is, the Syrian government must know about him. Its reality thus remains questionable.

The photos are accompanied by a report prepared by the London law firm Carter-Ruck & Co, and funded by Qatar (which supports the Syrian jihadist opposition). Published on January 20, 2014 by *CNN* and the British daily *The Guardian*, two days before the opening of peace negotiations on Syria in Geneva[730]. They will contribute to the discrediting of the Syrian government and the failure of the negotiations.

In 2014-2015, several media outlets (among others, *L'Express*, *Franceinfo* and *Le Soir*) accredited the CESAR photos by claiming that they had been authenticated, notably by the American FBI[731], and castigated the Syrian government for denying their authenticity. This is inaccurate and these media are lying by omission. In fact, the FBI has only stated that the photos are not montages, but it has not been able to certify their origin or the circumstances in which they were acquired[732].

Even if Laurent Fabius describes them as "irrefutable", the documents raise questions. In early December 2014, a report by Human Rights Watch (HRW) showed that 24,568 images (46%) depict Syrian soldiers and police officers who died in combat or as a result of attacks. This is a far cry from torture in Syrian jails. The remaining 28,707 photos are of 6,786 individuals whom HRW "*considers" to have* died in detention, but of whom only 27 could be identified on the basis of family statements, and who could therefore have been effectively tortured in Syrian jails[733]. But here again, questions remain as a number of cases of torture had been outsourced to Syria by the United States before 2011... Moreover, it is noted that a number of victims have the same registration number or - conversely - the same body is registered under several numbers.

In mid-December 2014, Human Rights Investigations (HRI) noted a number of inconsistencies and found that only 26,948 images had been provided by

729. Carter-Ruck Report, p. 12

730. It is called "Geneva II", from 22 to January 31, 2014.

731. "Syria: photos of César, photographer of the regime's torture, exposed", *lexpress.fr*, October 15, 2014; "Photos of "César": France files a complaint against the Syrian regime for "crimes against humanity"", *franceinfo*, September 30, 2015; Baudouin Loos, "Garance La Caisne: 'Les photos syriennes, l'image claire d'une machine de mort'", *lesoir.be*, December 16, 2015

732. Stav Ziv, "Syria Torture Photos 'Depict Real People and Events': FBI Report", *Newsweek*, July 22, 2015

733. "New Human Rights Watch Report and the Caesar photos", *Human Rights Investigations*, December 17, 2015

CESAR, with the rest coming from other unclear sources. Since then, the case appears to have stalled.

However, the international community has not been able to authenticate the photos, as *Amnesty International* admits[734], or to contact the mysterious CESAR[735]. So we don't know the "bottom line" of the story.

However, it seems rather strange that a government would seek to record its own crimes! In fact, it is more plausible that the government wanted to document the effects of terrorism and the methods of the rebellion, and that some of the photos come from this archive. The other photos are likely to have come from Western or Israeli intelligence services and may have been taken in Syria and Iraq.

Whatever the nature of the casualties, this may be a manipulative operation designed to provoke international intervention, like Benghazi in 2011. In the end, it failed to convince, and the US had to invent the 'Khorasan' group, in an attempt to force the hand of Congress, before the appearance of the EI provided the pretext for intervention. This is probably why the CESAR case was quickly forgotten.

On September 2, 2019, journalist Michel Apathie, on *LCI*, questions MP Thierry Mariani about his recent visit to Syria near Saydnaya prison. On the same day and on the same channel, journalist Thierry Moreau questions Nicolas Bay on the same subject. They refer to an Amnesty International report published in February 2017, which claims that the Syrian government hanged and "*exterminated*" between 5,000 and 13,000 prisoners between September 2011 and December 2015. Naturally, Michel Apathy will only mention the higher figure of what is only an estimate, as the methodology that leads to these figures is explained in the report itself:

> *During the first four months, it was usual to execute between seven and twenty people every ten to fifteen days. During the next 11 months, between 20 and 50 people were executed once a week, usually on Monday nights. Over the next six months, groups of 20 to 50 people were executed once or twice a week, usually on Mondays and/or Wednesdays. Testimonies from detainees suggest that executions took place at a similar - or even higher - rate at least until December 2015.*

This leads to the following calculation:

> *If between seven and twenty people were killed every ten to fifteen days from September to December 2011, the total number would be between 56 and*

734. "11,000 Reasons For Real Action in Syria", *Amnesty International*, January 23, 2014
735. "Syria defector's photos depict 'systematic torture and killing' of detainees", *CBC/Thomson Reuters*, January 21, 2014

240 people for this period. If between 20 and 50 people were killed every week between January and November 2012, the total number would be between 880 and 2,200 for that period. If between 20 and 50 people were killed in 222 executions (assuming that executions took place twice a week and once a week) between December 2012 and December 2015, the total number would be between 4,400 and 11,100 for this period. These calculations give a minimum figure of 5,336, rounded to the nearest thousand, and 13,540, rounded to the nearest thousand[736].

These figures are therefore a series of speculations and extrapolations based on "ifs", which are not confirmed by any facts. The lack of rigour, ethics and professionalism of journalists is becoming evident and borders on conspiracy.

Amnesty's sources are questionable to say the least: virtually all interviews were conducted in Turkey and by telephone with 'witnesses' based in Europe, Jordan and the US. Moreover, Amnesty was only able to identify 95 individuals who *may have been* in the prison, of whom 59 may have been transferred elsewhere, and 36 who *may have been* executed, but this is not known[737]. This is a long way from the facts.

This does not prevent the Western press, such as *Le Monde*[738], *Radio-Télévision Suisse*[739], *Jeune Afrique*[740], *France 24*[741], *Courrier international*[742], *La Presse du Canada*[743] or *La libre*[744] de Belgique from presenting certainties and sticking to the figure of 13,000. *L'Express* goes even further, stating "*no less than 13,000*[745]": propaganda in the service of political policy...

The report also presents some inconsistencies, such as the satellite photos of a military cemetery called "Martyrs' Cemetery", a strange name for burying victims who are allegedly enemies of the regime! Furthermore, the report states that death sentences must be approved by the Grand Mufti of Syria; this contradicts the secular Syrian Constitution and is not confirmed by any document. This incongruous reference to the Grand Mufti, at a time when the Grand Mufti

736. *Human Slaughterhouse - Mass Hangings And Extermination at Saydnaya Prison, Syria*, Amnesty International, February 2017, p.17
737. *Human Slaughterhouse... op. cit*, p. 30
738. "According to Amnesty, nearly 13,000 inmates have been killed in a Syrian prison in five years", *Le Monde/AFP*, February 7, 2017
739. "Syrian regime rejects report of mass hangings", *rts.ch*, February 8, 2017
740. Olivier Liffran, "Syria: the hell of Saidnaya government prison as told by Amnesty International", *Jeune Afrique*, February 7, 2017
741. "Syria: thousands of secret hangings in Saydnaya prison, denounces Amnesty", *france24.com*, February 7, 2017
742. "Syria. Mass hangings in Saidnaya prison", *Le Courrier International*, February 7, 2017
743. Maya Gebeily, "Damascus accused of hanging 13,000 people in five years", *La Presse/AFP*, February 6, 2017 (updated February 7, 2017)
744. "Syria: 13,000 people hanged in five years in a prison", *Lalibre.be/AFP*, February 7, 2017
745. "Syria: Thierry Mariani drank close to the prison of horror", *lexpress.fr*, September 2, 2019

of Jerusalem is reappearing in the Israeli media, suggests an attempt to create a parallel between Syria and Nazi Germany. A sort of Godwin point…

In reality, we know nothing: the report is a collection of assumptions and rumours based on prejudice. Like the CESAR report, its appearance just before a 'round' of peace negotiations in Geneva[746], imposes a certain caution, which the warmongers deliberately ignore.

6.8 "Khorasan" Group, "Imminent" Threat to the United States

As early as 2012, the United States is looking for a pretext to intervene in Syria and support the ASL with strikes. But after the lies to attack Iraq in 2003, such a decision is delicate. Article 1 of the US Constitution states that only Congress has the authority to declare war; but Article 2 authorises the president to respond militarily to an "imminent" or "sudden" threat, and when time is short. In order to be able to respond to terrorism without these constraints, the Authorisation for Use of Military Force (AUMF) Act was passed in 2001. It would become the US's preferred tool for justifying its interventions.

On 22 June 2014, when asked about the emergence of the Islamic State at a press conference, President Obama said that it could pose a threat in the "*medium to long term*", but that it was neither an immediate threat nor a necessary and sufficient condition for the United States to engage in external military operations without congressional approval[747]. On 10 July 2014, testifying before the US Senate, Jeh Johnson, Secretary of Homeland Security[748], stated that "*the United States is not aware of any particular threat from the Islamic State on US soil*[749]". His opinion was confirmed a few days later, in early September, by the director of the US National Counterterrorism Center[750], Matthew Olsen[751]. Thus, the EI does not constitute a sufficient threat for Congress to accept an intervention.

It was then that a terrorist group of unknown virulence appeared in the media in a very timely manner:

746. In this case: Geneva IV, from 23 February to March 3, 2017

747. Rory Carroll, "Obama: Isis could pose a 'medium and long-term threat' to the US", *The Guardian*, June 22, 2014

748. US Department of Homeland Security (DHS).

749. Doina Chiacu & Mark Hosenball, "U.S. says no precise threat to homeland from Islamic State", *Reuters*, August 29, 2014.

750. National Counterterrorism Center (NCTC)

751. Shane Harris, "United States Counterterrorism Chief Says Islamic State Is Not Planning an Attack on the U.S.", *Foreign Policy*, September 3, 2014.

While the Islamic State is attracting attention, another group of extremists in Syria - a mix of experienced jihadists from Afghanistan, Yemen, Syria and Europe - poses a more direct and imminent threat to the US, working with Yemeni bomb makers to target the US air force, says a US official. At the centre is a cell known as the Khorasan Group, a group of veteran al-Qaeda fighters from Afghanistan and Pakistan who have gone to Syria to connect with al-Qaeda's affiliate, the al-Nosrah Front.

The Khorasan militants did not go to Syria primarily to fight the government of President Bashar al-Assad, the US official said. But they were sent by al-Qaida leader Ayman al-Zawahiri to recruit Europeans and Americans, whose passports allow them to board US planes without attracting the attention of security officials.

In addition, according to classified US intelligence analysis, Khorasan militants have been working with Al Qaeda bomb makers in Yemen to test new methods of smuggling explosives through airport security. The fear is that Khorasan militants will provide these sophisticated explosives to their European recruits, so that they can introduce them on flights to the United States[752].

A few days later, *CBS News* reported:

The Islamic State of Iraq and the Levant (ISIL) may dominate the billboards and capture attention with its prolific propaganda, but CBS News' Bob Orr writes about another group in Syria - one that few have heard of because information about it has been kept secret - that is considered an urgent problem. Sources told CBS News that operatives and explosives experts from Osama bin Laden's former al Qaeda network could once again pose an immediate threat to the United States.

The sources confirm that the al-Qaeda cell is called "Khorasan" [...].

According to a CIA official, the threat posed by the new Syrian group is more dangerous than ISIL[753].

---

752. Ken Dilanian & Eileen Sullivan, "Syrian extremists may pose more direct threat to US than Islamic State", *Associated Press*, September 13, 2014.
753. "Al Qaeda's quiet plan to outdo ISIS and hit U.S.", *CBS News*, September 18, 2014.

On September 20, it was learned that the Khorasan group was led by Muhsin al-Fadhli (an Islamist close to OBL), who had allegedly participated in the preparation of the "9/11" attacks[754], and had financed the operation against the French ship M/V Limburg in 2002. A veteran of the wars in Chechnya and Afghanistan, al-Fadhli was killed in an American strike on July 8, 2015 at the age of 33, which means that he was already a senior member of the al-Qaeda hierarchy at barely 20 years of age, with colleagues two to three times his age. Possible, but doubtful.

The new group is credited with using "*explosive clothing*"[755]. US intelligence lends it an '*aspiration*' to carry out a '9/11' like attack and suggests a relationship with Pakistan, Afghanistan and Iran[756]. The fact that (Shiite) Iran is associated with Pakistan and Afghanistan in a jihadist project that is essentially Sunni in nature does not seem to disturb the experts. Yet it was on this basis that, to the surprise of all[757], on September 23, 2014, President Obama launched air strikes on Syrian territory:

> *Last night, we also carried out attacks to destroy plots against the United States by experienced al Qaeda operatives known as the Khorasan group. Once again, it must be clear to anyone who would seek to plot against America and harm Americans that we will not tolerate safe havens for terrorists who threaten our people*[758].

It is in self-defence, suggesting that Syria was providing sanctuary for terrorists planning actions against the United States. *The Washington Post*, citing Pentagon sources, mentions that the group was ready to implement "*imminent*" strikes against Europe or the US[759].

However, on the same day, doubts appeared and *Foreign Policy* magazine asked:

> *What concrete intelligence - if any - allowed the US to strike now? Officials who spoke to reporters about the strikes in Syria offered no information about a particular plot. Nor did they explain why the current threat,*

754. Mark Mazzetti, Michael S. Schmidt & Ben Hubbard, "U.S. Suspects More Direct Threats Beyond ISIS," September 20, 2014.
755. Josh Levs, Paul Cruickshank & Tim Lister, "Source: Al Qaeda group in Syria plotted attack against U.S. with explosive clothes", *CNN*, September 24, 2014.
756. Eli Lake, "Al Qaeda Plotters in Syria 'Went Dark'U.S. Spies Say," *The Daily Beast*, September 23, 2014.
757. Brett LoGiurato and Jeremy Bender, "Meet The Khorasan, The Terrorist Group That's Suddenly A Bigger Threat Than ISIS", *Business Insider*, September 23, 2014
758. "Statement by the President on Airstrikes in Syria", *The White House, Office of the Press Secretary*, September 23, 2014.
759. Terrence McCoy, "Targeted by U.S. airstrikes: The secretive al-Qaeda cell was plotting an imminent attack", *The Washington Post*, September 23, 2014.

which would have been described to members of Congress a year ago, is more dangerous now than it was in July, when Khorasan's efforts to recruit Westerners led to increased security checks at some foreign airports with direct flights to the US[760].

The article even quotes a US counter-terrorism official:

Khorasan intends to strike, but we don't know if their capabilities are equal to their desires[761].

The story quickly fizzled out. The *New York Times* reports that the group (which had prepared imminent attacks) had no definite targets or even concrete plans[762]. *CBS News* goes one better:

James Comey, the FBI director, and Rear Admiral John Kirby, the Pentagon spokesman, each acknowledged that the United States had no specific information about where or when the cell, known as the Khorasan group, chose to attack a Western target.

We can debate whether or not to hit them and whether it was too early or too late [...] I don't think we should debate that they were bad boys[763].

In late September 2014, an article in the *National Review* confirmed:

You have never heard of a group called Khorasan because there never was one. It was a name created by the administration, which had calculated that Khorasan - a region in the border area of Iran and Afghanistan - had enough links to the jihadist context that no one would question the word of the President[764].

Finally, on 2 October 2014, less than ten days after the start of the strikes in Syria, Vice President Joe Biden, in a speech at Harvard University, emphasised the absence of an existential threat:

The threat posed by violent extremism is real. And I want to say here on the campus of Harvard University: our response must be very serious, but we

760. Shane Harris, 'We're Not Sure Their Capabilities Match Their Desire', *Foreign Policy*, September 23, 2014.
761. Ibid.
762. Mark Mazzetti, "A Terror Cell That Avoided the Spotlight", *The New York Times*, September 24, 2014.
763. CBS News, "U.S. offers more nuanced take on Khorasan threat," *Associated Press*, September 25, 2014
764. Andrew C. McCarthy, "The Khorosan Groups Does Not Exist", *National Review*, September 27, 2014.

must keep it in perspective. The United States today faces threats that demand attention. But we do not face existential threats to our way of life or our security. Let me repeat: we face no existential threats - none - to our way of life or our security. You are twice as likely to be struck by lightning as you are to be hit by a terrorist event in the US[765].

Thus, the "Khorasan" group was only an American invention. But contrary to what Thierry Meyssan suggests in his book *Sous nos yeux*[766], it never physically existed. Like the Iraqi weapons of mass destruction twelve years earlier, it was only a pretext created from scratch to justify a military intervention in Syria. This demonstrates that in 2014, shortly after its emergence, the Islamic State did not pose a threat to the West and, in any case, not a threat sufficient for Congress to authorise intervention in Syria. In turn, the pretext invoked in 2014 by the Hollande government to carry out strikes in Iraq, and then in Syria, was equally fallacious, as we shall detail below.

On January 12, 2015, six months after the mention of this shadowy group, a group called 'Khorasan Province' emerged in Pakistan. Created from a dissident Taliban group, it has nothing to do with the "Khorasan" group and aligns itself with the Islamic State. It was put on the US list of foreign terrorist movements on January 16, 2016…

6.9 "Islamic State Dreams of recreating the Abissidian Caliphate[767]"

The idea that Islamists are using terrorism to serve a global expansionist agenda has been widely propagated by US neo-conservative circles since 2001. Widely taken up by Western politicians and media, it has become a "post-truth", the purpose of which is to hide the only real reason that has been systematically repeated by terrorist groups since the 1990s, but which is being sought to be concealed: Western interventions in the Middle East.

On September 10 and 11, 2006, the American television channel ABC broadcast a two-part docudrama, *The Path to 9/11*, which retraced the genesis of the attacks and was picked up by a large number of media around the world[768]. The most notable of these is a 'fatwa' allegedly written by OBL, including the following sentence

765. "Biden at Harvard: America "Faces No Existential Threat" From Islamic Terrorism", *YouTube*, October 5, 2014 (https://www.youtube.com/watch?v=dOZfom5rI2U)
766. Thierry Meyssan, *Sous nos yeux: Du 11 Septembre à Donald Trump…*, Éditions Demi-lune, Paris, March 21, 2017
767. Vincent Georis, "L'État islamique, enfant du chaos et des errements de l'Occident", *L'Echo*, November 21, 2015
768. In Europe, the programme will be broadcast in Belgium on VT4 (two parts: September 13, 2006 at 21:05 and September 20, 2006 at 21:05) and on RTL-TVI (in three parts on August 20, 2008 at 21:10, 22:00 and 22:50).

There will be no room for negotiation until America converts to Islam[769].

Suggesting that OBL would have declared a "holy war" against the United States until it is converted to Islam... an idea that does not appear in any of his fatwas[770].

Under the pretext of not encouraging their propaganda, the media systematically conceal the explanations of the terrorists themselves. The result is a lack of transparency about their real motives, which has led to confusion between Islam and Islamism. The result has been a fear of Islam (in French: islamophobie) that has widened the gap between communities, particularly in France.

In 2012, the European police annual terrorism report EUROPOL, in its 2013 edition, (thus covering 2012, before the Western strikes in Syria) notes that the aspirations of the Islamic State of Iraq (ISI) are exclusively local:

> *The Islamic State in Iraq*[771] *has emphasised the local nature of its struggle and has deliberately abandoned the ideology and imprint of al-Qaeda and its global jihad*[772].

In April 2013, after engaging in eastern Syria, and supporting Jabhat al-Nosrah, the EII attempted to absorb it and took *the* name Islamic State in Iraq and the Levant *(EIIL)* (Dawlah al-Islamiyyah fi'l-Eiraq wal-Sham)[773]. The relationship between the two groups has had its ups and downs. In March 2014, Ayman al-Zawahiri - considered OBL's successor - disapproved of the creation of a Caliphate and confirmed their division. There was another brief attempt to merge in late June 2014[774], just before the EIIL became simply the Islamic State (EI) (Dawlah al-Islamiyyah) on June 29. Operationally, the two groups are essentially divided by personal rivalries, even though EI propaganda refers to differences in the application of the Koran. But, as Abu Mohammed al-Jaulani, leader of Jabhat al-Nosrah, points out:

---

769. See "The Path to 9/11" FABRICATED a Fatwa Quote! My Pulitzer Submission", *YouTube*, October 5, 2008
770. 1996 Fatwa: "*Declaration of War against the Americans Occupying the Land of the Two Holy Places*" (https://en.wikisource.org/wiki/Osama_bin_Laden%27s_Declaration_of_War) (translated by the West Point Military Academy); 1998 Fatwa: Declaration of the World Islamic Front on "*Jihad against Jews and Crusaders*" (https://fas.org/irp/world/para/docs/980223-fatwa.htm)
771. Strictly speaking, this is in fact the Islamic State of Iraq *(Dawlat al-'Eiraq al-Islamiyah)* and not 'in' Iraq *(Dawlah al-Islamiyah fil-'Eiraq)*
772. *TE-SAT 2013 - EU Terrorism Situation and Trend Report*, European Police Office, 2013, p. 21 (https://www.europol.europa.eu/content/te-sat-2013-eu-terrorism-situation-and-trend-report)
773. It is the abbreviation DAIESh (pronounced 'DASH' by some French officials) that refers only to an earlier form of the Islamic State. It is interesting to note, however, that the Western use of the former abbreviation of the movement (ISIS, ISIL or DAIESh) tends to be used in the literature of the Islamists themselves, as was once the case with 'Al Qaeda'.
774. Al-Qaeda merges with Isis at Syria-Iraq border town, *The Telegraph/AFP*, June 25, 2014.

In any case, the Islamic State in Syria will be built by everyone, without excluding any party that has participated in the jihad and fighting in Syria[775].

The fear expressed by some of a Caliphate, which would take over the whole Mediterranean area by launching large-scale military operations, is unfounded. In fact, this idea emerged within the US government. In September 2004, in Lake Elmo, Vice President Dick Cheney first raised the notion of a Caliphate that would directly threaten Western Europe, which he then attributed to "al-Qaeda":

They talk about wanting to re-establish what you might call the Caliphate of the seventh century. It's the way the world was organised 1200-1300 years ago, when Islam or Muslims controlled everything from Portugal and Spain in the West; across the Mediterranean to North Africa; all of North Africa; the Middle East; all the way to the Balkans; the Central Asian republics; the southern tip of Russia; much of India; and all the way to modern Indonesia. In a sense, from Bali and Jakarta at one end to Madrid at the other[776].

The idea was taken up in a report by the US National Intelligence Council (NIC) - an advisory board, part of the Intelligence Community - published in December 2004. Entitled "Modelling the Future of the World", it presents four scenarios for the possible evolution of the world by 2020, including the reconstitution of the Caliphate. This report, which is only a hypothesis, will however be presented by the Bush administration - and in the first place by the Secretary of Defense Donald Rumsfeld - as being the objective of "Al-Qaeda[777]":

They found that the high resonance of the use of the word 'caliphate' [has] an impact of almost instinctive terror.

A map attributed to the Islamic State, depicting its vision of a Caliphate stretching across the northern half of the African continent, Asia from the Mediterranean to India, Spain, central European countries and the Balkans, can be found online[778]. *Business Insider* confirms that this map is a fantasy[779]. It was

775. "La fulgurante ascension du Front Al-Nosra en Syrie", lemonde.fr/AFP/Reuters, April 10, 2013 (http://www.lemonde.fr/proche-orient/article/2013/04/10/la-fulgurante-ascension-du-front-al-nosra-en-syrie_3157351_3218.html#0DgjKhluqIpSqzHa.99)

776. *Vice President's Remarks and Q&A at a BC'04 Roundtable in Lake Elmo, Minnesota*, Office of the Vice President, September 29, 2004

777. Elisabeth Bumiller, "21st-Century Warnings of a Threat Rooted in the 7th ", *The New York Times*, December 12, 2005.

778. http://www.vox.com/2014/7/10/5884593/9-questions-about-the-caliphate-you-were-too-embarrassed-to-ask

779. Jeremy Bender, "That ISIS Five Year Expansion Plan Map Is Fake", *Business Insider*, July 1st, 2014

taken from the Twitter account of the neo-conservative organisation American Third Position (A3P)[780] and published on July 3, 2014 by US broadcaster *ABC News* to illustrate the expected advance of the EI[781]. There is no evidence to link it to Islamic State planning. It is used by far-right circles and intelligence services to exaggerate the terrorist threat; as Swiss intelligence director Markus Seiler on May 4, 2015 to justify the need for a more intrusive intelligence law.[782]

In January 2018, in a documentary broadcast on *France 3* and entitled *Complotisme, les alibis de la terreur*[783], the philosopher Jacob Rogozinski states:

> *Jihadism is also a movement that aims at sovereignty, at world power. There is a dream behind it, a crazy dream no doubt, but a dream of creating a caliphate, which would be a global caliphate, which will take over Rome, which will take over Europe, which will defeat America, which will establish a global network of true believers, united behind an absolute sovereign power*[784].

One conspiracy is denounced by another conspiracy. This is absurd and disingenuous. That today's EI has made the Abbasid Caliphate of the ninth century (and not the Caliphate of Abissidia - which never existed!) a mythical model is undeniable. It is also likely that some people have the idea of reconstituting it, but that the EI uses terrorist action for this purpose is false: it has never claimed to want to impose Islam on the West by means of terrorism. Attributing global ambitions to it only serves to distract from its basic message: to stop the interventions it is targeted with. Moreover, assuming, hypothetically, that he has plans to reconstitute this Caliphate, his action should focus primarily on the Muslim world itself, with Saudi Arabia in the lead, and not on Western countries - such as France, Germany or Sweden - which have never been part of it.

In France, a communitarianism based on the confusion between two distinct processes has taken hold:

the extension of the land of Islam (Dar al-Islam), which will most certainly be carried out without violence, through emigration, in a process that began several decades ago. This is how Islam spread in North Africa between the 7th and 9th centuries. An approach based on opportunistic dynamics and a certain candour of Western society, which served the interests of European left-wing parties and organisations. It will be the result of increasing

780. See: https://twitter.com/Third_Position/status/478626230418173952/photo/1?ref_src=twsrc%5Etfw

781. Colleen Curry, "See the Terrifying ISIS Map Showing Its 5-Year Expansion Plan", *ABC News*, July 3, 2014.

782. Sylvain Besson, "La loi sur le renseignement signe le retour en grâce des services secrets suisses", *Le Temps*, August 31, 2016

783. Rudy Reichstadt & Georges Benayoun, "Complotisme, les alibis de la terreur", *YouTube*, January 24, 2018, (www.youtube.com/watch?v=d8e18NIqWiI)

784. Jacob Rogozinski in "Complotisme, les alibis de la terreur", *YouTube*, January 24, 2018 (www.youtube.com/watch?v=d8e18NIqWi) (31'20")

migration flows and investments from the Gulf monarchies into Western countries. It is a process that is more likely to involve the financing of football clubs than terrorism:

the use of terrorism to pressure Western countries to abandon military interventions in Muslim countries. This is what jihad theorists call "*deterrence operations*", which is exactly consistent with the meaning of the word "jihad" in its military sense. They know that you cannot subjugate a country through terrorism, but you can influence its politics. Generally speaking, revolutionary theories that advocate the use of terrorism use it as a "detonator" to trigger wider actions. With jihadists, however, there is no revolutionary "critical mass" capable of generating statehood as an extension of a terrorist campaign, not even in Iraq, Libya or Syria. Indeed, even in these countries, Western countries have had to take over from the jihadists in order to build the critical mass that was missing to initiate a revolutionary process. A fortiori, this critical mass does not exist in the West, despite sympathies for the EI.

Moreover, the extension of the EI in Africa is not the product of a colonisation from Syria, but of a rallying of orphaned Islamist groups (sometimes created by Western action, as in Libya or in the Sahel) in search of legitimacy (as in Tunisia, Libya or Egypt). This phenomenon is identical to what was observed with 'Al-Qaeda' ten years earlier.

The image of Islamism conquering its past is nothing more than a lie to mask terrorism that results from ill-considered interventionist policies.

6.10. "The United States Created the Islamic State"

As we have already seen after the attacks of September 11, 2001 with "Al-Qaeda", the creation of the Islamic State (EI) (*al-Dawlah al-Islamiyyah*) is often explained by a Machiavellian plan concocted between Washington DC and Tel Aviv for reasons as diverse as they are obscure. In support of this theory, it is recalled that Abu Bakr al-Baghdadi was incarcerated in Iraq, in the Camp Bucca prison in Iraq, considered an "academy" of jihadism, and that he was released by the Americans (by design) in December 2004. This is a perfect illustration of a conspiracy theory, created from known and verifiable elements, but interpreted and assembled to create an artificial image.

After the overthrow of Saddam Hussein with the help of the Shiite opposition, the Americans have not been able to set up a state that harmoniously brings together the different components of Iraqi society. They see themselves as "liberators" and do not understand that their mere presence creates a resistance movement[785]. They did not foresee that by giving power to the country's Shiite majority they would trigger the Sunni resistance that would lead to "Al-Qaeda" and its variants up to the EI. By the end of 2003, there was already an influx of hundreds of foreign jihadists into Iraq, as confirmed by Osama Kashmoula, governor of Nineveh province:

> *Now Iraq is open to all terrorists [...] We have arrested Iranians, Jordanians, Palestinians, Algerians - I don't know the number*[786].

The *International Herald Tribune* notes that this is not a coordinated flow, but the addition of individual initiatives[787], just like ten years later in Syria.

To deal with this situation, the Americans rushed to rebuild the security forces. Between June 2004 and September 2005, they hastily distributed some 185,000 AKM/AK-47 assault rifles, 170,000 pistols, 215,000 bulletproof vests and 140,000 helmets. Until December 2004, the weapons were not registered (!). In total, 110,000 assault rifles and more than 80,000 pistols were disseminated, without it being known to whom they were distributed[788]. In fact, they worked like amateurs: in Afghanistan, they lost track of some 465,000 small arms distributed to Afghan armed forces and other 'friendly' factions, according to a report by the Special Inspector-General for Afghanistan Reconstruction, published in July 2014[789].

The "strategy" of General Petraeus, applied since 2007, based on the financing of local Sunni militias has often been described as an "innovative solution". This is not the case. Exploiting local rivalries and loyalties to solve insurgency problems is as old as the hills and had already been used successfully in Vietnam and Laos by the French and then by the Americans. The difference - and not the least - is that in Iraq, loyalties are no longer based on political ideology, tribal power or money, but on power relations between religious or even tribal communities, which American strategists did not understand. Thus, in their desire to "divide and rule", the United States distributed arms very liberally to various Sunni armed groups, which would be known collectively as the "Awakening Movement" *or the* "Sons of Iraq". The same groups that would form the basis of what would later become the Islamic State.

---

785. "Press Briefing by Ari Fleischer, *Office of the Press Secretary*, March 28, 2003

786. Ann Scott Tyson, "Iraq battles its leaking borders", *The Christian Science Monitor*, July 6, 2004.

787. Don Van Natta Jr & Desmiond Butler, 'Hundreds of militant head to Iraq for Jihad', *International Herald Tribune*, November 3, 2003.

788. "US 'loses track' of Iraq weapons", *BBC News*, August 6, 2007 (accessed June 20, 2014).

789. Special Inspector General for Afghanistan Reconstruction, *SIGAR 14-84 Audit Report - Afghan National Security Forces: Actions Needed to Improve Weapons Accountability*, (SIGAR 14-84-AR/ANSF Weapons Accountability), July 2014

To this is added the idea of splitting the countries of the region and maintaining permanent instability in order to contribute to Israel's security; but it is unlikely to include the creation of international terrorist groups, even if the development of the EI on Syrian territory has conveniently served the interests of the US, France and Israel, as we have seen.

Thus, the claim that the United States deliberately created an organisation called 'Islamic State' dedicated to terrorism for foreign policy purposes is certainly conspiratorial. On the other hand, if one accepts that the United States and its Western allies have been overwhelmed by a situation of their own making, and that their strategies have fostered the emergence of particularly brutal armed groups, then one is close to the truth.

The EI has its roots in Iraq, in the Group of Unity and Jihad (Jama'at al-Tawhid wal-Djihad), which appeared on April 24, 2004 as a resistance group to the American occupation. This Iraqi origin, now denied by the French government which seeks to attribute the emergence of the EI to Bashar al-Assad, is however clearly assumed by the Islamists themselves, as Abu Musab al-Zarqawi affirmed in September 2004[790]:

> *The spark has appeared here in Iraq and its heat will continue to grow - if Allah permits - until it burns the Crusaders in Dabiq*[791].

On October 17 of the same year, the group decided to give itself a broader base and took *the* name Organisation of the Base of Jihad in Mesopotamia (OBDM) (*Tanzim Qaidat al-Jihad fi Bilad al-Rafidain*). The word 'base' ('Qaeda') is then immediately interpreted as a declaration of affiliation to 'al-Qaeda'. However, its genesis and objectives were different from OBL's original demands: it was no longer about forcing the United States to leave the holy land of Saudi Arabia, but about resistance against military occupation. In January 2006, OBDM leader Abu Musab al-Zarqawi expanded his group to include various Sunni groups, creating the Advisory Council of the Mujahideen in Iraq (*Majlis Shura al-Mujahidin fi'l-Eiraq*). In October 2006, four months after al-Zarqawi's death, his successor, Abu Hamza al-Muhajir, integrated his forces into a newly created group led by Abu Omar al-Baghdadi: the Islamic State of Iraq (ISI) (*Dawlat al 'Eiraq al-Islamiyyah*).

The idea behind the creation of the EII was to overcome tribal quarrels and to federate under a single banner - that of jihad - the various armed groups

790. *Dabiq Magazine*, No. 8, March 2015 (Jumada al-Akhira 1436), p. 2.

791. Dabiq is a small town of some 3,000 inhabitants in Syria, close to the Turkish border, where Muhammad predicted a final battle with the Turks. It is somewhat equivalent to Meggido in the Bible (some believe it is the same city) where the final battle (Armageddon) against Satan should take place. "Dabiq" is also the name chosen for the official magazine of the Islamic State.

that were dispersed in personal quarrels; a dynamic that the Taliban had used successfully in 1996, and that the EI will use in Syria, by 'phagocytising' the other armed Islamist groups. This is confirmed by a report from the Joint Intelligence Committee (JIC), where the head of intelligence analysis for the British government stated in July 2006:

> *The label 'jihadist' is becoming increasingly difficult to define: in many cases, the distinction between nationalists and jihadists is blurred. They increasingly share a common cause, being united by Shia sectarian violence*[792].

In March 2007, the JIC confirmed that the resistance to the US invasion was indeed behind the establishment of EII ("Al Qaeda in Iraq"), which later became the EI:

> *There is no shortage of suicide commandos. AQ-I [Al Qaeda in Iraq] is looking for high-profile attacks. We believe that AQ-I will try to expand its sectarian campaign wherever possible: suicide bombings in Kirkuk have increased sharply since October, when AQ-I declared the creation of the "Islamic State of Iraq" (including Kirkuk)*[793].

The mechanics of jihadist radicalisation were therefore well known, but for political reasons, they refused to take them into account. The French government will make exactly the same mistake ten years later. Moreover, the dynamic map of the Syrian war shows that the EI developed from a gradual, but rapid, shift in allegiance of the US and French-backed opposition[794].

The 'debunking' offered by *Radio France* in June 2018 denies - rightly - American responsibility, but on the basis of false arguments. Marie Peltier, from the University of Brussels, explains that "DAECH" has its origins in Iraq, but she carefully avoids specifying that it was a resistance to Western intervention, aimed primarily at the United States, but also at those who supported it later, such as France and Belgium, for example. Furthermore, it claims that the US would not have the means to create a terrorist organisation in a foreign country. This is obviously not true, as it created, armed and supported the armed Islamist opposition in Syria, which later became part of the EI[795].

---

792. Patrick Wintour, "Intelligence files support claims Iraq invasion helped spawn Isis", *The Guardian*, July 6, 2016
793. Patrick Wintour, "Intelligence files support claims Iraq invasion helped spawn Isis", *The Guardian*, July 6, 2016
794. "Syrian Civil War: Every Day", *NY Mapper/YouTube*, 17 March 2018
795. "Les idées claires: Daech a-t-il été créé par les États-Unis ?", *franceinfo/Radio France*, June 12, 2018 (updated June 13, 2018)

What Ms Peltier has not understood (or does not want to say) is that the situation of the Islamic State in Iraq and the Levant (EIIL or "DAECH") is not symmetrical: in Iraq, it threatens the stability of the central government in Baghdad and the embryonic Kurdish state set up by the United States and its Western allies; whereas in Syria, it is a useful ally in the fight against the "regime" of Bashar al-Assad.

In Syria, the Western interest was to have a sufficiently powerful, violent and radical rebel force to provoke a brutal response from the government, and thus justify its overthrow or force it to negotiate. So they watched the emergence of the EI, Machiavellianly, but mostly out of naivety and incompetence, and deliberately allowed it to develop in the belief that it would serve their purposes. Without measuring the consequences... Moreover, John Kerry himself admitted it in autumn 2016:

> *And we knew it [DAECH] was growing. We were watching. We saw that Daech was becoming more and more powerful and we thought that Assad was threatened. But we thought that we could probably get Assad to negotiate next. Instead of negotiating, he asked Putin for help*[796].

Thus, neither the US nor France 'created' the EI. But they have done everything to ensure that it develops in order to serve their immediate interests opportunistically[797]. This explains the confession of Lieutenant-General Michael Flynn, former Commander of the Joint Special Operations Command (USSOCOM) (2004-2007) and Director of the DIA at that time:

> *I think it was a deliberate decision [by the government]*[798] *!*

Moreover, the Americans knew from the beginning that the EI was financed and materially supported by Saudi Arabia and Qatar: in an email of August 19, 2014 sent by John Podesta to Hillary Clinton, then published by Wikileaks in 2016, it is stated:

> *We must use our traditional diplomatic and intelligence resources to pressure the governments of Qatar and Saudi Arabia, which provide clandestine*

796. John Kerry, Wikileaks recording of a meeting on September 22, 2016 ("Leaked audio of John Kerry's meeting with Syrian revolutionaries/UN (improved audio)", *YouTube*, October 4, 2016)
797. "Former DIA Chief Michael Flynn Says Rise of ISIS Was a "Willful Decision" of US Government", *YouTube*, October 6, 2015
798. "Ex-DIA boss Michael Flynn: White House took 'willful decision' to fund, train Syria Islamists ISIS", *YouTube*, August 23, 2015.

financial and logistical support to EIIL and other radical Sunni groups in the region[799].

This is not completely new, as Qatar had already armed the Islamists in Libya. All this information was known. But, obviously, you don't bite the hand that feeds you: Qatar and Saudi Arabia are then respectively the first and third client of France in terms of arms!

The responsibility of the West for the emergence of the EI in Syria is clear. However, it is not the product of superior intelligence (which would be a conspiracy!), but rather of their inability to manage the situation resulting from the decay of the Iraqi state.

Just after the January 2015 attacks, some commentators on social networks had noted that the virulence of the French discourse against the EI risked promoting it to the rank of the main defender of Islam against Western aggression. They were right, as Abu Bakr al-Baghdadi, the leader of the EI, himself confirms:

> *The sheer size of the forces amassed to fight the Islamic State is a testament to its strength and that it is on the right path*[800].

Through ignorance or design, people refuse to understand that the war on terror is asymmetric in nature. By hiding the messages of the EI, the media has only reinforced its notoriety and dramatically affected our understanding of jihadism. We are thus applying power-based strategies that work with criminal gangs, but have the opposite effect in a jihadist context.

In conclusion, the Americans became involved against the EI because it threatened to destabilise Iraq, with the idea of "pushing" it into Syria and weakening the Alawite power. France had no reason to become openly involved in Iraq, but it did so with the secret wish to switch at some point to Syria, where it was already operating clandestinely, in order to overthrow the government. As was perfectly foreseeable, terrorism gave it this opportunity, at the cost of more than 250 victims in metropolitan France. It is surprising that citizens and victims' associations did not turn against those who were really responsible for this situation: those who took these decisions, refusing to use democratic mechanisms to engage in adventures that *we knew* would put the lives of innocent people at stake.

---

799. wikileaks.org/podesta-emails/emailid/3774; Bethan McKernan. "Hillary Clinton emails leak: Wikileaks documents claim Democratic nominee 'thinks Saudi Arabia and Qatar fund Isis'", *The Independent*, October 11, 2016
800. Quote from a chat captured in April 2017.

6.11. "Israel Created the Islamic State"

The Islamic State (IS) has been portrayed as messianically driven, fighting the 'unbelievers', dedicated to rebuilding the Abbasid caliphate and - of course - anti-Semitic. Yet, despite its involvement in the Syrian conflict, Israel is spared by the EI. It does not take much more to draw the conclusion that there is a collusion between the two, and to deduce the most diverse conspiracy theories.

On the simplistic end of the conspiracy theory spectrum, some point to the similarity between 'ISIS', the English abbreviation for the EI, and 'ISIS' ('*Israeli Secret Intelligence Service*')[801]... all the more stupid as neither abbreviation is official! The next level is the claim that the leader of the EI, Abu Bakr Al-Baghdadi, was in fact an Israeli agent, whose real name is Simon Eliott. Attributed to Edward Snowden, the information actually comes from a Facebook post, without any source indicated. The Israelis would thus seek to create chaos and a partition of Syrian territory. That they have such an objective is more than likely, as we shall see, but that they have chosen this method to achieve it is a gratuitous allegation.

Nevertheless, the relationship between the EI and Israel is ambiguous. In September 2014, the Israeli government proclaimed that the EI and Hamas share the same ideology[802] in order to justify the brutality of its intervention in Gaza in August. But when the West mobilises against the EI, Israel is reluctant. In August 2015, the Israeli army listed Iran and Syria as its top threats, followed by Hamas and Hezbollah, while the EI was only mentioned at the end of the list, under the heading "and others" and not at all in the rest of the document[803].

In January 2016, Moshe Ya'alon, Minister of Defence, states:

> *In Syria, if I had the choice between Iran and the Islamic State, I would choose the Islamic State*[804].

Five months later, at a conference in Herzliyya, Israeli Major General Herzi Halevy, head of military intelligence (AMAN), declared that Israel did not want a situation where:

---

801. "ISIS = MOSSAD (Israeli Secret Intelligence Service) - 100% PROOF", *YouTube*, January 5, 2017

802. Yaara Shalom, "Netanyahu: Hamas, Islamic State share the same fanatic ideology", *ynetnews.com*, September 29, 2014

803. *Deterring Terror - How Israel Confronts the Next Generation of Threats*, Belfer Center for Science and International Affairs, Harvard Kennedy School, Cambridge (MA), August 2016

804. Yoav Zitun, Tova Tzimuki and Moran Azulay, 'Ya'alon: In choice between Iran and ISIS, I prefer ISIS', www.ynetnews.com, January 19, 2016; Judah Ari Gross, 'Ya'alon: I would prefer Islamic State to Iran in Syria', *The Times of Israel*, January 19, 2016.

[...] the EI has been defeated, it has been contained, its influence has been reduced; the superpowers have left the area and we are stuck with radical forces with Hezbollah and Iran[805] *[...]*

On November 27, 2016, in the Golan Heights, on the Syrian border, an Israeli patrol was attacked by jihadists from the *Yarmouk Martyrs Brigade* (*Liwa Shuhada al-Yarmouk*) associated with the EI[806]. Contrary to its usual policy, Israel did not retaliate. The incident is noted by the magazine *Le Point*[807]... But of course, a few months later, in April 2017, it will fail to mention that the EI would have apologised to the Jewish state by claiming to have struck it by mistake, according to the *Times of Israel*[808].

Moreover, it can be observed that the EI pocket that developed on the Israeli-Syrian border between 2017 and 2018, did not suffer any Western strikes[809]. Through local agreements, it even took over territory from 'moderate' groups, notably in the Daraa area in July 2018. In fact, Israel cooperates with Islamist movements such as Jabhat al-Nosrah or even the EI: it has armed and financed at least 12 jihadist groups, paid their fighters $75 per month, provided them with weapons, as well as funds to acquire equipment on the black market. Its objective is to keep the pro-Syrian militias away from the Israeli border[810].

This leniency towards the Islamists tends to confirm the hypothesis of a deliberate policy to maintain the Syrian territory in an unstable balance in the medium and long term. For Israel, the EI is a bulwark against Iranian influence and an ally in the fight against Hezbollah. This is confirmed by an Israeli think-tank - financed (among others) by Nato in the framework of its Mediterranean Dialogue[811] - in a report entitled *Destroying the Islamic State is a strategic mistake*, in which it postulates that the Islamic State "*can be a useful instrument to weaken Tehran's ambitious plan to dominate the Middle East*[812]". This is in line with the intellectual continuity of the Yinon report... Thus, while Israel certainly did not create the Islamic State, it benefits from its presence and a kind of unofficial and informal alliance.

805. Jason Ditz, "Israeli Intel Chief: We Don't Want ISIS Defeated in Syria", *Antiwar.com*, June 21, 2016; "Chief of Israeli Military Intelligence - 'Israel Doesn't Want Isis Defeated'", *YouTube*, May 1st, 2017

806. Aymenn Jawad Al-Tamimi, "The First Connections Between Liwa Shuhada' al-Yarmouk and Islamic State", www.aymennjawad.org, March 19, 2016

807. Armin Arefi, "Why Israel has (long) escaped from Daech", *Le Point*, November 29, 2016

808. Judah Ari Gross, "Ex-defense minister says IS 'apologized' to Israel for November clash", *The Times of Israel*, April 24, 2017 (http://www.timesofisrael.com ex-defense-minister-says-is -apologized-to-israel-for-november-clash/)

809. BBC, op.cit.

810. Elizabeth Tsurkov, "Inside Israel's Secret Program to Back Syrian Rebels", *Foreign Policy*, September 6, 2018

811. http://besacenter.org/about/international-support/#.XTX2cegzaUk

812. Prof. Efraim Inbar, *The Destruction of Islamic State is a Strategic Mistake*, Begin-Sadat Center for Strategic Studies, Perspectives Paper No. 352, August 2, 2016

Moreover, the EI has even declared war on the Palestinian Hamas because it is not fighting for religion but for a land[813]!... This highlights the "infoxes" propagated by the traditional media, such as *Le Figaro*, relaying the words of Anne-Clémentine Larroque, who puts all Islamic groups in the same basket[814]. This confirms that the Israeli-Palestinian conflict has nothing to do with religion, but is strictly territorial in nature.

Ironically, what we see as an almost existential threat in Europe is seen as insignificant in Israel. It's logical, the Israelis have understood that if left alone, the EI is not an essential threat. It's very simple: all they had to do was listen to what the British services had been saying since 2005... While in the West - and in France in particular - there is a tendency to hit hard at all those who might have, in one way or another, approved or even explained[815] the action of the EI, a much less scrupulous pragmatism prevails in Israel...

6.12. "France is in Iraq and Syria to Fight the Islamic State"

6.12.1. The context

In the aftermath of the Libyan conflict, France and the United States began to clandestinely support the revolution in Syria. In fact, according to General Dominique Delawarde[816], strikes on Syria had already been planned as early as January 2012[817], i.e. more than two years before the appearance of the Islamic State (EI) in Syria, at the end of June 2014!

Elected president in May 2012, François Hollande saw his popularity plummet quite rapidly and dramatically. In January 2013, however, the intervention in Mali (Operation SERVAL) seems to bring a respite to this fall. But the government continues to look for a credible pretext to officially intervene and overthrow Bashar al-Assad. In August, it will try to exploit the chemical attack in Ghouta to justify an armed intervention. But France does not have the capacity to act independently and Barack Obama does not commit himself: an unfavourable public opinion and the doubts of his intelligence services on

813. Iyad Abuheweila & Isabel Kershner, "Islamic State declares war on Hamas as Gaza families disown sons in Sinai", *The Irish Times*, January 11, 2018

814. Eugénie Bastié, "Hamas, Frères musulmans, djihadistes: les différents visages de l'islamisme", *lefigaro.fr*, August 8, 2014

815. "For Valls, there can be no possible 'explanation' for the acts of jihadists", *Le Figaro.fr*, January 9, 2016

816. General Dominique Delawarde is the former head of the situation-intelligence-electronic warfare office of the joint operational planning staff in the Paris region (Mohamed El-Ghazi, "Un général français: " François Hollande nous manipule", *Réseau international*, September 15, 2013)

817. Jean Guisnel, "Armes chimiques : Paris préparait une action militaire en Syrie depuis début 2012", *Le Point.fr*, September 20, 2013

the authorship of the attack compromise an approval of the Congress. In the absence of a proven threat, the Americans create the "*Khorasan Group*" out of thin air in order to justify an engagement in "self-defence".

6.12.2. The Strategy and Relevance of the Action

The war against the EI is only a pretext. The initial objective of the West was not to fight the EI, but to overthrow the Syrian government. The emergence and rise of the EIIL is the result of the US intervention in Iraq. It was because it threatened the fragile Iraqi and Kurdish states set up by the Americans that the US formed its international coalition. In a second phase, it was because the West was ineffective against the EI in Syria that Russia had to intervene. It was only after the 2015 attacks that France placed the terrorist group at the centre of its official discourse and used it as a pretext to pursue its objective of overthrowing the Syrian government.

In fact, the situation of *the* Islamic State in Iraq and the Levant (ISIL) is asymmetrical: in Iraq, it is disrupting the installation of a government set up by the United States and its Western allies, while in Syria, the ISIL is a useful ally in the fight against Bashar al-Assad's "regime" and Iranian influence. It is therefore treated differently in the two theatres. Moreover, in August 2016, the Begin-Sadat Center for Strategic Studies (BESA), an Israeli think-tank (funded by Canada, the United States and Nato, among others), published a paper explaining that destroying the Islamic State would be a "*strategic mistake*" and that cooperating with Russia against the EI is a "*strategic folly*" that only "*strengthens the Moscow-Tehran-Damascus axis*[818]". But of course, the European media avoids this delicate subject.

A US Defense Intelligence Agency (DIA) SECRET 'intelligence report' on the situation in Syria, dated August 5, 2012, clearly identifies the advantage of supporting Syrian Islamists despite the risks of an Islamic state emerging:

> *If the situation allows it, there is the possibility of establishing a declared or undeclared Salafist principality in Eastern Syria (Hasaka and Deir ez-Zor), and this is exactly what the countries supporting the opposition want in order to isolate the Syrian regime, which is seen as the strategic depth of Shiite expansion (Iraq and Iran)*[819].

818. Prof. Efraim Inbar, "The Destruction of Islamic State is a Strategic Mistake", *BESA Center Perspectives*, Paper No. 353, August 2, 2016

819. Brad Hoff, "West will facilitate rise of Islamic State "in order to isolate the Syrian regime: 2012 DIA document", *Foreign Policy Journal*, May 21, 2015; see also: http://www.judicialwatch.org/wp-content/uploads/2015/05/Pg.-291-Pgs.-287-293-JW-v-DOD-and-State-14-812-DOD-Release-2015-04-10-final-version11.pdf

The key to this strategy is a partition of Syria, of which there are several models. The most frequently mentioned is that of a break-up of Syria into a Kurdish state in the north-east, a Sunni state in the south-east and a Christian-Alawite state in the west of the country, on the coast. It recalls the Yinon Plan of 1982, already mentioned, and explains the convergence of Western and Israeli strategies. This idea is known, but it is hidden that it originated in Israel. It is even attributed to the Syrian government[820], as *Le Figaro*[821]! *France 24* goes further by saying that it is Bashar al-Assad's "*Plan B*"[822]. But this is a lie: the Syrian leader has never mentioned a partition of his country, but on the contrary, seeks to restore its integrity[823]. Moreover, the recapture of his territory in 2013 is proof of this. In fact, the notion of '*Plan B*' is that of the Obama administration: John Kerry, then Secretary of State, mentioned it during a hearing before the Senate Foreign Affairs Committee in February 2016[824]. It was taken up by Secretary of State Rex Tillerson at Stanford University on January 17, 2018, in line with the coalition's operational strategy[825].

This explains why, during the capture of Mosul in 2016, the coalition had left a free corridor for Islamic State fighters to reach Syria[826]. The website *Airwars.org* records the international coalition's air actions in the Middle East and their casualties[827]. If we superimpose the map of Western strikes and the map of the territories still held by the EI published by the *BBC*[828], we can see that there have been no strikes in the EI's regrouping areas in south-eastern Syria and that the coalition has clearly sought to 'channel' it towards this area. Moreover, it is strangely inactive when it comes to preventing the group from pushing towards Damascus[829]. Sometimes the Western coalition even strikes the Syrian army or the Christian allied forces facing it.

---

820. Laurent Lagneau, "For Mr. Ayrault, Damascus 'plays the partition card' of Syria", *OPEX360.com*, September 24, 2016

821. Isabelle Lasserre, "Khaddam: 'Assad plans the partition of Syria'", *lefigaro.fr*, January 25, 2012

822. Amara Makhoul-Yatim, "Towards a partition of Syria (second part)", *France24*, May 17, 2013 (updated May 31, 2013)

823. Margaret Brennan, "If Syria cease-fire fails, is there a Plan-B?", *CBS News*, February 25, 2016

824. Patrick Wintour, "John Kerry says partition of Syria could be part of 'plan B' if peace talks fail", *The Guardian*, February 23, 2016

825. Jeff Mackler, op.cit.

826. Simon Mabon, "Even if Mosul is liberated, it won't be the end of Islamic State", *The Conversation*, October 17, 2016

827. See airwars.org/data/.

828. Islamic State and the crisis in Iraq and Syria in maps, BBC News, March 28, 2018 (www.bbc.com/news/world-middle-east-27838034)

829. James Dobbins, Jeffrey Martini & Philip Gordon, "A Peace Plan for Syria", *Rand Corporation*, 2015 (Document PE-182-RC); Jeff Mackler, "The US Plan to Partition Syria", *Counterpunch*, February 9, 2018; Nafeez Mosaddeq Ahmed, "US military document reveals how the West opposed a democratic Syria", *mondiplo.com*, September 24, 2018

The most famous example took place on September 17, 2016, when American, Australian[830], Danish and British planes of the international coalition broke the ceasefire negotiated with Russia and struck the Syrian air base of Deir ez-Zor for 45 minutes, killing more than 80 Syrian soldiers. The garrison of the base is led by a Druze general and protects the (Sunni) city, which has been surrounded for more than two years by the EI, to the exclusion of any other rebel formation. The Western strikes allowed the EI to seize the Jabal al-Tharda heights, which dominate the base, making air supply to the base and Syrian strikes on the besiegers almost impossible[831].

Later, the Americans would explain that it was a simple mistake[832]. However, the excuse is a thin one. Firstly, because the Americans had made exactly the same 'mistake' a few months earlier[833]. Secondly, because irregularities highlighted by the US Central Command investigation report[834] and the Intelligence Veterans Association show that:

the Americans misled the Russians about the target locations, so that the Russians could not inform the Syrians that they were being targeted;

those responsible for the targeting ignored intelligence analysis that warned that the targeted positions were Syrian and not Islamic State;

there has been an abrupt shift from a planned targeting process to a 'dynamic targeting' (or 'opportunity shooting') mode with unplanned target selection[835].

As the UN notes, by the end of 2017, Western strikes have simply forced EI fighters to 'blend in' to the landscape[836] and continue their fight within other militant groups. This is also what explains the "radicalisation" of the "moderate" rebels protected and supported by the West.

830. "Australian jets involved in US-led air strike which killed dozens of Syrian soldiers, Defence confirms", *ABC Net*, September 18, 2016

831. According to the *Times of Israel*, the Russians managed, through electronic intelligence, to obtain enough evidence of collusion between Islamic State and Western forces to strike the offending command post with cruise missiles on September 20, killing several American, Qatari, Israeli and Turkish officers (Judah Ari Gross, "Russia: Mossad, other foreign agents killed in Aleppo strike", *The Times of Israel*, September 22, 2016). To what extent the latter information (which has hardly been reported in the Western press) is true is an open question. It should be noted, however, that in situations where clandestine actors are involved, the lack of reaction from the offending countries can be explained, without constituting "proof".

832. Anne Barnard & Mark Mazzetti, "U.S. Admits Airstrike in Syria, Meant to Hit ISIS, Killed Syrian Troops", *The New York Times*, September 17, 2016

833. "U.S. rejects Syrian claim state forces were targeted", *CBS News*, December 7, 2015

834. www.centcom.mil/Portals/6/media/REDACTED_FINAL_XSUM_Memorandum__29_Nov_16___CLEAR.pdf

835. Gareth Porter, "The 'Mistaken'US Airstrike on Syrian Troops", *consortiumnews.com*, December 7, 2016

836. *Eighth report of the Secretary-General on the threat posed by EIIL (Daech) to international peace and security and on the efforts of the United Nations to assist Member States in countering that threat*, United Nations, February 1st, 2019, (S/2019/103) para 5

Between December 2018 and March 2019, Donald Trump announced no less than 16 times[837] the defeat of the Islamic State. Yet it is still considered a threat[838]. In his report to Congress, the Inspector General of Operation INHERENT RESOLVE states that the IS is, in fact, believed to have between 14,000 and 18,000 'members' and 'fighters' (with no way to distinguish between the two[839]). But these figures are based on press reports and Brigadier General Yahya Rassoul, spokesman for the Joint Staff of the operation, says that they are "*greatly exaggerated*" and that:

> *Islamic State elements in these areas [NdA: Iraq and Syria] do not exceed a few dozen [people] deployed in small groups of three to five militants*[840].

In January 2015, after the attack on Charlie Hebdo, François Hollande declared:

> *You can murder men and women, but you never kill their ideas, on the contrary*[841].

He was right, but he failed to integrate this thinking into a coherent strategy against the EI. As a result, his strategy is directly responsible for the attacks that France has suffered. Finally, Abu Bakr al-Baghdadi was eliminated on October 27, 2019 in the Idlib pocket, controlled by militias trained by the Coalition's special forces and in an area that the West had done everything to protect from the actions of the Syrian army...[842]

6.13. "The White Helmets [...]: Neutral, Impartial and Apolitical[843]"

In 2014, most of the information on rebel areas came from a self-declared Syrian humanitarian non-governmental organisation: the White Helmets. Received and given a standing ovation by the National Assembly in Paris in 2016, they have strong support from France (notably from Foreign Minister

---

837. Ellen Mitchell, "16 times Trump said ISIS was defeated, or soon would be", *The Hill*, March 23, 2019
838. "IS 'caliphate' defeated but jihadist group remains a threat", *BBC News*, March 23, 2019
839. *Operation Inherent Resolve, Lead Inspector General Report To The United States Congress, April 1, 2019. June 30, 2019*, US Department Of Defense, August 2019, p. 15
840. Sangar Ali, 'Iraq rejects Pentagon's report claiming 14,000 ISIS fighters' presence in Iraq, Syria', *Kurdistan24.net*, August 12, 2019
841. "François Hollande: 'Charlie Hebdo lives and will live'", *BFM TV*, January 14, 2015
842. Courtney Kube, Dennis Romero, Hallie Jackson & Daniella Silva, "ISIS leader Abu Bakr al-Baghdadi killed in U.S. raid in Syria, Trump confirms," *NBC News*, October 27, 2019
843. *Le Temps*, August 27, 2016

Ayrault and President François Hollande), which supported their nomination for the Nobel Peace Prize in 2016[844].

Using the same logo and uniform as the Syrian Civil Defence (founded in 1953 and operating throughout Syria), the "White Helmets" are not recognised by the International Civil Defence Organisation (ICDO)[845] and do not answer the official Civil Defence emergency telephone number ("113"), which is accessible throughout Syria.

They were founded in March 2013 in Turkey[846] by James Le Mesurier, a British ex-military man. Their funding structure includes the Syria Campaign, the Netherlands-based NGO Mayday Rescue and the USAID-funded firm Chemonics[847], which collects donor funds and redistributes them to the field. Its main donors are the Netherlands with €4 million (2015)[848], the UK with £38.4 million (May 2918)[849] and the US with $33 million (May 2018)[850]. This does not prevent it from claiming that it is "*fiercely independent and has not accepted any funding from governments, corporations or anyone directly involved in the Syrian conflict*[851]"!

On 18 April 2016, despite these prestigious sponsorships, Raed Saleh, leader of the White Helmets, was turned away on arrival at Washington DC's Dulles Airport[852]. He was unable to attend the InterAction dinner, which was to honour the work of his organisation: his visa to enter the United States was revoked as he could pose a security risk[853]! In February 2017, a documentary film about the White Helmets won an Academy Award, but Raed Saleh was also unable to attend the awards ceremony. Officially, due to the situation in Syria[854].

In reality, the White Helmets only operate in areas hostile to the Syrian government and in the hands of Jabhat al-Nosrah[855]. Numerous videos show

---

844. The nomination of the White Helmets for the Nobel Peace Prize was supported by France, and its leaders were received at the Elysée Palace, without raising questions from French parliamentarians (Images for informed public only) (www.youtube.com/watch?v=1t8Wo8U2uF8&) (video removed)

845. See Article "International Civil Defence Organisation", Wikipedia

846. Presentation at "The Performance Theatre", "Lieutenant-General Sir Graeme Lamb; and James Le Mesurier, director of Mayday Rescue, Syria Civil Defence", *Vimeo,* Lisbon, June 26, 2015

847. https://syriacivildefense.org/our-partners (accessed February 15, 2019)

848. Rijksoverheid, *Nederland steunt Syrische reddingswerkers*, December 3, 2015

849. Karen McVeigh, "UK may increase aid to Syrian White Helmets after Trump pulls funding", *The Guardian*, May 10, 2018

850. Conor Finnegan, "Trump's Syria aid freeze hits 'White Helmets' rescue workers", *ABC News*, May 4, 2018

851. https://thesyriacampaign.org/about/

852. Natasha Bertrand, "A man who has helped save more than 40,000 lives in Syria was just denied entry into the US", *Business Insider*, April 20, 2016

853. Mark C. Toner, Spokesperson for the U.S. Department of State ("Daily Press Briefing - April 27, 2016", *YouTube/ U.S. Department of State*, April 27, 2016) (06'20")

854. "The White Helmets" Best Documentary Short Subject - Oscars 2017 | Full Backstage Interview", *Variety/ YouTube*, February 26, 2017 (02'10")

855. The al-Nosrah Front became the Levant Conquest Front (Jabhat Fath al-Sham) in January 2012, and then regrouped with other "moderate" rebel groups to form the Levant Liberation Assembly (Hayat Tahrir al-Sham) in

some of its members participating in the beheading of little Abdullah Issa by militants of the Nur al-Din al-Zinki Movement[856], or with weapons and an Islamist flag in hand. British journalist Vanessa Beeley posted videos on *YouTube* showing White Helmets participating in the making of the '*Mortars of Hell*', which project 'barrel bombs'[857]. Just after the recapture of East Aleppo, the young French development worker Pierre le Corf visited the White Helmets' headquarters and noted the collusion with Jabhat al-Nosrah[858]. This does not prevent Agnès Levallois, on *France 5,* from underlining the "*quite remarkable*" character of the organisation[859]... which will be allied with Turkey during its October 2019 offensive against the Syrian Kurds!

In March 2018, President Trump decided to freeze $200 million in funding for Syrian rebel movements, including the White Helmets[860]. The decision took effect in early May. However, in June, he backtracks in the name of collaboration with British and French intelligence and releases $6.6 million for the White Helmets[861]. In July 2018, cornered on the Golan Heights border, 422 White Helmets members with their families are quietly exfiltrated from Syria by Britain and some allies, with the help of Jordan and Israel, to remove them from the advance of Syrian forces[862]. Echoing his official Foreign Office statement[863], the former British ambassador to Syria (2003-2006) suggests that there are likely to be concerns that they could be questioned and provide information about chemical attacks[864].

Cooperation between the White Helmets and jihadist groups is widely seen as "conspiratorial" in the West[865]. Yet an examination of the Facebook accounts of 65 members of the White Helmets shows their close links with Jabhat al-Nosrah, Jound al-Aqsa, Ahrar al-Sham, Jaish al-Islam and the Islamic State[866].

January 2017.

856. "Syria White Helmets Hand In Hand with Al Qaeda", *YouTube*, January 22, 2017, (www.youtube.com/watch?v=OBkn78q_t_Q)

857. "White Helmet Equipment Used to Build Terrorist Hell Cannon?", *YouTube*, May 29, 2018

858. "ALEP: Pierre Le Corf visits WHITE HELMETS HQ", *YouTube*, March 11, 2017, (www.youtube.com/watch?v=ZWxQHPwoNMk)

859. Émission "C dans l'air", "Syrie : le coup de force de Poutine #cdanslair 28-09-2016", *YouTube/France 5*, September 28, 2016 (19'15")

860. Conor Finnegan, *op. cit.*

861. "U.S., Relenting, Releases Funding for Syrian 'White Helmets'", *The Wall Street Journal*, June 14, 2018

862. Seth J. Frantzman, "Israel Evacuates Hundreds of Syrian White Helmets in Humanitarian Effort", *The Jerusalem Post*, July 22, 2018

863. "Press release - Resettlement of White Helmets from Syria: statement", *Department for International Development, Foreign & Commonwealth Office*, July 22, 2018

864. Vanessa Beeley, "Former UK Ambassador Slams Government Statement on Syria's White Helmets", *Mint Pres News*, July 23, 2018

865. Nick Robins-Early, '5 Major Myths About Syria Debunked', *Huffington Post*, January 10, 2017 (updated January 11, 2017); Olivia Solon, 'How Syria's White Helmets became victims of an online propaganda machine', *The Guardian*, December 18, 2017

866. "White Helmets Exposed as Extremists: 65 Facebook profiles of Their Members", *Syrian War Blog*, November 14, 2017

The French government should explain which side it is actually supporting in this war…

In 2018, the Netherlands decided to stop its aid to Syrian rebels and the White Helmets after having given them a total of approximately €12.5 million. In an evaluation report presented to Parliament on 7 September, the Ministry of Foreign Affairs pointed out that the money paid to the White Helmets was not traceable in the field and was likely to have been used to acquire weapons. Furthermore, the Netherlands has judged the groups that the organisation supports on the ground as "unacceptable": it is the first Western country to acknowledge that its efforts have supported illegal and criminal activities[867]. But no mainstream French media relayed the Dutch decision.

At the end of 2019, Le Mesurier discovered a case of embezzlement within the White Helmets[868]. On November 11, 2019, he was found dead at the bottom of his building in Istanbul[869]. His death remains unexplained, but the British mainstream media attempts to rewrite his biography by erasing his links to the intelligence services and Mayday Rescue. [870]

6.14. "The Syrian Regime and Russia are Destroying Aleppo"

The recapture of East Aleppo has been widely presented in the West as a brutal battle against moderate rebels, victims of the Syrian government. At no point is there any mention of the fact that in 2012, at the beginning of the rebel presence in the city, when there was no fighting yet, nearly 600,000 inhabitants, i.e. the majority of the population, moved to West Aleppo preferring the government of Bashar al-Assad to the rebels supported by the West[871].

6.14.1. The Nature of the Opposition

In September 2016, *France 5* devoted a "C dans l'air" programme to the situation in Aleppo[872]. According to the 'experts' present, it is civil society that is opposing the Syrian government. According to Agnès Levallois, the forces

---

867. Ana van Es, "Nederland stopt steun aan Syrische oppositie wegens gebrekkig toezicht op hulpprojecten; Britse organisatie ontkent kritiek", *de Volkskrant*, September 10, 2018; "The Netherlands stops supporting Syrian rebels, ahead of Idlib offensive", *DutchNews.nl*, September 10, 2018

868. Janene Pieters, "Dutch accountant uncovers fraud behind Syria rescue organization White Helmets: report", *NLTimes.nl*, July 17, 2020; Ana van Es & Anneke Stoffelen, "Founder of Foundation behind White Helmets Admits Fraud", *De Volkskrant*, 17 July 2020

869. "White Helmets backer James Le Mesurier found dead in Turkey", *Middle East Eye*, November 11, 2019

870. Vanessa Beeley, "After His Mysterious Death, the Media Scrambles to Get its Story Straight About White Helmets Founder James Le Mesurier", *mintpressnews*, December 2, 2019

871. Vanessa Beeley in "Why Everything You Hear About Aleppo Is Wrong", *Ron Paul Liberty Report/YouTube*, September 29, 2016

872. Program "C dans l'air", "Syria: Putin's power grab #cdanslair 28-09-2016", *YouTube/France 5*, September 28, 2016

in Syria are divided between Bashar al-Assad's militias, the opposition and the Islamic State[873]! As the Islamic State is not present in East Aleppo, only the "*Bashar militias*" and the moderate opposition remain. This corresponds to a commonly accepted discourse on Syria, which aims to systematically minimise the importance of jihadist groups, in order to present a more 'acceptable' opposition and to remove any legitimacy to government action. For example, in October 2016, Staffan de Mistura, the UN special envoy for Syria, claimed that Jabhat Fath al-Sham had at most 900 fighters (or about 11% of rebel capacity) in East Aleppo[874]. This is disinformation. Already in 2012, the American journalist James Foley (who would be murdered by the Islamic State a few days later) noted:

> *Aleppo, a city of about 3 million people, was once the financial heart of Syria. As the situation continues to deteriorate, many civilians are losing patience with the increasingly violent and unrecognisable opposition - which is riddled with infighting and lack of structure, and deeply infiltrated by foreign fighters and terrorist groups*[875].

On 9 September 2016, the Americans and Russians concluded a ceasefire for East Aleppo. It was not negotiated with all parties, and the Americans - unlike the Russians - want to keep it secret[876]. One of its objectives is to separate the 'moderate' rebels from Islamist groups associated with 'al-Qaeda', notably the Army of Conquest (Jaish al-Fatah), (90% of which is made up of Jabhat Fath al-Sham *and* Ahrar al-Sham, another jihadist group), as well as to encourage the departure of civilians from the combat zone.

For the Americans, the objective is to "recover" the "moderate opposition" in order to continue the fight against the regime. The lie of a "moderate opposition" in East Aleppo appeared ten days after the signing of the agreement, when Mohammed al-Ghazi, leader of the *Tajammu Fastaqim Kama Umirt* (then a component of the so-called moderate "Free Syrian Army") announced that his group would not separate from the Islamists of the Fath al-Sham[877]. But this is not a surprise, because already in April, Colonel Steve Warren, American spokesman for Operation INHERENT RESOLVE, noted that Aleppo East

873. Agnès Levallois in the programme "C dans l'air", "Syria: Putin's power grab #cdanslair 28-09-2016", *YouTube/ France 5*, September 28, 2016 (55'35")
874. Tom Miles, "Aleppo's Jabhat Fateh al-Sham fighters far fewer than U.N. says: sources", *Reuters*, October 14, 2016
875. James Foley, "Syria: Rebels losing support among civilians in Aleppo", *Public Radio International*, October 16, 2012
876. Jim Lemuel Wilson, "US-Russia Syria agreement remains secret, Russian FM calls for publication", *Geopolmonitor*, September 2016 (archived)
877. OGN TV, "Will other Rebel Groups Turn their Backs on JFS (Nusra)", *YouTube*, September 17, 2016 (www.youtube.com/watch?v=CEmutmLr_Gs)

was in the hands of the Islamists of Jabhat Fath al-Sham (formerly: Jabhat al-Nosrah)[878].

Indeed, in January 2017, following the separation process, all rebel militias in East Aleppo finally regrouped under the authority of Hayat Tahrir al-Sham *(*Levant Liberation Assembly*) and* Harakat Ahrar al-Sham *(*Free Men's Movement of the Levant*)*[879], evacuated to the Idlib area. Both are considered to be terrorist movements associated with "al-Qaeda" with countless war crimes on their record[880]. Thus, contrary to what the 'experts' on 'C dans l'air' claimed, there were no 'moderates' among the fighters in East Aleppo.

6.14.2. The Strategy

During a programme on the situation in Aleppo on *France 5,* an "expert" claimed that the aim of the Syrian government was to starve the population and destroy it in order to empty the city of its inhabitants, a "*strategy that the Russians are used to*" (!!)[881]. This is both silly and false.

Of course, it fails to mention that in Shiite villages such as Foua, Kefraya, Madaya or Homs, which have been under siege for years, the rebels confiscate the humanitarian aid that arrives in the city, in order to sell it "at high prices" to buy arms and ammunition. After the capture of East Aleppo, the premises of the White Helmets and Jabhat al-Nosrah were found to contain vast stores of food and medicines taken from the population[882]. Furthermore, it does not mention the Syrian army's efforts to drop food to the besieged civilian population in order to bypass rebel checkpoints[883].

Our "experts" also fail to mention that the government has negotiated more than 13 agreements with rebel factions between 2014 and 2017 to evacuate

878. Defense Dept: "It's primarily al-Nusra who holds Aleppo.", *YouTube*, Apr 20, 2016 (www.youtube.com/watch?v=rfzjlq2HIEE)

879. Waleed Khaled al-Noufal, "Rebel factions merge with larger Islamist coalitions in response to infighting", *syriadirect.org*, January 31, 2017

880. Joining Hayat Tahrir al-Sham: Kataeb Suqour al-lzz (Maarshurin); Katiba al-Shahid Bi'ithnillah (unconfirmed); Katiba Shuhada al-Wastani (unconfirmed); Katibat Abu Jasem Huwayr; Katibat Ahfad Bani Umaya; Katibat Ahrar al-Janoub; Katibat al-Farouq (unconfirmed); Katibat al-Jihad Fisabilillah; Katibat al-Rasheed; Katibat al-Shahid Mohammad al-Asfoura (Helfaya); Katibat Ansar Banyas; Katibat Fursan al-Sham; Katibat Huthaifa Bin al-Yaman; Katibat Qawafel al-Shuhada (Khan Sheikhoun); Katibat Riah al-Janna ; Katibat Taliban; Katibat Usud al-Harb; Katibat Usud al-Rahman; Liwa Ahrar al-Jabal; Liwa al-Abbas; Liwa al-Haq; Liwa al-Qadisiyah; Liwa al-Tamkin (partial); Liwa Usud al-Rahman; Mujahidou Ashidaa; Siriat Usama Bin Zaid; Siriyat al-Aqsa; Siriyat al-Hamza.Joined Harakat Ahrar al-Sham: Katibat Majd al-Islam (Kiili); Katibat Shuhada al-Jabal; Katibat Suyuf al-Haq (Kiili); Katibat Usud al-Sunna; Liwa Ahrar al-Janoub; Liwa al-Karama; Liwa Khalid Bin al-Walid; Liwa Miqdad Bin Amro; Liwa Omar; Muj ahidi lbn Taimia. Shamia Front {West Aleppo); Sukour al-Sham; Tajamu Fastaqim Kama Umirt.

881. Agnès Levallois in the programme "C dans l'air", "Syria: Putin's power grab #cdanslair 28-09-2016", *YouTube/France 5*, September 28, 2016 (04'10")

882. "Syria rebel group 'deprived us of food', say Aleppo civilians", *Euronews/YouTube*, December 14, 2016

883. Laura Pitel, "Madaya: Convoy of food and medicine reaches the starving in besieged Syrian town". *The Independent*, January 11, 2016

encircled populations from combat zones[884]. In East Aleppo, the humanitarian corridors that the government has tried to set up since summer 2016 to allow the evacuation of civilians, are presented by Hala Kodmani as a trap to shoot down those who would dare to try to leave the rebel zone[885]. But of course, she does not specify that it is the rebels themselves who have refused these corridors[886] and that they - not the government - have placed snipers to discourage escapees: the civilians are 'merely' protection against Syrian army shelling[887].

Our "expert" does not yet know that in December 2016, it was these same "moderate" fighters who set fire to the buses that were to transport civilians evacuated from the villages of Foua and Kefraya to Aleppo[888]. And it was the same fighters who, in April 2017, blew up the buses carrying Shiite women and children on the same route, killing 126 people[889]; an attack that was described as a "*blunder*" (!) by the journalist Dan Cohen of *CNN*[890].

Agnès Levallois claims that it is the Russians who are leading the battle, but this is factually false: it is clearly the Syrian army alongside pro-government militias that is on the front line, while the Russian air force is only providing them with air support, together with the Syrian air force. It is only after the capture of East Aleppo that we will see Russian military personnel, notably to distribute food to the liberated population, and then in the operations of demining and depollution of the city.

Our "experts" on "C dans l'air" claim that the Syrian army is destroying hospitals so that civilians can no longer be treated and are forced to leave the city (probably to be shot by snipers?). The destruction of hospitals by the government seems to be a recurring theme in the propaganda in favour of the rebels, Thus the Andan hospital in North Aleppo was reportedly destroyed on February 3, 2016 by a Russian strike[891], but it may still have been damaged by subsequent strikes in July[892]. The same is true of the 'last paediatric hospital' in Aleppo, which was '*destroyed*' by the Syrian Air Force in June 2016[893], but probably not enough to

884. Mays Al-Shobassi, "Timeline: Syria's 13 'people evacuation' deals", *Aljazeera.com*, May 16, 2017

885. Hala Kodmani in the programme "C dans l'air", "Syria: Putin's power grab #cdanslair 28-09-2016", *YouTube/ France 5*, September 28, 2016 (19'00")

886. Christopher Cummins, "Syrian opposition rejects humanitarian corridors as a ploy to empty Aleppo", *Euronews*, July 29, 2016

887. Anne Barnard, "'I Saw My Father Dying': A View From Aleppo's Government-Held Side", *The New York Times*, November 4, 2016

888. "Aleppo battle: Rebels burn Syria evacuation buses", *BBC News*, December 18, 2016

889. "Bombing of evacuees near Aleppo claims at least 126 lives", *The Irish Times*, April 15, 2017 (updated April 16, 2017)

890. Jason Hanna, Salma Abdelaziz & Eyad Kourdi, "Syria: 126 killed as bomb hits buses with evacuees, *CNN*, April 16, 2017

891. "First responder: Last major north Aleppo hospital destroyed by Russian airstrike", *Syria Direct*, February 3, 2016

892. "Anadan Hospital Just Hit By Air Strike, Northern Aleppo", *Reliefweb*, July 30, 2016

893. "Jets bomb last children's hospital in rebel-held Aleppo", *Palestinian.com*, June 10, 2016

cease functioning, as it was partially destroyed in late July[894]. Similarly, in May 2016, several Western media outlets reported the death of Mohammed Wassim Mo'az, the '*last paediatrician*' in East Aleppo[895], in a Syrian strike. But in August, 15 doctors from East Aleppo, including 6 paediatricians, sent an open letter to President Obama[896].

According to Vanessa Beeley, a British freelance journalist who has spent several long periods in Syria and Aleppo, the Syrian government has even paid doctors to set up in East Aleppo to reinforce the medical staff[897].

There is nothing very sadly banal about this conflict, except that these jihadists were advised by Western military personnel, some of whom were reportedly captured by Syrian forces during the recapture of East Aleppo. On 19 December 2016, at a press conference, the Syrian ambassador to the UN gave the names of 14 foreign intelligence officers who had been surrounded in Aleppo by Syrian special forces. They include 1 American, 1 Israeli, 1 Turkish and 8 Saudi officers[898]. In fact, it clarifies a report by the US Army Veterans Association that 62 Turks, 22 Americans, 21 French, 16 British and 7 Israelis were captured by the Syrians[899]. They were probably only surrounded at this stage and not "captured", but the problem remains the same: Western officers were allegedly supporting jihadist factions in East Aleppo. This is what reportedly prompted the urgent adoption of Resolution 2328 by the UN Security Council to ensure the proper treatment of the survivors of East Aleppo[900].

Having determined once and for all that the 'bad guy' was Bashar al-Assad, everything else becomes acceptable and accepted… including the atrocities, which are carefully avoided in order to preserve the consistency of the official discourse.

In short, we are very poorly informed about the reality on the ground, and the mainstream media deliberately present only part of it. We have put the

894. "EXCLUSIVE: Four babies killed in attack on Aleppo's 'last children's hospital'", *Middle East Eye*, July 31, 2016
895. Margaret Chadbourn & Lena Masri Hospital, "Airstrike Kills Aleppo's Last Pediatrician, 3 Children and at Least 23 Others, Human Rights Group Says", *ABC News*, April 28, 2016; Tracy Wilkinson, "Airstrike on Aleppo hospital kills last pediatrician in Syria's largest city", *www.latimes.com*, April 28, 2016; Siobhán O'Grady, "One of Aleppo's Last Pediatricians Killed in Airstrike on MSF-Supported Hospital", *Foreign Policy*, April 28, 2016; Rose Troup Buchanan, "The Last Senior Pediatrician In Aleppo Was Killed In An Airstrike On A Syrian Hospital", *Buzzfeed.News*, April 29, 2016; Rick Noack & Tiffany Harness, "Aleppo lost one of its last pediatricians in latest hospital bombing", www.washingtonpost.com, April 29, 2016; Katie Reilly, "'Most Qualified Pediatrician' Killed in Airstrike on Syria Hospital", Time, April 30, 2016; Uri Friedman, "The Last Pediatrician in Aleppo*, *The Atlantic*, May 5, 2016
896. www.documentcloud.org/documents/3010504-Aleppo-Doctors-Open-Letter-to-President-Obama.html#document/p1
897. Vanessa Beeley in "Why Everything You Hear About Aleppo Is Wrong", *Ron Paul Liberty Report/YouTube*, September 29, 2016 (09'00")
898. "Syria Names Foreign Secret Agents Trapped in Aleppo", *YouTube*, December 19, 2016
899. http://www.veteranstoday.com/2016/12/17/breaking-syrian-special-forces-captured-14-us-coalition-officers-captured-in-aleppo/
900. "The situation in the Middle East (Syria)", United Nations *Security Council*, December 19, 2016 (S/RES/2328 (2016)

spotlight on the *France 5* programme "C dans l'air", but it is obviously not the only one to present a distorted image of reality. The "experts" only express professions of faith and act as advocates for groups that they do not really know, with a discourse that confirms the government's discourse.

6.15. "Putin is Not Seriously Fighting Daech and the Islamic State. This is Factually Certain[901]!"

6.15.1. The Reasons for Russian Involvement

From the outset, Russia's involvement was the subject of virulent criticism from the members of the coalition, led by France and the United States, who sought to demonstrate that the Russian intervention was not legitimate. First, they try to explain its motives by an expansionist desire[902] by resurrecting the old myth of the objective to recreate the Great Russia[903]. Secondly, by claiming that it does not target the Islamic State (EI)[904]. Some 'experts' are even surprised that Russia did not participate in the strikes against the Islamic State in Iraq[905]. This is manipulation, as the Islamic State was originally an Iraqi problem, created by the US and its deplorable management of the reconstruction of the Iraqi state.

In reality, it was the ineffectiveness of the West in fighting the EI that prompted the Russian intervention. In February 2016, Alexander Yakovenko, Russia's ambassador to Britain, revealed that the decision to intervene in Syria was made in the summer of 2015, when the EI reached the city of Palmyra. The Western coalition predicted that the EI would enter Damascus in October, and that the US would be able to establish a no-fly zone over the city. It was to prevent this, which would have handed the capital to the jihadists, that the Russians intervened[906]. Thus, the Western coalition allowed the EI to grow, in the hope that it would become such a threat to the Syrian government that it would be forced to negotiate, as confirmed by John Kerry, the US Secretary of State:

901. Frédéric Encel in the programme "C dans l'air", "Vladimir Putin: new master of the world? #cdanslair 30-11-2016", *YouTube/France 5*, November 30, 2016 (04'10")
902. Jannick Alimi, "Syria: how Putin is imposing his law on us", *leparisien.fr*, December 15, 2016
903. Program "C dans l'air", "Syria: advantage Putin #cdanslair 29-09-2015", *YouTube/France 5*, September 29, 2015 (46'50")
904. Frédéric Encel in the programme "C dans l'air", "Aleppo: Putin makes Bashar triumph #cdanslair 08-12-2016", *YouTube/France 5*, December 8, 2016 (29'45")
905. Pierre Servent in the programme "C dans l'air", "Syria: advantage Putin #cdanslair 29-09-2015", *YouTube/France 5*, September 29, 2015 (03'00")
906. Alexander Yakovenko, "Russia and the US are partners in trying to end the war in Syria", *The Evening Standard*, February 15, 2016

The reason why Russia got involved was because the EI was getting stronger. DAECH was threatening to reach Damascus and that's why Russia intervened. Because they didn't want a DAECH government and they were supporting Assad.

And we knew it [DAECH] was growing. We were watching. We saw that Daech was becoming more and more powerful and we thought that Assad was threatened. But we thought that we could probably manage, that Assad would negotiate afterwards. Instead of negotiating, he asked Putin for help[907].

Indeed, between August 2014 and March 2017, the Western coalition conducted a cumulative 6,000 strikes on five sites: Kobane, Manbij, Hasakah, Mosul and Sinjar. But in December 2016, when the Syrian army and Russian air forces were focused on retaking East Aleppo, the Western coalition deliberately allowed the Islamic State to retake Palmyra, an area with a total of only 28 strikes for the period 2014-2017[908]! Indeed, on March 24, 2016, State Department spokesman Mark Toner's embarrassed response to the question of whether it was a good thing to see the EI pushed back into Palmyra confirmed the ambiguity of the West[909].

An examination of the maps shows that Western (including French and Belgian) strikes then only target the EI insofar as it threatens other (Western-backed) rebel forces, and when it is not in contact with forces allied to the Syrian government[910]. It can be observed that the fastest territorial expansion of the EI took place between the end of 2014 and September 2015, with the beginning of the Western coalition's strikes in Syria. It was only from the end of 2015, after the start of the Russian intervention, that its territory began to contract[911]. Moreover, at the end of September 2015, Russia proposed the creation of an enlarged coalition to fight against the EI, which was shunned by the West. Dubbed the RSII (Russia-Syria-Iran-Iraq) Coalition, it established an intelligence exchange centre in Baghdad[912].

While since late 2017, the Islamic State has been confined to pockets of resistance in Homs governorate, there has been a dramatic decline in Western strikes. Since December 2017, following the Syrian government's successes against Islamist rebels, including the IS, the international coalition has conducted an

907. John Kerry, Wikileaks recording of a meeting on September 22, 2016 ("Leaked audio of John Kerry's meeting with Syrian revolutionaries/UN (improved audio)", *YouTube*, October 4, 2016)

908. https://airwars.org/data/

909. "Daily Press Briefing - March 24, 2016", *U.S. Department of State/YouTube*, March 24, 2016 (27'45")

910. See the dynamic maps of the war: https://syria.liveuamap.com/

911. See "The Syrian Civil War, every day", *YouTube* (updated daily)

912. "Iraq liaises with Syria, Russia and Iran to bomb ISIL", *Al-Jazeerah*, October 14, 2015

average of 22 strikes per month (less than one strike per day). By comparison, in the same period, the Russian Air Force has conducted an average of 215.5 strikes per month, i.e. about 7 strikes per day[913].

From the outset of the Russian intervention, the United States and France were quick to point to its destabilising nature. In reality, in Syria, it has only destabilised their ambitions in the region, because contrary to the Western approach, it is not based on the model of a "ménage à trois". The West has a propensity to mix things up and create inextricable situations, with opportunistic and temporary alliances dominated by the search for tactical success.

6.15.2. Russia's Interest

To think that Russia's involvement in Syria is simply to keep its military base in Tartus is a bit simplistic. The media are amnesiac: the prevailing Russophobia conveniently makes them forget that on October 7, 2007, Chechen Islamists formally created the Caucasus Emirate[914]. Its rallying to the EI, on June 23, 2015, was decisive in the Russian decision to engage in Syria[915].

In Syria, Russia has the advantage of clarity and strategic consistency. In terms of international law, unlike the West, it is intervening legally by virtue of a request for assistance from the Syrian government. A secret agreement between the two countries on August 26, 2015 defines the terms of this assistance. Moreover, in March 2016, after returning the advantage to the Syrian army, Vladimir Putin ordered a partial withdrawal of his contingent[916].

Chechens provided the intellectual and military backbone of the Islamic State. In order to explain the success of the Islamic State, an alliance between the jihadists and the former military of Saddam Hussein's army has been cited[917]. This is another lie. That former Iraqi military personnel are among the fighters of the Islamic State is very likely, but that is not the point: the Iraqi army was trained for "conventional" warfare; that is why it could be defeated so quickly in 1991 and 2003. Moreover, the Iraqi army had a very centralised and vertical leadership structure, whereas the Islamic State's was more decentralised, with flatter hierarchies. In fact, there is an attempt to justify a posteriori the accusations of collusion between "al-Qaeda" and the Iraqi government of 2003, and to

913. "US-led Coalition air and artillery strikes in Iraq and Syria", *airwars.org*, December 2018

914. See Jacques Baud, *Encyclopédie des terrorismeismes et des violences organisées*, Lavauzelle, 2009, pp. 1153-1168

915. Sarah Rainsford, "Islamic State may threaten Russia's Caucasus", *BBC News*, June 30, 2015; Mark Kramer, "The Return of Islamic State Fighters: The Impact on the Caucasus and Central Asia", www.ponarseurasia.org, August 2015

916. Denis Dyomkin & Suleiman Al-Khalidi, "Putin says Russians to start withdrawing from Syria, as peace talks resume", *Reuters*, March 14, 2016

917. Paul McLeary, "Why the Islamic State's generals are better than the Iraqi army's," *Slate.co.uk/Foreign Policy* (trans. Peggy Sastre), June 19, 2015

hide the failure of the exorbitant and ineffective training given by Nato to the Iraqi army between 2004 and 2011.

A close look at the tactics used by the EI shows that they have nothing to do with those of the former Iraqi army, but are derived from those developed by the jihadists in the wars in Chechnya and North Africa. With more than 4,000 fighters, the Chechen contingent is one of the most important organised structures of the EI. As the Counter-Terrorism Center at the West Point Military Academy notes, its experience in guerrilla warfare has been very useful in training fighters and bringing new combat and attack techniques to the Middle East[918].

Thus, for Russia, Syria constitutes a sort of glacis that allows it to fight the EI while keeping it away from national borders. This is a very different situation from that of France, which was not concerned by the threat of the EI before going to strike.

If we leave behind superficial and emotional analyses, we can see a remarkable coherence in the Russian approach, which is not found in the West. As far as the Middle East is concerned, the main axes of its strategy are 1) attacking Islamic terrorist groups where they live, rather than waiting for them to attack Russia; 2) avoiding a terrorist takeover of Syria, which it believes would be the most likely outcome of the violent overthrow of the Assad regime; 3) supporting a regime that has allowed it a military presence; 4) supporting the principle that ruling regimes should not be overthrown by outside forces; 5) expanding its role in the Middle East; and 6) challenging US unilateralism in the international system[919].

6.15.3. The Russian Strategy

At first glance, one might think that the Russian and coalition air forces have similar approaches and conduct strikes in support of the ground forces they support: the Syrian Army, Shiite forces and Christian forces for the Russians; Syrian and Kurdish rebels for the Western coalition. But the reality is more subtle, because in reality, for the Western coalition, the Islamic State is also an unnamed ally in the fight against the Syrian government.

Unlike the West, which operates in a form of "ménage à trois", Russia is in a binary relationship with its allies. By relying on the defence of the legal state, it has been able to adopt a more systematic strategy and synchronise its strikes with ground operations in an operative coherence. In fact, Russia is the only country to comply with the letter of UN Security Council Resolution 2254, and in particular its number 8:

918. Barak Barfi, "The Military Doctrine of the Islamic State and the Limits of Ba'athist Influence", *CTC Sentinel*, Combating Terrorism Center (West Point), February 19, 2016, pp. 18-22
919. Raymond Smith, "Understanding Russian Foreign Policy Today", *The Foreign Service Journal*, December 2016

[The Security Council] Calls upon Member States, as it has already done in resolution 2249 (2015), to prevent and suppress acts of terrorism committed in particular by the Islamic State of Iraq and the Levant (ISIL, also known as Daech) as well as by the al-Nosrah Front and all other individuals, groups, undertakings and entities associated with al-Qaida or the EIIL, and other terrorist groups that it has designated as such or that may subsequently be deemed to be such (...), and to eliminate the sanctuary they have created in large parts of the territories of Syria, and notes that the above-mentioned ceasefire will not apply to offensive or defensive actions directed against such individuals, groups, undertakings and entities[920] *[...]*

Russian strikes against the Islamists demonstrate planning according to clear operational objectives; whereas Coalition strikes are more dictated by opportunity and do not fit into an overall joint plan. For example, the latter have carefully avoided striking the EI's oil, even though it was known to be its main source of revenue[921] s. In November 2015, Michael Morell, former vice-director of the CIA, explained that the aim was to maintain an infrastructure for the reconstruction of the country and to protect the environment(!)[922]! It was finally the Russians who tackled it at the end of 2015.

Operationally, the Russian-Syrian engagement was methodical: starting from the west of the country, it pushed eastwards, avoiding leaving rebel pockets in its rear. In contrast, the approach of the coalition forces, with air action for the benefit of multiple actors, was less systematic and less sustainable.

Russian action in Syria has also had a significant regional impact. While Western interventions are clearly in response to their own national interests, Russia's involvement is based on an interest it shares with Syria. As a result, its credibility is considerable. So much so that Iraq is beginning to turn to Russia in its fight against the Islamic State[923]; a development that is linked to its categorical refusal to accept a US ground deployment on its soil[924].

920. Resolution 2254 (2015), Security Council, December 18, 2015 (S/RES/2254 (2015))

921. "ISIL Derives Significant Revenue from Oil Productions" Army Gen. Lloyd J. Austin III", *YouTube*, October 20, 2014

922. "CIA On ISIS Oil, *YouTube*, November 29, 2015

923. Ahmed Rasheed & Saif Hameed, "Iraq leans towards Russia in war on Islamic State", *Reuters*, October 7, 2015.

924. Rebecca Kheel, 'Iraqi government says it doesn't want US ground operations', *The Hill*, October 28, 2015.

6.16. " The Syrian Government uses Chemical Weapons Against its Own Population[925]"

6.16.1. The context

On 7 June 1981, Israel destroys the Iraqi nuclear power plant of Osirak by an air raid (Operation OPERA). The action was declared contrary to international law and in violation of the UN Charter, and prompted the UN Security Council to adopt Resolution 487. It enjoins the Hebrew State to place "*its nuclear facilities under the safeguards of the International Atomic Energy Agency*" (IAEA)[926]. But Israel refuses to implement it.

Syria then understands that thanks to American protection, Israel indirectly has a "second strike capability", which makes it the only country in the Middle East virtually capable of triggering a nuclear conflict. The threat is therefore serious and confirmed by regular Israeli attacks on Syrian territory. Syria is therefore seeking to equip itself with a deterrent capability. But, unlike Israel, it is a signatory of the Nuclear Non-Proliferation Treaty and respects the IAEA safeguard clauses. This is why it turned to chemical weapons, which were then also called the "poor man's atomic bomb".

Inspired by Soviet doctrine, its military doctrine has never considered chemical weapons as a "normal" means of combat, but as a weapon of mass destruction and last resort, as confirmed by a 1985 CIA TOP SECRET report, declassified in 2011[927]. According to this doctrine, chemical weapons are used in major operations, in support of a main effort.

Strategically, in a logic of deterrence, Syria maintains an ambiguous discourse on its real capabilities, while affirming, in July 2012, that they would only be used in case of "*external aggression*[928]". Moreover, Syria only acceded to the Chemical Weapons Convention (CWC) in September 2014 after receiving a commitment from Russia that it would provide protection against Israel's offensive ambitions.

6.16.2. The Chemical Attack in Ghouta (August 21, 2013)

Quite soon after the start of the insurgency in Syria, the idea that the Syrian regime might be using chemical weapons emerges in Israel. There are no

---

925. Ambassador François Delattre, in Marc Semo, "Syria: new accusations of chemical weapons use", *lemonde.fr*, February 7, 2018
926. S/RES/487 (1981) of June 19, 1981.
927. Office of Near Eastern and South Asian Analysis & Office of Scientific and Weapons Research, *Syria's Offensive Chemical Warfare Capability: An Intelligence Assessment*, Langley, VA: Central Intelligence Agency, November 1st, 1985, (TOP SECRET), declassified and published November 15, 2011, (available at: www.cia.gov/library/readingroom/document/cia-rdp86t00587r000400550004-2.)
928. Ian Black, "Syria insists chemical weapons would only be used against outside forces", *The Guardian*, July 24, 2012

concrete indications, but Israel views these weapons with suspicion, as its regular interventions on Syrian soil could one day be the last straw.

At this stage, the fears of Western intelligence services are directed more towards the rebels. Indeed, as soon as they took power in 2011, the new Libyan leaders provided the Syrian insurgents with weapons and fighters, which were transited through Turkey[929] with the explicit help of NATO countries[930]. But there are persistent rumours that chemical weapons have arrived in Syria from a depot captured by the Islamists in September 2011[931] in southern Libya[932]. Already in February 2011, the *Washington Post* feared that these weapons were getting into the hands of terrorists[933]. The *Guardian* reported with concern that Libya had 25 tonnes of mustard and about 1,400 tonnes of chemical weapons precursors that had not yet been destroyed: abandoned, they could pose a regional security problem if they fall "into the *hands of Islamist militants or rebels active in North Africa*[934] ". On social networks, photos showing Syrian rebels handing out gas masks appeared long before the international community mentioned this threat from the Syrian government. In June 2012, *RT (Russia Today)* even mentioned the possibility of chemical attacks by the rebels in order to provoke a Western intervention[935].

In July 2012, as the situation deteriorated, the government evacuated stocks of chemical weapons threatened by the rebellion[936]. But the secret nature of the operation opens the door to all kinds of speculation and the rebellion accuses the government of wanting to commit its chemical weapons[937]. For its part, Israel fears that they could fall into the hands of its enemies[938]. The next day, in order to reassure public opinion, the Syrian Foreign Ministry organised a press conference during which its spokesperson specified that chemical weapons "*if they existed*" would never be used against the Syrian people, but "*against an external aggression*[939]". *Radio Free Europe/Radio Liberty* (which was established by the CIA in 1949) reports that Syria promises not to use its chemical weapons against Syrians[940], and two days later *Voice of America* says that Syria is unlikely

929. Ruth Sherlock, "Libya's new rulers offer weapons to Syrian rebels", *telegraph.co.uk*, November 25, 2011
930. Tony Cartalucci, "The Libyan Election Farce", *Land Destroyer*, July 9, 2012.
931. Ian Black, "Libyan rebels discover Gaddafi's chemical weapons", *The Guardian*, September 22, 2011
932. Ben Ariel, "Libyan official: ISIS got our chemical weapons", *Arutz Sheva 7 (israelnationalnews.com)*, January 28, 2016
933. Jeff Stein, "Libya's poison gas unaffected by turmoil, official says", *The Washington Post*, February 28, 2011
934. "Libyan chemical weapons stockpiles intact, say inspectors", *The Guardian*, November 4, 2011
935. "Syrian rebels aim to use chemical weapons, blame Damascus", *RT*, June 10, 2012.
936. Eric Schmitt, "Syria Moving Parts of Chemical Arsenal, U.S. Says", *The New York Times*, July 14, 2012
937. "Rebels accuse Damascus of moving chemical weapons", *RTS Info*, 24 July 2012 (updated July 25, 2012)
938. Michael Bowman, "Netanyahu: Israel Prepared to Deal with Syrian Chemical Weapons", *Voice of America*, July 22, 2012
939. Dr. Jihad Makdissi, "Slaughtered terrorists of Arab nationalities", The Syria Diary / *YouTube*, July 23, 2012
940. "Damascus Pledges No Use Of Chemical Weapons Against Syrians, *RFE/RL*, July 23, 2012

to use its chemical weapons[941]. But the Europeans are trying to paint a much more ominous picture of Syria. Reuters states that it could "*use chemical weapons against foreigners*[942]" (implying that these could also be foreign fighters). The same is true in France, where some mainstream media are reporting that it is "*threatening to use chemical weapons*"[943]. In fact, the aim is to give a "black and white" image of the situation and to push the West to intervene.

This is when the "red line", defined by President Obama on August 20, 2012 during a press conference, comes into play. It is referred to as a warning to the Syrian government. But it is an "infox"! In fact, Obama is addressing more broadly *all the* actors in the conflict:

> *Question: Mr. President, could you give us your latest thoughts on the situation in Syria and, in particular, whether you are considering committing US forces, if only for the safety of the chemical weapons and whether you are confident that the chemical weapons are safe?*

> *Answer: (...) I have not yet given any order for military engagement in this situation. But your question about chemical and biological weapons is crucial. This is not just a problem for Syria; it concerns our close allies in the region, including Israel. It concerns us. We cannot have a situation where chemical or biological weapons fall into the hands of the wrong people.*

> *We have been very clear to the Assad regime, but also to other actors on the ground, that a red line for us is that we start to see a whole bunch of chemical weapons moving or being used. That would change my calculation. It would change my equation*[944].

The Americans know that the insurgency is dominated by Islamists[945] and their concern is the capacity of the Syrian government to ensure the security of chemical weapons in order to prevent them from falling into their hands.

941. Cecily Hilleary, "Experts: Syria Not Likely to Use Chemical Weapons", *Voice of America*, July 25, 2012
942. Erika Solomon & Mariam Karouny, "*Syria says could use chemical weapons against foreigners*", Reuters, July 23, 2012
943. Anne-Charlotte Dusseaulx, 'Damascus threatens to use chemical weapons', *Le Journal du Dimanche*, July 23, 2012 (updated June 19, 2017); M.-L. W., 'La Syrie menace d'utiliser des armes chimiques: la mise en garde d'Obama', *Le Parisien*, July 23, 2012.
944. "Remarks by the President to the White House Press Corps", *Office of the Press Secretary*, The White House, August 20, 2012; Glenn Kessler, "President Obama and the 'red line' on Syria's chemical weapons", *The Washington Post*, September 6, 2013
945. http://www.judicialwatch.org/wp-content/uploads/2015/05/Pg.-291-Pgs.-287-293-JW-v-DOD-and-State-14-812-DOD-Release-2015-04-10-final-version11.pdf

Moreover, the next day, when asked about the definition of the "red line" during a press briefing, the White House spokesman confirmed:

> *As the President said yesterday in relation to Syria, we are keeping a very close eye on the Syrian chemical weapons stockpile; that any use or attempted proliferation related to these chemical weapons would be a very serious matter and a serious mistake.*
>
> *The Syrian regime has important international obligations to manage its chemical weapons. And those who bear this responsibility will be held accountable for their actions and must comply with these international obligations*[946].

Thus, President Obama was addressing *all* actors in the Syrian conflict and apparently did not believe at that stage that the government intended to use its chemical weapons against the rebels. Indeed, at the same time, it refused to provide protective masks to the rebels for fear that they would use chemical weapons[947]. This is why the following year in Stockholm he denied having defined a red line in the way it was interpreted in the world:

> *I have not defined a red line. The world has defined a red line*[948].

So it was the media - in France in particular - that cheated and truncated the American president's message. They distorted the reading of it, and thus probably incited the use of chemical weapons. Indeed, the August 20 statement will be followed fairly quickly by unconfirmed reports of chemical weapons use in Syria.

On December 3, 2012, Hillary Clinton and Obama issued a warning to Syria[949], which responded the same day with a statement:

> *In response to statements by the US Secretary of State, who warned Syria against the use of chemical weapons, Syria has repeatedly stressed that it would not use such weapons, if available, against its population under any circumstances*[950].

946. "Press Gaggle by Principal Deputy Press Secretary Josh Earnest en route Columbus, OH, 8/21/2012" (aboard Air Force One), *Office of the Press Secretary*, The White House, August 21, 2012

947. Josh Rogin, 'Obama Refused to Send Gas Masks to Syrian Opposition for Over a Year', *The Daily Beast*, August 29, 2013 (updated July 11, 2017).

948. President Obama, Press conference in Stockholm, September 4, 2013

949. Peter Finn, "Obama warns Syria amid rising concern over chemical weapons", *The Washington Post*, December 3, 2012

950. "Syria says would not use chemical weapons against its people, *Reuters*, December 3, 2012

The explanation for this exchange comes on October 29, 2013, in the *Washington Post*, which publishes an extract from a 178-page TOP SECRET classified report on the intelligence services' budget, revealed by Edward Snowden. It reveals the existence of a network of sensors deployed near chemical weapons storage sites in Syria, which send data in real time to the satellites of the National Reconnaissance Office (NRO), which is responsible for satellite intelligence. They feed the American and Israeli warning systems to allow an immediate response in case of preparations for chemical attacks[951].

However, in December 2012, sensors had detected activity in the vicinity of some chemical weapons sites, but had not been able to determine the nature or perpetrators of the activity. In fact, after a siege of several months, Jabhat al-Nosrah, supported by the Muhajiri al-Sham, Majlis Shura al-Mujahideen *and* al-Battar phalanxes, seized the Darat Izza military base northwest of Aleppo, which includes, in addition to heavy weapons, a chemical weapons depot[952]. On December 8, the Syrian government informed the UN[953] that Jabhat al-Nosrah had also seized a chemical factory in Al-Safira, south-east of Aleppo, with nearly 200 tonnes of chlorine. At the same time, CNN reported that the Americans were training Syrian rebels in the storage of chemical weapons[954] ; this tends to confirm the concern of Obama and his services[955]. But in France, the traditional media and the official organs will not broadcast the information… the enemy is then Bashar al-Assad, even if it allows the jihadists to be strengthened. Moreover, none of the "*national assessments*" published later by the French government will mention that the rebels had chemical capabilities, as we shall see.

The first major (confirmed) 'attack' after Obama's warning was on Khan al-Assal on March 19, 2013. At this stage, despite the accusations of the French and American governments against the Syrian army, the use of chemical weapons by the rebels is hardly in doubt: the "*village is then under the control of the government*[956]" and Syrian soldiers are among the victims. The Syrian government appealed to the United Nations and *the* Organisation for the Prohibition of Chemical Weapons (OPCW) to request an international

951. Barton Gellman & Greg Miller, "'Black budget' summary details U.S. spy network's successes, failures and objectives", *Washington Post*, August 29, 2013

952. Harald Doornbos & Jenan Moussa, "How the Islamic State Seized a Chemical Weapons Stockpile", *Foreign Policy*, August 17, 2016 (reprinted in *Le Courrier International* in French: Harald Doornbos & Jenan Moussa, "Enquête. How Daech got its chemical weapons', *Le Courrier International / Foreign Policy*, September 9, 2016)

953. Michelle Nichols, "Syria 'genuinely worried' extremists could get chemical weapons", *Reuters*, December 17, 2012

954. Elise Labott, "Sources: U.S. helping underwrite Syrian rebel training on securing chemical weapons", *CNN*, December 9, 2012

955. Craig Whitlock & Carol Morello, "U.S. plans for possibility that Assad could lose control of chemical weapons cache", *The Washington Post*, December 16, 2012

956. Report of the UN Secretary-General to the Presidents of the General Assembly and the Security Council, December 13, 2013, (A/68/663-S/2013/735), p.32

commission of enquiry... a fact that the Western media, such as *BFMTV* and *France 5* - which have nevertheless broadcast several programmes on this subject - have obviously ignored...

On May 6, 2013, Carla del Ponte, a member of the UN Commission of Inquiry on Syria[957], told the *BBC* about the March and April 2013 attacks in Khan al-Assal[958]:

> *In particular the nerve agent: it appears from our investigation that it was used by the opposition, by the rebels. And we have no, no indication at all that the government, Syria, the Syrian government authority used chemical weapons*[959].

On July 9, 2013, Vladimir Churkin[960], Russia's ambassador to the UN, presented a 100-page report confirming the UN's accusations[961]: analysis of samples recovered from Khan al-Assal by an OPCW-accredited laboratory revealed the absence of stabiliser, which is found in prescription chemical weapons. In addition, a Bashair-3 missile, home-made by the rebel Bashair al-Nasr brigade[962], was used. Curiously, this event, which should inspire reasonable doubt, is not mentioned in any subsequent American or French analysis document. But in the programme "C dans l'air" of August 23, 2013, this will not prevent Frédéric Encel from evoking this attack as a precedent to blame the Syrian government for the Ghouta incident[963].

On May 30, 2013, a 2 kg canister of Sarin-type toxic chemical was discovered by Turkish security forces in Adana[964] in the flat of a Syrian Islamist affiliated to Jabhat al-Nosrah[965] one of the rebel groups supported by the US, Israel and France (!)

---

957. Full name: *International Independent Investigation Commission on the Syrian Arab Republic*. It was established by the UN Human Rights Council in 2011 and includes Mr Paulo Sérgio Pinheiro (Chair), Karen Koning Abu-Zayd, Vitit Muntarbhorn and Carla Del Ponte.
958. Damien McElroy and agencies, 'UN accuses Syrian rebels of chemical weapons use', *The Telegraph*, May 6, 2013.
959. "Leading UN investigator: 'Evidently Syrian Rebels used SARIN', *YouTube*, May 6, 2013
960. Tucker Reals, "Syria chemical weapons attack blamed on Assad, but where's the evidence?", *CBS News*, August 30, 2013; "Russia Presents Evidence Syrian Rebels Used Chemical Weapons", *RadioFreeEurope/RadioLiberty*, July 9, 2013
961. Matthew Schofield. "Russia gave UN 100-page report in July blaming Syrian rebels for Aleppo sarin attack", *McClatchy*, September 5, 2013
962. "Russian Inquiry to UN: Rebels, not Army, Behind Syria Aleppo Sarin Attack", *Information Clearing House/ RT*, July 10, 2013.
963. Frédéric Encel in the programme "C dans l'air", "Syrie La ligne rouge", *YouTube/France 5*, August 26, 2013 (05'54")
964. "Adana'da El Nusra'ya operasyon: iki kilo sarin gazı ele geçirildi", *Sol.org.tr*, May 30, 2013
965. OE Watch, "Turkey - Al Nusra With Sarin Gas?", *Foreign Military Studies Office*, Fort Leavenworth, (http://fmso.leavenworth.army.mil/OEWatch/201307/Turkey_02.html)

On June 20, a SECRET report by the US Defense Intelligence Agency (DIA) described the Islamists' chemical capabilities and confirmed that Jabhat al-Nosrah had the capacity to produce and use sarin-like nerve agents[966]:

> *Until now, the intelligence community has focused almost exclusively on chemical weapons stockpiles in Syria; the al-Nosrah Front is now attempting to create its own chemical weapons [...] The relative operational freedom of the al-Nosrah Front in Syria leads us to believe that the group's chemical weapons aspirations will be difficult to combat in the future*[967].

Thus, the hypothesis that the Syrian rebels received chemical weapons from the West, or at least that the West turned a blind eye to the development of such a capability, is realistic. In an interview with *Al-Jazeera* TV on June 10, 2013, Colonel Abd al-Basset al-Tawil, commander of *the* Free Syrian Army (FSA) Northern Front, gave the West one month to supply the FSA with heavy weapons or he would reveal the truth about chemical weapons[968]:

> *[...] In all sincerity, we would like a civilised state with Islamic law. Let me give you an example: we want our army to have a clear Islamic nature. I give the international community one month to give the rebels and the ASL the weapons and ammunition so that we can defeat this criminal regime. We give them one month. If we see that the international community continues to ignore our revolution, we will reveal all the evidence we have [on the use of chemical weapons]. I think you understand very well what I mean.*

Coincidence or not, nine days later, the press reported that the rebels received their first heavy weapons[969]... On July 7, as if to confirm the DIA report, the Syrian army discovered in Banias a clandestine laboratory intended for the manufacture of chemical toxins, where 281 drums containing "*enough* [toxics] *to destroy the entire country*[970]" were stored.

Two months later, on the night of August 20-21 2013, the chemical attack in Ghouta took place. Unlike the previous attacks, it affected an area under rebel control.

---

966. Seymour M. Hersh, "Whose sarin?", *London Review of Books*, Vol. 35 No. 24, December 19, 2013

967. Seymour M. Hersh, 'The Red Line and the Rat Line', *London Review of Books*, vol. 36 no. 8, April 17, 2014.

968. "FSA General Gives Int'l Community One Month to Provide Anti Tank, Anti Aircraft Weapons", *YouTube*, June 20, 2013, (www.youtube.com/watch?v=HYIdmlk2gAU)

969. Richard Spencer, "Syrian rebels get first heavy weapons on the front line of Aleppo", *The Telegraph*, June 19, 2013

970. Christof Lehmann, "Syrian Army seizes Massive Chemical Stockpile from Insurgents. Enough to Wipe out Entire Country", *NSNBC*, July 10, 2013.

The press and Western governments disseminate the information without analysis: *L'Express*, le *Point*, le *Journal du Dimanche*, *BFMTV* or *Franceinfo* report the words of Laurent Fabius, who sees a "*chemical massacre*"[971]. This is the pretext that Western governments were looking for to strike the Syrian government, although nothing indicates Damascus' responsibility. To give credibility to the event - which many doubt, at this stage - *Le Figaro* justifies it by the presence of a commando of 300 Israeli, Jordanian and CIA fighters coming from Jordan: an information taken up by most of the traditional media, such as *France 24*[972]... But in fact, no one has seen this commando and no trace of it will be found later: an "external aggression" is needed to explain the use of chemical weapons. This is disinformation.

British Prime Minister David Cameron orders the pre-deployment of a squadron to Cyprus. But on 29 August, the British Parliament refused to participate in the strikes. The same day, Obama asserts the guilt of the Syrian government, but his "services" are sceptical[973]. They quickly put forward the hypothesis that this was a "false-banner" operation aimed at incriminating President Bashar al-Assad[974]. Indeed, their sensor network did not detect any activity in the vicinity of the chemical weapons depots before the attack[975]. General Martin E. Dempsey, Chief of the *Joint Chiefs of Staff* (JCS)[976] doubts that the White House has real evidence of the Syrian government's guilt, and asks the DIA for more concrete information.

In fact, the Pentagon is generally opposed to intervention and is trying to convince President Obama, but is encountering the rigidity of the administration. In July 2013, in a presentation to the Senate Armed Services Committee, Dempsey advised against intervention, as attempts to overthrow Assad could only worsen the situation[977]. He relies on a confidential memo that confirms that aid to 'moderate' rebels has become aid to radical jihadist movements such as Jabhat al-Nosrah and the Islamic State in Iraq in the Levant (EIIL)[978]. In the summer of 2013, the JCS even took the initiative to share intelligence on the

---

971. "Syria: for Fabius, everything indicates that the regime committed a 'chemical massacre'" *LEXPRESS.fr/AFP*, August 24, 2013; "Fabius: 'There was a chemical massacre near Damascus'", *Le Point.fr/AFP*, August 24, 2013; E.C., "Fabius speaks of a 'chemical massacre' committed by the Assad regime", *lejdd.fr/AFP*, August 24, 2013 (updated June 19, 2017); M.T., "Syria: Fabius evokes a 'chemical massacre' perpetrated 'by Damascus'", *bfmtv.com*, August 24, 2013; "For Laurent Fabius, everything indicates that the Syrian regime has committed a 'chemical massacre'", *franceinfo/AFP*, August 24, 2013.

972. Isabelle Lasserre, "Syria: the anti-Assad operation has begun", *Le Figaro*, August 22, 2013; "According to 'Le Figaro', American-trained rebels are advancing towards Damascus", *France 24*, August 22, 2013.

973. Deb Riechmann & Kimberly Dozier, "Obama affirms Assad to blame, but officials say gas attack incomplete", *The Times of Israel*, August 29, 2013

974. Scott Baker, "Is the Syria Chemical Weapons Attack a false flag event?", *opednews.com*, September 11, 2013

975. Seymour M. Hersh, "Whose sarin?", *op. cit.*

976. Chief of the Joint Staff, (equivalent to the Chief of Staff of the Armed Forces, in France)

977. Mark Landler and Thom Shanker, 'Pentagon Lays out Options for U.S. Military Effort in Syria', *The New York Times*, July 22, 2013.

978. Seymour Hersh, 'Military to Military', *London Review of Books*, vol. 38 No. 1, January 7, 2016.

EIIL with German, Russian and Israeli services, in the hope that it would find its way to the Syrian government[979].

Furthermore, the operational context does not justify the use of chemical weapons by the Syrian army. Their tactical effects are difficult to predict and have serious strategic consequences. With Obama's "red line", the government would have had to be really cornered to use them. However, in July, General Dempsey[980] confirmed that Bashar al-Assad had regained the upper hand in May 2013 and was not cornered[981]. Unless one is a "conspiracy theorist", it is not clear why the Syrian army would have deliberately targeted civilians in an area that has no strategic importance. Moreover, such an attack by the government, only a few kilometres from Damascus, on the very day of the arrival of a UN mission charged with investigating - at its request - the Khan al-Assal incident, would have been particularly unwise!

On 30 August 2013, Barak Obama and John Kerry presented a White House summary[982], which stated that preparations for the attack had already been detected three days earlier. It triggers the anger of the Syrian opposition. In *Foreign Policy*, Razan Zaitouneh, a Syrian activist, says that "*it is incredible that they did nothing to warn people or try to stop the regime before the crime*"[983]! A controversy ensued, forcing the Office of the Director of National Intelligence (ODNI) to admit that in fact no clues had been detected before the incident and that the report was prepared after the fact on the basis of elements thought to be linked to the attack. Later, US officials would admit that the memo did not reflect the reports provided by the intelligence services[984]. It was therefore misinformation.

In order to commit the armed forces to Syria, the President must have the approval of Congress. An intelligence briefing is therefore provided to parliamentarians. It is based only on information from social networks, and members of the House Intelligence Committee will say that "*it doesn't prove anything at all*[985]". They ask for more information, but there will be none[986].

979. Gareth Porter, "US military leadership resisted Obama's bid for regime change in Syria, Libya", *Middle East Eye*, January 4, 2016

980. Richard Spencer, Aleppo and Ruth Sherlock, "Is Bashar al-Assad winning the civil war in Syria?", *The Telegraph*, May 23, 2013.

981. John Grady, "Testy Dempsey Reconfirmation Hearing Dominated by Syria", U.S. Naval Institute's News July 19, 2013

982. *Government Assessment of the Syrian Government's Use of Chemical Weapons on August 21, 2013*, The White House, Office of the Press Secretary, August 30, 2013

983. Shane Harris, 'U.S. Had Intel on Chemical Strike Before It Was Launched', *Foreign Policy*, August 30, 2013

984. Seymour M. Hersh, "Whose sarin?", *London Review of Books*, Vol. 35 No. 24, December 19, 2013

985. Scott Baker, "Congress Members Who Have Seen Classified Evidence About Syria Say It Fails to Prove Anything", *OpEdNews.com*, September 9, 2013

986. Alan Grayson, "On Syria Vote, Trust, but Verify", *The New York Times*, September 7, 2013

After the 'attack', Russian intelligence collected toxic samples and passed them on to the British services for analysis at Porton Down. The latter confirmed the presence of sarin. At the same time, the US DIA compared the 'signature' of the samples with those in the OPCW database, while the Syrian government provided additional data on the weapons in its possession. When the British Defence Staff provided the DIA with the results of the analysis, a British official said "*we have been set up*"[987]! The samples had the same "signature" as the toxic substances in the possession of the rebels[988]. For its part, the CIA, which analysed the situation separately, came to the same conclusion: the attacks did not come from the Syrian government. In this situation, Congress was certainly not going to give its consent to engage in strikes against Syria[989] and James Clapper, Director of National Intelligence, dissuaded Obama from engaging in strikes[990]. Obama will follow his advice[991] and leave the French government alone to call for intervention[992].

Washington's retreat leaves a bitter taste in France, where it is seen as a "betrayal". In the programme "C dans l'air" of September 29, 2015, Pierre Servent spoke of a president who "*reneged on his word*", thus leading to the "*weakening of the United States*[993]". A year later, in the same programme, while Agnès Levallois stated that the "*word of the leading international power [...] has lost all meaning*[994]", the journalist Frédéric Encel described this "*retreat*" as a "*catastrophic error*"[995]. An idea taken up by Nicole Bacharan in July 2019, who states that after this "*retreat*" Obama was "*swept away*" from the international scene[996]; then by Wassim Nasr in October 2019 to explain the disaster of the American policy[997]. Thus, on April 18, 2018, in the programme "C dans l'Air", General Vincent Desportes states:

---

987. Seymour M. Hersh, 'The Red Line and the Rat Line', *London Review of Books*, vol. 36 no. 8, April 17, 2014.
988. Alfred Hackensberger & Thorsten Jungholt, "Frieden mit Assad?", *Die Welt*, August 28, 2016; Alexander Mercouris. "Here's how US Intelligence warned Obama of doubts Assad was responsible for 2013 gas attack", *Defend Democracy Press*, August 30, 2016
989. Seymour M. Hersh, "Whose sarin?", *op. cit.*
990. Matthias von Hein, "Is Assad to blame for the chemical weapons attack in Syria?", *Deutsche Welle*, April 6, 2017
991. Thorsten Jungholt, "Frieden mit Assad?", *Die Welt*, August 28, 2016
992. Benjamin Barthe, Nathalie Guibert, Yves-Michel Riols & Christophe Ayad, "L'été où la France a presque fait la guerre en Syrie", *lemonde.fr*, February 2014
993. Pierre Servent in the programme "C dans l'air", "Syria: advantage Putin #cdanslair 29-09-2015", *YouTube/France 5*, September 29, 2015 (02'00")
994. Émission " C dans l'air ", " Syrie: le coup de force de Poutine #cdanslair 28-09-2016 ", *YouTube/France 5*, September 28, 2016 (25'35")
995. Frederic Encel in the programme "C dans l'air", "Aleppo: Putin makes Bashar triumph #cdanslair 08-12-2016", *YouTube/France 5*, December 8, 2016 (22'40")
996. Programme "C dans l'air", "Trump s'en va en guerre #cdanslair 05-07-2019", *YouTube/France 5*, July 5, 2019 (40'30")
997. Wassim Nasr in the programme "C dans l'air", "Syria / Turkey: the conflagration #cdanslair 14.10.2019", *YouTube/France 5*, October 15, 2019 (22'10")

Nations must be credible and feared. It is well known that the first consequence of the American non-intervention in 2013, was the seizure of Crimea by Mr Putin in 2014[998].

Their reading of the war in Syria reflects quite well the state of mind that reigned in France at the time, more aligned with Tel Aviv than Washington. It follows a logic that dates back to the First World War: striking is a way of showing one's power, whatever the conditions or the outcome. In reality, it is not the action itself that makes it credible, but its adequacy with reality: this is what cost the United States its credibility in 2003. In August 2013, Obama's "retreat" was an intelligence victory, and therefore a strength.

In France, people are convinced of Syria's guilt. On September 2, the General Secretariat for Defence and National Security (SGDSN) published a *National Synthesis of declassified intelligence*. An unusual approach. It is based on reports provided by the Directorate General of External Security (DGSE) and the Directorate of Military Intelligence (DRM), and aims to justify an intervention in Syria. After a very summary analysis, it concludes:

It is clear from the points of application of the attack that no one other than the regime could attack strategic positions for the opposition in this way.

Finally, we believe that the Syrian opposition does not have the capacity to conduct such a large-scale operation with chemical agents. No group belonging to the Syrian insurgency has, at this stage, the capacity to stockpile and use these agents, let alone in a similar proportion to that used on the night of August 21, 2013 in Damascus. These groups have neither the experience nor the know-how to deploy them, particularly through vectors such as those used in the August 21 attack[999].

Despite the lack of evidence, it generates a kind of fervour, and pseudo-intellectuals and strategists of all stripes follow one another in the media to call for an intervention.

Apart from circumstantial elements, the SGDSN note does not provide *any* factual elements - for example, satellite or electromagnetic intelligence - confirming the accusation. It is accompanied by six videos posted on the Ministry

998. General Vincent Desportes in the programme "C dans l'air", "Syria: after the strikes, the controversy #cdanslair 18.04.2018", *YouTube/France 5*, April 18, 2018 (28'35")
999. *National Intelligence Estimate - Syria's Chemical Programme - Cases of past use of chemical agents by the regime - Chemical attack conducted by the regime on August 21, 2013*, Paris, August 2013. (http://www.diplomatie.gouv.fr/fr/IMG/pdf/Syrie_Synthese_nationale_de_renseignement_declassifie_le_02_09_2013_cle01b7e8.pdf)

of Defence website[1000]. Like the White House memo a few days earlier, it is essentially based on information disseminated by the rebels on social networks. A Syrian NGO showed the inconsistencies. For example, some scenes were simply "borrowed" from the Rabiha al-Adawiya massacre... in Egypt, a few weeks earlier; nurses give injections to "corpses", while the same victims are filmed in several different places. The majority of the victims are children (most of them dressed, even though the attack took place at night), even though civilians have been evacuated from the area for several months already. Moreover, their parents seem to be absent from the victims and survivors[1001]. Moreover, the videos are removed from the site shortly after they are "debunked".

The number of 1,429 victims mentioned by John Kerry raised questions among American parliamentarians: its precision suggests an exact body count, but this is not the case and its origin remains obscure to this day[1002]. The summary of the French services mentions between 281 and 1,500 victims, while Médecins sans Frontières - which was on the spot - counted 355[1003]. According to the ASL office in Paris, the death toll even rose to 1,729[1004]. In the end, the exact number of victims will remain unknown, but only the number of 1,500 victims is retained[1005]. Although totally speculative, no one really tries to dispute it: it is a question of discrediting the Syrian government.

Technically, the French accusation is based on the characteristics of the Syrian army's 122mm artillery rockets, which have a maximum range of 20 km. But the rocket remnants found in Ghouta are of local manufacture, and are not compatible with the Syrian army's weapons[1006]. The Massachusetts Institute of Technology (MIT) in Boston was able to establish that these heavier rockets have completely different ballistics with a maximum range of 2.5-3 km, and could therefore only have been fired from areas then occupied by the rebels[1007]. These conclusions were later confirmed by further technical analysis[1008].

1000. See www.defense.gouv.fr/actualites/articles/programme-chimique-syrien-et-attaque-du-21-aout-2013

1001. Mother Agnes Miriam de la Croix et al, *The Chemical Attacks on East Ghouta - To Justify Military Right to Protect Intervention in Syria*, International Support Team for Mussalaha in Syria (ISTEAMS), Monastery of St. James, Syria, published by the International Institute for Peace, Justice and Human Rights (Geneva), September 15, 2013.

1002. Mark Hosenball, "Exclusive: U.S. total of Syrian gas deaths could include bomb casualties - sources", *Reuters*, September 13, 2013

1003. MSF, *Response to Government References to MSF Syria Statement*, August 27, 2013

1004. "Bodies still being found after alleged Syria chemical attack: opposition", *The Daily Star*, August 22, 2013; "Scientific report: it was not the Syrian army to use chemical weapons in Ghouta", *Vatican News*, January 8, 2016

1005. Hala Kodmani in the programme "C'dans l'air", "Syria: Putin's power grab", *YouTube*, September 28, 2016

1006. "Syria chemical attack: What we know", BBC News, September 24, 2013; See also "Terror gang in Aleppo fires hell cannon, February 2016", *YouTube*, March 26, 2019

1007. Richard Lloyd (Former UN Weapons Inspector) & Theodore A. Postol (Professor of Science, Technology, and National Security Policy, Massachusetts Institute of Technology), *Possible Implications of Faulty US Technical Intelligence in the Damascus Nerve Agent Attack of August 21, 2013*, MIT, Washington DC, January 14, 2014. https://s3.amazonaws.com/s3.documentcloud.org/documents/1006045/possible-implications-of-bad-intelligence.pdf

1008. Matthew Schofield, "New analysis of rocket used in Syria chemical attack undercuts U.S. claims", *McClatchy Foreign Staff*, Washington DC, January 15, 2014.

Furthermore, the SGDSN memo asserts the government origin of the sarin used based on samples found in Jobar and Saraqeb in April 2013. The problem is that in both cases, the OPCW had not been able to confirm that the toxic agent was of government origin[1009]. Furthermore, it completely obscures the fact that on August 24 in Jobar, chemical weapons were used against the Syrian army[1010], and therefore the rebels have chemical weapons. In its report of February 12, 2014, the Commission of Inquiry of the UN Human Rights Council confirms the similarities between the toxic weapons in Ghouta and those used against the Syrian army in Kahn al-Assal in March 2013:

> *With regard to the incident in Khan Al-Assal on March 19, the chemical agents used in this attack had the same unique characteristics as those used in Al-Ghouta*[1011].

Clearly, the government is trying to mislead its opinion in favour of an intervention in Syria. Belgian journalist Pierre Piccinin was held hostage in Syria and released on September 8, 2013. He claims to have overheard a conversation between two rebel officers confirming their responsibility in the chemical attack[1012]. But this first-hand testimony was lost in the prevailing disinformation...

No Western media mentions the fate of 200 women and children abducted in the region of Latakia between August 4 and August 18, 2013[1013], by various militias (including Ahrar al-Sham, the Islamic State in Iraq and the Levant, Jabhat al-Nosrah, Jaish al-Muhajirin wal-Ansar, Suqur al-Izz, supported by the West at the time) and who have never been found[1014]. There is a strong suspicion that the 'victims' of Ghouta were these Alawite children, 'sacrificed' to the rebel cause. Indeed, some individuals, who had been captured by rebel groups earlier, were identified in videos posted online on August 21[1015].

On August 27, 2013, in *Canal Plus*' "Grand Journal", to the question "*And there is nothing else possible but war?*" Bernard-Henri Lévy replied: "*But everything*

1009. https://unoda-web.s3.amazonaws.com/wp-content/uploads/2013/12/report.pdf (p. 38)

1010. Report of the UN Secretary-General to the Presidents of the General Assembly and the Security Council, December 13, 2013, (A/68/663-S/2013/735), p. 32

1011. *Human rights situations that require the Council's attention Report of the International Independent Investigation Commission on the Syrian Arab Republic,* Human Rights Council, United Nations General Assembly, Document A/HRC/25/65, February 12, 2014

1012. Rédaction Numérique de RTL, "Armes chimiques en Syrie : l'otage belge libéré dédouane le régime d'Assad", *RTL/AFP*, September 9, 2013.

1013. "Syria: Executions, Hostage Taking by Rebels", *Human Rights Watch*, October 10, 2013; *Report of the independent international commission of inquiry on the Syrian Arab Republic,* Human Rights Council, August 13, 2014, (A/HRC/27/60)

1014. "200 Civilians kidnapped by "rebels" from Latakia in August 2013 are still missing", *The Lemniscat,* January 25, 2014 (accessed April 4, 2017)

1015. Mother Agnes Miriam de la Croix et al, (*op. cit.*).

has been tried!" This is obviously false. On September 9, at a press conference, when asked how to get out of the crisis, John Kerry, then Secretary of State, replied:

> *(Bashar al-Assad) could hand over all his chemical weapons to the international community next week... But he is not about to do so, and it cannot be done, of course*[1016]*!*

The next day, Russian President Vladimir Putin surprises Western diplomacy by simply proposing the dismantling of Syria's chemical capabilities, based on discussions he had already had with Assad in 2012. On September 14, 2013, Russia and the United States reached an agreement to destroy Syria's chemical weapons under international supervision, and Syria acceded to the CWC. So not "*everything* had been *tried*"!

The Russian initiative caught the American and French 'war-mongers' off guard. Symptomatically, it is opposed by the rebels[1017], who see the prospect of a Western intervention receding.

On December 13, 2013, the UN published a report confirming that chemical weapons had been used, but not determining responsibility, as this was not its mandate[1018]. The West claims much, but demonstrates little; while the known facts tend to blame the rebels. Moreover, the context shows that only the rebels have an interest in creating a situation that could provoke an international intervention, as in Libya in 2011.

As for France, two possible conclusions can be drawn: either the "services" did not have the intelligence to support a political and military decision, and their conclusion is then the demonstration of a flagrant analytical deficit; or their synthesis does not reflect the actual state of their knowledge, but was written to influence public opinion, and thus "legitimise" an intervention that was illegal in the eyes of international law and illegitimate on the strategic level.

While many journalists and media in the US have tried to understand the real nature of the events, these inconsistencies have not resonated with the French media, which has been limited to reflecting the government's position.

6.16.3. The Chemical Attacks of 2014-2016

On June 23, 2014, OPCW Director-General Ahmet Üzümcü confirms in a statement that the last convoy of chemical weapons has left Syria[1019]. On

1016. Ibid.

1017. "Syrian rebels reject Russian proposal", *YouTube/euronews*, September 12, 2013

1018. United Nations Fact-Finding Mission on the Alleged Use of Chemical Weapons in the Syrian Arab Republic - Final Report, Document A/68/663, S/2013/735, December 13, 2013

1019. Announcement to media on last consignment of chemicals leaving Syria, (www.opcw.org/news/article/announcement-to-media-on-last-consignment-of-chemicals-leaving-syria/)

October 1st, 2014, the OPCW officially announced that the chemical weapons had left Syria, that the OPCW-UN Joint Mission had fulfilled its mandate, and that the Syrian government had met its obligations[1020]. As for the destruction of the toxins themselves, it will be announced as completed in January 2016[1021].

However, the use of chemical agents continues to be observed. Most often these are chlorine (which is not considered a chemical 'weapon' as such), but also phosgene, mustard gas, and sometimes nerve agents (sarin). Secretary of State John Kerry says he is "*absolutely certain*" that the Syrian government has used chemical weapons against its population[1022]. However, OPCW investigations have not confirmed the use of chlorine by the Syrian army[1023]. However, they do confirm the use of phosgene and chlorine between rebel forces[1024]. A confidential OPCW report published on October 29, 2015 even confirms the use of "mustard gas" - the common name for mustard gas[1025] - by the rebels[1026]. But in France and Belgium - more so than in the United States - the media, such as *Le Monde*[1027], *La Libre de Belgique*[1028] or *RTBF*[1029], simply ignore cases where the evidence points too clearly to the rebels.

In reality, the rebels are seeking to provoke a Western coalition intervention to overthrow the government. Clearly, they have chemical weapons, albeit crude ones. In November 2016, the *New York Times* cited a report by the London-based IHS Conflict Monitor, which found that the Islamic State had used chemical weapons more than 50 times in Iraq, thus invalidating the "analyses" of "experts" who appeared on American, French and Belgian public channels in 2017 to assert the opposite and unequivocally condemn the Syrian government[1030]! Blinded by the official discourse against the Syrian government, they simply deliberately exonerated the terrorists. Demonstrating what we have already seen: the fight against the Islamic State is variable geometry, and it is supported when it contributes to the objective of overthrowing the Syrian government.

1020. "OPCW-UN Joint Mission Draws to a Close", *OPCW* (Organisation for the Prohibition of Chemical Weapons Communiqué), October 1st, 2014

1021. "Destruction of declared Syrian chemical weapons completed", *OPCW News*, January 4, 2016

1022. Danielle Haynes, "John Kerry 'absolutely certain' Syria using chemical weapons on civilians", *UPI*, June 16, 2015

1023. Jerry Smith, "The challenge of assessing Syria's chemical weapons", *BBC News*, May 23, 2015

1024. Andrew V. Pestano, "U.N. confirms use of mustard, chlorine gas in Syrian civil war," *UPI*, November 8, 2015

1025. This is the same gas that was first used during the First World War at Ypres.

1026. Anthony Deutsch, "Exclusive: Chemical weapons used by fighters in Syria - sources", *Reuters*, November 6, 2015

1027. Benjamin Barthe, Jacques Follorou, Cécile Hennion & Yves-michel Riols, "Chlorine attacks in Syria: the evidence that embarrasses the West", *Le Monde*, June 4, 2014

1028. "En Syrie, 5 ans de chlore, de gaz moutarde et de gaz sarin", *La Libre.be*, January 23, 2018

1029. "Syria: the uses of chemical weapons in the conflict", *AFP/RTBF*, April 4, 2017

1030. Eric Schmitt, "ISIS Used Chemical Arms at Least 52 Times in Syria and Iraq, Report Says", The New York Times, November 21, 2016 (Accessed April 6, 2017)

6.16.4. The Chemical Attack in Khan Sheikhoun (April 4, 2017)

On April 4, 2017, in Khan Sheikhoun, a chemical incident resulted in the deaths of dozens of civilians, including many children. The nature of the attack is unclear. In fact, the only evidence incriminating the Syrian government is a strike by an Su-22 aircraft from the Shayrat base at the approximate time of the chemical attack.

On the ground, the rebel offensive on Homs has stabilised and a chemical bombardment in the Idlib region makes no sense operationally. Since the recapture of East Aleppo, the Syrian government's situation has improved overall, as it has been able to redistribute its forces to fight more effectively against the Islamic State and Hayat Tahrir al-Sham (formerly Jabhat al-Nosrah)[1031].

As in 2013, the Syrian government is far from being in a desperate situation and has no interest in risking Western intervention. On March 31, 2017, less than a week before the 'attack', Rex Tillerson, the US Secretary of State, had stated that Bashar al-Assad was not an obstacle to peace and that his fate should be a matter for the Syrian people. Moreover, on April 5 a conference on Syria was scheduled to take place in Brussels.

Naturally, the day after the strike, the American ambassador Nikki Haley accused Syria and Russia before the Security Council. On April 6, on *France 5*, Pascal Boniface, director of IRIS, asserted that "there is *no doubt about the use of chemical weapons*" and affirmed that "*Bashar al-Assad used chemical weapons to attack civilians*[1032]". Olivier Lepick, an "expert" on chemical weapons, says that there is no doubt about the nature of the weapon used and considers the Russian explanation "*unworthy*"[1033]. (In October 2001, he had already stated on Swiss television to the author of this book[1034] that the anthrax attack in the United States could only have been carried out by a state actor[1035], suggesting that Iraq could have been the instigator; although it was already known that this was false)! As for Agnès Levallois, she claims that Bashar al-Assad uses chemical weapons in order to avoid participating in a negotiation process, which he associates with the end of his regime[1036].

1031. *Levant Liberation Organisation* created on January 28, 2017 by the merger of several armed jihadist groups: Jabhat Fatah al-Sham (Front for the Conquest of the Levant), Harakat Nour al-Din al-Zinki (Harakat Nour al-Din al-Zinki Movement), Jabhat Ansar al-Dine (Front of the Partisans of Religion), Liwa al-Haq (Brigade of the Righteous), Jaish al-Sunnah (Army of the Sunnah).

1032. Pascal Boniface in the program "C dans l'air", "Syria: Trump découvre la guerre #cdanslair 06-04-2017", *YouTube/France 5*, April 6, 2017 (02'10")

1033. Olivier Lepick in the program "C dans l'air", "Syria: Trump découvre la guerre #cdanslair 06-04-2017", *YouTube/France 5*, April 6, 2017 (04'10")

1034. The author is a chemical and nuclear weapons expert trained at the NBC Defence Laboratory in Spiez, Switzerland.

1035. www.rts.ch/play/tv/19h30/video/peur-de-lanthrax-explications-scientifiques-et-politiques?id=1613745

1036. Agnès Levallois in the program "C dans l'air", "Syria: Trump découvre la guerre #cdanslair 06-04-2017", *YouTube/France 5*, April 6, 2017 (23'23")

In reality, at this stage, we don't know. The accusations of the "experts" are only circumstantial, based on the fact that Syria has possessed chemical weapons. They are thinking like Donald Trump, who launched strikes against the Shayrat airbase on April 7. Yet he has no evidence or conclusive proof[1037], as a White House memo of April 11 shows, which merely refutes Russian and Syrian arguments[1038].

In the following days, Professor Theodore A. Postol[1039], of the *Massachusetts Institute of Technology* (MIT), published a series of articles demonstrating that the White House memo was based on nothing more than evidence that could reasonably be assumed to have been "arranged"[1040]. Bashar al-Assad's responsibility can be decently questioned.

On April 26, 2017, the French Ministry of Foreign Affairs published a '*national assessment*' that blamed the Syrian government. It is based on the presence of chemical components similar to those observed in a homemade hand grenade used in Saraqeb in April 2013, which France had then attributed to the Syrian government[1041]. However, a UN report of December 12, 2013 noted that there was no certainty about the source of the Saraqeb munition[1042]. In July 2013, Moses Brown published a photo of a grenade rocket identical to the one from Saraqeb, found in Aleppo, in a Jabhat al-Nosrah base[1043]. Furthermore, the chemical evidence he relies on, namely the presence of hexamine and diisopropyl methylphosphonate (DIMP), is unproven, as Professor Postol demonstrates[1044].

By stating that the rebels have no means of engaging nerve agents (paragraph 3.a.1), the assessment note is simply misleading. In addition to the grenade mentioned above, Jabhat al-Nosrah is known to have seized stocks of chemical weapons before they were dismantled by the Syrian government in 2013-2014 (see above). In addition, on June 11, 2014, jihadists seized an old chemical weapons stockpile in Muthanna, Iraq[1045]! A UN report of December 13, 2013 on the use of

1037. "Syria war: Why was Shayrat airbase bombed?", *BBC News*, April 7, 2017

1038. "Declassified U.S. Report on Chemical Weapons Attack", *The New York Times*, April 11, 2017

1039. Professor Emeritus of Science, Technology, and National Security Policy, Massachusetts Institute of Technology

1040. Theodore A. Postol, "Video Evidence of False Claims Made in the White House Intelligence Report of April 11, 2017", *Sic Semper Tyrannis*, April 15, 2017; Theodore A. Postol, "A Critique of 'False and Misleading'White House Claims About Syria's Use of Lethal Gas", *Information Clearing House*, April 17, 2017; Theodore A. Postol, "A Quick Turnaround Assessment of the White House Intelligence Report Issued on April 11, 2017 About the Nerve Agent Attack in Khan Shaykhun, Syria", April 17, 2017.

1041. "Allegations of Use of Chemical Weapons in Syria Since 2012", *Annex to the National Assessment - Chemical Attack of 4 April 2017 (Khan Sheikhoun), Syrian Clandestine Chemical Programme*, April 25, 2017, p. 2

1042. https://unoda-web.s3.amazonaws.com/wp-content/uploads/2013/12/report.pdf (p. 38)

1043. http://brown-moses.blogspot.com/2013/07/more-on-gas-grenades-linked-to-chemical.html

1044. Theodore A. Postol, *The Flawed Chemical Analysis in the French Intelligence Report of April 26, 2017 Alleging a Syrian Government Sarin Nerve Agent Attack in Khan Sheikhoun of April 4, 2017*, April 30, 2017

1045. NdA: It had been declared to the UN by Saddam Hussein and had been controlled in 2003, but the Americans neglected to destroy it in more than ten years of presence! ("Isis seizes former chemical weapons plant in Iraq", *The Guardian*, July 9, 2014)

chemical weapons in Syria indicates at least three instances (March 19, August 24 and August 25, 2013) where chemical nerve weapons were used by rebels against the Syrian army[1046]. Furthermore, it is known that the Islamists had a chemical weapons production and engagement capability, as confirmed by John Parachini, former director of the RAND Corporation's Intelligence Policy Center[1047].

As for chlorine, it is known that in August 2012, Jabhat al-Nosrah[1048] seized the only Syrian chlorine gas factory in the vicinity of Aleppo[1049]. In December 2016, Syrian forces discovered large quantities of chlorine from Saudi Arabia in East Aleppo. Thus, contrary to French allegations, the rebels are in possession of chemical weapons that they produced (and stockpiled) themselves, including sarin, chlorine, phosgene[1050] and mustard. On October 29, 2015, three OPCW CONFIDENTIAL reports reported the use of chemical weapons (including mustard and chlorine) by the rebels in the same year[1051].

The national assessment refers to the use of binary chemical weapons. But this is not correct. In binary weapons, the toxic agent is packaged as two harmless products, in separate tanks, with a small explosive charge. During flight, a mechanism mixes them to produce the nerve agent that will be disseminated by the explosion. The advantage of such a munition is that it can be handled relatively safely. The disadvantage is that it is very ineffective, as the mixture is never optimal. This is why the US abandoned this technology in the early 1990s. It is *assumed* that Russia has been working on this technology. As for Syria, nothing is known. Rather, it is said to be stored separately and mixed when filling munitions just before a mission: a slow, tedious and detectable process. However, no independent mission has been able to collect samples of the toxic material on site: we are therefore in the realm of conjecture.

The military analysis of the situation as of April 4, 2017 is presented in a rather summary manner. On that day, the front line was 22-28 kilometres from Khan Sheikhoun. Under these conditions, it is difficult to understand why Syria would use 'last resort' weapons exclusively against civilians (women and children), at the risk of alienating the international community, while sparing jihadist forces.

1046. *United Nations Mission to Investigate Allegations of the Use of Chemical Weapons in the Syrian Arab Republic - Final report*, December 12, 2013

1047. John V. Parachini (former director of the RAND National Defense Research Institute's Intelligence Policy Center), "Keep Chemical Weapons Out of Terrorist Hands," *U.S. News & World Report*, September 23, 2016

1048. "Syrian Militants Have Access to Chlorine Gas: Plant Owner", *Nuclear Threat Initiative*, Washington DC, April 1st, 2013

1049. Aryn Baker, "Syria's Civil War: The Mystery Behind a Deadly Chemical Attack", *TIME Magazine*, April 1st, 2013

1050. It should be noted that some of the symptoms observed in Khan Sheikhoun are much more similar to those of phosgene than those of sarin.

1051. Anthony Deutsch, "Exclusive: Chemical weapons used by rebels in Syria - sources", *Reuters*, November 5, 2015

The assessment is accompanied by an annex that lists some 130 recorded chemical attacks in Syria. But under the guise of scientific neutrality, the list is misleading:

it omits many attacks already recorded by the UN[1052]. In particular, those that can be fairly clearly attributed to rebels because they targeted Syrian military personnel:

It also ignores attacks carried out by French and US-backed rebel groups, such as the one in Sheikh Maqsoud (East Aleppo), for which Jaish al-Islam itself has acknowledged responsibility[1053] !

it attributes only 3 chemical attacks to the Islamic State. On this basis, the Belgian news channel VRT will claim that the Syrian government is responsible for 98% of the chemical attacks[1054] ! Yet, in November 2016, the *New York Times* reported that the group had carried out 52, about 30% of which were in Syria[1055]...

it attributes the October 30, 2016 attack in al-Hamadaniyah (West Aleppo)[1056], to the Syrian "regime" although it was aimed at a government area. Is the Syrian army shooting itself?

Moreover, there is no contextual analysis. What would be the interest of the Syrian government to create such a provocation, against friendly populations, just after the American declarations not to target the government anymore, two days before a conference on Syria and while the operational situation in the Idlib-Hama region is rather favourable to it? Moreover, in this sector, the civilian population is essentially composed of Levantine Christians and Shiite Jaafari... Would Bashar al-Assad therefore attack the part of the population that is most favourable to him?

On June 29, the OPCW-UN Joint Investigative Mechanism (JIM) published its report on the incident[1057] and attributed responsibility to the Syrian government, despite the fact that the investigators did not have access to direct information and relied mainly on witness testimony. Russia[1058] and several

1052. *United Nations Mission to Investigate Allegations of the Use of Chemical Weapons in the Syrian Arab Republic - Final report*, December 12, 2013

1053. https://www.amnesty.org/en/latest/news/2016/05/syria-armed-opposition-groups-committing-war-crimes-in-aleppo-city/

1054. "Complot theory or international scandal? New document triggers controversy about Douma gas attack", *VRT-NWS*, May 30, 2019

1055. Eric Schmitt, "ISIS Used Chemical Arms at Least 52 Times in Syria and Iraq, Report Says", *The New York Times*, November 21, 2016

1056. Suleiman Al-Khalidi & Tom Perry, "Aleppo fighting spreads amid accusations of gas attack", *Reuters*, October 30, 2016

1057. *Report of the OPCW Fact-Finding Mission in Syria Regarding an Alleged Incident in Khan Shaykhun, Syrian Arab Republic, April 2017*, OPCW Technical Secretariat, June 29, 2017 (S/1510/2017)

1058. "Additional Assessment of the OPCW-UN Joint Investigative Mechanism Seventh Report", *Permanent Mis-*

organisations have found inconsistencies and "oversights" in the report, which is considered unprofessional[1059]. This is why Russia will want to replace the JIM with another mechanism, more strictly subordinated to the Security Council, which the West will consider as obstruction. We will come back to this later.

Once again, the Western version is flawed. In fact, the most likely and coherent version of the incident is probably the one proposed on June 25 by the American journalist Seymour Hersh, in the German newspaper *Die Welt*[1060]. Based on confidences from the DIA, the American military intelligence service, it tends to confirm the Syrian and Russian version, and illustrates the deep rift between the military and the White House.

Prior to the April 4 strike, the Russians had shared the SU-22's flight data with the Western coalition to avoid a collision. They had even communicated the objective of the mission: a two-storey building in which leaders of the two largest jihadist groups - Ahrar al-Sham and Jabhat al-Nosrah - were to meet to coordinate their action. The Russians were precise, allowing CIA operatives advising these groups to walk away. After the Syrian strike, the US damage assessment notes that the 250kg bomb explosion was followed by secondary explosions of fertilisers, insecticides and other chemicals stored by the rebels in the building and its immediate surroundings. It was the fumes from these chlorinated or organophosphate products that caused casualties with symptoms similar to those of chlorine or sarin.

It is likely that these chemicals were stored for later use, as the delivery of gas masks to Dr Shajul Islam on April 1st[1061] would suggest. This doctor settled in Khan Sheikhoun after being suspected by the British government of involvement in the abduction of two journalists in 2012, and then released for lack of evidence[1062].

The problem is that before the strike, the French services intercepted a message from the Syrians that mentioned a "special" weapon. Obsessed by the possible use of chemical weapons, they interpreted it as a "chemical bomb". However, it is a conventional bomb, but remote-controlled, provided by the Russians for the occasion, and which requires the adaptation of certain procedures. According to an American intelligence officer, this is how the "fairy *tale*" of the use of chemical

---

sion of the Russian Federation to the United Nations, November 13, 2017

1059. "The UN OPCW Joint Investigative Mechanism report regarding Khan Sheikhoun", *humanrightsinvestigations.org,* November 9, 2017

1060. Seymour M. Hersh, "Trump's Red Line", www.welt.de, June 25, 2017

1061. https://twitter.com/DrShajulIslam/status/848270456822145024 (see: http://archive.is/lnHXE, and: http://archive.is/GQoke)

1062. Martin Robinson, "Does this NHS doctor hold the key to identifying 'Jihadi John'? East London medic once accused of kidnapping journalists in Syria probed with his brother as hunt for world's most wanted man intensifies', *Daily Mail,* August 22, 2014; Robert Verkaik, "'Russia airstrikes are killing women and children… but MISSING ISIS': Struck off Brit NHS doctor accused of kidnapping Western hostages is treating bomb victims in Syria", *Daily Mail,* July 28, 2016

weapons in Khan Sheikhoun was born. The intelligence services immediately understood the situation and tried to explain it to Donald Trump. But the latter would not listen and ordered retaliatory strikes on April 7 [1063]. In the American magazine *Newsweek*, a former US intelligence contractor explains the fragility and contradictions in the accusations against Bashar al-Assad and the reasons that pushed Donald Trump to strike[1064]. In September 2017, journalist Gareth Porter notes that the facts reported by Seymour Hersh correspond with observations on the ground[1065].

In France, Emmanuel Macron's presidency heralded a more considered approach to engagement in the Middle East. In February 2018, underlining France's determination to strike Syria in the event of 'proven' use of chemical weapons against the Syrian population, he declared:

> *But today we do not have proof from our services that treaty-banned chemical weapons were used against the civilian population*[1066].

This suggested that the French services still had no evidence to confirm the use of chemical weapons by the Syrian government. The assertion echoed the statement by US Defence Secretary James Mattis, who said the same month that the US had *no* evidence of Syrian use of chemical weapons, including in 2013 and 2017[1067], while raising the possibility of a US retaliation in the event of an incursion[1068].

But the objective is not peace: it is the overthrow of the government and the partition of Syria.

6.16.5. The Chemical Attack in Douma (April 7, 2018)

At the beginning of February 2018, the noose was tightening on the rebels in Eastern Ghouta. Syrian strikes are apparently focusing on hospital infrastructure: '*13 hospitals targeted in 48 hours*', according to Patrick Cohen on *France 5*[1069]. Guest journalist Bernard Guetta says there is no Islamic State presence in the area (which is true), but suggests - along with Cohen - that the government is lying by claiming there are jihadists. This is false: they fail to mention that the area is held

1063. Seymour M. Hersh, "Trump's Red Line", www.welt.de, June 25, 2017
1064. Ian Wilkie, op.cit.
1065. Gareth Porter, "Have We Been Deceived Over Syrian Sarin Attack? Scrutinizing the Evidence in an Incident Trump Used to Justify Bombing Syria", *AlterNet*, September 11, 2017
1066. "Chemical weapons in Syria: Macron awaits 'proof' before striking the regime", *Le Journal du Dimanche (lejdd.fr)*, February 14, 2018
1067. Ian Wilkie, "Now Mattis Admits There Was No Evidence Assad Used Poison Gas on His People", *Newsweek*, February 8, 2018
1068. "US investigating possible sarin gas attacks in Syria: Defense Secretary Jim Mattis", *Egypt Independent/Deutsche Welle*, February 3, 2018
1069. "Humanitarian disaster in Syria - C à Vous - 21/02/2018", *France 5/YouTube*, February 21, 2018 (02'25")

by Faylaq al-Rahman, Ahrar al-Sham and Jaish al-Islam[1070], jihadist groups, which John Kerry claimed had committed "*shocking crimes... against innocent civilians, journalists and teachers*[1071]", and which are then holding the civilian population hostage. Ironically, these "rebels" that journalists are trying to protect will be the executioners of the Kurds in October 2019... We will come back to this.

On April 4, 2018, President Donald Trump announces that he has decided to withdraw US troops from Syria[1072]. On the same day, Steve Cox, an independent candidate for Congress from California, tweets:

> *If, after this announcement, we end up with headlines announcing a new gas attack by Assad against his own people, don't believe it.*
>
> *He may be a tyrant, but he is not an idiot. The US leaving his country is good for him and a gas attack would prevent the US from leaving*[1073].

Three days later - and one year after the Khan Sheikhoun incident - a "chemical attack" is reported in the Douma area (in Eastern Ghouta), in the Jaish al-Islam-held zone. Social networks broadcast images of what appears to be the aftermath of a chemical attack: semi-unconscious women and children and scenes of summary decontamination with water. Russia and Syria deny the use of chemical weapons.

In New York, in the Security Council, the United States, France and Great Britain react and accuse - once again - the Syrian government of using toxic agents against its own population and consider retaliation. The French ambassador François de Lattre even accuses Russia. Great intellectual honesty, because at this stage he knows nothing about it: he has no other elements than those coming from the "White Helmets". The attack itself has not been proven.

On April 10, some media still called it "alleged"[1074]. However, on *France 5*, Patrick Cohen described as "*revisionists*" those who question the reality of the chemical attack[1075] and Bernard-Henri Lévy deplored the fact that the West had

---

1070. Aron Lund, "Understanding Eastern Ghouta in Syria", *The Hew Humanitarian* (formerly IRIN), February 23, 2018

1071. John Kerry, Secretary of State, Aspen Institute, Aspen, Colorado June 28, 2016 (https://2009-2017.state.gov/secretary/remarks/2016/06/259165.htm)

1072. Karen Deyoung & Shane Harris, "Trump instructs military to begin planning for withdrawal from Syria", *The Washington Post*, April 4, 2018

1073. https://twitter.com/RealSteveCox/status/981539844546486272

1074. "Following the alleged chemical attack in Douma, Washington on Monday raised the threat of military action in Syria, addressing Moscow in particular. The Kremlin warned of "serious consequences" in the event of Western strikes.", *France 24*, April 10, 2018

1075. Patrick Cohen in the programme "C à Vous", "Faut-il faire la guerre en Syrie? - C à Vous - 10/04/2018", *France 5/YouTube*, April 10, 2018, (07'22")

not struck Syria earlier when "*we had the right to do so, we had the humanity, we had the military situation...*[1076]". This is a curious notion of law and humanity: one accuses on the basis of prejudice alone.

On April 12, on TF1, President Emmanuel Macron said he had "*evidence that chemical weapons were used by the regime of Bashar al-Assad*[1077]". But on the same day, James Mattis, the US Secretary of Defense, declared that the Americans had no proof and were still looking for it[1078]. Most likely, Macron is lying. Incidentally, the videos of this interview on *TF1* and *BFM TV* are removed from *YouTube*[1079]. It is clear that at this point Western intelligence services are clueless and the accusations against the Syrian government have no solid basis. An excellent debunking of the lies of the official discourse is presented by "TroubleFait" on *YouTube*[1080].

On April 13, the White House issued a press release claiming that the Syrian government had used Sarin-type toxins in Douma[1081]. It is with this certainty, but without evidence of actual Syrian government responsibility, that the US, France and Britain jointly conduct strikes on April 13-14, 2018[1082]. The OPCW experts mandated to investigate the Douma incident arrive in Damascus the day after the strikes (!), demonstrating that bombing had been carried out without any concrete evidence. They will start collecting samples on the 21st.

The strikes targeted a former missile storage base, a command bunker and the Syrian Scientific Studies and Research Center (CERS) in Barzeh near Damascus. The newspaper *La Croix* renamed it "Chemical and Biological Weapons Research and Development Centre[1083]" for the occasion, even though it has never been called that, but it is necessary to dramatise the image of the "bad guy"...

This is in the realm of influencing actions, the purpose of which is to justify a crime against international law. The OPCW has regularly monitored the ESRC since November 2016: the first inspection, held in 2017, did not identify any illegal activity[1084]. A second inspection in late 2017 confirmed that Syria had

1076. Bernard-Henri Lévy in the programme "C à Vous", "Faut-il faire la guerre en Syrie? - C à Vous - 10/04/2018", *France 5/YouTube*, April 10, 2018, (03'38")

1077. Cyril Fourneris, "Macron has 'evidence that chemical weapons were used by the Syrian regime'", *en.euronews.com*, April 12, 2018; "Douma - Syria, April 7, 2018", *YouTube/French Ministry for Europe and Foreign Affairs*, April 13, 2018

1078. David Martin, "U.S. 'looking for the actual evidence' of Syria chemical attack, Mattis says", *CBS News*, April 12, 2018.

1079. BFM TV, "Syria: Macron says he 'has proof' that chemical weapons were used", *YouTube*, April 12, 2018

1080. See TroubleFait, *Gassing in Syria*, May 2018

1081. *United States Assessment of the Assad Regime's Chemical Weapons Use*, The White House, Office of the Press Secretary, April 13, 2018

1082. See "Strikes destroyed a 'mysterious chemical laboratory' - which was under regular OPCW monitoring", *les-crises.fr*, April 16, 2018

1083. Gilles Biassette, Marie Verdier and Benjamin Quenelle, "Bilan nuancé des frappes sur la Syrie", *La Croix*, April 15, 2018

1084. OPCW Executive Council, *Report by The Director-General - First Inspections at The Barzah And Jamrayah*

destroyed its chemical weapons[1085] and renewed its conclusion on March 23, 2018[1086]. Despite some unanswered questions[1087], the Syrian government provided the inspectors with information that was considered complete and no illegal activity was found. Moreover, if there had been any doubts, the three Western powers could have requested a thorough inspection of the facility, which they did not.

Moreover, common sense would suggest that bombing a facility that produces chemical weapons would expose the civilian population to disaster, as a CERS employee noted in the aftermath of the strikes[1088]. So it was a lie from start to finish, and a senseless strike.

It is probably this lack of clear motives that leads the French government to justify itself after the fact with a new "*national assessment*[1089]". Published by the Ministry of Foreign Affairs, it sets out 3 reasons for the use of chemical weapons by the Syrian army[1090]:

chemical weapons are used to dislodge fighters who are holed up in shelters;

to punish the civilian population for supporting the rebels and to demonstrate that resistance is useless;

since 2012, Syrian forces have used chemical weapons in conjunction with conventional weapons.

She concludes:

> *France therefore considers (1) that, without doubt, a chemical attack was carried out against civilians in Douma on April 7, 2018, and (2) that there is no other plausible scenario than that of an action by the Syrian armed forces as part of an overall offensive in the Eastern Ghouta enclave*[1091].

This is disinformation. Indeed, the Douma area was then under the control of Jaish al-Islam, a group funded and supported by the Western coalition and Saudi

---

Syrian Scientific Studies And Research Centre Facilities In The Syrian Arab Republic In Accordance With Decision Ec-83/ Dec.5 (Dated November 11, 2016), Eighty-Fifth Session EC-85/DG.16, June 2, 2017

1085. OPCW, Executive Council, Note by The Director-General - Progress in The Elimination of The Syrian Chemical Weapons Programme, November 24, 2017

1086. OPCW, Executive Council, Note by The Director-General - Progress in The Elimination of The Syrian Chemical Weapons Programme, March 23, 2018

1087. Security Council Letter dated October 30, 2017 from the Secretary-General addressed to the President of the Security Council, S/2017/916, October 31, 2017

1088. "Syria: employees of a bombed centre assure that they were not producing chemical weapons", *AFP/Le Point*, April 14, 2018

1089. *National Assessment - Chemical attack of April 7, 2018 (Douma, Eastern Ghouta, Syria), Syrian Clandestine Chemical Program*, April 14, 2018

1090. *National Assessment - Chemical attack of April 7, 2018...* op. cit, (p. 3)

1091. *National Assessment - Chemical attack of April 7, 2018...* op.cit, (p.6)

Arabia[1092], which had already been accused in April 2016, of using chlorine to attack Kurdish forces in East Aleppo[1093] and had admitted responsibility[1094]. The British press mentions this precedent[1095], but not the French mainstream media. This means that the memo is lying when it states that:

> *The French services have no information to support the claim that the armed groups in Ghouta sought to acquire or had chemical weapons*[1096].

The only evidence mentioned in the note comes from social networks and from two NGOs, described as "usually reliable": the Syrian American Medical Society (SAMS) and the Union of Organizations for Medical Relief and Care (UOSSM). Both are funded by Western countries (notably the United States, France and Switzerland). The former is said to be run by members of the Muslim Brotherhood[1097], while the latter is close to the Free Syrian Army, which is now in the hands of the jihadists. After the recapture of East Aleppo, Pierre Le Corf, a young French humanitarian, showed that these two organisations occupied the same building as Jabhat al-Nosrah and Ahrar al-Sham[1098].

The sources of the document are "open", i.e. the same as those of Le *Monde*[1099] or Le *Figaro*[1100]. The photos of chemical weapons victims published in the "national assessment" were transmitted "*by a source*" of unverifiable (and probably unverified) origin. They show victims with breathing difficulties, foaming at the mouth. Symptoms that are not compatible with the toxins evoked in Douma, as the OPCW investigation will later show[1101]. Moreover, all accusations concerning the nature of the toxins, their use and the responsibility of the Syrian government are formulated in the conditional. Thus, the strikes against Syria were justified with unconfirmed information from unverified sources that later turned out to be false!

1092. Ian Black, "Syria crisis: Saudi Arabia to spend millions to train new rebel force", *The Guardian*, November 2, 2013
1093. Sirwan Kajjo, "Kurdish Officials: Rebels May Have Used Chemicals in Aleppo", *Voice of America*, April 8, 2016; Hisham Arafat, "Syrian rebels admit chemical use against Kurds", *Kurdistan24*, April 9, 2016
1094. https://www.amnesty.org/en/latest/news/2016/05/syria-armed-opposition-groups-committing-war-crimes-in-aleppo-city/
1095. Matt Drake, "Rebel group accusing Assad of gas attack 'USED CHEMICAL WEAPONS' against Kurds", www.express.co.uk, April 12, 2018
1096. *National Assessment - Chemical attack of April 7, 2018…* op.cit, (p.4)
1097. Max Blumenthal, ""Al Qaeda's MASH Unit": How the Syrian American Medical Society Is Selling Regime Change and Driving the US to War", *The Grayzone*, April 12, 2018
1098. "ALEP: Pierre Le Corf visits the WHITE HELMETS HQ", *YouTube*, March 11, 2017
1099. Gilles Paris, Marc Semo & Benjamin Barthe, "Chemical Carnage in Eastern Ghouta", *lemonde.fr*, April 9, 2018
1100. "Syria: suspicion of chemical weapons bombing in Douma", *le figaro.fr*, April 8, 2018
1101. *Note by the Technical Secretariat - Report of the Fact-Finding Mission Regarding the Incident of Alleged Use of Toxic Chemicals as a Weapon in Douma, Syrian Arab Republic, on April 7, 2018*, OPCW Technical Secretariat, March 1st, 2019 (S/1731/2019) Paragraph 8.98

In Britain, the *Guardian* reports on the claims of doctors on the ground of symptoms consistent with the effects of organophosphate toxins, of which sarin is one[1102]. The *Sun* goes further, claiming that it was a sarin gas attack with 70 victims[1103]. In the "C dans l'air" programmes of April 10 and 14 on *France 5*, Pierre Servent asserts that the Syrian army mixed chlorine and sarin in order to combine their effects[1104]. But he does not have a monopoly on disinformation: Raphaël Pitti, a doctor at UOSSM, told BFM TV that "a *substance was added to the chlorine (...) potentially sarin gas*[1105]", while the White House claims that the "Syrian regime" used chlorine and sarin weapons[1106]. This is simply outlandish.

As early as 1955, in a SECRET report, an American military laboratory demonstrated the incompatibility of the two toxins: since chlorine is a decontaminant for neurotoxins such as sarin, the effects of the latter would have been totally inhibited. Moreover, the combination of the two toxins would be too acidic to be stored in metal containers[1107]!...

That said, even if sarin is not considered a persistent agent, its volatility is random and its virulence requires an attacker to wear even minimal protection. However, in Douma, at the time when the "chemical toxins" were allegedly used, no particular preparation was observed among Syrian troops, who were only 400 metres from the "affected" areas[1108]... not exactly optimal!

The day after the strikes on the "*chemical weapons production and storage facilities*", no toxic fumes were detected. Civilian security personnel and civilians were walking around unprotected, as *CBS Weekend* News reporter Seth Doane reported[1109]. Moreover, in a mixture of unconsciousness and a desire to deceive, Arwa Damon, a *CNN* journalist in Syria, even went so far as to sniff (!) objects "*exposed to chemical toxins*" in order to confirm the attack[1110]!...

1102. Kareem Shaheen, "Syria: 500 Douma patients had chemical attack symptoms, reports say", *The Guardian*, April 11, 2018

1103. Lizzie Parry, 'A VICIOUS KILLER Deadly Sarin gas used in Syria chemical attack leaves victims foaming at the mouth before suffering seizures', *The Sun*, April 11, 2018

1104. Émission "C dans l'air", "Syrie: Trump et Macron prêts à frapper", *YouTube/France 5*, April 10, 2018 (06'00"); Emission "C dans l'air", "Syrie: Trump, Macron et May passent à l'attaque", *YouTube/France 5*, April 14, 2018 (04'20") (40'30")

1105. "Alleged chemical attack in Syria: deadly substance added to chlorine according to an NGO", BFM TV, April 9, 2018

1106. *United States Assessment of the Assad Regime's Chemical Weapons* Use, Office of the Press Secretary, The White House, April 13, 2018 (www.defense.gov/portals/1/features/2018/0418_syria/img/United-States-Assessment-of-the-Assad-Regime's-Chemical-Weapons-Use.pdf)

1107. Joseph Epstein, Virginia E. Bauer & Mary M. Demek, Medical Laboratories Research Report No. 379, *Reaction Of Sarin With Bleach In Dilute Aqueous Solution (U)*, Chemical Corps Medical Laboratories, July 1955 (SECRET, declassified 1980)

1108. James Harkin, "What happened in Douma? Searching for facts in the fog of Syria's propaganda war", *The Intercept*, February 9, 2019.

1109. CBS Evening News, "A look at the aftermath of Syria airstrike", *YouTube*, April 15, 2018

1110. CNN, "Suspected chemical attack survivors speak to CNN", *YouTube*, April 15, 2018

Thus demonstrating without wanting to (and by silliness), that there was strictly nothing to fear from these "contaminated" objects.

In the programme "C dans l'air" of April 14, Pierre Servent claims that chemical weapons are used to dislodge combatants. This is true in certain circumstances, but not here! He obviously knows nothing about the subject. Indeed, chlorine is a relatively dense and heavy gas, which "stagnates" in confined and low-lying spaces (cellars and underground) where air circulation is poor[1111]. This is why it was used in the First World War, so that it would 'flow' into the trenches. During the Algerian War, the French army dislodged NLA fighters in caves by using improvised chlorine with bleach and descaler[1112]. When the adversary is located in the upper floors to conduct harassment combat against troops in the streets (e.g. snipers), the use of chlorine does not really make sense, as it dissipates quickly to the lower floors. Yet in Douma in April 2018, the Syrian army retook an entire network of underground tunnels (which could even accommodate vehicles) without using a single chemical or chlorine projectile[1113]!

As with the previous "attacks", we note that the "victims" are only women and children, that they take place only in areas where the Syrian army is successful, that they do not affect journalists, fighters or "white helmets", and that their effects are simply neutralised with water! In other words: the Syrian government used tactically inappropriate weapons, in the wrong place and in insufficient quantity (only two projectiles), with the sole aim of drawing the attention of the international community?

Moreover, it would rather target the civilian population than the fighters? The national assessment states that it is a question of "*punishing the civilian population present in areas held by fighters opposed to the regime, and to provoke an effect of terror and panic on them, inciting them to surrender*[1114]", an argument taken up by the journalist Hala Kodmani[1115]. On *France 5*, Pierre Servent explains that Bashar al-Assad "*wants to show that he is the one who wins*[1116]"! These are totally gratuitous assertions, based on no demonstrable facts. In this case, why did he not use chemical weapons on the cities of Zabadani and Madaya in the hands of the jihadists since 2011?

1111. "Chlorine - Properties, *YouTube*, August 14, 2015

1112. Jean-Louis Brau, *Les armes de guérilla*, Balland, Paris 1974, p.137

1113. "Syrian Army captures large underground tunnel in E Ghouta", *YouTube*, April 16, 2018 (https://www.youtube.com/watch?v=PgGqwAwJL5M&feature=youtu.be)

1114. *National Assessment - Chemical attack of April 7, 2018 (Douma, Eastern Ghouta, Syria), Syrian Clandestine Chemical Program*, April 14, 2018, p. 4

1115. Hala Kodmani in "C dans l'air", "Syria: Trump, Macron and May go on the attack - Les questions SMS #cdanslair 14.04.2018", *YouTube/France 5*, April 14, 2018 (03'10")

1116. Pierre Servent in the programme "C dans l'air", "Syria: Trump and Macron ready to strike", *YouTube/France 5*, April 14, 2018 (38'20")

In fact, in early 2018, during the advance of Syrian forces into Ghouta, Jaish al-Islam was the only rebel group to refuse an agreement with the government. It is able to take this uncompromising stance thanks to the civilians it uses as hostages and human shields[1117]; an aspect totally obscured by the French media. In a *CBS Evening* News report, reporter Seth Doane interviews a Syrian woman, who confirms that the rebels have prevented civilians from leaving the combat zone[1118]. The report was shown on April 22, 2018 in the programme "C Politique", but without this sequence, which was cut by *France 5*'s "fact checkers"[1119]! Moreover, the national assessment and the "experts" of *France 5* and *France 24*[1120], are silent about the group's long history of human rights violations. Already in 2015, it had locked civilians (Assyrians and Christians) in cages mounted on vehicles deployed on locations likely to be hit by Syrian aircraft[1121]. In 2017, it captured between 3,500 and 5,000 hostages[1122] in Adra al-Omalia - an Alawite town next to Douma - to use them as bargaining chips[1123]: they are human shields in the primary sense of the word. Finally, in August 2013, Jaish al-Islam was already the main rebel group in Ghouta[1124]...

Thus, the explanation that Bashar al-Assad is seeking to "*punish the civilian population*", as the Macron government memo claims, or to "*terrorise children*", as Bernard-Henri Lévy asserts[1125], seems particularly absurd in this context. It is simply disinformation. On the contrary: during the Douma incident, the Syrian government was in the process of negotiating with Jaish al-Islam in order to free the civilians held hostage. It is the result of this negotiation that pushes the group to withdraw from Douma, not the alleged chemical attack: on April 8, *Reuters* announces that the group is allowed to leave the city in exchange for the release of

1117. Tamara Qiblawi, Judith Vonberg and Vasco Cotovio, "As thousands flee assaults in Syria, rebels won't let others out", *CNN*, March 16, 2018; Laure Stephan, "Avec la chute de la Ghouta orientale, les prisons rebelles commencent à livrer leurs secrets", *lemonde.fr*, March 28, 2018

1118. "Inside Douma, the site of apparent Syrian chemical attack", *CBS Evening News/YouTube*, April 16, 2018 (02'55")

1119. "Le bureau de vérif': fake news on chemical weapons in Syria - C Politique - 22/04/18", *France 5/YouTube*, April 23, 2018 (04'35")

1120. "War in Syria: Ghouta, a strategic recovery?", *France 24*, April 13, 2018

1121. Haidar Sumeri, "'Moderate rebels' in #Syria putting Alawite women in cages and using them as human shields. E. Ghouta.", *Twitter*, November 1st, 2015; Robert Mackey & Maher Samaan, "Caged Hostages From Syrian President's Sect Paraded Through Rebel-Held Suburb", *The New York Times*, November 1st, 2015; "Syrian rebels using caged civilian captives as 'human shields'", *The Telegraph/AFP*, November 2, 2015.

1122. according to estimates by the Syrian Observatory for Human Rights (OSDH) or the Syrian government

1123. "Amid resentment among their families, the regime ignores thousands of abductees from Adra Al-Omalia in return for speeding up the exit of Jaish Al-Islam from Douma", *Syrian Observatory for Human Rights*, April 10, 2018; Dania Akkad, Nadine Dahan & Zouhir Al-Shimale," Jaish al-Islam says it inflated hostage numbers, leaving Syrian families in the dark", *Middle East Eye*, April 13, 2018 (updated April 15, 2018)

1124. In fact, its name at the time was "Liwa al-Islam" (Brigade of Islam). It became "Jaish al-Islam" (Army of Islam) in September 2013.

1125. Bernard-Henri Lévy in the programme "C à Vous", "Faut-il faire la guerre en Syrie? - C à Vous - 10/04/2018", *France 5/YouTube*, April 10, 2018, (10'15")

the 3,500 hostages[1126]. On April 9, in Douma, this release was widely publicised by the government - like the previous releases - for propaganda purposes[1127]. The government had no interest in carrying out a chemical attack against a population whose liberation could serve its popularity! Naturally, the French media, which supports jihadist terrorism, will not show the images of these liberations...

The media's discretion on Jaish al-Islam can hardly be explained by ethics. Rather, it is to avoid shedding too much light on the 'rebels' that Western countries support. Indeed, in May 2016, France and its allies objected to Jaish al-Islam being put on the UN list of terrorist movements[1128]... and the group will be one of those committing crimes against the Kurds in October 2019[1129]! But, once again, the French media will superbly ignore the contradictions of French policy in the region.

Our "experts" and "journalists" have created facts based on their own prejudices. Western accusations are based exclusively on the assumption that the Syrian government is the only actor with access to chemical weapons, and that it is the only one who can project them. This is obviously false, as the use of chemical weapons (notably chlorine) has been reported on numerous occasions in Iraq and Syria during inter-factional fighting[1130]. When Pierre Servent states that only the Syrian government has the means to project chemical weapons, this is also untrue, as the rebels use heavy mortars that they manufacture themselves[1131].

In fact, in Douma, the very reality of an attack is open to debate: Russia, which had agents on the ground, claims that no attack took place, neither by the insurgents nor by the government. The British journalist Robert Fisk, from the *Independent* newspaper, collected the testimony of a doctor from the Douma hospital who confirmed that there had been no chemical attack[1132], but that the bombing had caused clouds of dust and made the atmosphere unbreathable in the underground tunnels where the civilian population had taken refuge; this would explain why the social networks only show women and children[1133]. His report is corroborated by Pearson Sharp, an American journalist working

---

1126. "Jaish al-Islam to leave Douma in return for releasing prisoners", *Reuters*, April 8, 2018; James Harkin, "What Happened In Douma? Searching for Facts in the Fog of Syria's Propaganda War", *The Intercept*, February 9, 2019

1127. "Syria: Douma hostages reunite with families after years in captivity", *Ruptly/YouTube,* April 9, 2018; "After rebels free hostages, Syrians search for loved ones", *France 24*, April 9, 2018; "Douma hostages tell of their 4+ years in captivity", *YouTube*, April 10, 2018

1128. "U.S., Britain, France block Russia bid to blacklist Syria rebels", *Reuters*, May 11, 2016

1129. *FACTSHEET - Factions in Turkish-backed "Free Syrian Army"*, Rojava Information Center, 2019; Meredith Tax, "Trump's Betrayal of Rojava", *Dissent Magazine*, October 15, 2019

1130. Eric Schmitt, "ISIS Used Chemical Arms at Least 52 Times in Syria and Iraq, Report Says", *The New York Times*, November 21, 2016

1131. See, for example: Andrew Illingworth, "VIDEO: Damascus militants rain down heavy mortar fire on Syrian Army troops", www.almasdarnews.com, July 13, 2017.

1132. "No evidence of chemical attack in Douma - doctor", www.aol.co.uk, April 17, 2018

1133. Robert Fisk, "The search for truth in the rubble of Douma - and one doctor's doubts over the chemical attack - Robert Fisk visits the Syria clinic at the centre of a global crisis", www.independent.co.uk, April 17, 2018

for *One America News Network* (a news channel considered rather favourable to Donald Trump), who went to the scene in the days following the alleged chemical attack. He claims that he could not find a single person in Douma who had heard of a chemical attack and that the civilians interviewed believe that it was a staged attack by Islamists in order to obtain a Western intervention[1134].

Thus, the rebels did not '*self-gas*', as Jean-Yves le Drian, Minister of Foreign Affairs, mendaciously ironises[1135]. They simply and opportunely knew how to exploit a non-event to 'create' a situation likely to provoke a foreign intervention. The images seen on social networks are probably not "montages", but an overdramatisation intended to mislead.

On April 15, 2018, the final communiqué of the Arab League Summit remains very nuanced on Syrian responsibility for the Douma incident:

> *We strongly condemn the use of chemical weapons against the friendly Syrian nation and demand an independent international investigation and the application of international law to those found responsible for the use of chemical weapons*[1136].

But the *Figaro* article on the summit does not reflect this caution and is based solely on the personal statement of the Saudi Arabian delegate, who stresses the "criminal" nature of the use of chemical weapons and suggests that it was carried out by the Syrian government[1137]. On *France 5*, in the programme "C dans l'air" of April 18, none of the experts present noted the caution of the Arab League or mentioned the possibility of alternative scenarios to the "official version"[1138]. The questioning of some members of the National Assembly was even treated with condescension, as a lack of solidarity.

In the United States, Republican Senator Rand Paul of the Foreign Affairs Committee, when asked on *CNN* whether sanctions should be imposed on Russia after the attack, replied:

> *Before talking about sanctions, we should first demonstrate that Russia is complicit in this attack. In fact, on this issue, I see this attack and I think: either Assad must be the stupidest dictator on the planet, or he didn't do it. I need proof that he did. The intelligence agencies claim to have it; but think about it! Does it make sense: he's been winning the war for the last few years;*

1134. "OAN Investigation Finds No Evidence of Chemical Weapon Attack in Syria", *One America News Network/ YouTube*, April 16, 2018

1135. "Le Drian: "Yes, there was a chemical attack on Douma", in Syria", *BFMTV*, April 16, 2018

1136. "Arab League Summit final statement condemns chemical attack, does not accuse Damascus", *AMN*, April 16, 2018

1137. "Arab league wants investigation into chemical weapons in Syria", *Le Figaro.fr/Reuters*, April 15, 2018.

1138. "Syria: after the strikes, the controversy", *YouTube*, April 18, 2018

the only thing that would galvanise the world to attack Assad directly would be a chemical attack[1139] *[...]*

But nobody tries to understand what the Syrian government's logic might be. In *Libération*, Luc Mathieu castigates Russian disinformation:

After the April 7 attack in Douma, the Kremlin flooded the media with false information. In November, it had already blocked the only UN mechanism that could investigate[1140].

The verification mechanism is also the subject of misinformation and we will come back to this below. Nevertheless, the Russian "blockage" clearly does not prevent a fact-finding mission (FFM) from being sent to the site on April 12. On site, the mission was unable to gain immediate access to the site. On April 16, in an address to the British Parliament, Theresa May accused the Syrian and Russian governments of preventing OPCW investigators from accessing the affected area[1141]. But she is lying: it was the decision of the UN Department of Safety and Security (UNDSS) officer on the ground[1142], in agreement with the Syrian authorities and the Russian military police. This version is confirmed in a communication from the OPCW Director General on April 18[1143] and in the interim report of the investigators[1144]. This did not prevent *Libération from* repeating the accusation on May 3[1145].

On April 26, a press conference was held at OPCW headquarters in The Hague with the allegedly 'gassed' 11-year-old Hassan Diab, who had been widely seen on social networks. But the French mainstream media simply ignore the event, while a French diplomat calls it an "*obscene charade*[1146]"!

On July 6, the OPCW published the interim report of the MEF, which found no traces of nerve agents in the environment or the blood of the alleged victims[1147]. Instead, it mentions scattered traces of chlorine (without concluding

1139. "Rand Paul Questions Douma Chemical Attack Narrative on CNN, *YouTube*, April 17, 2018

1140. Luc Mathieu, "Armes chimiques, mensonges toxiques", *liberation.fr*, May 3, 2018

1141. House of Commons Hansard, Syria, April 16, 2018, Volume 639

1142. Anthony Deutsch & Tom Perry, "U.N. team fired upon in Syria while visiting suspected chemical sites", *Reuters*, April 18, 2018

1143. "*Update by the Director-General on the Deployment of the OPCW Fact-Finding Mission to Douma, Syrian Arab Republic, to the Executive Council at Its Fifty-Ninth Meeting*", OPCW Executive Council, April 18, 2018 (EC-M-59/DG.2)

1144. *Note by the Technical Secretariat, Interim Report Of The OPCW Fact-Finding Mission In Syria Regarding The Incident Of Alleged Use Of Toxic Chemicals As A Weapon In Douma, Syrian Arab Republic, on April 7, 2018*, OPCW Technical Secretariat, Document, S/1645/2018, July 6, 2018 (para 6.1)

1145. Luc Mathieu, (*op. cit.*)

1146. "Conflict in Syria - Russia accused of staging an "obscene charade" at the OPCW", *rtl.be*, April 26, 2018

1147. *Note by the Technical Secretariat, Interim Report Of The OPCW...* (op. cit.) (p. 10) and "Annex 3 - Analysis Results" (pp. 15-18)

that it could have been used as a weapon, as chlorine is found in many everyday products)[1148]. At this stage, traces of chlorine are still being examined.

But this did not prevent the British *BBC* from publishing the headline on its website the next day: *The attack in Syria was chlorine…* a false report that was modified a few hours later into a text that was a little closer to the truth: *War in Syria: "Chlorine possible" at the site of the attack in Douma*[1149]. Furthermore, it asserts a strong presumption of the use of chemical weapons on targets where the OPCW has not been able to establish that they were actually used[1150].

In February 2019, *BBC* journalist Riam Dalati claims that the scene that circulated on social networks, showing women and children being "decontaminated" in the hospital in Douma, was only staged and that there were no victims of chemical weapons in the hospital. However, he remains evasive on the question of what actually happened[1151].

On March 1st, 2019, the OPCW published its final report[1152], which confirmed its interim report. Nothing really conclusive emerges: it is possible that chlorine was used, but no autopsy could be performed and the mission did not observe any symptoms that would confirm the use of chemical weapons. The absence of traces of nerve agents (sarin) is confirmed[1153]:

> *No organophosphate nerve agents, their degradation products or synthetic impurities were detected in the environmental samples prioritised for analysis or in plasma samples from presumed victims*[1154].

Therefore, the claims of the French government's "experts" and national assessment[1155] were outright lies. The US, British and French governments, and the media that blindly relayed their rhetoric, lied to cover up a war crime.

1148. *Note by the Technical Secretariat, Interim Report Of The OPCW Fact-Finding Mission In Syria Regarding The Incident Of Alleged Use Of Toxic Chemicals As A Weapon In Douma, Syrian Arab Republic, on April 7, 2018*, OPCW Technical Secretariat, Document, S/1645/2018, July 6, 2018

1149. "Syria war: 'Possible chlorine' at Douma attack site - watchdog", *BBC News*, July 7, 2018

1150. *Note by the Technical Secretariat, Interim Report Of The OPCW Fact-Finding Mission In Syria Regarding The Incident Of Alleged Use Of Toxic Chemicals As A Weapon In Douma, Syrian Arab Republic, on April 7, 2018*, OPCW Technical Secretariat, Document S/1645/2018, July 6, 2018

1151. "Russian Embassy Misleads on BBC Producer's Claim About Douma Hospital Video", *Polygraph.info*, February 20, 2019

1152. *Note by the Technical Secretariat - Report of the Fact-Finding Mission Regarding the Incident of Alleged Use of Toxic Chemicals as a Weapon in Douma, Syrian Arab Republic, on April 7, 2018*, OPCW Technical Secretariat, March 1st, 2019 (S/1731/2019)

1153. *Note by the Technical Secretariat* (op. cit.) Para 8.6, p. 13.

1154. *Note by the Technical Secretariat - Report of the Fact-Finding Mission Regarding the Incident of Alleged Use of Toxic Chemicals as a Weapon in Douma, Syrian Arab Republic, on April 7, 2018*, OPCW Technical Secretariat, March 1st, 2019 (S/1731/2019) Paragraph 2.7

1155. *National Assessment - Chemical attack of April 7, 2018* (op. cit.) p. 3

As for chlorine, traces of it were detected in many places, but their nature indicates that they could just as easily be cleaning products. In the room where a yellow cylinder was lying on a bed (the valve of which is intact, having passed through a concrete ceiling), no traces of chlorine were detected, except on a wooden slat[1156]. Furthermore, a similar cylinder was found by investigators in a nearby rebel workshop[1157].

But the case is not closed, because in May 2019, a document was "leaked", which analyses the two sites where the yellow cylinders were found. It is said to be part of a technical annex to the OPCW report, which was not published due to differing views within the organisation. The OPCW has confirmed that the document is authentic, but does not specify its status. Its author, Ian Henderson, concludes:

> *In summary, observations at the two sites, as well as subsequent analysis, suggest that there is a higher probability that the two cylinders were manually placed at these two locations rather than being dropped*[1158].

Initially, in order to minimise his testimony, Fernando Arias, Director General of the OPCW, claims that Henderson is only a casual employee of the OPCW, who was not part of the MEF, but conducted an independent investigation[1159]. This is not true, documents revealed in May 2020 prove that Ian Henderson was indeed part of the Mission, but his name did not appear in the original documents, as he was scheduled for another assignment[1160]. In fact, the official OPCW reports were manipulated and information that might have contradicted the official Western narrative was discarded, sparking a great deal of research to restore the truth[1161].

On 28 May, the OPCW Director sends a letter to the organisation's member countries expressing concern about the 'leaked' documents, without discussing their substance[1162]. On October 23, 2019, an OPCW whistleblower (probably a "*revisionist*"[1163]), confirms during a press conference that there was no chemical

---

1156. *Note by the Technical Secretariat* (op. cit.) Para 8.33, p. 17

1157. *Note by the Technical Secretariat* (op. cit.) Annex 8, p. 68

1158. Ian Henderson, *Engineering Assessment of two Cylinders Observed at the Duma Incident - Executive Summary, Draft for Internal Review*, Expanded Revision 1, UNCLASSIFIED - OPCW Sensitive, February 27, 2019

1159. "Leaked OPCW Report Raises New Questions About 2018 Chemical Attack in Douma, Syria", *Democracy Now*, May 23, 2019.

1160. Aaron Mate, "The Grayzone has obtained documents exposing numerous falsehoods and misleading claims by OPCW Director General Fernando Arias to degrade the reputation of Douma whistleblower Ian Henderson", *The Grayzone*, May 6, 2020

1161. Paul McKeigue, David Miller, Jake Mason, & Piers Robinson, *How the OPCW's investigation of the Duma incident was nobbled*, Working Group on Syria, Propaganda and Media, June 25, 2019

1162. *Remarks of the Director-General at the Briefing for States Parties on Syrian Arab Republic: Update on IIT-FFM-SSRC-DAT*, OPCW, May 28, 2019

1163. Patrick Cohen in the programme "C à Vous", "Faut-il faire la guerre en Syrie? - C à Vous - 10/04/2018 ",

attack in Douma: the measurements he had carried out on the spot showed that the chlorine levels

> *were comparable to and even lower than those given in the World Health Organization's guidelines on recommended permitted levels of trichlorophenol and other chlorinated organic chemicals in drinking water*[1164].

... and even *lower* than those measured outside the buildings! But his observations were deliberately ignored in the OPCW reports, obviously under pressure from the US. His June 22, 2018 email to his superior, Ambassador Robert Fairweather, was published by Wikileaks on November 23, 2019. In it, he expresses his "serious concerns" that the organisation's reports have been *doctored* to bolster the Western narrative against the Syrian government[1165]. The information was relayed by *BBC News* and several Anglo-Saxon media and NGOs[1166], but not by the French media.

In December 2019, WikiLeaks published several documents showing that the OPCW deliberately falsified its report on Douma at the request of the US and ordered all its staff to destroy information that would contradict the report. In particular, it reveals the minutes of an internal meeting of toxicologists who say that the symptoms seen on the videos are not consistent with the toxins mentioned in the reports and that they cannot be linked to known toxins. But these remarks will not appear in the final report[1167].

Thus, it appears that nothing happened in Douma, but that the jihadists were able to "create the event" with the complicity of the Western media. The Douma event tends to show two things: firstly, that politicians lie in order to cover up the attack for no reason and without a UN mandate from sovereign countries; secondly, that the intelligence services are not capable of assessing the situation on the ground...

Journalists and politicians whine about terrorist acts and humanitarian tragedies they have created out of dogmatism... In reality, no one is interested

---

France 5/YouTube, April 10, 2018, (07'22")

1164. Jonathan Steele, "The OPCW and Douma: Chemical Weapons Watchdog Accused of Evidence-Tampering by Its Own Inspectors," *Counterpunch*, November 15, 2019; "Jonathan Steele on Establishment Tales of a Chemical-Weapons Attack in Syria," *Fox News/YouTube*, November 26, 2019, (03'20").

1165. https://wikileaks.org/opcw-douma/document/Internal-OPCW-E-Mail/; Gunnar Hrafn Jónsson, "OPCW management accused of doctoring Syrian chemical weapons report", *Stundin*, November 24, 2019

1166. https://www.bbc.co.uk/sounds/play/w172wyjcsxxfg3w; "Panel Criticizes 'Unacceptable Practices' in the OPCW's investigation of the Alleged Chemical Attack in Douma, Syria on April 7th 2018", *Courage Foundation*, October 23, 2019 (https://couragefound.org/2019/10/opcw-panel-statement.); "OPCW-Inspektoren widersprechen offiziellem Abschlussbericht," *Internationalen Ärzte für die Verhütung des Atomkrieges/Ärzte in sozialer Verantwortung e.V. (IPPNW)*, October 23, 2019 (www.ippnw.de/startseite/artikel/de/opcw-inspektoren-widersprechen-offiz.html); "'Major Revelation' from OPCW whistleblower: Jonathan Steele speaking to the BBC," Tim Hayward Blog, October 27, 2019.

1167. https://wikileaks.org/opcw-douma/#OPCW-DOUMA - Release Part 04

in a solution in Syria: it is simply a matter of fracturing Syria to satisfy Israel, and distracting their publics from the domestic problems they cannot manage. In April 2018, the US, French and British governments are facing a crisis of credibility at home. In France, the government's proposed reforms are sparking protests and strikes; in Britain, the implementation of Brexit, the Windrush scandal, Amber Rudd's lies to a parliamentary committee are shaking up Theresa May's government; and in the US, Donald Trump is trying to establish the credibility of his foreign policy, particularly with regard to North Korea, which is "taunting" him. For all three, the temptation is great to seek 'success' outside the country, both to show their determination and to distract their publics.

6.16.6. Rule by Bad Faith

In April 2017, François Asselineau, a presidential candidate, expressed on *Franceinfo* his doubts about the accuracy of the information concerning the chemical attacks in Syria and suggested dialogue and restraint. He was violently taken to task by journalist Jean-Michel Aphatie and some of his colleagues, who asserted without qualification the guilt of the Syrian authorities and advocated the right to intervene, while a banner reading "*Asselineau, candidate of the conspiracy theorists?*" was displayed on the screen[1168]. This is an example of political exploitation of debatable facts, which are held as certainties. A total lack of intellectual honesty allows us to justify our violence and serves unmentionable ambitions. We do not try to understand events on the basis of facts, but on the basis of our prejudices.

Moreover, the chemical attack of November 24, 2018 against civilians in the city of Aleppo, then in the hands of the government, is barely mentioned in the French-language press: it contradicts the official discourse. The media then created doubt: the daily *La Croix* suggested that it was a manoeuvre by the "*pro-government media*"[1169] and *Paris Match* persisted in the logic that only the government had chemical weapons[1170]. We are at the roots of conspiracy!

On the set of "C dans l'air", they literally "invented" a "*Bashar al-Assad doctrine*", which would consist in terrorising the Sunni population (64% of the population) in order to replace it with "*foreign populations in Syria*"[1171]... The "Great Replacement" theory, Syrian version! Not only does this discourse

1168. See "Asselineau face à l'élite du journalisme - France Info 12/04/2017", *YouTube*, April 12, 2017, (20'50") (www.youtube.com/watch?v=3VhDvlNnIPs)
1169. Malo Tresca, "En Syrie, une attaque chimique aux conséquences incertaines", *La Croix*, November 26, 2018
1170. "À Alep, une centaine de cas de suffocations après une attaque aux 'gaz toxiques'", *Paris Match/ AFP*, November 25, 2018
1171. Agnès Levallois in the program "C dans l'air", "Syria: Trump discovers the war #cdanslair 06-04-2017", *YouTube/France 5*, April 6, 2017 (21'30")

have all the characteristics of conspiracy, but - ironically - it relays exactly the propaganda of the Islamic State[1172]!

In 2017, Pedro Agramunt, President of the Parliamentary Assembly of the Council of Europe (PACE), was forced to resign for going to Syria with Russian parliamentarians[1173] and being caught "*in a photo, next to someone who gassed his own people*[1174]"... a fact that is not even proven!

The mechanics of disinformation that turn a hypothesis into reality can have unexpected repercussions. Such is the case with a tweet from Alain Jakubowicz, honorary president of the LICRA, on April 15, 2018, linking questions about the Douma incident to the gas chambers of the Holocaust:

> *When the #FN asks for proof of the use of chemical weapons against civilians in #Syria it reminds me of the deniers who ask for proof of the existence of gas chambers*[1175].

A Godwin point to risk totally discrediting the question of the Holocaust and thus giving reason to those who doubt... Because in January 2020, Ian Henderson is heard by the Security Council and confirms "*that there was no chemical attack*" in Douma[1176]... The watered down, but inspiring...

6.16.7. The Role of "Red Lines"

Through their credulity, the West has encouraged the Islamists to repeat what worked so well with BHL in Libya, and to commit chemical weapons in order to push them to overthrow the government through air strikes. In such a context, defining a threshold for intervention gives the proponents of the use of violence the elements of a scenario to provoke it. Moreover, in October 2019, some media outlets, such as *L'Obs*, will try the same ploy against Turkey (which is not considered a country with chemical weapons)[1177].

An examination of the operations map shows that if the West were correct, the government would systematically avoid using its chemical weapons in its main lines of effort and in areas of strategic importance. Thus, Palmyra would have been an ideal site for these weapons, which do little damage and attack fighters without destroying infrastructure. Yet when it was retaken by the Islamic State in December 2016, the Syrian army only engaged conventional means there,

1172. "Yet the most fragile house is the spider's house", *Rumiyah*, no. 3, November 2016
1173. "Agramunt Resigns as PACE President after Syria Trip with Russian Lawmakers", *RFE/RL*, October 6, 2017
1174. Véronique Leblanc, "Following his much maligned meeting with Assad, the president of the Council of Europe must explain himself", *lalibre.be*, April 25, 2017
1175. Tweet from Alain Jakubowicz on Twitter, April 15, 2018 at 5:35 pm
1176. "Ian Henderson @ UN Jan. 20, 2020", *YouTube*, January 20, 2020
1177. "Kurdish children injured and burned in Syria, probably by 'chemical weapons'", *YouTube/ L'Obs*, October 17, 2019; "Kurds accuse Turkey of using unconventional weapons", *nouvelobs.com*, October 17, 2019

despite the strategic pressure being greater than in Ghouta, Douma or Khan Sheikhoun. And this, especially since the Western coalition - which had detected the Islamic State's counter-offensive - had refrained from striking! Would the Syrian government only use its strategic weapons in areas where it is in control of the situation with conventional forces? For the sole purpose of provoking the West?... this makes no sense.

Of the approximately 300[1178] incidents involving chemical weapons in Iraq and Syria, only three have triggered Western responses, with threats and/or direct interventions. Why have the others not had the same effect? Simply because they were directed against Syrian (or Kurdish) forces and carried out by rebel forces allied with the coalition, and identifying them would *ipso facto* have called into question the accusations against Bashar al-Assad.

The three cases that have been overexposed by the media show the same sequence, aimed at provoking a Western intervention of the "Libyan" type:

Triggering event	**Event**	**Most likely course of action**
Announcement of a "red line" intervention (August 20, 2012)	Ghouta (August 21, 2013)	Attack on the civilian population by rebel forces ("false flag" attack)
Donald Trump's statement that the overthrow of the Syrian regime is no longer a priority (March 30, 2017)[6] (see p. 398)	Khan Sheikhoun (April 4, 2017)	Exploitation by the rebels of an unforeseen incident (destruction of a stockpile of chemicals for an undefined use)
President Donald Trump's announcement to withdraw US forces from Syria (April 4, 2018)[7] (see p. 398)	Duma (April 7, 2018)	Opportunistic exploitation of the mechanical effects of artillery fire, which do not involve chemical weapons

Table 4- Likely scenarios for the 3 most publicised chemical incidents in Syria in the West.

In France, the mainstream and governmental media seem to have systematically pushed towards the use of violence, which ultimately benefited the Islamists.

1178. "Douma - Syria, April 7, 2018", *YouTube/French Ministry for Europe and Foreign Affairs*, April 13, 2018 (00'16")

6.17. " Russia Vetoes a UN Resolution Condemning the Chemical Attack in Syria[1179]"

On April 5, 2017, the day after the Khan Sheikhoun incident, France, Great Britain and the United States proposed a resolution to the Security Council that would condemn the Syrian government. They came up against the veto of Russia, which argued that at this stage, no serious investigation could confirm that it was responsible. The daily *Le Monde* even states that *"this is the eighth time since the beginning of the war in 2011 that Moscow has blocked any UN action against its Syrian ally*[1180].

The stakes are high, as this resolution would have opened the door to military intervention against Syria under Chapter VII of the UN Charter, as foreseen in number 21 of Resolution 2118 adopted in 2013, on the destruction of Syrian chemical weapons:

> *[...] that in the event of non-compliance with this resolution, including the unauthorised transfer or use of chemical weapons by anyone in the Syrian Arab Republic, it will impose measures under Chapter VII of the Charter of the United Nations ;*

Clearly, Russia is protecting its old Syrian ally, but this does not explain everything. In 2011, Russia and China did not use their veto power for Resolution 1973, which aimed to protect civilians in Libya. But the West had overstepped their mandate to attack and overthrow President Gaddafi, creating chaos in the region. Russia and China have become suspicious of repeated ill-conceived Western interventions without clear strategic objectives and using means disproportionate to the situation. They have realised that in the absence of a strategic counterweight, the West has gradually become comfortable with international law and the use of force and is generating instability in order to satisfy its own interests. Their position is to intervene only at the express request of the countries concerned (in accordance with the UN Charter) and to avoid participation in Western-led coalitions. A real information war then began on the use of the veto by Russia.

But at this point there are two questions:

a) the extension of the mandate of the OPCW-UN Joint Investigative Mechanism (JIM) established in August 2015. The JIM's mandate expires on

1179. "Russia vetoes UN resolution condemning chemical attack in Syria", Le *Monde.fr/AFP/Reuters*, April 13, 2017.

1180. "Russia vetoes UN resolution condemning chemical attack in Syria", Le Monde.fr/AFP/Reuters, April 13, 2017 (http://www.lemonde.fr/ameriques/article/2017/04/12/poutine-recoit-le-secretaire-d-etat-americain-tiller-son-dans-un-climat-tendu_5110366_3222.html)

November 17, 2017; but the Americans want to extend it already in April 2017, while Russia wants to see the Khan Sheikhoun investigation report first, due on October 26. Finally, the vote in the Security Council will take place on October 24. [1181]

b) the creation of a new investigative mechanism. The problem is that the OPCW fact-finding mission "*is not empowered to draw conclusions regarding who is responsible for the use of chemical weapons*[1182]". The US would prefer to have a mechanism that determines responsibility.

On April 10, 2018, the Western media[1183] castigate the Russian veto of a US resolution proposal. Yet that week, three resolution proposals were submitted to the UN Security Council (SC), all stopped by a veto[1184]:

> A US proposal provides for the establishment of an independent SC commission, which could "*identify to the fullest extent possible persons, entities, groups or governments that have perpetrated, organised or sponsored*" chemical attacks, without going to the scene;
>
> Two Russian proposals: the first was to set up a commission of enquiry under the authority of the SC, which would have appointed experts to work "*on the basis of credible, verified and corroborated evidence collected during site visits*", enabling it to determine responsibility; and the second proposed sending an OPCW commission of enquiry.

The problem with the US proposal is that it keeps the inspectors out of the sight of the SC, opening the door to manipulation. The Russian proposals, by keeping the authority of the UN, would have had the advantage of allowing an impartial approach to the evaluation of the situation and a possible condemnation of the culprits. But no one mentions the two American vetoes.

The Western media is trying to put the burden of international inaction on Russia alone. The interview of Adrien Quatennens by Jean-Jacques Bourdin on *BFM TV* is an excellent example of manipulation. The journalist literally tries to destabilise his guest by bombarding him with questions at a rapid pace. In reality, Bourdin does not know his subject and is simply trying to "demonstrate" Russian responsibility[1185]: he lies by deliberately omitting

1181. *Security Council Fails to Renew Mandate of Joint Investigative Mechanism on Chemical Weapons Use in Syria, as Permanent Member Casts Veto*, SC/13040, Security Council, October 24, 2017

1182. S/RES/2235 (2015)

1183. These include levif.be, lalibre.be, lecho.be, ouest-France.fr, 20minutes.fr, etc.

1184. "Syria: Security Council fails to adopt any of three draft resolutions on chemical weapons use", *UN Info*, April 10, 2018; "Three draft resolutions rejected in one meeting: Security Council spreads divisions over Syria chemical weapons issue", CS/13288, www.un.org, April 10, 2018

1185. "You don't know the subject", when Jean-Jacques Bourdin takes on Adrien Quatennens on Syria", *BFMTV*, April 11, 2018

to mention the Russian proposals and asserts exactly the opposite of what happened at the CS.

The only honest presentation of this issue is given on April 12, 2018 by Corinne Galacteros, on *RMC*[1186]... but it will receive almost no echo in the mainstream press. In fact, it is not about getting the truth, but about condemning the Syrian regime. This is manipulation.

6.18. Conclusions for the Syrian conflict

In March 2016, Alain Juillet, former Director of Intelligence at the DGSE, explained the Syrian conflict as a rivalry between Qatari and Iranian gas pipeline projects through Syria[1187]. This is not true. Attempts to destabilise Syria began long before these projects (2009). Moreover, the Qatari project was dependent on the shelved EU-funded NABUCCO project, while its main opponent was Saudi Arabia[1188], which did not allow the construction of the pipeline on its territory[1189].

The West entered the Syrian conflict with the stated aim of overthrowing the legal government and entered Syria in violation of the UN Charter. They therefore need to find legitimacy for these interventions. Initially, they convinced themselves that the revolution was driven by a democratic aspiration... As in Libya[1190], public opinion was misled about the nature of the demonstrations that triggered the crisis, about the nature of the rebels they were supporting, about the objectives they were trying to achieve and about the interests they were protecting.

In a second phase, the West realises that it has been playing with fire and that, as in Libya, the revolution is essentially Islamist and that the so-called 'moderate' forces were under the control of the Islamists from the start... with a downside: the emergence of the Islamic State and the spillover of the conflict into a terrorist campaign that directly affects them. Overthrowing the Syrian government becomes more complicated. The disinformation follows exactly the same pattern as in Iraq: the presence and use of banned weapons, collusion with terrorist movements and the massacres of civilians. Factual evidence is never

---

1186. Corinne Galacteros on RMC, "The reality of the Syrian conflict in front of Bourdin, by an expert in geopolitics! (12/04/18)", *YouTube*, April 12, 2018

1187. "Senate: End of the state lie about the origin of the war in Syria", *YouTube*, March 15, 2016

1188. Felix Imonti, "Qatar: Rich and Dangerous", *oiprice.com*, September 17, 2012

1189. Gareth Porter, 'The War Against the Assad Regime Is Not a "Pipeline War"', *truthout.org*, September 21, 2016

1190. Foreign Affairs Committee, *Libya: Examination of intervention and collapse and the UK's future policy options*, Third Report of Session 2016-17, House of Commons, September 14, 2016, p. 11

produced, only circumstantial. Information that disturbs and challenges the official discourse is hidden.

In January 2012, Israeli Defence Minister Ehud Barak predicted that Bashar al-Assad would be overthrown within weeks[1191]. Proof that Syria's close neighbour - whose intelligence services are considered by some to be the best in the world - knows very little about its own geostrategic environment.

The weakness of the Western position in the Middle East is that it is based on triangular relationships. Our Cartesian mind is quite comfortable with "friends of my friends are my friends" relationships but has more difficulty solving the equation when an enemy is in the triangle, unlike the Eastern mind. We saw this in October 2019, during the Turkish intervention in Syria. Our tendency to reduce these situations to a succession of bilateral relationships, with 'good guys and bad guys' leads us to the opposite of a holistic approach.

Why would President Assad attack his own people now? Why does his army, which is mainly Sunni, continue to support him? Why, when the rebels seized East Aleppo, did more than half a million people move to government protection in West Aleppo? Why does Bashar al-Assad, who "seeks to eliminate his people", let them communicate with the outside world via the Internet? Why do the majority of displaced people not move to rebel areas, but remain in government-controlled areas?

The West is now caught in the trap of its own disinformation. Despite what has been said about Bashar al-Assad, he now appears to be indispensable for discussing a peace process. And even if he were to disappear, no one knows who could replace him, because the most charismatic people in the region are undoubtedly Islamists: the cure would thus be worse than the disease, as was the case in Libya. The problem is that disinformation has made dialogue with Bashar al-Assad almost impossible.

Prejudice favours the Syrian opposition, but logic, doctrine and material facts tend to point to the good faith of the Syrian government, even if not everything is clear. The problem here is that by making decisions on vague and speculative grounds, Western governments have clearly escalated a situation and played recklessly with the lives of their citizens and international law. If the people of the West held their leaders and advisers to account, with the threat of being brought to justice, political decisions would probably be much more measured and in line with the facts. Otherwise, the Islamic State is vindicated, as it states in a video that the French population is more concerned about their welfare, overtime and time off work than knowing that their taxes are being used to finance wars that did not have to be fought[1192].

1191. Lahav Harkov, "Barak: Assad will be toppled within weeks", *The Jerusalem Post*, January 2, 2012

1192. Video in French: "*Leur coalition et notre terrorisme*" by the Islamic State, late July 2016 (04'00").

7. TERRORIST ATTACKS IN FRANCE

7.1. The context

In 2014, the West is not threatened by the Islamic State or any faction engaged in the war in Iraq or Syria and has no reason to intervene in Syria. This is what leads the US to create the fictitious group 'Khorasan' in the summer of 2014[1193].

The Islamic State and its Caliphate are established on June 29, 2014. The fighting between rival factions is brutal and the humanitarian situation is deteriorating rapidly and visibly. On August 10, 2014, questioned by *France 2* on France's action in Iraq, Foreign Minister Laurent Fabius even states:

> *Are we ourselves going to get involved militarily? The answer for the moment is no, I'm telling you clearly, because our doctrine is that we don't intervene unless there is a green light from the United Nations Security Council, and unless there is a direct threat to our nationals. But we welcome the work that the Americans are doing. That is the first point; and, in any case, there is no question of sending people on the ground*[1194].

However, French troops have already been engaged clandestinely in Syria since 2012. But it is to overthrow the Syrian government and not to fight against *the* Islamic State in Iraq and the Levant (EIIL), which shares the same objective as France.

On September 5, 2014, on the sidelines of the Nato Summit in Wales, the United States brought together nine countries[1195] in a coalition to fight the Islamic State first in Iraq and then in Syria, not to protect the West - which is not threatened - but to preserve the fragile stability of Iraq. Ten days later, at the Paris conference, this coalition was expanded by 18 countries[1196]. On

1193. See the chapter on Syria.
1194. Laurent Fabius in the 8 o'clock news, *Franceinfo*, August 10, 2014 (07'29")
1195. Australia, Canada, Denmark, France, Germany, Italy, Poland, Turkey, UK.
1196. Bahrain, Belgium, China, Czech Republic, Egypt, Iraq, Japan, Jordan, Kuwait, Lebanon, Oman, Qatar,

September 18, 2014, President Hollande announced that France would strike against terrorist groups in Iraq, at the request of the Iraqi government, despite the fact that France had not suffered any threats or attacks from the Islamic State until then. The next day, he confirmed that the first strikes were being carried out:

> *This morning at 9.40 am, in accordance with the orders I had given, Rafale aircraft pounded a target and completely destroyed it [...] In no case are there any French troops on the ground*[1197] *[...]*

At the Nato ministerial meeting in Brussels on December 4, 2014, the coalition is expanded by a further 33 countries[1198]. After the obscene images of throat slitting and beheadings, the language of firmness appeals. Nevertheless, the decision to carry out strikes in Syria without a mandate and without the endorsement of the UN Security Council - and therefore without international legality - was not justified by any direct threat to the West[1199].

7.2 "Let's Make No Mistake: Totalitarianism has Struck France not for What it Does, But for What It Is"[1200]

7.2.1. The Strategy of the Terrorists

The timing of the 2015 attacks was not entirely unpredictable. It followed several doctrinal articles in the jihadist literature on "*deterrence operations*[1201]", in the terminology of the Islamic State. A dispassionate examination of the jihadist attacks in Europe shows that they have been carried out with the same purpose: to push people to demand the withdrawal of their troops from the Middle East, as in Spain in 2004. But we refuse to understand this mechanism and the message conveyed by the media and journalists is exactly the opposite:

Netherlands, Norway, Russia, Saudi Arabia, Spain and United Arab Emirates

1197. First French bombing against Islamic State in Iraq, *Le Monde.fr/AFP/Reuters*, September 26, 2014.

1198. Albania, Austria, Bosnia and Herzegovina, Bulgaria, Croatia, Cyprus, Estonia, Finland, Georgia, Greece, Hungary, Iceland, Ireland, Kosovo, Latvia, Lithuania, Luxembourg, Macedonia, Moldova, Montenegro, Morocco, New Zealand, Portugal, Romania, Serbia, Singapore, Slovakia, Slovenia, South Korea, Somalia, Sweden, Taiwan and Ukraine.

1199. Jacqueline Klimas, 'Islamic State no threat to U.S. homeland: Air Force general', *The Washington Times*, July 14, 2015.

1200. Manuel Valls, November 19, 2015

1201. Abu Mu'sab al-Suri, 'The Jihadi Experience: The Strategy of Deterring with Terrorism', *Inspire Magazine*, No. 10, Spring 2013, p.22.

It is wrong to say that the attacks take place in France in response to and to put pressure on governments that intervene militarily in the Middle East[1202].

Yet in 2013, Abu Mu'sab al-Suri, the leading theorist of modern jihadist terrorism wrote in *Inspire* magazine:

[The resistance] must strive to create the impression that its arm is ready to reach out and strike anyone who is considering participating in an aggression. Generally, the majority of our enemies, from the general to the common soldier, are in fact cowards. And most of them can be deterred by a strong example, by striking and punishing a few. The desired effect of this deterrence is the withdrawal of those who are already engaged or to prevent those who are thinking of engaging[1203].

In May 2018, in his allegiance and claim video, before committing a knife attack, Khamzat Azimov conveys exactly the same message:

[...] You are the ones who started bombing the Islamic State, I am addressing France and its citizens, you are the ones who started killing Muslims, and then when we give you an answer, when we fight back, you cry. If you want this to stop, put pressure on your government! I am not the first to tell you this. Other brothers before me, who are on the ground there, have already told you this, but you refused to listen to[1204] *[...]*

The jihadists have understood that American public opinion - of all political persuasions - is very 'militarised' and generally in favour of external interventions. In Europe, however, the situation is quite different: the populations are more critical of these military adventures and therefore more vulnerable. This is the notion of the "*soft underbelly*", which Gilles Kepel associates - wrongly - with a hypothetical worldwide Islamic revolution... In Spain in 2004[1205], and then in Great Britain in 2005, the weak popular support of the government was a decision factor for the terrorists. But in ten years nobody has tried to understand their logic.

In 2013, 68% of French people were opposed to an intervention in Syria[1206] and at the end of 2014 the government's popularity rating stood at 15-20%[1207].

1202. Philippe Cohen-Grillet, Journalist, in "Le Grand Réferendum", *Sud-Radio*, March 23, 2017

1203. Abu Mu'sab al-Suri, "The Jihadi Experience: The Strategy of Deterring with Terrorism", *op. cit.*

1204. Verbatim excerpt from Khamzat Azimov's allegiance and claim video, *Amaq News Agency*, May 13, 2018

1205. See Abu Mu'sab al-Suri, "The Jihadi Experience - The Strategy of Deterring with Terrorism", *op.cit.*, p 23

1206. Antoine Goldet, "Public opinion opposed to intervention in Syria", www.liberation.fr, September 11, 2013

1207. Kocila Makdeche, "INFOGRAPHY. François Hollande's popularity at a level not seen since September 2012", *francetvinfo.fr*, December 2, 2015

By intervening in Iraq and Syria under these conditions, the Hollande government has literally made a "call of the foot" to the terrorists. On September 12, 2014, six days before President Hollande's declaration to engage in Syria, the *Washington Post* stated:

> *A more precise analysis would show that the US military intervention has enormous propaganda value for the Islamic State, helping it to rally other jihadists to its cause, perhaps even Salafists who have so far rejected its legitimacy*[1208].

This is exactly what happened. Furthermore, it should be noted that the expert does not automatically associate Salafism with jihadism as the media in France do.

7.2.2. The Claim of the Attacks

The myth of an attack on France "*for what it is and not for what it does*" serves to mask irresponsible government decisions. But, in turn, it serves the jihadists, who can thus demonstrate the bad faith of the government and its "hatred of Islam", feeding the process of radicalisation:

> *On Friday 19 September 2014 - more than three months before the Hyper Casher and Charlie Hebdo operations, and more than a year before the Paris and Saint-Denis operations - French Rafales bombed the Islamic State out of hatred for Islam and Sharia law, not in retaliation for attacks allegedly carried out by the Islamic State against France*[1209].

Moreover, Amédi Coulibaly's posthumous video and the claims of the January 2015 attacks do not refer to the 2005-2006 cartoons, nor to freedom of expression, nor to the conquest of the world, but to a response to bombings:

> *What we're doing right now is completely legitimate, given what they're doing [...] It's been well deserved for a long time. You attack the caliphate, you attack the Islamic State, we attack you. You can't attack and get nothing in return. So you play the victim, as if you don't understand what's going on, for a few deaths, while you and your coalition, you in the lead, almost even (sic), you regularly bomb there, you have invested forces, you kill civilians, you kill fighters, you kill... Why? Because we apply Sharia law? Even at home we are afraid to apply Sharia law now. You are the ones who decide*

1208. Ramzy Mardini, "The Islamic State threat is overstated", *The Washington Post*, September 12, 2014
1209. Dar al-Islam Magazine, No. 7, November 2015 (Safar 1437), p. 4.

what will happen on earth. [...] We are not going to let this happen. We are going to fight. Inch'a Allah[1210] *[...]*

The telephone interview given by Chérif Kouachi to *BFMTV*[1211] on January 9 is also very clear: no fight against Christianity or its destruction, but a "*revenge*" against the "*women and children killed in Iraq, Syria and Afghanistan*".

During the November 13, 2015 attack, survivors of the Bataclan claimed that one of the terrorists said:

> *You can thank President Hollande, because it is thanks to him that you are suffering this. We left our wives and children in Syria, under the bombs. We are part of the "Islamic State" and we are there to avenge our families and loved ones for the French intervention in Syria*[1212].

The claims of November 14, 2015, and later in the Islamic State's *Dabiq* and *Dar al-Islam* magazines in November 2015[1213] do not mention France's Christian character, democracy or way of life as justification for the attacks. Contrary to the rhetoric of the government and many "experts", the January and November 2015 operations in Paris had all the characteristics of "*deterrence operations*", aimed at forcing Western countries to stop their strikes, as the "official" organ of the Islamic State states:

> *I don't think it could be any clearer. So it is the indiscriminate French bombings that are the cause of this threat. A threat that was carried out on November 13, 2015 in Paris and Saint-Denis*[1214].

Date	Location	Author(s)	Reason given for the attack
22.03.2012	Toulouse	Mohamed Merah	French participation in Nato operations in Afghanistan and "The Jews killed our brothers and sisters in Palestine" (telephone claim on France24)[8(See Bibliography)]. The Jund al-Katibat al-Khilafah claim is "injustice and aggression in Palestine, Afghanistan and other Muslim countries".
24.09.2014	Tizi Ouzou	Jound al-Khalifah	Call for an immediate end to the French military operation CHAMMAL in Iraq

1210. Video in French, presented under an Italian title "Coulibaly rivendica le stragi Sono dell'Isis", *YouTube*, January 11, 2015

1211. "Exclu Message Interview Complete de Chérif Kouachi au journaliste de BFM TV 9 janvier 2015 10h", *YouTube*, January 9, 2015, (www.youtube.com/watch?v=KNFbfnPBKdY)

1212. Alexandre Fache, "Deux heures trente avec les terroristes du Bataclan", *L'Humanité*, November 17, 2015

1213. *Dabiq Magazine*, No. 12, 18 November 2015; *Dar al-Islam Magazine*, No. 7, November 2015

1214. *Dar al-Islam Magazine*, No. 7, November 2015 (Safar 1437), p. 4.

07.01.2015	Paris	Chérif Kouachi Saïd Kouachi	Bombing of women and children in Iraq, Syria and Afghanistan (telephone claim to BFM TV)
08.01.2015	Paris	Amédi Coulibaly	Western] attack on Caliphate, Islamic State… regular coalition bombing of civilians… (YouTube video claim)
13.11.2015	Paris	Multiple (Islamic State)	[…] For leading the crusade, insulting (sic) the Prophet, boasting about fighting Islam in France, and striking Muslims in the land of the Caliphate with their planes… (official claim)
22.03.2016	Brussels	Multiple (Islamic State)	[…] against the leadership of the crusader Belgium which has not stopped fighting Islam and Muslims (…) in response to their [the crusaders'] aggression against our state… (official claim of the Islamic State)
13.06.2016	Magnanville	Larossi Aballa	[…] Muslim lands are occupied […] 66 nations are fighting the Islamic State (video message)
14.07.2016	Nice	Mohamed Lahouaiej Bouhlel	[…] in response to calls to target citizens of nations fighting the Islamic State (claim / Amaq news agency)
26.07.2016	Saint-Etienne-du-Rouvray	Adel Kermiche Abdel Malik Petitjean	[…] in response to calls to target citizens of countries that belong to the coalition of crusaders (claim / Amaq news agency)
19.12.2016	Berlin	Anis Amri	[…] in response to the call to attack members of the coalition fighting the Islamic State (claim / Amaq news agency)
03.02.2017	Paris	Abdallah E-H (?)	No compromise, no return, there is no peace in war (terrorist's Twitter account) [no official claim].
22.03.2017	London	Khalid Masood	[…] in response to the call to target the nationals of the Crusader countries (French text) […in response to calls to target citizens of coalition countries. (English text)
06.06.2017	Paris	Farid Ikken	"This is for Syria!"
25.08.2017	Brussels	Haashi Ayaanle	[…in response to calls to target coalition states. (claim / Amaq News Agency)
13.05.2018	Paris	Khamzat Azimov	[…] you are the ones who started bombing the Islamic State […] you are the ones who started killing Muslims (video of allegiance and claim of responsibility / Amaq News Agency)
29.05.2018	Liege	Benjamin Herman	[…] in response to calls to target coalition countries (official claim/Amaq news agency)
12.12.2018	Strasbourg	Cherif Chekatt	[…]For our dead brothers in Syria (claim to a taxi driver); […] in response to the call to target citizens of the international coalition (claim / Amaq news agency)

Table 5 - Link between terrorist attacks in France and military operations in Iraq and Syria

In addition to this, the Western strikes are less surgical than they are said to be, as Colonel François-Régis Legrier has noted with courage and lucidity in Syria[1215]. Mosul was taken by the EI in 4 days, with 300-400 fighters, 2,600 dead[1216] and no major destruction; but it will be retaken by the Western coalition after a 9-month battle, with more than 100,000 fighters, around 18,500 dead, including 6,500 civilians and the destruction of half the city. Similarly, in 2013, the EI had taken Raqqa in 3 days and causing a total of 80 deaths; it would be retaken by the coalition in 2017 after 4 months of fighting and 3,500 deaths, including 1,500 civilians.

Collateral damage" then becomes an additional justification for terrorists:

> *Artillery, like terrorism, leads to the loss of non-combatant lives. A missile hitting a city, which is obviously not a precise weapon, is no different from a bomb in a city in a country that is at war with Muslims.*

> *... it is clear that Muslims are entitled to target populations in countries that are at war with Muslims, with bombs, guns or other forms of attack that inevitably lead to the death of non-combatants*[1217].

These "American-style" wars, i.e. with indiscriminate firefights, are the main factor of radicalisation in the West. But the Western media (mainly French-speaking) remain very discreet about this way of fighting and prefer to attribute it to the Syrian government. It is largely to avoid the dissemination of images of Western strikes that platforms such as Facebook, Twitter or YouTube have implemented filters and restrictive policies on content[1218].

Our 'remote' wars allow us to strike without risking the lives of Western soldiers, but are perceived as 'cowardly' wars:

> *Don't be cowards by attacking us with drones. Send us your troops instead, those we humiliated in Iraq*[1219]*!*

In 2015, Tom Pettinger, in the *Journal for Deradicalization*, observed:

1215. Clémence Labasse, "Conflict in Syria A French colonel criticises the Coalition's military strategy", *La Voix du Nord*, February 16, 2019

1216. To which must be added the deaths of 4,000 individuals eliminated by the EI afterwards. See more precise figures in the Wikipedia articles, "Fall of Mosul" and "Battle of Mosul (2016-2017)".

1217. *Inspire Magazine*, n°8, Fall 2011, p.42..

1218. Ben Norton, "Under US pressure, social media companies censor critical content and suspend Venezuelan, Iranian, and Syrian accounts", *The Grayzone*, January 12, 2020

1219. Islamic State spokesperson (http://dailycaller.com/2014/08/08/isis-threatens-america-we-will-raise-the-flag-of-allah-in-the-white-house/#ixzz3n1ziZgJ5)

In areas where the US drone programme has been engaged, there is a perception of a dishonourable, cowardly and unequal war, as air strikes are not associated with a risk to US personnel. For this reason 'there is an al-Qaeda acceptance' against such 'remote warfare' everywhere. Such a way of waging war generates a sense of invulnerability for those who intervene, and the sense of powerlessness of living under the threat of drones or air strikes can lead - especially when there are civilian casualties - to individualisation, and thus radicalisation, of individuals quickly, even for those who would previously have supported counter-terrorism measures[1220].

This is a factor of radicalisation that is totally ignored in France, fuelled by our way of waging war. Western countries did not understand that they were engaging in an asymmetrical combat: the use of force did not have the expected dissuasive effect - as in the logic of symmetrical conflicts - but on the contrary strengthened the posture of the Islamic State. This is exactly what is happening in Mali with Operation BARKHANE. After the death of 13 soldiers in November 2019, it was congratulated that they were doing "*the right things*", but nobody asked if the operation (or the French government) was doing "*the right things*"!

7.2.3. The Official Reactions

On November 19, 2015, before the National Assembly, Prime Minister Manuel Valls attempted to clear the government's responsibility for the motivation of the terrorists by stating:

Make no mistake: a totalitarianism has struck France not for what it does, but for what it is[1221].

Laurent Fabius, Minister of Foreign Affairs, spreads the idea that the country is the unjust victim of an indiscriminate campaign of terrorism:

We were among the first to fight against Daech because they are terrorists who want to destroy us. It is because they want to destroy us that we are in Syria. Moreover, the first attack against Charlie Hebdo, we were not in Syria. So it is really us, our existence that is targeted[1222].

1220. Tom Pettinger, *What is the Impact of Foreign Military Intervention on Radicalization?* Journal for Deradicalization, Winter 15/16, No. 5, pp. 92-114 (ISSN: 2363-9849)

1221. "Speech to the National Assembly - Manuel Valls: "A risk of chemical or bacteriological weapons"", www.parismatch.com, November 19, 2015 1

1222. "Laurent Fabius: 'We must unite and defeat these people'", interview by Jean-François Achilli, *France Info*, November 19, 2015

But these claims are misleading:

Fabius considers the Iraqi and Syrian parts of the Islamic State group ("DAECH") as two separate entities. This is patently false, especially since the French government has been the promoter of the name "DAECH", which stands for "Islamic State in Iraq *and* the Levant". In other words, bombing it in Iraq or Syria amounts to the same thing and this was the justification for the intervention in Iraq as early as September 2014;

Contrary to Fabius' assertion, the attack on *Charlie Hebdo* was not conceived or decided in Syria, since this action was sponsored and financed by the Arabian Peninsula Jihad Base (APJB) in Yemen, according to the admission of Chérif Kouachi, one of the perpetrators of the attack, to a *BFM TV* journalist on January 9, 2015:

> *I was sent myself, Chérif Kouachi by Al-Qaeda from Yemen (...) And that I went there and that it was Sheikh Anwar al-Awlaki who financed me (...) before he was killed*[1223].

Moreover, while Amedi Coulibaly is glorified in several issues of the Islamic State's *Dar al-Islam* magazine, the Kouachi brothers, perpetrators of the *Charlie Hebdo* attack, are never mentioned[1224].

The official communication carefully avoids any link between the strikes in Iraq and Syria and the attacks. To clear the authorities' responsibility, they even try to make people believe that the EI carried out attacks in Europe before the Western strikes in the Middle East, in order to give credence to the idea of "self-defence". This discourse is carried by some intellectuals, who claim that the terrorists struck France...

> *...when there was no military operation against them [...] The attacks of Daech were prior to any military action*[1225].

This is obviously not true. In May 2017, the report of a joint workshop of the DGSE and the Canadian Security and Intelligence Service (CSIS), attributed the attack on the Jewish Museum in Brussels (May 24, 2014) to the Islamic State, stating that it "*well predates the bombings against Daech by the US-led coalition,*

1223. "Exclu Message Interview Complete de Chérif Kouachi au journaliste de BFM TV 9 janvier 2015 10h", *YouTube*, January 9, 2015, (www.youtube.com/watch?v=KNFbfnPBKdY)
1224. See "The History of France's Enmity with Islam", *Dar al-Islam Magazine*, No. 2, February 2015 (Rabi al-thani 1436), p.10; "The Muslim's Security Rules", *Dar al-Islam Magazine*, No. 5, July-August 2015 (Shawwal 1436), p.33 ; 'Editorial', *Dar al-Islam Magazine*, No. 8, January 2016 (Rabi al-thani 1437), p. 4; 'Attacks - On the Prophetic Path - Part Two', *Dar al-Islam Magazine*, No. 10, August 2016 (Dhul Qidah 1437), p. 17.
1225. Jean-Pierre Filiu, *"C dans l'air"*, France 5, December 1st, 2016

starting in August 2014 in Iraq, and September in Syria[1226] ". This attribution is simply based on the discovery of an Islamist flag at Mehdi Nemmouche's home. However, not only is this flag identical to that of "Al-Qaeda" (and therefore does not allow an attribution to the EI), but the attack has never been claimed by the EI nor mentioned in its publications, which are nevertheless regularly used to glorify its actions[1227]. Although its imprimatur states that "*it is not an analytical document and does not represent the official position of any of the participating agencies*", this report is a perfect example of disinformation aimed at exonerating policymakers from their decisions.

7.2.4. The Treatment of the Attacks by the Media

After the November 13, 2015 attacks in Paris, the Islamic State's claim leaves little to the imagination:

> *[...] And France and those who follow its path must know that they remain the main targets of the Islamic State and will continue to smell the stench of death for taking the lead in the crusade, daring to insult our Prophet, boasting about fighting Islam in France and striking Muslims in the land of the Caliphate with their planes*[1228] *[...]*

However, hardly any mainstream media publish the full text of the claim: references to the Koran are retained, but the French strikes in Syria are carefully avoided.

In November 2016, *France 2* devoted a report to the genesis of the attacks. Entitled "*November 13: what we did not see*", it did not mention any link with the French strikes. For the authors (and the journalist Mohammed Sifaoui, who produced the report), the threat against France appeared as if by magic (two days after its first strikes), on September 21, 2014, through the voice of Abu Mohammed al-Adnani; and its first victim was Hervé Gourdel in Algeria[1229]. Why France? No answer. Thus, terrorism would have struck... for no reason.

By concealing the link with the French intervention in Iraq and Syria, we have transformed (predictable) terrorism into an unpredictable but inescapable phenomenon linked to the very nature of a faction of Islam: Wahhabism, Salafism and the Muslim Brotherhood. Thus, on *RT France,* Pierre Martinet, a former DGSE

1226. *Understanding Post-Daech*, Publication No. 2017-05-01, CSIS, May 2017

1227. To be perfectly accurate, Nemmouche is mentioned in issues 7 and 8 of the publication Dar al-Islam (November-December 2015 and January-February 2016), under the heading "*In the Words of the Enemy*", which presents Western journalists' views on terrorism.

1228. Islamic State's claim of responsibility for the attacks of November 13, 2015 (November 14, 2015)

1229. "13-November: what we failed to see", *France 2*, November 4, 2016 (https://fr.news.yahoo.com/13-novembre-lon-na-su-voir-103249266.html)

agent, affirms that they have largely infiltrated French society and are to be found in "*any stratum of society, doctors, lawyers (...) why not a judge, one day*[1230]..."

But in fact, he knows nothing about it and is only repeating what the press says. Because in reality, we don't know the importance of the Muslim Brotherhood in France: this movement is mainly present in the Near and Middle East, whereas the majority of Muslims in France come from the Maghreb or West Africa, where its prevalence - with the probable exception of Morocco - is very low. Moreover, no one recalls that the Muslim Brotherhood is banned in Saudi Arabia; nor that France and the United States supported the Free Syrian Army (FSA), the armed wing of the Syrian Muslim Brotherhood, in Turkey; nor does anyone explain why Saudi Arabia, which is quite comfortable with the West, would suddenly undertake to promote its state religion through violence in 2015. The Muslim Brotherhood may be a threat to Israel, certainly to Syria, but it is not clear why they would attack France.

We have thus virtually created an internal threat, based on elements that we are unable to verify. The real problem is not Islam, but the incoherent immigration policies pursued by the various governments over the past half-century, motivated by political squabbles and which have never resulted in a consistent integration strategy.

7.2.5. The Consequences of Disinformation

The terrorist attacks of 2015 and after are the consequence of two essential strategic mistakes: a) the lack of anticipation in engaging in a conflict without any real reason, and b) the lack of precautions taken to protect the population beforehand, when the terrorist risk was perfectly foreseeable.

When Russia engaged in Syria alongside the Syrian government, it simultaneously raised the level of its internal security in order to prevent attacks on its territory, because it knew that this could trigger a terrorist response. In France, the insistence that "*It is wrong to see Western military interventions as the main reason for jihadist terrorism*[1231]" has led to the neglect of upstream protection of the population. However, the Merah affair should have constituted an "early warning", in that it highlighted a link between events in the Middle East and the risk of terrorism, but there too, it was refused to be taken into account...

In August 2014, a poll on Islam in France, conducted by the British institute ICM Research on behalf of *Russia Today*, indicated that 27% of 18-24 year olds and 22% of 25-34 year olds had a "*favourable opinion of the Islamic State*". Relayed by the far-right media, it was quickly denigrated and forgotten: the

1230. "Pierre Martinet, ex-DGSE agent: 'Nothing is being done to stop Islamist ideology'", *RT France/YouTube*, January 22, 2020

1231. Bruno Tertrais, "Les interventions militaires, cause de terrorisme?", *Foundation for Strategic Research*, n°06/2016, February 15, 2016

figures frightened people and were perceived as Russian propaganda[1232]. However, beyond the polemic, it indicated a trend from which we have not been able to draw the consequences. The engagement in Iraq, then in Syria, was not accompanied by any communication campaign to change it. Curiously enough, even the victims' associations remained very complacent towards the state and did not address this issue.

By refusing to understand and state the real causes of radicalisation and attacks, we have no chance of solving the problem. If the strikes in Iraq had been correctly identified as a source of radicalisation and a possible motive for future attacks, would France have committed itself to Syria 8 months later, thus taking the risk of generating new attacks? One would have to be naive or stupid (or both) not to understand that the jihadists would let themselves be bombed without reacting. The image of jihadism given by the traditional media and certain journalists has largely contributed to this unpreparedness, and thus facilitated the work of the terrorists.

7.3. Conclusions for Terrorism in France

France's reasons for getting involved in Iraq and Syria in 2014-2015 are unclear. Moreover, they have evolved in the official discourse, passing successively from aid to the Yazidis (whom no one had thought of helping in 2004, against the exactions of the Kurds[1233]), to self-defence (whereas France had not suffered any attack by the Islamic State before September 2014), the overthrow of the 'Syrian regime' (a reason that has become obsolete due to a lack of strategy), the war against the Islamic State (which is an opportunistic reason, as we have seen) and finally in order to prevent terrorists from returning to Europe. The hypothesis of a political manoeuvre aimed at tightening national unity around an external threat therefore makes sense. For the government, then very unpopular and subject to numerous social movements, a scenario similar to the film *Men of Influence*[1234] does not seem totally unrealistic.

The problem is that by denying the terrorists any rationality, they are misleading all those who seek an adequate response to the problem. The French government is reacting like the Spanish government in 2004 and the British government in 2005, which lied to their parliaments and public opinion in

1232. Kocila Makdeche, "Are there really 15% of French people who support the Islamic State?", *francetvinfo.fr*, August 26, 2014

1233. *On Vulnerable Ground - Violence against Minority Communities in Nineveh Province's Disputed Territories*, Human Rights Watch, November 10, 2019

1234. "Wag the Dog is an American film directed by Barry Levinson, released in 1997.

order to hide the fact that the attacks were the consequence of a foreign policy that the population had overwhelmingly rejected.

In Spain, the people punished the Aznar government in the elections immediately following the Madrid bombing. In Britain, the war in Iraq is the subject of a Chilcot Inquiry[1235], whose conclusions are very clear and which some would like to see translated into an indictment of former Prime Minister Tony Blair for war crimes[1236].

But in France, after the attacks of 2015, the country tightened around its government to support it, without ever questioning interventions whose morality is questionable and whose implementation is carried out without strategy and without discerning their goals. Thus, from a terrorist threat, which stemmed from the inability to anticipate it before committing to Iraq and Syria, a second, more societal threat was created, inspired by a form of conspiracy. Salafism is described as violent in nature[1237], while the American intelligence services define it as "*a largely non-violent current in Islam*[1238] ".

In 2013, 68% of the French, 66% of the British, 63% of the Germans, 48-59% of the Americans and 52% of the Italians were opposed to an intervention in Syria[1239]; yet none of their governments listened to them, and the parliaments did not relay the voices of these majorities. Dozens of human lives would probably have been saved: fighting terrorism starts by not giving it the opportunity to appear… This is exactly what we are trying to hide.

Because the real reasons for jihadist terrorism were ignored, the communication was poor. In 2016, while France was responsible for only 4.7% of the international coalition's strikes[1240], it was in the front line of the terrorist threat. In fact, convinced that terrorism is an inescapable inevitability and seeking in foreign policy the success that was lacking at home, France was too "noisy" in its involvement in the Iraq-Syria conflict. The result was an overrated image of its involvement, which encouraged the terrorists.

Similarly, the use of the word 'Daech', which Islamists have never officially used, but which was promoted by the French government as early as 2015 because of its pejorative connotation in Arabic[1241], with the sole purpose of expressing contempt. Surprisingly, no attempt has been made in France to win the 'hearts

1235. http://www.iraqinquiry.org.uk/

1236. Christopher Hope, "Tony Blair 'could face war crimes charges' over Iraq War", *The Telegraph*, January 6, 2015.

1237. Mohammed Sifaoui in the programme "C à vous", "How to detect radicalisation? - C à Vous - 10/10/2019", *France 5/YouTube*, October 10, 2019 (05'45")

1238. *National Intelligence Estimate (NIE) NIE 2006-02R - Trends in Global Terrorism: Implications for the United States*, Office of the Director of National Intelligence (ODNI), April 2006 (SECRET-NOFORN), p.11 (declassified September 2011) ;

1239. Antoine Goldet, "Public opinion opposed to intervention in Syria", www.liberation.fr, September 11, 2013

1240. http://airwars.org/data/ (accessed on March 6, 2016)

1241. Armin Arefi, "Daesh-Islamic State: the name war has begun", *lepoint.fr*, September 22, 2014

and minds' of the radical fringe of its Muslim population, even though this is - at least partially - a domestic security issue. This casualness has even had repercussions within the armed forces[1242] and the intelligence services[1243]. In Britain, when 120 MPs urged him to use the word 'Daech', Tony Hall, Director General of the *BBC*, refused, explaining that the term is '*pejorative*' and '*would not preserve the impartiality of the* BBC[1244]'.

Thus, the victory against the EI in 2019 is only tactical in nature, achieved by 'brute force', by destroying its military component. This victory against terrorism is an optical illusion, as it has never managed to break through its logic and defeat it through strategy. As in the case of "Al Qaeda", the problem has been dealt with by "two-star corporals" and has not been solved, and it will reappear under another name. The same phenomenon as in the Sahel with operation BARKHANE...

The way we understand the problem determines the relevance of our solutions. This explains the failures of the various attempts to fight terrorism and radicalisation[1245]. In reality, those who decided to involve France in foreign wars for no reason (and those who advised them) are the same ones who divided it...

1242. *The French Military and Jihad*, Centre d'Analyse du Terrorisme, December 2019

1243. "Radicalisation: Sixteen people removed from the intelligence services since 2014, reveals Matignon", *20 Minutes / AFP*, January 21, 2020

1244. "UK questions Daech - BBC refuses to use the term "Daech" to describe the armed group", *lesechos.fr*, July 3, 2015. Editor's note: the BBC favours the term "*so-called Islamic State*"

1245. Mmes Esther Benbassa & Catherine Troendlé, *Rapport d'information fait au nom de la commission des lois constitutionnelles, de législation, du suffrage universel, du Règlement et d'administration générale (1) sur le désendoctrinement, le désembrigadement et la réinsertion des djihadistes en France et en Europe*, Senate - Extraordinary session of 2016-2017, July 12, 2017 (n° 633)

8. RUSSIA

8.1. The context

The author of this book has worked for many years on the study of the Soviet threat, watching for signs of political change in the press and media, for clues in the obituaries of leaders, for changes in the stocks of raw materials, for the frequency of space missions, for the flow of rail transport across the Polish and Czechoslovak borders, and for changes in the tone of state propaganda. A threat is always part of a context: something we have forgotten, because we systematically rewrite history.

The era of Boris Yeltsin was marked by a too rapid and uncontrolled liberalisation of society, which favoured a form of wild capitalism. What was left of the Soviet empire was taken over by unscrupulous oligarchs, who became shamelessly rich, opening the door to organised crime and corruption. At the same time, the United States took advantage of the situation to overturn the world order and international law in favour of murderous strategies with uncertain objectives.

The arrival in power of Vladimir Putin in March 2000 radically changed the situation. The oligarchs were hunted down and their fortunes confiscated[1246]. This will result in a first level of disinformation that will play on the antisemitic character of this hunt, as six of them are Jewish (Boris Berezovski, Vladimir Gusinsky, Alexander Smolensky, Mikhail Khodorkovski, Mikhail Friedman and Valery Malkin)[1247]. Most of these oligarchs find refuge in Great Britain, because of its great tolerance of funds that come to its financial centre. However, the world of high finance and that of organised crime are not always very far apart, as William Browder, managing director of the investment fund Hermitage Capital Management, confesses:

1246. Camille Grange, "Putin, or the hunt for the oligarch", *Le Journal International*, May 7, 2013
1247. Luke Harding, "The richer they come...", *The Guardian*, July 2, 2007

Unfortunately, London has become the global centre for money laundering and the reputation of Russian criminal organisations[1248].

President Putin quickly became the "bête noire" of the European intelligentsia: his time in the KGB explains "*his love for conspiracy theories*[1249]". He became responsible for everything: the Paris attacks in 2015[1250], the attack at Ankara airport on February 17, 2016[1251]; the head of the SBU, the Ukrainian security service, even attributed the Brussels attacks of March 22, 2016 to him[1252]; and a Ukrainian expert saw the Nice attack of July 14, 2016 as a way for Putin to strengthen his position in the ongoing discussions with John Kerry[1253]. In France, on the evening of the April 20, 2017 attack on the Champs Élysées, Christophe Girard, mayor of the 4th arrondissement of Paris (Socialist Party), did not hesitate to tweet:

Attack in France a few days before the presidential election. How strange! Go and ask Mr Putin for example[1254]

… a magnificent demonstration of imbecility, revealing a state of mind, symptomatic of an unenlightened political class with very little responsibility. Some will even claim that "*Putin is at the helm*[1255]" during the Yellow Vests demonstration of December 1st, 2018: "journalists" who would have worked wonders in the 1930s…

People like to present Vladimir Putin as a dictator who muzzles his opponents. *The Putin System is a* film by Jean-Michel Carré, whose many inaccuracies make it more a propaganda film than a documentary. It states that at the beginning of his career in the KGB, Putin "*participated in the hunt for dissidents*[1256]". This is a lie: he started in the 2nd Main Directorate (counter-intelligence), then in the 1st Main Directorate (foreign intelligence), before being posted to East Germany[1257]. Dissidents were then the business of the 5th Main Directorate.

1248. Robert Verkaik, "The truth behind McMafia: London is 'the jurisdiction of choice'for Russian crime gangs", I-News, January 5, 2018

1249. Quentin Peel, "Portrait of Vladimir Putin - President of the Russian Federation", *Insitut Montaigne*, blog, July 17, 2018

1250. Авраам Шмулевич, "Организовал Ли Путин Парижские Теракты?", *tsn.ua*, November 17, 2015

1251. ТСН, "До терактів у Туречині може бути причетна Росія", *YouTube*, February 21, 2016

1252. Новости Украины, "Глава СБУ Грицак - Придурок и Дегенерат", *YouTube*, March 24, 2016

1253. "Эксперт рассказал, как Керри убедил Путина не делать глупости", *glavnoe.ua*, July 15, 2016

1254. Text "tweeted" on 20 April 2017, at 21:47 - quickly deleted immediately afterwards.

1255. https://twitter.com/briceculturier/status/1068854748932128770?s=20

1256. "The Putin system - INFRARED", *France2/YouTube*, October 1st, 2015 (09'12")

1257. Official biography (http://eng.putin.kremlin.ru/)

Carré was probably inspired by the *Wikipedia* article (in French) which is wrong on this point[1258], and not by the English version, which is correct[1259].

Contrary to what Carré claims, Putin resigned from the KGB *before* the putsch of August 1991. After the putsch, the KGB did not fall into disgrace, but on the contrary came out of it stronger: only its head had participated in the putsch, but the structures did not follow it and opposed the putschists. The KGB had sensed the change long before the politicians in the East… and in the West.

Carré's film discusses Vladimir Putin's manifesto, published in late December 1999, which outlines his vision for Russia at the dawn of the 21st century. He cites some of the phrases: "*managed democracy*", "*vertical power*", "*dictatorship of law*" and says that he "*claims to be a champion of contradictory values such as liberalism and statism, democracy and dictatorship*[1260]". The problem is that none of these terms are found in the original text[1261]!

He is accused of regretting the former USSR and of having declared that "*the destruction of the USSR was the greatest geopolitical catastrophe in the history of the 20th century*[1262]". This sentence is periodically used in the media, such as *Le Monde*[1263], *Le Figaro*[1264] or *France 24*[1265], to illustrate his ambition to recover the "greatness" of the USSR. In fact, the phrase is taken from a speech of April 25, 2005, in which Putin regrets the *chaotic way in* which the transition to democracy took place:

> *[…] Above all, we must recognise that the collapse of the Soviet Union was a major geopolitical disaster of the century, which became a real tragedy for the Russian nation. Tens of millions of our citizens and compatriots found themselves outside Russian territory. Moreover, the epidemic of disintegration infected Russia itself. Everyone's economies melted away and old ideals were destroyed. Many institutions were dissolved or brutally reformed […]*[1266].

So this is not a disaster for Humanity, but for the everyday life of the Russian population: his sentence echoes a real nostalgia among the population, 11-13% of whose electorate remained faithful to the Communist Party, the first

1258. Wikipedia, Article "Vladimir Putin" (accessed August 5, 2019)
1259. Wikipedia, article "Vadimir Putin" (accessed August 5, 2019)
1260. "The Putin System - INFRARED", *France2/YouTube*, October 1st, 2015 (44'30")
1261. Владимир Путин, Россия на рубеже тысячелетий, Независимая газета, December 30, 1999; (English translation: https://pages.uoregon.edu/kimball/Putin.htm)
1262. "Comment un homme a changé la Russie", *la-croix.fr*, April 26, 2005
1263. "The fall of the Soviet empire, twenty-five years later", *lemonde.fr*, September 8, 2016
1264. "Vladimir Fedorovsky: "The fall of the USSR is still a trauma…", *lefigaro.fr*, December 16, 2016
1265. "Putin, the unavoidable boss of Russia", *France 24*, March 18, 2018
1266. *Annual Address to the Federal Assembly of the Russian Federation*, April 25, 2005, Kremlin, Moscow (http://en.kremlin.ru/events/president/transcripts/22931)

opposition party. At no point does Putin regret the old communist system: on the contrary, he pleads for a liberal economy.

His dream of a '*Greater Russia*' is often referred to in order to give a warlike image of the country[1267]. In 2016, Dutch Foreign Minister Halbe Zijlstra states:

> *In early 2006, I was in Vladimir Putin's dacha. I was able to hear Vladimir Putin explain what he meant by the term Great Russia, because what he wants is a return to Great Russia. He explained that for him, Greater Russia is Russia, Belarus, Ukraine and the Baltic States. And that it would also be nice to have Kazakhstan*[1268].

According to *Libération*, he even used the word "*annex*"[1269]. But, as four years earlier with former Polish minister Radoslaw Sikorski[1270], it turned out to be a fabricated lie, which led Zijlstra to resign in February 2018. However, it is interesting to note that while several Western media reported the resignation, some (such as *La Libre de Belgique*[1271], *Europe 1*[1272] or *RTBF*[1273]) carefully omitted to mention what the lie was about: it was necessary to avoid admitting that one was lying about Russia's desire for expansion… Daniel Cohn-Bendit tried to excuse Zijlstra, suggesting that Putin already had the annexation of Crimea in mind in order to satisfy his desire for a "*Greater Russia*"[1274]. An idea that persists: in 2017, RTBF writes:

> *Vladimir Putin had donned the robes of the restorer of "Greater Russia" by annexing the Ukrainian peninsula of Crimea*[1275].

In April 2018, in the same spirit, President Macron told *Fox News* that Putin wants a "*Greater Russia*"[1276], a message dear to the Anglo-Saxons, who like to see Russia as an enemy eager for conquest. This is a manipulation based on emotion, not fact. In Russian, the adjective "great" (Velikaya) has a qualitative,

1267. Marie Dousset, "Vladimir Putin, ready to do anything for "his" Great Russia, *geopolis.francetvinfo.fr*, August 22, 2013
1268. Antoine Mouteau, "Netherlands. Diplomacy chief resigns after lies about Putin", www.ouest-france.fr, February 13, 2018
1269. "After lying about a meeting with Putin, Dutch foreign minister resigns", *liberation.fr*, February 13, 2018
1270. Wiktor Szary, "Polish ex-minister quoted saying Putin offered to divide Ukraine with Poland", *Reuters*, October 20, 2014
1271. OleB, "The lying Dutch minister resigns", *La Libre.be*, February 13, 2018 (Updated February 14, 2018)
1272. "Netherlands: after lying about a meeting with Putin, the head of diplomacy resigns", *europe1.fr*, February 13, 2018
1273. Belga, "Dutch foreign minister resigns over lie", www.rtbf.be, February 13, 2018
1274. Daniel Cohn-Bendit in "Politics, lies and the great Russia", *Europe 1/YouTube*, February 14, 2018
1275. "Putin, the unavoidable boss of Russia", *rtbf.be/AFP*, December 6, 2017
1276. "President Macron on relations with the US, Syria and Russia", *Fox News/YouTube*, April 22, 2018.

not a quantitative or territorial dimension[1277]. Moreover, the term "*Great Russia*", used in the 16th century, covered only a part of Western Russia, i.e. roughly the Russian Tsarate, while Ukraine was "*Little Russia*". This is why in the 17th and 18th centuries people spoke of the "*Tsar of all the Russias*": Great Russia, Little Russia (Ukraine) and White Russia (Belarus)[1278]. Ironically, by combining inculture and bad faith, Westerners are dismantling their own lies...

In reality, the historical tendency to expansion that is attributed to Russia is primarily a Soviet attribute. In Marxist thinking, the USSR was in a *permanent* and *systemic* war with the West, which was part of the historical process of class struggle. Under Stalin the idea prevailed that the security of the Soviet Union would only be guaranteed by a victory of socialism over capitalism and thus a conquest of Europe. It was in order to prevent an imminent offensive against the whole of Western Europe that Nazi Germany felt compelled to attack the USSR on June 22, 1941, as former GRU agent Viktor Suvorov explains in his book *Icebreaker*[1279]. After Stalin's death, the idea of conquering the West in order to impose socialism gave way to the need to modernise society and the military apparatus. This is "peaceful coexistence".

But the fear of a Western attack remains. After three attempted invasions in two centuries (1812, 1918-1922 and 1941-1945) (not counting the 1917 Revolution, provoked by Germany), the Russians have retained a deep distrust of Westerners, who are also very aggressive in other parts of the world. This was the raison d'être of the Warsaw Pact, created after Nato: it was to constitute a "buffer zone" in case of external aggression, creating a protective glacis for the Soviet Union. It was the fear of a 'hole' in this shell that provoked the Soviet intervention in Prague in August 1968.

In 1990, the Russians understood that the end of communism was inevitable and did not try to oppose it; and that the "glacis" that protected them could no longer be achieved by coercion, but by forging economic links. For them, the end of the Cold War was an opportunity to get out of the war economy in which they found themselves and develop a "real" economy. This is why they quickly dissolved the Warsaw Pact and created the Commonwealth of Independent States (CIS) with broader ambitions.

For the West, it is the opposite problem: the end of the Cold War has brutally melted their military-industrial complex, generating concerns for the future of their defence capabilities. This largely explains their almost continuous involvement in military interventions.

1277. Anatoly Reshetnikov, "What Does Russia Mean When It Talks Greatness?", *E-International Relations*, May 20, 2018

1278. Wikipedia, article "Great Russia" (in English)

1279. Viktor Suvorov (Translated by Thomas B. Beattie), *Icebreaker - Who Started the Second World War?* Hamish Hamilton, London, 1990

8.2 "There was Never a Promise that NATO Would not Expand Eastward After the Fall of the Berlin Wall[1280]"

Since the fall of the Berlin Wall, with thirteen new members, Nato has become contiguous with Russia, reducing the strategic depth with which it could respond to an attack. Nato's official line is that no promises have been made on the Western side to keep Nato within its then limits. This is a lie.

Firstly, it should be understood that the end of the Cold War was more the result of the collapse of the socialist system on itself than of any action by the West. The idea that the West pushed the Soviet Union into a process of overspending (notably through the Strategic Defence Initiative (SDI), better known as '*Star Wars*') and thus caused the fall of the regime[1281] is a fanciful myth.

In fact, SDI was first mentioned in March 1983. At that time, it was just an ambitious research programme, requiring a massive redirection of industrial resources, which the United States launched but did not succeed in completing. Today, the 'experts' see it only as a technological challenge, but it was first and foremost a political-strategic challenge. SDI radically changed the logic of the Cold War: from a balance based on an offensive capability, we moved to a balance of power based on a defensive capability. Ronald Reagan even saw a global dimension to it: the logic only worked if these capabilities were shared. But his European allies, led by the United Kingdom, saw this as a dangerous and costly utopia and threw all their weight behind the Americans.

Unlike the US, the USSR lived in a war economy, where consumer goods were not a priority. Soviet leaders were aware that they had reached the limits of their capabilities[1282] and did not seek to engage in SDI. According to a CIA SECRET report declassified in 2014, the Kremlin leadership was considering increasing the number of its missiles rather than developing a new parallel system[1283]. Moreover, it is worth recalling that technology transfers were not one-way: many of the technologies required for SDI were in Soviet hands, particularly in the area of materials science. Thus, contrary to what Thierry Wolton[1284] and others assert, IDS did not cause a boom in the Soviet economy[1285]. In fact, apart from an abundance of often unworkable ideas, SDI did not bring any concrete results and was abandoned as early as 1993. Thirty years later, the Americans depend

1280. "NATO enlargement and Russia: myths and realities", *NATO Review*, 2014

1281. See Thierry Wolton, *Le KGB en France*, Grasset, August 28, 1987

1282. Andrew Cockburn, "The Threat: Inside The Soviet Military Machine", *Random House*, 1983

1283. Moscow's Response to US Plans for Missile Defense, web.archive.org/web/20170119110741/https://www.cia.gov/library/readingroom/docs/DOC_0006122438.pdf

1284. Thierry Wolton, *op. cit.*

1285. David E. Hoffman, "Mutually Assured Misperception on SDI", *Arms Control Today*, October 6, 2010

heavily on Russian titanium and technology for the construction of rocket engines and cruise missiles... despite the sanctions[1286]!

By the end of the 1980s, the Soviet system was deeply ill. The Chernobyl disaster triggered an awareness at all levels of the inefficiency of the administrative and political management mechanisms: it was the major event that led to the collapse of the USSR. It was in the wake of this event that the policy of transparency (glasnost) was launched in support of the restructuring efforts (perestroika) that had just been initiated. From then on, Western efforts to subvert the communist system had only a marginal effect and were overtaken by its failings. This is why the West was itself surprised by the events of 1989-90, as confirmed by General David Richards, the then Chief of the British Defence Staff: "*We had no idea*[1287]! The author himself - negotiating in Washington on the day of the 'fall of the Wall' - could see that neither the event nor its consequences had been imagined by American politicians. Thus, our sense of "victory" is usurped, and our contempt for Russia unjustified.

By November 1989, the idea of German reunification was in the air. But the Western establishment - particularly the intelligence services - did not believe in it: there was a fear that the USSR would oppose it. The Soviets had retained a deep-seated distrust of Germany, and the Group of Soviet Forces in Germany (GSFR) was the most powerful and modern contingent outside its territory. The prospect of a reunified Germany meant a return to the pre-war situation for Russia and could be the pretext for an intervention as in Prague in 1968[1288]: all Western intelligence services were put on alert.

On the other hand, the redeployment of the GFSA to the Soviet Union was a considerable effort in financial and strategic terms, but also - and above all - in emotional terms. This is why US Secretary of State James Baker started discussions with Mikhail Gorbachev at an early stage. On February 9, 1990, in order to calm his concerns, he assured Gorbachev that Nato "*would not move an inch to the East*[1289]". On May 17, 1990, in an address in Brussels, Manfred Wörner, Secretary General of Nato, confirmed:

> *The fact that we are prepared not to deploy a Nato army beyond German territory gives the Soviet Union a strong security guarantee*[1290].

1286. Tony Capaccio, "Replacing Russian Rocket Engine Isn't Easy, Pentagon Says", *Bloomberg*, May 1st, 2014.
1287. Rosie Laydon, 'Former British Military Chief 'Had No Idea' Berlin Wall Would Fall In 1989', www.forces.net, November 5, 2019
1288. Joshua Shifrinson, 'The Fall of the Berlin Wall Almost Ended in War', *Foreign Affairs*, November 23, 2019
1289. *Record of Conversation between Mikhail Gorbachev and James Baker*, February 9, 1990 (National Security Archive, The George Washington University, Washington DC) (https://nsarchive2.gwu.edu//dc.html?doc=4325680-Document-06-Record-of-conversation-between)
1290. Dave Majumdar, "Newly Declassified Documents: Gorbachev Told NATO Wouldn't Move Past East German Border", *The National Interest*, December 12, 2017

Today we have the feeling that the USSR, having "lost the Cold War", no longer had a say in world developments. This is not true. While it no longer had any influence on the winds of freedom blowing in the East, it had *de jure* veto power over German reunification as the winner of the Second World War. It was therefore with the assurances of President George H.W. Bush and James Baker, Chancellor Helmut Kohl and his Foreign Minister Hans-Dietrich Genscher, British Prime Minister Margaret Thatcher, her successor John Major and their Foreign Secretary Douglas Hurd, President François Mitterrand, but also CIA Director Robert Gates and Manfred Wörner, that Nato would not expand after the withdrawal of the GFSA, that Gorbachev agreed to German reunification[1291].

In Russia, the hope generated by the end of the communist regime was very real for the new leaders. The dissolution of the Warsaw Treaty in July 1991 was an opportunity for Russia to reflect on the new security architecture of the European continent. This is why Russia has remained very attached to the OSCE mechanism, to which it still attributes a major role today. The creation of the North Atlantic Cooperation Council (NACC) by NATO at the end of 1991 was welcomed with enthusiasm by the Russian authorities and public opinion. The Russian leaders, who saw the damage caused by communism, thought that a security architecture based on power relations was outdated and dreamed of a more cooperative system.

At this stage, the project of continental security cooperation was very popular in Russia, and did not exclude the idea of eventual NATO membership. Discussions in this direction took place in October 1993 between Boris Yeltsin and the American Secretary of State Warren Christopher, who remained reserved:

> *[...] we will in due course consider the question of membership as a longer-term possibility. There will be an evolution, based on the development of a habit of cooperation, but over time*[1292].

In 1954, the Soviet Union had already approached some influential Nato countries with a view to possible membership, but was turned down because - beyond political and emotional considerations - the West feared that it would completely block the decision-making mechanisms and make the Alliance inoperative[1293]. The raison d'être of NATO is to place its members under the

1291. Ibid.

1292. Warren Christopher's internal memorandum on his 22 October 1993 interview with Boris Yeltsin (declassified May 8, 2000) cited by Dave Majumdar, "How Bill Clinton Accidentally Started Another Cold War", *The American Conservative*, October 18, 2017

1293. "That time when the Soviet Union tried to join NATO in 1954", *euromaidanpress.com*, March 31, 2017; see also documents declassified by Nato: http://archives.nato.int/uploads/r/null/2/4/24086/C-R_54_14_ENG.pdf

nuclear protection of the United States. For the US, it is hardly conceivable to have the two main nuclear powers in the same alliance.

NATO's reaction did not meet the expectations of the Russian population, which withdrew into itself. In June 1994, the Russian government joined NATO's newly created Partnership for Peace (PfP) against public opinion. In 1997, in order to give the illusion that it wanted to integrate Russia, the foundations were laid for the NATO-Russia Council (NRC), which came into force in 2002. The NRC was intended to maintain a dialogue with Russia so that NATO's expansion would not be perceived as a threat. It was a rather cynical way of not implementing promises made to the leaders of the former USSR, as Bill Clinton summarised it:

> *What the Russians get out of this exceptional agreement that we are offering them is the opportunity to sit in the same room with NATO and join us whenever we all agree on something, but they have no way of stopping us from doing something they don't agree with. They can show their disapproval by leaving the room. And as a second big advantage, they get our promise that we will not put our military stuff with their former allies, who will now be our allies, unless we wake up one morning and decide to change our minds*[1294].

For the Eastern European countries, the situation is somewhat different. In their minds, membership of the European Union and NATO often go hand in hand: it is a question of ensuring their development in security. But their approach is more opportunistic than philosophical. For them, the values of democracy and human rights remain - despite everything - very secondary. Thus, despite certain constitutional and legal safeguards, their intelligence services have essentially remained security services and largely retain the legacy of their communist predecessors, as evidenced by their participation in the CIA's torture programme. Moreover, their involvement in conflicts such as Afghanistan and Iraq was motivated more by the modernisation of their armed forces than by humanistic values. They have earned the qualification of the "*new Europe*" by Donald Rumsfeld[1295]. The political crisis arising from the migrant flows in the Mediterranean (which they helped to create) illustrates this ambiguity. Just as during the Cold War, when these countries had often been even more communist and repressive than the Soviets themselves, they sought the protection of the United States, even if it meant sacrificing their honour.

1294. James Goldgeier and Michael McFaul, Power and Purpose: US Policy toward Russia after the Cold War, Washington 2003, pp. 204-205

1295. Mark Baker, "U.S.: Rumsfeld's 'Old' And 'New' Europe Touches On Uneasy Divide", *RFE/RL*, January 24, 2003

Often presented as a fanciful rumour propagated by Russia[1296], Western assurances of non-expansion of Nato are attested to by numerous newly declassified documents made public on December 12, 2017 by the National Security Archive at George Washington University[1297]. While it is true that they were never sealed by treaty, they were explicitly and openly formulated. The Russians are therefore justified in questioning Nato's word and intentions[1298].

8.3 "Russia Wants to Provoke NATO Forces"

The Americans have become experts in building threats out of thin air. In March 2016, US General Philip M. Breedlove, Supreme Allied Commander Europe, stated, without providing any justification:

> *Together, Russia and the Assad regime are deliberately militarising migration in an attempt to overwhelm European structures and break their resolve*[1299].

A Western delusion that was repeated the following year on the occasion of ZAPAD-2017, an exercise that is part of the manoeuvres regularly conducted by the Russian army and its allies. Before the exercise, Nato, the Western media (and Florence Parly) spoke of an attempt at intimidation[1300], or even preparations for a possible invasion of Europe[1301]. Some generals even suggest that the exercise could give Russia the opportunity to pre-position troops and equipment for a future aggression of Europe and NATO[1302]. Why? To what end? No answer. The Atlantic Council, a private institution dedicated to supporting NATO[1303], puts the figure at 100,000 participants[1304], well above the 13,000

1296. *Nato enlargement and Russia: myths and realities* (www.nato.int/docu/review/2014/Russia-Ukraine-Nato-crisis/Nato-enlargement-Russia/FR/index.htm)

1297. "Declassified documents show security assurances against NATO expansion to Soviet leaders from Baker, Bush, Genscher, Kohl, Gates, Mitterrand, Thatcher, Hurd, Major, and Woerner", *National Security Archive*, December 12, 2017, Washington D.C.

1298. Philippe Descamps, "Quand la Russie rêvait d'Europe - 'L'Otan ne s'étendendra pas un pouce vers l'est'", *Le Monde Diplomatique*, September 2018, pp. 10-11

1299. "NATO Commander: Russia uses Syrian refugees as 'weapon' against West", *DW.com*, March 2, 2016

1300. "France, Germany Denounce Russia's Strategy Of 'Intimidation,' Dispute Size Of War Games," *Radio Free Europe/Radio Liberty*, September 7, 2017

1301. "Ukrainian Minister of Defense: Russia can use the forthcoming Zapad-2017 military exercises to invade any European country", *uawire.org*, July 23, 2017

1302. Damien Sharkov, "Is Russia Using Belarus Wargame To Deploy Permanent Units Along Poland's Border?", *Newsweek*, August 23, 2017

1303. Ian Brzezinski & Nicholas Varangis, "The NATO-Russia Exercise Gap... Then, Now, & 2017", *Atlantic Council*, October 25, 2016

1304. Michael R. Gordon & Eric Schmitt, "Russia's Military Drills Near NATO Border Raise Fears of Aggression," *The New York Times*, July 31, 2017

notification threshold of the Vienna Document. Picked up by the Ukrainian website *InformNapalm.org*, this number "inspires" many European media[1305], but it is unfounded. We are back in the middle of the Cold War...

Russia announced 12,700 Russian and Belarusian participants and invited NATO observers to the manoeuvres[1306]. Jens Stoltenberg, NATO Secretary General, says he has "*every reason to believe that there will be significantly more participants than the number officially announced*[1307]". But he is lying. The official number will not be denied afterwards, despite the scrutiny of Western intelligence services. This does not prevent the journalist François Clémenceau from stating, in March 2018, on *France 5* that Russia seeks to "test" NATO's defences through its military presence and a lack of transparency in the military exercises[1308]. In fact, Russia strictly adheres to its international obligations, but some Eastern European countries, such as Poland and the Baltic States, deliberately 'inflate' Russian figures in order to justify a permanent deployment of Nato forces on their territory.

In 2017, during Nato manoeuvres in Lithuania, soldiers of the German contingent were accused of rape. However, it soon became clear that the crime had not taken place. On 16 February, the German magazine *Spiegel ran the* headline *Russia attacks Bundeswehr with fake news campaign*, but quickly corrected it to *Nato suspects Russia of being responsible for a false information campaign against the Bundeswehr*[1309]. The incident was widely reported in the German press. On the 18th, *Le Figaro* spoke of the destabilisation of "*the democratic balance by trying to orient public opinion*" and the concern of European leaders[1310]. However, it is known that the controversy arose from a single e-mail that arrived on February 14 at the office of the President of the Lithuanian Parliament and whose origin could not be determined[1311]. As for Russia's involvement, it is based only on the allegation of an anonymous "*NATO diplomat*"[1312].

1305. "Zapad-2017: how InformNapalm sent 100,000 Russian soldiers to Belarus", *informnapalm.org*, September 10, 2017
1306. "Столтенберг поприветствовал приглашение наблюдателей НАТО на 'Запад-2017'", *RIA Novosti*, March 13, 2017
1307. Teri Schultz, "NATO voices skepticism over size of Russia's Zapad military exercise", *dw.com*, September 14, 2017
1308. Programme "C dans l'air", "Putin: alone against all? #cdanslair 16.03.2018", *YouTube/France 5*, March 16, 2016 (59'20")
1309. Matthias Gebauer, "Nato vermutet Russland hinter Fake-News-Kampagne gegen Bundeswehr", *Spiegel Online*, February 16, 2017
1310. Nicolas Barotte, "Le développement des 'fake news' inquiète les leaders internationaux", *lefigaro.fr*, February 18, 2017
1311. "Lithuania/Otan: investigation into false rape accusations", *lefigaro.fr*, February 17, 2017
1312. "Eine E-Mail in Litauen ließ deutsche Medien Fake-News-Großalarm auslösen", *uebermedien.de*, February 28, 2017

In short: an incident that never happened, announced by a single anonymous email, is enough to accuse Russia, whose "*strategy aims to constantly blur the line between truth and falsehood*[1313]"! We are walking on our heads...

There are often references to "*provocations*" by Russian reconnaissance or fighter planes in the vicinity of Western airspace[1314], which Bruno Tertrais of the Foundation for Strategic Research describes as "*deliberate*[1315]". But this is not true. In fact, in March 2018, General Petr Pavel, Chairman of Nato's Military Committee, said that "*almost all interceptions*" were not due to hostile behaviour, but to human error:

> *[...] There have been no violations of the territory of the Baltic countries - not even of their airspace (...) So far we have not seen any real signs of aggressive behaviour against the Baltic countries or in the Black Sea region*[1316].

In fact, a sense of threat is being fostered that is totally irrational. Not only is it not based on any tangible facts, but it cannot even be explained why Russia would seek to provoke the West. Since the Ukrainian crisis, although no one has been able to demonstrate Russian military intervention, the spectre of invasion has fuelled the Western political imagination. In a Europe at peace, but at war with its budgetary balances, the Russian threat has become the "lifeline" of defence budgets... But it is also a way to create "national unity" or "Atlantic solidarity" in a troubled European context.

8.4 "Russia, Suspected of Attacks on US Siplomats in Cuba[1317]"

On August 9, 2017, at a State Department press conference, spokeswoman Heather Nauert informs that diplomats at the US embassy in Havana are complaining of various ailments and some have had to be repatriated. *TIME* magazine claims that these diplomats have been "injured" by an "acoustic

1313. Nicolas Barotte, *op. cit.*

1314. "VIDEO. Les incursions d'avions militaires russes en Europe en hausse en 2014", *Franceinfo*, February 9, 2015 (updated February 10, 2015); Philippe Bernard, Nathalie Guibert, Olivier Truc and Jean-Pierre Stroobants, "Les provocations calculées des vols militaires russes", *Le Monde*, February 6, 2015 (updated August 19, 2019)

1315. Nolwenn Leboyer, "Les incursions d'avions russes sont une provocation délibérée", *20Minutes.fr*, February 19, 2015 (updated February 20, 2015)

1316. Oriana Pawlyk, "Most Russian Plane Intercepts over Baltics Due to Error: NATO General", www.military.com, March 7, 2018

1317. Nora Gámez Torres, "Now Russia is suspected of attacks against diplomats in Cuba. Will U.S. strike back?", *Miami Herald*, September 11, 2018

weapon" that has been targeting them since the end of 2016[1318], and are suffering from serious ailments and even hearing loss[1319].

Experts were sent to the site and imaginations ran wild. There is talk of an 'acoustic cannon', similar to the system developed by the Germans in 1942 (which inspired Hergé for *The Sunflower Affair*). There was talk of a malfunctioning bug placed in the embassy: this probably referred to "The Thing", which had been discovered in 1952 in the American embassy in Moscow[1320], which was a totally passive device, subjected to constant microwave radiation and which sent back a signal modulated by the human voice.

CBS News reports that 60% of the diplomatic staff posted in Havana are being repatriated. The so-called "attacks" appear to be focused on intelligence officers under diplomatic cover[1321]! *Business Insider* will reveal that the affected individuals are suffering from brain damage and memory loss[1322].

However, neurologist Seth Horowitz says that "*there is no acoustic phenomenon in the world that can cause this type of symptom*[1323]". But the case is taken very seriously and its consequences are far from trivial. On 26 September 2017, Rex Tillerson, Secretary of State received his Cuban counterpart Bruno Rodriguez to discuss the matter[1324]. Three days later, he announced the reduction of the staff of the American embassy in Cuba, and on 3 October, fifteen Cuban diplomats were expelled due to "*Cuba's failure to protect American diplomatic personnel*[1325]".

On *FOX News*, citing a SIGINT report[1326], "expert" Dr Sebastian Gorka claims that Russia is behind the "attacks" in Havana and Beijing, and that the same weapons were used in Crimea[1327]. The presenter refers to a new type of weapon with a Russian fingerprint... without any proof[1328]!

1318. https://soundcloud.com/user-493247881/the-sound-in-havana#t=0:00; Josh Lederman & Michael Weissenstein (Associated Press), "What Americans heard in mysterious sonic attacks in Havana", *pbs.org*, October 12, 2017
1319. Kate Samuelson & Justin Worland, "U.S. Diplomats in Cuba Were Injured by a 'Sonic Weapon.' What Is That?", *Time Magazine*, August 10, 2017
1320. See Wikipedia article "The Thing (listening device)".
1321. "Cuba acoustic attacks targeted U.S. intelligence operatives", *CBS/AP*, October 2, 2017
1322. Kevin Loria, "A new study on the US officials who suffered brain injuries in Cuba makes their cases even more mysterious" *Business Insider*, February 16, 2018
1323. Kevin Loria, "Mysterious sonic weapons reportedly caused brain injuries in US diplomats in Cuba - here's what we know", www.businessinsider.com, August 24, 2017
1324. Josh Lederman & Matthew Lee, "Cuba tells Tillerson: No culpability in health 'attacks'", *AP*, September 27, 2017
1325. Rex W. Tillerson, "On the Expulsion of Cuban Officials From the United States," *U.S. Department of State*, October 3, 2017; Gardiner Harris, Julie Hirschfeld Davis & Ernesto Londoño, "U.S. Expels 15 Cuban Diplomats, in Latest Sign Détente May Be Ending," *The New York Times*, October 3, 2017
1326. Lia Eustachewich, "Russia suspected of mysterious attacks on US diplomats in Cuba", *New York Post*, September 11, 2018
1327. Fox Business, "Russia was behind US embassy attacks in Cuba, China: report", *YouTube*, September 11, 2018
1328. Doina Chiacu, Lesley Wroughton & Mark Hosenball, "Russia the main suspect in U.S. diplomats' illness in Cuba: NBC", *NBC News/Reuters*, September 11, 2018

In January 2019, the *New York Times* revealed that doctors were beginning to doubt the nature and even the existence of the 2017 symptoms[1329]. Until it is discovered that the key to the puzzle is probably... the mating call of a Caribbean cricket[1330]!

The Americans are used to this kind of accusation: on September 13, 1981, Alexander Haig, then Secretary of State, accused the Soviets of using mycotoxins in Afghanistan[1331]. But the analyses of the samples collected showed that they were... bee excrement[1332]! So as not to have to justify its ignorance and bad faith, the American government never wanted to declassify the file, which thus remains 'officially' unsolved!

The anecdote is amusing, but reveals several phenomena. First, the remarkable level of incompetence of the 'experts', who 'fit' facts (which were not even proven) to their prejudices. Secondly, the state of mind that dominates current international relations and which transforms events whose reasons, course and actors are unknown into certainties, with the sole aim of reinforcing predefined foreign policy objectives.

On an ethical level, it is surprising that no one - in the media or in the political world - has tried to understand what the purpose of this "attack" might have been. What would have been Cuba's interest in aggravating relations with its large neighbour, when they had just thawed after long diplomatic efforts, leading to the easing of an embargo that had been in place for more than fifty years?

8.5. "Putin's Hybrid War against the West[1333]"

Shortly before the 2019 European elections, *France 24* broadcast a report initially entitled *European elections: when Russia gets involved*[1334], then quickly changed to *European elections: what if Russia gets involved?*[1335] but with the same content: Russia seeks to weaken Europe through hybrid warfare[1336]. To support this assertion, *France 24* serves us propaganda worthy of the great hours of Pravda.

1329. Carl Zimmer, "The Sounds That Haunted U.S. Diplomats in Cuba? Lovelorn Crickets, Scientists Say", *The New York Times*, January 4, 2019

1330. Alexander L. Stubbs & Fernando Montealegre-Z, *Recording of "sonic attacks" on U.S. diplomats in Cuba spectrally matches the echoing call of a Caribbean cricket*, Biorxiv, January 4, 2019; "Sonic attack at the US embassy in Cuba: the surprising hypothesis of crickets", *Sciences et Avenir / AFP*, January 8, 2019

1331. Johnathan B. Tucker, "The 'Yellow Rain' controversy: Lessons for Arms Control Compliance", *The Nonproliferation Review*, Spring 2001

1332. "Yellow Rain Falls", *The New York Times*, September 3, 1987

1333. "Putin's hybrid war against the West", www.lecho.be, July 14, 2016

1334. "European elections: when Russia gets involved", *France 24/YouTube*, May 17, 2019

1335. "European elections: what if Russia gets involved?", *France 24/YouTube*, May 18, 2019

1336. Ibid (00'40")

All these accusations seem to fit into a coherent concept, described in a 2013 article entitled "*The Value of Science in Foresight*" by Valery Gherassimov, head of the Russian General Staff[1337]. It would outline a concept of 'hybrid warfare', which brings together cyberwarfare, terrorism, clandestine warfare, conventional warfare and, of course, information warfare.

The problem is that this concept does not exist, and Russia has neither theorised nor invoked it. It is a Western invention. In fact, Gherassimov analyses the recent evolution of conflicts (especially in the Middle East) and draws lessons on how to integrate them into military thinking. It is more a methodological approach than a description of how Russia would have integrated these lessons into its doctrine.

In 2014, during the Ukrainian crisis, the article was used as a key to reading by Western "experts" of all kinds, who embroidered around events in order to give them coherence. They explain a war they do not want to understand with a doctrine that does not exist.

In the wake of the Ukrainian propaganda, the mainstream media is having a field day[1338]. The West is thus artificially creating a Russian "doctrinal basis", which media such as *Le Temps*[1339] or *La Croix*[1340] use to explain and condemn Russia. The magazine *Le Point* goes even further by stating that the doctrine is "*validated by Vladimir Putin*" himself[1341].

There is an urban legend, dating from the Soviet era, that when Russians write about a military subject, it is because they have implemented it themselves. This is not true. Already during the Cold War, military doctrine was discussed in specialist journals. During the war in Afghanistan, there were real discussion forums where field officers could share their operational experience. Special forces ('spetsnaz') techniques, counter-terrorism and counter-insurgency methods were openly debated in the specialist press. Western concepts were openly discussed and dissected in the specialist literature, long before they were incorporated into doctrine.

In fact, it all stems from an article by Russia expert Mark Galeotti, who first commented on the Russian article to define the 'Gherassimov Doctrine', which was supposed to illustrate the Russian vision of hybrid warfare[1342]. But in 2018, noting the damage he had unwittingly caused by 'creating' the 'Gherassimov Doctrine', he apologised in *Foreign Policy* magazine:

1337. Валерий Герасимов, "Ценность науки в предвидении", Военнопромышленный курьер, February 26, 2013 (Gherassimov Valery, "The Value of Science in Foresight", *Military-Industrial Courier*, February 26, 2013)
1338. Elie Tenenbaum, "The Trap of Hybrid War", *IFRI*, October 2015
1339. Frédéric Koller, "Désinformation, l'offensive russe", *Le Temps*, December 27, 2016
1340. Olivier Tallès, "Bruxelles s'alarme de la désinformation russe", *La Croix*, May 4, 2017
1341. Marc Nexon, "Gherassimov, le général russe qui mène la guerre de l'information", *Le Point.fr*, March 2, 2017
1342. Mark Galeotti, "The 'Gerasimov Doctrine' and Russian Non-Linear War", *In Moscow's Shadows* (blog), July 6, 2014

I was the first to write about Russia's infamous high-tech military strategy. One small problem: it doesn't exist[1343].

He points out that Gherassimov's analysis of the Arab revolutions…

[…] was not a 'doctrine', in the Russian sense, for future adventures abroad: Gherassimov was trying to find a way to combat, not promote, such uprisings at home[1344].

In October 2019, the *New York Times* "revealed" the existence of the "secret" unit 29155. Based in the east of Moscow, it would have been discovered recently by the Western services and would be responsible for conducting the 'hybrid war' in Europe: its agents would be involved in the Skripal affair, or the attempted attack against the president of Montenegro in 2017[1345]. And that's not all: the GRU is said to have established a base in Haute-Savoie, not very far from the "spy nest" in Geneva. The daily *Le Temps* sees this as a new threat to Switzerland[1346]. We are in the midst of disinformation. However, this "*very secret"* unit is well known on the Internet[1347]: it is the 161st Intelligence Training Centre*, which* has been known for more than fifty years as a centre for tactical training, particularly in the field of foreign light weapons[1348].

The term "hybrid war" has become a "catch-all" in which all our perceptions are mixed up. Even Nato, which uses the term extensively to accuse Russia, is questioning its nature[1349]. The West has understood the Ukrainian crisis in the way it would have conducted itself. That is why their efforts to assist Ukrainian forces have not brought any substantial progress on the ground. Yet, if the Russians had really been operationally involved in the Donbass, as has been claimed, the crisis would probably have found a solution (good or bad) and not stagnated as it has since 2015.

We make exactly the same mistake with Russia as we do with jihadist terrorism: we attribute to the adversary a doctrine constructed from our own perceptions, assembling "facts" with our logic. As a result, we fail to enter the opponent's *real* logic and leave the initiative to him. This is why the West is held in check in all its theatres of operation, why the Israelis have been unable to

1343. Mark Galeotti, "I'm Sorry for Creating the 'Gerasimov Doctrine'", *Foreign Policy*, March 5, 2018
1344. Mark Galeotti, "I'm Sorry for Creating the 'Gerasimov Doctrine'", *Foreign Policy*, March 5, 2018
1345. Michael Schwirtz, "Top Secret Russian Unit Seeks to Destabilize Europe, Security Officials Say," *The New York Times*, October 8, 2019
1346. Frédéric Koller, "Ces espions russes qui aiment la Suisse", *Le Temps*, December 7, 2019
1347. https://twitter.com/leonidragozin/status/1181849700300972032
1348. Алексей Никольский, ""Элитная часть ГРУ" из статьи NY Times оказалась курсами для разведчиков," Ведомости, October 9, 2019, www.vedomosti.ru/politics/articles/2019/10/09/813253-elitnaya-chast-ny-dlya)
1349. Damien Van Puyvelde, "Does hybrid war really exist?", www.nato.int, May 7, 2015

control terrorism for more than sixty years, and why France fears the return of jihadists despite the 'defeat' of the Islamic State. You can't defeat an opponent you don't want to know...

8.6 "Moscow had Every Interest in Poisoning its Ex-Spy[1350]"

In 2006, photos of the emaciated face of Aleksander Litvinenko, a former agent of the Russian Federal Security Service (FSB), made the front page of British newspapers. Poisoned with Polonium-210, a highly radioactive material, the ex-spy died within weeks. The nature of the poison suggested direct intervention by Russian intelligence services, and in particular the FSB. As Litvinenko had links with the oligarch Boris Berezovsky, an opponent of Vladimir Putin, the idea of an elimination by the FSB fired the imagination.

In 2018, the poisoning of former Russian agent Sergei Skripal triggered a major political crisis between the UK and Russia, dragging Nato and the European Union into a controversy and disinformation not seen since the Cold War. The two cases highlight not only the bad faith of the West, but also a profound ignorance of the Russian intelligence services and how they operate.

Sergei Skripal was a colonel in the GRU, the Russian military intelligence service (equivalent to the Directorate of Military Intelligence - DRM - in France). In 1995, he was recruited by the British *Secret Intelligence Service* (SIS or MI-6), which 'bought' information from him for a total amount of some 100,000 dollars. Using "barium" (i.e. deliberately injected false information), the Russians detected the betrayal and Skripal was arrested in December 2004 in Moscow, where the investigation showed that he had sold the British the list of GRU agents operating in Europe. His treason is considered the most serious since that of Oleg Penkovsky in the early 1960s: he was tried in August 2006 and sentenced to 13 years in prison. But four years later, on July 9, 2010, he was exchanged with three other Western agents at Vienna airport for ten individuals accused of espionage in the United States[1351]. He was then housed in Salisbury, in the same city as his former handler, Pablo Miller.

On March 4, 2018, at 4.15pm, after having lunch in a pizzeria and feeding bread to ducks in a city park, Skripal and his daughter Yulia (who had arrived from Russia the previous day for a visit) became dizzy and collapsed on a bench. They are rescued by Sergeant Nick Bailey, who is off duty at the time and is at the scene. Both Skripal and Bailey showed signs of poisoning and were taken to

1350. Jean-Baptiste Naudet, "Pourquoi Moscou avait tout intérêt à empoisonner son ex-espion... et à ce que ça se sache", *l'Obs*, March 15, 2018

1351. Tom Parfitt in Moscow, Matthew Weaver & Richard Norton-Taylor, "Spy swap: US and Russia hand over agents in full media glare", *The Guardian*, July 9, 2010

hospital, where they were released in the following weeks. According to the British authorities, they were poisoned with a nerve agent - called "Novichok" - which was placed on the door handle of their house. The *Mirror*[1352] and the *Daily Mail*[1353] claim that three children were contaminated by the couple and that ducks died.

On March 12, when the investigation had just begun, Theresa May directly accused Russia in Parliament. Two days later, the government expels twenty-three Russian diplomats. On March 15, in a joint statement, Great Britain, France, Germany and the United States condemned the assassination attempt and demanded that Russia shed full light on the incident[1354]. At the same time, Nato in Brussels declared seven diplomats from the Russian representation *persona non grata*. Some twenty Western countries followed suit and a total of 153 Russian diplomats were expelled. Iceland declares that it will not send an official representative to the football World Cup in Russia[1355]. Portugal and Turkey, both Nato members, refrain from taking action against Russia in the absence of more convincing evidence[1356].

In the United States, Gina Haspel, then deputy director of the CIA, had a meeting with Donald Trump, and proposed that he take strong measures against Russia. In order to convince him, she showed him photos (provided by MI6) of the three 'poisoned' children and the dead birds[1357]. On March 26, Trump followed her recommendations and expelled sixty Russian diplomats - including twelve assigned to the United Nations - and ordered the closure of the Russian consulate in Seattle.

The problem is that no ducks died as a result of this affair, and the three children examined at the hospital were not suffering from any poisoning and were not ill[1358]! Gina Haspel thus lied to Trump. The *New York Times* article was quietly corrected on June 5, 2019, explaining that the CIA director had merely shown photos "*illustrating the consequences of nerve agent attacks, but which were not specific to the chemical attack in Britain*[1359]".

In early July 2018, the case rebounded with the announcement of two new victims at Amesbury: Dawn Sturgess (who would die) and Charlie Rowley,

1352. Alan Selby, 'Three children taken to hospital after poisoned Sergei Skripal handed them bread to feed ducks', *The Mirror*, March 24, 2018 (updated March 25, 2018)

1353. Gareth Davies, 'Three children were taken to hospital after Sergei Skripal gave them bread to feed ducks in the park where the Russian spy and his daughter were found poisoned', *dailymail.co.uk*, March 25, 2018

1354. "France, Germany, UK, US blame Moscow for ex-spy chemical attack - joint statement", *DW News*, March 15, 2018

1355. Julian Borger, Patrick Wintour & Heather Stewart, "Western allies expel scores of Russian diplomats over Skripal attack", *The Guardian*, March 27, 2018

1356. "Skripal affair: Turkey will not act against Russia 'on the basis of an allegation'", *Paris Match/AFP*, March 28, 2018

1357. Julian E. Barnes & Adam Goldman, "Gina Haspel Relies on Spy Skills to Connect With Trump. He Doesn't Always Listen," *The New York Times*, April 16, 2019.

1358. Steven Morris & Caroline Bannock, 'No children or ducks harmed by novichok, say health officials', *The Guardian*, April 18, 2019

1359. Julian E. Barnes & Adam Goldman, April 16, 2019 (*op. cit.*)

who were allegedly poisoned with the remaining poison, contained in a small bottle of perfume[1360]. But nothing is known about the bottle between March 4 and June 27, when it was found by Rowley. In short, we know nothing and understand nothing. This does not prevent the Home Secretary, Sajio Javid, from calling on Russia:

> *It is now time for the Russian state to come forward and explain exactly what happened*[1361]*!*

In August 2018, two tourists who arrived in Salisbury on March 2 and returned to Russia a few days later were identified by the British authorities as Russian intelligence agents and responsible for the assassination attempt.

The Western discourse is determined, but the case is far from clear, and many questions remain unanswered. For example, Skripal's handler, Pablo Miller, is also the associate of ex-agent Christopher Steele (the author of the incriminating 'dossier' on Donald Trump[1362]). Did Skripal contribute to the dossier in question[1363]? However, on 7 March 2018, the British government issued a '*DSMA-Notice*', a procedure that instructs the media to maintain silence on a sensitive matter[1364]. It is about "*intelligence personnel associated with the Skripal case*[1365]": it is about preventing the publication of the name of "Pablo Miller"… It is followed by a second *DSMA-Notice*, on March 14, which assimilates the publication of the identity of the protagonists to Russian propaganda[1366].

8.6.1. The Method

Even before the findings of an enquiry, Theresa May says there is "no *plausible alternative explanation*" for the fact that "it is *highly likely that Russia was responsible*"[1367].

But to deduce from the dangerousness of a product that only the Russian state is the user is profoundly dishonest. For we know that in 1994-95, the Russian mafia used chemical or highly radioactive products, such as caesium-137 and

1360. Lizzie Dearden, "Novichok poisoning latest: Couple in Amesbury exposed to toxin after handling contaminated item, police say", *The Independent*, July 6, 2018

1361. Danny Boyle, "Amesbury poisoning: Wiltshire police cannot rule out more people falling ill amid hunt for Novichok-tainted item", *The Telegraph*, July 6, 2018

1362. Tom Winter, "FBI releases documents showing payments to Trump dossier author Steele", www.nbcnews.com, August 3, 2018; Julia Macfarlane, "Former MI6 spy Christopher Steele, who compiled controversial dossier, breaks silence to criticise Trump", *ABC News*, October 10, 2018.

1363. Mark Duell & Richard Spillett, "Was poisoning in retaliation to Trump 'dirty dossier'? Kremlin double agent 'was close to consultant employed by former MI6 spy Christopher Steele'", *Daily Mail*, March 8, 2018

1364. See chapter Appendices: Censorship.

1365. http://powerbase.info/index.php/DSMA_notice_7_March_2018

1366. http://powerbase.info/index.php/DSMA_notice_14_March_2018

1367. Gabriela Baczynska & Elizabeth Piper, "EU leaders agree with Theresa May that Russia was behind the Sergei Skripal nerve agent attack", *Business Insider/Reuters*, March 22, 2018

cobalt-60, on at least six occasions to eliminate individuals[1368]. As for 'Novichok', none of the Western mainstream media noted that it had already been used by the Russian mafia to murder Ivan Kivelidi, an executive of Rosbusinessbank, in 1995[1369]. The Russian government had prosecuted Leonid Rink, a former Soviet laboratory employee who had worked on Novichok, for diverting small amounts of the drug for sale to Latvian mafia members as early as 1994[1370]. Hypotheses involving other actors, such as organised crime, have been deliberately ruled out[1371], although links between the Skripal case and Russian mafia racketeering and money laundering activities have been detected[1372]. Russian criminal organisations - which are very active in the UK - are not only involved in financial activities, but also in violent score-settling. Since the early 2000s, there have been no fewer than 14 unexplained murders of Russian citizens in the UK[1373].

The very spectacular and well-publicised poisoning of Alexander Litvinenko in 2006 is often cited as a reference. This former FSB agent and specialist in the fight against organised crime had been called in by Boris Berezovsky to fight Russian mafia factions that were harassing him in London. Although the report of the British Commission of Inquiry (Owen Report)[1374] points the finger at the Russian government, it provides no evidence of this and admits that its conclusions are "circumstantial" (i.e. based on circumstances, not facts)[1375]. He considers the FSB's involvement[1376] "*highly probable*" and Putin's approval[1377] "*likely*". Clearly, these are assumptions. Today, the most likely - and most consistent - hypothesis is that of a "contract" executed by a mafia[1378].

8.6.2. The Role of the Services

As a preliminary remark, we note that the Western 'experts', apart from a few expressions taken from the press, know very little about the way in which the intelligence services in general, and the Russians in particular, operate. Thus, the

1368. Jacques Baud, *La Guerre asymétrique ou la défaite du vainqueur*, Éditions du Rocher, 2003, p. 62
1369. Роман Шлейнов, "Новичок" уже убивал", Новая газета, March 22, 2018
1370. Reuters Staff, "Secret trial shows risks of nerve agent theft in post-Soviet chaos: experts", *Reuters*, March 14, 2018
1371. Gareth Porter, 'UK Government Overlooks Russian Mob's Use of Novichok for Assassination', *mintpressnews.com*, April 18, 2018
1372. David Wooding, "Russian mafia 'is using scheme meant for UK farmers to launder £60bn of dirty money'", *The Sun*, April 29, 2018
1373. Diana Swain, "How journalism prompted a closer look at 14 deaths in the U.K. with Russian connections", *CBC News*, March 17, 2018
1374. *The Litvinenko Inquiry - Report into the death of Alexander Litvinenko*, Chairman: Sir Robert Owen, Her Majesty's Stationery Office, January 2016 (figures 9.145 and 9.199)
1375. William Dunkerley, 'Six reasons you can't take the Litvinenko report seriously', *The Guardian*, February 5, 2016
1376. *The Litvinenko Inquiry*, *op. cit.* figure 9.200
1377. *The Litvinenko Inquiry*, *op. cit.* para 9.215
1378. Justin Raimondo, "Did the Russian Mafia Kill Alexander Litvinenko?", *antiwar.com*, December 27, 2006

journalist François Clémenceau claims that during the Cold War there was an "*unwritten code*" between Western and Soviet services to cooperate on a certain number of files, and to spare the families of agents when it came to carrying out eliminations[1379]. This is pure fantasy.

Today, clandestine action abroad - such as an elimination - would not be the responsibility of the FSB (responsible for internal security) or the GRU (responsible for military intelligence), but of *Directorate S* of the SVR (the equivalent of the French DGSE) which has clandestine networks abroad. The problem is that the SVR is so discreet that our media and politicians do not know about it... and accuse those they do know.

Moreover, if - as the British services claim - the Russians had been monitoring Yulia Skripal's phone for several months[1380], it is surprising that they waited for her visit to Britain to attempt this assassination and thus unnecessarily complicate the operation.

As for the "executors", we remain in the realm of conjecture. In August 2018, the British authorities identified two Russians - who arrived in Britain on March 2 and then returned to Russia - and claimed that they were agents of the Russian intelligence services and could be the perpetrators of the assassination attempt. On September 13, 2018, the two "agents" Alexander Petrov and Ruslan Boshirov gave an interview to the Russian television channel RT. Despite their gauche appearance, their statements correspond to the facts: according to the British police, they arrived in Salisbury on March 4 at 11.48 a.m. and could not have placed the poison before noon. Yet it is known that the Skripals did not return to their home after midday. Surveillance cameras - ubiquitous in Britain - did not record the presence of the two "agents" within 150 metres of the Skripals' home. In short, there is no confirmation that they were involved in the case.

Founded by Eliot Higgins - an ex-employee of a women's lingerie manufacturer - the Bellingcat website specialises in conflict analysis based on open sources. Known for its pro-Western positions, it is frequently commissioned by governments to support or legitimise official positions. But his working methods are not as rigorous as he is said to be. On September 26, 2018, he claimed that Ruslan Boshirov was in fact Colonel Anatoly Chepiga of the military intelligence service (GRU). In its "20 heures" of September 27, *TF1* announced that the British site had "*formally identified*" Chepiga, who had served in the Spetsnaz (the Russian elite troops) and had been decorated in 2004 for his actions in Afghanistan. But this is not true. In fact, Bellingcat arrived at this conclusion

1379. Programme "C dans l'air", "Putin: alone against all? #cdanslair 16.03.2018", *YouTube/France 5*, March 16, 2018 (08'40")

1380. Samuel Osborne, "Ex-spy Sergei Skripal and daughter were 'under Russian surveillance' months before Salisbury poisoning", www.independent.co.uk, July 5, 2018

through a succession of approximations: they did not try to find out who Boshirov was, but looked for an individual with a corresponding profile. Thus, Bellingcat began by establishing the typical profile of a Russian military intelligence officer, and then looked for a character who could match it. This was done by selecting a military unit where it was thought such an officer might have been trained, and then searching the media (newspaper articles, archival documents and the like) for mentions of individuals who fit the profile, which led to Chepiga[1381]. In reality, Bellingcat states that its search yielded several possible candidates and that Tchepiga's identity is not certain, so TF1 is lying when it claims that there is a formal identification.

8.6.3. The Background

The elimination of Georgi Markov on September 11, 1978 in London is often mentioned to explain the elimination of Skripal by Russia. But here again, we are in the approximation. First of all, contrary to what some "specialists" claim, it was carried out by the Bulgarian security services and not by the Soviet KGB.

Secondly, it is important to note at this point that, contrary to what the cinema suggests, the secret services do not take revenge: the political risk of a revenge operation is such that its benefit is often nil. Thus, since the beginning of the Cold War, more than sixty agents of Soviet or Russian services have 'passed' to the West. Some of them have even been highly publicised in the media, such as Oleg Kalugin[1382], Vladimir Rezun[1383], Oleg Gordievsky[1384] or Vassili Mitrokhin[1385], and have undoubtedly provided the Western services with even more valuable information than Skripal. Yet they were not eliminated.

The example of Oleg Penkovsky, a GRU colonel who had provided Western services with files on nuclear engagement procedures in the early 1960s, is also readily cited. This information proved particularly useful in the outcome of the Cuban missile crisis in October 1962. Discovered and arrested, he was tried and sentenced to death. According to a legend - which has never been confirmed - he was burnt alive, so that his death would serve as an example. In any case, he was "eliminated" in the USSR itself, in application of a judgment, and not by killers abroad.

1381. Bellingcat Investigation Team, "Skripal Suspect Boshirov Identified as GRU Colonel Anatoliy Chepiga", *Bellingcat*, September 26, 2018

1382. Katie Cella, "Famous KGB Spies: Where Are They Now?", *Foreign Policy*, June 18, 2012

1383. Luke Harding, "'Will they forgive me? No': ex-Soviet spy Viktor Suvorov speaks out', *The Guardian*, December 29, 2018

1384. Ofer Aderet, "How Double Agent Oleg Gordievsky Changed the Course of History", *Haaretz*, September 21, 2019

1385. Ronen Bergman, "The KGB's Middle East Files: Leaking thousands of documents", *Ynetnews.com*, October 28, 2016

With the exception of the Israeli services, which have made revenge a point of doctrine against terrorism, the services only take such a risk to eliminate direct and immediate threats. This was the case with Stepan Bandera[1386], leader of the Ukrainian Insurgent Army (UPA), a pro-Nazi underground organisation created during the Second World War to fight the Soviets. Until the early 1960s, it carried out guerrilla operations in Ukraine with political and material support from the United States, Britain and France. On 15 October 1959, Bandera was eliminated by the KGB, the day after a coordination meeting with the German secret service (BND), which was aimed at intensifying clandestine operations in Ukraine.

In all cases, the 'eliminations' were carried out in a discreet manner. In the Bandera case, the nature of the weapon is only known because the killer, Bogdan Stashinsky, 'moved' to the West immediately after his crime. As for the assassination of Georgi Markov, we still do not know how he was killed: the 'Bulgarian umbrella' was never found. It is therefore only a hypothesis, probable, but never confirmed, based on the claims of an ex-KGB agent, who claimed that such a weapon existed. But in fact, we know nothing about it.

8.6.4. The Objective

The first question that comes to mind is: "For what purpose? The use of a poison that immediately identifies Russia automatically gives the crime a political dimension. Yet neither the official British discourse, nor Western governments, nor the mainstream media, which serve as their sounding board, have been able to provide a coherent answer or plausible reason. In its annual report on the security of Switzerland, the Swiss Strategic Intelligence Service (SRC) states:

> *The Russian regime wanted to signal that the West and traitors should beware. The subsequent Russian disinformation campaign followed the existing pattern of similar influence operations, aimed at driving a wedge between EU members, negatively influencing relations between Europe and the US, and spreading insecurity, fear and mistrust globally*[1387].

This is obviously not true: the official British line is slavishly repeated. Prime Minister Theresa May claims that Vladimir Putin is trying to "*divide Europe*"[1388];

1386. Stepan Bandera (1909-1959) Hero of the Ukrainian resistance against the USSR at the head of the Organization of Ukrainian Nationalists (OUN) and notorious collaborator of the Nazis during the Second World War, will become the symbolic figure of the Maïdan events in 2014.

1387. *The Security of Switzerland 2019 - Situation Report*, Federal Intelligence Service (FIS), February-March 2019, p. 22

1388. Julian Borger, Patrick Wintour & Heather Stewart, "Western allies expel scores of Russian diplomats over Skripal attack", *The Guardian*, March 27, 2018

an explanation taken up by Jens Stoltenberg, Secretary General of Nato[1389]. First of all, it is not clear how the elimination of an ex-Russian agent could "*divide Europe*", let alone "*relations between the EU and the US*". But assuming this is true, what would be the point? With the Ukrainian crisis still unresolved, the Syrian file still open and sanctions piling up, the Russian president's strategy would defy logic. Yet everything shows that he is remarkably rational in his decisions. Europe is already divided on many issues, including Russia. The best way to unify it would be to give it a common enemy. The Brexit referendum - decided by David Cameron - certainly contributed much more surely to the division of Europe!

Moreover, in June 2018, Putin on an official visit to Austria declared:

> *We have an interest in a united and prosperous EU, because the EU is our most important trading and economic partner. And the more problems there are in the EU, the greater the risks and uncertainties for us. On the contrary, we must develop cooperation with the EU. (...) We do not aim to divide anything or anyone in the EU*[1390].

The assumption of "punishment" or "revenge" by the Russian government is doubtful. Firstly, if his treason had been deemed so serious, he would have been sentenced to death, like Oleg Penkovsky. Such trials are usually held behind closed doors and away from the media because of their confidentiality, so it would have been easier, especially if the judiciary is '*known to be in the service of the Kremlin*', as the Belgian newspaper *Le Soir* claims[1391]. Secondly, the Russians could have eliminated him discreetly during his detention between 2004 and 2010: nobody would have noticed the disappearance of a second-rate spy. Third, if the Russians chose to release him in 2010, it is reasonable to assume that he was no longer a threat to them and it is not clear why they would have waited another eight years to eliminate him permanently.

In fact, our judgements are based on prejudices and we create false coherences. After the Ukrainian crisis, the idea was promoted that Vladimir Putin was prepared to take any risk to satisfy his whims. So the killing of an ex-agent in the UK becomes quite coherent. Yet, in his speeches, interviews and other public appearances, Vladimir Putin appears considerably more measured and consistent than the Western leaders who have created chaos in the Middle East, Libya and the Sahel, by misusing the international law they claim to defend...

1389. "EU, NATO Chide Russia on Skripal Poisoning, Slow Response", *RFE/RL*, March 19, 2018
1390. "Putin wants a 'united and prosperous' European Union", *levif.be*, June 4, 2018
1391. "Russia: Khodorkovsky caught by Putin's justice", *lesoir.be*, December 23, 2015

8.6.5. The Nature and Origin of the Poison

Western accusations are based on the nature and supposed origin of the poison. In the programme "C dans l'air" of June 2, 2018, the journalist Jean-Dominique Merchet claims that the poison allegedly administered to Skripal, "Novichok", is of Russian origin and that the only question is at what political level its use on British soil was decided[1392]. This is untrue, but he has an excuse because the British government has done everything possible to mislead the international community.

Novichok" ("Novice") is said to be the nickname given to a range of toxic chemicals developed experimentally in the USSR during the 1970s-1980s under the generic code name FOLIANT, the main ones being: Substance-33, A-230, A-232, A-234, A-242 and A-262[1393]. However, the very existence of a "Novichok" development programme is disputed by Russia[1394] and by some Western experts[1395]: in fact, it plays on words and on a confusion with the development of another category of toxic agents called "GV". Without getting into this very technical debate, we will use the term "Novichok" as it is understood in the West.

Novichok' was developed in the 1970s and 1980s by the Chikhany (Russia) and Nukus (now Uzbekistan) laboratories for production at the Pavlodar Laboratory (now in Kazakhstan). However, in 1987, these facilities were converted to the production of chemical agents for civilian use. In December 1991, Kazakhstan declared its independence and the Pavlodar site was dismantled under US supervision. All sites involved in the development, testing or production of Novichok were dismantled. According to the German newspapers *Süddeutsche Zeitung* and *Die Zeit*, in the early 1990s the German intelligence service, BND, managed to obtain samples of 'Novichok' and have them analysed in several Nato countries[1396], including Germany[1397], the USA, Great Britain and Czechoslovakia, for the purpose of research and development of antidotes. In addition, according to Nikolai Kovalev, a former FSB director and Duma deputy, Novichok was stored in Ukraine[1398]. It is also known that it was synthesised as early as 1998 by the

---

1392. Programme "C dans l'air: Espionnage: des services pas si secrets", *YouTube/France 5*, June 2, 2018

1393. Peter R. Chai, Bryan D. Hayes, Timothy B. Erickson & Edward W. Boyer (2018) Novichok agents: a historical, current, and toxicological perspective, Toxicology Communications, 2:1, 45-48, DOI: 10.1080/24734306.2018.1475151

1394. "Zakharova about the Moscow's response to London's actions", *Rossiya24/YouTube*, March 18, 2018

1395. Paul McKeigue, Jake Mason & Piers Robinson, "Update to briefing note 'Doubts about Novichoks'", *Tim-hayward*, April 1st, 2018

1396. Samuel Osborne, "Germany obtained novichok nerve agent sample in 1990s, reports say", *The Independent*, May 17, 2018

1397. Alexander Pearson, "Skripal poisoning: Germany got Novichok chemical sample from Russia in 1990s", www.dw.com, May 17, 2018

1398. Tony Wesolowsky, "A Timeline Of Russia's Changing Story On Skripal Poisoning", *Radio Free Europe / Radio Liberty*, March 21, 2018

American chemical weapons laboratory at Edgewood[1399] and that its chemical formula was made public in 2009 in the United States by Vil Mirzayanov, one of the product's developers[1400]. Therefore, the categorical attribution of Novichok to Russia is questionable.

Indeed, the Porton Down laboratory, which is responsible for chemical weapons research in Britain and which analysed the samples collected by the police, was able to identify the substance, but said it was unable to say who produced it or who used it.

This did not stop Boris Johnson, then Foreign Secretary, on March 20, 2018, from lying that Gary Aitkenhead, Director of Porton Down, had told him that the substance came from Russia. The minister's words were echoed in a tweet posted by the Foreign Office two days later. But on April 4, 2018, Aitkenhead clarified that because of its mandate and capabilities, the laboratory could only identify the composition of the product, but not where it came from or where it was manufactured[1401]. Immediately after this interview, the Foreign Office tweet was surreptitiously deleted[1402].

On March 22, the British ambassador to Russia holds a presentation to the diplomatic community in Moscow in which he states:

> *... there is no doubt that the weapon used in the attack was a military grade nerve agent of the Novichok series. This has been confirmed by specialists, our specialists. An Organisation for the Prohibition of Chemical Weapons mission is currently in the UK to independently confirm this analysis.*
>
> *There is also no doubt that Novichok was manufactured in Russia by the Russian state*[1403].

But the official transcript, on the British Foreign Office website, will be slightly changed to:

> *There is also no doubt that Novichok was manufactured in Russia by the Russian state*[1404].

1399. Karel Knip, "'Unknown'newcomer novichok was long known", *nrc.nl*, March 21, 2018

1400. Vil S. Mirzayanov, *State Secrets: An Insider's Chronicle of the Russian Chemical Weapons Program*, Outskirts Press, Inc, 2009

1401. "Sky News Interview with Porton Down lab's chief exec, *YouTube*, April 4, 2018

1402. "Foreign Office deletes tweet claiming Salisbury nerve agent made in Russia", *SkyNews*, April 4, 2018

1403. Foreign & Commonwealth Office, "Briefing on the UK government's response to the Salisbury attack", *YouTube*, 22 March 2018 (video) (00'20")

1404. "British Ambassador to Russia briefing on the Salisbury attack: March 22, 2018", www.gov.uk, March 22, 2018

... even though it says "*transcript of the speech, exactly as it was given*"(!) Moreover, formally, it was the Soviet Union and not Russia that developed "Novichok".

On 16 March, former British ambassador Craig Murray wrote on his blog that the government had tried to pressure the Porton Down director to confirm the Russian origin of the toxin. But Gary Aitkenhead only agreed to a compromise wording, which refers to a toxic "*of a type developed by Russia*", and excludes the words "*produced*" or "*manufactured*", while remaining ambiguous[1405]. This is the phrase Teresa May uses on March 12, 2018 in Parliament, naming Russia as a '*highly likely*' culprit:

> *It is now clear that Mr Skripal and his daughter were poisoned with a military grade nerve agent of a type developed by Russia*[1406].

These same words will be used in a joint statement by the United States, Britain, Germany and France on March 15, condemning Russia's action, an hour before new sanctions are to be adopted:

> *This use of a military grade nerve agent, of a type developed by Russia, is the first offensive use of a nerve agent in Europe since the Second World War*[1407].

On March 22, 2018, an application is submitted to the UK court for a ruling - to be approved - on whether the OPCW could be allowed to obtain blood samples from Sergei Skripal and his daughter to identify the chemical agent used. In his ruling, the judge states:

> *Blood samples from Sergei Skripal and Yulia Skripal were analysed and the results indicated exposure to a nerve agent or related compound. The samples tested positive for the presence of a Novichok class nerve agent or a closely related agent*[1408].

The terms "*related compound*" and "*related agent*" suggest that there is some doubt about the nature of the poison itself. Indeed, in April 2018, OPCW Director Ahmet Üzümcü confirmed that "Novichok" could be "*produced in any country with some expertise in chemistry*[1409]".

1405. "Of A Type Developed By Liars", www.craigmurray.org.uk, March 16, 2018
1406. "PM Commons statement on Salisbury incident: 12 March 2018", gov.uk, March 12, 2018
1407. Alex Ward, "The US and 3 allies are blaming Russia for nerve agent attack on ex-spy", www.vox.com, March 15, 2018
1408. Approved Judgment, Royal Courts of Justice, Strand, London, WC2A 2LL, March 22, 2018
1409. (Interview in English) "Глава ОЗХО: Вещество, которым отравили Скрипалей, могло быть

To complicate matters, the laboratory in Spiez, Switzerland, to which the Organisation for the Prohibition of Chemical Weapons (OPCW) entrusted samples provided by Britain, concluded that the toxic agent used was "3-Quinclidinyl benzilate". Better known as BZ, this is a toxic substance manufactured in Britain and the United States and stockpiled by some Nato countries[1410] ! But this conclusion is not included in the OPCW's final report… Foreign Minister Lavrov is concerned and accuses the OPCW of manipulation[1411]. But there is an explanation: it would only be BZ precursors used as "control samples" in the analysis protocol[1412]. In fact, it was the leak of partial information that misled Russia. Taken to task on Twitter, the Spiez laboratory defends itself with an ellipsis:

> *[…] But we can repeat what we said ten days ago: we have no doubt that Porton Down has identified Novichok. PD - like Spiez - is a designated OPCW laboratory. The verification standards are so rigid that the results can be trusted*[1413].

Thus, hiding behind the OPCW's rules of procedure, the Spiez laboratory neither confirms nor denies Russia's claims, without providing any details on the nature of its findings. Moreover, its cryptic wording suggests that the product identified by Porton Down is not the same as the one allegedly used against Skripal.

The toxicity of Novichok is reportedly five to eight times greater than that of VX, which has a lethal dose by the skin of 10 mg[1414]. According to Nikolai Volodin, one of the engineers who worked on the design of Novichok, exposure to minute doses leads to instant death[1415]. Vil Mirzayanov states that there is no known treatment for Novichok[1416].

However, the Skripals remained symptom-free for several hours (assuming they were poisoned at home) to half an hour (if they were hit in the pizzeria) and the three people who were infected that day have all recovered. Sergeant Nick Bailey, who was at the scene but did not have direct contact with the two Russians[1417], appears to have been poisoned as well. The doctor who treated

---

произведено в любой стране!", *YouTube*, April 23, 2018 (www.youtube.com/watch?v=OhGLJ82rAFs)

1410. "Russia: Swiss lab analysis shows nerve agent designed in West", *New York Post/AP*, April 14, 2018

1411. "Moscow accuses OPCW of manipulating Skripal probe", *24News/AFP*, April 14, 2018

1412. Mike Corder, "Britain Spy Case: Watchdog Rejects Russia Nerve Agent Claim", *U.S. News & World Report*, April 18, 2018

1413. twitter.com/SpiezLab/status/985243574123057152

1414. NdA: This is the "LD50", the lethal dose for 50% of the people affected.

1415. Павел Каныгин, "Новичок" - это слишком для одного Скрипаля", Новая газета, March 22, 2018

1416. Joseph Ax, "Only Russia could be behind U.K. poison attack -toxin's co-developer", *Reuters*, March 13, 2018

1417. James Fielding, Paul Thompson, Richard Spillett, Mark Duell & Lara Keay, 'Police probe whether Russian spy was poisoned with nerve agent at his own house as it emerges 21 people were hospitalised after attack and sick detective 'didn't have direct contact with Skripals', *Daily Mail*, March 8, 2018 (updated March 10, 2018)

Yulia Skripal in hospital for about half an hour was completely unaffected by the toxic agent and claims that there was no nerve agent on Skripal's body[1418]. Furthermore, while the Times on March 14 claimed that the Skripal case had "*left 40 people requiring treatment*"[1419], on March 16 a National Health Service emergency medicine consultant wrote to readers claiming that "*no patients showed any symptoms of nerve agent poisoning in Salisbury and there were only three cases of serious poisoning*[1420]". Furthermore, the first report from the hospital after the victims were admitted was of Fentanyl poisoning, as reported by *Radio Free Europe/Radio Liberty* in September 2018, without mentioning 'Novichok'[1421]. The *Salisbury Journal* of March 5 also mentions possible Fentanyl poisoning[1422].

Finally, on April 12, 2018, the OPCW published its conclusions, based on the samples taken at the scene and the samples submitted to it. The public version of the document does not mention a "nerve agent", but only a "chemical toxicant". It states that the sample analysed by the OPCW would be of "*high purity*" in "*the almost complete absence of impurities*[1423]". In this field, impurities are like "fingerprints" that make it possible to identify the origin of a product. Novichoks are very unstable, and it is almost impossible for a sample to remain "pure" after several days on a doorknob or in the blood of victims before being analysed. A lack of impurity could mean that the samples came directly from a laboratory and not from swabs.

The silence of the British and Western authorities on this issue suggests that the analysis could not confirm Russian guilt. But factually, we don't know.

According to some experts, the only plausible explanation for these apparent inconsistencies is that Skripal and his daughter suffered food poisoning from seafood in the pizzeria where they had lunch. The symptoms described in the press are similar to those of poisoning by paralytic shellfish poisoning (PSP), also known as saxitoxin (STX) produced by marine micro-organisms[1424]. This hypothesis could explain the cryptic formula of the Spiez laboratory, which suggests that the substance analysed by Porton Down is not the same as the one that poisoned the couple. It would also explain the poisoning of Sergeant

1418. "Russian spy: Salisbury attack was 'brazen and reckless'", *BBC News*, March 8, 2018

1419. "Salisbury poison exposure leaves almost 40 needing treatment", *The Times*, March 14, 2018

1420. Fiona Hamilton, John Simpson & Deborah Haynes, "Russia: Salisbury poison fears allayed by doctor", *The Times*, March 16, 2018

1421. Ron Synovitz, "Name Your Poison: Exotic Toxins Fell Kremlin Foes", *Radio Free Europe/Radio Liberty*, September 18, 2018

1422. "Man found critically ill at Maltings in Salisbury man is former Russian spy Sergei Skripal", www.salisburyjournal.co.uk, March 5, 2018.

1423. *Note By The Technical Secretariat - Summary Of The Report On Activities Carried Out In Support Of A Request For Technical Assistance By The United Kingdom Of Great Britain And Northern Ireland* (Technical Assistance Visit TAV/02/18), OPCW Technical Secretariat, (S/1612/2018), April 12, 2018

1424. STX is a nerve agent, which the US had attempted to weaponise in the 1960s for special operations. During its investigation into the CIA's clandestine activities in 1975, the Church Commission discovered that the Agency kept a stockpile of it. (We are not suggesting here that the CIA was involved in the Skripal case!)

Bailey, who was in the vicinity of the pizzeria, but not on duty at the time of the incident, but whose schedule has not been confirmed by the British government.

8.6.6. Conclusions for the Skripal Case

On the France 5 programme "C dans l'air" on March 16, 2018, the "experts" expressed no doubt that Vladimir Putin was directly involved[1425]. However, the British accusation is only circumstantial. It is not based on facts, but on potentialities and hypotheses, as Theresa May herself explained on March 14, 2018:

> *On the basis of [its] capability, coupled with its history of state-sponsored assassinations - including against former intelligence officers whom they regard as legitimate targets - the British government concluded that it was highly likely that Russia was responsible for this irresponsible and despicable act*[1426].

It is a pattern that follows exactly that of conspiracy theories: elements are put together based on prejudice, not fact. By combining the same elements in different ways, one could just as easily accuse Britain of the same crime. Which is what some have done...

Theresa May immediately dramatised the incident and invoked Nato solidarity, even though the full details were not yet known. By treating it as a '*chemical attack*' on Britain, not just a poisoning, it was deliberately placed in the higher register of an international conflict.

But here again, Westerners are inconsistent. The Chemical Weapons Convention (CWC) is invoked, but its procedures for resolving disputes are not applied: in the event of a "*situation that would be considered ambiguous or that gives rise to concern about possible non-compliance*", the state asked for a clarification has ten days to respond[1427]. But here, Britain gave Russia only 24 hours[1428]. Furthermore, it refused to provide details of the incident, as well as poison and blood samples requested by Russia in order to take a position[1429]. It is as if there is a fear of a different truth.

Britain has thus applied a strategy of tension, which might suggest a 'Wag the Dog' syndrome, aimed at creating national unity and international solidarity around an 'external attack'. This does not necessarily mean that the British government poisoned the Skripals, but that it opportunely exploited

1425. Programme "C dans l'air", "Putin: alone against all? #cdanslair 16.03.2018", *YouTube/France 5*, March 16, 2018 (16'00")
1426. Theresa May, March 14, 2018 (Quoted in presentation to the British Embassy in Moscow to the diplomatic corps, March 22, 2018)
1427. Article IX - Consultations, Cooperation and Fact-finding
1428. Joe Watts, "Russian spy attack: Vladimir Putin has 24 hours to explain how deadly nerve agent was used on UK soil, says Theresa May", *The Independent*, March 12, 2018
1429. Chris Harris, "Russia has 'no right' to see nerve agent samples", *euronews*, March 22, 2018

the incident for political purposes. Some cite the example of Operation HADES, organised by the German Bundesnachrichtendienst (BND) in 1994, which was designed to make it appear that Russia was involved in plutonium trafficking in order to encourage the Bundestag to give it more resources[1430]. In addition to international condemnation, Russia was then pushed to tighten the security of its nuclear repositories with the help of the United States.

So, contrary to what the British claim, there are plausible alternatives to their accusations. The problem is that 'reasonable doubt' is systematically avoided. The field of doubt is so vast that only bad faith provides certainty. As in Afghanistan, Iraq, Libya and Syria, our so-called 'rule of law' states are satisfied with vague presumptions to engage in conflicts whose outcome they do not know. They are supported by traditional and state-run media (such as *France 24*, *France 5*, *BFM TV*, etc.) which are totally aligned with the official versions, without any critical spirit with regard to very incomplete information.

In 2016, the geostrategic context is tense: the Ukrainian crisis is dragging on, the West is losing its footing in the Middle East, the British government is overwhelmed by the Brexit, social movements are beginning to undermine Macron's presidency, Nato has doubts about transatlantic relations and the European spirit is cracking under the pressure of immigration. It is hard not to see the rush of the Western response - when we don't even know the exact nature of the poison - as an attempt to distract public opinion from their domestic problems.

8.7. Russia Paid the Taliban to Injure American Troops in Afghanistan[1431]

On May 26, 2020, Donald Trump stated his intention to fulfil his campaign promise to withdraw US troops from Afghanistan[1432]. Joe Biden, his Democratic presidential rival[1433], and a small group of Republicans (Lincoln Project[1434]) oppose the withdrawal and accuse the president of being on Putin's payroll. On June 26, 2020, the *New York Times* and the *Washington Post* claimed that Russia

1430. "Panik Made in Pullach", *Der Spiegel*, April 10, 1995

1431. Thomas Romanacce, "La Russie accusé d'avoir payé des Talibans pour tuer des soldats américains", capital.fr, July 7, 2020

1432. Barbara Starr, "Pentagon commanders drawing up options for early Afghanistan troop withdrawal," *CNN*, May 26, 2020; Thomas Gibbons-Neff & Julian E. Barnes, "Trump Wants Troops in Afghanistan Home by Election Day. The Pentagon Is Drawing Up Plans," *The New York Times*, May 26, 2020.

1433. Andrew O'Reilly, "Biden accuses Trump of 'dereliction of duty' over Russia bounty reports in first press briefing in nearly 3 months", *Fox News*, June 1st, 2020

1434. https://lincolnproject.us/

was paying bounties to the Taliban to kill Americans[1435]. The White House is thus forced to back down.[1436]

Yet the story is far from proven: is Vladimir Putin trying to pay the Taliban for what they have been doing for twenty years, in order to slow down the departure of the Americans, which the whole region (including Russia) wants? In fact, General Frank McKenzie, head of the US Central Command, does not believe this, and has not even taken additional protective measures[1437]. A week later, the National Intelligence Council (NIC) published a report questioning the claims of the two newspapers: the CIA and the National Counterterrorism Center (NCC) have only moderate confidence in the information, while the National Security Agency (NSA) has only low confidence[1438].

In fact, the only people indicted for helping the Taliban conduct operations against U.S. forces were… Americans, in December 2019[1439].

8.8. Conclusions on Russia

The accusations against Putin remain systematically vague and lacking in substance. As is often the case, they are limited to innuendo and rumours, but never provide any facts. Thus, in June 2017, the broadcasting on *France 3* of Oliver Stone's documentary on Putin triggered the ire of journalist Vincent Jauvert, who judged the film "*scandalous*" and denounced the "*multiple lies*" it contained. However, he did not provide any factual evidence of a lie or help to re-establish the truth[1440].

In fact, it is easy to imagine that the Russian democratic tradition is more rustic than in Switzerland, for example. But this is not enough to define a dictatorship, as it is tried to portray. In 2019, before the elections to the Moscow Duma, where 20,000-50,000 demonstrators demanded 'free elections', the French media were alerted. Headlines such as *27 candidates have been excluded* (*Le Figaro*) or *Authorities exclude opposition candidates* (*Le Monde*) suggest that

1435. Charlie Savage, Eric Schmitt & Michael Schwirtz, "Russia Secretly Offered Afghan Militants Bounties to Kill U.S. Troops, Intelligence Says," *The New York Times*, June 26, 2020; "Russian operation targeted coalition troops in Afghanistan, intelligence finds," *The Washington Post*, June 26, 2020

1436. David S. Cloud, "White House tentatively agrees to leave some troops in Afghanistan past U.S. election", *The Los Angeles Times*, July 2, 2020

1437. Lolita C. Baldor, 'US general skeptical that bounties led to troops' deaths', AP/msn.com, July 7, 2020; Luis Martinez, 'Top Pentagon officials say Russian bounty program not corroborated', *abcnews*, July 10, 2020.

1438. Charlie Savage, Rukmini Callimachi, Eric Schmitt & Adam Goldman, "New Administration Memo Seeks to Foster Doubts About Suspected Russian Bounties", *The New York Times*, July 3, 2020

1439. Tim Ryan, "US Contractors Accused of Funding Taliban Attacks Against American Troops," *courthousenews.com*, December 27, 2019; https://www.courthousenews.com/wp-content/uploads/2019/12/Anti-terrorism-lawsuit.pdf

1440. Vincent Jauvert, "Oliver Stone's scandalous documentary on Vladimir Putin", *TéléObs*, June 25, 2017

the validation of candidacies is discretionary[1441]. The BBC claims that the candidates were "*ignored*" and "*treated as if they were insignificant*[1442]". This is simply not true. In fact, it is a problem of validation of candidacies: as in France for the presidential elections, candidates must have a certain number of signatures to participate. Unlike in France, where the candidate must have the signatures of 500 *elected officials*, a Russian non-party candidate must have the signatures of 5,000 *ordinary citizens, which does* not seem too much to ask in a city of 12 million inhabitants. Naturally, these signatures are checked by an electoral commission to avoid fraud, and despite a 10% tolerance, some candidates did not reach the required number. Those who demonstrated in Moscow were of multiple persuasions, ranging from the far right to the far left, some of whom did not even try to collect the signatures...

During his meeting with Emmanuel Macron at the Fort de Brégançon in August 2019, when asked about these demonstrations, Putin replied to the press:

> *It is not only in Russia that there are events of this type. It is not very convenient to say it, I am invited here, but you knew that there were the Yellow Vests demonstrations and according to our calculations, I believe that there are nearly 11 people who died, there are more than 2000 people who were injured. There are notably police officers who have been injured. We wouldn't want to*[1443]*... [...]*

This version will be repeated in Belgium. But in France, on *LCI*, the translation becomes:

> *It's not just happening in Russia. I'm invited by the French president and I'm uncomfortable saying this, but you all know that during the Yellow Vests protests you had several dozen people who were injured. There were police officers who were injured. We don't want*[1444]*... [...]*

...and on *RMC:*

> *This kind of situation does not only happen in Russia. We know what happened during the Yellow Vests protests. We don't want*[1445]*... [...]*

1441. "En Russie, les autorités excluent des candidats d'opposition aux élections locales à Moscou", Le Monde, June 16, 2019

1442. "Moscow protests: What's behind the rallies in Russia?", *BBC News*, August 13, 2019

1443. "Joint statement by Vladimir Putin and Emmanuel Macron in Brégançon", *RT France/YouTube*, August 19, 2019 (42'00")

1444. "Putin mentions the injured of the Yellow Vests in front of Macron", *LCI/YouTube*, August 20, 2019

1445. "The tense standoff between Putin and Macron over the 'yellow waistcoats'", *RMC/YouTube*, August 20, 2019

To put it plainly, Russia has been stigmatised for 3,000 arrests during demonstrations, some of which were unauthorised, while in France the actions of the "Gilets jaunes" have been erased from the mainstream media since May 2019: too much light is avoided on the 11 deaths, more than 4,000 injured (including 24 with eye sores) and more than 12,000 arrests[1446]...

The "Russian threat" has become a real tool of manipulation: it allows to distract public opinion from the errors of domestic politics, to give credibility to Western support for the Islamists against the Syrian government, to justify an increase in defence budgets and to discredit an opposition.[1447]

In February 2020, it is suggested that Russia (and thus, Vladimir Putin) is involved in the release of Benjamin Griveaux's "intimate" video[1448]! For what purpose? No answer. To what end would Russia, in trouble with Europe, take the risk of getting involved in the election of a mayor (even that of Paris), to harm a candidate whose electoral campaign has been dismal since its beginning[1449] and "*doomed to failure*[1450]"? With "it is *said that...*", a journalist from *LCI* even suggests that Piotr Pavlensky - the author of the leak - benefited from a "*form of complaisance*" from the Russian police and would be a "*character who practices duplicity*[1451]..." However, Cedric O, Secretary of State for Digital Affairs, says he has "*no information to suggest that there could be anything other than personal action*" and that he has "*no evidence or clues to suggest that Russia was involved*[1452]". So: nothing. Susan Rice, the US ambassador to the UN, even claims that Russia was behind the demonstrations after the murder of George Floyd in June 2020[1453]! Between contradictions and lies, the myths that are created around Russia correspond exactly to the definition of conspiracy and are only a means of masking the incompetence of Western leaders without honour and dignity.

1446. "Mobilization, injuries, arrests... 6 months of yellow waistcoats in figures", *CNews*, May 15, 2019 (Updated May 17, 2019)

1447. "For Vladimir Putin, François Fillon is a 'great professional'", *LEXPRESS.fr/AFP*, November 23, 2016; "François Fillon's pro-Russian positions worry Germany", *Le Point*, November 28, 2016

1448. Nicolas Scheffer, "VIDEO - 'On n'est pas couché': 'What suits Putin is the mess we are in'", *RTL.fr*, February 23, 2020

1449. Pierre Lepelletier, "Municipales: la campagne cauchemar de Griveaux résumée en cinq épisodes", *LeFigaro.fr*, February 14, 2020

1450. "Elections municipales 2020: la campagne de Benjamin Griveaux à Paris inquiète les macronistes", *lemonde.fr*, January 23, 2020

1451. "Piotr Pavlenski in custody", *LCI/YouTube*, February 17, 2020

1452. "Affaire Griveaux: Pavlenski a-t-il été manipulé et jusqu'où ?", *AFP/Le Point*, February 17, 2020

1453. Barbara Boland, "Obama's former national security adviser offered no evidence for her bizarre claim", *The American Conservative*, June 1st, 2020

9. THE UKRAINIAN CRISIS

9.1. The context

The controversial etymology of the name "Ukraine", sometimes explained as a peripheral country, sometimes as the cradle of Russian culture, reflects its complexity. Situated on the borders of Poland, the Ottoman Empire and Russia, its capital dominated the "Kievan Rus" (or "Kievan Russia"), which gave birth to Russia, with which it shares its destiny. Ukraine did not emerge as a state until after the First World War, just before being incorporated into the Soviet Union. It was not until 1991, after the fall of communism, that it became a truly independent country.

A significant event in its history was the famine that affected it in 1932-1933 and left its mark on the Ukrainian collective consciousness. Known as the "holodomor" ("holod": hunger; "mor": plague), it is estimated to have killed between 4 and 7 million people and is considered in Ukraine as a genocide, often compared to the Jewish "holocaust". Despite its magnitude, which makes it perhaps the largest massacre in history, it remains largely ignored in the West and its character as 'genocide' is disputed. Whatever the reality, the over-representation of Jews in the leadership of the Communist Party and the NKVD[1454] left the Ukrainian population feeling that they had orchestrated the Holodomor. The result was a deep hatred both against the power in Moscow and against the Jews, which has fuelled Ukrainian nationalism to this day[1455].

It is therefore hardly surprising that Ukrainian nationalists (as in other Eastern European countries) retained a certain sympathy for Germany, which had helped them fight the Soviet regime. Add to this the liberation of Kharkov against the Red Army by the 2nd SS Panzer Division '*Das Reich*' in 1943, and

1454. Timothy Snyder, professor at Yale University, estimates that 40% of the NKVD and more than 50% of the Communist Party leadership in the 1920s and 1930s were Jewish (Timothy Snyder, *Bloodlands: Europe Between Hitler and Stalin*, 2010).
1455. Lev Golinkin, "Violent Anti-Semitism Is Gripping Ukraine - And The Government Is Standing Idly By", *The Forward*, May 20, 2018

you have the main ingredients of a near-veneration of the Ukrainian far right for the Third Reich. Thus, alongside the 500,000 or so Ukrainians who joined the partisans against the German occupation, the nationalists, whose largest faction was led by Stepan Bandera, took advantage of the German presence to set up an anti-communist resistance that continued to operate until the early 1960s, with the help of NATO.

This past - or its perception - explains the takeover of the "*Wolfsangel*" rune, which was the symbol of the "*Das Reich*" Division, by the elite Ukrainian AZOV battalion[1456], created in May 2014, and guilty of numerous abuses and war crimes, according to the OSCE[1457]. The nature of the problem is best illustrated by the remark of an AZOV battalion fighter:

> *Putin is not even a Russian. He is a Jew*[1458] *!*

The film *Le système Poutine* by Carré presents a conspiracy-type construction around the Ukrainian legislative elections of March 2006 which were allegedly manipulated by Russia[1459]. In fact, in the 2004 presidential elections, after a very close first round (39.9% against 39.26%) Viktor Yushchenko won the second round against Viktor Yanukovych with 52% against 44%.

But he does not have the strength to put together a governing coalition without his former opponent for the parliamentary elections. The film suggests that Russia stopped gas deliveries on January 1st, 2006 in order to put pressure on the parliamentary elections. This is not true[1460]. It cannot be ruled out that the interruption had been planned several months earlier, but the main reason was the diversion of gas destined for European countries by the Ukrainian state company *Neftgaz*[1461]. Contrary to what the film suggests, it is not a question of imposing a prime minister on Ukraine[1462], but of finding a solution to the corruption that prevails there. Moreover, the problem continued in the following years, leading Russia to build pipelines in the Baltic and Black Seas to bypass Ukraine.

In February 2010, Viktor Yanukovych became President of Ukraine after a "*transparent and honest*" election that "*offered an impressive demonstration of democracy*" according to Joao Soares, President of the OSCE Parliamentary

1456. NdA: The Azov Battalion became a regiment in January 2015.
1457. *War crimes of the armed forces and security forces of Ukraine: torture and inhuman treatment (Second report)*, The Foundation for the Study of Democracy, 2015 (http://www.osce.org/pc/233896?download=true)
1458. Shaun Walker, "Azov fighters are Ukraine's greatest weapon and may be its greatest threat", *The Guardian*, September 10, 2014
1459. "The Putin System - INFRARED", *France2/YouTube*, October 1st, 2015 (1h10'05")
1460. See Wikipedia, Article "2005-06 Russia-Ukraine gas dispute
1461. "Ukraine 'stealing Europe's gas', *BBCNews*, January 2, 2006
1462. "Press Conference Following Talks with President of Ukraine Viktor Yushchenko", *en.kremlin.ru*, January 11, 2006

Assembly[1463]. But the far-right nationalist opposition is making great strides. It is mainly represented by the *Svoboda* party, known until 2004 as the Social Nationalist Party *of Ukraine*, in reference to the German National Socialist Party[1464]! It is led by Oleh Tyahnybok, who had been excluded from President Viktor Yushchenko's parliamentary faction because he called for a fight against the "*Jewish-Moscow mafia*", and had co-signed an open letter, entitled *Stop the criminal activities of the organised Jewish community* in 2005[1465].

In August 2012, the "Kivalov-Kolesnichenko" law[1466] came into force, which guarantees the use of regional languages as official languages. It triggers the anger of nationalists, who see it as an attempt to "Russify" Ukraine.

In October 2012, the BBC reported on the worrying rise of *Svoboda*, which surprised many by entering parliament with just over 10% of the vote. Although an "American official" later claims that since the elections *Svoboda* has moderated its position considerably[1467], the European Parliament adopts a resolution on the situation in Ukraine on 12 December which states:

> *[...] 8. Is concerned about the rise in nationalist sentiment in Ukraine, which has resulted in support for the "Svoboda" party, which is one of the two new parties entering the Verkhovna Rada; recalls that racist, anti-Semitic and xenophobic views are contrary to the fundamental values and principles of the European Union and therefore calls on the democratic parties in the Verkhovna Rada not to associate, endorse or form coalitions with this party*[1468]*;*

But during and after Euromaidan, Europeans are not bothered by the ubiquitous presence of *Svoboda* flags and portraits of Stepan Bandera - a notorious Nazi collaborator - at party events[1469]. In fact, these pro-Nazi tendencies are presented as Russian propaganda in the Western media[1470]. Ironically, on February 9, 2014, Bernard-Henri Lévy addressed a crowd studded with flags of *Svoboda* and its 'armed wing', the *Pravi Sektor*... but he would claim not to have '*seen any neo-Nazis* there'[1471]! Despite attempts to downplay the importance of neo-Nazis

---

1463. "Ukraine: OSCE recognises the proper conduct of the election", *Le Monde.fr/AFP*, February 8, 2010
1464. "The Right Wing's Role in Ukrainian Protests, *Spiegel Online*, January 27, 2014
1465. David Stern, "Svoboda: The rise of Ukraine's ultra-nationalists", *BBC News*, December 26, 2012
1466. *Law on the bases of the state language policy*, (Закон "Об основах государственной языковой политики") of August 10, 2012
1467. Sabina Zawadzki, Mark Hosenball & Stephen Grey, "INSIGHT - In Ukraine, nationalists gain influence - and scrutiny", *Reuters*, March 7, 2014
1468. *European Parliament resolution of December 13, 2012 on the situation in Ukraine* (2012/2889(RSP)
1469. Max Blumenthal, "Is the U.S. Backing Neo-Nazis in Ukraine?", *AlterNet*, February 24, 2014
1470. Joshua Keating, "In Ukraine, fascists versus Nazis?", *Slate.fr*, February 22, 2014; "Russia is winning the propaganda war. Except in France," *Slate.fr*, June 2, 2014
1471. "Ukraine: Entscheidet sich Europas Schicksal auf dem Maidan?", *euronews (deutsch)/YouTube*, February 9, 2014

in Ukraine[1472], the development of violent antisemitism there is alarming[1473]: in 2018, the Ukrainian parliament even instituted an official day of remembrance for Stepan Bandera[1474].

In December 2013, Senator John McCain met with Tyahnybok and promised him financial aid for the AZOV battalion, which was then the spearhead of the nationalist right[1475]. The nationalist and far-right character of the Ukrainian government was systematically concealed in the Western media. The flow of neo-Nazi volunteers from France, Great Britain and Canada did not provoke any reaction in Europe: the media and governments carefully ignored these abuses (and crimes), which would have delegitimised support for Ukraine against Russia. Ironically, after McCain's death in 2018, the *Washington Post paid* tribute to the "*Champion of Human Rights*" with a photo showing him alongside Tyahnybok[1476], who had been denied entry to the United States in June 2013... for anti-Semitism[1477]!

In 2017, the FBI indicted four members of the AZOV regiment for training American right-wing supremacists from the highly anti-Semitic *Rise Above* movement[1478]. Despite several attempts by Congress to ban military aid to far-right militias, it was not until 2018 that the Pentagon stopped supporting the training of its fighters.

Geopolitically, since the end of the Cold War, Ukraine has remained an issue for both the West and the Russians. While Russia is trying to maintain the ties that existed with the former USSR republics, the West is trying to draw them into its sphere of influence. Like other Eastern European countries, Ukraine sees its economic future in integration into the Western community. It is part of Nato's Euro-Atlantic Partnership Council (EAPC) and aspires to join the Alliance. Nato is reluctant to take this step in order to avoid confrontation with Russia, which would interpret it as a hostile gesture.

On the political and economic level, the EU is working to forge closer ties with Ukraine. But its approach is ideological and at the origin of the Euromaidan revolution:

1472. *Antisemitism in Ukraine*, DIDR-OFPRA, January 7, 2015

1473. Lev Golinkin, "Violent Anti-Semitism Is Gripping Ukraine - And The Government Is Standing Idly By", *The Forward*, May 20, 2018

1474. Cnaan Liphshiz, "Ukraine celebrates Nazi collaborator, bans book critical of pogrom leader", *The Times of Israel*, December 27, 2018

1475. Laurent Brayard, "Nazis in Ukraine: From the Nachtigall to the Azov Battalion", *arretsurinfo.ch*, March 10, 2015

1476. Jennifer Rubin, "The human rights community lost a champion", *The Washington Post*, August 27, 2018

1477. "Ultranationalist Ukrainian political party leaders banned from U.S.", *Jewish Telegraphic Agency*, June 27, 2013

1478. Max Blumenthal, "US-Funded Neo-Nazis in Ukraine Mentor US White Supremacists", consortiumnews.com, November 17, 2018

Ukraine is a very fragmented country, with multiple identities, and cannot make a clear-cut choice, either in favour of the West or of Russia. One of Brussels' mistakes was to ask it to do so and to turn its back on Russia, a suicidal option for the country[1479].

In the *Washington Post*, Henry Kissinger notes that the European Union "*helped turn a negotiation into a crisis*[1480]". To sum up: European diplomacy saw Ukraine as a border between East and West, while Russia saw it as a bridge[1481].

An agreement is negotiated between Ukraine and the EU. At the end of 2013, the European side turned a deaf ear to Ukrainian requests to postpone the signing of the agreement to a later date in order to better study its compatibility with the customs union proposed by Russia[1482] and to better prepare the Ukrainian economy for this situation. Indeed, the Ukrainian economy - strongly linked to Russia - was weakened by a free trade agreement with the EU. The suspension sought by Ukraine was therefore only temporary, but was presented by the Western press and the Ukrainian opposition as a refusal to move closer to Europe under Russian pressure[1483]. Ukrainian public opinion, which had been promised visas or salary increases, was quickly polarised and its discontent exploited.

Ironically, after taking power, the new authorities in Kiev had to delay the entry into force of the agreement until January 1st, 2017. Indeed, economic sanctions have made it difficult for Ukraine to benefit from its agreement with the EU: its products are not sold in Europe because they are not competitive or unsuitable for the market, while the products it used to sell in Russia (especially in the arms sector) are now unsellable. Its situation has therefore deteriorated overall. Thus, European intransigence has not only contributed to the split in the country by pushing nationalist parties to power, but has also put the Ukrainian economy in a dead end.

In fact, Europe has used Ukraine for the benefit of a policy with no real objective[1484]. As Henry Kissinger rightly notes:

1479. Comments by Arnaud Dubien, director of the Franco-Russian Observatory, funded by the Franco-Russian Chamber of Commerce in "UE-Ukraine: "Moscou a remporté une nouvelle bataille géopolitique"", *Le Monde.fr*, November 22, 2013

1480. Henry A. Kissinger, "How the Ukraine Crisis Ends", *The Washington Post*, March 5, 2014

1481. Federico Santopinto, *From free trade to the Ukrainian crisis - The EU facing its mistakes*, GRIP, Brussels, April 14, 2014

1482. "Azarov: Ukraine could cooperate with Customs Union and EU", *Kiyv Post*, December 17, 2012

1483. AFP, 'L'Ukraine renonce à l'accord d'association avec l'UE', *Libération*, November 21, 2013; Lucas Roxo, 'Pourquoi l'Ukraine dit non à l'Europe', *Radio France/Franceinfo*, November 29, 2013 (updated on May 2, 2014); RTL/AFP, 'L'Ukraine refuse toujours de signer un accord avec l'UE', *RTL.fr*, November 29, 2013

1484. Seumas Milne, "It's not Russia that's pushed Ukraine to the brink of war", *The Guardian*, April 30, 2014

(…) the demonisation of Vladimir Putin is not a policy; it is an alibi for not having one[1485].

After the overthrow of President Yanukovych on February 22, 2014, Western media and governments defended the legitimacy of the new authorities by all means. In his speech to parliament on March 4, 2014, British Foreign Secretary William Hague states:

Former President Yanukovych left office and then left the country, and the decisions to replace him with an interim president were taken by the Rada, the Ukrainian parliament, by the very large majorities required by the Constitution, including with the support of President Yanukovych's former Party of Regions, so it is wrong to question the legitimacy of the new authorities[1486].

He is lying. Firstly, the change of government did not meet the situations in which a president can be deposed, as defined by Article 108 of the Constitution, nor the manner of doing so, as defined by Article 111. Moreover, the decree for the removal of Yanukovych was adopted with 328 votes out of 450 (72.8%), while the required majority was 75%[1487]: nothing was respected. To achieve this result, the new authorities abolished the Constitutional Court and started criminal proceedings against its members.

Secondly, it was the language issue that triggered the revolt of Russian-speaking populations in Crimea and Donbass. On February 23, 2014, as soon as they came to power, the Ukrainian nationalists decided to repeal the Kivalov-Kolesnichenko law of 2012 on regional languages. Ukrainian is now the only officially recognised language, and Russian is stripped of its status as an official language in 13 of the country's 27 regions: not only will official documents be written only in Ukrainian, but Russian will also disappear from schools.

On February 24, Ms Astrid Thors, OSCE High Commissioner on National Minorities, warned the new Ukrainian government against "*quick decisions that could lead to an escalation of the situation*" in a context where "*languages are a divisive issue*"[1488]. It was clear then that this decision would add fuel to the fire.

It was a sad repetition of the Sudetenland crisis three quarters of a century later. It was triggered by the anger of the German minority, whose language had been banned contrary to the provisions of the Versailles and St. Germain

1485. Henry A. Kissinger, op.cit.

1486. Ibid. and House of Commons report, March 4, 2014, column 736

1487. David Morrison, "How William Hague Deceived the House of Commons on Ukraine", www.huffington-post.co.uk, March 10, 2014 (updated May 9, 2014)

1488. http://www.osce.org/hcnm/115643

treaties, provoking German intervention. Ironically, when Bernard-Henri Lévy addressed the population of Kiev on March 2, 2014, he explained that '*Hitler (...) argued that the Sudeten Germans spoke German in order to invade Czechoslovakia*[1489]', when in fact it was precisely the abolition of this right that caused the crisis. It was exactly the same phenomenon that occurred in Poland at the beginning of 1939, against the German-speaking minority, several villages of which were massacred, forcing 80,000 people into exile even before the war began. Superimposed on the Danzig question, it was one of the forgotten triggers of the Second World War.

People talk about democracy and interpret the Euromaidan demonstrations as an expression of it. But it is not so clear-cut. A poll conducted between January 24 and February 1st, 2014 by the Social and Marketing Research Centre (SOCIS) and *the* International Institute of Sociology in Kiev shows that, while 47.7% of the population are rather in favour of *the spirit of* the demonstrations, 46.1% are not; and that 63.3% would prefer negotiations against 20.1% who would like to continue the demonstrations and 11.1% are in favour of force. Furthermore, in the event of a presidential election in February, 29.5% of voters would choose Yanukovych in first place, while Poroshenko would only come third with 18.6% of the vote[1490].

The nationalists obviously target the Russian speakers, who are the most numerous, but also other minorities. After the adoption of the education law in 2017, they receive support from neighbouring countries. Hungary is calling for the restoration of Magyar language education for the Hungarian minority[1491] and the deployment of OSCE monitors in Transcarpathia to prevent atrocities committed by nationalists[1492]. Ironically, Ukraine, which wanted to move closer to Nato by distancing itself from Russia, is caught at its own game: the Hungarian government is holding back its support for Ukraine's EU bid and blocking the Nato-Ukraine Commission (NUC) meeting in December 2017[1493], while Galicia is calling for autonomy[1494]. Poland and Romania, which have supported several projects with Ukraine in the framework of Nato, are

1489. "March 2, 2014, BHL, Kiev, second address at the Maidan", *YouTube*, March 5, 2014

1490. Дані спільного загальноукраїнського соціологічного дослідження Центру соціальних та маркетингових досліджень "СОЦИС" та Київського міжнародного інститу соціології, February 7, 2014 (https://archive.is/20140207104534/http://www.socis.kiev.ua/ua/press/dani-spilnoho-zahalnoukrajinskoho-sotsiolohichnoho-doslidzhennja-tsentru-sotsialnykh-ta-marketyn.html); see also Wikipedia, article "Opinion polling for the 2014 Ukrainian presidential election"

1491. Péter Krekó & Patrik Szicherle, "Why Is Hungary Blocking Ukraine's Western Integration?", *Atlantic Council*, January 16, 2018

1492. "Hungary's FM: OSCE should deploy observers to Ukraine's Transcarpathia region", *abouthungary.hu*, December 8, 2017

1493. MTI, "Szijjártó: Magyarország nem tudja támogatni Ukrajna integrációs törekvéseit", *Lokal*, October 27, 2017

1494. "Во Львове митинговали за автономию Галичины", *Korrespondent. net*, July 18, 2015

marking time and maintaining a façade of support only because of the United States[1495]. But here again, the French media are silent: the division in Europe must come from Russia, not from Ukraine!

On February 11, 2015, in Minsk (Belarus), Ukrainian, Russian, French and German leaders signed an agreement on a set of 13 measures concerning the war in Donbass (Minsk II agreement). Among these, the French media (such as *Wikipedia*[1496] or *Le Parisien*[1497]) mention the resumption of the control of the Russian-Ukrainian border by Kiev (article 9). But they do not mention the conditions for its application, namely the prior adoption of a constitutional reform granting autonomy to the Lugansk and Donetsk regions (Article 11), the organisation of local elections (Article 12) and a complete amnesty (Article 5). The full text of the agreement (to which Britain is not a party) can be found on the *Financial Times* website[1498]. With a far-right majority, the Ukrainian parliament has failed to adopt a constitution that grants autonomy to its provinces. This makes it appear that the Russian-speaking side is not fulfilling its obligations, while it is Ukraine that is dragging its feet in this matter.

9.2 "Russia Invades Crimea[1499]"

Russia's annexation of Crimea in 2014 was rejected by Western countries and remains the main stated reason for the hardening of relations between the West and Russia. Editorials castigating President Putin's expansionist policy have proliferated, but more often than not they obscure part of the issue, focusing on the illegitimacy of the Russian legacy in Crimea, the fate of the Tatars and their deportation under Soviet rule. As is often the case, false realities are created from truncated realities and deliberate omissions. For few have noted that Ukraine had, over the previous twenty years, trampled on Crimea's rights, and no one in Europe had cared.

Arriving in the 13th century with the Mongols, the Tatars reigned in the peninsula until the 15th century, when the Ottoman Empire created the Khanate of Crimea. Its main economic activity was the slave trade for the Muslim world. In the 18th century, following the Russo-Turkish war, Crimea was ceded to Russia, which abolished slavery and encouraged the return of populations that had fled the peninsula to escape it.

1495. Andrzej Sadecki, Tomasz Piechal & Tomasz Dąborowski, "Ukraine: a blow against the national minorities' school system", *Center for Eastern Studies*, Warsaw, September 27, 2017

1496. en.wikipedia.org/wiki/Minsk_II

1497. "Crisis in Ukraine: what the Minsk 2 agreement says", www.leparisien.fr, February 12, 2015

1498. "Full text of the Minsk agreement", www.ft.com, February 12, 2015

1499. Claude-Marie Vadrot (Blog), "La Russie envahit la Crimée sous les applaudissements (gênés) de Jean-Luc Mélenchon", *politis.fr*, March 2, 2014

Today, the plight of the Tatar community is frequently used to stigmatise Russia's role. In 2016, the Eurovision Grand Prix was awarded to the Ukrainian singer Jamala, who sang about the deportation of Tatars by the Soviets in 1944. The website *Geopolis* explains that "*a minority of Tatars apparently collaborated with the Nazis*"[1500]. The word 'apparently' tends to suggest that this could be false information: the role of collaboration with the Nazis is relativised and minimised, the better to castigate Russia, as in the newspaper *La Croix*[1501].

In fact, the several tens of thousands of voluntarily enlisted Tatars formed 7 large units of the Waffen SS[1502]. In 1944, after having surrounded them in Crimea, Stalin wanted to move them away from the front by deporting them to the east. They were not allowed to return to Crimea until the early 1980s.

In 1954, to celebrate the 300th anniversary of Ukraine's attachment to Russia, Nikita Khrushchev (who was Ukrainian) offered Crimea to Ukraine. But the significance of the event was only symbolic, as the effective authority remained in Moscow.

On January 20, 1991, well before the independence of Ukraine, as the end of the USSR was felt to be coming, the Crimeans were invited to choose by referendum whether to remain with Kiev or to return to the pre-1954 situation and be administered by Moscow. They decided by 93.6%[1503] to be attached to Moscow, and Crimea was declared an autonomous Soviet Socialist Republic. This was the first referendum on autonomy in the USSR. Two months later, on 17 March, Moscow organised a referendum on remaining in the Union, which was accepted by Ukraine. But on 24 August, the Kiev Rada adopted a decree for the independence of Ukraine, which was ratified by a referendum on December 1st. The participation of the Crimeans was low and very divided, because for them the problem had already been settled: Crimea was autonomous.

After Ukraine's independence, Crimea sought to maintain its status. On February 26, 1992, the Crimean parliament proclaimed the "Republic of Crimea" with the agreement of the Ukrainian government, which granted it the status of a self-governing republic. On May 5, 1992, Crimea declared its independence and adopted its constitution[1504]. This decision was to be confirmed by a popular referendum scheduled for August 2, 1992. However, on May 13, the

---

1500. Jacques Deveaux, "Who are the Tatars sung by Jamala, the Eurovision winning singer?", *Geopolis*, May 15, 2016

1501. Olivier Tallès, "Les Tatars de Crimée sous la pression de Moscou", *La Croix*, September 13, 2017

1502. The Tatar volunteers formed 7 militias and units attached to the Waffen-SS: SS-Waffengruppe Idel-Ural, Waffen-Gebirgs-Brigade der SS (Tatar Nr. 1), 30. Waffen-Grenadier-Division der SS (russische Nr. 2), Wolgatatarische Legion, Tataren-Gebirgsjäger-Regiment der SS, Waffen-Gruppe Krim, Schutzmannschaft Battalion. In all, it can be estimated that 40,000-60,000 Tatars fought with the German forces.

1503. NdA: with a participation of 81.3% of the population.

1504. On May 6, it is clarified that Crimea is part of Ukrainian territory.

Ukrainian Parliament annulled the declaration of independence and ordered the Parliament of the Republic of Crimea to do the same.

Negotiations between the governments of Crimea and Ukraine followed, and in June 1992 it was agreed that Crimea would have a degree of administrative and territorial autonomy within Ukraine. This status allows Crimea to decide independently on matters referred by the Constitutional Council of Ukraine.

In May 1994, the Crimean parliament decided to revert to the May 1992 constitution, and in September the Crimean president decided to formulate a new constitution. But on March 17, 1995, the Ukrainian parliament decided to abolish the 1992 constitution and Crimea was governed in an authoritarian manner by presidential decrees from Kiev. An event that was hardly reported by the Western media. This situation led the Crimean Parliament to formulate a second constitution in October of the same year establishing the Autonomous Republic of Crimea, which was ratified by the Crimean Parliament on October 21, 1998 and confirmed by the Ukrainian Parliament on December 23, 1998.

This back and forth by the Kiev government and the concerns of the Russian-speaking minority led to the signing of a Treaty of Friendship between Ukraine and Russia on May 31, 1997[1505]. The fear of a secession of Crimea led Ukraine to include the principle of the inviolability of borders. But in return, and this will be decisive in 2014, it guarantees "*the protection of the ethnic, cultural, linguistic and religious originality of national minorities on their territory*".

In 2014, the "Euromaidan" riots, largely supported by the West, brought the Ukrainian nationalists to power. Their decision on February 23, to "downgrade" the Russian language was a bombshell in Crimea: 65% of the population were Russian speakers and the 1997 treaty was broken. On the 27th, the Crimean regional parliament in Simferopol was stormed. Already at this stage, the vocabulary used by the Western media indicates the trend: *Le Monde* speaks of "*pro-Russian activists*[1506]", while Russia has no involvement at this stage.

Violence between Russian speakers and Ukrainian nationalists is on the rise, and incidents, sometimes tragic, fuel disinformation on both sides. The use of paramilitary militias by the new authorities in Kiev to restore order leads to the creation of Russian-speaking popular protection militias.

A set of three treaties signed in 1997 between Ukraine and Russia[1507] (updated in 2010 and valid until 2042), allowed the latter to station up to 25,000 personnel in Crimea. In 2014, only 20,000 military personnel are stationed there. In order to prevent the garrisons from being caught up in riots,

1505. https://apps.dtic.mil/dtic/tr/fulltext/u2/a341002.pdf

1506. "The crisis in Ukraine", *Le Monde*, February 27, 2014

1507. See Wikipedia article "Partition Treaty on the Status and Conditions of the Black Sea Fleet

Russian troops are deployed around their bases and at certain strategic points, in accordance with the provisions of the treaty. Nato played on words and spoke of an invasion, despite the absence of any indication of reinforcements arriving in the peninsula.

While the new authorities in Kiev were legitimate for the people of Lviv, they were not legitimate for the people of Crimea. The Ukrainian army is territorially structured and many of its soldiers in Crimea are Russian-speaking. Thus, when the government ordered them to repress the demonstrations, 20,000 of the 22,000 Ukrainian military personnel stationed in Crimea refused to intervene against their compatriots and rallied to the demonstrators, as Ivan Vinnik, a deputy in the Rada, later confirmed[1508]. In addition to these soldiers, there were about 15,000 Russian-speaking members of the police, the Security Service (SBU) and the border guards[1509]. This makes a total of 35,000 defectors, to which will be added about 4,000 hunters and members of shooting societies, and 15,000 members of the territorial reserve. All these 'military' in disparate uniforms, whose Ukrainian insignia were torn off to avoid confusion, became what the West identified as Russian special forces and nicknamed 'little green men'.

Throughout eastern Ukraine, Russian-speaking populations demonstrated their discontent, but the new authorities in Kiev were unable to control the situation. In Crimea, faced with the rise in violence between Russian speakers and loyalists at the end of February, and with the forces of law and order no longer able to fulfil their mission, Putin instructed his troops to intervene to restore order and avoid violence.

The March 2014 referendum asks Crimean voters to choose between returning to the 1992 Constitution (i.e., broad autonomy) or joining Russia. They chose the latter, which corresponds to their decision of January 1991.

The issue of Crimea is therefore less trivial than it seems. In response to Western accusations of violating the principle of the intangibility of borders, Russia is countering the case of Kosovo in 2008. For the West, the case of Crimea is an annexation by force, while Kosovo is an expression of the right of peoples to self-determination… But to make this distinction, Western politicians and media had to erase the January 1991 referendum[1510], thus distorting the reading of history. Thus, NATO[1511], the "*Policy Paper*" devoted to the Crimean affair by

1508. Евгений Мураев и Иван Виник, народные депутаты, в "Вечернем прайме" телеканала "112 Украина", August 4, 2016 (https://112.ua/video/evgeniy-muraev-i-ivan-vinnik-narodnye-deputaty-v-vechernem-prayme-telekanala-112-ukraina-04082016-206216.html)

1509. "Ukrainian defectors in occupied Crimea sidelined, relocated", www.unian.info, October 5, 2017

1510. "Russia, Ukraine and international law", Question d'Europe n° 344, *Robert Schuman Foundation*, February 16, 2015

1511. *North Atlantic Council Statement on Crimea*, Press Release (2019) 039, Nato, March 18, 2019 (updated March 22, 2019)

the Robert Schuman Foundation does not devote even a word to it[1512] ; nor does IFRI's foreign policy review[1513] or Arnaud Dubien, in *Le Monde*, even though he is the director of *the* Franco-Russian Observatory[1514]. On the site *laregledujeu.org*, in an article devoted to the "*1991 referendum*", Gilles Hertzog - a fellow traveller of BHL - omits the January and March polls... more convenient to condemn Russia!

9.3 "Russia invaded Ukraine[1515]"

Today, Russia is attributed with an expansionism that belonged to the USSR. With the abandonment of communism, Russia today has neither an ideological basis nor geostrategic reasons for an expansionist doctrine. This no doubt explains why the Western media is looking for justifications in Vladimir Putin's psychology...

In a resolution adopted in September 2014, the European Parliament speaks of "*direct military intervention*", ceasefire violations "*mainly by regular Russian troops*" and claims that Russia has "*increased its military presence on Ukrainian territory*"[1516], although there is no evidence to support these accusations! The terms "intervention" and "invasion" are alternated in order to cast doubt on the actual Russian presence in eastern Ukraine[1517]. In fact, with a clear lack of integrity, the media are adding fuel to the fire.

The only material "proof" of the presence of the Russian army in Ukraine produced by Nato was the satellite photo of 4 (!) "Russian" armoured howitzers[1518]. However, not only were the vehicles not formally identified, but they were only *assumed to* be Russian, as NATO saw no other possible explanation: the same "default" judgement that we saw in Syria or in the Skripal affair. In fact, it was deliberately "ignored" that elements of a Russian-speaking Ukrainian artillery battalion equipped with Russian-origin equipment had just "crossed

1512. Anna Dolya, "The annexation of Crimea: lessons for European security", *Robert Schuman Foundation*, Question d'Europe, n° 382, February 22, 2016

1513. Catherine Iffly, "Quelles perspectives pour la Crimée", *Politique étrangère*, IFRI, n° 2-2017

1514. Hélène Sallon (moderator), "Le coup de force de Poutine en Crimée s'inscrit dans une volonté de marchandage", *Le Monde*, March 3, 2014 (updated March 4, 2014)

1515. Emmanuel Macron, during his press conference at the end of the G7, on May 27, 2017 ("Ukraine: Macron promises a 'demanding' exchange without 'concessions' with Putin", *Europe 1*, May 27, 2017); "Putin - Macron: les dossiers qui fâchent", *BFMTV*, May 29, 2017; "Vladimir Putin: Emmanuel Macron, prêt à engager un 'rapport de force'", *Le Point*, May 29, 2017

1516. *European Parliament resolution of September 18, 2014 on the situation in Ukraine and the state of EU-Russia relations (2014/2841(RSP)*, Strasbourg, September 18, 2014

1517. Wikipedia, Article "Russian military intervention in Ukraine (2014-present)" (accessed May 15, 2019)

1518. NATO releases satellite imagery showing Russian combat troops inside Ukraine, August 28, 2014, (http://www.nato.int/cps/en/natohq/photos_112202.htm)

over" to the rebel side, becoming the "KALMIUS" battalion, and that it was in the area covered by the photo in August 2014[1519].

In September 2014, in an article entitled "*When Putin threatens to invade Eastern Europe*", the magazine *Le Point*, reported Vladimir Putin's words, which he reportedly said to Ukrainian President Petro Poroshenko:

> *If I wanted to, Russian troops could be in two days not only in Kiev, but also in Riga, Vilnius, Tallinn, Warsaw and Bucharest.*

According to José Manuel Barroso, he also declared: "*If I want to, in a fortnight I will take Kiev*". *Le Point* sees it as "*threatening remarks [...] aimed directly at European countries*[1520]". But the words have obviously been taken out of context. What Putin, who was accused of intervening in Ukraine for the benefit of the Donbass autonomists, meant was that if Russia were really involved, the conflict would not be "dragged out" in this way and would already be "settled". This was not a threat, but rather a demonstration of the inanity of the accusations.

For no one - not even European politicians - has tried to find out why Russia would be prepared to take the considerable political risk of attacking Ukraine (with 4 artillery pieces!)... without even giving itself the means to win. Let's remember that in 1943, in the same area, the Red Army faced the German army with nearly 7,500 tanks and 45,000 artillery pieces!

In March 2015, Republican Senator James Inhofe tried to convince his counterparts to authorise the sale of arms to Ukraine. In support of his plea, he presented the MPs with photographs showing Russian military columns... taken during the Georgian crisis six years earlier[1521]! He later claimed that he had been misled by the Ukrainian embassy that had provided the photographs. In fact, such documents on an invasion of Ukraine do not exist. This is puzzling... but the European media 'walks' (among the mainstream media, hardly anyone but *franceinfo* picks up the deception[1522]). The absence of actual observations of Russian troops in Ukraine is itself becoming a source of disinformation. Thus, CNN asserts that the Russian army has mobile crematoria, intended to burn the bodies of its soldiers who died in combat and to erase the traces of its passage. The aim is to hide the intervention from the Russian people, who would immediately rebel if they learned the truth[1523]!

1519. Confidential source.
1520. "When Putin threatens to invade Eastern Europe", *Le Point*, September 18, 2014
1521. Antoine Krempf, "Six-year-old photos show Russian invasion of Ukraine", *Radio France*, March 5, 2015
1522. Antoine Krempf, "Six-year-old photos show Russian invasion of Ukraine", www.francetvinfo.fr, March 5, 2015
1523. "Shocking News 2015 Russia is burning its Own Soldiers in Ukraine Mobile Crematorium", *CNN/YouTube*, July 4, 2015

In June 2015, in an interview with *Corriere della Sera*, Petro Poroshenko claimed that Russia had 200,000 troops stationed in Ukraine[1524]. In September, before the UN General Assembly in New York, he stated that

> *We are forced to fight the trained and armed troops of the Russian Federation. Heavy weapons and military equipment are concentrated in the occupied territories in such quantities that the armies of the majority of UN member states could only dream of them*[1525].

He is lying. On January 29 that year, General Viktor Muzhenko, head of the Ukrainian General Staff, claimed that the Ukrainian army was not fighting Russian troops and that only individual Russian fighters had been observed[1526]. This was later corroborated by General Vasyl Hrytsak, head of the SBU, in October 2015, confessing that since the beginning of the fighting in eastern Ukraine, only 56 Russian servicemen had been observed[1527].

Indeed, Russian citizens wearing military uniforms were captured by Ukrainian security forces, but they were young soldiers who were going to join the Donbass insurgents in solidarity during their military leave. Apart from the fact that they were wearing uniforms from the war in Afghanistan, the individuals shown in the Ukrainian videos appeared very young, disoriented and far from the profile of seasoned spetsnaz who would be sent to an external theatre for clandestine actions. This also explains why the Russians killed in Ukraine 'off duty' were buried without military honours. A similar phenomenon had already been observed during the war in the Balkans, when Swiss soldiers went from Ticino to Bosnia to "shoot up" with their ordinance weapons during weekends! Yet this is the basis on which Ukraine and Nato claim that Russia has deployed troops in Ukraine.

Moreover, if there were the number of military personnel put forward by Poroshenko, i.e. 75 military units, including 45 ground force units - as presented to the Nato Parliamentary Assembly in Istanbul on November 19, 2016[1528] - one should observe logistical columns for the operational support of these units and bases for the troops. However, the American observation satellites have not detected anything... Neither has the OSCE observation mission, whose deputy head, Alexander Hug, admitted to *Foreign Policy* magazine in 2018 that no direct observation confirms the engagement of Russian troops in Ukraine[1529].

1524. Giuseppe Sarcina, "Ukraine's Poroshenko: "Putin the Pact-Breaker"", *Corriere della Sera*, June 30, 2015
1525. Programme "C dans l'air du 02-10-2015: Syria: Putin Attacks", *YouTube/France 5*, November 10, 2015 (46'10")
1526. "No Russian Troops in Ukraine says Kiev General", *YouTube*, February 1st, 2015
1527. "Only 56 Russians Fought in Ukraine- says Ukraine's State Security (SBU)", *YouTube*, February 7, 2016
1528. "The 75 Russian military units at war in Ukraine", *Euromaidan Press*, November 23, 2019
1529. Amy Mackinnon, "Counting the Dead in Europe's Forgotten War", *Foreign Policy*, October 25, 2018

Desperately lacking evidence, the Western discourse falls back on the distribution of medals to Russian servicemen as early as 2014[1530], based on a report by Bellingcat[1531], an organisation of highly questionable impartiality. But here too, it is a lie, as it fails to mention that these were medals awarded to military personnel engaged in Syria. Not only did Russia have intelligence activities there (as evidenced by the capture of a GRU electronic listening post in the Golan Heights region in 2014[1532]), but its military personnel who participated in the elimination of Syrian chemical weapons were awarded medals between 2013 and 2015, as confirmed by the very "pro-Ukrainian" website *informnapalm.org*[1533].

The Western media present the successes of the autonomists as proof of Russian assistance. This ignores several facts. Firstly, it is not mentioned that the Ukrainian army units were organised territorially and composed of troops of the same language up to brigade level. It is therefore easy to understand that in the Russian-speaking areas, many soldiers (and even entire units) preferred to go over to the side of the autonomists with arms and baggage. This explains the modern equipment of the rebels.

Secondly, Ukraine claims to be conducting an "Anti-Terrorist Operation" (ATO), but it conducts its operations as if it were a conventional war against a structured and conventionally armed opponent. The Ukrainian staffs, too rigid and stuck in a doctrinaire approach to the art of operations, suffered from the enemy without managing to impose themselves. An examination of the course of the fighting in 2014-2016 in the Donbass shows that the Ukrainian general staff systematically and mechanically applied the same operational patterns. However, the war waged by the autonomists is very similar to what we observe in the Sahel: highly mobile operations conducted with light means. With a more flexible and less doctrinaire approach, the rebels were able to exploit the inertia of the Ukrainian forces to 'trap' them repeatedly.

Thirdly, the Ukrainian army is in a deplorable state. In four years, 2,700 soldiers have died *outside of* combat situations (accidents, drugs, mishandling of weapons, murders and suicides)[1534]. In fact, the army is undermined by the corruption of its cadres and no longer enjoys the support of the population. According to a UK Home Office report, in the March-April 2014 recall of reservists, 70 per cent did *not* turn up for the first session, 80 per cent for the second, 90 per cent for the third and 95 per cent for the fourth[1535]. In October-

1530. Paul Roderick Gregory, "Russian Combat Medals Put Lie To Putin's Claim Of No Russian Troops In Ukraine", *Forbes*, September 6, 2016

1531. "Russia's War in Ukraine: The Medals and Treacherous Numbers, *Bellingcat*, August 31, 2016

1532. Lazar Berman, "Rebels find joint Russian-Syrian spy site near Golan Heights", *The Times of Israel*, October 8, 2014

1533. "Russian medal standings in military operation in Syria. Part 1", *informnapalm.org*, April 12, 2016

1534. "На Донбассе небоевые потери ВСУ составили 2700 человек, - Матиос", focus.ua, October 27, 2018

1535. *Country Policy and Information Note - Ukraine: Military service*, Version 4.0, Home Office, April 2017

November 2017, 70% of conscripts did not turn up for the '*Autumn 2017*' recall campaign[1536]. This is without counting suicides and desertions (often to autonomists), which reached up to 30% of the workforce in the ATO area[1537].

In terms of strategy, Ukraine is a textbook case. The training and advice provided by the Nato military has only made the situation worse. Strategies based on the balance of power favoured by Nato are inadequate. No attempt is made to win the "hearts and minds" of the autonomists. On the contrary, the aim is to punish them even more. Encouraged by Western sanctions, the Ukrainian government has cut off all economic aid, funding (e.g. for the reconstruction of cities and infrastructure), social support (payment of pensions, social benefits, etc.) and banned all banking activity in the autonomous areas. In short, it is acting as if the population of Donbass were that of a foreign and enemy country. In doing so, he has placed himself in an asymmetrical situation. His strategy is backfiring: it is Russian companies and banks that are now providing these services. By trying to isolate the autonomists, the Kiev government has pushed them into the arms of Russia. NATO has learned nothing from its war in Afghanistan!

9.4. Conclusions for Ukraine

From the beginning of the crisis, despite the evidence of a popular conflict, Nato and Western countries see Moscow's hand. On April 13, 2014, Samantha Power, US ambassador to the UN, says on *ABC News*:

> *It's professional, coordinated. There is nothing popular about it*[1538]*!*

She is lying. All the information available at this stage indicates the opposite. Moreover, in July 2019, a report by the International Crisis Group (financed by several European countries and the Open Society Foundation), confirms the spontaneous nature of the conflict, far from the set-ups attributed to Russia:

> *The conflict in eastern Ukraine began as a popular movement. [...]*

1536. "ВСУ заявили о 70% неявки во время осеннего призыва", *iPress.ua*, December 13, 2017

1537. *Fact Finding Mission Report - Ukraine*, Office français de protection des réfugiés et apatrides (OFPRA) and Bundesamt für Fremdenwesen und Asyl (BFA), May 2017 (p. 36); Mikhail Klikushin, "Why Are So Many Ukrainian Soldiers Committing Suicide?", *Observer.com*, June 30, 2017

1538. https://www.facebook.com/bbcnews/videos/10151987042927217/; Paul Roderick Gregory, "You Tube Shatters Russian Lies About Troops In Ukraine: Putin Denies Truth To Obama", *Forbes*, April 14, 2014.

> *The demonstrations were organised by local citizens claiming to represent the Russian-speaking majority in the region. They were concerned both about the political and economic consequences of the new government in Kiev and about the government's later abandoned measures to prevent the official use of the Russian language throughout the country*[1539].

The impact of the linguistic dimension is regularly downplayed in the Western media, when it is not simply ignored: apart from giving legitimacy to the revolt of the populations concerned, it would highlight the 'social-nationalist' character of the new Ukrainian regime.

The Western press and media have "surfed" on our lack of knowledge of languages, cultures and domestic situations in Russia and its neighbours to convey a message aligned with Washington. Public opinion has been subtly conditioned by cheating on vocabulary and facts. For example, the French media systematically refer to the Donbass rebels as "*pro-Russian separatists*", whereas they should be called "Russian-speaking autonomists" (because - at least initially - they were not trying to "leave" Ukraine)[1540].

The misinformation surrounding the Ukrainian crisis is largely based on Cold War prejudices, with the result that it leads us to accept a nationalist far-right regime in Kiev. This position certainly suits the United States and NATO supporters, but does it correspond to our European values? For as in other Eastern European countries where hatred of Russia feeds an Atlanticist fervour, nationalism takes on pre-war overtones.

Our media's relentless attack on Russia tends to blind us to the real nature of those we support. This is true in Syria, but also in Ukraine where the international community is failing to curb (or even stimulating) endemic corruption[1541]. Propagated by personalities such as John McCain, and "intellectuals" such as Bernard-Henri Lévy, ignorance of realities and ethnocentrism have contributed to sinking Ukraine into its problems. Institutions, such as NATO or the Geneva Centre for the Democratic Control of Armed Forces (DCAF), involved in the fight against corruption and for good governance are too ideologically influenced to bring about concrete and lasting results.

1539. *Rebels without a Cause: Russia's Proxies in Eastern Ukraine*, International Crisis Group, Europe Report N° 254, July 16, 2019, p. 2

1540. See, for example: "Ukraine: pro-Russian separatists proclaim the birth of 'Little Russia'", *RTBF/Agencies*, July 18, 2017; Benoît Vitkine, "Ukraine: exchange of numerous prisoners between Kiev and the separatists", *Le Monde*, December 27, 2017; Sébastien Gobert, "Ukraine: coup d'état en terre séparatiste à Lougansk", *RFI*, November 22, 2017; "Les séparatistes pro-russes veulent remplacer l'Ukraine", *Euronews*, July 18, 2017; "Pourquoi Macron choisit Poutine #cdanslair 09.09.2019', *YouTube/France 5*, September 10, 2019 (34'22")

1541. Adrian Karatnycky & Alexander J. Motyl, "How Western Anticorruption Policy Is Failing Ukraine", *Foreign Affairs*, May 29, 2018

10. CYBERWARFARE AND INTERFERENCE ATTEMPTS

10.1. The context

On April 27, 2007, after the Estonian authorities undertook to move a monument to Soviet fighters against Nazi Germany, the country was completely paralysed by an unprecedented computer attack. The mainstream media immediately blamed Russia[1542], claiming that even if the government was not directly involved, the action could not have taken place without Kremlin approval! It even goes as far as to suggest an extension of the scope of Nato's Article 5[1543]!

On the basis of purely speculative evidence, it is claimed that "*the attack on Estonia was indeed initiated by pro-Russian services*[1544]". But what is a "*pro-Russian service*"? Is it a Russian service (i.e. an official, and by implication "secret", body)? Or a body that is independent of Russia (e.g. Estonian), but which is pro-Russian? As for the term "insider", it suggests the existence of a plan and an organisation. Swiss *Radio and Television* unreservedly denounces the responsibility of the Russian government[1545].

However, this is far from proven: of the 3,700 IP addresses that triggered the attack, 2,900 were Russian, 200 Ukrainian, 130 Latvian and 95 German[1546]. According to Mikko Hyppönen, an expert from the Finnish IT security firm F-Secure:

1542. Sylviane Pasquier, "Estonia: la main de Moscou", *L'Express*, May 16, 2007; Kertu Ruus, "Cyber War I: Estonia Attacked from Russia", *European Affairs*, volume IX, Nr 1-2, Winter/Spring, 2008; Benoît Vitkine, "L'Estonie, première cybervictime de Moscou", *Le Monde*, March 14, 2017

1543. James A. Lewis, *The "Korean" Cyber Attacks and Their Implications for Cyber Conflict*, Center for Strategic and International Studies, October 2009

1544. Olivier Robillart, "L'attaque contre l'Estonie était bien initiée par les services pro-russes", *silicon.fr*, March 13, 2009

1545. "A Russian-Estonian cyberwar triggered", *rts.ch*, August 6, 2007 (updated January 31, 2013)

1546. Santeri Taskinen, Mari Nikkarinen and Shankar Lal, "The Estonian Cyberwar", April 21, 2017 (https://mycourses.aalto.fi/pluginfile.php/457047/mod_folder/content/0/Kyber%20Crystal.pdf?forcedownload=1)

In practice, there is only one IP address that leads to a government computer. It is of course possible that an attack was also launched from there, but the person involved could be anyone from a caretaker in a government department to someone higher up[1547].

So we don't know. There is no evidence of the involvement of Russian official bodies[1548] and everything points to civil society action. Moreover, neither the European Commission nor NATO[1549] confirm Russia's involvement. In the end, only one culprit was identified: a young Russian activist from the youth movement "Nachi" - a Russian patriotic organisation that fights against "*oligarchs, anti-Semites, Nazis and liberals*" - who acted independently.

In December 2016, the United States accused Russia of causing a power outage in Vermont: Department of Homeland Security (DHS) experts linked the attack to the GRIZZLY STEPPE entity, allegedly linked to the FSB (Russian internal security service)[1550]. The *Washington Post* article, which revealed the affair, grew by the hour. The information was relayed by *Europe 1*, *RTBF* and *RTL*[1551]. But in the end, it turned out that the problem came from a laptop, disconnected from the electricity company's network, with malware that had not been implanted by Russians[1552]! The *Washington Post* discreetly corrected its article, but not the French media...

Beyond the almost caricatural accusations against Russia, this case illustrates the difficulty of attributing criminal activities on the Net, and the danger of assimilating them to acts of 'physical' warfare as the Pentagon does[1553]: a simple individual could thus push states into war[1554]. More seriously, *National Security Presidential Memorandum 13*, signed by President Trump in June 2018 authorises Cyber Command to conduct offensive operations without presidential or congressional approval. Thus, the US cyber attack on the Russian power grid in

1547. Nate Anderson, "Massive DDoS attacks target Estonia; Russia accused", *arstechnica.com*, May 14, 2007
1548. Sean Michael Kerner, "Estonia Under Russian Cyber Attack?", *internetnews.com*, May 18, 2007
1549. Cyberattacks - A Chronological Overview (https://www.nato.int/docu/review/2013/Cyber/timeline/FR/index.htm) (accessed October 1st, 2019)
1550. Juliet Eilperin & Adam Entous, "Russian hackers penetrated U.S. electricity grid through a utility in Vermont, U.S. officials say", *The Washington Post*, December 30, 2016; *GRIZZLY STEPPE - Russian Malicious Cyber Activity*, National Cybersecurity and Communications Integration Center/FBI, December 29, 2016 (Ref: JAR-16-20296A)
1551. "United States: Russian hackers have penetrated the electricity grid", *AFP/Europe1.fr*, December 31, 2016; "Russian hackers have penetrated the US electricity grid", *Belga/RTBF.be*, December 31, 2016; "Russian hackers have penetrated the US electricity grid", *Belga/RTL.be*, December 31, 2016
1552. Glenn Greenwald, "Russia Hysteria Infects WashPost Again: False Story About Hacking U.S. Electric Grid", *The Intercept*, December 31, 2016; Kalev Leetaru, "'Fake News' And How The Washington Post Rewrote Its Story On Russian Hacking Of The Power Grid", *Forbes*, January 1st, 2017.
1553. John Hudson, "Pentagon: Cyber Attacks Are Acts of War", *The Atlantic*, May 31, 2011; Siobhan Gorman & Julian E. Barnes, "Cyber Combat: Act of War", *The Wall Street Journal*, May 31, 2011
1554. Eric Schlosser, 'World War Three, by Mistake', *The New Yorker*, December 23, 2016

June 2019[1555], conducted without any prior political approval[1556], could legally be considered an "*act of war*"!

As we shall see, the accusations against Russia cannot be proven by facts. They all present the same mechanics of conspiracy: an assembly of interpretations and suspicions and disjointed facts into a project guided by Vladimir Putin. In the run-up to the 2019 European elections, they are being used to discredit the 'sovereignist' parties. Thus, on May 21, 2019, on *France 24*, the journalist Julie Dungelhoeff evokes a "*Russian interference*" in Austria[1557]. She refers to the "Ibizagate" which involved Heinz-Christian Strache, Austrian vice-chancellor (and leader of the far-right FPÖ party), trapped in a corruption sting[1558], where one of the protagonists posed as the niece of Russian oligarch Igor Makarov. Recorded on July 24, 2017, the video was not released until May 17, 2019, just before the European elections, however. It shows that Strache was prepared to obtain illegal financing (in this case from a Russian businessman, who has no niece...). However, there is no '*interference*' (since it is a staged event[1559]), nor - a fortiori - any involvement of the Russian government. Thus, it certainly shows that the politician was corrupt, but not that "*Austria was always a default choice for Russia*[1560]"... This is manipulation...

10.2 "Russia Tried to Influence the US Election"

The election of Donald Trump in 2016 will certainly go down in history for the hysteria it unleashed. In fact, on both sides, the party apparatuses are not fully convinced of their candidate. Donald Trump was not the favourite candidate of the Republicans and he owes his nomination more to the weakness of his opponents than to his own qualities: he is a choice by default. As for Hillary Clinton, her nomination to the Democratic Party was the result of internal shenanigans, to keep out Bernie Sanders - the candidate "outside" the system - who threatened her. As Donna Brazile, acting chair of the Democratic National Committee (DNC), later admitted, Hillary Clinton had secured control of the DNC's strategy in exchange for funding, which enabled her

1555. Edward Moyer, "US Cyber Command powers up attacks against Russia's electrical grid", *C-Net*, June 15, 2019

1556. David E. Sanger & Nicole Perlroth, "U.S. Escalates Online Attacks on Russia's Power Grid," *The New York Times*, June 15, 2019; Dave Lindorff, "US Cyber Attack on Russia's Power Grid is an 'Act of War'(According to the US)," *Dissident Voice*, June 16, 2019

1557. "European elections: can Russia influence the vote?", *France 24/YouTube*, May 21, 2019 (00'42")

1558. "Ibizagate: what we know about the video", *24heures.ch*, May 27, 2019

1559. "Austria: the far right trapped in a video", *RFI*, May 18, 2019

1560. Sébastian Seibt, "'Ibiza-gate': the FPÖ and Russia, special partners for a decade", *France 24*, May 21, 2019

to win the party's nomination[1561]. This manipulation was later confirmed by Democratic Senator Elisabeth Warren[1562] and caused many Democratic voters to change their minds…

A large part of the American national press is rather favourable to the Democrats. Up until the eve of the election, the polls gave Hillary Clinton a 4-point lead over Donald Trump (48% to 44%)[1563] and some even announced her victory as 99% inevitable[1564]. Trump's election is therefore a brutal disillusionment. His personality, his conflicting links with the media, and a foreign policy that clearly deviates from the line drawn by his predecessors, have encouraged attempts to delegitimise his election, with the idea of an impeachment procedure in the background.

Between August 2015 and November 2016, several events - real or supposed - combine to form what will become 'Russiagate'; with the double effect of masking political manoeuvring within the Democratic Party and discrediting (and then, after the elections, delegitimising) Donald Trump. This is a particularly technical and complex case, where assumptions dominate. It is divided into four main 'strands':

Voter influence through social networks;

the release of nearly 50,000 emails from the NEC (including private emails from Hillary Clinton and her campaign manager John Podesta);

penetration of the electronic voting system to alter or influence the results;

contacts between Donald Trump's campaign team and Russia in order to develop a common strategy ("collusion").

In May 2017, Robert S. Mueller, is commissioned to investigate possible collusion between Russia and Donald Trump's campaign team. His report is published in April 2019[1565] and concludes that Russia interfered in the 2016 presidential election, but that there is no evidence of this, nor of possible collusion with Donald Trump's campaign team. In fact, it reflects the embarrassment of the establishment.

10.2.1. Influencing Voters through Social Networks

The Mueller Report claims that Russia tried to influence minds through "*a social media campaign*". For this purpose, it used the services of the Internet Research Agency (IRA) - nicknamed the "troll factory" in the West - a

1561. Donna Brazile, "Inside Hillary Clinton's Secret Takeover of the DNC", *Politico Magazine*, November 2, 2017
1562. "Elizabeth Warren agrees Democratic race 'rigged' for Clinton", *BBC News*, November 3, 2017
1563. "US election poll tracker: Who is ahead - Clinton or Trump?", *BBC News*, November 8, 2016
1564. Rachael Revesz, "Survey finds Hillary Clinton has 'more than 99% chance'of winning election over Donald Trump", www.independent.co.uk, November 5, 2016
1565. Robert S. Mueller, III, *Report On The Investigation Into Russian Interference In The 2016 Presidential Election*, Department of Justice, Washington, D.C., March 2019

private structure with ill-defined contours, which some media outlets such as *France24*[1566], *Europe1*[1567], *BFMTV*[1568] or the debunkage site *Stopfake*[1569] claim to be linked to the Kremlin (by the fact that it is allegedly financed by Evgueny Prigogine, the Kremlin's caterer).

According to Facebook's analysis, "Russians" spent $100,000 on approximately 3,517 ads between June 2015 and May 2017[1570]. The Computational Propaganda Research Project at Oxford University estimates this amount at $73,711[1571]; including $46,000 before the election. An investigation by Google found that "*operatives*" bought ads for $4,700 "*using accounts suspected of being linked to the Russian government*". In addition, Google found $53,000 worth of politically motivated ads whose payments were linked to Russia, but "it is unclear *whether they were linked to the Russian government*": $7,000 was spent to promote a documentary called *You've Been Trumped* against Donald J. Trump, and $36,000 to question whether President Barack Obama should resign. Other amounts were used to promote Obama's message[1572].

Thus, not only did the Russian government - against all odds - propagandise against Trump instead, but the amounts seem small compared to the $81 million spent on Facebook ads by the two candidates[1573]. In the three states where the election was held (Wisconsin, Michigan and Pennsylvania), the Russians spent a total of $3,102 on ads (most of it during the primaries); and a few hundred dollars before the election[1574]! According to Facebook, about 10 million people saw at least one of the ads paid for by Russians, 44% of them before the election and 56% after, while about 25% were targeted to specific profiles and were never seen by anyone[1575]. In other words: a negligible impact.

1566. "European elections: when Russia gets involved", *France 24/YouTube*, May 17, 2019
1567. "Soupçons d'ingérence russe: Twitter a fermé 1 000 nouveaux comptes", *Europe1.fr*, January 20, 2018
1568. "Soupçons d'ingérence russe: Twitter a fermé 1 000 nouveaux comptes", *bfmbusiness.bfmtv.com*, January 20, 2018
1569. "Twitter found several thousand Twitter accounts associated with Kremlin 'troll factories'", *Stopfake.org*, January 20, 2018
1570. Richard Nieva, "Facebook sold ads to Russian-linked accounts during election", *CNet.com*, September 6, 2017
1571. Philip N. Howard, Bharath Ganesh & Dimitra Liotsiou, *The IRA, Social Media and Political Polarization in the United States, 2012-2018*, Computational Propaganda Research Project, University of Oxford, December 2018
1572. Daisuke Wakabayashi, "Google Finds Accounts Connected to Russia Bought Election Ads", *The New York Times*, October 9, 2017
1573. Josh Constine, "Trump and Clinton spent $81M on US election Facebook ads, Russian agency $46K", *TechCrunch*, November 2017
1574. Aaron Maté, 'New Studies Show Pundits Are Wrong About Russian Social-Media Involvement in US Politics', *The Nation*, December 28, 2018; Thomas Ferguson, Paul Jorgensen & Jie Chen, *Industrial Structure and Party Competition in an Age of Hunger Games: Donald Trump and the 2016 Presidential Election*, Working Paper No. 66, Institute for New Economic Thinking, January 2018
1575. Elliot Schrage (FB Vice President of Policy and Communications), "Hard Questions: Russian Ads Delivered to Congress", *newsroom.fb.com*, October 2, 2017

In a report commissioned by the Senate Intelligence Committee (SSCI)[1576], New Knowledge found that only 11% of IRA 'posts' had political content, of which only 33% triggered an associated action ('*engagements*'). Posts naming Clinton or Trump accounted for only 6% of tweets, 18% of posts on Instagram and 7% of posts on Facebook[1577]. Thus, not only was the bulk of the advertising not political in nature, but only a very small proportion (277) touched on the key states that were crucial to Trump's victory.

The IRA has even used the Pokémon Go game, allowing players to name their characters after victims of police brutality in the US[1578]! The Russian "troll" ad, which was the most seen by Americans was "*Back the Badge*": a pro-police ad[1579]! Posted online on October 19, 2016, it was viewed more than 1.3 million times and received 73,063 "clicks".

New Knowledge and investigative journalist Aaron Maté find that in reality the IRA's strategy was more like digital marketing than influence. Far from having the configuration of a sophisticated propaganda operation, it was a much simpler job, operating with "click traps" designed to make money[1580].

Moreover, there is no evidence of links between the IRA and the Kremlin. Robert Mueller's February 2018 indictment against the IRA does not mention any links to the Russian government[1581]. Furthermore, in July 2019, in an opinion and accompanying order, Federal Judge Dabney L. Friedrich criticised the Mueller Report for suggesting that influence activities "*were undertaken on behalf of, if not at the direction of, the Russian government*", when there is no evidence linking the IRA to the Russian government and therefore the term "*active measures*" is inappropriate[1582]. From this perspective, the claims of *France24, BFMTV* and others are conspiracy theories.

10.2.2. The Publication of the NEC Emails

The second main operation that the Mueller Report attributes to Russia would have been the release of hacked emails. According to FBI Director James Comey, the "Bureau" had suspected possible intrusions into the DNC's servers as early as

1576. Senate Select Committee on Intelligence (SSCI)

1577. Renee DiResta, Dr Kris Shaffer, Becky Ruppel, David Sullivan, Robert Matney, Ryan Fox, Dr Jonathan Albright & Ben Johnson, *The Tactics & Tropes of the Internet Research Agency*, New Knowledge, 2018, p. 76.

1578. Renee DiResta, Dr Kris Shaffer, Becky Ruppel, David Sullivan, Robert Matney, Ryan Fox, Dr Jonathan Albright & Ben Johnson, *The Tactics & Tropes of the Internet Research Agency*, New Knowledge, 2018; Glenn Fleishman, "Russia Even Used Pokémon Go to Hack the 2016 Election. Here's How", *Fortune.com*, December 18, 2018

1579. Alfred Ng, "This was the most viewed Facebook ad bought by Russian trolls", *CNet*, May 10, 2018

1580. Aaron Maté, 'New Studies Show Pundits Are Wrong About Russian Social-Media Involvement in US Politics', *The Nation*, December 28, 2018

1581. Robert S. Mueller III, *United States of America vs. Internet Research Agency LLC, Indictment*, February 16, 2018 (Document No. 18 U.S.C. §§ 2, 371, 1349, 1028A)

1582. Dabney L. Friedrich, *United States Of America V. Concord Management & Consulting Llc, Memorandum Opinion & Order*, Document No. 18-cr-32-2 (DLF), July 1st, 2019

August 2015, and had informed his campaign staff. But these were only suspicions, supported by no facts, which did not attract the attention of party officials[1583].

On June 12, 2016, Julian Assange's announcement that WikiLeaks would soon publish emails "*related to Hillary Clinton*" is probably the major turning point in this case. In fact, at this stage, Hillary Clinton is already under investigation by the FBI for using private messaging to exchange classified official information, and WikiLeaks has already published 30,322 of her emails in March[1584]. But we are six weeks away from the Democratic convention scheduled for July 25-28, and these new revelations risk damaging the candidate by exposing the way she won the party's nomination against Bernie Sanders.

On June 14, CrowdStrike, a computer security firm urgently commissioned by the NEC, announced that it had discovered malware on the NEC's servers, with indications that Russian hackers might be involved. The next day, a mysterious 'Guccifer 2.0' appeared and claimed to be the hacker who had planted the malware and published a document bearing Russian 'fingerprints'[1585]. Among these fingerprints are the first names "Feliks Edmundovitch"[1586] which would "confirm" the involvement of Russian services (!) Later, the FBI will claim that Guccifer 2.0 is an officer of the GRU (the Russian military intelligence service)[1587], although he claims to be Romanian[1588]. However, there are many inconsistencies: the first document he publishes as "proof" does not come from the CND, but from John Podesta's emails[1589]; he uses an email service (AOL.fr) that reveals his IP address; he uses a server that is not secured by the GRU; he uses a Russian VPN service, but whose IP address is taken by default and is not hidden; his activities were recorded in the US East Coast time zone; and so on[1590]. In fact, to this day, no one knows exactly who is behind Guccifer 2.0, but it is known that it is a hoax.

The Veteran Intelligence Professionals for Sanity (VIPS) association, which brings together former analysts from the main American intelligence agencies, including William Binney, former technical director of the NSA[1591], explained in

1583. Hearing of FBI Director James Comey (Samuel Ezerzer, "FBI James Comey 'The DNC denied FBI access to computers hacked by Russians'", *YouTube*, March 30, 2017)

1584. These include 50,547 pages of documents exchanged between June 30, 2010 and August 12, 2014, and 7,570 documents sent by Hillary Clinton, while she was Secretary of State, between 2009 and 2013. (Mark Tran, "WikiLeaks to publish more Hillary Clinton emails - Julian Assange", *The Guardian*, June 12, 2016)

1585. https://guccifer2.wordpress.com/2016/06/15/dnc/; VIPS, "Intel Vets Challenge 'Russia Hack'Evidence", *consortiumnews.com*, July 24, 2017

1586. First names of Dzerzhinsky, founder of the Russian security services in 1917.

1587. Julien Rebucci, "Who is really Guccifer 2.0, suspected of Russian hacking of the US Democratic Party?", *lesinrocks.com*, March 26, 2018

1588. "How Russia-linked hackers stole the Democrats' emails and destabilised Hillary Clinton's campaign", *abc news*, November 4, 2017 (updated November 5, 2017)

1589. https://theforensicator.wordpress.com/did-guccifer-2-plant-his-russian-fingerprints/

1590. See: Adam Carter, 'Guccifer 2.0: Evidence Versus GRU Attribution', December 20, 2019; Tim Leonard, 'Guccifer 2.0's Hidden Agenda', *Consortium News*, May 21, 2020

1591. William Binney, NSA's Technical Director for Global Geopolitical and Military Analysis and creator of the

an open letter in July 2017 that there had been no hacking, but a leak, and saw these events as a manoeuvre by the Democratic Party to discredit the revelations of *WikiLeaks*[1592].

On July 22, 2016, Wikileaks published a first set of NEC emails, followed on October 7 by the publication of emails from Hillary Clinton's campaign manager John Podesta. How they reached WikiLeaks remains controversial. WikiLeaks claims to have received them from an informant, while the US administration claims that they were obtained illegally by "hacking" the NEC's computer network.

It is known that the emails published by WikiLeaks were downloaded on July 5, 2016, at a speed of 1,976 MB in 87 seconds. According to VIPS computer intelligence specialists, such a speed would only be possible by direct transfer to a medium such as a USB stick, ruling out theft by hacking the network[1593]. Clearly, this was not a case of hackers (Russian or otherwise), but a leak from a whistleblower within the NEC. Assange confirmed this version to Dana Rohrabacher (Republican - California), member of the House of Representatives[1594]. Thus, contrary to what François Clémenceau asserted in the programme "C dans l'air" of February 27, 2019[1595], and the *France 24* newspaper of February 24, 2020, it is not known who downloaded these files, but it is very unlikely that this was done from Russia.

One incident, which went almost unnoticed in Europe, is probably linked to this case: on July 10, 2016, a young CND staff member, Seth Rich, was killed in Washington DC, shot several times in the back, in a deserted street. The official version speaks of an armed robbery gone wrong, although nothing was taken from the victim. The rumour spread fairly quickly that Seth Rich was the source of the emails published by WikiLeaks. The case took on a momentum of its own. On August 9, 2016, in an interview with a Dutch television station, Julian Assange suggested quite strongly that Rich was the source of the documents[1596] and offered $20,000 for any information leading to the arrest of his killer[1597]. In line with his source protection policy, however, he does not explicitly state that Seth Rich was his source.

According to Michael Isikoff, on *Yahoo News*, this is a conspiracy theory created - obviously! - by the Russian Foreign Intelligence Service (SVR)[1598]. An accusation

agency's Center for Automated Signals Intelligence Research.

1592. VIPS, "Intel Vets Challenge 'Russia Hack' Evidence", *consortiumnews.com*, July 24, 2017

1593. See the detailed explanation by William Binney, former NSA technical director, and Larry Johnson, former CIA officer, "Why The DNC Was Not Hacked By The Russians," *Information Clearing House*, February 15, 2019

1594. Manu Raju & Zachary Cohen, "A GOP congressman's lonely quest defending Julian Assange", *CNN*, May 23, 2018

1595. François Clémenceau in the programme "C dans l'air", "Korea: Trump aims for the Nobel Peace Prize! #cdanslair", *YouTube/France 5*, February 28, 2019 (55'20")

1596. Nieuwsuur, "Julian Assange on Seth Rich", *WikiLeaks*, August 9, 2018

1597. Nick Allen, "WikiLeaks offers $20,000 reward over murder of Democrat staffer Seth Rich", *The Telegraph*, August 10, 2016

1598. Michael Isikoff, "Exclusive: The true origins of the Seth Rich conspiracy theory," *Yahoo News*, July 9, 2019

taken up by the *Conspiracy Watch* website[1599]. But it is not true. The *Washington Post* notes that in the hours following Rich's death, conspiracy theories abounded on social networks, already suggesting the involvement of the Clinton team, well *before* the appearance of a mysterious "note" from the SVR[1600], which does not seem to exist.

In an August 2017 telephone conversation, Seymour Hersh, a journalist with close ties to the intelligence community, asserts that the NEC emails were not 'hacked', but passed to WikiLeaks after downloading[1601]. He suggests that Seth Rich is the source of the leak, without establishing a link with the murder[1602] which, curiously and despite suspicions, will not be investigated… Thus, to this day, we know nothing, neither of the perpetrators of the crime, nor of their motives, nor if Rich is indeed the author of the leaks; but the accusation against Russia is taking on water.

In February 2020, the media reported that "*Donald Trump offered the Wikileaks founder a pardon if he said Russia was not involved in the leak of internal US Democratic Party emails*[1603] ". The information apparently comes from *SkyNews*[1604]: it aims to discredit Julian Assange and defuse the "risk" of his revelations. But it is a lie. In fact, MP Dana Rohrabacher has offered to intercede on Assange's behalf if he would disclose the source of the leaked NEC emails[1605].

Unusually for a case of this importance, the FBI never had access to the original data, only to that provided by CrowdStrike. Testifying before a Congressional committee, FBI Director James Comey stated that despite repeated requests, access to the CND's servers was systematically denied to his departments[1606]; while CND spokesman Eric Walker denied that the FBI had made any such requests[1607]. It would later emerge that for its investigation, the FBI only received three redacted drafts from CrowdStrike, with the firm never producing a full final report[1608]. Stranger still, in December 2017, it will be revealed by Donna Brazile that after the leak was discovered, the NEC made replicas of the servers (for submission to the FBI) and destroyed the original devices[1609]!

1599. "The origins of the Seth Rich murder conspiracy theory", *Conspiracy Watch*, July 16, 2019
1600. Philip Bump, "Don't blame the Seth Rich conspiracy on Russians. Blame Americans," *The Washington Post*, July 9, 2019.
1601. Joe Lauria, "A New Twist in Seth Rich Murder Case", *Consortium News*, August 8, 2017
1602. Audio 2, *Rod Wheeler/YouTube*, July 11, 2017
1603. "Trump would have offered to pardon Assange if he exonerated Russia", *AFP/LaLibre.be*, February 19, 2020; Amaelle Guiton, "Assange wants to seek asylum in France", *Libération*, February 20, 2020
1604. https://twitter.com/SkyNews/status/1230193529114243073
1605. https://twitter.com/Timcast/status/1230526801820241927
1606. "The DNC Denied The FBI Access To Their Servers To Look For Russian Hacking", *YouTube*, January 10, 2017
1607. Ali Watkins, "The FBI Never Asked For Access To Hacked Computer Servers", *BuzzFeed News*, January 4, 2017
1608. Ray McGovern, "FBI Never Saw CrowdStrike Unredacted or Final Report on Alleged Russian Hacking Because None Was Produced," *Consortium News*, June 17, 2019; *Government's Response To Defendant's Motion To Compel Unredacted Crowdstrike Reports*, District Court For The District Of Columbia, Criminal Document No. 19-cr-18-ABJ, May 31, 2019
1609. Nicholas Ballasy, "Brazile: After Hacking, DNC Replicated Server for FBI Then 'Destroyed' Machines",

However, CrowdStrike is a private firm that regularly works for the Democratic Party[1610], and the risk that its impartiality will be compromised by conflicts of interest is great. It is surprising that after the Wikileaks announcement of June 12, 2016, the NEC did not turn to the FBI but to a private actor, whose reliability is controversial. Nevertheless, the firm attributes the 'attack' to a group of hackers called FANCY BEAR[1611].

In the end, the CND 'hack' has never been seriously and impartially investigated, and the very basis of the accusations is open to question[1612]. The NSA, which is responsible for IT security, has all the tools to detect an intrusion into the NEC servers, yet it is surprisingly absent from the discussions[1613]. On May 7, 2020, the Parliamentary Intelligence Committee decided to declassify and publish a number of hearings of Russiagate witnesses[1614], including that of Shawn Henry, president of CrowdStrike. He states that he had "*no concrete evidence that data was exfiltrated from the NEC, but indications that it was exfiltrated*". The term "exfiltrated" leaves two possibilities open: that the data was taken from outside (hacking) or that it was downloaded onto a local medium (USB stick). Asked about these '*indications*', he confesses '*that the data was prepared to be exfiltrated, [they just] didn't have the evidence that it actually left*[1615]'. What he describes suggests that the data (emails) was gathered before being 'exfiltrated', indicating a download type method and not a hack. Clearly: we don't know, and the accusations against Russia are just speculation.

Assumptions became facts, which both obscured corrupt practices within the Democratic Party and provided the basis for the eventual impeachment of Donald Trump.

10.2.3. The Penetration of the Electronic Voting System

During the Democratic primaries, an anomalous difference between the results and exit polls reportedly showed that Hillary Clinton would have performed better overall in states where the voting machines were easier to hack[1616]. Although these 'correlations' do not demonstrate fraud, their repetition

---

PJMedia, December 13, 2017

1610. See, for example: *President Obama Announces More Key Administration Posts*, The White House, Office of the Press Secretary, April 13, 2016

1611. It is also known as PAWN STORM, SEDNIT, TSAR TEAM (FireEye), STRONTIUM (Microsoft), SOFACY GROUP (Kaspersky) and APT28 (Mandiant).

1612. ""What Happened To The DNC Servers?" President Trump Demands To See Evidence Of Russia Hacking", *YouTube*, July 16, 2018

1613. Robert Mackey, "If Russian Intelligence Did Hack the DNC, the NSA Would Know, Snowden Says," *The Intercept*, July 26, 2016

1614. https://intelligence.house.gov/russiainvestigation/

1615. *Interview Of: Shawn Henry*, Permanent Select Committee On Intelligence U.S. House Of Representatives, Washington, D.C., December 5, 2017

1616. Doug Johnson Hatlem, "Clinton Does Best Where Voting Machines Flunk Hacking Tests: Hillary Clinton vs. Bernie Sanders Election Fraud Allegations", www.counterpunch.org, May 16, 2016

is a source of suspicion[1617] and highlights the risk of Russian interference, which will not be confirmed.

On September 29, 2016, on the basis of "*well-informed sources*", the US press revealed that Russia had penetrated the electronic voting systems of "*almost half*" of the states[1618]. But this is a lie. The information comes from a draft report by the Department of Homeland Security *(DHS)* and the Office of the Director of National Intelligence (ODNI)[1619] to be released on October 7, 2016, but it is much less assertive. It simply states that 21 states could "*potentially be targeted by Russian government cyber actors*". In other words, this is a "possibility", not even a probability. As with all of this, the memo is not based on facts or evidence, but on circumstantial evidence; in this case, "*consistency with* Russian *methods and motivations*[1620]". However, it states that the intelligence agencies are "*not in a position to attribute this activity to the Russian government*[1621]".

In October 2019, the report of the Senate Intelligence Committee will confirm that there is no indication that the electoral rolls have been altered[1622].

10.2.4. The Perception of the American Intelligence Services

In early December 2016, the *Washington Post* reported on a CIA analysis suggesting Russian interference in the US presidential election[1623]. The mere fact that the information comes from the CIA gives it global credibility. However, this is not an official CIA report, but a discussion moderated by a CIA official. The ODNI then issued a memo and launched an investigation into the matter at the request of President Obama[1624].

Few media outlets note that the information is not confirmed by the National Security Agency (NSA) (responsible for cybersecurity), James Comey, Director of the FBI (responsible for counter-intelligence), or General James Clapper, Director of National Intelligence (who oversees and coordinates the activities of the Intelligence Community), who note, but do not dispute, the total absence

1617. See the Democratic primary table with potential fraud (docs.google.com/spreadsheets/d/1sGxtIofohrj3POp-wq-85Id2_fYKgvgoWbPZacZw0XlY/edit#gid=1476097125)
1618. Mike Levine & Pierre Thomas, "Russian Hackers Targeted Nearly Half of States' Voter Registration Systems, Successfully Infiltrated 4", *ABC News*, September 29, 2016
1619. Office of the Director of National Intelligence (ODNI)
1620. DHS & ODNI, *Joint Statement from the Department Of Homeland Security and Office of the Director of National Intelligence on Election Security*, DHS Press Office, October 7, 2016 (1st paragraph)
1621. Ibid (2nd paragraph)
1622. *Report of The Select Committee on Intelligence United States Senate on Russian Active Measures Campaigns and Interference in The 2016 U.S. Election - Volume 1: Russian Efforts Against Election Infrastructure with Additional Views*, 116th Congress, 1st Session, Senate Report, October 8, 2019, p.5
1623. Adam Entous, Ellen Nakashima and Greg Miller, "Secret CIA assessment says Russia was trying to help Trump win White House", *The Washington Post*, December 9, 2016
1624. Director of National Intelligence, *Statement on Requests for Additional Information on Russian Interference in the 2016 Presidential Election*, Washington, DC 20511, December 16, 2016

of evidence[1625]. In addition, six former senior intelligence officials refute the accusations against Russia in a statement[1626].

Despite these reservations, some mainstream media, such as *RTBF*, do not hesitate to turn doubts into certainties, following the model of conspiracy and claim that the "*support of FBI boss James Comey, as well as James Clapper, head of the Directorate of Intelligence (DNI), solidly supports the opinion of the CIA*[1627] "... exactly the opposite of reality! *Europe 1* even asserts - without any factual elements - that Putin himself would have "*given instructions on how to filter and use the messages stolen from the Democrats after the hacking*[1628]". We are in the middle of disinformation.

On January 6, 2017, a new report is published by the ODNI on alleged Russian interference attempts. Its first '*key judgement*' is to '*assess that Putin and the Russian government aspire to help candidate Trump*[1629]'. After five pages of 'analysis' and another five pages reporting on RT's criticism of the US, he presents an 'Appendix B'. It provides a grid that quantifies the likelihood of the information given in the document as follows:

Probability	Variation9	English Vocabulary (official)	French translation
100 %	-10 %	Almost certainly, Nearly certain	Almost certain
80 %	±10 %	Very likely, Highly probable	Very likely
70 %	±10 %	Likely, Likely	Likely
50 %	±10 %	Roughly even chances, Roughly even odds	Approximately equal chances
35 %	±10 %	Unlikely, Improbable	Unlikely
18 %	±10 %	Very unlikely, Highly Improbable	Very unlikely
5 %	±5 %	Almost no chance, remote	Almost no chance

Table 6 - Expressions of probability in the analyses of the US Office of the Director of National Intelligence (2017)

1625. Mark Hosenball & Jonathan Landay, "Exclusive: Top U.S. spy agency has not embraced CIA assessment on Russia hacking", *Reuters*, December 13, 2016; Rebecca Savransky, "US spy chiefs not sold on CIA assessment of Russian hacking: report", *The Hill*, December 13, 2016 ;

1626. "US Intel Vets Dispute Russia Hacking Claims", *consortiumnews.com*, December 12, 2016

1627. "FBI believes in Russian intervention in the US election", *7sur7.be*, December 16, 2012; "USA: FBI also believes in Russian intervention in the US election", *rtbf.be*, December 16, 2016

1628. "American elections: Putin personally involved in hacking?", *Europe 1*, December 15, 2016

1629. Intelligence Community Assessment (ICA), *Background to "Assessing Russian Activities and Intentions in Recent US Elections": The Analytic Process and Cyber Incident Attribution*, Annex B, Office of the Director of National Intelligence, ICA 2017-01D, January 6, 2017, p.ii.

It is accompanied by an assessment of the confidence in the claims made in the document[1630]:

English expression	French translation	Official interpretation
High confidence	High confidence	High confidence generally indicates that judgements are based on high quality information and multiple sources. High confidence in a judgment does not imply that the product is a fact or a certainty; such judgments may be wrong.
Moderate confidence	Moderate confidence	Moderate confidence means that the information is based on credible sources and is plausible, but is not of sufficient quality or sufficiently corroborated to ensure a high level of confidence.
Low confidence	Low confidence	Low confidence means that the credibility of the information and/or its plausibility is uncertain and that the information is too fragmentary and insufficiently corroborated to provide a basis for sound analysis, or that the reliability of sources is questionable.

Table 7 - Expressions used by the US Office of the Director of National Intelligence to indicate confidence in a judgment (2017)

It is worth noting that in relation to the notion of '*high confidence*' - which appears seven times in the report - the ODNI makes it clear that it can refer to false judgements!

The presence of such grids in the appendix of an intelligence report is not common. The report was probably intended to satisfy both the departing Obama administration and the new Trump administration that was being installed, and the services were thus able, by an elegant pirouette, to relativise a message they did not really believe in. It is also noticeable that the European media hardly mentioned these grids and repeated the accusations without any nuance.

And that's not all. On January 7, 2017, the newspaper *Libération* stated:

> *At a Senate hearing on Thursday, the 17 spy agencies believe that "only the most senior Russian officials could have authorised the theft and publication of election-related data"*[1631].

1630. Intelligence Community Assessment (ICA), *Background to "Assessing Russian Activities and Intentions in Recent US Elections": The Analytic Process and Cyber Incident Attribution*, Office of the Director of National Intelligence, ICA 2017-01D, Annex B, January 6, 2017, p. 13

1631. Estelle Pattée, "American intelligence services reaffirm Russia's interference in the presidential election", *liberation.fr*, January 5, 2017

This suggests that *all* intelligence services approve of the report's conclusions. *BFMTV* goes further, stating that "*Putin's involvement is confirmed*[1632]". In June 2017, journalist Megyn Kelly threw the accusation at Vladimir Putin during her interview on *NBC News*[1633]. Even the prestigious *New York Times* accuses Trump of...

> *still refuses to acknowledge a key fact agreed upon by 17 US intelligence agencies and now overseen by him: Russia orchestrated the attacks and did so to help him get elected*[1634].

These are lies. Four days later, the editors corrected the article to say that only four agencies had supported the accusation against Russia: the ODNI, the CIA, the FBI and the NSA.

In fact, James Clapper adopted the same stratagem as Donald Rumsfeld in 2002: he had the report written by analysts chosen from within a few intelligence agencies[1635], leaving out the more "reserved" services on the issue, such as the Military Intelligence Agency (DIA). However, even among these "selected" services, there is no unanimity: while the CIA and the FBI have "*high confidence*" in Russia's involvement, the NSA (the only agency capable of scrutinising cyberspace) has only "*moderate confidence*[1636]". In intelligence jargon: "*we have no evidence*".

On January 18, Barak Obama admitted that the report was "*inconclusive*" on the issue of hacking and how WikiLeaks had gained access to Democratic Party emails[1637]. But here again, the media will not pick up on this...

In March 2017, the US FBI indicted two Russian FSB agents for recruiting hackers to "steal" the data of some 500 million Yahoo email accounts in 2014. Their targets were "*Russian journalists, Russian and US government officials; employees of a major Russian cybersecurity company, 'as well as employees of webmail and access providers in Russia and the United States'*". This information is already normally available to the FSB under Russian law. During the press conference, Mary McCord, the acting deputy US attorney general, claims that the hackers were working for the Russian FSB, and therefore with the government's blessing. However, McCord concedes that there is a complete lack of evidence on this issue and that at this stage these are only accusations based on presumptions[1638].

1632. "United States: Putin's involvement in the election confirmed", *BFMTV*, January 6, 2017

1633. "FULL Unedited Interview of Putin With NBC's Megyn Kelly," *NBC News/YouTube*, June 8, 2017

1634. Maggie Haberman, "Trump's Deflections and Denials on Russia Frustrate Even His Allies", *The New York Times*, June 25, 2017

1635. Ray McGovern, "A Look Back at Clapper's Jan. 2017 'Assessment'on Russia-gate", *consortiumnews.com*, January 7, 2019

1636. Intelligence Community Assessment (ICA), *Background... op.cit.* p.ii.

1637. "Obama's Last News Conference: Full Transcript and Video", *The New York Times*, January 18, 2017

1638. http://www.worldbulletin.net/news/186327/russias-fsb-hired-criminal-hackers-to-attack-yahoo

For if the FBI document does speak of two FSB agents, it seems to ignore that they were working for their own account at the time. The first, Major Dmitry Dokuchaev, had even been arrested by the FSB in December 2016 for treason and accused of having worked for the CIA[1639]. The second, Igor A. Sushchin, worked for a Russian financial group. By making it appear that they were still working for the FSB - and failing to say that they were considered criminals by Russia - the FBI and the US press[1640] suggest that the Russian government was behind the hacking. As for the hackers, it is suggested that they were among the 35 Russian diplomats expelled in December 2016 by the Obama administration after the suspected intrusion into the Democratic Party server[1641].

There are attempts to substantiate the thesis of Russian interference in the election by trying to demonstrate hyperactivity in cyberspace. The official accusations repeat the claims of private companies such as FireEye and CrowdStrike, which are known for 'finding' hackers where the government wants to find them: in 2014, it was China and since 2016, it is Russia[1642]. In this case, the 'Russian interference' in the American election is attributed to two entities, which the Americans have named FANCY BEAR and COZY BEAR, and which are said to be GRU and FSB offices.

On July 13, 2018, the Department of Justice indicted 12 Russian citizens suspected of belonging to GRU Units 26165 and 74455[1643], which are associated with FANCY BEAR. But the indictment raises some questions. First of all, these units are designated by their postal numbers, which are openly accessible and used for mail delivery while concealing their real designation; a system used for all military formations since the Soviet era. It is clear that the American services do not know these units, nor their exact place in the GRU structure. The little that is known is that they are specialised in cryptology[1644], a discipline that has nothing to do with hacking. On the other hand, surprisingly enough, they know the full names of hackers whose hacking skills are questionable. For example, the only 'accused' who could be associated with unit 26165 is Viktor Borisovitch Netyksho, who has a PhD in mathematics applied to complex computer networks[1645]. Another defendant, Boris Alekseyevich Antonov, has

1639. "Second FSB Agent Arrested for Treason Revealed as Notorious Hacker", *The Moscow times*, January 27, 2017

1640. One example among many: David Gilbert and Noah Kulwin, "The U.S. government says Russia recruited a notorious cybercriminal for Yahoo hack", *Vice News*, March 15, 2017

1641. Cathy Burke, "Two Expelled Russian Diplomats Among FBI's Most Wanted", *Newsmax*, December 29, 2016

1642. Jeffrey Carr, "Was Yahoo a sanctioned FSB operation or a rogue operation?", *Medium.com*, March 16, 2017

1643. https://www.justice.gov/file/1080281/download

1644. Шевякин Александр Петрович - Система безопасности СССР. Читать книгу онлайн. Страница - *30*, (https://unotices.com/book.php?id=132685&page=30)

1645. https://www.dissercat.com/content/vosstanovlenie-parametrov-diskretnykh-ustroistv-osnovannoe-na-pereotsenke-veroyatnostei-s-is

developed a patented method of storing and processing explosives[1646]... a rather different field!

In fact, we don't know. The methodology used is the same as that of Bellingcat for the Skripal affair: a profile of the entities or individuals thought to be guilty is established, and then information is sought that 'fits' with the initial hypotheses. For an honest examination of the traces left by the hackers tends to show that they are Ukrainian, and would even have helped the commission of enquiry into the crash of flight MH-17 in July 2017[1647]!

In December 2016, *CrowdStrike* claimed that the hacker entity FANCY BEAR (allegedly associated with Russian military intelligence) had penetrated the Ukrainian artillery fire control network to plant malware, causing significant losses[1648]. The information is a bit 'big', but some European mainstream media reported it anyway, such as the *Swiss Radio-Television*[1649] or the newspaper *Libération*[1650]. It turned out that the information was false and had to be withdrawn[1651].

The presence of the United States in virtually every conflict on the planet makes its Department of Defense the primary cyber challenge for thousands of hackers around the world. In 2018, the Pentagon was blocking about 36 million attacks per day[1652]. That Russian services are involved in these attacks is very likely, but the link between them and the presidential election is purely speculative and has never been demonstrated[1653]. In December 2016, the National Cybersecurity and Communications Integration Center (NCCIC) published a summary accusing the GRIZZLY STEPPE entity of hacking into the emails of prominent Democratic Party figures, such as John Podesta[1654]. However, the data published by the NCCIC, allows to determine that GRIZZLY STEPPE is... Ukrainian[1655]!

1646. http://www.freepatent.ru/patents/2031896

1647. Petri Krohn, "Did a Ukrainian University Student Create Grizzly Steppe?", *off-guardian.org*, January 9, 2017; George Eliason, "Why the Evidence Mueller Has for the Indicting 13 Russian Nationals is Fraudulent", *off-guardian.org*, June 5, 2018; George Eliason, "Who is Fancy Bear and Who Are They Working for?", *off-guardian.org*, June 25, 2018

1648. *Use of FANCY BEAR android malware in tracking of Ukrainian field artillery units*, CrowdStrike, December 22, 2016

1649. "Russian Democratic Party hackers targeted Ukrainian military", *rts.ch*, December 22, 2016

1650. Amaelle Guiton, "Les Russes donnent des sueurs froides sur le front numérique", *liberation.fr*, December 30, 2016

1651. The old report was published on December 22, 2016 and the corrected report on March 23, 2017 (Oleksiy Kuzmenko & Pete Cobus, "Cyber Firm Rewrites Part of Disputed Russian Hacking Report", *Voice of America (VOA)*, March 24, 2017)

1652. Frank R. Konkel, "Pentagon Thwarts 36 Million Email Breach Attempts Daily," *Nextgov.com*, January 11, 2018

1653. Matthew Cole, Richard Esposito, Sam Biddle & Ryan Grim, "Top-Secret NSA Report Details Russian Hacking Effort Days Before 2016 Election", *The Intercept*, June 5, 2017

1654. *GRIZZLY STEPPE - Russian Malicious Cyber Activity*, NCCIC/FBI, December 29, 2016 (Reference: JAR-16-20296A)

1655. Petri Krohn, "Did a Ukrainian University Student Create Grizzly Steppe?", *Off-Guardian*, January 9, 2017

The bad faith is coupled with a profound lack of understanding of the Russian intelligence and security services. The latter have very specific remits and areas of activity. The GRU is a defence intelligence service and focuses on military assessments, such as the NATO presence in Eastern Europe, the situation in Ukraine, Central Asia and Syria. The FSB deals with internal security issues, like the DGSI in France, which obviously does not exclude it having a presence abroad (like the DGSI or the American FBI) but its attention is focused on threats that would affect the internal situation in Russia. It is not in their remit to monitor or influence a presidential campaign, which must be subject to rigorous strategic monitoring.

Moreover, it is difficult to see why foreign interference of this magnitude would be conducted by two separate intelligence agencies. In reality, it would be a task for the foreign intelligence service, the SVR, which provides strategic, political and cyberspace intelligence[1656]. It is the equivalent of the DGSE in France or the CIA in the United States, but it is never mentioned… partly because it has not been found to have any link with interference, and partly - more prosaically - because, unlike the GRU and the FSB, it is very little known to journalists!

The accusations against Russia are based on four clues: a) the hacking software was in Russian, b) the keyboards used were in Cyrillic, c) the time zone of the hackers corresponded to that of Moscow and c) the IP address was based in Russia. Thus, FireEye has associated APT28 with the Russian government simply because it operates during St Petersburg and Moscow business hours!

Moreover, the version of the malware used by the hacker(s) was more than a year and a half old and had not been updated. Not only would one expect Russia to have the capacity to develop specific software, but it is hardly conceivable that it would risk using obsolete software developed in Ukraine[1657] to carry out operations of this importance.

It seems rather surprising that services specialising in cyberwarfare operations would openly display their IP addresses and use keyboards whose signatures can be easily detected! The DHS and ODNI review of 876 IP addresses shows that they are based in 59 countries, most of them (15%) are TOR (anonymised and accessible by anyone) and US. Russian IP addresses are only in third place - after the US - followed closely by the Netherlands, Germany and France[1658]. Clearly, the links to the Russian government are totally speculative and France could just as easily have been blamed.

In March 2017, WikiLeaks published several thousand CIA documents under the name "VAULT 7", which show that the US agency created an internal

1656. Sluzhba Vnechnei Razvedki: Foreign Intelligence Service
1657. Mark Maunder, "US Govt Data Shows Russia Used Outdated Ukrainian PHP Malware", *Wordfence*, December 30, 2016
1658. Ibid.

group, designated OMBRAGE, responsible for developing computer tools, such as MARBLE FRAMEWORK[1659], that allow hacking operations to be carried out involving foreign countries (under a "false banner"), emulating these activities in several languages (including Chinese, Russian, Korean, Arabic, and Farsi[1660]) such as here[1661]. According to VAULT 7, this software was used in 2015 and 2016[1662]. It should also be remembered that no one has mentioned the hypothesis - just as possible and probable - of an operation carried out from the United States by the Republican Party[1663], nor that the CIA had already infiltrated the French presidential elections in 2012[1664]! However, these documents do not make it possible to affirm that the CIA was behind the actions against the Democratic Party[1665], but they do make the accusations against Russia more fragile.

In June 2017, as part of its investigation, the Senate Intelligence Committee interviewed three senior officials from the Department of Homeland Security[1666]. When asked whether there was any evidence to show that '*the votes of Americans were distorted in any way*', they all answered '*no*[1667]'. It should be noted in passing that during these hearings, reference was systematically made to '*the Russians*', without specifying whether they were isolated individuals or institutions.

On February 16, 2018, the indictment of 13 Russian nationals by the Department of Justice for interfering in the US presidential election reignited the rumours against Russia. However, unlike the January 2017 report, the indictment does not link the "conspiracy" to the Russian government or mention any violation of US election laws. It also notes that these activities were aimed at supporting the candidacies of Donald Trump, Bernie Sanders and Jill Stein (without however explaining how and for what purpose) and that they would have started in 2014[1668]... when Trump's candidacy was not even being considered!

1659. WikiLeaks.org/ciav7p1/cms/page_14588467.html

1660. Stephanie Dube Dwilson, "WikiLeaks Vault 7 Part 3 Reveals CIA Tool Might Mask Hacks as Russian, Chinese, Arabic", *Heavy.com*, March 31, 2017

1661. Jacques Cheminat, "Marble Framework: the treacherous double game of CIA hackers", *silicon.fr*, March 31, 2017

1662. Catalin Cimpanu, "WikiLeaks Dumps Source Code of CIA Tool Called Marble", *Bleeping Computer*, April 1st, 2017

1663. Aaron Blake, "The dangerous and irresistible GOP conspiracy theory that explains away Trump's Russia problem", *The Washington Post*, March 10, 2017

1664. Press Release, "The CIA's mission letter for the 2012 French presidential election", *WikiLeaks*, February 16, 2017

1665. Kim Zetter, "WikiLeaks Files Show the CIA Repurposing Hacking Code to Save Time, Not to Frame Russia", *The Intercept*, March 8, 2017

1666. They are Dr Samuel Liles, Director of the Office of Intelligence and Analysis, Ms Jeannette Manafra, Deputy Director of Cybersecurity and Communications, and Mr Bill Priestap, Deputy Director of Counterintelligence.

1667. *PBS NewsHou*, "Senate Intelligence Committee hearing on Russia election interference", *YouTube*, June 21, 2017

1668. *"Grand Jury Indicts Thirteen Russian Individuals and Three Russian Companies for Scheme to Interfere in the United States Political System"*, Office of Public Affairs, Department of Justice, February 16, 2016

10.2.5. The Collusion of Donald Trump's Team with Russia

Donald Trump's campaign team is accused of having been in contact with Russian agents in order to coordinate a strategy. There is talk of compromising documents (the media is fond of the term "kompromat") from the Kremlin to "blackmail" Trump[1669]. In February 2017, the *New York Times* claimed that Trump's team had regular contact with "*Russian intelligence officers*[1670]", which was denied four months later by Robert Mueller, the FBI deputy, before the *Senate Intelligence Committee*[1671]. Trump's lawyer, Michael Cohen, reportedly went to Prague to meet with Russian agents and pay them to hack into the CND's servers. This gives rise to the idea of "collusion" between Trump and Putin, which some call a "*conspiracy*[1672]". There are even suspicions that Trump is a "*Russian agent*[1673]"! In *US News*, columnist Michael Fuchs states:

> *We cannot exclude the possibility that the President of the United States of America is an agent - willing or otherwise - of a hostile foreign power*[1674].

At the origin of these accusations, a classified file, collected by Christopher Steele - an ex-British agent - on behalf of a private intelligence agency - Fusion GPS - and transmitted to the FBI. On October 21, 2016, before the judge in charge of counter-intelligence surveillance (FISA[1675]), the FBI swore that Steele's information "*was corroborated*[1676]". The press overreacted[1677], but this was not true. In fact, the accusations were discussed with some members of the administration ten days before the report was published[1678]. The news site *Buzzfeed* published a report claiming that Michael Cohen lied to the congressional committee at the behest of Donald Trump[1679]; but it turned out that the site had fabricated[1680].

1669. "Moscow holds sensitive information on Trump, says US intelligence", *France 24,* January 11, 2017
1670. Michael S. Schmidt, Mark Mazzetti, Matt Apuzzo, "Trump Campaign Aides Had Repeated Contacts with Russian Intelligence," *The New York Times*, February 14, 2017
1671. Erik Wemple, "'In the main, it was not true': Comey denounces New York Times story", *The Washington Post*, June 8, 2017
1672. Greg Miller, "Trump has hidden details of his encounters with Putin from White House officials", www.independent.co.uk, January 13, 2019
1673. "FBI suspects Donald Trump of being a Russian agent", *AFP/Le Point*, January 13, 2019 (updated January 14, 2019)
1674. Michael H. Fuchs, "POTUS: Compromised?", *USNews*, December 28, 2017
1675. Foreign Intelligence Surveillance Act
1676. John Solomon, 'FBI's Steele story falls apart: False intel and media contacts were flagged before FISA', *The Hill*, May 9, 2019
1677. Sonam Sheth, "Evidence corroborating a key dossier allegation against Michael Cohen is stacking up", *Business Insider*, December 27, 2018
1678. John Solomon, 'FBI's Steele story falls apart: False intel and media contacts were flagged before FISA', *The Hill*, May 9, 2019
1679. "Donald Trump asked his ex-lawyer to lie to Congress, according to BuzzFeed", *RFI*, January 19, 2019
1680. Estelle Pattée, "Affaire Buzzfeed: " Si les médias disent "on est transparents, donc on sort tout", c'est la fin des

On March 22, 2018, the Senate Intelligence Committee published its first report. Classified as TOP SECRET, it concludes that there was no collusion between Donald Trump's campaign and Russia[1681]. But it received almost no coverage in the French-speaking press. It was only in December 2018 that some media reported Trump's denials: a way of discrediting the Commission's conclusions by putting them in Trump's mouth[1682].

Finally, in March 2019, after 27 months of investigation, the Mueller report established that none of the most serious accusations against Donald Trump could be verified[1683]. The financing of the Steele Report[1684] has not been formally established, despite consistent evidence (including bank statements[1685]) that points to Hillary Clinton's campaign team and the DNC[1686].

This psychodrama fuels the perception that Russia is trying to attack the United States. This is evidenced by the arrest on July 15, 2018 of Mariia Butina, a 29-year-old Russian woman domiciled in the United States and an activist with the *National Rifle Association* (NRA). Arrested on charges of "*conspiracy*" and "*acting as a foreign agent*", she is accused of attempting to establish unofficial links with US politicians and organisations, including organising Russian-American "friendship and dialogue" dinners, contacting US officials and using her personal contacts to promote Russian interests[1687].

The FBI's affidavit is reminiscent of the heyday of McCarthyism: argued with "*I think*" or "*in my experience*", it provides no facts[1688]. *Euronews* headlines *Une agent russe présumée plaide coupable*[1689], the magazine *l'Express* calls her a "*spy*"[1690], and the media *20 Minutes* claims that she has been "*charged with espionage*[1691]", the magazine *Le Point* claims that she "*pleaded guilty to being a Russian agent*[1692]",

médias " ", *liberation.fr*, January 12, 2017

1681. House Permanent Select Committee on Intelligence, *Report on Russian Active Measures*, (TOP SECRET - Declassified), March 22, 2018

1682. "Russian investigation: 'No collusion' claims Trump after a cascade of revelations", *AFP/Le Point*, December 8, 2018; Belga, "Russian interference in the USA: 'No collusion' between his campaign team and Moscow, claims Trump", *sudinfo.be*, December 9, 2018

1683. Alan Cullison & Dustin Volz, "Mueller Report Dismisses Many Steele Dossier Claims," *The Wall Street Journal*, April 19, 2019

1684. https://www.influencewatch.org/for-profit/fusion-gps/

1685. Tyler Durden, "Nunes: Fusion GPS Bank Records Show Payments From Clinton Campaign & DNC," *zerohedge.com*, September 5, 2019

1686. Rosalind S. Helderman, Adam Entous & Devlin Barrett, "Clinton campaign, DNC paid for research that led to Russia dossier", *The Washington Post*, October 14, 2017

1687. *Russian National Charged in Conspiracy to Act as an Agent of the Russian Federation Within the United States*, Department of Justice, Office of Public Affairs, July 16, 2018

1688. See www.justice.gov/opa/press-release/file/1080766/download and Wikipedia, "Russian interference in the 2016 United States elections"

1689. Anne-Lise Fantino, "United States: alleged Russian agent pleads guilty", *en.euronews.com*, December 11, 2018

1690. Lucas Godignon/AFP, "Les deux vies de Maria Butina, étudiante et espionne russe", *lexpress.fr*, July 18, 2018

1691. "United States: Russian woman close to NRA charged with espionage", *20 Minutes/AFP*, July 17, 2018

1692. "États-Unis: 18 mois de prison pour une agente russe coupable d'ingérence", *Le Point*, April 26, 2019

Paris Match and *Europe 1* underline the fact that the young Russian was not part of the Russian services, but claim that she practiced "*light espionage*" (!) and "*was part of a Kremlin plot*[1693]".

But these are lies and conspiracies, because the charges against her do not mention espionage or membership of an intelligence structure[1694]. In reality, she is charged with participating in lobbying activities as a foreigner, without being duly registered as required by US law, which makes her guilty of "*conspiracy*". But she is 'conspiring' alone, as she has no 'accomplices'. In fact, naively, she aspired to improve US-Russia relations and had written a concept in March 2015 called the "*Diplomacy Project*" aimed at revitalizing ties between the two countries "*through official institutions*" and social events. Ironically, Mariia Butina is also politically active in Russia, in the party of... Alexei Navalny, an opponent of Vladimir Putin[1695]! She was finally released in October 2019 after being tortured and held incommunicado for several months.

The West has gone mad!

California Democratic Congressman Adam Schiff, chairman of the House Intelligence Committee, summarises the accusations of collusion against Donald Trump's campaign team and Russia, despite the release of the Mueller Report. Each of these is refuted by investigative journalist Aaron Maté, in a video made for *The Grayzone*, an independent US media outlet, which we reprint here[1696]:

> *The Russians offered Donald Trump to smear the Democratic candidate.* This is not true. This is an email sent by Rob Goldstone, a Briton who is an agent for a Russian pop star, to Donald Trump Junior, offering him a meeting with a Russian lawyer, who allegedly had compromising documents on Hillary Clinton. In fact, none of the protagonists in this affair are official or remotely linked to the Russian government, nor sponsored by it[1697].
>
> *Paul Manafort, a member of Donald Trump's campaign team, allegedly gave information to a Russian oligarch.* This is not true. The accusation is based on an email between Manafort and one of his colleagues about how he could exploit his position to get close to Russian oligarch Oleg Deripaska, to whom he owed money. In reality, there was no exchange of benefits between the

1693. "Aux États-Unis, 18 mois de prison pour Maria Butina, agent russe coupable d'ingérence", *Paris Match/AFP*, April 26, 2019; "États-Unis: 18 mois de prison pour une agente russe coupable d'ingérence", *Europe 1*, April 26, 2019

1694. *Criminal Complaint*, United States District Court for the District of Columbia, July 14, 2018 (www.justice.gov/opa/press-release/file/1080761/download)

1695. "Давайте проголосуем, раз уж можно голосовать", *navalny.com*, May 6, 2014

1696. Aaron Maté, "Congressman Adam Schiff's Russiagate Delusions Are Not Okay", *The Grayzone*, April 10, 2019

1697. "Rob Goldstone on His Infamous Russia Email: 'I Had No Idea What I Was Talking About'", *npr.com*, September 25, 2018

two men in relation to the Trump campaign[1698]. Paul Manafort's indictments have nothing to do with the campaign, but with tax issues related to his lobbying activities in Ukraine… against Russia[1699]!

A member of Trump's campaign team allegedly provided polls on voting intentions to Russian intelligence agents. The person in question is Konstantin V. Kilimnik, a Russian-Ukrainian, who is accused of having "links" with Russian intelligence agencies. In reality, we know nothing about this. Robert Mueller himself admits that the FBI has never been able to prove these accusations[1700].

Donald Trump is said to have approved of Russia hacking into Hillary Clinton's emails (the BBC even claims that he "*encouraged*" Russia to do so[1701]!). This is not true. In fact, this accusation comes from a speech by Donald Trump in which he refers to the 30,000 emails that Hillary Clinton evaded official controls by using a private server while she was Secretary of State. He quipped that "*Russia, China or any other country*" would be wrong not to take advantage of this indiscipline.

Trump's son-in-law allegedly tried to establish a secret communication channel with Moscow using Russian facilities. Misinformation. In fact, a few days after Donald Trump's election, Jared Kushner made contact with the Russian embassy, in order to exchange information about Syria. This exchange required a secure line, which neither the campaign team nor the Russian embassy had, so nothing was done until President Trump's inauguration[1702]. Kushner has not been charged with lying to Mueller or Congress.

Candidate Trump has reportedly authorised a member of his campaign team to make contact with WikiLeaks. Misinformation. Indeed, after the announcement of the forthcoming publication of Democratic Party emails, Roger Stone contacted WikiLeaks, in order to find out the content of these emails; and after July 22, Steve Bannon allegedly asked Stone for details of the following disclosures. In fact, this shows that these disclosures were independent of the Trump team, and that they had no knowledge of the operation. Moreover,

1698. Aaron Blake, "A Russian oligarch offers a significant denial in the Mueller probe", *The Washington Post*, February 12, 2019

1699. Graham Stack, "Everything you know about Paul Manafort is wrong", www.kyivpost.com, September 17, 2018

1700. Kenneth P. Vogel & Andrew E. Kramer, "Russian Spy or Hustling Political Operative? The Enigmatic Figure at the Heart of Mueller's Inquiry," *The New York Times*, February 23, 2019.

1701. Ashley Parker & David E. Sanger, "Donald Trump Calls on Russia to Find Hillary Clinton's Missing Emails", *The New York Times*, July 27, 2016; BBC News, "Donald Trump 'encourages Russia to hack Clinton emails' BBC News", *YouTube*, July 28, 2016

1702. Mehreen Khan, "Kushner denies setting up secret 'back channel' with Moscow", *Financial Times*, July 24, 2017

the 'collusion' between WikiLeaks and Russian intelligence services has always been refuted by Julian Assange.

Donald Trump's future National Security Advisor tried to make contact with the Russians, in order to weaken US sanctions, and allegedly lied to the FBI about these contacts. This is a lie. In fact, in the weeks following Donald Trump's election, General Michael Flynn, the future National Security Advisor, did make contact with Russian Ambassador Sergei Kislyak. But it was not about US sanctions, but about thwarting an Obama administration resolution in the UN Security Council to condemn Israeli settlements in the occupied territories[1703]. Trump was responding to a request from Netanyahu to influence the UN decision[1704]. The Russian ambassador refused. So the only collusion here is with… Israel! After the rumours about Russian interference in the elections, the Obama administration took a series of new sanctions against Russia. Michael Flynn then got back in touch with the Russian ambassador to reassure him about Trump's intentions after he took office. The transcripts of the phone conversations are known, and it is known that there was no transaction between the Trump team and the Russian government.

Trump wanted to build a tower in Moscow and sought to ingratiate himself with the government. Misinformation. In fact, as his lawyer Michael Cohen testified before the Congressional Committee, Trump thought that if he didn't win this election, it would give him great publicity, and he planned to build a tower in that case. In the end, no concrete steps or payments were made for this construction.

10.2.6. Conclusions for Russiagate

As the months go by, the Russian interference in the American presidential election appears to be a gigantic hoax. In the first instance, the Democrats' challenge is to ensure the legitimacy of the primary result in favour of Hillary Clinton; and in the second instance, after the shock of an election whose outcome no one had obviously foreseen, the party seeks to delegitimise President Trump. For example, the media focused on the attacks on the DNC, but little mention was made of the fact that the Republican National Committee (RNC) had also been subject to cyber attacks[1705]. Similarly, they

1703. Aaron Maté, "The Trump Team Definitely Colluded With a Foreign Power-Just Not the One You Think", *The Nation*, December 5, 2017; Kevin Breuninger & Dan Mangan, "Michael Flynn transcripts released, calls with Russian diplomat detailed", *CNBC*, May 29, 2020

1704. Kate O'Keeffe & Farnaz Fassihi, "Inside the Trump Team's Push on Israel Vote That Mike Flynn Lied About", *The Wall Street Journal*, January 5, 2018

1705. See William Bastone, "RNC E-Mail Was, In Fact, Hacked By Russians," *The Smoking Gun*, December 13, 2016; Paul Sperry, "Mueller All but Ignores the Other Russian Hack Target: the GOP," *RealClearInvestigations*, July 17, 2018

focused on how the DNC emails were obtained, but neglected their content, which could have been devastating for the Democratic Party. In the end, Russiagate was a masterful way of masking the weaknesses of the Democratic candidate and her strategy.

The French reading of the American presidential election is based on linear thinking, influenced by its own political culture, where the impact of a campaign strategy is weak. However, in the American system of Great Electors, which gives the states different weight, strategy is of considerable importance. For example, the *ABC News* website *FiveThirtyEight* compared the strategies of the two candidates[1706]. Among other things, it found that Wisconsin was a key state but that Hillary Clinton did not visit it once during the campaign[1707]. In fact, the Democratic candidate abandoned states that she took for granted, while the Trump team focused on states that could 'bring her the most'.

The single largest documented manipulation of the 2016 US election resulted from an $800,000 contract between John Bolton and the British firm Cambridge Analytica, aimed at influencing the electorate in key states. Using data on more than 50 million potential voters, sold by Facebook, the firm enabled more precise and effective targeting of voters by Donald Trump's team in the final days of the campaign[1708].

During the 2017 Senate elections, the Alabama Democratic Party attempted a similar manipulation, which received almost no coverage in the French-language media. Pudimentarily called an "experiment", it was revealed by the *New York Times.* Carried out by the firm New Knowledge, it aimed to promote the Democratic candidate by creating fake Republican accounts on Facebook and Twitter, and using thousands of fake Russian bots to suggest that Republican Roy Moore was backed by Russia[1709]. He was defeated by 22,000 votes, even though the state had not had a Democratic senator since 1992. The newspaper *Le Monde* saw this as a defeat for Trump, but did not mention this 'cheating'[1710]. Probably rightly so, because according to the *Times*, his $100,000 budget "*was probably too small to have a significant effect on the election*", the total cost of which amounted to $51 million. Yet during the presidential election, "the Russians"

1706. Walt Hickey, "Which Tipping-Point States Favor Trump?", *fivethirtyeight.com*, November 2, 2016

1707. Christophe Deroubaix, "L'abstention frappe plus Clinton que Trump", *humanite.fr*, November 10, 2016

1708. Sabrina Siddiqui, "Cambridge Analytica's US election work may violate law, legal complaint argues", *The Guardian*, March 27, 2018

1709. Alan Blinder, Scott Shane, 'Secret Experiment in Alabama Senate Race Imitated Russian Tactics', *The New York Times*, December 19, 2018; Tony Romm, Craig Timberg & Aaron C Davis, 'Billionaire LinkedIn co-founder apologises for funding 'Russian-style' disinformation group in Alabama Senate race', *The Independent*, December 27, 2018; Adriana Cohen, 'Democrats' fake data scheme in Alabama casts doubt on James Comey investigation', *The Boston Herald*, December 30, 2018 (accessed January 30, 2019).

1710. "En Alabama, la victoire démocrate est un revers politique majeur pour Trump", *Le Monde / AFP*, December 13, 2017

invested less than $100,000 in Facebook, a drop in the bucket compared to the $2.4 billion spent by the two presidential candidates.

In October 2019, the Senate Intelligence Committee published its final report. The report relays simplistic prejudices alongside gratuitous assertions, but nevertheless confirms that:

> *The overwhelming majority of the content disseminated by the IRA did not express clear support for any of the presidential candidates*[1711].

A month later, the *Journal of the American Academy of Sciences* published an in-depth study of 'tweets' during the election campaign, which concluded that the accounts created by the IRA had no impact on voter behaviour[1712]. All indications are that Russiagate is merely the 'hysterisation' of a 'click-trap' campaign run by groups of computer scientists in Russia and Romania to make money[1713]. If the Russian government had indeed interfered in the election, it is not clear why and how Russia would have leveraged this work, since there is no evidence that it was rigged.

It is rather pathetic that the country that has probably instigated the most coups in the world, that has been the most involved - including criminally - in the affairs of other countries, that has supported and organised terrorist acts, and that has attempted to assassinate Fidel Castro 638 times[1714] (!), is now whining about the possibility that others might interfere in its affairs[1715].

1711. *(U) Report of the Select Committee on Intelligence on Russian Active Measures Campaigns and Interference in the 2016 U.S. Election*, Volume II: Russia's Use of Social Media, October 2019, p. 32

1712. Christopher A. Bail, Brian Guay, Emily Maloney, Aidan Combs, D. Sunshine Hillygus, Friedolin Merhout, Deen Freelon, and Alexander Volfovsky (eds. By Arild Underdal), *Assessing the Russian Internet Research Agency's impact on the political attitudes and behaviors of American Twitter users in late 2017*, approved October 22, 2019 (www.pnas.org/cgi/doi/10.1073/pnas.1906420116)

1713. Hunt Allcott and Matthew Gentzkow, "Social Media and Fake News in the 2016 Election", *Journal of Economic Perspectives*, Volume 31, No. 2, Spring 2017, pp 211-236

1714. Duncan Campbell, "638 ways to kill Castro", *The Guardian*, August 3, 2006; "How Castro survived 638 very cunning assassination attempts", www.abc.net.au, November 28, 2016

1715. List of countries where the United States intervened militarily or attempted to actively influence a political process through clandestine actions: China (1945-46), France (1948-1950), Italy (1948-1952), Syria (1949), Korea (1950-53), China (1950-53), Iran (1953), Guatemala (1954), Tibet (1950-), Indonesia (1958), Cuba (1959-), Congo (1960-65), Iraq (1960-63), Dominican Republic (1961), Vietnam (1961-1975), Brazil (1964), Congo (1964), Guatemala (1964), Laos (1964-73), Dominican Republic (1965-66), Peru (1965), Greece (1967), Guatemala (1967-69), Cambodia (1969-70), Chile (1970-73) Argentina (1976), Turkey (1980), Poland (1980-81), El Salvador (1981-92), Nicaragua (1981-90), Cambodia (1980-95), Angola (1980), Lebanon (1982-84), Grenada (1983), Philippines (1986), Libya (1986), Iran (1987-88), Libya (1989) Panama (1989-90), Iraq (1991), Kuwait (1991), Somalia (1992-94), Iraq (1992-96), Bosnia (1995), Iran (1998), Sudan (1998), Afghanistan (1998), Serbia (1999), Afghanistan (2001), Iraq (2003-), Somalia (2006-2007), Libya (2011-), Syria (2011-)

10.3 "Russia Influenced the British Vote on Brexit"

On June 23, 2016, in a historic vote, 51.9% of British voters decided to leave the European Union. Since 2014, polls had shown a very divided public opinion on the European question[1716]. For European political elites, 'common sense' could only be in favour of Europe; thus, the result is interpreted as a disavowal. The fear that the phenomenon would be repeated elsewhere led the 'experts' and other European governments, including France, to dramatise the '*leap into the unknown*' and to predict disaster. The fear is very real, since in January 2018, President Macron confessed to the BBC that the French would probably agree to leave Europe if they were consulted by referendum[1717].

An explanation for this unexpected decision must therefore be found quickly... Initially, false promises are mentioned, such as the reallocation of European contributions to British social security. Secondly, in the wake of the "Russiagate" in the United States, the search is on for the "bad guys". Russia naturally comes to mind. The British Parliament's report on disinformation and the exploitation of fake news notes:

> *In November 2017, the Prime Minister accused Russia of interfering in the elections and spreading "fake news" in order to "use information as a weapon" and sow discord in the West*[1718].

But he concludes:

> *However, we would like to reiterate that the Government has not had evidence of the successful use of disinformation by foreign actors, including Russia, to influence UK democratic processes*[1719].

Asked what the term 'successful' means, the British Secretary of State replied:

> *We have found nothing to persuade us that Russia's interference had a material impact on the way people choose to vote in elections. It is not that they did not try, but we have not seen evidence of such a material impact*[1720].

1716. See Wikipedia, "List of polls on the referendum on the United Kingdom's continued membership of the European Union".

1717. "Macron says France would 'probably' vote to leave EU if country held referendum", *YouTube*, January 21, 2018; Silvia Amaro, "France would have voted to leave EU too if in UK's situation, French leader Macron says", CNBC, January 22, 2018.

1718. *Disinformation and 'fake news'- Interim Report: Government Response to the Committee's Fifth Report of Session 2017-19*, Document HC 1630, House of Commons, October 23, 2018, (p. 16)

1719. *Disinformation and 'fake news'- Interim Report: Government Response to the Committee's Fifth Report of Session 2017-19*, Document HC 1630, House of Commons, October 23, 2018, (p. 16)

1720. *Disinformation and 'fake news': Final Report*, Paragraph 241, www.parliament.uk, 2017

In short: we don't know, but no impact has been observed. As for social networks, Simon Milner, Facebook's policy director for the Middle East and Africa, said:

> *We didn't see, in the last general election, the Brexit vote or the 2015 general election, any investigative journalism - for example - that would have suggested that many campaigns were being funded by third parties. [...] There is no evidence that this is happening*[1721].

In June 2019, Nick Clegg, former deputy prime minister, MP and deputy head of Facebook, confirmed that there was "*absolutely no evidence*" that Russia had influenced the vote, and that the social network had seen "no *significant attempts by external forces*" to do so, while noting that "*the roots of British Euroscepticism run deep*[1722]", and therefore there was no need for Russian intervention[1723].

As for Twitter, 419 accounts - considered to be based in Russia - issued 3,468 "tweets" on the subject of Brexit, 78% of which were made *after* the vote[1724]! But this does not prevent the newspaper *Libération from* claiming that there was Russian interference in the vote, without giving a single element that confirms it[1725]. Apart from general considerations on actions attributed to Russia (such as a power failure on election day), the journalist creates a confusion between what "comes from Russia" and what would be carried out by the Russian government.

The case rebounds in July 2020, as Britain faces post-CoVid-19 difficulties. The accusations against Russia resurface, echoed by the international press[1726]. But no one is pointing out that these accusations are based on hot air. In Parliament, Dominic Raab, the Foreign Secretary, said:

> *Although there is no evidence of a broad-based Russian campaign against the general election, any attempt to interfere in our democratic processes is totally unacceptable*[1727].

1721. *Disinformation and 'fake news': Final Report,* Paragraph 251, www.parliament.uk, 2017

1722. "Facebook: Nick Clegg says 'no evidence' of Russian interference in Brexit vote", *BBC News,* June 24, 2019

1723. Chris Baynes, 'Facebook found 'no evidence'of Russian meddling in Brexit vote, says lobbyist Nick Clegg', *The Independent,* June 24, 2019

1724. Robert Booth, Matthew Weaver, Alex Hern, Stacee Smith & Shaun Walker, 'Russia used hundreds of fake accounts to tweet about Brexit, data shows', *The Guardian,* November 14, 2017

1725. Sonia Delesalle-Stolper, "Brexit: la Russie aussi y a mettre le doigt, révélent les grandes oreilles britanniques", *Libération,* November 15, 2017

1726. Cécile Ducourtieux, "Le Royaume-Uni accuse la Russie de cyberattaques et d'interférences dans ses élections", *Le Monde,* July 16, 2020 (updated, July 17, 2020); Alexandre Counis, "Brexit: le gouvernement britannique accusé d'avoir sous-estimé le risque d'ingérence russe dans la campagne de 2016", *Les Echos,* July 21, 2020; "Ingérence russe: des députés britanniques demandent une enquête sur la campagne du Brexit", *France24,* July 21, 2020.

1727. *Dominic Raab (Secretary of State for Foreign and Commonwealth Affairs) - Cyber Security: Update: Written statement - HCWS384,* www.parliament.uk, 16 July 2020

Once again, a problem is being created out of thin air. In reality, Russia's interference is a cover for the traditional Euroscepticism of the British people and the complete lack of a European strategy for dealing with the refugee crisis between 2014 and 2016. Western elites are woefully lacking in imagination when it comes to developing strategies, whether in the political or military sphere.

10.4 "Russia Tried to Influence Macron's Election"

The hysteria created in the United States by the hypothesis of Russian intervention in the American elections has not spared France. In fact, we are riding the wave created by the election of Donald Trump, fuelled by the speculations of Richard Ferrand in February 2017[1728] and of Mounir Mahjoubi, IT manager of the En Marche campaign[1729]. *BFM TV* unequivocally points the finger at Russia[1730], while by Ferrand's own admission, the "*2,000 attacks [...] very clearly come from Ukraine*[1731]". As for the reasons for such interference, Ferrand maintains that Putin is seeking to extend his influence[1732]... To what end and how? No answer. This is silly.

This distortion of the facts allows the media to kill two birds with one stone: against Trump and against Russia, while opening the door to accusations about the Brexit referendum and Emmanuel Macron's campaign[1733]! An illustration of the 'post-truth' phenomenon...

In fact, in February 2017, candidate Macron is neck and neck with Fillon, but he has no programme and his electorate is still fragile. An Ifop poll shows that his electorate is the least convinced of his choice[1734]. It is therefore necessary to strengthen him and give him a stature by showing that he is the target of Russia. Ferrand's accusations have no technical basis: interviewed on the ".pol" platform, he gives the runaround and brings only circumstantial elements. He

1728. Richard Ferrand, "Don't let Russia destabilise the presidential election in France", *lemonde.fr*, February 14, 2017

1729. Martin Untersinger, "En marche! denounces "organised" and "convergent" computer attacks", *lemonde.fr*, February 14, 2017

1730. "The site of "En Marche!" again victim of a Russian attack", *BFM TV*, February 14, 2017

1731. "When hacking threatens the presidential election", *France 3 (www.francetvinfo.fr)*, February 16, 2017 (updated March 30, 2017). NdA: the expression "*very clearly*" is spoken by Ferrand (see video), but is not included in the text quote!

1732. "Richard Ferrand takes aim at Russia after computer attacks on Macron", *The Huffington Post/YouTube*, February 16, 2017

1733. "La campagne d'Emmanuel Macron dans le cible de pirates russes", *Lemonde.fr*, April 25, 2017

1734. Arnaud Focraud, "Présidentielle: pourquoi les sondages sont incapables de prévoir l'affiche du second tour", *Le Journal du Dimanche*, April 18, 2017 (updated July 27, 2017); Julien Absalon, "Présidentielle 2017: Macron doit composer avec un électorat friable", *RTL*, March 6, 2017

specifies that even if it were a "*publicity stunt*", he would not admit it[1735]! This is simply childish.

On May 5, 2017, two days before the second round of the presidential elections, the En Marche movement announced that it had been the subject of a computer attack and that some 20,000 emails had been hacked. Immediately, Russian interference was mentioned. The British newspaper *The Independent* quotes Vitali Kremez, director of the IT security firm "Flashpoint", who claims that the hackers belong to the entity FANCY BEAR[1736], which allegedly attacked the American Democratic Party in 2016. But in fact, we don't know. An analysis produced by *slate.fr* shows that the origin of the leaks is probably in France and that in addition to the "leaked" emails, there are also forgeries that do not come from the hacking in question[1737]. The American magazine *Forbes*[1738] is investigating and has the same doubts about Russia's responsibility. The "Macronleaks" could therefore be a machination orchestrated in France itself.

In June, Guillaume Poupard, director of the French National Agency for Information Systems Security (ANSSI), responsible for cybersecurity in France, stated that "*there is no evidence to suggest that Russia is behind this attack*[1739]". He told the *Associated Press* that the attack does not have the characteristics of a state action, that there is nothing to link it to Russia, and that it "*could even have been carried out by an isolated individual*[1740]". So: nothing.

However, the report drawn up jointly by the Centre for Analysis, Forecasting and Strategy (CAPS) of the French Ministry of Foreign Affairs and the Strategic Research Institute of the Military Academy (IRSEM) of the French Ministry of the Armed Forces in 2018 does not mention these observations, and states that those responsible for the leaks are 'with *relative certainty [...] linked to Russian interests*[1741]'. Media such as *Le Parisien*[1742] and *Le Monde*[1743] will return to the 'Russian threat' during the European elections... without providing any factual elements. In Belgium, the daily *La Libre* goes so far as to claim that the same

1735. "Macron and Russia: Richard Ferrand denies any com' stunt by En Marche!", *lelab.europe1.fr*, February 16, 2017

1736. Lizzie Dearden, "Emmanuel Macron email leaks 'linked to Russian-backed hackers who attacked Democratic National Committee'", *The Independent*, May 6, 2017

1737. Jean-Marc Manach, "We examined the 'Macron Leaks' for you, here's what we found", *slate.fr*, May 9, 2017

1738. Thomas Brewster, "Did Russia Hack Macron? The Evidence Is Far From Conclusive", *Forbes*, May 8, 2017

1739. Louis Adam, "MacronLeaks: l'Anssi ne confirme pas la piste russe", *ZDNet*, June 2, 2017; Louis Adam, "Macronleaks: Alors M.Poupard, c'est la Russie?", www.zdnet.fr, June 8, 2017

1740. John Leicester, "AP Interview: France warns of risk of war in cyberspace", *AP News*, June 1st, 2017

1741. Jean-Baptiste Jeangène Vilmer, Alexandre Escorcia, Marine Guillaume & Janaina Herrera, *Les manipulations de l'information*, CAPS/IRSEM, Paris, August 2018

1742. Henri Vernet & Ava Djamshidi, "Comment la Russie veut influencer sur les élections européennes", *leparisien.fr*, February 27, 2019

1743. Agathe Dahyot, "'MacronLeaks': almost all the tracks lead to the East", *lemonde.fr*, June 15, 2019

actors attacked the telephone operator Proximus and NATO[1744]. But no one mentions the fact that one of the tracks leads to… the United States[1745]!

During Vladimir Putin's visit in May 2017, Emmanuel Macron did not mention these alleged cyber attacks[1746]. Instead, he accuses the Russian media *Sputnik* and *RT* of having "*produced untruths*" during the French presidential campaign. But he is lying. For they did not 'produce' them, at most they relayed false news produced in France itself, as demonstrated by a debunking of *Libération*[1747].

In all likelihood, the Russian government did not interfere in the French campaign, but a doubt has been generated that will be 'dragged out' until the 2019 European elections. Despite some factual errors, *France-Culture* is one of the few French media to offer a more honest analysis of the situation[1748]. The affair resurfaced in December[1749] - without any new element - and was taken up by Emmanuel Macron in February 2020 during thc Munich Security Conference[1750].

Moreover, if there had really been interference, no doubt a true democracy would have invalidated the election!… In fact, this is just speculation. If a law on fake news had been in force during the 2017 presidential election, La République en Marche (LREM) would certainly have been the first victim… In fact, this is simply a way of creating stature at the expense of Russia, without any concrete evidence.

10.5. Conclusions on "Russian Interference"

As it stands, it is neither possible nor honest to say with certainty that Russia is behind attempts at interference. In fact, we do not know, although the available evidence points towards overdramatisation and Western disinformation. Assuming that Russia is the main suspect, the first question to ask is: to what end?

The idea of Russia "*trying to divide*" Europe seems to be a self-sufficient explanation. In fact, these allegations are based on a rather simplistic

1744. Christophe Lamfalussy, "Macronleaks: Les pirates sont les mêmes que ceux qui se sont attaqués à Proximus et à l'Otan", LaLibre.be, April 27, 2017 (Updated May 6, 2017)
1745. "Russland im Verdacht - eine Spur führt in die USA", www.20min.ch, May 6, 2017
1746. Corentin Durand, "Macron and Putin: when denouncing fake news overshadows Russian cyberwar", *numerama.com*, May 30, 2017
1747. Vincent Coquaz, "Did RT and Sputnik relay fake news during the campaign as En Marche says?", *Check-News.fr*, June 6, 2018
1748. Philippe Reltien and Cellule investigation de Radio France, "La menace d'une ingérence russe plane-t-elle sur les élections européennes?", *France-Culture*, March 22, 2019
1749. "Russian military intelligence behind hacking of Macron's campaign, according to Le Monde", *AFP/RTBF. be*, December 7, 2019
1750. "Macron: Russia will continue to "try to destabilise" the West", *Rfi.fr*, February 15, 2020 (updated February 16, 2020)

interpretation of Soviet policy and its extrapolation to the present day (since Putin was a KGB agent!).

Until the 20th Communist Party Congress, the USSR considered war with the West inevitable. But from 1956 onwards, with the principle of *peaceful coexistence*, it was considered 'avoidable', but the risk remained. In this context, Soviet disinformation was always linked to very concrete objectives, and not to generic aims, as it is presented today. It followed two main axes: a) to show the Soviet population that their system was superior to the other (in order to encourage them to accept living in a war economy); b) to decouple Europe from the United States (in order to take away its nuclear "umbrella"). This is why the USSR was then rather in favour of a European defence (without Germany)[1751], and supported the pacifist and anti-nuclear movements (which would become "The Greens" in Germany[1752]).

The tendency to convert shades of grey into a binary image (white/black) leads to misunderstandings. In 2017, Marine Le Pen's visit to Vladimir Putin triggered a rhetoric illustrated by Frans Timmermans, Vice-President of the European Commission:

> *The reason Putin supports the far right in Europe is because he knows it weakens and divides us*[1753].

However, it can be seen that the European countries with the most conservative policies (Poland and Hungary) are precisely those that are most fiercely opposed to Russia. The statement is therefore strictly political and aims to influence politics in France, but does not reflect reality. The real problem is that neither the media nor politicians have understood the mechanisms that generate populism (vulgarly called "extreme right").

It can be observed that in almost all countries where Russian interference has been mentioned, the government is caught up in domestic political problems: the issue of linguistic minorities (Baltic countries and Ukraine), mistakes in electoral strategy (the Democratic Party in the United States and France) or poor management of current affairs (in Britain, Sweden and France).

In France since the end of 2018, the "Yellow Vests" have been making news every Saturday in the streets. Such longevity is unprecedented and fuelled by unclear strategies and clumsy communication by the government. In fact, no one has tried to understand the movement: there have been partisan and emotional

1751. *Soviet Views on the "Western European" Movement,* Directorate of Intelligence, CIA, November 30, 1984 (https://www.cia.gov/library/readingroom/docs/CIA-RDP85T00287R001401130001-3.pdf)

1752. Christiane Falbisaner, "Le mouvement de la paix en République Fédérale d'Allemagne", *Autres Temps - Les cahiers du christianisme social,* N° 4, 1984, pp. 72-81

1753. "According to the EU, Putin supports the far right to divide Europe", *RTBF/Belga,* March 30, 2017

readings of the phenomenon, all political tendencies included, and - as is often the case - we have to go to Anglo-Saxon commentators to get a more dispassionate reading[1754]. The lack of understanding here is linked to incompetence, and is difficult to defend: Russia is therefore blamed! An article in the *Times*[1755] of London helps the French media to explain that "*Russia is stirring up protest*"[1756], to "*amplify the divisions*[1757]". With what aim? No answer! In reality, we don't know, as Kevin Limonier, lecturer at the French Institute of Geopolitics at the University of Paris 8, explains on *France-Culture*:

> *For all we know today, Russian interference in the Gilets jaunes movement is fairly minimal to non-existent. There is sympathy for the Russian media among the Gilets jaunes, but we have not seen anything more*[1758].

In France, as in the case of "Russiagate", accusations such as "*we think that...*", "*it could be that...*", "*it is possible...*", etc. become certainties. Hypotheses are assembled on the basis of prejudices dating back to the Cold War, such as "*disinformation is a strong tradition in Russia*[1759]", without providing any evidence to support it. This is the method of conspiracy theory: what "Russians" do becomes an action of "Russia", therefore of the government, and therefore a decision of Vladimir Putin himself... In reality, the politicians who spread these rumours do not hold democracy in high esteem: they simply use it for their own ends...

On the other hand, the American interference in the 1975 referendum on Britain's membership of the European Union is not reported[1760]... More recently, on June 7, 2019, the *Washington Post* reported that Mike Pompeo openly declared that he would do everything in his power to prevent Labour leader Jeremy Corbyn from becoming Prime Minister of Britain[1761]! Yet no French mainstream media will report this interference... Demonstrating that the independence of our media is not a given.

1754. See for example: "Yellow Vests Update: CNN Says They Are Creating Chaos, But Are They?", *Collective Evolution/YouTube*, December 14, 2018

1755. Rhys Blakely, "Russian accounts fuel French outrage online", *The Times*, December 8, 2018

1756. Marianne Enault, "Gilets jaunes: est-elle la Russie derrière de faux comptes qui attisent la contestation sur les réseaux sociaux ?", *Le Journal du Dimanche*, December 9, 2018; Julien Duriez, "Gilets jaunes, des comptes russes attisent les braises sur Twitter", *La Croix*, December 10, 2018

1757. Florian Delafoi, "In the shadow of the 'yellow waistcoats', the Russian threat", *Le Temps*, December 10, 2018

1758. "Macronleaks: was there Russian interference in the French presidential election?", *France-Culture*, December 10, 2019

1759. Henri Vernet & Ava Djamshidi, "Comment la Russie veut influencer sur les élections européennes", *leparisien.fr*, February 27, 2019

1760. Luise Hemmer Pihl, "CIA supported British 1975 Yes to EU", *euobserver.com*, August 18, 2001

1761. Alex Tiffin, 'Mike Pompeo Threatens To Intervene In British Democracy To Stop Corbyn Becoming Prime Minister', *Medium.com*, June 10, 2019

11. NORTH KOREA

11.1 "The North Koreans Have Never Lived Up to their Commitments to Stop Working on their Nuclear Weapon[1762]"

At the Singapore summit on June 12, 2018, Donald Trump and Kim Jung-Un sign a roadmap for normalisation between the two countries. Virtually all commentators claim that North Korea (DPRK[1763]) has never lived up to its commitments until then. But it is carefully hushed up that the root of the problem lies in the fact that the US has *never* fulfilled its obligations.

US intelligence agencies have been interested in the DPRK's nuclear capabilities since the 1980s. But their analyses have remained highly inconsistent, based more on the fluctuations of US foreign policy than on hard facts[1764]. In May 1983, a CIA SECRET report admitted:

> *We have no reason to believe that the North Koreans have the facilities and equipment to develop and test nuclear weapons*[1765].

Indeed, in December 1985, the DPRK joined the Nuclear Non-Proliferation Treaty (NPT). In fact, according to a CIA *East Asia Brief* dated December 27, the Soviets helped the DPRK build a reactor on condition that it joined the NPT[1766]. From 1989 onwards, the US administration accused the Pyong Yang regime of running a clandestine weapons programme, but in fact nothing was

1762. Pierre Haski, "Why war has become possible with North Korea", *Le Nouvel Observateur*, August 7, 2017 (www.nouvelobs.com/editos-et-chroniques/20170807.OBS3090/pourquoi-la-guerre-est-devenue-possible-avec-la-coree-du-nord.html)
1763. Democratic People's Republic of Korea
1764. Jonathan D. Pollack, "The United States, North Korea, and the End of the Agreed Framework", *Naval War College Review*, Vol. 56, No. 3, Summer 2003
1765. *À 10-Years Projection of Possible Events of Nuclear Proliferation Concern*, Directorate of Intelligence, CIA, May 1983, p. 5
1766. https://nsarchive2.gwu.edu/NSAEBB/NSAEBB87/nk06.pdf

known about it. In accordance with its strategy of dissuasion, Pyongyang - like Israel - maintains doubts on this subject.

In 1994, the Clinton administration began negotiations with the North Korean regime to dismantle its nuclear programme in exchange for economic aid. An *Agreed Framework* was signed on October 21, 1994. It provides for the freezing of the activities of the Yongbyon nuclear complex and the reprocessing of plutonium. In exchange, the United States undertook to relax oil restrictions and to build two light water reactors to replace the existing ones and allow the development of civilian energy. The first was to be built within three months and the second after Korea returned its nuclear fuel to international control. At the same time, the two countries were to re-establish diplomatic relations with an exchange of embassies.

The DPRK respects its part of the agreement, but the United States does not: the first oil deliveries are very late, South Korea and Japan, which were supposed to finance the first light water reactor, did not do so, and the American Congress did not want to contribute. So, no reactors… As for the diplomatic aspect: in 2018, the United States has still not recognised North Korea as a sovereign state…[1767]

The issue of uranium enrichment facilities is also raised in this dossier. The NPT allows the production of low-enriched uranium (LEU) (which Article IV describes as an "*inalienable right*"), but prohibits the production of highly enriched uranium (HEU), which is used for nuclear weapons. Although the Agreed Framework does not contain any provisions on the issue of uranium enrichment, it refers to the January 1992 Joint Declaration of the Two Koreas on the Denuclearisation of the Korean Peninsula[1768], which prohibits "*uranium enrichment facilities*" but does not specify whether they are LEU or HEU.

Initially, North Korea strictly implemented the provisions of the Agreed Framework and abandoned its plutonium research programme, but after four years, seeing that the Americans were not fulfilling their end of the bargain, it resumed uranium enrichment activities.

In 2001, with the arrival of the Bush administration, the tone changed. In January 2002, in his State of the Union address, President Bush included North Korea in his "Axis of Evil". But his attention turned to another target: Iraq. The diplomatic contacts initiated under the Clinton presidency and the Framework Agreement were formally abandoned:

> *We do not negotiate with evil, we destroy it*[1769]*!*

1767. Fred Kaplan, "Sorry, Trump, but Talking to North Korea Has Worked", *Slate.com*, October 10, 2017

1768. *Joint Declaration on the Denuclearization of the Korean Peninsula*, signed on January 20, 1992, entered into force on February 19, 1992.

1769. Fred Kaplan, op.cit.

In October 2002, James Kelly, Assistant Secretary of State for the Far East and Pacific, visiting Pyongyang, accused the regime of conducting a secret weapons-grade uranium enrichment (HEU) programme in breach of the 1994 Agreed Framework. No longer feeling bound by the agreement, the United States stopped oil deliveries on November 14, 2002.

Two factors explain the US reversal. First, the rapprochement between the DPRK and its main Asian partners had aroused its mistrust: the Koreas' plan to build a railway between the North and the South in April 2002, and the rapprochement efforts led by Japanese Prime Minister Junichiro Koizumi - without the 'knowledge' of the United States - which culminated in his visit to Pyongyang in September 2002. The Bush administration feared that its foreign policy would be dictated by the agendas of its partners[1770]. This is why the US initially dragged its feet and refused to clear the demilitarised zone along the railway line.

The second factor is that the 2002 US accusations are fragile. A CIA report dated November 19, 2002 and submitted to members of Congress[1771] shows that the intelligence services have only a very partial view of the situation in the country, based mainly on hearsay and approximations. The analyses tend to ignore the distinction between LEU and HEU. Reports are imprecise, couched in terms of probability or potential, but without any indication of their reality in practice: among the possible interpretations, the worst one was systematically adopted. This is the technique known as "worst case", which we will see again with Iraq and then Iran a few years later.

The DPRK then found itself in a situation quite similar to that of Iraq: the possibility of an American attack became likely. Logically enough, it retaliated by resuming its enrichment activities, which it had frozen since 1994, and withdrew from the NPT on January 10, 2003. It will however continue to accept inspections by the International Atomic Energy Agency (IAEA). In June 2004, the United States proposed a regional initiative supported by six countries (including China) for the denuclearisation of the peninsula, but put as a precondition the obligation for the DPRK to officially confess that it was carrying out prohibited enrichment activities... which it naturally refused, dooming the initiative to failure. The US accusations have never been proven, as Zhou Wenzhong, Chinese Vice Foreign Minister, pointed out on June 7, 2004:

> *So far, the US has not presented convincing evidence that the uranium (enrichment) programme exists. We don't know if it exists*[1772].

1770. Jonathan D. Pollack, *op. cit.*

1771. https://fas.org/nuke/guide/dprk/nuke/cia111902.html

1772. Selig S. Harrison, "Did North Korea Cheat?", *Foreign Affairs*, January/February 2005

The DPRK tests its first nuclear device on October 9, 2006. Two days later, the Ministry of Foreign Affairs states that

> *(its) nuclear test was entirely due to the US nuclear threat, sanctions and pressure (and that it) was obliged to prove that it possessed nuclear weapons in order to protect its sovereignty*[1773].

The communiqué states that North Korea "*maintains its commitment to denuclearise the peninsula through dialogue and negotiations*". The Bush team then realised that it had completely destabilised the situation and tried to backtrack. A new agreement was reached in early 2007, but it was poorly crafted and hastily negotiated and ineffective.

Curiously enough, while it is now known how the Bush administration manipulated information in order to attack Iraq, no one questioned his assessment of the situation in North Korea, which was aimed at denigrating Bill Clinton's policy[1774].

It was essentially American bully-boy behaviour that pushed North Korea away from its international commitments. In fact, the DPRK only advanced in nuclear technology (in terms of testing, ballistic missile development and fusion technology) after the Americans rejected diplomatic solutions. The Americans were unable to anticipate the reaction of the North Korean leadership, just as they were unable to understand that of the Islamists. The gunboat policy that marked American foreign policy and worked until the beginning of the 20th century is now outdated, but it is still supported by a number of subservient allies such as Britain, Poland, the Czech Republic and - newly - France.

Unlike the West, North Korea has learned the lessons of 2002. The North Korean leader's approach to the Singapore summit is remarkable for its finesse and skill in imposing his own agenda on the Americans. Having realised that the Americans were afraid of being "double-crossed by the right" by their Asian allies, Kim Yong-Un approached them: this is what made Donald Trump change his mind, who had initially said he did not want to meet him.

The West operates with the same mentality that led to the First and Second World Wars: victory is conceived as in a football match. For example, after the Singapore summit, some commentators castigated Trump's proposal to freeze exercise activities with South Korea, using the example of the TEAM SPIRIT exercises in 1992, which the US had agreed to suspend in exchange for IAEA inspections. These inspections were relatively effective and detected that the DPRK was keeping bomb-making material. But as the DPRK resisted further

1773. B. Dan Wood, *Presidential Saber Rattling: Causes and Consequences*, Cambridge University Press, Cambridge, October 2012, p. 127

1774. Selig S. Harrison, "Did North Korea Cheat?", *Foreign Affairs*, January/February 2005

inspections, the US unilaterally decided to reinstate the exercises, prompting Pyongyang to refuse all inspections. The best is the enemy of the good: the Americans were suddenly blind[1775].

The Americans are incapable of strategies that are not based on a balance of power. This is why they are unable to fight asymmetric adversaries. Thus, when General James Mattis, then Secretary of Defense, calls on the North Koreans to "*stop considering any action that could lead to the end of its regime and the destruction of its people*[1776]", he tends to stiffen them. Indeed, they have not forgotten that during the Korean War, the Americans - according to General LeMay, then commander of the *Strategic Air Command* - destroyed 20% of the North and South Korean population[1777]!

Military exercises are traditionally a way of camouflaging war preparations, and can easily become their starting point. However, the US-Korean manoeuvres (TEAM SPIRIT, KEY RESOLVE or FOAL EAGLE) are not only defence exercises, but also invasion exercises against North Korea[1778]. They therefore result each time in a rise in the level of alert in North Korea, which mobilises resources that are essential to the economy. However, these exercises are usually - and deliberately - conducted in April-May (during the planting season) or August (during the rice harvest), when agriculture is most labour intensive. In the 1990s, this timing contributed (through the lack of fertiliser, due to sanctions) to shortages and famine. One of the ways in which the North Korean leadership has responded to this problem is through the so-called "*byongjin*" policy, which relies on nuclear deterrence to ease the pressure on its economy[1779].

The West has a constant propensity to seek conflict. At the Singapore summit, Donald Trump and Kim Jong-Un agreed on a four-step 'roadmap':

1. The United States and the DPRK are committed to building a new U.S.-DPRK relationship consistent with the desire of the peoples of both countries for peace and prosperity.

2. The United States and the DPRK will work together to establish a lasting and stable peace regime on the Korean Peninsula.

3. Reaffirming the Panmunjom Declaration of April 27, 2018, the DPRK is committed to working towards the complete denuclearisation of the Korean Peninsula.

1775. "The Danger of Fake History", *38 North.com*, August 18, 2017

1776. Elizabeth Mclaughlin, "Mattis warns North Korea of 'end of its regime,' 'destruction of its people'," *ABC News*, August 9, 2017

1777. Richard H. Kohn & Joseph P. Harahan (Eds), *Strategic Air Warfare*, Office of Air Force History, United States Air Force, Washington, D.C., 1988

1778. Charlotte Beale, "South Korean and US forces stage 'blitzkrieg' simulation of North Korea beach landing", *The Independent*, March 12, 2016

1779. Wikipedia, article "Byongjin"

4. The United States and the DPRK commit to recovering the remains of POW/MIAs and immediately repatriating those already identified[1780].

In fact, it is a "freeze for freeze" agreement: the Americans refrain from conducting large-scale exercises, and the North Koreans stop testing missiles and nuclear weapons.

But at the Hanoi summit in February 2019, sanctions are still in place, no steps have been taken to open embassies and no peace agreement has been signed. The DPRK has destroyed test tunnels and dismantled a missile test range, and returned the remains of US military personnel. But on the US side, nothing has been done to make the roadmap a reality.

Even the most conservative analysts understood this roadmap as a sequencing of activities[1781]. But in February 2019, Donald Trump reversed the order of what had been agreed and said that sanctions would be lifted only after the dismantling of nuclear facilities[1782]. The North Koreans then held an impromptu press conference to clarify that they were not asking for all sanctions to be lifted at this stage, but only five[1783]. In fact, the Americans had already unilaterally changed the rules of the game. On August 28, 2018, while introducing his new special envoy for North Korea, Mike Pompeo announced that he would "*lead our efforts to achieve President Trump's goal of the final and fully verified denuclearisation of North Korea, as agreed by Chairman Kim Jong-Un*[1784]". But this is not true: the North Korean leader committed to "*work towards complete denuclearisation*" (similar to the wording of Article VI of the Nuclear Non-Proliferation Treaty), with no mention of verification. Moreover, it refers to the whole of the "*Korean Peninsula*" and not just "*North Korea*".

This American stiffening - and failure - is the work of John Bolton, who does not want an agreement[1785]. But in France, people try to blame it on Pyongyang's exaggerated expectations. The debate between "experts" on *France 24* is symptomatic of interpretations based on professions of faith and where the facts play only a secondary role: at no time are the differences on sequencing, which are at the heart of the problem, mentioned[1786].

1780. "READ: Full text of Trump-Kim signed statement", *CNN*, June 12, 2018

1781. Duyeon Kim, "Pompeo Has to Learn Pyongyang's Rules", *Foreign Policy*, July 30, 2018

1782. Alex Ward, "Read the full transcript of Trump's North Korea summit press conference in Vietnam", *Vox*, February 28, 2019

1783. "(2nd LD) (US-NK summit) N.K. seeks partial lifting of sanctions: foreign minister", *en.yna.co.kr*, March 1st, 2019

1784. Michael R. Pompeo, "Remarks on the Appointment of Special Representative for North Korea Stephen Biegun", www.state.gov, August 23, 2018

1785. Tom O'connor, "Donald Trump's North Korea Deal Fell Apart Because of John 'Bomb-'Em' Bolton, Experts Say," *Newsweek*, February 28, 2019

1786. "Second Kim-Trump summit in Vietnam: no agreement, the failure of Trump diplomacy?", *France 24*, February 28, 2019

In the second half of 2019, North Korea's missile launches are widely reported in the press, suggesting that North Korea is not living up to its commitments[1787]. But this is not true. In fact, it was the Americans who broke the agreement in August by conducting the '19-2 DONG MAENG' exercise, aimed at an occupation of North Korea[1788].

But the Western media follow the Trump administration's disinformation quite faithfully - and slavishly. Thus, on May 31, 2019, the 8 p.m. news programme on *France 2* announced that the North Korean "dictator" "*would have had collaborators executed*", notably Kim Hyok-chol, in order to "*take revenge*". The journalist Thomas Sotto (who also hosts a fact-checking programme for young people on *France 4*) certainly uses conditionals, but the message remains affirmative. The traditional press, such as *Le Monde, Le Parisien, France 24*, the *New York Times*, the *Wall Street Journal*, and many others, follow without verifying the information[1789]. It was launched by *Bloomberg*, relaying the South Korean far-right newspaper *Chosun Ilbo*:

> *North Korea executed its special envoy to the United States on espionage charges as its president Kim Jong-Un, staged a purge of the country's top nuclear negotiators after his second summit with President Trump failed, a leading Korean daily reported on Friday.*

But this is not true: on the same day, Kim Hyok-Chol is seen in public while attending a performance by his wife. Bloomberg then rushed to discreetly correct his article[1790]. He was followed by the *New York Times, CNN* and *Reuters*, who discreetly corrected the story without acknowledging their mistake.

However, this is not the first time the Western media has done this. In August 2013, the magazine *Marie-Claire* announced that on August 20 Kim Jong-Un had had 'pop stars' executed, including his girlfriend Hyon Song-Wol[1791]. It was followed by *Le Point*[1792] and - naturally - by *BFMTV*[1793] via the traditional

1787. "North Korea tested a new missile, possibly launched from a submarine," *LEXPRESS.fr / AFP*, October 3, 2019; "New North Korean test of a multiple missile launcher," *Le Figaro / AFP*, October 31, 2019

1788. Yang Seung-sik, "S.Korea, U.S. to Practice Stabilizing N.Korea", *Chosun Ilbo*, August 9, 2019

1789. "North Korea: Kim Jong-Un reportedly had negotiators from failed Hanoi summit executed", *leparisien.fr*, May 31, 2019; "North Korea 'executed' officials after failed Trump summit: report", *News Wires/france24.com*, May 31, 2019; Choe Sang-hun & Edward Wong, 'North Korean Negotiator's Downfall Was Sealed When Trump-Kim Summit Collapsed', *The New York Times*, May 31, 2019; 'Kim Jong Un executes officials after failed Trump summit - News', *Reuters Top News/Twitter*, May 31, 2019; Andrew Jeong & Dasl Yoon, 'North Korea Executed Members of Nuclear-Negotiating Team', *The Wall Street Journal*, May 31, 2019; 'Was North Korea's Chief Negotiator Shot? ", *Mediapart*, June 1st, 2019.

1790. Shinhye Kang & Jihye Lee, "North Korea Executed Envoy Over Trump-Kim Summit, Chosun Reports," *Bloomberg*, May 31, 2019

1791. "Kim Jong-un's ex-girlfriend executed for dancing!", *marieclaire.fr*, August 2013

1792. "Kim Jong-un allegedly had his ex-girlfriend shot", *Lepoint.fr*, August 29, 2013 (updated August 30, 2013)

1793. "North Korea: Kim Jong-un allegedly had his ex-girlfriend executed", *BFMTV*, August 30, 2013

Anglo-Saxon press, such as *The Telegraph*[1794], *USA Today*[1795] or *CNBC*, which stated that she had been shot[1796]... but she would reappear a few months later on television[1797]! In June 2019, the British newspaper *The Mirror* will note that reports of her disappearance had been "*greatly exaggerated*[1798]"!... To say the least!... In fact, all of these media outlets based themselves, without verifying them, on the claims of the *North Korea Strategy Center*, a think-tank based in South Korea. But none of them will apologise to their readers...

In May 2015, *BFMTV* announced that Kim Jong-Un had his aunt Kim Kyong-Hui poisoned in May 2014 because she opposed the construction of an "acquaparc"[1799]! The information was picked up by *Le Point*, *RTL* and several other media[1800]. The Western media thus decided that she had been eliminated by the "regime": the wording is generally in the conditional tense in French-speaking countries, but more categorical in English-speaking countries[1801]. In reality, Kim Kyong-Hui had simply disappeared from the media and in January 2020, she reappeared in public alongside Kim Jong-Un[1802], and some even suggest that she has a new role within the regime[1803].

In February 2016, the Western media announced the elimination of General Ri Yong-Gil, Chief of Staff of the People's Army[1804]... but he reappeared a few months later, at the Communist Party Congress[1805]... with a promotion[1806]! For once, *France24* was one of the rare media to question these false information[1807].

But these repeated fake news stories show that the media are not learning and improving their analytical skills. In April 2020, for example, it was rumoured

---

1794. Julian Ryall, "Kim Jong-un's ex-lover 'executed by firing squad'", *The Telegraph*, August 29, 2013
1795. Kate Seamons, "Report: Kim Jong Un's ex-girlfriend executed", *USA Today*, August 29, 2013
1796. "Death by firing squad for Kim Jong Un's ex, *CNBC*, August 29, 2013 (updated September 3, 2013)
1797. Damien McElroy, "'Executed' Kim Jong-Un girlfriend reappears on North Korea television", *The Telegraph*, May 17, 2014; Ariel Zilber, "Back from the dead! Kim Jong-un's pop star ex-girlfriend is seen alongside North Korean dictator in public after reports she was executed by firing squad for making a sex tape", *dailymail.co.uk*, June 9, 2019
1798. Andrew Gilpin, 'Kim Jong-un's pop star ex seen despite reports she was executed for making a sex tape', *mirror.co.uk*, June 10, 2019
1799. "North Korea: Kim Jong-Un is said to have had his aunt poisoned", *BFM TV*, May 12, 2015
1800. "North Korea: Kim Jong-un's serial executions", *Le Point*, May 13, 2015; Ryad Ouslimani, "Kim Jong Un would have had his aunt poisoned", *RTL.fr*, May 12, 2015 (updated May 13, 2015)
1801. Paula Hancocks, 'North Korean leader ordered aunt to be poisoned, defector says', *CNN*, May 12, 2015; David Blair, 'North Korea's leader Kim Jong-un 'poisoned his aunt'', *The Telegraph*, May 12, 2015
1802. "Kim Jong-un's aunt reappears in public, six years after assassination rumours", *BFM TV*, January 27, 2020; Justin McCurry, "Kim Jong-un's aunt reappears, six years after purge rumours", *The Guardian*, January 27, 2020
1803. "North Korean leader Kim Jong-un's aunt reappears after six years", *BBC News*, January 26, 2020
1804. "North Korea's army chief of staff reportedly executed", *lapresse.ca*, February 10, 2016
1805. Junzhi Zheng, "North Korea: General Ri Yong-gil has been resurrected", *lefigaro.fr*, May 11, 2016
1806. Laura Bicker, "North Korea execution reports - why we should be cautious", *BBC News*, May 31, 2019
1807. Charlotte Boitiaux, "La Corée du Nord, pays de tous les fantasmes médiatiques", *France24*, May 15, 2015 (updated May 22, 2015)

that Kim Jong-Un had died. There is even talk that he was a victim of the coronavirus. This will of course prove to be false[1808]...

Kim Jong-Un is portrayed as temperamental, unpredictable and irrational. This is not true. Koreans are rational, but we do not make the effort to understand them. As in Iraq, Iran, Ukraine or Syria, our prejudices have become certainties, which we use to decide. In reality, Westerners, mainly to please the United States, but also because of their inability to produce independent intelligence analysis, tend to align themselves with the American position. This tendency is almost institutionalised within Nato.

1808. Justin McCurry, "Kim Yo-jong: the sister of Kim Jong-un, fast 'becoming his alter ego'", *The Guardian*, April 20, 2020; Jim Sciutto, Joshua Berlinger, Yoonjung Seo, Kylie Atwood & Zachary Cohen, "US monitoring intelligence that North Korean leader is in grave danger after surgery", *CNN*, April 21, 2020; Justin McCurry, "South Korea and China play down Kim Jong-un's ill-health claims", *The Guardian*, April 21, 2020; "North Korea: Kim Jong-un dead and replaced by a look-alike, the new crazy rumour', *Midi Libre*, May 6, 2020; 'Is Kim Jong-Un dead? Voici le nouveau détail étrange qui vient relancer les rumeurs sur le décès du leader de la Corée du Nord", *Sudinfo.be*, May 20, 2020

12. VENEZUELA

12.1. The context

As an oil-producing country and a founding member of the Organisation of Petroleum Producing Countries (OPEC), Venezuela has long been of interest to the United States. Until the mid-1970s, the black gold was exploited by American companies. In 1975, however, a wave of nationalisations brought together the various operations into a national company, "Petroleos de Venezuela S.A." (PDVSA). But the centre-right governments that held power until the 1990s benefited from the country's wealth without developing or diversifying an economy atrophied around oil. As a result, Venezuela depends on oil for more than 95% of its income.

In December 1998, after two years in prison for trying to seize power in 1992, Hugo Chávez was elected President of the Republic. This marked the beginning of the "Bolivarian Revolution", which reappropriated oil revenues for the benefit of the population. A period of growth followed that no previous government had achieved. The gross national product per capita, which had stagnated between $1,000 and $4,000 for decades, rose to $13,500 in 2010[1809]. Poverty is reduced from 70.8% (1996) to 21% (2010), while extreme poverty falls from 40% (1996) to 7.3% (2010). Child malnutrition falls from 7.7% (1990) to 2.9% (2012). Dependence on imported food products falls from 90% (1980) to 30% (2012)[1810].

In the last decade of the 20th century, the US was absorbed in the aftermath of the Gulf War (1991) and '9/11', with a foreign policy focused on the Middle East and North Africa. Apart from a coup d'état that temporarily overthrew Chávez in 2002[1811], the United States is abandoning the subcontinent, which

1809. Figures: *Worldbank*
1810. Carles Muntaner, Joan Benach & Maria Paez Victor, "The Achievements of Hugo Chavez", *Counterpunch*, December 14, 2012
1811. "Hugo Chávez Departs", *The New York Times*, April 13, 2002

is tilting almost entirely to the left in Venezuela's wake: Chile (March 2000), Brazil (January 2003), Argentina (May 2003), Bolivia (January 2006), Ecuador (January 2007), Paraguay (August 2008), Uruguay (March 2010) and Peru (July 2011). One of the consequences of this shift to the left, dubbed the "pink tide", has been the arrival of other players, such as China, which is taking advantage of this "vacuum" to aggressively move into the continent.

During Barak Obama's second term, the US strategy in the Middle East is facing increasing difficulties. The US is unable to integrate its military operations into a coherent and holistic strategy, resulting in a stiffening of Turkey and instability that is causing the US to change its focus.

Priorities were refocused on the American continent, which began a new shift to the right: Paraguay (August 2013), Chile (March 2014), Uruguay (March 2015), Argentina (December 2015), Brazil (May 2016), Peru (July 2016). This swing of the pendulum is compounded by the deaths of two mythical figures of the South American left: Hugo Chávez (March 2013) and Fidel Castro (November 2016). Donald Trump took office at the beginning of 2017 and is continuing his predecessor's efforts to restore American power in the region.

In 2013, Chávez's designated successor, Nicolas Maduro, was elected with 50.61% of the vote. The result was close and his opponent contested the outcome. An initial audit of 54% of the votes shows that there are no irregularities. The audit of the remaining 46%, demanded by the opposition, confirmed the results of the election, and on 19 April Maduro was inaugurated[1812].

In May 2014, the US Congress adopted a first wave of sanctions against personalities who allegedly do not respect human rights. This is the beginning of a cascade of financial sanctions that complicate international transactions and contribute to shortages (especially of medicines). In March 2015, President Obama signed an executive order describing Venezuela as a "*threat to U.S. national security and foreign policy*[1813]".

The increase in the price of oil from 2000 onwards is the reason for the economic success and popularity of Chavez and then, by ricochet, of Maduro. But it has a perverse effect: it does not require the development of production infrastructures. The importance of this weakness will become apparent when Venezuela is forced to modernise them.

In 2014, the price of a barrel began to fall, but it was not until it reached 30 dollars that the first inflection in the Venezuelan production curve appeared, exactly like the curve in Colombia. The real problem appeared on August 4, 2017, with the adoption by the Trump administration of a package of sanctions that prohibited Venezuela from accessing the financial market: not only could it no

1812. "Venezuela audit confirms Nicolas Maduro electoral victory", *BBC News*, June 12, 2013

1813. Executive Order 13692 "Blocking Property and Suspending Entry of Certain Persons Contributing to the Situation in Venezuela", March 8, 2015.

longer obtain financing on the US market, but the oil revenues of its national oil company CITGO could no longer be repatriated. According to Mark Weisbrot, deputy director of the *Center for Economic Research and Policy* in Washington DC, this is a deliberate move to prevent the country's economic recovery[1814]. In order to escape the sanctions, Venezuela is now trying to sell its oil in yuan.

This rapid economic deterioration naturally has an impact on the political life of the country. In the 2016 parliamentary elections, three opposition MPs were elected as a result of fraud[1815]. A Supreme Court ruling postponed their nomination to clarify the conditions of their election and called for a new vote in their constituencies[1816]. The problem is that with these three MPs, the opposition had the 2/3 of the votes needed to control the parliament. In July, the National Assembly decided to keep the three MPs anyway. This led to a dialogue of the deaf in which the National Assembly no longer recognised the legitimacy of the Supreme Court, resulting in a complete paralysis of the institutions.

In 2017, in order to unblock the situation, the government decided to set up a Constituent Assembly (without dissolving the National Assembly, as was sometimes claimed in the Western press). The choice of this instrument is highly questionable and was certainly misunderstood in the West. In fact, it was the only way the Constitution offered to form a kind of arbitration, with the aim of re-establishing a dialogue between institutions that no longer communicate. The opposition, as well as international observers, is invited to participate in the Constituent election. Finally, in July 2017, the three parliamentarians concerned resigned as a sign of appeasement[1817].

Following the 2017 riots, a negotiation process between the government and the opposition was initiated under the arbitration of former Spanish Prime Minister Jose Luis Rodriguez Zapatero. The opposition platform has two main demands: the anticipation of the presidential elections (traditionally scheduled for December 2018) and the presence of United Nations observers to ensure the smooth running of the electoral process. In return, the opposition had to commit to working with the government to lift the American, Canadian and European sanctions.

The discussions are taking place in the Dominican Republic. Both parties set the date for the presidential election for April 22, 2018. The government-together with Henri Falcon, a member of the opposition and a candidate in the

1814. Mark Weisbrot, "Trump's Sanctions Make Economic Recovery in Venezuela Nearly Impossible", *The Nation*, September 7, 2017

1815. "Venezuela: three opposition lawmakers resign in concession to Maduro", *Reuters/The Guardian*, November 16, 2016

1816. "Venezuela congress swears in three politicians barred by supreme court", *Associated Press/The Guardian*, January 6, 2016

1817. "Venezuela: un coup de plus contre la démocratie", *lemonde.fr*, July 29, 2017 (Updated July 31, 2017); "Venezuela: le Parlement se réunit malgré sa dissolution de fait", *mediapart.fr*, August 20, 2017.

election[1818] - then made a request to Antonio Guterres, Secretary General of the United Nations, for an observation mission[1819]. On February 6, 2018, when everything was ready for the signing of the agreement, the opposition delegation abruptly decided to withdraw from the negotiations (according to some, after a phone call from an American personality), and urged Guterres not to send observers, under the pretext that the electoral process would be rigged and that the presence of observers would only legitimise the fraud[1820].

In order to allow more time for negotiation and to allow the opposition to organise itself, the Maduro government then postponed the date of the elections to May 20. But the opposition announced that it would boycott the election. A strategy that is difficult to understand, as experience shows that the best way to contest elections is to participate in them and then denounce the fraud. A Brookings Institution study published in 2010, which analysed 171 cases of electoral boycotts, concluded that this is the worst strategy: it tends to strengthen the parties that participate, weaken those that abstain and is not enough to make the election appear illegitimate. In fact, it is better to participate, even if one expects it to be rigged[1821].

But here the problem is different: the reality is that the opposition is fragmented and feels it is not ready for a presidential election. The boycott was probably only meant to mask this fragmentation. This boycott will be downplayed later in the European media, which is a mouthpiece for US policy.

In fact, in March 2018, the most serious polls show that the opposition (and in particular the Table of Democratic Unity (MUD) from which Juan Guaidó will emerge) is in free fall, while the popularity of Nicolas Maduro - who is not the favourite at this stage - is increasing. It is estimated that the call for a boycott of the polls by the opposition would be followed by only 12.3% of the population and that 77.6% plan to vote[1822].

On May 20, with a boycott by part of the opposition, Nicolas Maduro was elected with 67.8% of the vote and an abstention of 46%, i.e. 31% of eligible votes; more than Obama in 2012 and Trump in 2016[1823]. Although his victory was clearly predictable, the government will be accused of rigging the vote.

However, the election was monitored by several hundred foreign observers, including José Luis Zapatero, former Spanish Prime Minister, Marcos Cipriani,

1818. "Venezuela in plea to UN to send observers for election", *AFP*, March 13, 2018

1819. "UN Rapporteur: US Sanctions Cause Death in Venezuela, www.therealnews.com, March 14, 2018

1820. "Venezuela opposition asks U.N. not to send observers to May vote", *Reuters*, March 12, 2018; "Venezuela in plea to UN to send observers for election", *AFP*, March 13, 2018

1821. Matthew Frankel, *Threaten but Participate: Why Election Boycotts Are a Bad Idea*, Policy Paper, No. 19, March 2010, The Brookings Institution

1822. "Venezuela & Ecuador This Week, *Torino Capital LLC*, February 26, 2018

1823. Alan MacLeod, "Media Delegitimize Venezuelan Elections Amid Complete Unanimity of Outlook", *FAIR*, May 23, 2018

former Cypriot Foreign Minister and Jean-Pierre Bel, former President of the Senate in France, and representatives of South American and European civil society. Moreover, an audit of 53% of the votes - as required by law - was carried out after the election and confirmed the legality of the vote. In fact, even the American press notes that the United States is doing everything to undermine the electoral process and delegitimise the Venezuelan government[1824]; a lucidity that cannot be found in the French-speaking media.

On January 10, 2019, Maduro's swearing-in for his new term triggers - unwillingly - the international campaign to remove him from office. On 23 January, Juan Guaidó, president of the National Assembly, proclaimed himself president of the country and very quickly gathered the support of a large number of Western countries, in the wake of the Trump administration. He relies on the "illegitimacy" of the 2018 election to justify his "takeover" of power.

12.2 "Venezuela is Sinking into Dictatorship[1825]"

The Venezuelan crisis provides a striking example of an attempted 'coup by influence', not dissimilar to what was implemented before the Iraq war, but with a greater weight of economic factors.

12.2.1. The Role of the United States

In May 2018, *voltairenet.org* published a document dated February 23, attributed to the US Southern Command (SOUTHCOM) and entitled *Plan to Overthrow the Dictatorship of the Venezuelan "MASTERSTROKE"*[1826]. A year later, as the US increased pressure on Venezuela, it resurfaced[1827]. But it is most likely a fake: the terminology used, the format of the document and its structure do not conform to US military practice and standards, especially at this level of command.

However, it would be wrong to ignore the role of the United States in the crisis. At the beginning of 2019, *France 5* devoted three "*C dans l'air*" programmes to the Venezuelan crisis, which reflect the position of the French media quite well. At no point do the 'experts' elaborate on the role of the United States. On the January 25 programme, the hypothesis of an American attempt to destabilise the situation is dismissed out of hand and Maduro's accusations are described as "*largely fallacious*[1828]". Yet in July 2017, at the Aspen Security Forum

1824. Mark Weisbrot, 'Behind the Scenes in Venezuela', *US News & World Report*, March 3, 2018
1825. "Venezuela sinks into dictatorship", *Le Monde*, August 21, 2017
1826. http://web.archive.org/web/20180514190031/https://www.voltairenet.org/article201100.html
1827. Eric Zuesse, "Leaked: USA's Feb 2018 Plan for Coup in Venezuela", *Off-Guardian*, May 2, 2019
1828. Émission "C dans l'air", "Venezuela: la crise qui divise le monde #cdanslair 25.01.2019", *YouTube/France 5*, January 26, 2019 (20'00")

in Colorado, Mike Pompeo, then CIA director, let slip that he was working with Mexico and Colombia on the issue of regime change in Venezuela[1829]. Moreover, in September 2018, during his address to the United Nations General Assembly, Donald Trump called on the international community to "join with *the United States in calling for the restoration of democracy in Venezuela*[1830]".

Nor do any of these 'experts' mention the threats made in November 2018 by National Security Adviser John Bolton to fight the '*Troika of Tyranny*[1831]', echoing George W. Bush's '*Axis of Evil*' fifteen years earlier. Nor do any mention the discussions between the US government and rebel Venezuelan military in early 2018 to depose President Maduro by force[1832], an option raised at a February 2018 press conference by then Secretary of State Rex Tillerson[1833]. It could explain the mysterious attempt to attack Maduro with two explosive drones 6 months later[1834].

At no time do the "experts" on "C dans l'air" mention Mike Pompeo's appointment of Elliott Abrams as "special envoy for Venezuela" on January 25, 2019. This ex-diplomat, "former" of the clandestine operations in Central America, had organised the illegal financing of the Contras in Nicaragua, cleared those responsible for war crimes in El Salvador[1835], was perjured in front of the investigative commissions of the Congress and was one of the actors of the coup d'état of 2002 against Hugo Chavez[1836].

The French media has been very quiet about efforts to thwart any cooperation with China and Russia[1837]. Moreover, it is silent on the situation in Honduras, which is the opposite and where the US government is trying to keep its protégé in power[1838].

1829. The Aspen Institute, *Aspen Security Forum 2017 - The View from Langley*, Aspen, Colorado, July 20, 2017; Andrew Buncombe, "CIA chief hints agency is working to change Venezuelan government", *The Independent*, July 25, 2017

1830. Lesley Wroughton & Brian Ellsworth, "U.S. sanctions Venezuela officials, Trump slams Maduro", *Reuters*, September 25, 2018

1831. Josh Rogin, "Bolton promises to confront Latin America's 'Troika of Tyranny'", *Washington Post*, November 1st, 2018

1832. Nicholas Casey & Ernesto Londoño, "Trump Administration Discussed Coup Plans With Rebel Venezuelan Officers", *The New York Times*, September 8, 2018

1833. Jon Herskovitz, "Tillerson raises prospect of Venezuela military ouster of Maduro", *Reuters*, February 2, 2018

1834. Christoph Koettl & Barbara Marcolini, "A Closer Look at the Drone Attack on Maduro in Venezuela", *The New York Times*, August 10, 2018

1835. Julian Borger, "US diplomat convicted over Iran-Contra appointed special envoy for Venezuela", *The Guardian*, January 26, 2019

1836. Ed Vulliamy, "Venezuela coup linked to Bush team", *The Guardian*, April 21, 2002

1837. Barbara Starr, Ryan Browne & Zachary Cohen, "Pentagon developing military options to deter Russian, Chinese influence in Venezuela", *CNN*, April 15, 2019

1838. Lee Fang & Danielle Mackey, "The President Of Honduras Is Deploying U.S.-Trained Forces Against Election Protesters", *The Intercept*, December 3, 2017; Sarah Kinosian, "US recognises re-election of Honduras president despite fraud allegations", *The Guardian*, December 22, 2017; Linda Cooper & James Hodge, "US backs questionable election in Honduras, supports dictatorship, opposition says", *National Catholic Reporter*, December 28, 2017.

12.2.2. An Economic Disaster

Regarding the economic situation, the "experts" of course mention the mismanagement and unfortunate choices made by President Nicolas Maduro, minimise the role of his predecessors and remain surprisingly silent on the US sanctions. During the three "C dans l'air" programmes devoted to Venezuela in early 2019, the US sanctions since 1999 and their real impact are not mentioned once, despite the presence of an economist on the set! The British newspaper *The Independent* mentions their illegal nature and their deadly consequences on the population[1839]. A UN report on the situation in Venezuela states that the US sanctions are illegal because they were never approved by the UN Security Council, had been condemned on March 23, 2018 by the Human Rights Council, and could fall into the category of 'crimes against humanity' under Article 7 of the Rome Treaty[1840].

But in France, the American line is still followed. On May 2, on *France 5*, the journalist Saraï Suarez went even further by affirming that it is a "*strategy of the [Venezuelan] government*" which aims to keep people busy surviving so that they don't think about rebelling[1841]! We are in the middle of a conspiracy!

Many countries are dependent on a single economic sector, have poor management and political transition problems. Yet they do not have the inflation rates and shortages of Venezuela. The comparison between Colombia and Venezuela shows that the difference lies in the sanctions[1842], whose impact is regularly downplayed by the Western media[1843].

While Venezuela has the largest oil reserves in the world, and has consistently paid its debts, the sanctions prevent it from accessing financial markets. Thus, the risk associated with its ability to pay has been artificially increased, even since the recovery in oil prices. According to the Colombia-based Latin American Strategic Geopolitical Centre (CELAG), the JPMorgan bank has set Venezuela's risk coefficient at 4,820 points, 38 times the value assigned to Chile, which has the same debt-to-gross national product ratio. Furthermore, the sanctions regime already put in place under the Obama presidency, and renewed by the Trump administration, makes companies or financial institutions (public and

1839. Michael Selby-Green, 'Venezuela crisis: Former UN rapporteur says US sanctions are killing citizens', *The Independent*, January 26, 2019

1840. *Report of the Independent Expert on the promotion of a democratic and equitable international order on his mission to the Bolivarian Republic of Venezuela and Ecuador*, Document A/HRC/39/47/Add.1, August 3, 2018 (submitted to the 39th session of the UN Human Rights Council, September 10-28, 2018)

1841. Sarai Suarez in the programme "C dans l'air", "Venezuela: Trump prêt à intervenir ? #cdanslair 02.05.2019", *YouTube/France 5*, May 3, 2019 (11'42")

1842. Joe Emersberger, "Trump's Economic Sanctions Have Cost Venezuela About $6bn Since August 2017," *Venezuelanalysis.com*, September 27, 2018

1843. See Michel De Grandi & Raphael Bloch, "Brussels adopts a series of sanctions against Venezuela", *lesechos.fr*, November 13, 2017; Francisco Rodríguez (Translated by Pierre Marti), "Si les sanctions financières augmentent, le Venezuela court à la catastrophe humanitaire", *slate.fr*, January 18, 2018

private) that collaborate with Venezuela liable to punishment. Thus, many banks (Citibank, Commerzbank, Deutsche Bank) have unilaterally (and often without prior notice) cancelled contracts with Venezuela. CITGO, the national oil company based in the United States, cannot send Venezuela the proceeds from the sale of oil products on the US market, an estimated 9-10 billion dollars[1844].

Our 'experts' are always talking about the hyperinflation that is affecting the country. The figure of 1,000,000% for 2018 is mentioned, but it is not true. This figure is a projection of momentary inflation over a full year. The real figure is much lower - although still extremely high - and is around 80,000%. Moreover, they fail to mention that it is due to the inability to access international financial instruments due to sanctions imposed by the Trump administration, pushing the government to produce money to cover a growing budget deficit.

Nor do they mention that the scarcity of certain consumer goods due to sanctions contributed to the phenomenon of arbitrage. This phenomenon was already known in occupied Europe during the Second World War, where unscrupulous individuals stockpiled goods in order to create a shortage, speculating on price increases and thus amplifying the inflationary fever. Furthermore, no 'expert' mentions the impact of sanctions on financial instruments, which prevented the government from taking measures to curb hyperinflation[1845].

Moreover, while 'conventional' economic crises follow known and quasi-mathematical mechanisms - even if they are not always well controlled - the Venezuelan crisis changes in nature over time. The countermeasures taken by the government cannot take effect because they are systematically "caught up" by a new sanction. For example, the Maduro government tried to curb inflation by creating a currency (the 'Petro') whose value is linked to the value of oil; but the US immediately banned its use by US citizens and companies[1846]. Whether or not this was an appropriate remedy is open to debate, but this example clearly illustrates that the Venezuelan crisis is externally driven.

Nothing very surprising here, as the scenario follows exactly the US Army's unconventional warfare manual, which describes the use of financial weapons to bring down governments[1847]. In essence, the strategy is the same as the one used since World War II: attacking the civilian population in order to make them rebel against their government. This is the logic of the embargo against Iraq since 1990, of the air strikes in Serbia in 1999, in Iraq in 2003, and in Syria in 2015:

1844. Alfred de Zayas in Empire Files, "An Ocean of Lies on Venezuela: Abby Martin & UN Rapporteur Expose Coup," *YouTube*, February 22, 2019

1845. Mark Weisbrot & Jeffrey Sachs, *Economic Sanctions as Collective Punishment: The Case of Venezuela*, Center for Economic and Policy Research, Washington DC, April 2019, p. 20

1846. Executive Order 13827 of March 19, 2018. The Wikipedia article on the Petro in French only states that it is "supposed to circumvent US sanctions". The English version of the article is more correct.

1847. *FM 3-05.130, Army Special Operations Forces Unconventional Warfare*, HQ - Department of the Army, September 2008, numbers 2-40 ff.

it is a matter of creating an untenable situation for the civilian population and making the government responsible for it:

> *Since the embargo was imposed on Iraq on August 6 [1990] after the invasion of Kuwait, the US has resisted any relaxation in the belief that by making life difficult for the Iraqi people, it will encourage them to overthrow Saddam Hussein from power*[1848].

It is absolutely the same strategy as that of the Islamic State, except that instead of bombs, consumer goods are suppressed.

On April 24, 2019, the State Department publishes a list of measures taken against the government of Venezuela. It is quickly removed from the website, but a copy remains (forgotten?) on the website of the US embassy in Brazil[1849]. It shows that the US is trying to asphyxiate the country, long before Juan Guaidó's arrival. It mentions as a "result", the drop in oil production and the inability of Venezuelans to sell it on the market, and confirms that CITGO's oil revenues were transferred by the US to Guaidó. In fact, nothing very new for those who seriously follow the situation, but it underlines the "conspiracy of silence" seen in the mainstream media on the sanctions.

In a report on the "20 heures", *France 2* even states that the economic crisis is a way for the government to get the support of the population[1850] (!). Naturally, no mention is made of the Local Supply and Production Committees (CLAP) programme, created in 2016 by President Maduro to provide basic necessities to the most disadvantaged.

In May 2019, after Juan Guaidó's failure to mobilise the people and take power, the Trump administration tries new measures: sanctions hit the CLAP programme, under the pretext that it would be a means of money laundering[1851]. But here again, the European mainstream media remains silent on the consequences...

12.2.3. The Role of the Western Media

What is striking here is not really the way the Americans handle their foreign policy; it is the lack of perspective of the European press and media, which willingly vilify the US president, but explicitly support companies that contravene international law and the rule of law. For example, in January 2019, the open letter sent to Donald Trump by 70 US political, academic and press

1848. Paul H. Lewis, 'After The War; U.N. Survey Calls Iraq's War Damage Near-Apocalyptic', *New York Times*, March 22, 1991.
1849. https://br.usembassy.gov/western-hemisphere-fact-sheet-u-s-actions-on-venezuela/
1850. "Food shortage in Venezuela", *France 2/YouTube*, May 20, 2018
1851. Matt Spetalnick, "U.S. reads sanctions, charges over Venezuela food program: sources", *Reuters*, May 22, 2019

figures[1852] warning him about US interference in Venezuela received virtually no coverage in the European media.

The experts of "C dans l'air" try to minimize the importance of the American involvement in the crisis: the journalist François-Xavier Freland explains it by an "*armchair anti-Americanism*". It is an intellectual dishonesty: in the magazine *US News*, the American economist Max Weisbrot, demonstrates that the United States has spared no effort to undermine the 2018 elections[1853]. Of course, at this point, he cannot yet know that in March 2019, throughout his Latin American tour, Juan Guaidó will be accompanied by the Under Secretary of State, Kimberly Breier, ex-CIA analyst and Latin American specialist[1854]. A fact that none of the mainstream media has seen fit to report…

Since the beginning of the 19th century, the Monroe Doctrine has made Latin America the exclusive backyard of the United States ("America's backyard"): "America for Americans". It was supplemented at the beginning of the 20th century by Theodore Roosevelt's "Big Stick" doctrine, which gave him the right to strike at any country whose policies did not suit American interests. To this day, they explain US interventions in Central America and it would be surprising if the socialist government of Venezuela were an exception.

But the problem is not only political. On January 24, 2019, John Bolton, Donald Trump's national security adviser, said on *Fox News*:

> *If US oil companies could actually invest and produce oil capacity in Venezuela, it would make a big economic difference to the US*[1855].

Nor does anyone mention that shortly after recognising Juan Guaidó as president, the Trump administration imposed sanctions that give him de facto authority over the revenues of the US-based Venezuelan oil industry. Treasury Secretary Steven Mnuchin has even said that sanctions against PDVSA could be lifted if the firm recognises Juan Guaidó's authority[1856]. Clearly, this is about bringing the country to its knees: Mnuchin announces that the US has taken steps with Saudi Arabia to stabilise the price of oil while Venezuelan production is halted[1857].

Efforts to encourage armed subversion in the country are still difficult to assess. On February 7, the US news agency McClatchy reported that the

1852. "Open Letter by Over 70 Scholars and Experts Condemns US-Backed Coup Attempt in Venezuela", www.commondreams.org, January 24, 2019.
1853. Mark Weisbrot, "Behind the Scenes in Venezuela", *US News*, March 3, 2018
1854. "Who Is US Intelligence Official Advising Guaido on His 'Regional Tour'", *www.telesurenglish.net*
1855. "US coup in Venezuela motivated by oil and corporate interests - Neocon John Bolton spills the beans", *YouTube*, January 29, 2019
1856. Irina Slav, "U.S. Treasury Specifies Sanctions on Venezuelan Oil Imports", *oilprice.com*, February 1st, 2019
1857. Phil Flynn, "The Venezuela Oil Options", www.moneyshow.com, January 29, 2019

Venezuelan government had intercepted a shipment of arms and ammunition on a plane belonging to North Carolina-based 21Air, two of whose executives were associated with CIA flights in the early 2000s[1858]. In total, 21Air made around 40 flights between the two countries from January 11, the day after Maduro was sworn in.[1859]

12.2.4. Juan Guaidó and the Nature of the Opposition

Guaidó's self-proclamation as president of the Republic was presented in the media as spontaneous. This is not the case, and in Venezuela the majority of opposition parties do not support it[1860]. In fact, it is the result of long negotiations with the United States, which were held partly in Puerto Rico. On the programme "C dans l'air" on January 25, experts were asked about Trump's surprisingly quick recognition of Guaidó. But none of them really answer, nor do they mention that on January 22 - the day before he declared himself president - Juan Guaidó had a telephone conversation with US Vice President Mike Pence, who gave him the "green light" and assured him of US support should he take power. Yet the very rapid succession of events surrounding this self-proclamation suggests a high level of coordination, which the *Wall Street Journal* explains:

> *The overnight call set in motion a plan developed secretly over the previous weeks, accompanied by discussions between US officials, allies, parliamentarians and Venezuelan opposition figures, including Guaidó himself*[1861].

This is why, within minutes, Donald Trump recognises the new 'president' and grants him 20 million dollars in humanitarian aid. It will arrive at the Colombian border in the following weeks. We will come back to this.

The same pattern is then found as at the beginning of the insurgency in Syria to present the "regime". In "C dans l'air", Philippe Dessertine claims that the police are firing live ammunition into the crowd[1862], but the available documents do not show a deliberate policy, as he suggests. The videos show the military using riot guns, which appear to use rubber bullets. The *Washington Post* puts it into perspective:

1858. Whitney Webb, "US Air Freight Company that Smuggled Weapons Into Venezuela Linked to CIA 'Black Site' Renditions," *Mint Press News*, February 13, 2019

1859. Tim Johnson, "Venezuela says plane from Miami delivered weapons for use by enemies of Maduro", www.mcclatchydc.com, February 7, 2019

1860. "Capriles: Partidos de oposición no apoyaban autojuramentación de Guaidó", *Notitarde*, February 2 2019

1861. Jessica Donati & Vivian Salama, "Pence Pledged U.S. Backing Before Venezuela Opposition Leader's Move", *The Wall Street Journal*, January 25, 2019

1862. Programme "C dans l'air", "Venezuela: la crise qui divise le monde #cdanslair 25.01.2019", *YouTube/France 5*, January 26, 2019 (24'15")

[...] the security forces have mostly used non-lethal force to suppress them. As a result, violence is common, but deaths are relatively rare.

[And yes, people die. Shoot rubber pellets at a person at very close range or point a tear gas canister directly at their chest, and you will kill them. One hundred and two people died in the last wave of protests, about one a day. That's 102 too many, of course... and yet it's also far, far fewer than it could have been.

[...] The security forces have understood that the use of live ammunition during demonstrations is prohibited. The few demonstrators who were killed by police bullets seem to have been truly isolated incidents: officers who felt threatened in the midst of chaotic demonstrations panicked and drew their weapons. Significantly, the regime actually filed a complaint against them[1863].

In the absence of reliable and unbiased data, it is difficult to draw conclusions, but it is clear that not all victims are the sole responsibility of law enforcement.

The approach to the crisis by Western countries, including the United States, Canada, France, Belgium and many others, tends to reinforce radical positions and a hardening of the actors, as it is partisan in its essence. As for the initiative of Mexico and Uruguay (joined by Bolivia, Costa Rica and Ecuador[1864]) coordinated with the European Union "Contact Group"[1865] (supported by Emmanuel Macron[1866]), it is rejected by Guaidó, who refuses any dialogue with the government, claiming that it is simply a matter of Maduro buying time[1867]. But this refusal to negotiate is not mentioned by anyone, not by Jean-Yves LeDrian, nor by the "experts" gathered on the set of Le *Figaro* on February 4[1868], nor by any of the experts on "C dans l'air" on February 6, and it has been concealed by the whole of the traditional French press: it is necessary to avoid presenting Guaidó as a "hawk".

Because Juan Guaidó is not well known. A poll conducted in Venezuela the day after his self-proclamation shows that more than 80% of the population has never heard of him[1869]. As for the portrait painted by the traditional international press, it is, to say the least, very "modest". The Wikipedia article on him speaks for

1863. Francisco Toro, "Is Venezuela on the verge of civil war?", *Washington Post*, July 24, 2017

1864. "Europeans, Latin Americans to meet on Venezuela crisis", *News24/AFP*, February 8, 2019

1865. "Europe creates contact group on Venezuela", www.lecho.be, January 31, 2019

1866. Tweet of February 4, 2019 (09:51)

1867. "Venezuela crisis: Guaido rejects talks with Maduro", *BBC News*, January 26, 2019; Sinikka Tarvainen, "Venezuela's Guaido rejects mediation by 'neutral' countries", DPA International, February 1st, 2019

1868. "Venezuela: a-t-ôn raison de reconnaître Juan Gaido ?", *video.lefigaro.fr*, February 4, 2018

1869. George Ciccariello-Maher, "Venezuela: Call It What It Is-a Coup", *The Nation*, January 25, 2019

itself: he is presented as a rebellious intellectual who is close to the people. This is not the case. In 2007, after studying at the Andres Bello Catholic University in Caracas, he took a course in governance and political management in the United States, at George Washington University, under the tutelage of Venezuelan economist Luis Enrique Berrizbeitia, one of Latin America's leading neoliberal economists and former executive director of the International Monetary Fund (IMF), who worked for many years for the Venezuelan government overthrown by Chávez. In 2009, he joined the Popular Will party ("*Voluntad Popular*"), created and led by Leopoldo Lopez, and affiliated to the Socialist International. British Labour MP Rachel Reeves even claims that it is a "sister socialist" party[1870]. But this is only a facade, as it remains discreet about its rather astonishing positioning described by Wikipedia (French version, until February 28): "*Extreme right, right, centre right, centre left*"[1871] (in fact, this "positioning" has been the subject of no less than 8 changes on Wikipedia between February 5 and March 6, 2019, testifying to the political vagueness in which it is situated[1872])

Our image of the Venezuelan opposition, presented by the media as united behind Juan Guaidó, against Maduro, is largely biased[1873]. The journalist François-Xavier Freland, claims that it is united[1874]. This is not true. In 2008, a common platform (MUD[1875]) was created to bring the opposition together under a single banner to counter Hugo Chavez. But by 2016, it began to fall apart, and the movement accelerated in 2017[1876]. In 2018, it broke up into three smaller platforms. The one in which People's Will is today is itself divided and has not even managed to find a name for itself. Thus, contrary to what the pro-American propaganda presents, Guaidó does not represent the whole opposition, but only a small part: the most radical. Moreover, in June 2019, after the failure of the attempted popular uprising on April 30, Mike Pompeo will admit that it is practically impossible to unify the opposition[1877].

Indeed, in its 2018 study of the Venezuelan opposition, the International Crisis Group (ICG) does not mention Juan Guaidó's name once. Instead, it notes the internal struggles of the MUD and the range of tendencies it comprises: from the far right to the far left[1878]. In fact, the different components of the

1870. "BBC Politics Live, *YouTube*, January 29, 2019 (33'15")

1871. Wikipedia article "People's Will (party)", accessed February 19, 2019.

1872. "People's Will (party): Version history", *Wikipedia*, accessed March 31, 2019

1873. "Venezuelan opposition, led by Guaidó, marches to convince army", *rtbf.be*, January 30 2019

1874. François-Xavier Freland in the programme "C dans l'air", "Venezuela: la crise qui divise le monde #cdanslair 25.01.2019", *YouTube/France 5*, January 26, 2019 (15'50")

1875. Mesa de la Unidad Democrática (Democratic Unity Table)

1876. Alonso Moleiro, "La alianza opositora venezolana certifica su fin", *El Pais*, October 24, 2018

1877. John Hudson, "Exclusive: In secret recording, Pompeo opens up about Venezuelan opposition, says keeping it united 'has proven devilishly difficult'", *The Washington Post*, June 5, 2019

1878. *Friendly Fire: Venezuela's Opposition Turmoil*, Crisis Group Latin America Report N°71, International Crisis Group, Brussels, November 23, 2018

MUD have never managed to agree on a clear political and economic line. Their opposition strategy is far from unanimous: some, like Popular Will, are opposed to any dialogue, while others are more in favour of collaboration with the government[1879]. The inconsistencies of the opposition - sometimes boycotting, sometimes participating in elections - have made it unpopular and favoured the government alliance (as in the October 2017 regional elections)[1880].

As for the internal situation in the country, journalist François-Xavier Freland says that "you *rarely see the crowd around Maduro*[1881]". This is not true, and it is precisely what some see as a risk of confrontation, or even civil war, in the event of a coup de force. In the absence of figures, it is difficult to say which one is mobilising more activists, but it is certain that Maduro has broad popular support, contrary to what he claims, and as we will see in May. The number of supporters mobilised for the US aid distribution at the Colombian border on February 23, 2019 gives an indication of the problem. Juan Guaidó had called for a million volunteers, and British billionaire Richard Branson had organised a concert near the distribution site where over 250,000 spectators were expected. But on the day, there were only a few hundred activists on the Tienditas Bridge and the concert attracted only about 20,000 people. The *Washington Post*, published a glowing article about the event[1882]; but it was quickly withdrawn and replaced by another one that no longer mentioned the 200,000 spectators[1883], and then by a third and final version, which no longer even mentioned the Branson concert[1884].

In June 2019, the *PanAm Post* of Miami revealed that the money collected for humanitarian purposes by Richard Branson, including funds from international organisations, had been squandered by Juan Guaidó's confidants in hotels, luxury clothes and with prostitutes[1885]... The British billionaire issued a press release declining any responsibility. Obviously, the French media remain very discreet about these misappropriations, as with the images of Guaidó's motorcade being

1879. Steve Ellner, "After Elections, Intransigence in Venezuela", *nacla.org*, May 25, 2018

1880. See Wikipedia, article "2017 Venezuelan regional elections".

1881. François-Xavier Freland in the programme "C dans l'air", "Venezuela: la crise qui divise le monde #cdanslair 25.01.2019", *YouTube/France 5*, January 26, 2019 (15'50")

1882. The original article could still be seen on Mercury News: Anthony Faiola, Dylan Baddour and Mariana Zuñiga, "Guaidó and supporters prepare to defy Maduro's blockade of aid in Venezuela", *The Washington Post/ Mercury News*, February 23, 2019

1883. Mariana Zuñiga, Anthony Faiola and Dylan Baddour, "Amid chaos and defiance, Venezuelan opposition faces off against security forces as Maduro digs in", www.washingtonpost.com, February 23, 2019 (http://archive.is/qM6Ie#selection-734.0-1475.22)

1884. Mariana Zuñiga, "Amid chaos and defiance, Venezuelan opposition faces off against security forces as Maduro digs in", www.washingtonpost.com, February 23, 2019

1885. Orlando Avendaño, 'Enviados de Guaidó se apropian de fondos para ayuda humanitaria en Colombia', *PanAm Post*, June 18, 2019; Dan Cohen, 'From coup leaders to con artists: Juan Guaidó's gang exposed for massive humanitarian aid fraud', *The Grayzone*, June 17, 2019

forced by the crowd to backtrack as he wants to enter a popular district of Caracas in March 2019[1886].

As for the claim by one of the "experts" on "C dans l'air" that Guaidó was "*elected*" to the post of president of the National Assembly[1887], it is inaccurate[1888]. This was a pre-arranged election, as the four parties making up the MUD had decided on a rotating presidency. When Popular Will's turn came, its president, Leopoldo Lopez, was under house arrest and could not take on the role, as was his running mate, Freddy Guevara, who was prosecuted and took refuge in the Chilean embassy. Next on the list of 'next in line' was Juan Andrés Mejía, but for reasons that are still unclear at this stage, it was the next in line, Juan Guaidó, who got the job. So when *FOX News* in May 2019 talks about a '*duly elected president*[1889]', it is a lie.

In the programme "C dans l'air" of February 6, Ms Andréïna Flores, judged Guaidó's self-proclamation to be constitutional because Maduro's election was illegitimate; in particular because it had been brought forward by seven months[1890]. But she fails to mention that the date was brought forward at the request of… the opposition[1891]! Moreover, Article 233 of the Constitution does indeed allow the President of the National Assembly to be interim President, but only in the event of a permanent vacancy of power due to resignation, illness, accident or death[1892], and not when elections are contested, which is the case here. Moreover, it does not say that the interim president can only hold this position for a maximum of 30 days, in order to organise elections… which Guaidó did not even attempt to do, since he proclaimed himself president! Naturally, none of the "experts" on the set pointed out these unconstitutionalities…

But the US and the Venezuelan opposition apparently saw this problem because at the end of February 2019, the National Assembly took the decision that the interim would only start after Maduro's departure[1893]! In sum, Guaidó is president by an interim that has not begun: legality is being adjusted to 'fit' with illegality; an adjustment made necessary by the fact that the expected popular uprising against Maduro has not taken place.

1886. "Guaido Kicked Out From Working Class Neighborhood", *videos.telesurenglish.net*, March 30, 2019
1887. Pascal Boniface in the programme "C dans l'air", "Venezuela: pourquoi tout le monde s'en mêle ? #cdanslair 06.02.2019", *YouTube/France 5*, February 7, 2019 (18'30")
1888. "Au Venezuela, Juan Guaido, chef de l'opposition par hasard, "président" par effraction", *lemonde.fr*, January 25, 2019
1889. Sean Hannity, "Venezuela shows how socialism always culminates", *FOX News*, May 2, 2019
1890. Andréïna Flores in the programme "C dans l'air", "Venezuela: pourquoi tout le monde s'en mêle ? #cdanslair 06.02.2019", *YouTube/France 5*, February 7, 2019 (19'10")
1891. "Venezuela opposition weighs election run after talks end, *BBC News*, February 8, 2018
1892. https://venezuelanalysis.com/constitution
1893. "Briefing with Special Representative for Venezuela Abrams", *U.S. Department of State/YouTube*, March 15, 2019

If the UN continues to recognise Maduro, it is not because "*on the UN side (...) there is no democratic principle that applies*[1894]", but simply because the organisation does not recognise governments, but states. A principle usually applied by France... which makes Emmanuel Macron's recognition of Guaidó an anomalous practice[1895]. But here again, no 'expert' will point out this contradiction.

The infographics produced to illustrate international support for the two Venezuelan 'presidents', which are supposed to provide clarity, contribute to Western propaganda. For example, the map produced by *franceinfo/AFP*[1896] shows that Maduro is only supported by countries considered autocratic such as Russia, China, Turkey, Cuba and Bolivia. But it carefully avoids mentioning India[1897] and South Africa[1898], which could provide an element of "democratic" support for Maduro.

In March 2019, a series of blackouts affected the Venezuelan electricity network, with images of them playing over and over on our national media. This is not the first time, and there is talk of a failure to maintain the network. It is possible. But no one mentions the astonishing similarity of the events to a plan drawn up in September 2010 by the Centre for Applied Nonviolent Action and Strategies[1899] (CANVAS), which proposes regime change in Venezuela by provoking a popular uprising triggered by electricity cuts[1900]. Incidentally, the location of the 2019 incidents is exactly the one indicated in the 2010 report to create a blackout: the Guri dam, where the Simon Bolivar power plant is located[1901]. For the record: based in Belgrade, CANVAS is an NGO funded by *the* International Republican Institute (IRI) in Washington DC and the Open Society Foundation (OSF) and has been very active in Ukraine, where it trained the Euromaidan protesters.

On March 7, before the Senate Foreign Relations Subcommittee, Republican Senator Marco Rubio called on the US to bring about regime change through a combination of three measures: 'widespread unrest', support for the Venezuelan

---

1894. Pascal Boniface in the programme "C dans l'air", "Venezuela: pourquoi tout le monde s'en mêle ? #cdanslair 06.02.2019", *YouTube/France 5*, February 7, 2019

1895. "France's practice is to maintain diplomatic relations not with governments but with states. Thus, it does not perform a formal act of recognition when a new government is established following a change of regime. This is a constant position. (Jean François-Poncet, Minister of Foreign Affairs, March 16, 1979). Quoted in *Sydney Conference (2018) - Recognition/Non-Recognition In International Law*, Final Report; 'Venezuela: Macron Recognises Oppositionist Juan Guaido as "President in Charge"', *Marianne*, February 4, 2019

1896. "Venezuela: Juan Guaido ou Nicolas Maduro ? Discover which countries support them", franceinfo/AFP, February 6, 2019

1897. "India Refuses to Join US in Recognising Venezuela's Guaido as Interim President", *thewire.in*, January 25, 2019

1898. Qaanitah Hunter, "SA backs beleaguered Venezuelan President Nicholas Maduro", www.timeslive.co.za, January 26, 2019

1899. In English: Center for Applied Nonviolent Action and Strategies (CANVAS)

1900. "Analysis of the situation in Venezuela, September 2010. (DRAFT)", *CANVAS Analytic Department*, September 2010 (wikileaks.org/gifiles/docs/21/218642_vz-elections-.html)

1901. Ricardo Vaz, "Venezuela Suffers Major Power Outages After Alleged Cyber Attack," *venezuelanalysis.com*, March 10, 2019

military and elites, and international pressure[1902]. At 5pm, an unexplained incident affects the Simon Bolivar hydroelectric plant; and 18 minutes later, while Venezuelan authorities have yet to identify the nature of the problem[1903], Rubio tweets about the event, stating that the backup generators are down[1904]! While it is not clear whether this was a deliberate action, there is room for doubt! On March 26, addressing the National Assembly, Guaidó stated that "[…] *the end of darkness will come definitively with the end of the usurpation*", which the government interpreted as an admission of sabotage[1905].

Bias pushes to incoherence. In February 2019, while President Macron recognises the legitimacy of Juan Guaidó and joins an ultimatum against President Maduro, he recalls his ambassador to Rome, after Luigi Di Maio, the Italian deputy prime minister, met with representatives of the "yellow waistcoats" in France[1906]. So we accept interference in the internal politics of other countries, but we do not tolerate it at home!

This issue has nothing to do with democracy or the rule of law. It is a classic conflict of regional hegemony, treated in a binary mode, as the Americans like it, with 'good guys' and 'bad guys'. There is no doubt that the US administration is acting according to a plan. It is difficult to distinguish between the naivety and bad faith - not to say 'willingness to deceive' - of journalists who refuse to see the American influence in Central American countries.

Thus, on February 17, 2019, during the riots against Haitian President Joven Moise, five Americans, two Serbs and one Haitian were arrested in Port-au-Prince with weapons almost identical to those captured in Venezuela[1907]. Among them are two ex-Navy SEALs, a former Marine Corps pilot, a former military policeman and ex-member of Blackwater and an employee of Patriot Group Services (PGS), a subcontractor of the US Department of Homeland Security. They claim to be "on a *mission for the government*[1908]". Three days later, they were extradited to the United States, where they were not prosecuted[1909]. In fact, no

1902. Marco Rubio in "Senate Hearing On Venezuela", *MoxNews/YouTube*, March 7, 2019 (2h14'25")

1903. Ricardo Vaz, "Venezuela Suffers Major Power Outages After Alleged Cyber Attack," *venezuelanalysis.com*, March 10, 2019

1904. https://twitter.com/marcorubio/status/1103782022537977857

1905. "Gustavo Villapol: Guaidó confesó estar detrás del sabotaje eléctrico", *vtv.gob.ve*, March 27, 2019

1906. "France can't digest Italian visit to Yellow Vests", *Euronews*, February 7, 2018

1907. Alexander Rubinstein, "Haitian Authorities Arrest Americans Transporting Cache of Weapons amid Uprising," www.mintpressnews.com, February 18, 2019

1908. Jacqueline Charles, "Haitian police arrest five Americans who claimed they were on a 'government mission'", *Miami Herald*, February 18, 2019 (updated February 19, 2019); Tamar Lapin, "Americans arrested in Haiti claiming to be on 'government mission' return to US", New York Post, February 20, 2019

1909. Jacqueline Charles, David Ovalle & Jay Weaver, "Americans arrested in Haiti with arsenal of guns won't face U.S. charges", *Miami Herald*, February 21, 2019; Leah McDonald, "Mystery as group of U.S. 'mercenaries' armed with arsenal of weapons, drones and satellite phones are arrested in Haiti for 'targeting Government's executive branch' and sent home on American Airlines but 'WON'T face charges'", *Dailymail.Com / Associated Press*, February 22, 2019 (updated February 23, 2019)

one knows exactly why they were in Haiti, but it is clear that the US is keeping a close eye on domestic developments.

In fact, the mainstream media is behaving like the "useful idiots", serving the bad faith and foolishness of high ranking US officials like John Bolton and Elliott Abrams, who have only succeeded in sowing chaos around the world. As Alfred de Zayas said during a presentation on the situation in Venezuela: "*We are swimming in an ocean of lies*[1910]!" As before the wars in Iraq, Afghanistan, Libya nd Syria, one discerns with the Western media a form of what the Germans call "*Schadenfreude*[1911]". It allows them to "sell", to the detriment of the truth and the lives of civilian populations…

12.2.5. The Blocking of "Humanitarian" Aid

The humanitarian aid promised by Donald Trump arrives in Colombia in February and is scheduled to enter Venezuela on the 23rd. The Venezuelan government sees this as a propaganda operation and does not allow it. The international media castigate the decision, but do not mention the reasons for it[1912]. Technically, aid can be qualified as humanitarian if it is "*neutral, impartial and independent*"[1913]. However, in this case, the aid does not meet any of these criteria: its sole purpose is to be a propaganda tool for Guaidó. Moreover, the United Nations warns the United States against this politicisation[1914]. Furthermore, Christoph Harnisch, head of the International Committee of the Red Cross (ICRC) delegation in Colombia, states that the ICRC considers US aid to be a government action and will not participate in its distribution[1915].

The International Crisis Group confirms that the Venezuelan government is not obliged to accept US aid:

> *Under international law, governments must accept the distribution of food and medical supplies when the survival of a population is threatened, but only if the aid is exclusively humanitarian and impartial in nature. However, this aid operation is essentially political and is aimed at undermining Maduro and bringing about a change of government. Jeremy Konyndyk, the former head of US foreign disaster assistance, tweeted, "Aid blocked at the border*

1910. "The Grayzone testifies at the UN - 'Humanitarian crisis in Venezuela: Propaganda vs. reality'", *The Grayzone / YouTube*, March 19, 2019

1911. Literally: "joy in the misfortune of others".

1912. Émission " C dans l'air ", " Venezuela: pourquoi tout le monde s'en mêle ? #cdanslair 06.02.2019", *YouTube/ France 5*, February 7, 2019 (58'00")

1913. Denise Plattner, "The neutrality of the ICRC and the neutrality of humanitarian assistance", *International Review of the Red Cross*, 818, April 30, 1996

1914. Michelle Nichols, "U.N. warns against politicizing humanitarian aid in Venezuela", *Reuters*, February 6, 2019

1915. Patrick Bèle, "Venezuela: Guaido calls on the army to disobey", *lefigaro.fr*, February 11, 2019

while US officials castigate the government is there only for a political show and not for humanitarian purposes." [1916]

Moreover, the US president is threatening to retaliate against the Venezuelan military if they obey their government by blocking US aid at the border[1917].

Media outlets such as *BFMTV*, *Euronews*[1918] and *the Express*[1919] are trying to make it appear that President Maduro is preventing humanitarian aid from reaching his people:

> *In Venezuela, humanitarian aid has still not been able to enter the country. Nicolas Maduro is opposed to the arrival of this aid, sent in particular by the United States*[1920] *(...)*

The "*in particular*" suggests that Maduro is opposed to *all* humanitarian aid. This is a misleading formulation, intended to make it appear that Maduro is seeking to starve his population[1921]. In reality, aid from the ICRC, Russia, China or the European Union regularly enters the country. It is only American aid - politicised for the benefit of Guaidó[1922] - that is blocked.

France24 ironises that President Maduro is linking this aid to an attempt at military intervention:

> *Nicolas Maduro still refuses the entry of humanitarian aid into the country. He sees it as a preamble to an invasion of the country*[1923].

The magazine *L'Express* publishes a video in which it is claimed that Maduro "*considers the arrival of the American humanitarian convoys as an attempted military invasion*[1924]". But here too, the story is manipulated: it is not about the US military hiding behind sacks of rice, but about the exploitation of this aid for partisan purposes and interference. This being the case, in March 2019, the American media *Bloomberg News* revealed that ex-Venezuelan soldiers under the

1916. Phil Gunson, "High Noon over Humanitarian Aid at Venezuela's Border", *International Crisis Group*, February 22, 2019

1917. Harriet Alexander, "Donald Trump threatens Venezuela's military if aid is blocked from entering country", www.telegraph.co.uk, February 19, 2019

1918. Euronews, "In Venezuela, the army prevents the entry of humanitarian aid", *YouTube*, February 23, 2019

1919. L'Express, "Venezuela: humanitarian aid blocked by Maduro", *YouTube*, February 25, 2019

1920. "Venezuela: 'It's time to overthrow the tyrant', says Juan Guaido representative to military", *rmc.bfmtv.com*, February 9, 2019

1921. Sarai Suarez in the programme "C dans l'air", "Venezuela: Trump prêt à intervenir ? #cdanslair 02.05.2019", *YouTube/France 5*, May 3, 2019 (11'42")

1922. Michelle Nichols, "U.N. warns against politicizing humanitarian aid in Venezuela", *Reuters*, February 6, 2019

1923. France 24 News, March 1st, 2019

1924. "Venezuela: aide humanitaire bloquée par Maduro", *L'Express/YouTube*, February 25, 2019 (01'44")

command of ex-General Cliver Alcalá had prepared to make a coup de force in the wake of the "humanitarian" convoy, in order to push government troops to join the opposition; but the Colombian government, not wanting to be involved, had interrupted the operation[1925]. This information was obviously not relayed by the French media...

Mike Pompeo calls Maduro a "*sick tyrant*" because he opposes the entry of American aid. But obviously, no media recall that in the 1990s, the American embargo against Iraq caused the death of tens of thousands of children (without the figure of 500,000 mentioned at the time disturbing the American ambassador Madeleine Albright[1926]); that in 2005, George Bush refused Venezuelan humanitarian aid after Hurricane Katrina[1927]; that in Yemen, the international coalition is preventing humanitarian aid from reaching the victims[1928]; and that American sanctions are preventing the entry of medicines into Venezuela.[1929]

In France, the media present the shortage of medicines as a consequence of Maduro's policy. In February 2018, the magazine *Science & Vie*, devoted an article to this subject without mentioning once the impact of sanctions[1930]. Yet, in July 2017, Citibank blocked the payment of 300,000 doses of insulin. In August 2017, the company EUROCLEAR, blocked a payment from the Venezuelan government of $1.65 billion for the purchase of food and medicines; in November 2017, the Colombian government blocked the supply of malaria drugs just after the start of an epidemic: in May 2018, it was dialysis equipment worth $9 million that was blocked in turn[1931]. A UN report of August 2018 describes Venezuela as 'under siege' due to the effect of US sanctions, which cause casualties through malnutrition and lack of medicines:

> *Modern economic sanctions and blockades are comparable to medieval sieges of cities with the intention of forcing them to surrender*[1932].

So this is indeed a militarisation of humanitarian aid. In April 2019, a report by the Center for Economic and Policy Research, based in Washington DC,

1925. Ethan Bronner & David Wainer, "Heavily Armed Soldiers Aborted a Plan to Enter Venezuela by Force," *Bloomberg News*, March 6, 2019

1926. 60 Minutes, Madeleine Albright, *newmedia7/YouTube*, August 5, 2016

1927. Duncan Campbell, "Bush rejects Chávez aid", *The Guardian*, September 7, 2005

1928. "Yemen: Coalition blocking humanitarian aid puts civilians at risk," *Human Rights Watch*, September 27, 2017.

1929. Moises Rendon, *Are Sanctions Working in Venezuela?* CSIS Brief, Center for Strategic & International Studies, September 3, 2019; Michael Fox, 'The human cost of the US sanctions on Venezuela', www.dw.com, October 1st, 2019

1930. "Pénurie de 95 % des médicaments au Venezuela", *Sciences et Avenir / AFP*, February 12, 2018

1931. Unidad Debates Económicos, "Las Consecuencias Económicas Del Boicot A Venezuela", *celag.org*, February 8, 2019

1932. *Report of the Independent Expert on the promotion of a democratic and equitable international order on his mission to the Bolivarian Republic of Venezuela and Ecuador*, Document A/HRC/39/47/Add.1, August 3, 2018 (submitted to the 39th session of the UN Human Rights Council, September 10-28, 2018), p.14.

confirmed that US sanctions had caused the deaths of 40,000 people between August 2017 and December 2018[1933]. But these reports will have virtually no resonance in France, where President Macron faithfully follows Donald Trump's policies...

The images of the Tienditas bridge blocked by containers are repeated. Mainstream media, such as *CNN*[1934] and *RFi*[1935] claim that the bridge was purposely blocked by the military to prevent humanitarian aid from arriving and *France24* relays Mike Pompeo's tweets[1936]. However, the bridge, which was completed in 2015, was never put into service due to deteriorating relations with Colombia and barriers and concrete blocks were placed by... Colombia in 2016[1937], it was only in 2018 that containers were placed by Venezuela on its side of the border. *BBC News, which initially followed* the US administration's lead, has now realised its mistake and corrected the relevant page on its website[1938]. It was therefore known for a long time that "humanitarian aid" would not be able to cross this bridge. Moreover...

> *We forget to mention that there is another one not far away, the Bolivar bridge: it too is between the two countries, but it is open, in both directions. And you can cross it. On foot, but it happens. With lots of people carrying lots of things*[1939].

The humanitarian convoy is therefore just a propaganda operation: it was probably never really the idea to send humanitarian aid, but simply to show that Maduro was preventing aid from reaching his people. Thus, Western exaggerations give an opportunity to *RT* - rather systematically accused of spreading fake news - to set the record straight[1940].

Finally, on February 23, Juan Guaidó tried to get the announced convoy through. But there were clashes and one of the trucks was set on fire. At first, the Western media accused the Maduro government of setting the vehicle on fire. On its Facebook page, *Canada's La Presse* shows an image of the incident with

---

1933. Mark Weisbrot & Jeffrey Sachs, *Economic Sanctions as Collective Punishment: The Case of Venezuela*, Center for Economic and Policy Research, Washington DC, April 2019, p. 11

1934. Isa Soares, Natalie Gallón & Kara Fox, "Venezuela blocks border bridge where aid is set to arrive", *CNN*, February 6, 2019

1935. "Venezuela: 30 tonnes of humanitarian aid blocked at the border", *RFI*, February 7, 2019

1936. "Violence on Venezuela's borders where humanitarian aid remains blocked", *France24*, February 23, 2019 (modified on February 24, 2019)

1937. "Tienditas, el puente de 40 millones de dólares que no han estrenado", *La Opinión*, February 5, 2016; Justin Emery, "The Tienditas Bridge "blockade", *Medium*, February 8, 2019

1938. "Venezuela crisis: Pompeo demands aid corridor opened", *BBC News*, February 6, 2019

1939. Jean-Marc Four, "In Venezuela as elsewhere, humanitarian aid is never politically neutral", *France Inter*, February 21, 2019

1940. "A bridge too far: US claims Venezuela blocked aid deliveries... at a crossing that was never open", *RT*, February 12, 2019

the caption "*A truck carrying humanitarian aid was set on fire Saturday at the border with Colombia by Venezuelan police and army*"[1941]. On *FOX News*, Mike Pompeo states:

> *The Lima Group, the OAS and the European countries, the whole world has witnessed the devastation caused in Venezuela by Maduro, this sick tyrant, who denies food to hungry Venezuelans and medicine to sick Venezuelans. Burning trucks with...- This is the worst of the worst of a tyrant. I think the Venezuelan people see that. We saw yesterday the army start to see it too*[1942].

But this is not true: it is only a question of adding fuel to the fire - literally. A video of the incident, posted on the YouTube channel of former US Republican Senator Ron Paul, shows very clearly that it was a Guaidó supporter who set the truck on fire (probably unintentionally) with a Molotov cocktail[1943]. Some media quickly change their articles, others use ambiguous wording that suggests the responsibility of the Venezuelan military, such as *Franceinfo* - which reproduces Guaidó's tweet accusing the military[1944] - or *Le Figaro*[1945]. None of them then indicate that the fire was caused by a Guaidó supporter. The *New York Times* is probably the only "major" newspaper to study the videos and question the official version[1946].

12.2.6. The April 2019 "Coup"

On April 30, 2019, Juan Guaidó announces "*the final phase of Operation Freedom*[1947]" and calls on the population and the armed forces to rise up against the government.

The disinformation starts with the definition of what looks like an attempted "coup". In the programme 'C dans l'air', Frédéric Encel rejects this appellation because Guaidó is '*supported by the parliament*', Maduro's social policy is '*erratic*' and he '*does not call for the seizure of power by force of arms*'[1948].

1941. www.facebook.com/LaPresseFB/videos/venezuela-un-camion-daide-humanitaire-incendié-par-la-police/276078426639570/

1942. *Fox News*, February 24, 2019 (Jason Hopkins, "Mike Pompeo Blasts 'Sick Tyrant' Maduro for Denying Aid to Starving Venezuelans", *The Daily Caller*, February 24, 2019)

1943. Liberty Report, "Venezuela False Flag: Who Burned The Aid Truck?", *YouTube*, February 25, 2019

1944. "VIDEO. Crisis in Venezuela: trucks loaded with humanitarian aid burned near the Colombian border", *franceinfo / AFP*, February 24, 2019

1945. "Venezuela: un camion d'aide incendié à la frontière colombienne", *Le Figaro.fr / AFP*, February 23, 2019

1946. Nicholas Casey, Christoph Koettl & Deborah Acosta, "Footage Contradicts U.S. Claim That Nicolás Maduro Burned Aid Convoy", *The New York Times*, March 10, 2019

1947. Mariana Zuñiga, "Venezuela's Maduro denies Pompeo's claim that he sought to escape to Cuba after day of clashes that left 1 dead, dozens hurt", *The Washington Post*, April 30, 2019

1948. Frédéric Encel in the programme "C dans l'air", "Venezuela: Trump prêt à intervenir ? #cdanslair 02.05.2019", *YouTube/France 5*, May 3, 2019 (06'45")

This is the position of the Trump administration. The logic is that Juan Guaidó is "interim president", since he is supported by the parliament, and therefore he cannot make a "coup" against his own position. Moreover, in March 2019, Robert Palladino, deputy spokesman for the State Department, instructed the press to stop using the term "*self-proclaimed president*", but to use the term "*interim president*[1949]". In the United States, more than in Europe, the mainstream media adopt the 'official' term. Thus the very notion of a 'coup' becomes questionable: it is simply a matter of restoring Guaidó's legitimacy. The mainstream media then find euphemisms: The *Washington Post* speaks of "an *opposition-led challenge covered by the military*[1950]", *CBS News* speaks of "an *uprising*[1951]", the *New York Times of* "a *protest*[1952]" and Bloomberg of "a *risky bet*[1953]". Bloomberg goes even further, with the headline *A coup in Venezuela? It's best not to use that word in this situation* and There *is no coup in Venezuela*[1954].

On April 30, 2019, there are two rallies in Caracas: one by supporters of Juan Guaidó and one by supporters of the government; but the international media only picks up on the opposition demonstration. The repeated announcement of the possible defection of high-ranking military personnel had encouraged insurgents to try to enter the La Carlota military base in Caracas to rally the armed forces. CNN reporter Jake Tapper tweets that the government military is firing on the crowd. Problem: he uses photos of pro-Guaidó soldiers, clearly recognisable by their blue armbands[1955]! The media is playing a loop of images of armoured national guard vehicles ramming into the demonstrators. This could be an outbreak of violence, as we have seen elsewhere in the world; but no one mentions that Guaidó supporters stole identical vehicles the same morning[1956] and that they could have used them to stir up tension. In fact, we don't know anything about it, but no media outlet is in any doubt.

At the end of the day, the attempt to unite the people and the armed forces around Juan Guaidó is a total failure. *USA Today* reports:

1949. Robert Palladino, "Department Press Briefing - March 5, 2019", *Department Press Briefing*, Washington DC, March 5, 2019

1950. Michael Robinson Chavez, "In photos: Opposition-led, military-backed challenge underway in Venezuela", *The Washington Post*, May 1st, 2019

1951. Camilo Montoya-Galvez, Sarah Lynch Baldwin, "Venezuela's Maduro proclaims 'defeat' of uprising led by opposition leader", *CBS News*, April 30, 2019

1952. "Return of Firebrand Opposition Leader Lopez Energizes Venezuelan Protests", *Reuters/The New York Times*, April 30, 2019

1953. Andrew Rosati, Alex Vasquez & Patricia Laya, "Guaido's High-Risk Gamble Flops as Maduro Keeps Grip on Military," *Bloomberg/Yahoo News*, May 1st, 2019

1954. David Papadopoulos, "A Coup in Venezuela? That Word Is Best Avoided in This Situation", *Bloomberg*, April 30, 2019; Eli Lake, "There Is No Coup in Venezuela", *Bloomberg*, April 30, 2019

1955. https://twitter.com/AlanRMacLeod/status/1123591698469277697

1956. https://twitter.com/ThomasVLinge/status/1123211270654779392

Guaidó saw it as the perfect time for Venezuelans to take back their democracy once and for all. But as the hours ticked by, he found himself alone on a highway bridge with the same small group of soldiers with whom he recklessly tried to spark a military uprising[1957].

In fact, the situation presented by the Western media was played out in a rectangle of 200 m by 500 m to the north of the La Carlota base, whose garrison will remain loyal to the government.

For their part, the Americans react by disseminating false information. On the one hand, it is a question of creating an insurrectionary dynamic, and on the other hand of explaining why the expected - and announced - popular uprising is not happening, while putting forward pretexts for a possible military option. Thus, Mike Pompeo announced on social networks that President Maduro was preparing to leave the country to seek refuge in Cuba, but that he had been dissuaded at the last minute by Moscow[1958]. Mario Diaz-Balart, a Republican congressman from Florida, claims that Venezuela could have nuclear weapons and would be ready to fire them against the US[1959]. While Donald Trump is threatening Cuba with a "total and complete" embargo if…

[If] Cuban troops and militia do NOT immediately cease military or other operations aimed at causing the death and destruction of the Constitution of Venezuela[1960].

National Security Adviser John Bolton - who is no longer one lie away - says the Venezuelan army was prevented from reaching Guaidó by the 20,000 Cuban military deployed in Venezuela to support Maduro[1961]. In the evening, John Bolton states:

We believe that the Cubans were very instrumental in supporting Maduro today with the Russians - this is certainly speculation in Caracas. We think this demonstrates why Venezuela must be led by the people of Venezuela and not by outside forces[1962].

1957. Joshua Goodman & Christopher Torchia, "How the Venezuelan 'coup' didn't get beyond street demonstrations supporting Juan Guaido," *Associated Press/USA Today*, May 1st, 2019
1958. "Pompeo Says Russia Dissuaded Maduro From Fleeing Venezuela", *Radio Free Europe/ Radio Liberty*, April 30, 2019
1959. Jerry Iannelli, "Miami Rep. Mario Diaz-Balart Claims, Without Evidence, That Venezuela Might Nuke U.S.," *Miami New Times*, May 1st, 2019
1960. https://twitter.com/realDonaldTrump/status/1123333506346749952
1961. Adam Taylor, "How many Cuban troops are there in Venezuela? The U.S. says over 20,000. Cuba says zero", The Washington Post, May 2, 2019
1962. "WATCH LIVE: Bolton to discuss situation in Venezuela", *PBS NewsHour/YouTube*, April 30, 2019 (02'00")

We are in the midst of delirium! Thus, speculations, rumours and "what we believe" generate a certainty: this is exactly the pattern of "fake news" that is fed to us by the mainstream media in support of risky policies.

In the end, the failure is very clear: Guaidó clearly does not have the support of the majority of the population, contrary to what the mainstream press says. But it is also likely that the Venezuelan government has played a more sophisticated game than it appears. In his April 30 press briefing, Bolton mentions that Defence Minister Vladimir Padrino, Supreme Court judge Maikel Moreno (the one who had requested the lifting of Juan Guaidó's parliamentary immunity[1963]), Presidential Guard commander Ivan Rafael Hernandez Dala had already been approached by the opposition and had promised their support[1964]. It is not impossible that the Venezuelan government deliberately 'leaked' information suggesting that major defections were imminent, in order to push Guaidó into a premature and doomed attempt. The "release" of Leopoldo Lopez - the historic leader of Popular Will, whose legitimacy is greater than Guaidó's - could be part of this scheme, in order to discredit Guaidó in the eyes of the West. For in Venezuela, the opposition is far from unanimous behind Guaidó.

This is compounded by his selfies in February 2019 at the Colombian border with members of the Rastrojos, a group linked to the far-right Autodefensas Unidas de Colombia (AUC) in Colombia and known for its cocaine trafficking activities[1965]. They helped him to cross the border illegally and provide him with protection in Colombia.

Finally, the *New York Times*, which used the title of "*interim president*" abandoned it[1966]: Guaidó's failure confirms the disinformation served up by the Western press and the failure of the American strategy.

Ironically, the military personnel who defected to Guaidó in April and sought asylum in the US have since been interned in immigration camps[1967]...

In January 2020, Juan Guaidó's mandate expires. On January 5, for the election of the president of the National Assembly, the moderate opposition joins the chavist majority against Juan Guaidó. Luis Parra, a member of the right-wing opposition (Primero Justicia party), was elected to the presidency of the Parliamentary Assembly. Franklin Duarte (Christian-conservative COPEI

1963. "The Latest: Venezuela judge seeks to strip Guaido's immunity", *Associated Press*, April 1st, 2019

1964. "WATCH LIVE: Bolton to discuss situation in Venezuela", *PBS NewsHour/YouTube*, April 30, 2019 (01'15"); "Bolton presses key aides to Venezuela's Maduro to abandon him", *Reuters*, April 30, 2019

1965. "Venezuela investigates Guaido over photo with suspected Colombian criminals", Reuters, September 13, 2019; Tom Phillips & Joe Parkin Daniels, "Opposition leader plays down images but analysts say they could prove highly damaging", *The Guardian*, September 14, 2019

1966. Anatoly Kurmanaev, "Venezuela's Opposition Leader Juan Guaidó May Negotiate With Maduro", *The New York Times*, May 21, 2019

1967. Alan Macleod, "Pro-Coup Venezuelan Soldiers Who Fled to the US Now Locked Up in ICE Detention Center," *Mint Press News*, December 27, 2019

party) was elected vice-president, José Gregorio Goyo Noriega (Voluntad Popular party) was elected second vice-president, and Negal Morales (from the neo-liberal Acción Democrática party) was elected secretary of the Assembly. The election of four opposition members to head the National Assembly thus belies Western accusations of a government takeover of the legislature.

Of course, the Western media declared the election illegitimate and the US adopted sanctions against the newly elected[1968]. *France 24* claims that Parra "*proclaimed himself president of the parliament*" and that "*José Guaidó was prevented from entering the hemicycle*[1969]". This is not true: the American alternative media *The Grayzone* filmed the election minute by minute: everything clearly went constitutionally[1970]. Probably knowing that he would not have enough votes to be elected, Guaidó clearly did everything possible to be absent from the vote, in order to contest it…

In fact Guaidó is highly contested, even within his own party. Two days after the election, he resigned from his party, probably anticipating his ouster.

On April 29, in a press conference, Mike Pompeo showed surprising optimism about relations between the two countries:

> *[…]. In Venezuela, I am pleased to report that the multilateral effort to restore democracy continues to gain momentum. I have asked my team to update our plans for the reopening of the U.S. Embassy in Caracas so that we are ready. As soon as Maduro steps down, I am confident that we will raise our flag again in Caracas*[1971].

On May 1st, John Bolton tweets:

> *To date, the large foreign military presence in Venezuela denies the will of the people. The strongest possible sanctions must remain until the peaceful transition of power & @jguaido, [and that] the legitimate interim president of Venezuela and the Venezuelan people are firmly in control*[1972].

The explanation comes four days later, on May 3, 2020, in the middle of the coronavirus crisis: American mercenaries and ex-Venezuelan military are

1968. "Asamblea Nacional: EE.UU. sanciona a Luis Parra, el diputado que se proclamó "presidente" del Parlamento de Venezuela en lugar de Juan Guaidó", *BBC News*, January 13, 2020

1969. "Venezuela: Juan Guaido at the door, an elected opposition official proclaims himself president of the Parliament", *France 24*, January 5, 2020

1970. Orlenys Ortiz, "Cómo Juan Guaidó perdió el control de la Asamblea Nacional en Venezuela", *The Grayzone*, January 20, 2020

1971. *Secretary Michael R. Pompeo At a Press Availability - Remarks to the Press*, Press Briefing Room, state.gov, April 29, 2020

1972. https://twitter.com/AmbJohnBolton/status/1256015581511331847

captured while trying to infiltrate Venezuela. In fact, Juan Guaidó's popularity in Venezuela is very low[1973] and he cannot count on either the military or the people to overthrow the government. So he tries to operate with mercenaries and mandates Sivercorp, a private military company that employs former members of the US Special Forces. The contract was published by the *Washington Post*: the GIDEON operation aimed at "*capturing/detaining/eliminating*" President Maduro for $212.9 million, with the support of AC-130 Gunship aircraft and armed drones[1974]. Moreover, it appears that the mercenary group was to be institutionalised after the takeover and become a kind of 'death squad'. No Western country will condemn this coup attempt.

12.3 Conclusions for Venezuela

The Venezuelan crisis illustrates the dangerous drift of militarising human rights and humanitarian emergencies to justify intervention and regime change in a country. Here, the humanitarian crisis was created out of thin air by sanctions and then amplified by the Western mainstream media to legitimise intervention.

It is very likely that Venezuela is not a model of democracy and that its government is corrupt. But our assessments are clearly skewed. The real situation is probably less caricatured than the one presented to us by the establishment media. The Anglo-Saxon media are generally more critical and inquisitive, even if a large proportion of them follow the US policy line.

Beyond what one may think of Venezuela and its politics, it is disturbing that one can base foreign policy on such fragile and questionable accusations. Clearly, Western countries - and European ones in particular - are subservient to US policy. Yet their geographical distance and economic weight would allow them to play a moderating role in crises that - as with Iran - have more psychopathological than factual causes. A fundamental problem here in Europe, as in Switzerland (which has joined the sanctions), is the lack of independent analytical intelligence capabilities.

1973. Kejal Vyas, "Venezuela's Juan Guaidó Slips Into Colombia for Regional Conference", *The Wall Street Journal*, January 19, 2020

1974. "Read the attachments to the General Services Agreement between the Venezuelan opposition and Silvercorp", *The Washington Post*, May 7, 2020

13. CONCLUSIONS

We have learned nothing: today's conflicts start as they did sixty years ago and wars are fought with the same principles as a hundred years ago. Literally. Technology has evolved, but we are still applying doctrines based on power relations, exactly as in the First World War. We have multiplied multilateral platforms for conflict resolution, but dominated by the United States, they are run without intelligence. Our leaders are less and less thoughtful, more attached to their image on Facebook than to the mark they will leave on history. As for our values, between the use of torture, interference in the internal affairs of others, the violation (or non-compliance) of treaties we have signed, and the deception of public opinion, they seem to have no meaning except in the financial vocabulary. As for the people, they accept rather meekly to be manipulated, until their "pocket" is concerned...

13.1. An Intelligence Problem

The primary role of intelligence is to provide relevant elements for decision-making at the political, strategic, operative and tactical (operational) levels. It is therefore an essential tool of the rule of law, where the decision is not discretionary but rational, based on the interests of the nation and not on particular interests. Its analytical product must constitute a reference, which must help the decision-maker to free himself from misinformation, rumours and, therefore, from external influences. This is why, to be relevant, intelligence must remain non-partisan and enlighten the decision while staying away from political bickering.

The inability of Western intelligence services to analyse situations objectively and factually is a vulnerability on two levels. The first is the disproportionate influence of the American, British and Israeli services, which are said to have far superior analytical capabilities. The second is that a rumour or the action of a group of individuals could well lead to a major conflict. Our services lack the method and experience to understand strategic realities.

Faced with the complexity of security problems, Western services have sought answers in the accumulation of data. Paradoxically, however, data has become their weakness. Pseudo-experts attribute this to the growing inability of the services to process the mass of information. This is incorrect: the problem is their inability to see the bigger picture. Focusing on the 'trees' means that the 'forest' is no longer visible, as Vladimir Putin rightly observes when evaluating his services:

> *We are better than the United States because we don't have the same means as them*[1975].

On the fringes of the work of the services, the intervention of former "agents" in the media is often misleading. This is the case of a Belgian "expert", generally presented in the French-speaking media as a former "agent of the DGSE", but who, in reality, has never been a member of the "services", but a simple "informer" (in police jargon: an "informant"), paid to provide "*information*" (not "*intelligence*"). Sometimes we get the opinion of a former Service Action, who thinks he is an analyst. But they are not analysts: they give their opinion, wrapped in the credibility of an organisation to which they did not belong and whose methodology they do not master. The media play with the credulity of the public. In fact, in the "big" intelligence services, each individual sees only a small part of the information or its exploitation: it is only at the level of senior management that a global view is possible. This is very different in a "small" service...

13.2. The Cure Worse than the Disease?

Our understanding of the 'infox' phenomenon is simplistic. This is evidenced by the debunker tools available on the Net, such as the French government's "*On te manipule.fr*"[1976], or NATO's "*The News Hero*"[1977], which it is difficult not to describe as "stupid".

To combat the problem, governments tend to blame social networks and delegate a form of censorship to them. Thus, Google, Facebook, *Le Monde*, *Libération*, the European Union or NATO propose "fact-checkers". But in the absence of precise criteria and a rigorous methodology, these tools become a way of stigmatising deviant thoughts[1978].

1975. "Conversations with Mr Putin 2-4", *France 3*, (31'15")
1976. www.gouvernement.fr/on-te-manipule
1977. http://www.natowatch.org/newsbriefs/2018/nato-centre-launches-news-hero-game-antidote-fake-news
1978. Julia Kassem, "YouTube Censors Accounts Reporting Truth About Syria's Idlib", *Mint Press News*, September 12 2018.

The European Union's fact-checker[1979] has become a veritable disinformation site directed against Russia[1980]. The method is quite simple: from a piece of information gleaned from a pro-Russian site, it formulates a "rebuttal" based on another fact, which - often - does not invalidate the original information, but a very similar one. For example, on August 2, 2019, *euvsdisinfo.eu* pinned the Spanish version of *Sputnik*[1981] for stating that

> *US President Donald Trump has threatened to release thousands of members of the Islamic State terrorist group captured in Syria if European countries do not take them back*[1982].

It accuses the Russian media of distorting a tweet from Trump on February 16 about the fate of 800 Islamic State fighters[1983]. The tweet is real, but the European site is lying, because on August 2, in a 'press briefing', Trump stated almost word for word what *Sputnik* claims[1984]. This 'fact-checking' then becomes a form of manipulation.

In the same spirit, the European site denies the Russian-speaking Ukrainian media *politnavigator.net*[1985], which claims about the investigation into the destruction of flight Malaysia Airlines MH-17:

> *Malaysia does not have full access to all information concerning the [MH17] investigation, although it is invited to participate in the investigation of this disaster*[1986].

In fact, *euvsdisinfo.eu is* lying by omission and pretends to be unaware that there are *two* simultaneous investigations into MH17: (a) an investigation by the Dutch Safety Office (OVV) under the aegis of the International Civil Aviation Organization (ICAO) whose objective "*is the prevention of accidents and similar incidents*" and not "*to question the responsibilities or liabilities of any party*"; (b) another investigation, conducted by the Joint Investigation Team (JIT), under the aegis of Europol and Eurojust, of a criminal nature, which aims to determine the responsibilities for the incident. In the former, Malaysia is present in its own right; but in the latter, it has only been invited to provide an observer, but

1979. https://euvsdisinfo.eu/
1980. https://eeas.europa.eu/sites/eeas/files/dr_47_final.pdf
1981. "¿Pueden miles de miembros de ISIS invadir Europa?", *Sputnik*, August 2, 2019
1982. https://euvsdisinfo.eu/report/trump-threatens-to-release-thousands-of-isis-members-in-europe/
1983. https://twitter.com/realDonaldTrump/status/1096980408401625088
1984. Richard Hall, 'Trump threatens to release thousands of Isis fighters 'to Europe'', *The Independent*, August 2, 2019 (video)
1985. https://euvsdisinfo.eu/report/malaysia-was-sidelined-from-mh17-investigation/
1986. Ольга Козаченко, "Малайзию не допускают к расследованию катастрофы MH17", politnavigator.net, August 1st, 2019

receives neither reports nor conclusions, for reasons that remain unclear, perhaps because of its more 'political' nature. So the Russian-speaking media was right.

Fact checking should be based on... facts. For example, the website *euractiv.fr* describes the estimate of 11 million Muslims in France by the Russian media *Rossiya 1 as* a "*far-fetched*" statistic and "*almost three times the real figure*"[1987]. But what is the "*real figure*"? In reality, we don't know, because it is forbidden to count the religious affiliation of individuals in France, and there are only estimates[1988]. This "fact-checking" therefore becomes an infox in itself.

As for the automatic "fact checkers" of social networks, they are not capable of judging the substance of information. They "decide" on the basis of algorithms fed by user behaviour, with perverse effects. For example, in September 2016, Facebook censored Norwegian Prime Minister Erna Solberg for posting a photo of a girl running naked to escape napalm bombing during the Vietnam War in 1972[1989]. The social network also censored Gustave Courbet's painting *The Origin of the World*[1990], and more recently a series of paintings by Rubens[1991].

Efforts to debunk infomercials - particularly by some mainstream media - sometimes have the perverse effect of inhibiting the public's critical faculties. Indeed, they tend to place all false information on the same level, whereas the real problem is not the false information itself, but its impact on the decision-making process. Whether President Macron is gay or not is of no importance whatsoever, but the way Vladimir Putin or Bashar al-Assad is presented determines the way we conduct foreign policy...

The Fondation Jean-Jaurès, in collaboration with IFOP and Conspiracy Watch, has conducted two studies - published in 2017 and 2019[1992] - on conspiracy theories among the French population. They show the danger of politicising the issue of fake news by staying on the surface of things: we then risk using the same procedures as those used in the Middle Ages to combat witchcraft, or during the Prague trials in 1948-1949. Apart from the banality of certain "*major lessons*" such as "*the more a conspiracy statement is known, the more statistical chances it has of being believed*[1993]", the study becomes manipulative. It relates

1987. Cécile Barbière, "La Russie championne de la manipulation de l'information", *euractiv.fr*, September 10, 2018

1988. See Wikipedia, article "Islam in France"; Agnès De Féo, "Why these data on the number of Muslims in Europe are not reliable", *slate.fr*, December 20, 2017; Rémi Banet & Benoît Fauchet, "20 million Muslims in France? Ils sont environ 4 fois moins, selon les estimations les plus sérieuses", *Factuel/AFP*, May 17, 2018

1989. Clarisse Martin, "Facebook reverses its censorship of the famous photo of the little girl burned during the Vietnam War", *rtl.fr/AFP*, September 9, 2016.

1990. Matthieu Mondoloni, "Facebook and "The Origin of the World": "Facebook does not distinguish between nudity, pornography and a work of art", *Radio France*, February 1st, 2018 (updated February 2, 2018)

1991. Christopher Carbone, "Facebook censorship: Nude paintings by Rubens run afoul of social network", *Fox News*, July 24, 2018

1992. *Enquête sur le complotisme*, IFOP for the Jean-Jaurès Foundation and Conspiracy Watch, December 2017; *Enquête sur le complotisme - Vague 2*, IFOP for the Jean-Jaurès Foundation and Conspiracy Watch, January 2019

1993. Rudy Reichstadt, 'Complotism Survey 2019: Les Grands Enseignements', *jean-jaures.org*, February 6, 2019

issues of minor importance - such as the death of Lady Di, the flatness of the earth or the fact that Americans have not been to the moon - to "*the importance attached to living in a democracy*[1994]".

The very design of the surveys makes the interpretation of the results problematic. For example, when asked whether or not to agree with the statement "*the Illuminati are a secret organisation that seeks to manipulate the population*[1995]", the possible answers do not imply that one believes that they are actually doing so. Yet the magazine *Le Point* does not hesitate to draw the conclusion that "*one in four French people think that the Illuminati manipulate us*[1996]". This is obviously a lie: "seeking to" does not mean that we do, and the "we" is a clarification that the initial question did not mention at all. In this case, *Le Point* would be more of a "conspiracy theorist"!

The questions themselves are misleading: they ask for an opinion on the proposition: "*Only a handful of insiders are able to decipher the conspiracy signs that have been written on banknotes, logos of famous brands or in music videos*[1997]". Thus, it is claimed that '*conspiracy signs [...] have been written*' on banknotes; it is therefore logical to assume that only insiders can understand them. To get a meaningful answer, one should have asked whether 'it is *believed that signs have been written...*'

The authors play on ambiguities to conjure up "conspiracy theories", with the aim of establishing a correlation between adherence to a "conspiracy theory" and doubt about democracy. For example, the statement "*international drug trafficking is actually controlled by the CIA*[1998]" is most likely false when expressed in this way, but it is not unrelated to reality. As far back as 1993, the *New York Times* claimed that the CIA's links to the drug trade go back to its inception[1999]. Indeed, the CIA has been - and still is - involved in many drug deals. At the end of the 1940s, in exchange for fighting the communist unions in Marseille, the CIA allowed the Italian and Corsican mafias to continue their drug trafficking: the famous "French connection". Later, in Indochina, inspired by the strategy of the French SDECE, which had financed the production and distribution

1994. Rudy Reichstadt, "Enquête (...) (op.cit.)
1995. *Enquête sur le complotisme - Vague 2*, IFOP for the Fondation Jean-Jaurès and Conspiracy Watch, January 2019, p. 71
1996. Thomas Mahler, "Un français sur quatre pense que les Illuminati nous manipulent", *Le Point*, February 6, 2019
1997. *Enquête sur le complotisme - Vague 2*, IFOP for the Fondation Jean-Jaurès and Conspiracy Watch, January 2019, p. 71
1998. *Enquête sur le complotisme - Vague 2*, IFOP for the Fondation Jean-Jaurès and Conspiracy Watch, January 2019, p. 71
1999. Larry Collins, "The CIA Drug Connection Is as Old as the Agency," *The New York Times*, December 3, 1993; CovertAction Information Bulletin, *CIA and Drugs*, No. 28, June 1st, 1987, CIA-RDP90-00845R000100170001-8.pdf (Publicly available June 3, 2010); Jon Schwarz, "Oliver North Worked With Cocaine Traffickers to Arm Terrorists. Now He'll Be President of the NRA," *The Intercept*, May 28, 2018.

of drugs to obtain the support of the Hmong tribes ("Operation X"), the CIA effectively supported the opium producers of the "Golden Triangle" in the 1960s and 1970s (Operation PAPER), in order to create a bulwark against the advance of communism in South-East Asia and organised the transport of drugs. In Latin America, the CIA applied the same strategy by supporting coca producers in order to counter the establishment of Marxist maquis... before turning against them after the failure of the communist guerrillas[2000]. In Afghanistan, the Taliban had reduced opium production to an all-time low of 74 tons by October 2001[2001], but by the end of 2018 it had reached 6,400 tons[2002], or 82% of global production[2003]. Despite the fact that eradicating drug production was one of the objectives of their intervention in Afghanistan[2004], the West has been unable to find an alternative. In fact, the Americans and Nato have turned a blind eye and even protected[2005] this illicit crop in order to prevent local warlords from allying themselves with the Taliban. In 2010, Nato even turned down a Russian offer to eradicate opium plantations, with its then spokesman James Appathurai saying:

> *We cannot be in a situation where we remove the only source of income for people living in the second poorest country in the world without being able to offer them an alternative*[2006].

To claim that the international drug trade is controlled by the CIA is certainly an exaggeration, but to doubt the ethics of the US and international institutions in this regard is far from irrational!

Similarly, the claim that "*some of the white trails created by passing aircraft in the sky are composed of chemicals deliberately released for secret reasons*[2007]" is also based on real facts. On September 26-27, 1950, the US Navy secretly released biological agents over San Francisco Bay[2008] (Operation SEA SPRAY)

2000. Cristina Maza, "The CIA Was Behind a Massive Drug Trafficking Operation in Argentina, Russian Drug Smuggler Claims", *Newsweek*, March 1st, 2018

2001. Raphael F. Perl (Foreign Affairs, Defense, and Trade Division), *Taliban and the Drug Trade*, Congressional Research Service, Report RS21041, October 5, 2001 (available at https://file.wikileaks.org/file/crs/RS21041.pdf).

2002. *Afghanistan Opium Survey 2018 - Cultivation and Production*, UN Office on Drugs and Crime, November 2018, p. 7

2003. *World Drug Report 2019 - Global Overview of Drug Demand and Supply (Booklet 2)*, United Nations Office on Drugs and Crime, June 2019, p. 44

2004. "Britain to support Afghanistan's bid to eradicate poppy growing, Blair tells World Service listeners", *BBC*, April 5, 2001

2005. "US/NATO Troops Patrolling Opium Poppy Fields in Afghanistan", *publicintelligence.net*, May 21, 2010

2006. David Brunnstrom, "NATO rejects Russian call for Afghan poppy spraying", *Reuters*, March 24, 2010

2007. *Enquête sur le complotisme*, IFOP for the Fondation Jean-Jaurès and Conspiracy Watch, December 2017, p. 44

2008. See Wikipedia, Article "Serratia marcescens".

to test the vulnerability of an urban area[2009]. The operation was not revealed until 1976, but it was replicated in other countries, including Britain in the early 1970s[2010]. In 1977, the US military confessed to having conducted 239 experiments involving the release of biological agents on populations between 1949 and 1969[2011]. Obviously, the *contrails* seen in the sky behind aircraft are not related to chemical weapons, and it is highly unlikely that such experiments are still being conducted today, but the fear of them is not entirely irrational either.

The *France 24* media was created to carry the French government's message abroad, particularly in Africa. Its programme "Contre-Faits" is intended as a tool to fight against infoxes. It tries to pass off Florian Philippot's assertion that "*40% of French people are for Frexit*[2012]" as an infox. The information is perfectly true[2013], but the media argues on a different subject: the outcome of a possible election by adding the abstention rate[2014]. It thus distorts the initial statement in order to denigrate its author: it is manipulation.

On *France 4,* the January 19, 2019 programme in the *Escape News* series, entitled *Vladimir Poutine: le tsar de l'infox? aims to* stimulate a critical approach to information among young people. The host suggests putting together snippets of sentences from articles in Le *Monde* and *RT* on the repression of demonstrations in Russia. But the result is sentences that do not appear in either of the two original texts and are simply intended to highlight Vladimir Putin's "repressive regime"... Debunking is clearly being used for the purpose of influence.

Labelling deviant thinking as 'conspiracy' is not innocent. In the United States, in order to prevent terrorist acts and mass killings, the FBI is currently implementing systems to detect individuals who may *be* guilty of such acts[2015]. This is based on the idea that they have a 'mental disorder', detected by algorithms based on mass surveillance[2016]. Deviant elements, alternative political thinking or belief in conspiracy theories are seen as manifestations of mental disorder,

---

2009. Bernadette Tansey, "Serratia has dark history in region / Army test in 1950 may have changed microbial ecology", *sfgate.com*, October 31, 2004; Helen Thompson, "In 1950, the U.S. Released a Bioweapon in San Francisco", *smithsonian.com*, July 6, 2015

2010. Antony Barnett, "Millions were in germ war tests", *The Guardian*, April 21, 2002

2011. George C. Wilson, 'Army Conducted 239 Secret, Open-Air Germ Warfare Tests', *The Washington Post*, March 9, 1977

2012. "Florian Philippot: '40% of French people are for Frexit'", *sudradio.fr*, February 8, 2019

2013. *Les Français et le référendum d'initiative citoyenne*, Ifop pour Valeurs Actuelles, JF/PC N° 116120, January 2019; Romain Pichon, "40 % des Français veulent sortir de l'Union européenne", *rattrapages-actu.fr*, April 25, 2019

2014. Caroline De Camaret & Roxane Runel, "Do 40% of French people want a Frexit?", *Contre-Faits, France 24*, June 12, 2019

2015. Cora Currier & Murtaza Hussain, "48 Questions the FBI Uses to Determine if Someone Is a Likely Terrorist", *the Intercept*, February 13, 2017

2016. Leandra Bernstein, "FBI seeks tools to monitor social media, 'detect mass shooters before they strike'", *WLJA.com*, August 7 2019

and thus potentially of terrorist radicalisation[2017]. We are not far from Patrick Cohen's "sick brains" and the psychiatric hospitals that made the reputation of the Soviet system!

Understanding these complex environments with their asymmetric logics is clearly beyond the reach of the media and our 'elites', who use outdated and overly simple reading grids. Thus, in August 2019, the killings in Dayton and El Paso were immediately associated with the 'extreme right'. *France-Culture* refers to the El Paso killer's manifesto "*as an echo of Donald Trump's incendiary speeches*[2018]". However, the Dayton killer was left-wing, his manifesto predates the election of Donald Trump and he had expressed his intention to vote for the Democratic candidate Elizabeth Warren[2019]!

The media willingly claims the role of the "fourth estate", but does not assume it and becomes the blind relay of power. Journalists increasingly function as editorialists: instead of facts, they provide professions of faith. Thus, there is a surprising homogeneity of information in the traditional press. Subjects such as Russia, Syria, Europe, immigration or the Yellow Vests[2020], are treated in the same way by the same experts and journalists who rotate from one media to another[2021]. By the summer of 2019, the 'acts' of the gilets jaunes, and the unrest in Honduras and Haiti, have been neglected by the French media in favour of the protests in Hong Kong. It is therefore not very surprising that the Yellow Vests crisis has revealed "*a growing hatred against journalists*[2022]". They are then - rightly or wrongly - perceived as propaganda organs of the government (*LCI, France 2, France 3*) or of the establishment (*BFM TV*)[2023].

As we have seen in this book, the Anglo-Saxon media offer a much wider diversity, with a journalistic culture more oriented towards research and investigation, without seeking controversy. The *Bureau of Investigative Journalism, WikiLeaks, The Grayzone* or *The Intercept, for* example, balance our perception of reality. In France, certain media such as *Acrimed* or *Mediapart*

2017. *Anti-Government, Identity Based, and Fringe Political Conspiracy Theories Very Likely Motivate Some Domestic Extremists to Commit Criminal, Sometimes Violent Activity* (UNCLASSIFIED//LA W ENFORCEMENT SENSITIVE), FY 19 Intelligence Bulletin, FBI Phoenix Field Office, May 30, 2019; Jana Winter, "Exclusive: FBI document warns conspiracy theories are a new domestic terrorism threat," *Yahoo News*, August 1st, 2019; Yaron Steinbuch, "FBI: Conspiracy theory 'extremists' are a terror threat," *New York Post*, August 1st, 2019

2018. "El Paso and Dayton shootings: Donald Trump accused of being a dangerous arsonist", *France-Culture*, August 5, 2019

2019. Alex Kasprak, "Was Dayton Mass Shooter a Self-Described 'Pro-Satan Leftist Who Supported Elizabeth Warren'?", *Snopes*, August 5, 2019

2020. Maxime Friot, "Journalist: author or content provider?", *Acrimed*, August 12, 2019

2021. Jérémy de Rugy, "C dans l'air", chatter between friends on public service, *Acrimed*, May 5, 2014

2022. https://rsf.org/fr/france

2023. "'Gilets jaunes': we have counted the attacks on journalists since the beginning of the movement", *franceinfo*, January 19, 2019 (updated on January 20, 2019)

also have this "gadfly" function, which is essential to the work of researchers and analysts.

13.3. A Problem of Democracy

It would be wrong to believe that fake news masks a will. That would be a "conspiracy" interpretation. In fact, the opposite is true: we act without understanding the situation or in haste, and then, in order to hide the errors of governance, we invoke fake news. As a classified presentation by the UK's Joint Threat Research Intelligence Group (JTRIG) on influence operations states:

People make decisions for emotional reasons, not rational ones[2024].

This is what happened during the coronavirus crisis in most countries: by ignoring the Chinese experiences, precious time was lost in preparing for the crisis, and emergency measures (generalized containment) had to be taken with catastrophic consequences.

The real problem is not the 'infoxes' that 'get the buzz', but the subtle distortions of facts that lead our democracies down the wrong path. Our opinions are deliberately distorted by assumptions or mere suspicions, framed in such a way that they appear as established facts.

By wanting to listen to everyone, democracy hears no one. There is no longer a hierarchy of problems and we want to solve them all at the same time. The notions of general and particular interest become confused. Everything tends to have the same importance, and political decision-making is increasingly complex. This growing difficulty of Western governments to provide coherent answers to complex problems leads them to simplify their discourse and to discard "parasitic" information.

Thus, the image of an intellectual and paternalistic 'elite' was forged, which alone would be capable of mastering issues that the 'little' people were not able to understand. As a prelude to totalitarian temptations, consciously or not, politicians and editorialists have taken on the mission of 'guiding' the ignorant crowd and removing the '*sick minds*': they do not trust democracy. Thus, when asked whether the free trade treaty with Canada should be put to a referendum, journalist Christophe Barbier replies:

2024. *The Art of Deception: Training for a New Generation of Online Covert Operations*, Joint Threat Research Intelligence Group (SECRET//SI//REL TO USA FVEY), February 2014.

[...] Those who are already in an extremely ideological conflict will be given a political instrument, the referendum, which will trigger civil wars[2025].

Under these conditions, Switzerland would have had more than 200 civil wars since the end of the 19th century! Whether on the question of Europe[2026] or the privatisation of Paris airports (ADP), the voice of the people is not listened to, because they are afraid of its verdict.

On February 15, 2003, the largest anti-war demonstration ever held in London was attended by two million people, according to its organisers[2027]. Despite this, Tony Blair will go into Iraq knowing that the charges against Saddam Hussein were false[2028]. Ten years later, the majority of the population and the Republican opposition[2029] are opposed to an American intervention in Syria[2030]; this leads Barak Obama to promise on *CNN* that there will be no American troops on the ground[2031]. A commitment that he repeated 16 times[2032]... but did not keep. In France, an IFOP poll conducted for *Le Figaro* states that 68% of the French population is opposed to an intervention in Syria[2033]. But fifteen months later, President Hollande decided to intervene in Iraq and then in Syria... Unable to solve their domestic problems, Western governments took refuge in military adventurism. This was the case with Bill Clinton in 1998 - whose strikes provided the motive and model for "9/11" - and with Donald Trump's assassination of Qassem Soleimani. Having decided on the basis of lies, one must continue to lie to escape the verdict of the ballot box.

The 2019 Jean-Jaurès/IFOP poll shows that for 29% of French people "*it is acceptable to distort information to protect the interests of the state*"[2034]. Paradoxically, this very undemocratic spirit is most prevalent with La République en Marche (LREM) (44%) and is at a minimum in 'extremist'

2025. Christophe Barbier, in the programme "C dans l'air", "Globalisation: should we say no to CETA? #cdanslair 22.07.2019", *YouTube/France 5*, July 23, 2019 (1h03'40")

2026. "Macron says France would 'probably' vote to leave EU if country held referendum", *YouTube*, January 21, 2018; Silvia Amaro, "France would have voted to leave EU too if in UK's situation, French leader Macron says", CNBC, January 22, 2018.

2027. "Anti-war protest Britain's biggest demo", *MailOnline, Daily Mail*, February 15, 2003

2028. Richard Norton-Taylor & Nicholas Watt, 'No 10 knew: Iraq no threat', *The Guardian*, August 19, 2003; Kara Vickery & Charles Miranda, 'Chilcot report finds 2003 Iraq war unnecessary, Saddam Hussein was 'no imminent threat", *News Corp Australia Network*, July 7, 2016

2029. John Harwood & Jonathan Weisman, House Republicans Say Voters Oppose Intervention, *The New York Times*, September 6, 2013

2030. Andy Sullivan, "U.S. public opposes Syria intervention as Obama presses Congress", *Reuters*, September 3, 2013

2031. CNN, "Obama: No boots on the ground in Syria", *YouTube*, September 10, 2013

2032. Gregory Korte, "16 times Obama said there would be no boots on the ground in Syria", *USA Today*, October 31, 2015

2033. Antoine Goldet, "Les opinions publiques opposées à une intervention en Syrie", *Libération*, September 11, 2013

2034. *Investigating Conspiracy*, *op. cit*, p. 50

parties such as Debout la France (DF) and France Insoumise (FI) (22%). For example, Sibeth Ndiaye, the French government spokeswoman, admits that she is prepared to lie to protect the president (even if she had his private life in mind[2035]). In other words, a significant part of the population accepts that the truth is hidden from them. We are at the antipodes of the rule of law, which everyone claims to be.

The problem with democracy is that we don't believe in it...

2035. Pauline Moullot, "Did Sibeth Ndiaye really say 'I assume perfectly well to lie to protect the president'?", www.liberation.fr, April 2, 2019

BIOGRAPHY

Jacques Baud holds a master's degree in econometrics and post-graduate degrees in International Security Policy and International Relations from the Graduate Institute of International Studies in Geneva. He is a former agent of the Swiss secret service. He holds the rank of colonel. Expert in chemical and nuclear weapons. Served the United Nations as advisor to the *Zairian Contingent for the Security of the* Rwanda Refugee *Camps* for the UNHCR in Zaire (Congo). While at the UN Headquarters in New York, he designed and established the *Geneva International Centre for Humanitarian Demining* (GICHD) and the *Information Management System for Mine Action (IMSMA),* now deployed in over 60 countries. It has established demining programmes in Chad, Sudan, Somalia and Ethiopia. He helped establish the concept of intelligence for UN peacekeeping operations and headed the first UN Joint *Mission Analysis Centre (JMAC)* in Sudan. He was also Head of Doctrine for UN Peacekeeping Operations in New York, Director of the Research Department of the *International Peace Support Training Centre (IPSTC)* in Nairobi for the African Union, and Head of Small Arms and Light Weapons Control at NATO in Brussels. He is the author of numerous books on intelligence, asymmetric warfare and terrorism.

MAIN PUBLICATIONS

- *Encyclopedia of Terrorism and Organized Violence*, Ed. Lavauzelle, Paris, France, 2009, pp. 1300
- *Jihad - Asymmetry between misunderstanding and fanaticism*, Ed. Lavauzelle, Paris, France, 2009, pp. 250
- *Le renseignement et la lutte contre le terrorisme*, Ed. Lavauzelle, Paris, France, 2005, pp. 450
- *Encyclopaedia of Terrorism and Political Violence*, Ed. Lavauzelle, Paris, France, 2005, pp. 750 (Ministry of the Interior "Akropolis" Prize).
- *La guerre asymétrique ou la défaite du vainqueur*, Ed. du Rocher, Paris, France, 2003, pp.250
- *Encyclopedia of Intelligence and Secret Services*, Lavauzelle, Paris, France, 3rd Ed. 2002, pp. 750
- *Forces Spéciales du Traité de Varsovie 1917-2000*, Ed. L'Harmattan, Paris, France, 2002, pp.200
- *Warsaw Pact Weapons Handbook*, Paladin Press, Boulder (CO), USA, 1989, pp.100

NOTES IN THE TABLES

Note 1 of table p.39. Only rounded figures are quoted here.

Note 2 in table p.89. This refers to the Canadian parliament's decision to participate in the strikes in Iraq ("ISIS mission: MPs approve Canada's air combat role", *CBCNews*, October 8, 2014)

Note 3 in table p.89. Decision taken in September 2014 to send 300 instructors to train Kurdish fighters. They will be followed by about 60 special forces instructors to train Iraqi forces for the recapture of Mosul. The actual date of deployment has not been communicated.

Note 4 in table p.89. Finland announced its contribution to the international coalition in Iraq in September 2014. Initially limited to humanitarian aid, the Finnish contribution quickly included arms deliveries to the Kurds (Hoshmand Sadq, "Seven Countries to sell weapons to Kurds", *BasNews - Erbil*, August 14, 2014), then the deployment of a contingent to train Kurdish fighters as of August 2015 and then a deployment of military advisers during the battle of Mosul as of August 2016 ("Finland's Training Contributes To Troops' Capabilities in Iraq", *Global Coalition*, April 25, 2017). After the attack in Turku in 2017, no European or French media reported this participation.

Note 5 in table p.89. Patrick Wintour, "Britain carries out first Syria airstrikes after MPs approve action against Isis", *The Guardian*, December 3, 2015

Note 6 in table p.234. AFP, "US says Assad's overthrow no longer a priority", *dailymail.co.uk*, March 30, 2017

Note 7 of table p.234. Julie Hirschfeld Davis, "Trump Drops Push for Immediate Withdrawal of Troops from Syria," *The New York Times*, April 4, 2018

8. "Toulouse: the suspect is said to be called Mohammed Merah", *Slate.fr*, March 21, 2012

9. Approximate variation estimated by the author: the original report only gives this variation with colour gradients.

Printed in the USA
CPSIA information can be obtained
at www.ICGtesting.com
LVHW081943020524
779197LV00011B/355